THE SACRED BOOKS OF THE EAST

Translated by

VARIOUS ORIENTAL SCHOLARS

Edited by

F. MAX MÜLLER

Vol. 26

SACRED BOOKS OF THE EAST

(50 VOLUMES)

Series Editor : *F. Max-Müller*

ISBN: 978-81-208-0101-1 (Set)

These volumes of the Sacred Books of the East series include translations of all the most important works of the seven non-Christian religions that have exercised a profound influence on the civilisations of the continent of Asia. The Vedic Brahmanic system claims 21 volumes, Buddhism 10, and Jainism 2; 8 volumes comprise Sacred Books of the Parsis; 2 volumes represent Islam; and 6 the two main indigenous systems of China. Translated by twenty leading authorities in their respective fields, the volumes have been edited by the late F. Max Müller. The inception, publication and the compilation of these books cover almost 34 years.

I. BUDDHISM

Vol. 49: Buddhist Mahayana Texts (2 Parts)
Vol. 11: Buddhist Suttas
Vol. 10: The Dhammapada and Sutta Nipata
Vols. 35 & 36: The Questions of King Milinda (2 Parts)
Vol. 21: The Saddharma Pundarika or the Lotus of the True Law
Vols. 13, 17 & 20: Vinaya Texts (3 Parts)

II. CHINESE

Vol. 19: The Fo-Sho-Hing-Tsan-King
Vols. 3, 16, 27, 28, 39 & 40: The Sacred Books of China (6 Parts)

III. A GENERAL INDEX

Vol. 50: A General Index to the Names and Subject-matter of the Sacred Books of the East

IV. ISLAM

Vols. 6 & 9: The Qur'an (2 Parts)

V. JAINISM

Vols. 22 & 45: The Jaina Sutras (2 Parts)

VI. PARSIS

Vols. 5, 18, 24, 37 & 47: Pahlavi Texts (5 Parts)
Vols. 4, 23 & 31: The Zend-Avesta (3 Parts)

VII. VEDIC-BRAHMANIC SYSTEM

Vol. 8: The Bhagavadgita with the Sanatsujatiya and the Anugita
Vols. 29 & 30: The Grihya-Sutras: Rules of Vedic Domestic Ceremonies (2 Parts)
Vol. 42: Hymns of the Atharva Veda together with Extracts from the Ritual Books and the Commentaries
Vol. 7: The Institutes of Vishnu
Vol. 25: The Laws of Manu
Vol. 33: The Minor Law Books
Vols. 2 & 14: The Sacred Laws of the Aryas as Taught in the Schools of Apastamba, Gautama, Vasishtha and Baudhayana (2 Parts)
Vols. 12, 26, 41, 43 & 44: The Satapatha Brahmana According to the Text of the Madhyandina School (5 Parts)
Vols. 1 & 15: The Upanishads (2 Parts)
Vols. 34 & 38: The Vedanta Sutras (2 Parts)
Vol. 48: The Vedanta-Sutras (with the commentary by Ramanuja)
Vols. 32 & 46: Vedic Hymns (2 Parts)

THE
ŚATAPATHA-BRĀHMAṆA

According to the Text of the
Mādhyandina School

Translated by
JULIUS EGGELING

PART II
BOOKS III AND IV

MOTILAL BANARSIDASS PUBLISHERS
PRIVATE LIMITED • DELHI

8th Reprint: Delhi, 2011
First Published by the Clarendon Press, 1885

ISBN: 978-81-208-0127-1

MOTILAL BANARSIDASS
41 U.A. Bungalow Road, Jawahar Nagar, Delhi 110 007
8 Mahalaxmi Chamber, 22 Bhulabhai Desai Road, Mumbai 400 026
203 Royapettah High Road, Mylapore, Chennai 600 004
236, 9th Main III Block, Jayanagar, Bangalore 560 011
Sanas Plaza, 1302 Baji Rao Road, Pune 411 002
8 Camac Street, Kolkata 700 017
Ashok Rajpath, Patna 800 004
Chowk, Varanasi 221 001

UNESCO COLLECTION OF REPRESENTATIVE WORKS— Indian Series
This book has been accepted in the Indian Translation Series of the UNESCO Collection of Representative Works, jointly sponsored by the United Nations Educational Scientific and Cultural Organization (UNESCO) and the Government of India

Printed in India

By Jainendra Prakash Jain at Shri Jainendra Press,
A-45 Naraina, Phase-I, New Delhi 110 028
and Published by Narendra Prakash Jain for
Motilal Banarsidass Publishers Private Limited,
Bungalow Road, Delhi 110 007

RASHTRAPATI BHAVAN,
NEW DELHI-4
June 10, 1962

I am very glad to know that the Sacred Books of the East, published years ago by the Clarendon Press, Oxford, which have been out-of-print for a number of years, will now be available to all students of religion and philosophy. The enterprise of the publishers is commendable and I hope the books will be widely read.

S. RADHAKRISHNAN

PREFATORY NOTE TO THE NEW EDITION

Since 1948 the United Nations Educational, Scientific and Cultural Organisation (UNESCO), upon the recommendation of the General Assembly of the United Nations, has been concerned with facilitating the translation of the works most representative of the culture of certain of its Member States, and, in particular, those of Asia.

One of the major difficulties confronting this programme is the lack of translators having both the qualifications and the time to undertake translations of the many outstanding books meriting publication. To help overcome this difficulty in part, UNESCO's advisers in this field (a panel of experts convened every other year by the International Council for Philosophy and Humanistic Studies), have recommended that many worthwhile translations published during the 19th century, and now impossible to find except in a limited number of libraries, should be brought back into print in low-priced editions, for the use of students and of the general public. The experts also pointed out that in certain cases, even though there might be in existence more recent and more accurate translations endowed with a more modern apparatus of scholarship, a number of pioneer works of the greatest value and interest to students of Eastern religions also merited republication.

This point of view was warmly endorsed by the Indian National Academy of Letters (Sahitya Akademi), and the Indian National Commission for UNESCO.

It is in the spirit of these recommendations that this work from the famous series "Sacred Books of the East" is now once again being made available to the general public as part of the UNESCO Collection of Representative Works.

PUBLISHER'S NOTE

First, the man distinguished between eternal and perishable. Later he discovered within himself the germ of the Eternal. This discovery was an epoch in the history of the human mind and the *East was the first to discover it.*

To watch in the Sacred Books of the East the dawn of this religious consciousness of man, must always remain one of the most inspiring and hallowing sights in the whole history of the world. In order to have a solid foundation for a comparative study of the Religions of the East, we must have before all things, complete and thoroughly faithful translation of their Sacred Books in which some of the ancient sayings were preserved because they were so true and so striking that they could not be forgotten. They contained eternal truths, expressed for the first time in human language.

With profoundest reverence for Dr. S. Radhakrishnan, President of India, who inspired us for the task; our deep sense of gratitude for Dr. C. D. Deshmukh & Dr. D. S. Kothari, for encouraging assistance; esteemed appreciation of UNESCO for the warm endorsement of the cause; and finally with indebtedness to Dr. H. Rau, Director, Max Müller Bhawan, New Delhi, in procuring us the texts of the Series for reprint, we humbly conclude.

CONTENTS.

PAGE

Introduction xi

THIRD KÂ*N*D*A*.

A. Day (or Days) of Preparation.

Dîkshâ, or Consecration 1

Prâya*n*îyesh*t*i, or Opening Sacrifice 47

Hira*n*yavatî-âhuti, or Offering with Gold; and Homage to Soma-cow 52

Purchase of Soma-plants 63

Procession and Entrance of King Soma . . 75

Subrahma*n*yâ-litany 81

Âtithya, or Guest-meal to King Soma 85

Tânûnaptra, or Covenant of Tanûnapât . . . 93

Avântara-dîkshâ, or Intermediary Consecration . . 97

Upasada*h*, or Homages (sieges) 104

Preparation of Soma-altar with High-altar . . . 111

Agni-pra*n*ayana, or Leading Forward of the Fire to the High-altar 121

Construction of Sheds, and Preparation of Pressing-place and Dhish*n*ya-hearths 126

Havirdhâna, or Cart-shed 126

Uparava, or Sound-holes 135

Sadas, or Tent 140

Dhish*n*ya-hearths 148

Vaisar*g*ina-offerings, and Leading Forward of Agni and Soma (to Âgnîdhra) 155

Animal Sacrifice 162

Setting up of Sacrificial Stake 162

Slaying of Victim 178

Oblations:—

Fore-offerings with Âprî-verses 184

Offering of Omentum (vapâ) 190

Pa*s*u-puro*d*â*s*a, or Cake-offering 199

Cutting and offering of Flesh-portions . . 201

PAGE
Offering of gravy (vasâ) 205
Offering to Vanaspati 208
After-offerings 210
Purificatory Bath, &c. 215
Ekâdasinî, or Set of Eleven Victims . . 217
Vasatîvarî-water 222
B. Day of Soma-feast.
Prâtar-anuvâka, or Morning-prayer; and Preparatory Ceremonies 226
Prâtah-savana, or Morning-pressing:—
Preliminary Pressing 238
Nigrâbhyâ-water 242
Nigrâbha-formula 245

FOURTH KÂNDA.

Upâmsu-graha 248
Great Pressing:—
Antaryâma-graha 257
Aindravâyava-graha 265
Maitrâvaruna-graha 265
Âsvina-graha 272
Sukra- and Manthi-grahas 278
Âgrayana-graha 288
Ukthya-graha 292
Vaisvânara- and Dhruva-grahas 298
Viprud-homa, or Oblation of Drops 305
Bahishpavamâna-stotra 307
Âsvina-graha 312
Offering of Savanîya-purodâsâh 314
Ritu-grahas, or Libations to the Seasons . 318
Aindrâgna-graha 322
Vaisvadeva-graha 323
Âgya-sastra 325
Mâdhyandina-savana, or Midday-pressing 331
Sukra and Manthin; Âgrayana and Ukthya-grahas 332
Marutvatîya-grahas 334
Mâhendra-graha 338
Dakshinâ-homas 340

PAGE
Tr*i*tîya-savana, or Evening-pressing 350
Â*s*vina-graha 351
Âgraya*n*a-graha 355
Sâvitra-graha 357
Vai*s*vadeva-graha 359
Offering of *k*aru (rice-pap) to Soma 363
Pâtnîvata-graha 365
Âgnimâruta-*s*astra 369
Hâriyo*g*ana-graha 370
Concluding Ceremonies 374
Samish*t*aya*g*us 374
Avabh*ri*tha, or Purificatory Bath 378
Udayanîya-ish*t*i 386
Udavasânîyâ-ish*t*i, or Completing Oblation . . 389
Offering of Barren Cow 391
C. Additional Forms of Soma-sacrifice.
Sho*d*a*s*in 397
Dvâda*s*âha 402
Atigrâhyas 402
Avakâ*s*as 409
Trirâtra sahasradakshi*n*a 414
Dvâda*s*âha vyû*dh*a-*kh*andas 418
A*ms*u-graha 423
Gavâm ayanam 426
Mahâvratîya-graha 429
Brahma-sâman 434
Dîkshâ, or Consecration, for Sacrificial Sessions . 440
Sattrotthâna, or Rising from a Session . . . 447
*K*aturhot*ri*-formulas 452
Brahmodya 452

INDEX TO PARTS I AND II (VOLS. XII AND XXVI) . . 457
Additions and Corrections 474
Plan of Sacrificial Ground 475

Transliteration of Oriental Alphabets adopted for the Translations of the Sacred Books of the East . . 477

INTRODUCTION.

The contents of the third and fourth books of the *S*atapatha-brâhma*n*a form an important chapter of its dogmatic explanation of the sacrificial ceremonial. This portion of the work treats of the ordinary forms of the most sacred of Vedic sacrificial rites, the Soma-sacrifice. The exposition of the Soma-ritual also includes an account of the animal offering which, though it may be performed as an independent sacrifice, more usually constitutes an integral part of the Saumya-adhvara.

Since F. Windischmann, in his treatise 'Ueber den Somacultus der Arier' (1846), pointed out the remarkable similarity of conceptions prevalent among the ancient Indians and Iranians in regard to the Soma, both from a sacrificial and a mythological point of view, this subject has repeatedly engaged the attention of scholars. In A. Kuhn's masterly essay, 'Die Herabkunft des Feuers und des Göttertranks' (1859), the Soma-myth was thoroughly investigated, and its roots were traced far back into the Indo-European antiquity. Within the last few years the entire Rig-vedic conceptions regarding Soma have, for the first time, been subjected to a searching examination in M. A. Bergaigne's 'La Religion Védique.' This book forms an important contribution to the interpretation of the Vedic hymns; and though the combinations and theories put forth by the author may not always commend themselves to scholars generally, there can be no doubt that his enquiries exhibit a rare analytic faculty, and have yielded a mass of new and valuable suggestions.

Among the numerous features which the Vedic Âryans had in common with their Iranian kinsmen, and from which it is supposed that an intimate connection must have subsisted between these two easternmost branches of the Indo-European stock for some time after they had become separated from their western brethren, the Soma cult and myth are not the least striking. Both the Vedic soma and the Zend haoma—derived from the root su (Zend hu), 'to press, produce'—denote in the first place a spirituous liquor extracted from a certain plant, described as growing on the mountains; the words being then naturally applied to the plant itself. But the Rig-veda, not less than the Avesta, distinguishes between an earthly and a celestial Soma; and it is precisely the relation between these two, or the descent of the heavenly Soma to the world of men, which forms the central element of the Soma-myth. To the childlike intellect of the primitive Âryan which knew not how to account for the manifold strange and awe-inspiring phenomena of nature otherwise than by peopling the universe with a thousand divine agents, the potent juice of the Soma-plant which endowed the feeble mortal with godlike powers, and for a time freed him from earthly cares and troubles, seemed a veritable god, not less worthy of adoration than the wielder of the thunderbolt, the roaring wind, or the vivifying orb of day. The same magic powers are, upon the whole, ascribed to Soma by the Indian and Persian bards: to both of them he is the wise friend and mighty protector of his votary, the inspirer of heroic deeds of arms as well as of the flights of fancy and song, the bestower of health, long life, and even immortality. The divine personality of Soma, it is true, is, even for Vedic imagery, of an extremely vague and shadowy character; but it is difficult to see what plastic conception there could be of a deity whose chief activity apparently consists in mingling his fiery male nature with the teeming waters of the sky, and the swelling sap of plants. The principal cause, however, of the vagueness of Soma's personality, and the source of considerable difficulties in explaining many of the Vedic conceptions of this deity, is his twofold nature as a fiery liquor, or liquid fire,—that is to say, his fluid and his fiery or luminous nature.

The Soma, with whom the worshipper is chiefly concerned, is the Soma-plant, and the juice extracted from it for the holy service. This is the earthly Soma, or, so to speak, the Avatâr of the divine Soma. The latter, on the other hand, is a luminous deity, a source of light and life. In the Brâhma*n*as, Soma, in this respect, has become completely identified with the Moon, whose varying phases, and temporary obscuration at the time of new-moon, favoured the mystic notions of his serving as food[1] to the Gods and Fathers (Manes); and of his periodical descents to the earth, with the view of sexual union with the waters and plants, and his own regeneration[2]. Though this identification appears already clearly in several passages of the *Ri*k, Vedic scholars seem mostly inclined to refer this conception to a secondary stage of development[3]. According to Professor Roth, indeed, this identification would have no other mythological foundation than the coincidence of notions which finds its expression in the term i n d u[4] (commonly used for Soma, and in the later language for the moon), viz. as 'a drop' and 'a spark (drop of light).' This is not unlikely, but it does not of course help us to settle the point as to how that term came ultimately to be applied exclusively to the moon among heavenly luminaries. To the Vedic poet it is rather the sun that appears, if not identical, at any rate closely connected, with the divine Soma. The fact was first pointed out by Grassmann[5], who proposed to identify Pavamâna, the 'pure-streamed, sparkling' Soma, with the, apparently solar, deity Puemuno of the

---

[1] Or, as the vessel containing the divine Soma, the drink conferring immortality.

[2] See, for instance, *S*at. Br. I, 6, 4, 5 seq. Possibly also the shape of the 'horned moon' may have facilitated the attribution to that luminary of a bull-like nature such as is ascribed to Soma; though a similar attribution, it is true, is made in the case of other heavenly objects whose outward appearance offers no such points of comparison.

[3] M. A. Barth, The Vedic Religions, p. 27, on the other hand, is of opinion that this identification goes back to Indo-European times.

[4] St. Petersburg Dict. s. v. According to A. Kuhn, the two myths of the descent of Fire and of the divine Liquor spring from one and the same conception, whence the spark of fire is conceived as a drop. 'Herabkunft,' p. 161.

[5] Kuhn's Zeitsch. f. Vergl. Spr. XVI, p. 183 seq.

Iguvian tablets. M. Bergaigne has also carefully collected the passages of the *Ri*k in which Soma appears either compared or identified with the sun. Although a mere comparison of Indu-Soma with the sun can scarcely be considered sufficient evidence on this point, since such a comparison might naturally enough suggest itself even to one who had the identity of Soma and the moon in his mind, there still remain not a few passages where no such ambiguity seems possible. Somewhat peculiar are the relations between Soma and Sûrya's daughter (probably the Dawn), alluded to several times[1] in the *Ri*k. In one passage (IX, 1, 6) she is said to pass Sûrya through the perpetual filter (*s*a*s*vat vâra); whilst in another (IX, 113, 8) 'Sûrya's daughter brought the bull (Soma?), reared by Par*g*anya (the cloud); the Gandharvas seized him and put him, as sap, into the Soma (plant?).' A combination of this female bearer of Soma with the eagle (or falcon) who carried off Soma (IV, 27, &c.) seems to have supplied the form of the myth, current in the Brâhma*n*as, according to which Gâyatrî fetched Soma from heaven. The hymn X, 85[2], on the other hand, celebrates the marriage ceremony of Soma and Sûryâ, at which the two A*s*vins act as bride'smen, and Agni as the leader of the bridal procession to the bridegroom's home.

There are, however, other passages in the Rig-veda, in which Soma, so far from being identified with the sun, seems to be regarded as some sovereign power which originates or controls that luminary, as well as the other lights of heaven. Thus in Rig-veda IX, 61, 16 Soma is represented as producing (*g*anayan) the bright light belonging to all men; in IX, 97, 41 as producing the light in the sun (a*g*anayat sûrye *g*yotir indu*h*); in IX, 28, 5; 37, 4 as causing the sun to shine (ro*k*ayan); in IX, 86, 22; 107, 7 as making him rise (â-rohayan) in the sky; in IX, 63, 6

[1] M. Bergaigne, II, p. 249, identifies with Sûrya's daughter the girl (? Apâlâ) who, going to the water, found Soma, and took him home, saying, 'I'll press thee for Indra!' On this hymn see Prof. Aufrecht, Ind. Stud. IV, 1 seq.

[2] On this hymn see A. Weber, Ind. Stud. V, 178 seq.; J. Ehni, Zeitsch. der D. M. G. XXXIII, p. 166 seq.

the celestial waters, or the heavenly cows, too long confined by malicious demons in their mountain strongholds; or, after a time of tempest and gloom, one longed to see again the bright sky and the golden sunlight, to cheer life and ripen the crops: in which case it was a struggle for the recovery of the heavenly light.

The relation in which Soma stands to Indra is mainly that of the fiery beverage, the welcome draughts of which give the warrior god the requisite strength and nerve for battling with the demons of drought and darkness. Indra's favourite weapon is the thousand-spiked, iron or golden thunderbolt, the lightning. But inasmuch as it is Soma that enables Indra effectually to wield his weapon, the poet might, by a bold, yet perfectly natural, metaphor, identify the potent drink with the terrible bolt. This identification is indeed met with in several passages of the *Ri*k[1], notably in IX, 47, 3, 'When his song of praise is brought forth, then Soma, the powerful (indriya) liquor, becomes the thousand-fold-winning thunderbolt;' in IX, 72, 7, 'Indra's thunder-bolt, the bountiful (vibhûvasu) bull, the exhilarating Soma clarifies itself in a manner pleasing to the heart;' and in IX, 77, 1, 'This sweet (Soma) has roared in the tub, Indra's thunderbolt, more beautiful than the beautiful one[2].' Not less natural is the simile implied in epithets, properly applying to Indra,—such as 'v*ri*trahan' (slayer of V*ri*tra), and 'godâ' (cow-giver),—when applied to Soma, who helps him to make good those titles of his; just as one can understand their being occasionally applied to Agni, the sacrificial fire, as the medium through which the libations reach Indra. A similar kind of poetic figure is involved in passages representing Soma as exercising an influence, not on Indra himself, but on the weapons wielded by him[3];

[1] Cf. A. Bergaigne, Religion Védique, II, 253. In the Brâhma*n*as it is not Soma, but the pressing-stone, that is identified with the Va*g*ra.

[2] Prof. Ludwig proposes to read 'va*g*rât' instead of 'va*g*ro,' thus 'more beautiful than Indra's beautiful thunderbolt.' But even if we retain the received reading, 'vapusha*h*' might refer to the (real) thunderbolt; though, of course, it may also be taken as referring either to the sun, or to Agni, or to some other deity or heavenly object.

[3] Cf. A. Bergaigne, II, 251.

such as VIII, 76, 9, 'O Indra, drink the pressed Soma, . . . sharpening the thunderbolt with its strength;' or IX, 96, 12, where Soma is called upon to join Indra, and produce weapons for him (*g*anayâyudhâni); or VIII, 15, 7, where the Soma-cup (dhisha*n*â) is said to whet Indra's power, his daring and intelligence, as well as the desirable thunderbolt.

But, while most scholars will probably be content to apply this kind of interpretation to cases of an apparent identification of Soma and the Va*g*ra such as those referred to, M. Bergaigne is evidently in favour of their identity pure and simple. Now, it cannot be denied that the authors of some of those passages may really have intended to represent Soma as virtually or actually the same as the thunderbolt; but even if that were so, we should hardly be justified in assuming this identity to have been anything like a settled and universally accepted conception in the times of the hymns. There surely is some danger in treating a miscellaneous collection like the Rig-veda, as if it were a uniform and homogeneous production, and in generalizing from one or two isolated passages. In this respect I cannot help thinking that M. Bergaigne has often gone farther than many scholars will be prepared to follow him. Thus another of his favourite theories seems to be the ultimate identity of Soma and Agni. But close as the relations of these two deities undoubtedly are, and even admitting that they may occasionally have been the object of those syncretist tendencies which we see so often at work in the mythological speculations of the *Ri*shis, nevertheless I cannot but think that to the generality of Vedic poets Agni and Soma were perfectly distinct deities, as distinct from each other as the two visible objects which represent them on earth. Indeed, M. Bergaigne himself has to admit (I, 167) that, 'as the fire and beverage were in reality distinct on earth, this distinction was inevitably extended sometimes to their divine forms.' But if such is the case, and if they are actually invoked together in one and the same hymn, should one not think that even in those divine forms of theirs they must at least have been regarded as two different manifestations of the same divinity?

Soma makes his descent to the earth in showers of rain, amid thunder and lightning. Here a new problem presents itself: in this strife of elements, what is the exact phenomenon in which we are to recognise the divine Soma as temporarily embodied? It used to be taken for granted that the rain of the thunderstorm must be so regarded, being as it were the atmospheric counterpart of the earthly Soma drops, expressed from the juicy stalk and flowing into the vat. M. Bergaigne, however, has put forward the theory that it is not the rain, but the lightning, that really represents Soma; and has tried to show, with no little ingenuity, that several passages of the *Ri*k can only, or at any rate most naturally, be explained by the light of his theory. Now, according to an old myth, frequently alluded to in the hymns, Soma was brought down to the earth by an eagle or falcon (*s*yena). Thus we read in I, 93, 6, 'Mâtari*s*van has brought down the one (Agni) from the sky, and the *S*yena has churned the other (Soma) from the (celestial) rock.' A. Kuhn saw in this bird only another form of Indra who, in two passages (I, 32, 14; X, 99, 8), is indeed directly likened to a *S*yena. On the other hand, this identification is rendered doubtful by two other passages (I, 80, 2; IV, 18, 13), in which the *S*yena is represented as bringing the Soma to Indra himself. Here, then, is a veritable crux. M. Bergaigne does not hesitate to cut the knot by identifying the Soma-bearing bird with the lightning; and the lightning again being to him no other than Soma, the myth thus resolves itself into the rather commonplace fact that Soma takes himself down to the earth. He only needed to go a step further by identifying Soma, not only with Agni and the lightning, but also with Indra himself, and the phantasmagory would have been complete. Indeed, one of M. Bergaigne's disciples, M. Koulikovski, has already come very near supplying this deficiency, when he remarks (Revue de Linguistique, XVIII, p. 3), that in the hymn IV, 26 'we have to do with a twofold personage, composed of the attributes of Indra and Soma.'

Now, if this myth were a purely Indian one, one might be content to relegate it to the category of Vedic 'paradoxes' to the vindication of which M. Bergaigne declares himself ready to devote his life. But as there can be no reasonable doubt that the myth goes back to Indo-European times, and that its object is simply to account for the mysterious effect of spirituous liquor or the 'fire-water,' so to speak, I for one find it impossible to accept M. Bergaigne's explanation of this myth, at least so far as the identification of Soma and the lightning is concerned[1]. On the other hand, his theory undoubtedly receives a considerable amount of support from the fact that the Soma is frequently compared with the *S*yena. But we saw that the same term is applied to Indra, as it also is to the Maruts (X, 92, 6), to the A*s*vins (IV, 74, 9; VIII, 73, 4), and to Sûrya (V, 45, 9); and there is in my opinion no evidence to show that this comparison has any connection with the myth which makes the fiery liquor to be brought down by a *S*yena. Moreover, wherever that comparison occurs, it undoubtedly applies to the Pavamâna, or the drops or streams of Soma flowing through the filter into the vat; and I can see no reason why we should not consider the showers of rain as the exact counterpart of the clarifying Soma. But, of course, the real divine Soma is not the rain-drop itself, any more than he is the drop of juice expressed from the Soma-plant; but he is the spark of celestial fire enclosed in the drop. It would seem, then, that, as the masses of cloud overspread the sky, Soma, the heavenly light, is conceived as entering into union with the celestial cows or waters, released by the thunderbolt from their mountain keep, and coming down with them to the earth.

[1] For the same reason I find it impossible to accept M. Bergaigne's interpretation of the hymn IV, 27, put forward at the end of his work (vol. iii, p. 322 seq.). According to that interpretation, Soma, in the first verse, declares that he himself flew forth from his prison as an eagle; and then, in the second verse—as it were reproving those who might imagine the eagle to be a different being from himself—he adds, 'It was not he (the eagle) that bore me away with ease, but I triumphed by my own cleverness and bravery!' I am afraid this critical specimen of the feathered tribe will not find many admirers among

But while I find it impossible, as regards the myth of the Soma-bearing bird, to identify with M. Bergaigne the winged bearer (probably the lightning) with its burden, the Soma; the descent of the fiery god is pictured in various other ways, and it might still be possible that one or other poet had conceived of the bull-like Soma, as the lightning, uniting with the heavenly cows in their earthward course, so that before reaching the earth the rain-drops would be impregnated with Soma's essence, and would, in fact, be of the same nature as the Soma-juice. I am not prepared, therefore, entirely to reject the identification of Soma with the lightning; only I do not think that any one of the crucial passages adduced by M. Bergaigne in favour of that identity necessarily requires the interpretation he proposes. Thus, in IX, 41, 3, 'The sound of the mighty Pavamâna (the clarifying Soma) is heard like that of the rain: the lightnings pass in the sky,' it surely seems rather far-fetched to take the lightning, instead of the rain, to be the object with which Soma is compared, merely because in the same hymn Soma is also compared with the sun and the heavenly river Rasâ. The same may be said of IX, 108, 11, 'That joy-pouring (mada-*k*yut) thousand-streamed bull they have milked out from the sky,' and several other passages. The verse IX, 87, 8, divo na vidyut stanayanty abhrai*h*, somasya te pavata indra dhârâ, 'Thy stream of Soma, O Indra, clarifies itself, as (does) the thundering lightning of the sky by means of the clouds,' is more favourable to

prosaic Sanskritists. I should prefer, with Prof. Roth, to read 'nir ádîyat' instead of 'nir adîyam,' unless it were possible to read '*s*yena*g*avásâ' instead of '*s*yenó *g*avásâ.' M. Koulikovski, in the paper referred to, throws the hymns IV, 26 and 27 together, and takes them as a sort of mytho-critical controversy between the god Soma and some other person (perhaps the author himself), advocating two different versions of the Soma-myth, viz. Soma contending that it was himself who brought the divine plant, while his interlocutor ('who has the last word in the hymn') maintains that it was brought by a falcon. Thus, according to this scholar, the falcon was already (!) distinguished from Soma; and these two hymns 'are, as it were, an echo of a religious, or rather mythological dispute, which had divided the theologians of the Vedic epoch.' Perhaps Prof. Oldenberg's theory of Âkhyâta-hymns, or detached pieces of poetry connected by prose narratives, might have a chance with these hymns.

M. Bergaigne's view, as may also be the doubtful passage, V, 84, 3, yat te abhrasya vidyuto divo varshanti v*ri*sh*t*aya*h*, 'When the rains of the cloud rain thee (O earth) lightnings from the sky (?).' As regards VII, 69, 6, addressed to the A*s*vins, 'Come, ye two men, to our libations this day, like two thirsty bulls to the lightning,' M. Bergaigne (I, 168) thinks that the identification of Soma with the lightning can alone explain this passage; since it would be impossible to imagine that the two bulls could anticipate the falling of rain from the appearance of the lightning. Though a poetic figure like this hardly bears such critical handling, perhaps M. Bergaigne will allow me to ask whether, if the passage had read, 'Come ye hither to our libations, like two bulls to the thunder [1],' he would have thought it so very bold a figure for a Vedic poet to use?

The most important of all passages, however, undoubtedly is IX, 84, 3: â yo gobhi*h* s*rig*yata oshadhîshu . . . . â vidyutâ pavate dhârayâ suta*h*, indra*m* somo mâdayan daivya*m g*anam. M. Bergaigne translates (I, 172) the first pâda by 'Lui qui est répandu avec les vaches (i. e. the rain-drops) dans les plantes,' which, of course, fits either view equally well; the only question being, whether Soma is already united with the rain-drops when they are poured forth by the clouds, or whether, in the shape of lightning, he is still separate from them. The third pâda, M. Bergaigne remarks (I, 170), may be boldly (hardiment) translated by 'Il se clarifie, exprimé en un torrent qui est l'éclair.' This rendering, if correct, would doubtless settle the point; but to my mind it is not only a very doubtful, but a highly improbable explanation. What I believe to be the true interpretation of the passage had been given by Prof. Ludwig two years before the publication of M. Bergaigne's volume, viz. 'Expressed in a stream, he clarifies himself by the lightning—Soma who exhilarates (or inebriates) Indra and the divine race.' It will be seen that this alters the case completely. The lightning would be

[1] Cp. IX, 100, 3: 'Send forth mind-yoked thought, as the thunder sends forth rain.'

compared with the filter of white sheep's wool, through which the Soma-juice percolates into the vat. The same simile, in my opinion, is implied wherever the formula pavate (â) v*ri*sh*t*im, 'he clarifies himself into rain,' is used (IX, 49, 1; 3; 65, 3; 24; 96, 14; 108, 10). And, in truth, the simile seems to me a very striking one; but we must not, of course, think of single flashes of lightning such as we are accustomed to in our northern climes (and as are doubtless implied in the Vedic conception of the Va*g*ra or thunderbolt), but of that continuous and widespread electric illumination (vi-dyut) which forms a characteristic feature of the monsoon, when the showers of rain seem to flow through an immense space of light[1].

---

[1] For a description of this phenomenon in the districts where we must imagine the Vedic poets to have composed their hymns, see Elphinstone, Account of the Kingdom of Cabool, p. 126 seq.

I cannot forbear here to quote a few extracts from a graphic description of the setting in of the monsoon in India proper, given in the Rev. H. Caunter's Oriental Annual (1834):—'There was a slight haze upon the distant waters which seemed gradually to thicken, although not to a density sufficient to refract the rays of the sun, which still flooded the broad sea with one unvarying mass of glowing light .... Towards the afternoon, the aspect of the sky began to change; the horizon gathered blackness, and the sun, which had risen so brightly, had evidently culminated in darkness, and to have his splendour veiled from human sight by a long, gloomy period of storm and turbulence. Masses of heavy clouds appeared to rise from the sea, black and portentous, accompanied by sudden gusts of wind, that suddenly died away, being succeeded by an intense, death-like stillness, as if the air were in a state of utter stagnation, and its vital properties arrested. It seemed no longer to circulate, until again agitated by the brief but mighty gusts which swept fiercely along, like the giant heralds of the sky. Meanwhile the lower circle of the heavens looked a deep brassy red, from the partial reflection of the sunbeams upon the thick clouds, which had now everywhere overspread it .... From the house which we occupied we could behold the setting in of the monsoon in all its grand and terrific sublimity. The wind, with a force which nothing could resist, bent the tufted heads of the tall, slim cocoa-nut trees almost to the earth, flinging the light sand into the air in eddying vortices, until the rain had either so increased its gravity, or beaten it into a mass, as to prevent the wind from raising it. The pale lightning streamed from the clouds in broad sheets of flame, which appeared to encircle the heavens as if every element had been converted into fire, and the world was on the eve of a general conflagration, whilst the peal, which instantly followed, was like the explosion of a gunpowder-magazine, or the discharge of artillery in the gorge of a mountain, where the repercussion of surrounding hills multiplies with terrific energy its deep and astounding echoes. The heavens seemed to be

The striking coincidences between the Vedic Agnishtoma and the Homa ceremony of the Pârsîs, pointed out by Martin Haug (Ait. Br. I, p. 59 seq.), leave no doubt as to the complete development of the Soma-ritual in its essential features before the separation of the Indo-Iranians. The exact identity of the plant from which their sacred liquor was prepared is still somewhat doubtful. An official inquiry which has been set on foot in consequence of two papers published by Prof. Roth (Journal of Germ. Or. Soc. 1881 and 1883), and translated by Mr. C. J. Lyall, secretary to the Chief Commissioner of Assam, and which, it is understood, is now carried on, on the part of the Government of India, by Dr. Aitchison, botanist to the Afghan Boundary Commission, will probably ere long settle the matter once for all. The appearance of the first official blue-book on the subject has already led to a renewed discussion of the matter, in the columns of a weekly journal[1], in which Profs. Max Müller and R. v. Roth, as well as several distinguished botanists, especially Drs. J. G. Baker and W. T. Thiselton Dyer, have taken part. Of especial interest in this discussion is a letter[2], by Mr. A. Houttum-Schindler, dated Teheran, December 20, 1884, in which an account is given of the plant from which the present Pârsîs of Kermân and Yezd obtain their Hûm juice, and which they assert to be the very same

one vast reservoir of flame, which was propelled from its voluminous bed by some invisible but omnipotent agency, and threatened to fling its fiery ruin upon everything around. In some parts, however, of the pitchy vapour by which the skies were by this time completely overspread, the lightning was seen only occasionally to glimmer in faint streaks of light, as if struggling, but unable, to escape from its prison, igniting, but too weak to burst, the impervious bosoms of those capacious magazines in which it was at once engendered and pent up. So heavy and continuous was the rain, that scarcely anything, save those vivid bursts of light which nothing could arrest or resist, was perceptible through it . . . . Day after day the same scene was repeated with somewhat less violence, though at intervals the might of the hurricane was truly appalling . . . . The breaking up of the monsoon is frequently even more violent, if possible, than its setting in, and this happened to be the case during the first season after my arrival in India. It was truly stupendous, and I shall never cease to remember it to the latest moment of my existence.'

[1] The Academy, Oct. 25, 1884—Feb. 14, 1885.

[2] Ibid., Jan. 31, 1885.

as the Haoma of the Avesta. The Hûm shrub, according to this description, grows to the height of four feet, and consists of circular fleshy stalks (the thickest being about a finger thick) of whitish colour, with light brown streaks. The juice was milky, of a greenish white colour, and had a sweetish taste. Mr. Schindler was, however, told that, after being kept for a few days, it turned sour and, like the stalks, became yellowish brown. The stalks break easily at the joints, and then form small cylindrical pieces. They had lost their leaves, which are said to be small and formed like those of the jessamine. This description, according to the above naturalists, would seem to agree tolerably well with the *Sarcostemma* (akin to the common milk-weed), or some other group of *Asclepiads*, such as the *Periploca aphylla* which, as Mr. Baker states, has been traced by Dr. Haussknecht to 3000 feet in the mountains of Persia, and, according to Dr. Aitchison, is common also in Afghanistan. A quotation from a medical Sanskrit work, to which attention was drawn by Prof. Max Müller many years ago, states that, 'the creeper, called Soma, is dark, sour, without leaves, milky, fleshy on the surface; it destroys (or causes) phlegm, produces vomiting, and is eaten by goats.' The foul, sour smell of the Soma-juice is also alluded to in our Brâhma*n*a (see the present volume, p. 266). According to Prof. Spiegel[1], the Pârsîs of Bombay obtain their Homa from Kermân, whither they send their priests from time to time to get it. The plant at present used by the Hindu priests of the Dekhan, on the other hand, according to Haug, is not the Soma of the Vedas, but appears to belong to the same order. 'It grows (he informs us, Ait. Br. II, 489) on hills in the neighbourhood of Poona to the height of about four to five feet, and forms a kind of bush, consisting of a certain number of shoots, all coming from the same root; their stem is solid like wood; the bark grayish; they are without leaves; the sap appears whitish, has a very stringent taste, is bitter, but not sour: it is a very nasty drink, and has some intoxicating effect. I tasted it several times, but

[1] Eranische Alterthumskunde, III, p. 572.

it was impossible for me to drink more than some teaspoonfuls.' In fact, several varieties of Sarcostemma or Asclepiads[1], somewhat different from those of Persia and Afghanistan, which are not to be found so far south, seem to have been, and indeed seem still to be, made use of for the Soma-sacrifice. And notwithstanding the objections raised by Dr. G. Watt, in his useful 'Notes,' appended to the translation of Professor Roth's papers, every probability seems to me to be in favour of the identity of the original Soma-plant with the shrub, the stalks of which are used by the Pârsîs in preparing their Hûm juice, or with some other plant of the same genus. It certainly would seem to have been a plant with soft, succulent stems. Dr. Watt remarks, 'We know of no instance of a succulent plant retaining, for weeks or months, its sap within isolated twigs, and, indeed, we can recall but few plants which could withstand, even for a day or two, the dry climate of India, so as to retain the sap within their isolated and cut twigs.' But, though at the time of the Vedic hymns fresh and juicy plants were probably used for the preparation of the sacred drink, in later times, when the plants had to be conveyed some considerable distance into India, the withered and shrunk plants were apparently found, with the admixture of water and other ingredients, to serve the same purpose. For we know from the description given in the Sûtras, that water was poured on the plants previously to their being beaten with the pressing-stones. This moistening or steeping is called âpyâyanam, or 'the making (the plants) swell.' After being then well beaten and bruised, they were thrown into the vat, or rather trough, partly filled with water, and were pressed out with the hand. Dr. Watt thinks Professor Roth ought rather to have published briefly the leading passages in the hymns descriptive of the plant, from which naturalists might have drawn their own conclusions. One might as well ask a Hebrew

[1] Especially *Sarcostemma intermedium, S. brevistigma,* and *S. viminale* (or Asclepias acida). See R. Roth, Zeitsch. der D. Morg. Ges. vol. xxxv, p. 681 seq.

scholar to give accurate descriptions of the 'lily of the valley' to enable the botanist to identify and classify the lovely flower which delighted the heart of ki g Solomon. It is exactly the want of an accurate knowledge of the nature of the Soma-plant which prevents the Vedic scholar from being able to understand some of the few material allusions to it. Thus the term a*m*s*u, commonly applied to the Soma-plant, used to be taken to mean simply 'plant' or 'sprig, shoot;' but Professor Roth seems now inclined, perhaps rightly, to take it as referring to the internode, or cylindrical piece between two joints of the stem. The substitutes approved of by the *S*atapatha-brâhma*n*a, in case no genuine Soma-plants can be obtained, will be found enumerated at pp. 421-422 of the present volume. A description of these plants, so far as they have been identified, is given in Professor Roth's paper.

I cannot conclude these remarks without expressing my hearty thanks to those scholars who have done me the honour of reviewing the first volume of this work. To Professor Whitney I feel especially indebted for his most careful examination of my translation, and the searching, yet appreciative, criticism he has been good enough to apply to it. I shall feel content, if the present volume finds at least one reader as conscientious and painstaking. While I agree with most of Prof. Whitney's suggestions[1], there are one or two points raised by him, and these perhaps of the more important, on which I have been unable to take his view; and as some of these points involve renderings adhered to in the present volume, I take the opportunity here briefly to advert to them.

The most important of these points probably is my rendering of the term kapâla by 'potsherd,' instead of 'cup, dish,' as proposed by Prof. Whitney. Instead of speaking of a sacrificial cake on eleven or twelve potsherds, we are to call it a cake on so many cups or dishes. The term

[1] American Journal of Philology, vol. iii, pp. 391-410; Proceedings of the American Oriental Society, October 1882, p. xiv seq.

'potsherd' no doubt is somewhat awkward, and, had it been possible, I should have preferred to use the simple obsolete word 'shard' or 'sherd' for it; but I decidedly object to either 'cup' or 'dish.' I gather from his suggestion, that we take entirely different views of the purpose and nature of the kapâla. I have to reject the proposed renderings for the very reason for which they commend themselves to Prof. Whitney, namely, because they imply so many vessels complete in themselves. He asks, whether I suppose 'that the Brahmans made their offerings on fragments of broken pottery?' Well, I certainly believe that the kapâlas are meant to represent the fragments of a broken dish. The sacrificial cake is to be baked on a dish, but for symbolic reasons this dish is supposed to be broken up into a number of pieces or kapâlas. The symbolic significance of this seems to be a twofold one. On the one hand, the dish is to resemble the human skull. Hence we read *S*at. Br. I, 2, 1, 2, 'The cake is the head of Ya*gñ*a (the sacrifice, and symbolically the sacrificer himself); for those potsherds (kapâlâni) are what the skull-bones (*s*îrsh*n*a*h* kapâlâni) are, and the ground rice is nothing else than the brain.' On the other hand, the kapâlas are usually arranged (see Part I, p. 34, note) in such a manner as to produce a fancied resemblance to the (upper[1]) shell of the tortoise, which is a symbol of the sky, as the tortoise itself represents the universe. Thus with cakes on a single kapâla, the latter is indeed a complete dish. In the same way the term kapâla, in the singular, is occasionally applied to the skull, as well as to the upper and the lower case of the tortoise, e. g. *S*at. Br. VII, 5, 1, 2: 'That lower kapâla of it (the tortoise) is this world, for that (kapâla) is firmly established, and firmly established is this world; and that upper (kapâla) is yonder sky, for it has its ends turned down, and so has that sky its ends turned down; and that which is between is that atmosphere: verily that same (tortoise) represents these worlds.' More usually, however, the term is applied to the single

[1] Or perhaps the lower shell which represents the earth, being as it were a symbol of firmness and safety.

bones of the skull (and the plates of the tortoise-case). Hence the Medinî says (lânta 71), kapâlo 'strî *s*iro-'sthni syâd, gha*t*âde*h* *s*akale, vra*g*e,—kapâla may be used in the sense of 'head-bone,' in that of 'fragment of a pot,' &c., and in the sense of 'collection.'

Professor Whitney takes exception to my occasionally translating âtman by 'body,'—an inaccuracy, he remarks, that might easily be avoided. I do not quite understand on what grounds he objects to this rendering. The original meaning of âtman doubtless is (breath) 'self, soul;' but surely there can be no question that it also commonly means 'body, trunk,' in contradistinction to the limbs, wings, &c. Thus we read *S*at. Br. IV, 1, 2, 25, 'The sacrifice is fashioned like a bird: the Upâ*ms*u and Antaryâma are its wings, and the Upâ*ms*usavana is its body[1].'

My rendering of 'videgho ha mâthava*h*' (I, 4, 1, 10) by 'Mâthava the (king of) Videgha,' instead of 'Videgha (the) Mâthava,' is rightly objected to. Indeed, I had already taken occasion, in the introduction to the same volume (I, p. xli, note 4), to make that correction.

Prof. Whitney's remarks on 'yûpena yopayitvâ' are adverted to at p. 36, note 1 of the present volume; as are also those on 'ed' at p. 265, note 2. In regard to the latter point he rather does me wrong by supposing that I apparently regarded the particle (or particles) 'ed' (for which the Kâ*n*va text seems to read 'â hi') as a verb-form from the root 'i,' to go. The fact is that I followed Prof. Weber (Ind. Stud. IX, p. 249) in taking it to be a popular expression, with a verb of motion understood, somewhat in the sense of the German 'hin;' e.g. 'Shall we go there?'—'Hin denn!' i.e. 'Let us go then.'

My translation of II, 4, 2, 19 is not quite approved of by

[1] Professor Max Müller has been kind enough to send me a number of passages from Upanishads and Âra*n*yakas, in which âtman has the sense of 'body, trunk,' and is usually explained in the commentaries by *s*arîra (âtmâna*h* = *s*arîrâvayavâ*h*, B*ri*hadâr. Up. I, 1, 2, 7). The adverb adhyâtmam, he remarks, always means 'with reference to the body;' cf. Taitt. Up. I, 7; *S*at. Br. IV, 1, 3, 1, the present volume, p. 265, note 1.

Prof. Whitney. There offering is made severally to the sacrificer's grandfather and great-grandfather with the formula 'N. N., this for thee!' to which some authorities add 'and for those who come after thee.' This addition is rejected by the author on the ground that 'svayam vai teshâm saha yeshâm saha,' which I translated by 'since he himself is one of those to whom [it would be offered] in common.' Prof. Whitney takes exception to this, remarking that in that case, the phrase 'and those who (come) after thee' might be added, without any reason to the contrary. But he forgets one important point, namely, that it would be a fatal thing for the sacrificer in this way to associate himself with the departed ancestors, and even make offering to himself along with them: it would simply mean that 'he would straightway go to yonder world,' that he would not live his fulness of days. The clause under discussion is elliptic, its literal translation being 'Himself surely (is) of those withal of whom (he is) withal.' This may either be taken in the sense in which I took it (see also St. Petersb. Dict. s.v. saha); or in a general way, 'He surely is one of those with whom he associates himself;' i.e. he would himself be a dead man.

In the legend of Manu and the Flood (I, 8, 1, 1 seq.) I find it impossible to accept Prof. Delbrück's conjecture, which Prof. Whitney thinks the best and only acceptable one, viz. that (in par. 4) the sentence 'sasvad ha ghasha âsa, sa hi gyeshtham vardhate' is an interpolated gloss. My reason for not accepting it is the fact that the passage occurs likewise in the Kânva recension, and is thus authenticated for so comparatively early a period that the difficulty of accounting for the interpolation might be even greater than that of the interpretation of the passage itself. Professor Ludwig, in his kindly notice in 'Göttinger Gel. Anz.' 1883, proposes to take sasvat in the sense of πάντως: 'It quite so (i.e. in accordance with the prediction) became a large fish.' Prof. Max Müller has again translated this legend in his 'India, what can it teach us?' p. 134 seq., where he renders this passage by 'He became soon a large fish (*gh*asha), for such a fish grows largest.' I am still inclined to take *gh*asha as the name of some kind of fish, real or mythic.

Professor Whitney once more discusses the vexed question as to the real meaning of '*G*âtávedas,' and thinks the translation 'Wesen-kenner,' 'being-knower,' or 'he who knoweth [all] beings' to be unacceptable. He remarks that 'The word may, indeed, fairly be regarded as an obscure one: that is to say, it is very strange that an appellation so frequently applied to Agni should not have its meanings distinctly pointed out, either by its applicableness, or by parallel expressions used in the descriptions of the same god or in ascriptions made to him; but no such explanation has been found obtainable from the Vedic writings.' It is no doubt a fact that at the time of Yâska—who (7, 19) proposes five different derivations of the term, the first of which is the one given above, viz. *g*âtâni veda, 'he knows (the things) that are born'—the real meaning of the compound was unknown; and even at the time of the hymns the epithet seems to have been understood in different ways. That the meaning 'knower of beings' was, at any rate, one of those commonly assigned to '*G*âtavedas' by the Vedic poets, seems to me, however, sufficiently manifest from a number of parallel expressions used in reference to Agni, such as Rig-veda VI, 15, 13, vi*s*vâ veda *g*animâ *g*âtavedâ*h*[1], '*G*âtavedas knows all races (or existences);' I, 70, 1, â daivyâni vratâ *k*ikitvân â manushyasya *g*anasya *g*anma, 'he who minds the divine ordinances, and the race of the human kind;' ib. 3, devânâm *g*anma martâ*ms* *k*a vidvân, 'knowing the race of gods and the men;' I, 189, 1, vi*s*vâni vayunâni vidvân, 'knowing all works;' ib. 7, tvam tân agna ubhayân v vidvân veshi, &c. On the other hand, in *S*at. Br. IX, 5, 1, 68, the term is explained by *g*âta*m* *g*âta*m* vindate; he takes possession of being after being, or of whatsoever is born. How easily terms such as *G*âtavedas and Wesen-

[1] See Grassmann, Wörterbuch s. v.; M. Bergaigne, III, 334, takes this passage to supply the etymology of the word.

kenner (knower of beings) may assume different meanings, may be seen from Mr. Peile's remark (Notes on the Nalopâkhyânam, p. 23), '*G*âtavedas, the Vedic epithet of Agni, is described as the "knower of the essence" (*g*âta), Grassmann, Dict. s. v.'

For the first chapter of the third book, treating of the ceremony of consecration, I have had the advantage of availing myself of the German translation, published by Dr. B. Lindner in his pamphlet, 'Die Dîkshâ,' Leipzig, 1878.

*S*ATAPATHA-BRÂHMA*N*A.

THIRD KÂ*ND*A.

THE AGNISH*T*OMA.

THE DÎKSHÂ, OR CONSECRATION.

FIRST ADHYÂYA. FIRST BRÂHMA*N*A.

1. They choose a place of worship. Let them choose (the place) which lies highest, and above which no other part of the ground rises[1]; for it was from thence that the gods ascended to heaven, and he who is consecrated indeed ascends to the gods. He thus sacrifices on a place of worship frequented by the gods; but were any other part of the ground to rise above it, he would indeed be lowered while sacrificing: let them therefore choose (the place) which lies highest.

2. While being high, that place should be even; and being even, it should be firm; and being firm, it should incline towards the east, since the east is the quarter of the gods; or else it should incline

[1] Abhi-*s*î, 'to lie or rise above,' with Sây. Dr. Lindner takes bhûme*h* as abl., and translates 'whereon nothing but earth lies.' The Kâ*n*va rec. has bhûme*h* (gen.) likewise in the preceding clause: 'tad yad eva varshish*th*am bhûmes tad eva devaya*g*ana*m* syâd yatrânyad bhûmer nâbhi*s*ayîteto vai devâ, &c.' The gods evidently ascended to heaven from the highest spot of the earth, and so is the sacrificer to choose the highest available place. See Kâty. VII, 1, 11 scholl.; Lâ*t*y. S. I, 1, 17, 'na *k*âsya sthalataram (higher place) adûre syât.'

towards the north, since the north is the quarter of men. It should rise somewhat towards the south, that being the quarter of the Fathers. Were it to incline towards the south, the sacrifice would quickly go to yonder world; but in this way the sacrificer lives long: let it therefore rise somewhat towards the south.

3. Let not the measure of the sacrificial ground be exceeded on the east side, since such an excess would be in favour of his spiteful enemy. It may be so in the south, and also in the north; but that place of worship alone is thoroughly efficient where the measure of the sacrificial ground is exceeded in the west; for to him (who possesses such a one) the higher[1] worship of the gods readily inclines. So much as to the place of worship.

4. Now Yâgñavalkya spake,—'We went to choose a place of worship for Vârshnya[2]. Sâtyayagña then said, "Verily, this whole earth is divine: on whatever part thereof one may sacrifice (for any

[1] Or 'subsequent;' a play on the word 'uttara,' which has the meanings 'upper (superior), later, and left (north).' Dr. Lindner takes it in the sense of 'from the north.' Possibly uttara also refers to the Soma-altars (uttara vedi and uttara-vedi) to be prepared later on (see III, 5, 1, 1 seq.) on the eastern part of the sacrificial ground.

[2] The Kânva text reads,—Accordingly Yâgñavalkya spake, 'Vârshna intended to sacrifice (ayakshyata). Thus we went (ayama!) to look for a place of worship.' He who is known as Sâtyayagñi said, 'Verily, this whole earth is divine: a place of worship there is wheresoever one sacrifices on it, after enclosing it with a yagus.' And thus indeed he thought, but the officiating priests doubtless constitute the (real) place (medium) of worship: where wise (priests) perform the sacrifice in due form, there alone no failure takes place. That (other definition) is not the characteristic of the place of worship. (Without final iti.)

one), after enclosing (and consecrating) it with a sacrificial formula, there is a place of worship."

5. 'It is, however, the officiating priests that constitute the place (or medium) of worship: wheresoever wise and learned Brâhmans, versed in sacred lore, perform the sacrifice, there no failure takes place: that (place of worship) we consider the nearest (to the gods)[1].'

6. On this (ground) they erect either a hall or a shed, with the top-beams running from west to east[2]; for the east is the quarter of the gods, and from the east westwards the gods approach men: that is why one offers to them while standing with his face towards the east.

7. For this reason one must not sleep with his

[1] That is to say, one who employs such skilled Brâhmans for his officiating priests (*ri*tvi*g*) may use sacrificial ground of any description. Kâty. VII, 1, 18.

[2] Prâ*k*îna-va*ms*a (prâg-va*ms*a, K.). The 'va*ms*as' are the horizontal beams supported by the four corner-posts. In the first place two cross-beams are fastened on the corner-posts, to serve as the lintels of the eastern and western doors. Across them tie-beams are then laid, running from west to east, on which mats are spread by way of a roof or ceiling. The term 'prâ*k*îna-va*ms*a' refers to these upper beams (upari-va*ms*a), and especially to the central beam (p*ri*sh*th*a-va*ms*a or madhyavala) the ends of which rest on the middle of the lintels of the eastern and western doors; cf. Sâya*n*a on Taitt. S. I, 2, 1 (vol. i, pp. 279, 286); Kâty. VII, 1, 20 scholl. Inside the Prâ*k*îna-va*ms*a there is the Âhavanîya fire immediately facing the east door; the Gârhapatya fire facing the west door; between the two the altar; and south of the latter the Dakshi*n*âgni. The shed (vimita) is to be erected on the back (west) part of the sacrificial ground, after the roots have been dug up. It is described as a square structure of ten (or twelve) cubits, somewhat higher in front than at the back; with doors on each side (except, optionally, on the north). The *s*âlâ, or hall, is to measure twenty cubits by ten. Kâty. VII, 1, 19–24 comm.

head towards the west, lest he should sleep stretching (his legs) towards the gods. The southern quarter belongs to the Fathers; and the western one to the snakes; and that faultless one is the one where the gods ascended (to heaven); and the northern quarter belongs to men. Hence in human (practice) a hall or shed is constructed with the top-beams running from south to north, because the north is the quarter of men. It is only for a consecrated, not for an unconsecrated person that it is (constructed) with the top-beams running from west to east.

8. They enclose it on every side, lest it should rain upon (the sacrificer, while being consecrated): this, at least, is (the reason for doing so in) the rainy season[1]. He who is consecrated, truly draws nigh to the gods, and becomes one of the deities. Now the gods are secreted from men, and secret also is what is enclosed on every side: this is why they enclose it on every side.

9. Not every one may enter it, but only a Brâhman, or a Râganya, or a Vaisya, for these are able to sacrifice.

10. Let him not commune with every one; for he who is consecrated draws nigh to the gods, and becomes one of the deities. Now the gods do not commune with every one, but only with a Brâhman, or a Râganya, or a Vaisya; for these are able to sacrifice. Should there be occasion for him to converse with a Sûdra, let him say to one of those, 'Tell this one so and so! tell this one so and so!'

[1] (?) Iti nv eva varshâh. The same particles occur III, 2, 1, 11. The Kânva text has,—'lest it should freeze in winter, lest it should pour in the rainy season, and lest there should be burning heat in summer.'

This is the rule of conduct for the consecrated in such a case.

11. In the first place, having taken the two churning-sticks in his hand, he approves of the hall. Taking hold of the chief post of the front (east) side, he pronounces this sacrificial formula (Vâg. S. IV, 1), 'We have come to this place of worship on earth, wherein all the gods delighted.' Thereby that (place of worship) of his becomes acceptable to all the gods, as well as to the learned Brâhmans versed in sacred lore; and that (place of worship) of his, which those Brâhmans versed in sacred lore see with their eyes, becomes acceptable to them.

12. And when he says, 'Wherein all the gods delighted,' thereby it becomes acceptable for him to all the gods. 'Crossing over by means of the *rik* and sâman, and by the yagus;' by means of the *rik* and sâman, and the yagus, indeed, they reach the end of the sacrifice: 'May I reach the end of the sacrifice!' he thereby says. 'May we rejoice in increase of substance and in sap!' Increase of substance doubtless means abundance, and abundance means prosperity: he thereby invokes a blessing. 'May we rejoice in sap,' he says, because people say of one who enjoys prosperity and attains to the highest distinction, that 'he rejoices in sap;' therefore he says, 'May we rejoice in sap!'

SECOND BRÂHMANA.

1. Let him perform the rite of consecration (dîkshâ)[1] in the afternoon. Previously to the shaving

[1] The rite described in the following paragraphs is called apsudîkshâ, or 'consecration in water.'

of his hair and beard he may eat of what he likes, or whatever comes to hand; for hereafter his food consists of fast-milk (vrata) only. But, if he does not care to eat, he need not eat anything.

2. Thereupon they enclose a place[1] north of the hall, and place a vessel of water in it. Beside this the barber takes up his position. He (the sacrificer) then shaves his hair and beard, and cuts his nails. For impure, indeed, is that part of man where water does not reach him. Now at the hair and beard, and at the nails the water does not reach him: hence when he shaves his hair and beard, and cuts his nails, he does so in order that he may be consecrated after becoming pure.

3. Now some shave themselves all over, in order that they may be consecrated after becoming pure all over; but let him not do this. For even by shaving the hair of his head and his beard, and by cutting his nails, he becomes pure: let him therefore shave only the hair of his head and his beard, and cut his nails.

4. In the first place he cuts his nails, first of the right hand—for in human (practice) those of the left hand (are cut) first, but with the gods in this manner. First (he cuts those) of the thumbs—for in human (practice) those of the little fingers (are cut) first, but with the gods in this manner.

5. He first passes (the comb) through his right whisker—for in human (practice they comb) first the left whisker, but with the gods in this manner.

6. His right whisker he moistens first, with the text, 'May these divine waters be propitious

[1] It is to be square and covered in on all sides with mats, and with a door on the east side. Kâty. VII, 1, 25 scholl.

unto me! The reason why he says, 'May these divine waters be propitious unto me,' is this: the waters are a thunderbolt, for the waters are indeed a thunderbolt; hence wherever these waters flow they produce a hollow, and whatever they come near that they destroy (lit. burn up). Hereby, then, he appeases that same thunderbolt; and thus appeased, that thunderbolt does not injure him. This is why he says, 'May these divine waters be propitious unto me!'

7. Thereupon he lays a stalk of sacrificial grass on (the hair of the whisker), with the text, 'O plant, protect me!' For the razor is a thunderbolt, and thus that thunderbolt, the razor, does not injure him. Thereto he applies the razor, with the text, 'O knife, injure him not!' for the razor is a thunderbolt, and thus that thunderbolt, the razor, does not injure him.

8. Having cut off (part of the stalk and hair), he throws it into the vessel of water. Silently he moistens the left whisker; silently he lays the stalk of grass on it; and having silently applied the razor thereto and cut through (it and the hair), he throws them into the vessel of water.

9. He then hands the razor to the barber, and the latter shaves off the hair and beard. When he has shaved the hair and beard[1],—

[1] The text has, 'when he shaves (vapati) the hair and beard [when he shaves himself (vapate), K.] he bathes.' According to this it would seem that he does not bathe unless he shaves (?). See, however, Kâty. VII, 2, 22, where the shaving is said to be optional, but not so, according to the commentary, the bathing. There seems also to be some doubt as to where the bathing is to take place. While, according to Karka, the sacrificer is to bathe in the vessel of water in the tent; according to other authorities he is to

10. He bathes. For impure, indeed, is man: he is foul[1] within, in that he speaks untruth;—and water is pure: he thinks, 'May I be consecrated, after becoming pure;'—and water is cleansing: he thinks, 'May I become consecrated after being cleansed!' This is the reason why he bathes.

11. He bathes, with the text (Vâg. S. IV, 2; Rigveda X, 17, 10), 'May the waters, the mothers, cleanse us!' whereby he says, 'May they cleanse[2]!' 'May the purifiers of ghee purify us with (heavenly) ghee!' For he, indeed, is thoroughly purified whom they have purified with ghee[3]: accordingly he says, 'May the purifiers of ghee purify us with ghee!'—'For they, the divine, take away all taint;' now 'all' means 'every,' and 'taint' means what is impure; for they do take away from him every impurity: therefore he says, 'For they, the divine, take away all taint.'

12. He steps out (from the water) towards the north-east[4], with the text, 'Cleansed and pure

---

do so in some tank, or other kind of bathing-place of standing water. Cf. Taitt. S. VI, 1, 1, tîrthe snâti, tîrtham eva samânânâm bhavati.

[1] I now take pûti (with Dr. Lindner) in the sense of 'foul, filthy, fetid,' and would correct the passage (I, 1, 1, 1) accordingly. Professor Ludwig (Göttinger Gel. Anz. 1883, p. 49) proposes to take pûti in the sense of 'pure,' both here and in I, 1, 1, 1.

[2] The Kânva recension has the better reading, 'For they, indeed, now cleanse him when he bathes.' According to Taitt. S. VI, 1, 1, 3, he also sips (asnâti) some water with the view of internal purification.

[3] Lit. 'for that indeed is well purified, whom they purified (i. e. when they purify anybody) with ghee.' The imperfect is rather strange. See also III, 1, 3, 22. The Kânvas read, 'For that, indeed, is well purified what is purified (yad pûyate) with ghee.'

[4] Prâṅ ivodaṅ = uttarapûrvârdham, Kâty. VII, 2, 15, i. e. 'towards the north with a slight turn to the east.' Dr. Lindner takes 'udaṅ'

I go forth from them;' for cleansed and pure he indeed goes forth from them.

13. He then puts on a (linen) garment, for completeness' sake: it is indeed his own skin he thereby puts on himself. Now that same skin which belongs to the cow was originally on man.

14. The gods spake, 'Verily, the cow supports everything here (on earth); come, let us put on the cow that skin which is now on man: therewith she will be able to endure rain and cold and heat.'

15. Accordingly, having flayed man, they put that skin on the cow, and therewith she now endures rain and cold and heat.

16. For man was indeed flayed; and hence whereever a stalk of grass or some other object cuts him, the blood trickles out. They then put that skin, the garment, on him; and for this reason none but man wears a garment, it having been put on him as his skin. Hence also one should take care to be properly clad, so that he may be completely endued with his own skin. Hence also people like to see even an ugly person properly clad, since he is endued with his own skin.

17. Let him, then, not be naked in the presence of a cow. For the cow knows that she wears his skin, and runs away for fear lest he should take the skin from her. Hence also cows draw fondly near to one who is properly clad.

18. Now the woof of this cloth belongs to Agni, and the warp to Vâyu[1], the thrum to the Fathers,

---

as meant to explain the preposition 'vi.' This, however, does not account for the 'iva.'

[1] Agne*h* paryâso bhavati, vâyor anu*kh*âdo (?). The Black Yagus

the fore-edge[1] to the snakes, the threads to the All-gods, and the meshes to the asterisms. For thus indeed all the deities are concerned therein; and hence it is the garment of the consecrated.

19. Let it (if possible) be a new one[2], for the sake of unimpaired vigour. Let him (the Adhvaryu) tell (the Pratiprasthâtri) to beat it, in order that whatsoever part of it an unclean woman has spun or woven may become clean. And if it be a new one, let him sprinkle it with water, so that it become clean. Or let him be consecrated in one which is laid aside to be worn (daily) after bathing, without being soaked (in some sharp cleansing substance)[3].

20. He puts it round him, with the text, 'Thou art the covering[4] of consecration and penance;' heretofore, indeed, this was the covering of him as one unconsecrated, but now it is that of consecration and penance: hence he says, 'thou art the covering of consecration and penance.' 'I put thee on, the kindly and auspicious;' whereby he means to say, 'I put thee on, the kindly and pleasing one;'—

(T. S. VI, 1, 1) reads, agnes tûshâdhânam (salâkopadhânam tûshâh, tatra tantûnâm pûranam tûshâdhânam; Sây.), vâyor vâtapânam (vâyunâ soshanam vâtapânam, S.). The warp (prâkînatâna) and woof (otu), on the other hand, are by the Black Yagus ascribed to the Âdityas and Visve Devâh respectively.

[1] Praghâta, apparently the closely-woven part at both ends of the cloth from whence the loose threads of the nîvi, or unwoven fringe (thrum), come out. The Black Yagus ascribes it to the plants.

[2] Literally, 'unbeaten (ahata), unwashed.'

[3] That is to say, if it be not a new garment, it should be one that has not been washed by a washerman (with mautra, &c.), but worn daily after bathing.

[4] Or, outward form, tanu. Its meaning sometimes comes very near to that of 'skin,' assigned to it by the lexicographers. Cf. III, 2, 2, 20; 4, 3, 9.

'fostering a fair appearance;' for evil indeed is that appearance which he has heretofore fostered while unconsecrated; but now (he fosters) a fair appearance: therefore he says, 'fostering a fair appearance.'

21. He (the Adhvaryu) then makes him enter the hall. Let him not eat (the flesh) of either the cow or the ox; for the cow and the ox doubtless support everything here on earth. The gods spake, 'Verily, the cow and the ox support everything here: come, let us bestow on the cow and the ox whatever vigour belongs to other species[1]!' Accordingly they bestowed on the cow and the ox whatever vigour belonged to other species (of animals); and therefore the cow and the ox eat most. Hence, were one to eat (the flesh) of an ox or a cow, there would be, as it were, an eating of everything, or, as it were, a going on to the end (or, to destruction). Such a one indeed would be likely to be born (again) as a strange being, (as one of whom there is) evil report, such as 'he has expelled an embryo from a woman,' 'he has committed a sin[2];' let him therefore not eat (the flesh) of the cow and the ox. Nevertheless Yâgñavalkya said, 'I, for one, eat it, provided that it is tender.'

---

[1] Vayasâm, cf. III, 3, 3, 3. The Kânva rec. has 'yad anyeshâm vayasâm vîryam yad anyeshâm pasûnâm.'

[2] A different translation of this passage is proposed by Professor Delbrück (Synt. Forsch. III, p. 25); but the Kânva text (sâ tam hesvaro 'dbhutam abhiganitor gâyâyâ vâ garbham niravadhîd yad veti tad u hovâka) shows that we have here, as frequently, to supply îsvarah to the infinitive in tos. The Kânva yad vâ ('or some such thing') would also seem to indicate that we ought to translate:—(as of one of whom) there is evil report: 'he has committed some such (iti) sin as the producing of abortion.'

THIRD BRÂHMANA.

1. Having brought water forward[1], he takes out (the material for) a cake on eleven potsherds for Agni and Vishnu; for Agni is all the deities, since it is in Agni that offering is made to all the deities. Moreover Agni is the lower half, and Vishnu is the upper half of the sacrifice: 'I will become consecrated after encompassing all the deities, after encompassing the entire sacrifice,' thus he thinks, and hence there is a cake on eleven potsherds for Agni and Vishnu.

2. Some then offer a rice-pap to the Âdityas. This is referred to (in the passage, Rig-veda X, 72, 8), 'There are eight sons of Aditi who were born from her body; with seven she went to the gods, but Mârtânda[2] she cast off.'

3. Now Aditi had eight sons. But those that are called 'the gods, sons of Aditi,' were only seven, for the eighth, Mârtânda, she brought forth unformed[3]: it was a mere lump of bodily matter[4], as broad as it was high. Some, however, say that he was of the size of a man.

4. The gods, sons of Aditi, then spake, 'That

---

[1] Viz. the so-called 'pranîtâh,' see part i, p. 9 note. The offering, described in the following paragraphs, is called the Dîkshanîyeshti, 'Consecration offering.' As to the formulas used at the offering, see Ait. Br. I, 4 seq.

[2] The bird, Vishnu, the sun.

[3] Or, the eighth she brought forth undeveloped, as a mârtânda (? either a bird, or, more probably, in accordance with Taitt. S. VI, 5, 6, 1,=vyriddham ândam, 'an abortive egg'). See Rig-veda Sanhitâ, translated by M. M., p. 239.

[4] Sandegha; the St. Petersburg Dict. takes it in the sense of 'doubt, uncertainty,' in this passage.

which was born after us[1] must not be lost: come, let us fashion it.' They accordingly fashioned it as this man is fashioned. The flesh which was cut off him, and thrown down in a lump, became the elephant: hence they say that one must not accept an elephant (as a gift)[2], since the elephant has sprung from man. Now he whom they thus fashioned was Vivasvat, the Âditya (or the sun); and of him (came) these creatures.

5. He spake, 'Among my offspring he shall be successful who shall offer that rice-pap to the Âdityas.' Accordingly he alone succeeds who offers that rice-pap to the Âdityas. Only that (cake) to Agni and Vish*n*u is, however, generally approved.

6. There are seventeen kindling-verses for it[3]. In a low voice he offers to the two deities. There are five fore-offerings and three after-offerings. For the sake of completeness they perform the patnîsa*m*yâ*g*as[4]; but he offers no samish*t*ayag*u*s, lest, having put on that garment of the consecrated, he should reach the end of the sacrifice before its completion; for the samish*t*ayag*u*s is the end of the sacrifice.

7. He (the sacrificer) then gets himself anointed (with fresh butter), while standing east of the hall. For, having been flayed, man is sore; and by getting himself anointed, he becomes healed of his soreness: for man's skin is on the cow, and that fresh butter

---

[1] Or, perhaps, after the manner of us (anu).

[2] Muir, O. S. T. IV, 15, reads 'parigr*i*h*n*îyât' instead of 'pratigr*i*h*n*îyât,' and translates, 'let no one catch an elephant, for an elephant partakes of the nature of man.'

[3] For the ordinary eleven Sâmidhenîs (raised to the number of fifteen by repetitions of the first and last verses), see part i, p. 102, and for the two additional ones (dhâyyâ), ib. p. 112 note.

[4] See part i, p. 256; for the Samish*t*ayag*u*s, ib. p. 262.

also comes from the cow. He (the Adhvaryu) thus supplies him with his own skin, and for this reason he gets himself anointed.

8. It is fresh butter,—for melted butter (ghee) belongs to the gods, and creamy butter[1] to men. Here, on the other hand, it is neither ghee nor creamy butter; it should rather be both ghee and creamy butter, for the sake of unimpaired vigour: by means of that which is of unimpaired vigour he accordingly makes him of unimpaired vigour.

9. He anoints him from the head down to the feet in accordance with the tendency of the hair, with the text (Vâg. S. IV, 3), 'Thou art the sap of the great ones.' The 'great ones,' doubtless, is one of the names of those cows, and their sap indeed it is: therefore he says, 'thou art the sap of the great ones.' 'Thou art life-giving: give me light!' There is nothing obscure in this.

10. Thereupon he anoints the eyes. 'Sore, indeed, is the eye of man; mine is sound,' so spake Yâgñavalkya. Dim-eyed, indeed, he was (heretofore); and the secretion of his eyes was matter. He now makes his eyes sound by anointing them.

11. Now, when the gods slew the Asura-Rakshas, Sushna[2], the Dânava, falling backward entered into the eyes of men: he is that pupil of the eye, and

[1] Phânta, explained as the first particles of butter that appear in churning (?). The Kânva recension, on the other hand, reads 'âgyam nishpântam' (!) instead. Cf. Taitt. S. VI, 1, 1, 4, Ghritam devânâm, mastu pitrinâm, nishpakvam (i.e. surabhi ghritam, 'well-seasoned butter,' Sây.) manushyânâm; tad vai etat sarvadevatyam yan navanîtam; also Ait. Br. I, 3, âgyam vai devânâm, surabhi ghritam manushyânâm, âyutam pitrinâm, navanîtam garbhânâm; with Haug's note, Transl. p. 8.

[2] The Kânva text (MSS. O. W.) reads Sisna.

looks like a young lad[1]. Against him he (the sacrificer), now that he enters on the sacrifice, raises a rampart of stone all round himself, for the ointment is (produced from) stone.

12. It is such as comes from mount Trikakud; for when Indra slew Vritra he transformed that eye of his (Vritra's) into the mount Trikakud[2]. The reason, then, why (ointment) from mount Trikakud (is used), is that he thereby puts eye into eye. Should he be unable to obtain any Traikakuda ointment, any other than Traikakuda may be used; for one and the same, indeed, is the significance of the ointment.

13. He anoints (the eyes) with a reed-stalk, for the reed is a thunderbolt. It is one with a tuft, in order to chase away the evil spirits[3]. For rootless,

---

[1] Sa esha kanînakah kumâraka iva paribhâsate. A play on the word kanînaka, which has the double meaning of 'youth' and 'pupil of the eye.' The St. Petersburg Dict. assigns also to kumâraka the meaning of 'ball of the eye' in this (the only) passage. The Kânva recension reads, Sa esha kumâraka iva kanînakâyâm (? both 'maiden' and 'pupil of the eye').

[2] 'Indra slew Vritra, his eye-ball fell away, it became collyrium.' Taitt. S. VI, 1, 1, 5.

[3] Professor Delbrück, S. F. III, 27, takes it thus, 'He brushes the eye with the end of a reed, for the reed is a thunderbolt capable of repelling mischief.' But, if 'virakshastâyai' belonged to what precedes, it would probably have to be construed with 'sareshikayâ 'nakti,' the clause with 'vai,' giving the reason, being inserted parenthetically; while, in an idiomatic rendering, it would have to be placed at the end: He anoints the eyes with a reed-stalk in order to chase away the evil spirits, the reed being a thunderbolt. This abstract dative of purpose is very common; it being generally construed with what precedes, as, for instance, I, 1, 4, 1; 3, 2, 8; 5, 3, 8; 15; III, 1, 2, 13; 19; 3, 6; 8; and, with a parenthetic clause with 'vai' intervening, III, 2, 1, 13; IV, 5, 7, 7. Not less common is the analogous construction with a clause with 'ned'

indeed, and unfettered on both sides, the Rakshas roams along the air; even as man here roams along the air[1], rootless and unfettered on both sides: the reason, then, why it is (a reed-stalk) with a tuft, is to chase away the evil spirits.

14. The right eye he anoints first; for in human practice the left (eye is anointed) first, but with the gods (it is done) thus.

15. He anoints it with the text, 'Thou art the eye-ball of V*ri*tra,'—for V*ri*tra's eye-ball it indeed is;—'Eye-giving thou art: give me the eye!' in this there is nothing obscure.

16. The right eye he anoints once with the sacrificial formula, once silently; and the left one he anoints once with the formula, twice silently: thus he makes the left (or upper) one superior[2].

17. And the reason why he anoints five times, is that the sacrifice is of equal measure with the year, and five seasons there are in the year: he thus obtains possession of the latter in five (divisions), and therefore he anoints five times.

18. He then purifies him with a cleanser (pavitra, strainer) of sacred grass; for impure, indeed, is man:—he is foul within in that he speaks untruth;—and sacred grass is pure: 'Having become pure, I shall be consecrated,' thus he thinks;—and the stalks of sacred grass are a means of cleansing,—

('lest such an event should happen') instead of the dative of the abstract, cf. I, 2, 1, 8; 9; IV, 5, 9, 3.

[1] I now take this passage differently from my interpretation of I, 1, 2, 4 ('and, in order that this man may move about the air, rootless and unfettered in both directions'). See also IV, 1, 1, 20.

[2] 'Tad uttaram evaitad uttarâvat karoti;' 'uttarấm évaitad úttaram karoti,' Kâ*n*va recension. Cf. p. 2, note 1.

'Having become cleansed, I shall be consecrated,' thus he thinks; and therefore he purifies him with a cleanser of sacred grass.

19. It may consist of one (stalk of grass); for that blower (or purifier, the Wind) is one only, and in accordance with his nature is this (cleanser): hence it may consist of one (stalk).

20. Or there may be three (stalks); for one, indeed, is that blower, but on entering into man he becomes threefold, to wit, the out-breathing, the in-breathing, and the through-breathing[1], and in accordance with his measure is this (cleanser): hence there may be three (stalks).

21. Or there may be seven (stalks[2]); for there are seven vital airs of the head: hence there may be seven (stalks). There may even be thrice seven,—one and twenty: such indeed is perfection.

22. He purifies him with seven (stalks) each time, with the text (Vâg. S. IV, 4), 'May the Lord of thought purify me!' The lord of thought doubtless is Pragâpati[3]: he thereby means to say, 'May Pragâpati purify me!' 'May the lord of speech purify me!' The lord of speech doubtless is Pragâpati[4]: he thereby means to say, 'May Pragâpati purify me!' 'May the divine Savitri purify me,'—for well purified indeed is he whom the divine

[1] See part i, p. 19, note 2.

[2] The Taitt. S. VI, 1, 1 allows the option between (one), 2, 3, 5, 6, 7, 9, and 21 stalks; while the Ait. Br. I, 3 mentions only the highest number.

[3] The Kânva text adds, sa hi kittânâm îshte, 'for he rules over the thoughts.'

[4] The Kânvas read, ayam vâva vâkpatir yo 'yam pavate, tad enam esha punâti, 'the lord of speech doubtless is that blower (purifier, the wind): hence it is he that purifies him.'

Savitri has purified[1]; therefore he says, 'May the divine Savitri purify me!'—'with a flawless cleanser;' for that blower (the wind) is indeed a flawless cleanser: 'with that one,' he means to say; 'with the rays of the sun;' for they, the rays of the sun, are indeed purifiers; therefore he says, 'with the rays of the sun.'

23. 'O Lord of the pavitra' (means of purification),—for he (who is consecrated) is indeed the lord of the pavitra,—'of thee, purified by the pavitra,—for he is indeed purified by the pavitra;—'with whatsoever desire I purify myself, may I be able to effect it!' whereby he says, 'May I reach the end of the sacrifice!'

24. He then makes him pronounce the beginning of the benedictions (Vâg. S. IV, 5), 'We approach you, O gods, for desirable goods, at the opening of the sacrifice; we call on you, O gods, for holy[2] blessings.' Thereby the officiating priests invoke on him those blessings which are their own.

25. He (the sacrificer) then bends his fingers inwards, viz. the two (little fingers), with the text (Vâg. S. IV, 6), 'Hail, from the mind (I take hold of) the sacrifice!'—the two (nameless or ring fingers) with, 'Hail, from the wide ether!'—the two (middle fingers) with, 'Hail, from the sky and earth!'—with, 'Hail, from the wind, I take hold (of the sacrifice)!' he clenches both fists[3]. Not visibly

[1] See p. 8, note 3.

[2] I take yagñiyâsah as acc. pl. fem., as does Mahîdh. Perhaps it ought to be translated 'for prayers proper at the sacrifice,' whereby he makes sure that each priest uses his own proper prayers during the sacrifice.

[3] For the symbolic meaning of the closing of the hands, see III, 2, 1, 6; Ait. Br. I, 3, 20.

indeed is the sacrifice to be taken hold of, as is either this staff or the garment,—but invisible indeed are the gods, invisible is the sacrifice.

26. Now when he says, 'Hail, from the mind (I take hold of) the sacrifice,' he takes hold of it from the mind;—in saying, 'From the wide ether,' he takes hold of it from the ether;—in saying, 'From heaven and earth,' he takes hold of it from those two, heaven and earth, on which this entire universe rests;—and in saying, 'From the wind I take hold of (the sacrifice)'—the wind being the sacrifice—he takes hold of the sacrifice directly.

27. And when he calls, 'Hail! Hail[1]!'—the 'Svâhâ' being the sacrifice—he thereby appropriates the sacrifice. Here now he restrains his speech; the sacrifice being speech: he thereby appropriates[2] the sacrifice.

28. He (the Adhvaryu) then makes him enter the hall. He walks along the back of the Âhavanîya and the front of the Gârhapatya[3],—this is his passage until the Soma pressing. The reason why this is his passage until the Soma pressing is this. The fire is the womb of the sacrifice, and the consecrated is an embryo; and the embryo moves about

[1] That is, 'svâhâ' in each formula. The Samhitâ has twice 'svâhâ' in the last formula (svâhâ vâtâd ârabhe svâhâ), to which this might refer, but neither recension of the Brâhmana mentions the final 'svâhâ.'

[2] Literally, 'he takes within him' (as the speech confined within him through silence).

[3] That is, he enters the hall by the front (east) door, then walks along the north side of the Âhavanîya and altar, and passes between the Gârhapatya and altar to his seat south of the Âhavanîya. The Pratiprasthâtri then silently anoints and purifies the Dîkshita's wife and leads her into the hall, either by the front or back door.

within the womb. And since he (the sacrificer) moves about there (between the fires), and now turns round and now back, therefore these embryos move about, and now turn round and now back. Hence this is his passage till the Soma pressing.

FOURTH BRÂHMAṆA.

1. All formulas of the consecration are audgrabhaṇa (elevatory), since he who is consecrated elevates himself (ud-grabh) from this world to the world of the gods. He elevates himself by means of these same formulas, and therefore they say that all formulas of the consecration are 'audgrabhaṇa.' Now they also (specially) designate these intermediate ones as 'audgrabhaṇa,' because these are libations[1], and a libation is a sacrifice. For the muttering of a sacrificial formula is an occult (form of sacrifice), but a libation is a direct (form of) sacrifice: hence it is by this same sacrifice that he elevates himself from this world to the world of the gods.

2. And again, the three libations which he makes with the dipping-spoon (sruva) are said to be 'âdhîtayagus[2].' The fourth libation is made for the sake of completeness; while the fifth, which is made with the offering-spoon (sruk, viz. the guhû), is the real audgrabhaṇa-libation: for he makes it with an

[1] While all the formulas of the Dîkshâ are supposed to be of an 'elevatory (audgrabhaṇa)' character, the designation 'audgrabhaṇâni (yagûṃshi, or elevatory formulas)' is specially applied to the five libations described in the succeeding paragraphs. The Kâṇva text reads,—atha yad etâny avântarâm audgrabhaṇânîty âkhyâyanta âhutayo hy etâ âhutir hy eva yagñaḥ paroksham iva hi tad yad yagur gapaty etena hi tad yagñenodgṛibhṇîte.

[2] I. e. yagus for some 'meditated' object.

anushtubh verse, and the anushtubh is speech, and the sacrifice also is speech.

3. By means of the sacrifice the gods obtained that supreme authority which they now wield. They spake, 'How may this (world) of ours be unattainable by men!' They then sipped the sap of the sacrifice, as bees would suck out honey; and having drained the sacrifice and effaced its traces by means of the sacrificial stake, they disappeared: and because they effaced (scattered, yopaya) therewith, therefore it is called yûpa (stake).

4. Now this was heard by the *Ri*shis. They collected the sacrifice, just as this sacrifice is collected (prepared)[1]; for even so does he now collect the sacrifice, when he offers those (audgrabha*n*a) libations.

5. He offers five libations, because the sacrifice is commensurate to the year, and there are five seasons in the year: thus he gains it (the year) in five (divisions), and therefore he makes five libations.

6. Now then of the oblation (Vâg. S. IV, 7): 'To the Purpose, to the Impulse, to Agni, hail!' At the outset he indeed purposes to sacrifice. What part of the sacrifice (is contained) in this (first libation), that he now collects and makes his own.

7. 'To Wisdom, to Thought, to Agni, hail!' with wisdom and thought he indeed conceives that he may sacrifice. What part of the sacrifice (is contained) in this (second libation), that he now collects and makes his own.

8. 'To Initiation, to Penance, to Agni, hail!' This is merely uttered, but no libation is made.

---

[1] Sam-bh*ri*; on the technical meaning of this verb (to equip, prepare) and the noun sambhâra, see part i, p. 276, note 1.

9. 'To Sarasvatî, to Pûshan, to Agni, hail!' Now Sarasvatî is speech, and the sacrifice also is speech. And Pûshan represents cattle, because Pûshan means prosperity (push*t*i), and cattle also means prosperity, since the sacrifice means cattle. What part of the sacrifice (is contained) in this (third libation), that he now collects and makes his own.

10. As to this they say, 'These (three) libations are offered indefinitely; they are unestablished, without a god: therein is neither Indra, nor Soma, nor Agni.'

11. 'To the Purpose, to the Impulse, to Agni, hail!'—not any one (god we obtain) from this[1]! But Agni surely is definite, Agni is established: when he offers in Agni (the fire), surely those (libations) are thereby made definite, are thereby established: for this reason he offers at all libations with, 'To Agni, hail!' Moreover, these libations are called 'âdhîtaya*g*û*m*shi.'

12. 'To the Purpose, to the Impulse, to Agni, hail!' he says; for by his own mind he purposes to sacrifice, and from his own mind he impels it (the sacrifice) when he performs it: these two deities—the Purpose and the Impulse—are meditated upon (âdhîta) in his mind.

13. 'To Wisdom, to Thought, to Agni, hail!' he says; for with wisdom and thought he indeed conceives that he may sacrifice: these two deities—

[1] This last sentence has probably to be taken ironically. In the Kâ*n*va text it seems to form part of the objection raised: Sa yat sarveshv agnaye svâheti *g*uhoty anaddheva vâ etâ âhutayo hûyante 'pratish*th*itâ iva na hi kasyai *k*ana devatâyai hûyante ‖ âkutyai pra-yu*g*a iti tan nâgnir nendro na somo, medhâyai manasa iti nâto 'nyatara*k* *k*anaivam eva sarveshv, agnir uvâ addhâ . . .

Wisdom and Thought—are meditated upon in his mind.

14. 'To Sarasvatî, to Pûshan, to Agni, hail!' he says; for Sarasvatî is speech, and the sacrifice also is speech: this deity—Speech—is meditated upon in his mind. Pûshan, on the other hand, means cattle, for Pûshan means prosperity (push*t*i), and cattle means prosperity, since the sacrifice means cattle: hence cattle are meditated upon in his mind. And because these deities are meditated upon (â-dhîta) in his mind, therefore (these libations) are called âdhîtaya*g*û*m*shi.

15. He then offers the fourth libation, with the text, 'Ye divine, vast, all-soothing Waters! Heaven and Earth, wide Ether! let us render homage unto B*ri*haspati with offering, hail!' This (libation) truly is nearer to the sacrifice, since he praises the waters, and water is sacrifice. 'Heaven and Earth! wide Ether!' he says, because he thereby praises the worlds. 'Let us render homage unto B*ri*haspati, with offering, hail!' he says; for B*ri*haspati is the Brahman, and the sacrifice also is the Brahman: for this reason also this (libation) is nearer to the sacrifice.

16. But the fifth libation which he makes with the offering-spoon (sru*k*), doubtless is the veritable sacrifice; for he offers it with an anush*t*ubh (verse), and the anush*t*ubh is speech and so is the sacrifice.

17. In the first place he pours the butter, which remains in the dhruvâ, into the *g*uhû. He then ladles with the sruva three times butter from the melting-pot into the *g*uhû: with what he takes the third time he fills the sruva[1].

[1] The third time he holds the sruva over the *g*uhû and pours

18. He offers, with the text (Vâg. S. IV, 8; Rig-veda V, 50, 1), 'May every mortal espouse the friendship of the divine guide! every one prayeth for wealth: let him choose glory, that he may prosper, hail!'

19. Now this (verse and libation) consists of five parts in respect of deities[1]: 'visvo devasya' refers to the Visve Devâh; 'netur' to Savitri; 'marto vurîta' to Mitra; 'dyumnam vrinîta' to Brihaspati, since Brihaspati means dyumna (glory); and 'pushyase' (for prospering) refers to Pûshan.

20. This (libation), then, consists of five parts, in respect of deities;—fivefold is the sacrifice, fivefold the animal victim, and five seasons there are in the year: the latter he accordingly gains by this (libation) consisting of five parts in respect of deities.

21. He offers this libation with an anushtubh verse, because the anushtubh is speech, and the sacrifice is speech; so that he thereby obtains the real sacrifice.

22. As to this they say, 'Let him offer only this one: for whatever object the others are offered, that object he gains even by this one.' And, indeed[2], if

ghee from the pot into the sruva, so as to fill it; after which he pours it from the sruva into the guhû. Kâty. VII, 3, 18 comm.

[1] The Taitt. S. (VI, 1, 2, 5) divides the couplet into its four pâdas, which it assigns to Savitri, the Fathers, the Visve Devâh, and Pûshan respectively. The various reading 'visve' of the Black Yagus, instead of 'visvah,' is very remarkable.

[2] The author here states, in his own words, the reasons (by 'vai') which have led the teachers referred to to maintain that by offering this one oblation one gains all the objects in view. The Kânva text includes the entire passage regarding the fivefold division of the formula and oblation (pars. 19–21) in the argument of those teachers. For a detailed description of the pûrnâhuti, or full-offering,

he offers only this one, he would offer a full-offering; and the full means everything: hence he gains everything by this (oblation). And by filling the dipping-spoon (sruva), he fills the offering-spoon (guhû), and the latter he offers full. This, however, is a mere statement (of others' views)[1]; but all (five) libations are offered.

23. He offers this one with an anushtubh verse. Being an anushtubh verse, it consists of thirty-one syllables. Now there are ten fingers, ten toes, ten vital airs, and the thirty-first is the body wherein those vital airs are contained; for this much constitutes man, and the sacrifice is a man, the sacrifice is of the same proportion as a man[2]. Thus, whatever the extent of the sacrifice, whatever its measure, to that extent he takes possession of it by means of this (libation), when he offers it with an anushtubh verse of thirty-one syllables.

SECOND ADHYÂYA. FIRST BRÂHMANA.

1. South of the Âhavanîya he spreads two black antelope skins on the ground, with the neck parts towards the east: thereon he consecrates him. If there are two (skins), they are an image of these two worlds (heaven and earth), and thus he consecrates him on these two worlds.

---

see part i, p. 302, note 2. A similar view, that the full-offering renders other oblations unnecessary, is there given (II, 2, 1, 5).

[1] Saishâ mîmâmsaiva, 'This, however, is mere speculation,' Kânva recension.

[2] See I, 2, 5, 14, with note. The sacrifice represents the sacrificer himself, and thus he makes sure of his offering up his entire Self, and obtaining a new divine Self, and a place among the immortals.

2. They are joined (fitted) together along their edge[1], for these two worlds are also, as it were, joined together at their edge. At the hind part they are fastened together through holes: thus, after uniting (mithunîkritya) these two worlds, he consecrates him thereon.

3. But if there be only one (skin), then it is an image of these (three) worlds; then he consecrates him on these (three) worlds. Those (hairs) which are white are an image of the sky; those which are black are (an image) of this (earth);—or, if he likes, conversely: those which are black are an image of the sky, and those which are white are (an image) of this (earth). Those which are of a brownish yellow colour[2], are an image of the atmosphere. Thus he consecrates him on these (three) worlds.

4. And let him, in that case, turn in the hind end (of the skin)[3]: thus, after uniting these worlds with each other, he consecrates him thereon.

5. He then squats down behind the two skins, with his face towards the east and with bent (right) knee; and while touching them thus[4] at a place

---

[1] The two skins are fitted together at the inner sides, and stretched along the ground by means of wooden pins driven into the ground and passed through holes all round the edge of the skins; the hairy sides of the latter remaining outside (above and below). At their hind parts they are tacked together by 'means of a thong passed through the holes and tied together in a loop.'

[2] Yâny eva babhrûnîva harîni. The Kânva text reads, Yâny eva madhye babhrûni vâ harîni vâ, 'those in the centre (or between the black and white) which are either brown or yellow (grey).

[3] According to Kâty. VII, 3, 21 it would seem that the two hind feet, or one of them, should be doubled up (at the joint) and sewed under. According to the Sûtras of the Black Yagus, on the other hand, the right fore-foot is turned under.

[4] According to the Sûtras of the Black Yagus, he is to touch at

where the white and black (hair) join, he mutters (Vâ*g*. S. IV, 9), 'Ye are the images of the *Rik* and Sâman;'—an image doubtless is what is conformable[1]: 'Ye are conformable to the *rik*s and sâmans' he thereby means to say.

6. 'I touch you.' Now, he who is consecrated becomes an embryo, and enters into the metres: hence he has his hands closed, since embryos have their hands closed.

7. And when he says, 'I touch you,' he means to say, 'I enter into you.' 'Do ye guard me up to the goal of this sacrifice!' whereby he says, 'Do ye protect me until the completion of this sacrifice!'

8. He then kneels down with his right knee (on the skin), with the text, 'Thou art a refuge: afford me refuge!' for the skin (*k*arma) of the black deer it is indeed among men, but among the gods it is a refuge (*s*arma): therefore he says, 'Thou art a refuge: afford me refuge.' 'Homage be to thee: injure me not!' Now he who raises himself upon the sacrifice[1] doubtless raises himself to one that is his better; for the black deer skin is a (means of) sacrifice. Hereby, now, he propitiates that sacrifice, and thus that sacrifice does not injure him: for this reason he says, 'Homage be to thee: injure me not!'

9. He must indeed sit down first on the hind part (of the skin). Were he, on the other hand, to sit down at once in the middle (of the skin), and were

---

the same time the white hair with his thumb and the black with his fore-finger. Sây. on Taitt. S. I, 2, 2 (vol. i, p. 297).

[1] *S*reyâ*m*sa*m* vâ esha upâdhirohati yo manushya*h* san ya*gñ*am upâdhirohati. Kâ*n*va recension.

any one there to curse him, saying, 'He shall either become demented or fall down headlong!' then that would indeed come to pass. Let him therefore first sit down on the hind part (of the skin).

10. He then girds himself with the zone. For once upon a time when the Aṅgiras were consecrated, they were seized with weakness, for they had prepared no other food but fast-milk. They then perceived this (source of) strength (viz. the zone), and this (source of) strength they put in (or round) the middle of their body as a (means of attaining) completion: and thereby they attained completion. And so does he now put that (source of) strength in the middle of his body and thereby attain completion.

11. It is made of hemp. Hempen it is in order to be soft. Now when Pragâpati, having become an embryo, sprung forth from that sacrifice, that which was nearest to him, the amnion, became hempen threads: hence they smell putrid. And that which was the outer membrane (and placenta) became the garment of the consecrated. Now the amnion lies under the outer membrane, and hence that (zone) is worn under the garment. And in like manner as Pragâpati, having become an embryo, sprung forth from that sacrifice, so does he become an embryo and spring forth from that sacrifice.

12. It (the cord) is a triple one, because food is threefold, food being cattle. (Moreover) the father and mother (are two), and that which is born is a third: hence it is a triple (cord).

13. It is intertwined with a shoot of reed (muñga) grass, for the sake of chasing away the evil spirits, the reed being a thunderbolt. It is plaited after

the manner of a braid of hair. For were it to be twisted[1] sunwise (from left to right) as any other cords, it would be human; and were it twisted contrary to the course of the sun, it would be sacred to the Fathers: hence it is plaited after the manner of a braid of hair.

14. He girds himself with it, with the text (Vâg. S. IV, 10), 'Thou art the strength of the Aṅgiras,'—for the Aṅgiras perceived this (source of) strength;—'soft as wool, bestow thou strength on me!' there is nothing obscure in this.

15. He then tucks up the end of his (nether) garment, with the text, 'Thou art Soma's tuck.' For heretofore it was the tuck of him, the unconsecrated; but now that he is consecrated, it is that of Soma[2]: therefore he says, 'Thou art Soma's tuck.'

16. He then wraps up (his head)[3]. For he who is consecrated becomes an embryo; and embryos are enveloped both by the amnion and the outer membrane: therefore he covers (his head).

17. He covers himself, with the text, 'Thou art Vishnu's refuge, the refuge of the sacrificer.' He who is consecrated indeed becomes both Vishnu and a sacrificer; for when he is consecrated, he is Vishnu; and when he sacrifices, he is the sacrificer: therefore he says, 'Thou art Vishnu's refuge, the refuge of the sacrificer.'

18. Thereupon he ties a black deer's horn to the

---

[1] Twisted and plaited is here expressed by the same term 'srishta.'

[2] Literally, but now (it being that) of (him) the consecrated, (it is that) of Soma.

[3] With his upper garment, or, according to others, with a turban. Kâty. VII, 3, 28 scholl.

end (of his garment[1]). Now the gods and the Asuras, both of them sprung from Pra*g*âpati, entered upon their father Pra*g*âpati's inheritance: the gods came in for the Mind and the Asuras for Speech. Thereby the gods came in for the sacrifice and Asuras for speech; the gods for yonder (heaven) and the Asuras for this (earth).

19. The gods said to Ya*gñ*a (m., the sacrifice), 'That Vâ*k* (f., speech) is a woman: beckon her, and she will certainly call thee to her.' Or it may be, he himself thought, 'That Vâ*k* is a woman: I will beckon her and she will certainly call me to her.' He accordingly beckoned her. She, however, at first disdained him from the distance: and hence a woman, when beckoned by a man, at first disdains him from the distance. He said, 'She has disdained me from the distance.'

20. They said, 'Do but beckon her, reverend sir, and she will certainly call thee to her.' He beckoned her; but she only replied to him, as it were, by shaking her head: and hence a woman, when beckoned by a man, only replies to him, as it were, by shaking her head. He said, 'She has only replied to me by shaking her head.'

21. They said, 'Do but beckon her, reverend sir, and she will certainly call thee to her.' He beckoned her, and she called him to her; and hence a woman at last calls the man to her. He said, 'She has indeed called me.'

[1] The Mâdhyandinas tied the horn to the unwoven end (thrum, da*s*â) of the nether garment which was tucked through (par. 15) and then allowed to hang down in front. The Kâ*n*vas, on the other hand, tied it to the hem of the upper garment (uttarasi*k*e! Kâ*n*va text); cf. Kâty. VII, 3, 29 scholl.

22. The gods reflected, 'That Vâk being a woman, we must take care lest she should allure him[1].—Say to her, "Come hither to me where I stand!" and report to us her having come.' She then went up to where he was standing. Hence a woman goes to a man who stays in a well-trimmed (house). He reported to them her having come, saying, 'She has indeed come.'

23. The gods then cut her off from the Asuras; and having gained possession of her and enveloped her completely in fire, they offered her up as a holocaust, it being an offering of the gods[2]. And in that they offered her with an anushtubh verse, thereby they made her their own; and the Asuras, being deprived of speech, were undone, crying, 'He 'lavah! he 'lavah[3]!

[1] Yoshâ vâ iyam vâg yad enam na yuvitâ. The St. Petersburg Dict. (s. v. yu) takes it differently, 'That Vâk is indeed a woman, since she does not wish to draw him towards herself (i. e. since she does not want him to come near her).' Sâyana, on the other hand, explains it elliptically, 'Since she has not joined him (no confidence can be placed in her).' The Kânva text reads: Ta u ha devâ bibhayâm kakrur yoshâ vâ iyam iti yad vâ enam na yuvîteti. Perhaps in our passage also we should read 'yuvîta' (as proposed by Delbrück, Syntact. Forschungen III, p. 79), and translate, 'Verily that Vâk is a woman: (it is to be feared) that she will [or, it is to be hoped that she will not] allure him [viz. so that Yagña also would fall to the share of the Asuras];' 'Dass sie ihn nur nicht an sich fesselt!' For similar elliptic constructions with yad and the optative, see paragraphs 26 and 27; and II, 2, 4, 3 ['Dass er mich nur nicht auffrisst!']; IV, 3, 5, 3 ('Dass uns nur die Rakshas nichts zu Leide thun!'); IV, 6, 9, 1. One would expect an 'iti' here.

[2] And therefore requiring no priests' portion &c. to be taken from it.

[3] According to Sâyana, 'He 'lavo' stands for 'He 'rayo (i. e. ho, the spiteful (enemies))!' which the Asuras were unable to pronounce correctly. The Kânva text, however, reads, te hâttavâko 'surâ hailo haila ity etâm ha vâkam vadantah parâbabhûvuh; (? i. e. He

24. Such was the unintelligible speech which they then uttered,—and he (who speaks thus) is a Mlekha (barbarian). Hence let no Brâhman speak barbarous language, since such is the speech of the Asuras. Thus alone he deprives his spiteful enemies of speech; and whosoever knows this, his enemies, being deprived of speech, are undone.

25. That Yagña (sacrifice) lusted after Vâk (speech[1]), thinking, 'May I pair with her!' He united with her.

26. Indra then thought within himself, 'Surely a great monster will spring from this union of Yagña and Vâk: [I must take care] lest it should get the better of me.' Indra himself then became an embryo and entered into that union.

27. Now when he was born after a year's time, he thought within himself, 'Verily of great vigour is this womb which has contained me: [I must take care] that no great monster shall be born from it after me, lest it should get the better of me!'

28. Having seized and pressed it tightly, he tore it off and put it on the head of Yagña (sacrifice[2]);—for the black (antelope) is the sacrifice: the black deer skin is the same as that sacrifice, and the black deer's horn is the same as that womb. And because it was by pressing it tightly together that Indra tore out (the womb), therefore it (the horn) is bound tightly (to the end of the garment); and as Indra,

ilâ, 'ho, speech.') A third version of this passage seems to be referred to in the Mahâbhâshya (Kielh.), p. 2.

[1] Compare the corresponding legend about Yagña and Dakshinâ (priests' fee), Taitt. S. VI, 1, 3, 6.

[2] 'Yagñasya sîrshan;' one would expect 'krishna(sâra)sya sîrshan.' The Taitt. S. reads 'tâm mrigeshu ny adadhât.'

having become an embryo, sprang from that union, so is he (the sacrificer), after becoming an embryo, born from that union (of the skin and the horn).

29. He ties it (to the end of the garment) with the open part upwards, for it is in this way that the womb bears the embryo. He then touches with it his forehead close over the right eyebrow, with the text, 'Thou art Indra's womb,'—for it is indeed Indra's womb, since in entering it he enters thereby[1], and in being born he is born therefrom: therefore he says, 'Thou art Indra's womb.'

30. Thereupon he draws (with the horn) the ('easterly') line, with the text, 'Make the crops full-eared!' Thereby he produces the sacrifice; for when there is a good year, then there is abundant (material) for sacrifice; but when there is a bad year, then there is not even enough for himself: hence he thereby produces the sacrifice.

31. And let not the consecrated henceforth scratch himself either with a chip of wood or with his nail. For he who is consecrated becomes an embryo; and were any one to scratch an embryo either with a chip of wood or his nail, thereby expelling it, it would die[2]. Thereafter the consecrated would be liable to be affected with the itch; and—offspring (retas) coming after the consecrated—that offspring would then also be liable to be born with the itch. Now his

---

[1] In the Kânva text 'ata*h* (therewith)' refers to the head of the sacrificer,—sa ya*k kh*irasta upaspr*is*aty ato vâ enâm etad agre pravi*s*an pravi*s*aty ato vâ agre *g*âyamâno *g*âyate tasmâ*k kh*irasta upaspr*is*ati.

[2] Apâsyan mrityet=apaga*kkh*an mr*i*tim prâpnuyât, Sây.—? apâsyet, 'he would force it out and it would die.' The Kâ*n*va text has merely 'ayam mr*i*tyet (!).'

own womb[1] does not injure its offspring, and that black deer's horn being indeed his own womb, that (horn) does not injure him; and therefore the consecrated should scratch himself with the black deer's horn and with nothing but the black deer's horn.

32. He (the Adhvaryu) then hands to him a staff, for driving away the evil spirits,—the staff being a thunderbolt.

33. It is of Udumbara wood (Ficus Glomerata), for him to obtain food and strength,—the Udumbara means food and strength: therefore it is of Udumbara wood.

34. It reaches up to his mouth,—for so far extends his strength: as great as his strength is, so great it (the staff) is when it reaches up to his mouth.

35. He makes it stand upright, with the text, 'Stand up, O tree, erect; guard me from injury on to the goal of this sacrifice!' whereby he means to say, 'Standing erect, protect me till the completion of this sacrifice!'

36. It is only now that some bend the fingers inward[2] and restrain their speech, because, they argue, only from now will he not have to mutter anything. But let him not do so; for in like manner as if one were to try to overtake some one who runs away, but could not overtake him, so does he not overtake the sacrifice. Let him therefore turn in his fingers and restrain his speech on that (former) occasion.

37. And when the consecrated (after restraining his speech) utters either a *rik*, or a sâman, or a ya*g*us[3],

---

[1] That is, the womb from which he (the sacrificer) is born.

[2] II, 1, 3, 25.

[3] Viz. in muttering the formulas mentioned above, III, 2, 1, 5 seq.

he thereby takes a firmer and firmer hold of the sacrifice: let him therefore turn in his fingers and restrain his speech on that (former) occasion.

38. And when he restrains his speech—speech being sacrifice—he thereby appropriates the sacrifice to himself[1]. But when, from speech restrained, he utters any sound (foreign to the sacrifice), then that sacrifice, being set free, flies away. In that case, then, let him mutter either a *rik* or a yagus addressed to Vishnu, for Vishnu is the sacrifice: thereby he again gets hold of the sacrifice; and this is the atonement for that (transgression).

39. Thereupon some one[2] calls out, 'Consecrated is this Brâhman, consecrated is this Brâhman:' him, being thus announced, he thereby announces to the gods: 'Of great vigour is this one who has obtained the sacrifice; he has become one of yours: protect him!' this is what he means to say. Thrice he says it, for threefold is the sacrifice.

40. And as to his saying, 'Brâhman,' uncertain, as it were, is his origin heretofore[3]; for the Rakshas, they say, pursue women here on earth, and so the Rakshas implant their seed therein. But he, forsooth, is truly born, who is born of the Brahman (neut.), of the sacrifice: wherefore let him address even a Râganya, or a Vaisya, as Brâhman, since he who is born of the sacrifice is born of the Brahman (and hence a Brâhmana). Wherefore they say, 'Let no one slay a sacrificer of Soma; for by (slaying) a Soma-sacrificer he becomes guilty of a heinous sin[4]!'

[1] Or, puts it in himself, encloses it within himself.

[2] That is, some one other than the Adhvaryu, viz. the Pratiprasthâtri or some other person, Kâty. VII, 4, 11 scholl.

[3] That is, inasmuch as he may be of Rakshas origin

[4] Viz. of the crime of Brâhmanicide (brahmahatyâ).

Second Brâhma*n*a.

1. He maintains silence; and silently he remains seated till sunset. The reason why he maintains silence is this:

2. By means of the sacrifice the gods gained that supreme authority which they now wield. They spake, 'How can this (world) of ours be made unattainable to men?' They sipped the sap of the sacrifice, even as bees would suck out honey; and having drained the sacrifice and scattered it by means of the sacrificial post, they disappeared: and because they scattered (yopaya, viz. the sacrifice) therewith, therefore it is called yûpa (post)[1].

3. Now this was heard by the *Ri*shis. They collected the sacrifice. As that sacrifice was collected (prepared)[2], so does he who is consecrated collect the sacrifice (by keeping his speech within him),—for the sacrifice is speech.

---

[1] Professor Whitney (American Journal of Philology, III, p. 402) proposes to take yopaya here in the sense of 'to set up an obstacle, to block or bar the way.' He remarks, 'How the setting up of a post should operate to "efface traces" cannot easily be made to appear.' I am not aware that any one has supposed that it was by the 'setting up' of the post that the traces of the sacrifice were obliterated. From what follows—'They collected the sacrifice'—it seems to me pretty clear that our author at any rate connects 'yopaya' with the root yu, to mix, stir about, and hence to efface the traces by mixing with the ground, or by scattering about. This causative was evidently no longer a living form, but resorted to for etymological purposes.

[2] Or, perhaps, They collected the sacrifice in the same way as this (present) sacrifice has been collected. See, however, the corresponding passage III, 2, 2, 29; 4, 3, 16. The Kâ*n*va text is clearer: Ta*m* yathâ yatharshayo ya*gñam* samabhara*m*s tathâya*m* ya*gñah* sambh*ri*to yatho vai tad *ri*shayo ya*gñam* samabharann evam u vâ esha etad ya*gñam* sambharati yo dîkshate.

4. When the sun has set, he breaks silence. Now Pragâpati is the year, since the sacrifice is Pragâpati; and the year is day and night, since these two revolving produce it. He has been consecrated during the day, and he has gained the night: as great as the sacrifice is, as great as is its extent, to that extent has he gained it before he breaks silence.

5. Some, however, make him break his silence on seeing the (first) star[1], arguing that then the sun has actually set. But let him not do so, for what would become of them if it were cloudy? Let him therefore break silence as soon as he thinks the sun has set.

6. Now, some make him break silence by the formula, 'Earth! ether! sky!' arguing that thereby they strengthen the sacrifice, they heal the sacrifice. But let him not do so; for he who breaks silence with that (formula) does not strengthen the sacrifice, does not heal the sacrifice.

7. Let him rather break silence with this one (Vâg. S. IV, 11), 'Prepare ye the fast-food! prepare ye the fast-food! [prepare ye the fast-food!] Agni is the Brahman, Agni is the sacrifice; the tree is meet for the sacrifice.' For this indeed is his sacrifice, this is his havis-offering at this (rite of consecration), even as the Agnihotra was heretofore[2]. In thus preparing the (Soma) sacrifice by means of the sacrifice, he establishes the sacrifice

---

[1] 'After pointing out (some) stars [nakshatrâni darsayitvâ],' Kânva recension. Cf. Taitt. S. VI, 1, 4, 4, 'when the stars have risen, he breaks silence with "Prepare the fast-food!"'

[2] That is to say, the eating of the fast-food, consisting chiefly of milk, takes, as it were, the place of the Agnihotra, or evening and morning sacrifice, which he is not allowed to perform during the time of his consecration.

in the sacrifice, and carries on the sacrifice by means of the sacrifice; for (the partaking of) that fast-food is indeed carried on by him till the pressing of the Soma. Thrice he pronounces (the first words[1]), for threefold is the sacrifice.

8. Moreover, he breaks silence, after turning round towards the fire. He, on the other hand, who breaks silence with any other (formula) but this[2], does not strengthen the sacrifice, does not heal the sacrifice. In pronouncing the first (part of the formula)[3] he utters the truth of speech[4].

9. 'Agni is the Brahman' (neut.), he says, for Agni is indeed the Brahman (sacerdotium);—'Agni is the sacrifice,' for Agni is indeed the sacrifice;—'the tree is meet for the sacrifice,' for trees[5] are indeed meet for the sacrifice, since men could not sacrifice, if there were no trees: therefore he says, 'the tree is meet for the sacrifice.'

10. Thereupon they cook the fast-food for him. For he who is consecrated draws nigh to the gods and becomes one of the deities. But the sacrificial food of the gods must be cooked, and not uncooked: hence they cook it, and he partakes of that fast-milk

[1] Viz. the injunction 'Prepare ye the fast-food!' which is indeed read thrice in the Kânva text, where the arrangement of these paragraphs is much clearer.

[2] Thus Sây. 'ato 'nyena, bhûr bhuvah suvar ityanena' (MS. I. O. 657). Dr. Lindner makes atah refer to Agni. The Kânva text begins the passage, corresponding to paragraphs 7 and 8: 'So 'gnim îkshamâno visrigate vratam krinuta (thrice) etad vâ etasya havir esha yagño yad vratam.'

[3] That is, the words 'Agni is the Brahman.'

[4] Viz. because 'the Brahman (neut.) is the truth (or essence, satyam),' Sây.

[5] Viz. trees from which sacrificial implements, fire-wood, the sacrificial stake, &c., are obtained.

(vrata) and does not offer it in the fire. The reason why he eats the fast-food and does not offer it in the fire is this:

11. By means of the sacrifice the gods gained that supreme authority which they now wield. They spake, 'How can this (world) of ours be made unattainable to men?' They sipped the sap of the sacrifice, even as bees would suck out honey; and having drained the sacrifice and scattered it by means of the sacrificial post, they disappeared. And because they scattered (yopaya) therewith, therefore it is called yûpa (post).

12. Now this was heard by the *Ri*shis. They collected the sacrifice. As that sacrifice was collected, so does he who is consecrated now become the sacrifice, for it is he that carries it on, that produces it. And whatever (sap) of the sacrifice was sucked out and drained, that he now restores again by sipping the fast-milk and not offering it in the fire; for, assuredly, were he to offer it in the fire, he would not replenish (the sacrifice). But let him, nevertheless, think (that he does so) sacrificing and not the reverse.

13. For, verily, these vital airs are born of the mind, endowed with mind[1], of intelligent power[2]: Agni is speech; Mitra and Varu*n*a are the out-breathing and the in-breathing; Âditya (the sun) is the eye; and the All-gods are the ear,—it is unto these deities that offering is thereby made by him.

14. Now, some add both rice and barley to the first (day's) fast-milk, arguing,—"By means of these two substances (rasa) we restore what part of the sacrifice was sucked out and drained; and, should

[1] Manoyug (?), 'mind-yoked,' i.e. having thoughts for their team.
[2] Cf. paragraph 18.

the vrata-cow yield no milk, he may prepare his fast-food of whichever of these (cereals) he pleases; and thus both the rice and the barley are 'taken hold of' by him." But let him not do this; for he who adds both rice and barley (to the milk) neither replenishes the sacrifice nor heals it. Let him therefore add only the one or the other (cereal). Both the rice and barley doubtless form his (havis) material for offering (at the New and Full-moon Sacrifice), and when they do so become his material for offering, then they are also 'taken hold of[1]' by him. Should the vrata-cow yield no milk, let him prepare the fast-food of whichever of them he pleases.

15. Some, again, add to the first (day's) fast-food (vrata) all manner of vegetables and fragrant (seasoning), arguing,—'If disease were to befall him, he might cure it by whatever thereof he pleases, as if he cured it by the fast-milk[2].' But let him not

[1] Anvârabdha has here the usual sacrificial meaning of 'taken hold of (from behind),' with perhaps something of that of 'taken (as medicine=einnehmen).' Thus at the invocation of the I*d*â, the sacrificer has to touch (anv-ârabh) the i*d*â from behind, thereby keeping up his connection, and identifying himself, with the sacrifice. Cf. part i, p. 228, note 1; and III, 2, 4, 15. Hence the author, making use of the term suggested by those he criticises, argues that as both kinds of material have already been used and therefore touched (anvârabdha) by him at the New and Full-moon Sacrifice (Sâya*n*a), they have therefore been taken possession of by him. It is possible, though scarcely likely, that the verb may have reference here to the anvârambha*n*îyâ ish*t*i,—or preliminary ceremony of the first performance of the New and Full-moon Sacrifice,—with which the present use of these cereals would, in that case, be identified, as that of the vrata-milk was with the Agnihotra (cf. paragraph 7 above). The Kâ*n*va text has the verb â-rabh instead, yathâ havishârabdhena bhishagyed ity evam etat.

[2] That is to say, though the restoration might be due to the medicinal properties of some of those ingredients, it could be ascribed to the milk.

do this, lest he should do what is inauspicious to the sacrifice; for those people do at the sacrifice what is a human act, and inauspicious to the sacrifice assuredly is that which is human. If any disease were to befall him who is consecrated, let him cure it wherewith he pleases; for completion is proper[1].

16. He (the Adhvaryu) hands the fast-food to him, after letting the ordinary (meal-)time pass,—viz. the evening-milk in the latter part of the night, and the morning-milk in the afternoon,—for the sake of distinction: he thereby distinguishes the divine from the human.

17. And when he is about to hand the fast-food to him he makes him touch water[2], with the text, 'For protection we direct our thoughts to divine devotion, the source of supreme mercy[3], the bestower of glory and the bearer of sacrifices[4]: may it prosper our ways, according to our desire!' Heretofore, indeed, it was for a human meal that he cleansed himself, but now it is for the sake of divine devotion: therefore he says, 'For the sake of assistance we turn our thoughts to divine devotion, the source of supreme mercy, the bestower of glory, the bearer of sacrifices: may it

[1] Sâyana takes this to mean, that, as above all the consummation of the sacrifice is desirable, one should in case of disease cure it by any of those drugs without their being taken (anvârabdha) sacrificially, or as part of the sacrificial performance.

[2] According to the Kânva text, the sacrificer first washes himself (nenikte) and then sips water (âkâmati); and having drunk the fast-milk, he touches water (apa upasprisati).

[3] Or, perhaps, 'we meditate on the divine intelligence, the most merciful.'

[4] Yagñavâhasam ('bringing, or bearing, worship'); thus also Taitt. S. I, 2, 2. The Kânva text reads visvadhâyasam, 'all-nourishing, all-sustaining.'

prosper our ways, according to our desire!' Whenever, being about to take the fast-food, he touches water, let him touch it with this same (formula).

18. Thereupon he drinks the fast-food, with the text, 'May the gods favour us, they who are born of the mind, and endowed with mind[1], and of intelligent power! may they protect us! Hail to them!' Thus that (fast-food) comes to be for him (by means of the Svâhâ) as an oblation consecrated by the Vashat.

19. Having drank the fast-food, he touches his navel[2], with the text (Vâg. S. IV, 12), 'Ye waters that have been drank, may ye become palatable and auspicious within us! may they prove agreeable to us, freeing us from disease and weakness and sin,—they the divine, the immortal, the holy!' Now, he who is consecrated draws nigh to the gods and becomes one of the deities; but the sacrificial food of the gods is not increased (with other material): hence, if in handing the fast-food (to the consecrated) he increases it (with other milk), he commits a fault and breaks the fast. This (formula), however, is the atonement for that (transgression), and thus that fault is not committed by him, and he does not break the fast (or vow): therefore he says, 'Ye waters....!' Whenever, after drinking the fast-food, he touches his navel, let him touch it with this (formula); for who

[1] See p. 39, note 2. The Kânva text here again identifies the divinities referred to in the text with the vital airs.

[2] Having eaten and touched water, he strokes his belly (udaram abhimrisate), Kânv. The Kânva text renders the meaning quite clear: Uta vai tîvram vratam bhavati tat kshudrataram asad iti vopotsiñkaty, alpam vâ bhavati tad bhûyaskâmyopotsiñkati.

knows whether (or not) he who hands the fast-food (to the consecrated) increases it (with other milk)[1]!

20. When he intends to pass urine, he takes up a clod of earth or some other object by means of the deer's horn, with the text (Vâg. S. IV, 13), 'This (O Earth) is thy covering meet for worship.' For this earth truly is divine, and serves as a place for the worship of the gods: it must not be defiled by him who is consecrated. Having lifted up this its sacrificially pure covering[2], he now relieves himself on its impure body, with the formula, 'I discharge not offspring, but waters,'—for so indeed he does[3]; 'delivering from trouble, and consecrated by Svâhâ,'—for they do indeed deliver from trouble what is pressed together inside: therefore he says, 'delivering from trouble,'—'consecrated by Svâhâ, enter ye the earth!' whereby he means to say, 'Having become offerings, do ye enter the earth, appeased!'

21. Thereupon he throws the clod of earth down again, with the text, 'Unite with the earth!' for truly this earth is divine, and serves as a place for the worship of the gods: it must not be defiled by him who is consecrated. Having lifted up this its

---

[1] No other fresh milk is to be added to that obtained by one milking of the vratadughâ (fast-milk) cow (Kâty. VII, 4, 29); but the preceding formula is to be muttered in order to obviate any evil consequences arising from a possible secret breach of this rule, on the part of him who hands the milk to the sacrificer. Dr. Lindner takes upotsi*k* in the sense of 'to spill,' but I find no authority for this rendering, which neither the prep. upa, nor abhi (in the equivalent abhyutsi*k*) would seem to admit of.

[2] See p. 10, note 4.

[3] 'Ubhaya*m* vâ ata ety âpa*s* *k*a reta*s* *k*a; sa etad apa eva mu*ñk*ati na pra*g*âm.'

sacrificially pure covering, he has relieved himself on its impure body, and now restores to it this its pure covering: therefore he says, 'Unite with the earth!'

22. He then gives himself up to Agni (the fire) for protection and lies down to sleep. For he who is consecrated draws nigh to the gods and becomes one of the deities; but the gods do not sleep, while to him sleeplessness is not vouchsafed; and Agni being Lord of vows to the gods, it is to him that he now commits himself and lies down to sleep, with the text (Vâ*g*. S. IV, 14), 'O Agni, be thou a good waker: may we thoroughly refresh ourselves!' whereby he says, 'O Agni, wake thou: we are going to sleep!'—'Guard us unremittingly!' whereby he means to say, 'protect us heedfully!'—'Make us awake again!' whereby he means to say, 'Order so that, having rested here, we may awake safely.'

23. And when he has slept and does not wish to fall asleep again, (the Adhvaryu) makes him mutter the text (Vâ*g*. S. IV, 15), 'Thought and life have come back to me, breath and soul have come back to me, eye and ear have come back to me;' for all these depart from him when he sleeps; the breath alone does not; and after he has slept he again unites with them: therefore he says, 'Thought and life have come back to me . . .'—'May Agni Vai*s*vânara, the unassailable preserver of lives, preserve us from mishap and shame!' whereby he means to say, 'May Agni save us from whatever mistake (may be committed) on this occasion, either by sleep or otherwise:' this is why he says, 'May Agni Vai*s*vânara, the unassailable preserver of lives, preserve us from mishap and shame!'

24. For, when he who is consecrated utters any-

thing that is foreign to the vow, or when he becomes angry, he commits a fault and breaks his vow, since suppression of anger behoves him who is consecrated. Now, Agni is the Lord of vows among the gods,—it is to him therefore that he resorts (Vâg. S. IV, 16; Rig-veda VIII, 11, 7): 'Thou, O Agni, art the divine guardian of vows among men, to whom praise is due at the sacrifices.' This, then, is his atonement for that (transgression); and thus that fault is not committed by him, and he does not break his vow: therefore he says, 'Thou, O Agni, art the divine guardian of vows among men, to whom praise is due at the sacrifices.'

25. And whatever (gift) people offer to him[1], thereon he (the Adhvaryu) makes him pronounce the text, 'Bestow this much, O Soma, bring more!' for Soma indeed it is that appropriates for the consecrated whatever people offer to him: when he says, 'Bestow this much, O Soma,' he means to say, 'Bestow this much on us, O Soma;' and by 'Bring more,' he means to say, 'Fetch more for us!'—'The divine Savit*ri*, the bestower of wealth, hath bestowed wealth on us;' whereby that (gift) comes to be impelled by Savit*ri* with a view to (further) gifts.

26. Before sunset he (the Adhvaryu) says, 'Consecrated, restrain thy speech!' and after sunset he releases speech. Before sunrise he says, 'Consecrated, restrain thy speech!' and after sunrise he releases

[1] 'And if they were to bring him either a garment or a cow, let him address it with the text—.' Kâ*n*va text. According to some authorities the Dîkshita is to go about for twelve days begging his means of subsistence, and whatever he obtains he is to touch and consecrate by the above text. Kâty. VII, 5, 3, comm.

his speech,—for the sake of continuity: with the night he continues the day, and with the day the night.

27. Let not the sun set on him while abiding elsewhere (than the hall); nor let the sun rise on him while asleep. For were the sun to set on him while abiding elsewhere, he (the sun) would cut him off from the night; and were the sun to rise on him while asleep, he would cut him off from the day: there is no atonement for this, hence it must by all means be avoided. Prior to the purificatory bath he should not enter water, nor should it rain upon him; for it is improper that he should enter water, or that it should rain upon him, before the purificatory bath. Moreover, he speaks his speech falteringly, and not effusively after the manner of ordinary speech[1]. The reason why he speaks his speech falteringly and not after the manner of ordinary speech is this:

28. By means of the sacrifice the gods gained that supreme authority which they now wield. They spake, 'How can this (world) of ours be made unattainable to men?' They sipped the sap of the sacrifice, even as bees would suck out honey; and having drained the sacrifice and scattered it by means of the sacrificial post, they disappeared. And because they scattered (yopaya) therewith, therefore it is called yûpa (post).

29. Now this was heard by the *Ri*shis. They collected the sacrifice; and as that sacrifice was collected, so does he who is consecrated now collect the sacrifice (by keeping back his speech),—for the sacrifice is speech. And whatever part of the sacrifice

[1] Literally, 'Falteringly (i.e. hesitatingly, cautiously) he speaks speech, not human effusive (speech).'

was then sucked out and drained, that he now restores again by speaking his speech falteringly and not effusively after the manner of ordinary speech. For were he to speak effusively after the manner of ordinary speech, he would not restore (the sap of the sacrifice): therefore he speaks his speech falteringly and not effusively after the manner of ordinary speech.

30. He verily anoints himself,—it is for speech that he anoints himself[1], since he anoints himself for the sacrifice, and the sacrifice is speech. Dhîkshita (the anointed) doubtless is the same as dîkshita (the consecrated).

THE PRÂYANÎYESHTI, OR OPENING-SACRIFICE.

THIRD BRÂHMANA.

1. He prepares the Prâyanîya rice-pap for Aditi. Now while the gods were spreading (performing) the sacrifice on this (earth) they excluded her (the earth) from the sacrifice. She thought, 'How is it that, in spreading the sacrifice on me, they should exclude me from the sacrifice?' and confounded their sacrifice: they knew not that sacrifice.

[1] Dhîkshate, apparently the desiderative of dih (Weber, in St. Petersb. Dict. s. v.) Cf. III, 1, 3, 7 seq. The construction (especially the first hi) is rather peculiar. This paragraph apparently is to supply further proof why he should be cautious in his speech, and the words 'sa vai dhîkshate' have to be taken parenthetically: 'He speaks his speech cautiously....; for (anointing himself as he does) he anoints himself for speech, &c.' The Kânva text offers less difficulty: Atha yad dhîkshito nâma vâke vâ esha etad dhîkshate, yagñâya hi dhîkshate, yagño hi vâk, tasmâd dhîkshito nâma, dhîkshito ha vai nâmaitad yad dîkshita ity âhuh. Sâyana's comment (MS.) is not very satisfactory: Vâkam yagñasâdhanatvena prasamsati; sa vai dhîkshita iti prasangâd dhîkshitasabdam nirvakti dhîkshito ha vâ iti yasmâd dîkshita iti nâma tâdrisî dîkshâ vâk sâdhyeti vâk srutih.

2. They said, 'How comes it that our sacrifice was confounded, when we spread it on this (earth)? how is it that we know it not?'

3. They said, 'In spreading the sacrifice on her, we have excluded her from the sacrifice: it is she that has confounded our sacrifice,—let us have recourse to her!'

4. They said, 'When we were spreading the sacrifice on thee, how was it that it became confounded, that we know it not?'

5. She said, 'While spreading the sacrifice on me, ye have excluded me from the sacrifice: that was why I have confounded your sacrifice. Set ye aside a share for me; then ye shall see the sacrifice, then ye shall know it!'

6. 'So be it!' said the gods: 'Thine, forsooth, shall be the opening (prâyanîya[1]), and thine the concluding (udayanîya) oblation!' This is why both the Prâyanîya and the Udayanîya (pap) belong

[1] At IV, 5, 1, 2, the name prâyanîya is derived from pra-i, to go forth, because by means of this offering they, as it were, go forth to buy the Soma. Similarly, udayanîya is explained as the offering he performs after coming out (ud-i) from the bath. In Ait. Br. I, 7, on the other hand, the name prâyanîya is explained as that by means of which sacrificers go forward (pra-i) to the heavenly world. In the Soma sacrifice, the Prâyanîyâ and Udayanîyâ may be said to correspond to the Fore-offerings and After-offerings (prayâga and anuyâga) of the New and Full-moon Sacrifice; though, of course, the Fore- and After-offerings form part of the prâyanîyâ and udayanîyâ, as ishtis. But they are peculiar in this respect, that offering is made at both to the very same deities, and that the invitatory prayers (anuvâkyâ) of the prâyanîyeshti form the offering-prayers (yâgyâ) of the udayanîyeshti, and vice versâ. For these formulas, see Âsval. Srautas. IV, 3; Haug, Ait. Br. Transl. p. 16. The offering formula of the oblation to Aditi at the Prâyanîyâ (and invitatory formula at the Udayanîyâ), strange to say, is not a Rik-verse, but one from the Atharvan (VII, 6, 2).

to Aditi; for Aditi truly is this (earth). Thereupon they saw and spread the sacrifice.

7. Hence, when he prepares the Prâya*n*îya rice-pap for Aditi, he does so for the purpose of his seeing the sacrifice: 'After seeing the sacrifice I shall buy (the Soma) and spread that (sacrifice);' thus thinking he prepares the Prâya*n*îya pap for Aditi. The sacrificial food had been prepared, but offering had not yet been made to the deity (Aditi),—

8. When Pathyâ Svasti[1] appeared to them. They offered to her, for Pathyâ Svasti (the wishing of 'a happy journey') is speech, and the sacrifice also is speech. Thereby they perceived the sacrifice and spread it.

9. Thereupon Agni appeared to them: they offered to him; whereby they perceived that part of the sacrifice which was of Agni's nature. Now of Agni's nature is what is dry in the sacrifice: that they thereby perceived and spread.

10. Then Soma appeared to them: they offered to him; whereby they perceived that part of the sacrifice which was of Soma's nature. Now of Soma's nature is what is moist in the sacrifice: that they thereby perceived and spread.

11. Then Savit*ri* appeared to them: they offered to him. Now Savit*ri* represents cattle, and the sacrifice also means cattle: hence they thereby perceived and spread the sacrifice. Thereupon they offered to the deity (Aditi), for whom the sacrificial food had been prepared.

12. It is to these same five deities, then, that he offers. For that sacrifice, when thrown into dis-

[1] I. e. 'welfare on the road, or a happy journey,' a genius of well-being and prosperity.

order, was in five parts; and by means of those five deities they recognised it.

13. The seasons became confounded, the five: by means of those same five deities they recognised them.

14. The regions became confounded, the five: by means of those same five deities they recognised them.

15. Through Pathyâ Svasti they recognised the northern (upper) region: wherefore speech sounds higher here[1] among the Kuru-Pañkâlas; for she (Pathyâ Svasti) is in reality speech, and through her they recognised the northern region, and to her belongs the northern region.

16. Through Agni they recognised the eastern region: wherefore they take out Agni from behind towards the east[2], and render homage to him; for through him they recognised the eastern region, and to him belongs the eastern region.

17. Through Soma they recognised the southern region: hence, after the Soma has been bought, they drive it round on the south side; and hence they say that Soma is sacred to the Fathers; for through him they recognised the southern region, and to him belongs the southern region.

18. Through Savit*ri* they recognised the western region, for Savit*ri* is yonder burning (sun): wherefore he goes towards the west, for through him they recognised the western region, and to him belongs the western region.

[1] Atra, ? 'there.' In the St. Petersb. Dict. uttarâhi is here taken in the sense of 'in the north,' instead of 'higher.' See also part i, pref. p. xlii, note 1; Weber, Ind. Stud. I, p. 191.

[2] That is, from the Gârhapatya to the Âhavanîya fire-place.

19. Through Aditi they recognised the upper region, for Aditi is this (earth): wherefore the plants and trees grow upwards on her; for through her they recognised the upper region, and to her belongs the upper region.

20. The hospitable reception[1] (of King Soma) verily is the head of the sacrifice, and the opening and closing oblations are its arms. But the arms are on both sides of the head, and hence those two oblations, the Prâyanîya and Udayanîya, are made on both sides of (before and after) the reception.

21. Now, they say that whatever is done at the Prâyanîya should be done at the Udayanîya[2], and the barhis (grass-covering of the altar), which is used at the Prâyanîya, is also used at the Udayanîya: he lays it aside, after removing it (from the altar). The pot (in which the rice-pap was cooked) he puts aside with the parched remains of dough, and (so he does) the pot-ladle after wiping it. And the priests who officiate during the Prâyanîya, officiate also at the Udayanîya. And because of this identical performance at the sacrifice the two arms are alike and of the same shape.

22. But let him not do it in this way. Let him rather[3] (at the proper time) throw both the barhis and the pot-ladle after (the prastara, into the fire[4]), and let him put the pot aside after rinsing it. The priests who officiate during the Prâyanîya, officiate also at the Udayanîya; but should they (in the

[1] See III, 4, 1.

[2] See p. 48, note 1. For the Udayanîya, see IV, 5, 1.

[3] Or, perhaps, 'let him, if he chooses (kâmam) . . .;' see Kâty. VII, 5, 16–19; cf. also note on III, 2, 4, 14.

[4] See I, 8, 3, 19; 9, 2, 29.

mean time) have departed this life, others may officiate instead. It is because he offers to the same deities, and the same oblations, that the two arms are alike and of the same shape.

23. To five deities he offers at the Prâyanîya, and to five at the Udayanîya: hence there are five fingers here and five there. This (Prâyanîya offering) ends with the Samyu. They perform no Patnîsamyâgas[1]. For the arms are on the fore-part of the body, and the fore-part of the sacrifice he perfects by this (opening ceremony). This is why it ends with the Samyu, and why no Patnîsamyâgas are performed.

HIRANYAVATÎ-ÂHUTI, OR OFFERING WITH GOLD; AND HOMAGE TO THE SOMA-COW.

FOURTH BRÂHMANA.

1. Now Soma was in the sky, and the gods were here on earth. The gods desired,—'Would that Soma came to us: we might sacrifice with him, when come.' They created those two illusions, Suparnî and Kadrû. In the chapter on the hearths (dhishnya[2]) it is set forth how that affair of Suparnî and Kadrû came to pass.

2. Gâyatrî flew up to Soma for them. While she was carrying him off, the Gandharva Visvâvasu stole him from her. The gods were aware of this,—'Soma has indeed been removed from yonder (sky), but he comes not to us, for the Gandharvas have stolen him.'

[1] For the Samyuvâka, see I, 9, 1, 24; for the Patnîsamyâgas, I, 9, 2, 1 seq.

[2] See III, 6, 2, 2 seq.

3. They said, 'The Gandharvas are fond of women: let us send Vâk (speech) to them, and she will return to us together with Soma.' They sent Vâk to them, and she returned to them together with Soma.

4. The Gandharvas came after her and said, 'Soma (shall be) yours, and Vâk ours[1]!' 'So be it!' said the gods; 'but if she would rather come hither, do not ye carry her off by force: let us woo her!' They accordingly wooed her.

5. The Gandharvas recited the Vedas to her, saying, 'See how we know it, see how we know it[2]!'

6. The gods then created the lute and sat playing and singing, saying, 'Thus we will sing to thee, thus we will amuse thee!' She turned to the gods; but, in truth, she turned to them vainly, since she turned away from those, engaged in praising and praying, to dance and song. Wherefore even to this day women are given to vain things: for it was on this wise that Vâk turned thereto, and other women do as she did. And hence it is to him who dances and sings that they most readily take a fancy[3].

7. Both Soma and Vâk were thus with the gods. Now, when he buys Soma he does so in order that he may sacrifice with him, when obtained, for his (own) obtainment (of heavenly bliss[4]); for he who

[1] 'Yours (shall be) Soma, and ours Vâk, wherewith you bought (Soma) from us.' Kânva text.

[2] The G. proclaimed the sacrifice and Veda to her, saying, 'Thus we know the sacrifice, thus we know (the Veda); mighty are we.' Kânva text.

[3] 'And hence it is to him who is given to vain things, who dances and sings, that women are most attached.' Kânva text.

[4] Literally, 'that he may sacrifice with the arrived (guest) for his own arrival (? in the world of the gods).'

sacrifices with Soma that has not been bought, sacrifices with Soma that has not been (properly) obtained[1].

8. In the first place he pours the butter, which remains in the dhruvâ spoon, in four parts into the *g*uhû; and having tied a piece of gold with a blade of the altar-grass[2], and laid it down (in the *g*uhû), he offers (the butter), thinking, 'I will offer with pure milk;' for milk and gold are of the same origin, since both have sprung from Agni's seed[3].

9. He lays down the piece of gold, with the text (Vâ*g*. S. IV, 17), 'This (butter) is thy body, O shining (Agni)! this (gold) is thy light,'—for that gold is indeed light:—'unite therewith and obtain splendour!' When he says, 'Unite therewith,' he means to say, 'Mingle therewith;' and when he says, 'Obtain splendour,'—splendour meaning Soma,—he means to say, 'Obtain Soma.'

10. And as the gods then sent her (Vâ*k*) to Soma, so does he now send her to Soma; and the cow for which the Soma is bought being in reality Vâ*k*, it is her he gratifies by this offering, thinking, 'With her, when gratified, I shall buy the Soma.'

11. He offers, with the text, 'Thou art the singer of praises[4],'—for this (word '*g*û*h*'), the 'singer of praises,' is one of her (Vâ*k*'s) names;—'upholden by the Mind,'—this speech of ours

---

[1] Lit. 'with Soma that has not come' (to him as a guest), so that the guest-offering (âtithya, III, 4, 1) could not take place.

[2] Because of this piece of gold, the offering here described is called Hira*n*yavatî-âhuti, or 'offering with gold.'

[3] See II, 1, 1, 5; 3, 1, 15.

[4] The author seems to take *g*û*h* here as nom. of *g*ur=gur (g*ri*, gir), cf. *g*ûr*ni*. Some of the native dictionaries give *g*û as one of the names of Sarasvatî. The St. Petersb. Dict. takes it here in the sense of 'drängend, treibend (pressing forward).'

is indeed upheld by the mind, because the Mind goes before[1] Speech (and prompts her), 'Speak thus! say not this!' for, were it not for the Mind, Speech would indeed talk incoherently: for this reason he says, 'Upholden by the Mind.'

12. 'Well-pleasing to Vishnu,' whereby he means to say, 'Well-pleasing to Soma whom we approach[2].' [He proceeds, Vâg. S. IV, 18], 'Inspired by thee of true inspiration,' whereby he means to say, 'Be thou of true inspiration! go thou to Soma for us!'—'May I obtain a support for my body, Svâhâ!' for he who reaches the end of the sacrifice, indeed obtains a support for his body: hence he thereby means to say, 'May I reach the end of the sacrifice!'

13. Thereupon he takes out the piece of gold (from the spoon), whereby he bestows gold on men; but were he to offer (the butter) together with the gold, he would doubtless cast the gold away from men, and no gold would then be gained among men.

14. He takes it out, with the text, 'Thou art pure, thou art shining, thou art immortal, thou art sacred to all the gods.' When, having offered the whole milk, he now says, 'Thou art pure . . . ,' it is indeed pure, and shining, and immortal, and sacred to all the gods. Having loosened the grass-blade, he throws it on the barhis, and ties a string round the gold[3].

15. Having then taken butter a second time in

---

[1] Mano hîdam purastâd vâkas karati, Kânva text.

[2] To whom we send you, K.

[3] The concluding ceremonies of the Prâyanîya (see III, 2, 3, 23) are now performed; the offering of the Barhis being optional, as the barhis may be used again for the Udayanîya (ib. 22). Kâty VII, 6, 11 comm.

four parts, he says, 'Sacrificer, hold on behind[1]!' They open the (south and east)[2] doors of the hall (and walk out). On the right side (of the front door) approaches the Soma-cow[3]: (by having) her thus put forward[4], he has sent her forth (to Soma); for the Soma-cow is in reality Vâ*k*: it is her he has gratified by this offering, thinking, 'With her, when gratified, I will buy Soma.'

16. Having gone up to her, he (the Adhvaryu) salutes her, with the text (Vâ*g*. S. IV, 19), 'Thou art thought, thou art the mind,'—for speech, doubtless, speaks in accordance with thought, with the mind[5];—'Thou art intelligence, thou art the Dakshi*n*â[6],'—for it is by means of their respective intelligence[7] that people seek to make their living, either by reciting (the Veda), or by readiness of speech[8], or by songs: therefore he says, 'Thou art intelligence;' and 'Dakshi*n*â' (gift to the priests) he calls her, because she is indeed the Dak-

---

[1] According to the Kâ*n*vas, the Adhvaryu's formula is,—Ihi, Ya*g*amâna, 'Go, Sacrificer!' In Kâty. VII, 6, 12 only the above formula is mentioned.

[2] The eastern door is for the Adhvaryu (and Sacrificer) and the southern for the Pratiprasthât*ri*.

[3] Soma-kraya*n*î, 'the cow for which the Soma is bought.'

[4] Prahita*m* seems to be taken here in the double sense of 'put forward or in front' (from pra-dhâ) and despatched (from pra-hi).

[5] 'In accordance with the thought of the mind,' manaso vai *k*ittam anu vâg vadati, K.

[6] The omission of 'asi' in the Brâhma*n*a is curious; the Kâ*n*va text has correctly 'dakshi*n*âsi.'

[7] Dhiyâ-dhiyâ, or rather 'by means of this their respective genius (in regard to speech).' Dhî seems to mean 'thought expressed by speech,' hence often 'prayer, hymn;' cf. III, 5, „ 11.

[8] Prakâmodya, rather either 'fondness for talk' or 'effusive speech.' It seems to refer to story-tellers (? amusing speech).

shinâ;—'Thou art supreme, thou art worthy of worship,'—for she is indeed supreme and worthy of worship;—'Thou art Aditi, the double-headed,'—inasmuch as, through her (Vâk, speech), he speaks the right thing wrongly, and puts last what comes first, and first what comes last, therefore she is double-headed: that is why he says, 'Thou art Aditi, the double-headed[1].'

17. 'Be thou for us successful (in going) forward and successful (in coming) back!' when he says, 'Be thou for us successful (in going) forward,' he means to say, 'Go to (fetch) Soma for us!' and when he says, 'Be thou successful (in coming) back,' he means to say, 'Come back to us with Soma!' This is why he says, 'Be thou for us successful (in going) forward and successful (in coming) back!'

18. 'May Mitra bind thee by the foot!' For that rope, doubtless, is of Varuna; and were she (the cow) tied with a rope, she would be (under the power) of Varuna. And, on the other hand, were she not tied at all, she would be uncontrolled. Now that which is of Mitra is not of Varuna; and as (a cow), if tied with a rope, is under control, so it is in the case of this one when he says, 'May Mitra bind thee by the foot!'

19. 'May Pûshan guard thy paths!' Now Pûshan is this Earth, and for whomsoever she is the guardian of his paths[2], he stumbles not at any time: therefore he says, 'May Pûshan guard thy paths!'

20. 'For Indra as the supreme guide;'—whereby he says, 'May she be well-guarded!' [He

[1] In Taitt. S. VI, 1, 7, 5, this epithet is explained by the fact that both the prâyanîya and the udayanîya belong to Aditi.

[2] 'And her he thereby makes the guardian on his path,' imâm evâsmâ etad adhvani goptâram karoti, K.

proceeds, Vâg. S. IV, 20], 'May thy mother grant thee permission, thy father, thine own brother, thy fellow in the herd!' whereby he says, 'Go thou for us to fetch Soma, with the permission of all thy kin.'—'O goddess, go to the god,'—for it is indeed as a goddess, as Vâk, that she goes to a god, to Soma: therefore he says, 'O goddess, go to the god;'—'To Soma for the sake of Indra!' Indra truly is the deity of the sacrifice: therefore he says, 'To Soma for the sake of Indra.' 'May Rudra guide thee back!' this he says for her safety, for cattle cannot pass beyond Rudra[1]. 'Hail to thee! come back, with Soma for thy companion!' whereby he says, 'Hail to thee, come back to us together with Soma!'

21. Even as, at that time, the gods sent her to Soma, and she returned to them together with Soma, so does he now send her to Soma, and she returns to him together with Soma.

22. And as the gods then wooed her with the Gandharvas, and she turned to the gods, so does the sacrificer now woo her, and she turns to the sacrificer. They lead her (the Soma-cow) northwards round (to the place where the Soma is to be sold); for the north is the quarter of men, and hence it is that of the sacrificer: for this reason they lead her northwards round.

Third Adhyâya. First Brâhmana.

1. He follows her, stepping into seven foot-prints of hers[2]; he thereby takes possession of her: that

[1] Rudra rules over these (cows); the cattle do not pass beyond (nâtiyanti) him; and thus she does not pass beyond him: therefore he says, 'May Rudra turn thee back!' Kânva text.

[2] Viz. into seven foot-prints of her right fore-foot. According to

is why he steps into seven of her foot-prints. For when the metres were produced from Vâk (speech), the one consisting of seven feet, the Sakvarî, was the last (highest) of them. It is that (metre) he now draws down towards himself from above: this is why he steps into seven of her foot-prints.

2. It is as Vâk[1] that he steps into them; (with the text, Vâg. S. IV, 21), 'Thou art a Vasvî, thou art Aditi, thou art an Âdityâ, thou art a Rudrâ, thou art Kandrâ; for she is indeed a Vasvî and Aditi, an Âdityâ, a Rudrâ, Kandrâ. 'May Brihaspati make thee rest in happiness!'—Brihaspati being the Brahman, he thereby means to say, 'May Brihaspati lead thee hither by means of the good (work)[2]!' 'Rudra, together with the Vasus, is well-pleased with thee:' this he says to secure her (the cow's) safety, for cattle cannot pass beyond Rudra.

3. They now sit down[3] round the seventh foot-print; and having laid down the piece of gold in the foot-print, he offers. For offering is made on nothing but fire, and the gold has sprung from Agni's seed: and thus that offering of his is indeed made over

---

Taitt. S. VI, 1, 8, 1 he steps into six foot-prints and offers on the seventh. According to Kâty. VII, 6, 17 they pass (or overstep, atikram) six foot-prints and sit down round the seventh.

[1] Literally, 'by a form (rûpena) of Vâk (speech),' viz. the text which is pronounced.

[2] This can scarcely be the correct reading. The Kânva text has the more acceptable reading, 'Brihaspati being the Brahman, and felicity the sacrifice, he thereby says, "May the Brahman make thee rest (or delight, ramayatu) in the good (work), the sacrifice!"'

[3] According to the comm. on Kâty. VII, 6, 17 the Brahman and the Sacrificer are to sit on the south, the Adhvaryu on the west, and the Neshtri on the north side of the foot-print.

the fire. And the clarified butter being a thunderbolt, he now delivers her (the cow) by means of that thunderbolt, the butter; and by delivering her he makes her his own.

4. He (the Adhvaryu) offers (with the text, Vâg. S. IV, 22), 'On Aditi's head I pour thee;' for Aditi being this earth, it is on the head of the latter that he offers;—'on the worshipping-ground of the earth'—for on the worshipping-ground of the earth he indeed offers;—'Thou art Idâ's foot-print, filled with butter, Hail!' for Idâ being the cow[1], he indeed offers on the cow's foot-print; and 'filled with butter, Hail!' he says, because it indeed becomes filled with butter when offered upon.

5. Thereupon he takes the wooden sword and draws lines round (the foot-print): the wooden sword being a thunderbolt, it is with the thunderbolt that he draws round it. Thrice he draws round it, so that he encompasses it on all sides with a threefold thunderbolt, for no one to trespass upon it.

6. He draws the lines (with the texts), 'Rejoice in us!' whereby he means to say, 'Rejoice in the sacrificer!' Having then, by tracing, cut out the foot-print all round[2], he throws it into the pan, with, 'In us is thy kinship,' whereby he means to say, 'In the sacrificer is thy kinship.'

7. He then pours some water on (the place whence the earth has been removed). Wherever in digging they hurt her (the earth) and knock off anything

[1] See the legend, part i, p. 216 seq.; especially I, 8, 1, 7; 20; and p. 216, note 3.

[2] According to the comm. on Kâty. VII, 6, 20, it would rather seem that he scratches with the sphya all over the foot-print and then takes out the loose dust (pâmsûn) and throws it into the pan.

from her,—water being (a means of) soothing,—that he now soothes by means of water, that he heals by means of water: that is why he pours water thereon.

8. He then hands (the dust of) the foot-print to the sacrificer, with, 'In thee is wealth,'—wealth meaning cattle, he thereby means to say, 'in thee is cattle.' The sacrificer receives it with, 'With me[1] is wealth,'—wealth meaning cattle, he thereby means to say, 'with me is cattle.'

9. The Adhvaryu then touches himself (near the heart), with, 'May we not be deprived of prosperity!' Thus the Adhvaryu does not exclude himself from (the possession of) cattle.

10. Thereupon they hand (the dust of) the foot-print over to the (sacrificer's) wife. The house being the wife's resting-place, he thereby establishes her in that safe resting-place, the house: for this reason he hands over the (earth of the) foot-print to the wife.

11. The Nesh*tri* makes her say, 'Thine, thine[2] is wealth;' whereupon he causes her to be looked at by the Soma-cow. Now, Soma is a male, and the wife is a female, and that Soma-cow becomes here (exchanged for) Soma: a productive union is thus effected;—this is why he causes her to be looked at by the Soma-cow.

12. He causes her to be looked at (while she pronounces the text, Vâ*g*. S. IV, 23), 'I have seen eye to eye with the divine intelligence, with the far-seeing Dakshi*n*â: take

---

[1] The Kâ*n*va text (Sa*m*hitâ and Br.) has asme instead of me.

[2] See St. Petersb. Dict. s. v. totas. The Kâ*n*va text explains it similarly: 'tvayi tvayi pa*s*ava*h*.' The Taitt. S. VI, 1, 8, 5 has 'Tote râya*h*'—"Thine (?) is wealth" thus for the wife, for she, the wife, is one half of himself.'

not my life from me, neither will I take thine; may I obtain a hero[1] in thy sight!' She thereby asks a blessing: a hero meaning a son, she thereby means to say, 'May I obtain a son in thy sight!'

13. One that is brown, with red-brown eyes, is (fit to be) a Soma-cow. For when Indra and Vishnu divided a thousand (cows) into three parts, there was one left[2], and her they caused to propagate herself in three kinds; and hence, even now, if any one were to divide a thousand by three, one would remain over.

14. The brown one, with red-brown eyes, is the Soma-cow; and that ruddy one is the Vritra-killer's (Indra's) own, whom the king here chooses for himself[3] after winning the battle; and the ruddy one with reddish-white eyes[4] is the Fathers' own whom they slay here for the Fathers.

15. Let, then, the brown one, with red-brown eyes, be the Soma-cow. And if he be unable to obtain a brown one with red-brown eyes, let it be a dark-red[5] one. And if he be unable to obtain a dark-red one, let it be a ruddy one, one of the

---

[1] The Kânva text reads 'may I obtain heroes.'

[2] This arithmetical feat of Indra and Vishnu is apparently already referred to in Rig-veda VI, 69, 8, though nothing is said there as to the difficulty regarding the odd cow. The threefold division seems to refer to Vishnu's three steps, by which (as the sun) he measures the sky; or to the division of the universe into the three worlds (?). See also Ait. Br. VI, 15.

[3] Or, drives forth (from the enemy's stables). The red cows are compared with the red clouds, which appear after the thunderstorm (i. e. after king Indra's battle with Vritra).

[4] Sâyana takes 'syetâkshî' as 'black-eyed (krishnalokanâ).'

[5] 'Arunâ;' the Kânva text adds, 'for that one nearest to it (the brown one, or Soma-cow proper) in appearance.'

Vritra-killer's own. But let him nowise turn his fancy upon a ruddy one with reddish-white eyes.

16. Let it be one that is not impregnated. For that Soma-cow is in reality Vâk, and this Vâk (speech) is of unimpaired vigour; and of unimpaired vigour is one not (yet) impregnated: let it therefore be one not impregnated. Let it be one that is neither tailless, nor hornless, nor one-eyed, nor earless[1], nor specially marked, nor seven-hoofed[2];—for such a one is uniform, and uniform is this speech.

THE BUYING OF SOMA.

SECOND BRÂHMANA.

1. Having thrown the (earth of the) foot-print (into the pan), he (the Adhvaryu) washes his hands. Now as to why he washes his hands;—clarified butter being a thunderbolt, and the Soma being seed, he washes his hands lest[3] he should injure the seed, Soma, with the thunderbolt, the ghee.

2. Thereupon he ties the piece of gold to this (finger[4]). Now, twofold indeed is this (universe),—there is no third,—the truth and the untruth: the gods are the truth and men are the untruth. And gold having sprung from Agni's seed, he ties the gold to this (finger), in order that he may touch the twigs (of the Soma) with the truth, that he may handle the Soma by means of the truth.

[1] 'Akarnâ;' the Kânva text has 'anupârshtakarnâ (one whose ears are not perforated ?),' and instead of 'alakshitâ (not specially marked),' it reads 'asronâ (aslonâ), not lame.'

[2] That is, with one hoof undivided (seven-toed).

[3] The construction in the original is as usual in the oratio directa.

[4] Viz. to the nameless (or ring) finger. Kâty. VII, 6, 27.

3. He then orders (the sacrificer's men), 'Bring thou the Soma-cloth! bring thou the Soma-wrapper! bring thou the head-band!' Let some shining (cloth) be the Soma-cloth; for this is to be his (king Soma's[1]) garment, and shining indeed is his garment: and whosoever serves him with a shining (garment), he truly shines. But he who says, '(Bring) anything whatsoever,' he will indeed be anything whatsoever: let the Soma-cloth, therefore, be some splendid (cloth), and the Soma-wrapper one of any kind.

4. If he can get a head-band, let there be a head-band; but if he cannot get a head-band, let him cut off from the Soma-wrapper a piece two or three fingers long, to serve as the head-band. Either the Adhvaryu or the Sacrificer takes the Soma-cloth, and some one or other the Soma-wrapper.

5. Now, in the first place, they pick the king (Soma). A pitcher of water is placed close to him, and a Brâhman sits beside him[2]. Thither they (the priests and sacrificer) now proceed eastward.

6. While they go there, he (the Adhvaryu) makes

---

[1] I do not think 'asya' could refer to the sacrificer, in opposition to 'etasya' (Soma); nor can the latter be construed with the following relative clause 'sa yo . . .' The Kânva text reads, Tad yad eva sobhanatamam tat somopanahanam syâd, vâso hy asyaitad bhavati; sa yo haitak khobhanatamam kurute, sobhate haiva sah, &c.

[2] The Pratiprasthâtri, in the first place, takes the Soma-plants (from the seller) and puts them on an ox-hide, dyed red and spread on the ground at the place (in the east of the hall) where the 'sounding-holes' will be dug (see III, 5, 4, 1 seq.). The seller of the Soma, who is to be either of the Kutsa tribe or a Sûdra, then picks the Soma, breaking the plants at the joints. A jar filled with water is placed in front of the Soma, and a Brâhman (or the assistant of the Brahman, viz. the Brâhmanâkhamsin) sits down by the (right or south) side of the Soma. Kâty. VII, 6, 1-6.

(the sacrificer) say the text (Vâg. S. IV, 24), 'Say thou, for me, unto Soma, "This is thy gâyatrî-part (bhâga)[1]!" Say thou, for me, unto Soma, "This is thy trishtubh-part!" Say thou, for me, unto Soma, "This is thy gayatî-part!" Say thou, for me, unto Soma, "Obtain thou the supreme sovereignty of the names of metres!"' Now, when he (king Soma) is bought, he is bought for one (destination[2])—for the sovereignty of the metres, for the supreme sovereignty of the metres; and when they press him, they slay him: hereby now he says to him, 'It is for the sovereignty of the metres, for the supreme sovereignty of the metres that I buy thee, not for slaying thee.' Having gone there, he sits down (behind the Soma) with his face towards the east.

7. He touches (the Soma-plants), with, 'Ours thou art,'—thereby he (Soma), now that he has come (as a guest), becomes as it were one of his (the sacrificer's) own (people): for this reason he says, 'Ours thou art;'—'Thy pure (juice) is meet for the draught,' for he will indeed take therefrom the 'pure draught[3].' 'Let the pickers pick thee!' this he says for the sake of completeness.

8. Now some, on noticing any straw or (piece of) wood (among the Soma-plants), throw it away. But let him not do this; for—the Soma being the nobility and the other plants the common people, and the

[1] The three parts refer to the three Savanas, at which the respective metres are used. See IV, 3, 2, 7 seq.

[2] Bhâgam appears to have been lost here, since a play on that word seems to be intended, which might perhaps be reproduced by 'lot.' It is given both at the Kânva text and at III, 4, 1, 7.

[3] For the Sukra-graha, see IV, 2, 1, 1 seq.

people being the nobleman's food—it would be just as if one were to take hold of and pull out some (food) he has put in his mouth, and throw it away. Hence let him merely touch it, with, 'Let the pickers pick thee!' Those pickers of his do indeed pick it.

9. He then spreads the cloth (over the ox-hide), either twofold or fourfold, with the fringe towards the east or north. Thereon he metes out the king (Soma); and because he metes out the king, therefore there is a measure,—both the measure among men and whatever other measure there is.

10. He metes out, with a verse to Savit*ri*; for Savit*ri* is the impeller of the gods, and so that (Soma) becomes for him impelled by Savit*ri* to the purchase.

11. He metes out with an ati*kh*andas-verse; for that one, viz. the ati*kh*andas[1], embraces all metres; and so that (Soma) is meted out for him by means of all the metres: therefore he metes out with an ati*kh*andas-verse.

12. He metes out, with the text (Vâ*g*. S. IV, 25), 'Unto that divine Savit*ri* within the two bowls[2], the sage, I sing praises, to him of true

[1] Ati*kh*andas ('over-metre') is the generic name for the metres which number more than forty-eight syllables: hence it is said to include all the other metres which consist of fewer syllables. See VIII, 6, 2, 13, where the term is explained by 'atti-*kh*andâ*h* (metre-eater).'

[2] Or, that divine invigorator of the two 'o*n*i.' According to the St. Petersb. Dict., 'o*n*i' would seem to refer to two parts of the Soma-press. Professor Ludwig takes it to mean 'press-arm' and the 'arm' generally, which suits very well some of the passages in which the word occurs. Here, in the loc. or gen. case, it can scarcely mean 'arms' (though Savit*ri*'s two arms are often referred to as dispelling the darkness and keeping asunder the spaces, cf. Rig-veda II, 38, 2; IV, 53, 3; 4; VI, 71, 1; 5; VII, 45, 2), but apparently refers to 'heaven and earth' being thus equivalent to

impulse, the bestower of treasures, the wise and thoughtful friend;—he at whose impulse the resplendent light shone high, the golden-handed sage hath measured the ether with his form.'

13. Therewith[1] he metes out (the Soma) with all (five fingers), therewith with four, therewith with three, therewith with two, therewith with one; therewith with one, therewith with two, therewith with three, therewith with four, therewith with all (fingers); having laid (the two hands) together[2] he throws (Soma) thereon with the joined open hands.

14. He metes out while bending up and bending down (the fingers). The reason why he metes out in bending (the fingers) up and down is that he thereby makes those fingers of separate existence, and therefore they are born separate (from each other); and as to his meting out with all (fingers) together, these (fingers) are to be born, as it were, united. This is why he metes out in bending (the fingers) up and down.

15. And, again, as to his meting out in bending them up and down,—he thereby renders them of varied power, and hence these (fingers) are of varied

the two *k*amû (originally the two receptacles or bowls into which the pressed Soma flows) in Rig-veda III, 55, 20.

[1] Viz. with the same formula, repeating it each time. The meting out of the Soma is done with the fingers of the right hand, first with all five, and then successively turning in one (beginning with the thumb), till the little finger remains with which he takes Soma twice, whereupon he again successively releases the fingers.

[2] There is some doubt as to whether this refers to the preceding 'with all (viz. ten fingers);' or whether he is to take for the tenth time some Soma with the five fingers of the right hand, and then once more (without muttering the text) with the joined hands. See Kâty. VII, 7, 18, 19. The text seems to be purposely vague.

power. That is why he metes out in bending them up and down.

16. And, again, as to his meting out in bending them up and down,—he thereby harnesses a virâg[1] (to ply) thitherwards and hitherwards: going thitherwards, namely, it conveys the sacrifice to the gods, and coming hitherwards it assists men. This is why he metes out in bending (the fingers) up and down.

17. And as to his meting out ten times,—the virâg is of ten syllables, and the Soma is of virâg nature: for this reason he metes out ten times.

18. Having gathered up the ends of the Soma-cloth, he (the Adhvaryu) ties them together by means of the head-band, with, 'For descendants (I tie) thee;'—for it is indeed for (the purpose of obtaining) descendants that he buys it (Soma): what (part of man) here is, as it were, compressed between the head and the shoulders, that he thereby makes it to be for him (the sacrificer)[2].

19. He then makes a finger-hole in the middle (of the knot), with the text, 'Let the descendants breathe after thee!' For, in compressing (the cloth), he, as it were, strangles him (Soma and the sacrificer) and renders him breathless; hereby now he emits his breath from inside, and after him breathing the descendants also breathe: for this reason he says, 'Let the descendants breathe after thee.' Thereupon he hands him (Soma) to the Soma-seller. Now, then, of the bargain.

[1] The virâg (the 'shining' or 'ruling' metre) consists of (generally three or four) pâdas of ten syllables each: hence it is here connected with the ten metings out of Soma.

[2] The Soma representing offspring, he gives the bundle a shape resembling the human body.

THIRD BRÂHMA*N*A.

1. He bargains for the king (Soma); and because he bargains for the king, therefore any and everything is vendible here. He says, 'Soma-seller, is thy king Soma for sale?'—'He is for sale,' says the Soma-seller.—'I will buy him of thee!'—'Buy him!' says the Soma-seller.—'I will buy him of thee for one-sixteenth (of the cow).'—'King Soma, surely, is worth more than that!' says the Soma-seller.—'Yea, King Soma is worth more than that; but great, surely, is the greatness of the cow,' says the Adhvaryu.

2. 'From the cow (comes) fresh milk, from her boiled milk, from her cream, from her sour curds, from her sour cream, from her curdled milk, from her butter, from her ghee, from her clotted curds, from her whey:

3. I will buy him of thee for one hoof[1]!'—'King Soma, surely, is worth more than that!' says the Soma-seller.—'Yea, King Soma is worth more than that, but great, surely, is the greatness of the cow,' replies the Adhvaryu; and, having (each time) enumerated the same ten virtues, he says, 'I will buy him of thee for one foot,'—'for half (the cow),'—'for the cow!'—'King Soma has been bought!' says the Soma-seller, 'name the kinds!'

4. He (the Adhvaryu) says, 'Gold is thine, a cloth is thine, a goat is thine, a milch cow is thine, a pair of kine is thine, three other (cows) are thine!' And because they first bargain and afterwards come to terms, therefore about any and everything that is for sale here, people first bargain and afterwards

[1] That is, for one-eighth of a cow, each foot consisting of two hoofs (or toes, *s*apha).

come to terms. And the reason why only the Adhvaryu enumerates the virtues of the cow, and not the Soma-seller those of the Soma, is that Soma is already glorified, since Soma is a god. And the Adhvaryu thereby glorifies the cow, thinking, 'Seeing her virtues he shall buy her!' This is why only the Adhvaryu enumerates the virtues of the cow, and not the Soma-seller those of the Soma.

5. And as to his bargaining five times:—the sacrifice being of equal measure with the year, and there being five seasons in the year, he thus obtains it (the sacrifice, Soma) in five (divisions), and therefore he bargains five times.

6. He then makes (the sacrificer) say on the gold[1] (Vâg. S. IV, 26), 'Thee, the pure, I buy with the pure,' for he indeed buys the pure with the pure, when (he buys) Soma with gold;—'the brilliant with the brilliant,' for he indeed buys the brilliant with the brilliant, when (he buys) Soma with gold;—'the immortal with the immortal,' for he indeed buys the immortal with the immortal, when (he buys) Soma with gold.

7. He then tempts[2] the Soma-seller (with the gold): 'In compensation[3] for thy cow,' whereby he means to say, 'With the sacrificer (be) thy cow!'

---

[1] That is, according to Kâty. VII, 8, 5, in making him touch the gold. The Kânva text has, 'Thereupon he buys him (Soma) with gold.'

[2] Or, according to the commentaries, 'he frightens the Soma-seller (by threatening to take back the money).'

[3] ? Sagme (? compact), explained by the commentators as meaning the sacrificer. Perhaps it may mean, 'one of the parties to an agreement,' and hence here the sacrificer as the bargainee. The Kânva text reads, He then takes it back again (punar âdatte) with 'Sagme te goh,' and throws it down with 'Ours thy gold.'

He then draws it (the gold) back towards the sacrificer, and throws it down, with, 'Ours be thy gold!' whereby he (the sacrificer) takes unto himself the vital energy, and the Soma-seller gets only the body. Thereupon the Soma-seller takes it[1].

8. He then makes him (the sacrificer) say on the she-goat, which stands facing the west, 'Thou art the bodily form of fervour,'—that she-goat was indeed produced as the bodily form of fervour, of Pra*g*âpati; hence he says, 'Thou art the bodily form of fervour,'—'Pra*g*âpati's kind,' because she brings forth three times in the year, therefore she is Pra*g*âpati's kind. 'Thou art bought with the most excellent animal,' because she brings forth three times in the year, she is the most excellent of animals. 'May I increase with a thousandfold increase!' Thereby he implores a blessing: a thousand meaning abundance, he thereby means to say, 'May I obtain abundance!'

9. With that (text) he gives the she-goat, with that he takes the king[2]; for a*g*â (goat) doubtless

[1] According to some authorities, the gold is again taken away forcibly from the Soma-seller by the Adhvaryu, after the sacrificer has uncovered his head (paragraph 12), and the seller is driven away by blows with a speckled cane. Kâty. VII, 8, 27. According to Âpastamba (ib.), he buys off the Soma-cow with another cow, and then dismisses her to the cow-pen; and if the Soma-seller objects, he is to be beaten with a speckled cane. The Mânava-sûtra merely says, that they are to give the Soma-seller something for compensation. The whole transaction was evidently a feigned purchase, symbolising the acquisition of the Soma by the gods from the Gandharvas. The real bargain was probably concluded before the sacrificial performance. See also Haug, Ait. Br. Transl. p. 59, note 2.

[2] While making over the she-goat to the Soma-seller with his left hand, he receives the Soma with the right.

means the same as âgâ (driving thither[1]), since it is through her (the she-goat) that he finally drives him (Soma) thither. It is thus in a mystic sense that they call her 'agâ.'

10. He takes the king, with the text (Vâg. S. IV, 27), 'Come to us, a friend, bestowing good friends!' whereby he means to say, 'Come to us, as a kind and propitious one!' Having pushed back the garment on the sacrificer's right thigh, he lays him (Soma) down thereon, with the text, 'Seat thee on Indra's right thigh,'—for he, the sacrificer, is at present Indra[2]: therefore he says, 'Seat thee on Indra's right thigh;'—'willing on the willing,' whereby he means to say, 'beloved on the beloved one;'—'tender on the tender!' whereby he means to say, 'propitious on the propitious one.'

11. Thereupon he (the sacrificer) assigns (to the Gandharvas) the objects constituting the purchase price for the Soma, with the text, 'O Svâna, Bhrâga, Aṅghâri, Bambhâri, Hasta, Suhasta, Krisânu! these are your wages for Soma: keep them! may they not fail you!' Now those (Gandharvas) are instead of the hearth-mounds—these being the names of the hearth-mounds—it is these very (names) that he thereby has assigned to them[3].

---

[1] Sâyana takes â-ag in the sense of 'to go to, to come' (âgâ, the comer); because the sacrificer through her comes to Soma.

[2] See part i, introduction, p. xix, note 4.

[3] 'For those same Gandharvas, the overseers of the Guardians of Soma, they are (meant) in lieu of those (? hearth-mounds), for those are their names: it is to them that he thereby assigns those (objects constituting the purchase-price), and thus he becomes debtless towards them.' Kânva text. See also part i, p. 183, note 2.

12. He now uncovers (his head[1]); for he who is consecrated becomes an embryo, and embryos are enveloped both in the amnion and the outer membrane: him (the sacrificer or sacrifice) he has now brought forth, and therefore he uncovers himself. Now it is he (Soma[2]) that becomes an embryo, and therefore he is enveloped, since embryos are, as it were, enveloped both in the amnion and the outer membrane.

13. He then makes (the sacrificer) say the text (Vâg. S. IV, 28), 'Keep me, O Agni, from evil ways! let me share in the right ways.' Now he (Soma) approaches him while he is seated, and when he has come, he rises: thereby he does wrong and breaks the vow. This, then, is his expiation of that (transgression), and thus no wrong is thereby done, and he breaks not the vow: therefore he says, 'Keep me, O Agni, from evil ways! let me share in the right ways!'

14. Having then taken the king, he rises, with the text, 'With new life, with good life, am I risen after the immortals;' for he who rises after the bought Soma, rises indeed after the immortal: therefore he says, 'With new life, with good life, am I risen after the immortals.'

15. Thereupon he takes the king and goes towards the car, with the text (Vâg. S. IV, 29), 'We have

---

[1] See III, 2, 1, 16. His wife does the same.

[2] According to a former passage (III, 1, 2, 28), the sacrificer is supposed to remain in the embryonic state till the pressing of the Soma. The Kânva recension reads, 'Sa etam yagñam agîganat sa esha garbho bhavaty â sutyâyâh;' where 'agîganat' seems to mean 'he has begotten.' I am not quite certain whether Soma himself is really implied. See III, 3, 4, 6.

entered upon the path that leadeth to well-being, free from danger; whereon he escheweth all haters, and meeteth with good[1].'

16. Now, once on a time, the gods, while performing sacrifice, were afraid of an attack from the Asura-Rakshas. They perceived that prayer for a safe journey; and having warded off the evil spirits by means of that prayer, they attained well-being in the safe and foeless shelter of that prayer. And so does he now ward off the evil spirits by means of that prayer, and attain well-being in the safe and foeless shelter of that prayer. For this reason he says, 'We have entered upon the path that leadeth to well-being, free from danger; whereon he escheweth all haters and meeteth with good.'

17. They carry him thus[2], and (afterwards) drive him about on the cart; whereby they exalt him: for this reason they carry the seed on their head (to the field), and bring in (the corn) on the cart.

18. Now the reason why he buys (the Soma) near water[3] is that—water meaning sap—he thereby buys Soma sapful; and as to there being gold, he thereby buys him lustrous; and as to there being a cloth, he thereby buys him with his skin; and as to there being a she-goat, he thereby buys him fervid; and as to there being a milch cow, he thereby buys him with the milk to be mixed with him; and as to there being a pair (of kine), he thereby buys him with a mate.—He should buy him with ten (objects), and

[1] Compare the slightly different verse, Rig-veda VI, 51, 16.

[2] The sacrificer carries the bundle of Soma on his hand resting on his head.

[3] Viz. the vessel of water mentioned III, 1, 2, 2.

not with other than ten, for the virâg consists of ten syllables, and Soma is of virâg nature: therefore he should buy him with ten (objects) and not with other than ten.

PROCESSION AND ENTRANCE OF KING SOMA.

FOURTH BRÂHMANA.

1. In the enclosed space (of the cart)[1] he (the Adhvaryu) lays down the black deer-skin, with the text (Vâg. S. IV, 30), 'Thou art Aditi's skin;' its significance is the same (as before)[2]. Thereon he places him (Soma), with, 'Seat thee on Aditi's seat!' for Aditi being this (earth), and she being indeed a safe resting-place, he thereby places him on that safe resting-place: therefore he says, 'Seat thee on Aditi's seat!'

2. He then makes (the sacrificer) say, after touching (the Soma), 'The bull hath propped the sky, the welkin[3].' For, when the gods were spreading the sacrifice, they were afraid of an attack on the part of the Asura-Rakshas. Now by what he says, 'The bull hath propped the sky, the welkin,'

[1] The cart stands south of the place where the purchase of Soma took place, with the shafts towards the east, fitted with all the appliances, and yoked with a pair of oxen. The antelope skin is spread with the hairy side upwards, and the neck part towards the east.

[2] See I, 1, 4, 1 seq. The Kânva text has: 'the significance of this yagus is the same.'

[3] In Rig-veda VIII, 42, 1, this verse relates to Varuna. In adapting it to the present sacrificial requirements, 'vrishabho (rishabho, K.) antariksham' has been substituted for the original 'asuro visvavedâh;' Soma being meant by 'the bull.'

thereby they rendered it (the sacrifice or Soma) superior to the deadly shaft[1].

3. 'He hath measured the breadth of the earth;'—thus he gains through him (Soma) these worlds, for there is no slayer, no deadly shaft for him by whom these worlds have been gained: therefore he says, 'He hath measured the breadth of the earth.'

4. 'As all-ruler hath he taken his seat over all things existing (bhuvana);'—thus he gains through him this All, for there is no slayer, no deadly shaft for him by whom this All has been gained: therefore he says, 'As all-ruler hath he taken his seat over all things existing.'

5. 'Verily, all these are Varu*n*a's ordinances;'—thereby he makes here everything whatsoever obedient to him, and every one that is refractory: therefore he says, 'Verily, all these are Varu*n*a's ordinances.'

6. Thereupon he wraps (the Soma) up in the Soma-wrapper, lest the evil spirits should touch him. For this one doubtless is an embryo, and hidden (tiras), as it were, are embryos, and hidden also is that (which is) wrapped up;—hidden, as it were, are the gods to men, and hidden is that which is wrapped up: therefore he wraps him up.

7. He wraps him up, with the text (Vâ*g*. S. IV, 31; Rig-veda V, 85, 2), 'Over the woods he hath stretched the welkin,' for over the woods, over the tops of the trees, that welkin (or air) is indeed stretched;—'strength (hath he laid) into the coursers, milk into the kine,'—strength means

[1] Or, superior to (beyond the reach of) the slayer (or the blow), '*g*yâyâ*m*sa*m* vadhât.'

manliness and the coursers are the men: he thereby bestows manliness upon men; and 'milk into the kine' he says, because this milk is indeed contained in the kine;—'Into the hearts Varuna (hath laid) wisdom, into the homesteads[1] fire;' for into the hearts that wisdom, the swiftness of thought, has indeed entered; and 'into the homesteads fire' he says, because that fire is in the homesteads, with the people;—'Into the heaven hath he placed the Sun, and Soma upon the rock;' for that sun is indeed placed in the heaven; and 'Soma on the rock' he says, because Soma is in the mountains. This is why he says, 'In the heaven hath he placed the Sun, and Soma upon the rock.'

8. If there are two deer-skins[2], he then puts up the other by way of a flag[3];—and if there is only one, he cuts off the neck of the deer-skin and puts it up by way of a flag;—with the text (Vâg. S. IV, 32), 'Mount thou the eye of Sûrya, the eye-ball of Agni, where thou fliest along with the dappled (horses), shining through the wise (Sûrya).' He thereby places Sûrya (the sun) in front, thinking, 'May Sûrya, in front, ward off the evil spirits!' They now drive (Soma) about on a safe (cart), unmolested by evil spirits.

9. At the fore-part of the shafts two boards have been put up: between them the Subrâhmanyâ[4]

[1] 'Into the waters (apsu),' Rig-veda.

[2] See III, 2, 1, 1 seq.

[3] He is to fasten it to a staff fixed to the pole of the cart near the yoke. Kâty. VII, 9, 9.

[4] The Subrâhmanyâ is one of the assistants of the Udgâtri (chanter of Sâma-hymns). He stands on the ground between the two shafts in front of the yoke; the two planks, according to Sâyana, reaching up to his chin.

stands and drives. He (Soma), indeed, is too high for (the driver) mounting beside him, for who is worthy of mounting beside him? Therefore he drives while standing between (the boards).

10. He drives with a palâsa branch. Now when Gâyatrî flew towards Soma[1], a footless archer aiming at her while she was carrying him off, severed one of the feathers (or leaves, parna), either of Gâyatrî or of king Soma; and on falling down it became a parna (palâsa) tree; whence its name parna. 'May that which was there of the Soma nature, be here also now!' so he thinks, and for this reason he drives with a palâsa branch.

11. He urges on the two oxen. If they be both black, or if either of them be black, then let him know that it will rain, that Parganya will have abundance of rain that year: such indeed is science.

12. He (the Adhvaryu) first yokes them, with the text (Vâg. S. IV, 33), 'Ye oxen, come hither, patient of the yoke!' for they are indeed oxen, and they are patient of the yoke;—'Let yourselves be yoked, tearless!' for they are now being yoked; and tearless means unscathed;—'not man-slaying,' this means 'not doing wrong;'—'speeding the Brahman,' for they are indeed speeders of the Brahman (worship, or the priests);—'Go ye happily to the sacrificer's dwelling!' this he says in order that the evil spirits may not injure them on the way.

13. Having then gone round to the back (of the

[1] See I, 7, 1, 1; part i, p. 183. According to Ait. Br. III, 26, Krisânu the Soma-keeper's arrow cut off one of the talons of Gâyatrî's left foot, which was turned into a porcupine.

cart) and taken hold of the drag[1], he says (to the Hotri)[2], 'Recite to the bought Soma!' or, '—to Soma, now driven about!' whichever way he pleases.

14. He then makes (the sacrificer[3]) say the text (Vâg. S. IV, 34), 'Thou art gracious unto me, go forth, O Lord of the world—,' for he (Soma) is indeed gracious to him, wherefore he heeds no other but him. Even his (Soma's own) kings[4] come (to

[1] Apâlamba, a piece of wood fastened to the back part of the cart to prevent its running backwards when going up-hill; or, according to others, a rope used for retarding the progress of the cart in going down-hill. Kâty. VII, 9, 15 comm. The cart stands with the oxen towards the east; it is then wheeled round towards the right to the west and driven to the hall, in front of which it is turned towards the north; the Soma being then taken down. See Ait. Br. I, 14.

[2] The duties of the Hotri, while the Soma-cart is driven to the hall, are set forth Âsv. Srautas. IV, 4: He stands three feet behind the cart between the two wheel tracks, and throws thrice dust towards the south with the fore-part of his foot without moving the heel, with the formula, 'Thou art wise, thou art intelligent, thou upholding all things: drive away the danger arising from men!' Thereupon, after uttering the sound 'Him,' he recites eight verses, or, the first and last being recited thrice each, in all twelve verses. Cf. Ait. Br. I, 13. He first remains standing in the same place and recites thrice the first verse. Then in following the cart he recites the five following verses. The cart having now stopped, he walks round it on its right (south) side, and while looking on the Soma follows it while it is placed on the throne. He then touches it and completes his recitation by the last two verses. The first of these two verses is the same which the sacrificer is to mutter (with the Adhvaryu) while Soma is carried into the hall, and which is given in paragraph 30.

[3] While the Soma is driven to the hall, the sacrificer has to hold on to it from behind.

[4] 'Asya râgânah sabhâgâh;'—Soma seems to be compared here with an emperor or overlord of kings (adhirâgo râgñâm, V, 4, 2, 2), who is holding a royal court (râgasabhâ), or a Darbar, to which the under-kings are flocking. Sâyana seems to interpret the passage differently: apy asya râgânah iti sabhâgâ ity anena râgñâm anatikra-

him) to attend the assembly, and he is the first to salute the kings, for he is gracious. This is why he says, 'Thou art gracious.' 'Go forth, O Lord of the world,' he says, because he (Soma) is the lord of beings. 'To all dwellings,' 'all dwellings' doubtless means the limbs; with reference to his limbs he says this, 'May no prowling enemies meet thee! may no waylayers meet thee! May no malicious wolves meet thee!' this he says lest the evil spirits should meet him on his way.

15. 'Having become a falcon, fly away!' he thereby makes him fly forward after becoming a falcon; for the evil spirits fly not after what is fearful: now he, the falcon, forsooth is the most fearful, the strongest of birds, and as such a one he makes him (Soma) fly forwards when he says, 'Having become a falcon, fly away!'

16. Now they (can) only hit his body[1]. 'Go to the sacrificer's dwelling,—that is the place prepared for us.' In this there is nothing obscure.

---

manîyam uktam bhavati; api sambhâvanâyâm madhuparkam âha 'râgñe kâkâryasvasurapitrivyamâtulânam keti' (Âsv. Grihyas. I, 24) sambhâvanîyânâm madhye râgñâm prathamato nirdisena (!) sreshthyâvagamâd itarapûgyopalakshakatvenâpy asya râgâna iti nirdesa iti mantavyam, râgña âgatân svayam prahva eva san pûrvas tebhyah prâg evâbhivadati vâgvyavahâram karoti. The Kânva text reads: For he is his gracious lord, therefore he heeds not even a king; and yet (?) he is the first to salute the kings: thus he is indeed gracious to him: 'esha vâ etasya bhadro bhavati, tasmâd esha na râgânam kanâdriyate 'tho pûrvo râgño 'bhivadati tathâsyaisha eva bhadro bhavati (!).'

[1] Or, they can only shoot after his body, 'sarîram evânvavahanti.' The Kânva text has 'athâsyedam sarîram evânasâ 'nvâvahanti,' i.e. 'Now they only bring his body with the cart.' The MS. of Sâyana also has 'anvâvahanti,' but it explains it by 'syenîbhâvâd upâdeyasya sârâmsasya bâdhâbhâvâd dhantâ sarîram evânugatya hanti nâtmânam.'

17. Thereupon he recites the Subrahma*n*yâ litany. Even as one would say to those for whom he intends to prepare a meal, 'On such and such a day I will prepare a meal for you;' so does he thereby announce the sacrifice to the gods. 'Subrahma*n*yôm! Subrahma*n*yôm! Subrahma*n*yôm!' thus he calls, for the Brahman indeed moves the gods onward. Thrice he says it, because the sacrifice is threefold.

18. 'Come, O Indra!' Indra is the deity of the sacrifice: therefore he says, 'Come, O Indra!' 'Come, O lord of the bay steeds! Ram of Medhâtithi[1]! Wife of V*ri*sha*n*as*v*a[2]! Bestriding buffalo! Lover of Ahalyâ[3]!' Thereby he wishes him joy in those affairs of his.

[1] This myth, according to which Indra was supposed to have assumed the form of a ram and to have carried off Medhâtithi, the Kâ*n*va (or, according to others, to have robbed him of his Soma), appears to be alluded to in Rig-veda VIII, 2, 40. On the possible connection of the myth with the Greek one of Ganymede, see Weber, Ind. Stud. IX, p. 40. Sâya*n*a does not explain the Subrahma*n*yâ formula, but remarks, that he has already done so in the Sâma-brâhma*n*a (viz. in the Sha*d*vi*ms*a).

[2] According to Rig-veda I, 51, 13, Indra became the wife (menâ) of V*ri*sha*n*as*v*a (Mena); the reason for this transformation being, according to the Sha*d*vi*ms*a Br., that he was in love with Menâ or Menakâ, the daughter of that king (or sage). Ind. Stud. I, p. 38. The later explanation of the simple statement of the Rik seems of doubtful authenticity, unless the choice of the word menâ for 'wife' was intended by the bard as an allusion to the name of the king's daughter. It is more likely that the myth alluded to in the Rik had been forgotten at the time of the Brâhma*n*as, and a new version of it was invented, based on the 'menâ' of the original. Haug, Transl. Ait. Br. p. 383, takes Menâ here as a name.

[3] This is another of Indra's love-myths about which very little is known. Ahalyâ (Maitreyî) is said to have been the wife of the *Ri*shi Gautama (or of Kau*s*ika, according to Sha*d*v. Br.) and to have been loved by Indra.

19. 'O Kausika[1], Brâhman, thou who callest thee Gautama[2].' Just so has this (formula) been devised in these days by Âruni, to wit, 'thou who callest thee Gautama:' he may say it, if he choose, and if he does not choose, he need not attend to it[3]. 'In so and so many days, to the Soma-feast,' (stating) in how many days from hence the pressing is to be.

20. 'Ye gods and priests, come hither[4]!' This he says to the gods and Brâhmans, because it is of these two, the gods and Brâhmans, that he has need.

21. Thereupon the Pratiprasthâtri steps up to the front of the hall with the victim for Agni and Soma. Now Agni and Soma have seized him, who consecrates himself, between their jaws, for that consecration-offering above[5] belongs to Agni and Vishnu, and Vishnu, forsooth, is no other than

[1] According to Sâyana on Rig-veda I, 10, 11 (where Indra is called Kausika, 'favourable to the Kusikas') Kusika desired to have a son equal to Indra, whence the latter was born as Kusika's son Gâthin (Gâdhin). Differently Sây. on Taitt. Âr. I, 12, 4.

[2] The Shadv. Br. (Ind. Stud. I, p. 38) explains this as follows:—The Gods and Asuras were at war with each other. Gotama was performing austerities between them. Indra went up to him and said, 'Go out as our spy.' 'I cannot,' he replied. 'Then I will go in your form.' 'As thou thinkest fit!' And because he (Indra) went about in the form of Gotama, passing himself off as Gotama, therefore he says, 'thou who callest thee Gotama.'

[3] The Kânva text also states that this last portion of the formula was devised by Âruni, but nothing is said as to its use being optional.

[4] For variations of this concluding part of the Subrahmanyâ in different schools, see Lâty. Sr. I, 3, 3 seq.; also notes to III, 9, 3, 10; IV, 9, 6, 25; Haug, Transl. Ait. Br. p. 383.

[5] See III, 1, 3, 1 seq.

Soma, and the offering is he himself who is consecrated: thus they have seized him between their jaws; and by this victim he now redeems himself[1].

22. Now, some take a firebrand from the Âhavanîya, saying, 'Here is Agni, and here is Soma: with these two thus being together we will redeem ourselves.' But let him not do this; for wheresoever these two are, there they are indeed together.

23. It (the victim) is two-coloured, because it belongs to two deities: 'For the sake of concord between the two deities let it be a black-spotted (buck)!' they say; 'for that is most like those two (gods).' If he be unable to obtain a black-spotted buck, it may be a red-spotted one.

24. Thereon he makes (the sacrificer) say (Vâg. S. IV, 35; Rig-veda X, 37, 1), 'Homage be to the eye of Mitra and Varuna! perform ye diligently this holy service to the god! sing ye unto the far-seeing, god-born light, to Sûrya, the son of the sky!' Thereby he renders homage to it (the victim) and makes it a token of the covenant.

25. The Adhvaryu then removes the Soma-wrapper. With (Vâg. S. IV, 36) 'Thou art Varuna's stay,' he props (the cart) with the prop. With 'Ye two are the rest of Varuna's stay,' he pulls out the two wedges. The reason why he says, 'Ye two are the rest of Varuna's stay[2],' is that he, the bought Soma, now indeed is of Varuna[3].

[1] 'By this victim he redeems himself, the victim, and with that redeemed self, now his own, he sacrifices.' Kânva rec.

[2] Skambha visarganî ('support or pin of the prop') is taken by Sâyana in the sense of 'offshoot of the prop' or 'that which is let go (srishta) by the prop.'

[3] I.e. belongs to Varuna or is of Varuna's nature (varunyo

26. Thereupon four men take up the king's throne; two men, it is true, take it up for the human king, but four take up this for him who rules over everything here.

27. It is of udumbara wood—udumbara meaning sap and food—for (the sacrificer's) obtainment of sap and food: therefore it is of udumbara wood.

28. It reaches up to his navel, for it is there that the food settles, and Soma is food: therefore it reaches up to his navel. Moreover, there is the seat of the seed, and Soma is seed: therefore it reaches up to his navel.

29. He (the Adhvaryu) touches it with, 'Thou art the rightful seat (*ri*tasadanî) of Varu*n*a!' He then spreads on it the black deerskin with, 'Thou art the rightful seat (*ri*tasadanam) of Varu*n*a!' and places him (Soma) thereon with, 'Seat thee on the rightful seat of Varu*n*a!' The reason why he says, 'Seat thee on the rightful seat of Varu*n*a,' is that he (Soma) is now of Varu*n*a's nature.

30. Thereupon he makes him (king Soma) enter the hall; and in making him enter, he causes (the sacrificer) to say (Vâ*g*. S. IV, 37; Rig-veda I, 91, 19), 'Whatsoever powers of thine they worship with offering, may they all encompass the sacrifice[1]! Go forth to our dwellings, O Soma, prospering our homes, ever helpful, bestowing abundance of men, not slaying our

bhavati). Sâya*n*a (if the MS. is correct) takes it in the sense of 'is Varu*n*a himself,' etasmin krîtâvasare somo varu*n*o bhavati.

[1] Or, 'may the sacrifice encompass them all,' if, with Grassmann and Ludwig, we read '*yag*ña*h*' instead of '*yag*ñam.' This verse is likewise recited (? at the same time) by the Hot*ri*, see p. 79, note 2.

men!' dwellings meaning houses, he thereby means to say, 'Go forth to our houses, kind, propitious, not doing evil.'

31. Some now pour out a vessel of water beside him, saying that this would be as one would bring water for a king that has come to him. But let him not do this, for they (who do this) do at the sacrifice what is human, and inauspicious for the sacrifice forsooth is that which is human: let him therefore not pour out water, lest he should do at the sacrifice what is inauspicious.

THE ÂTITHYA, OR GUEST-OFFERING

(HOSPITABLE RECEPTION GIVEN TO KING SOMA).

FOURTH ADHYÂYA. FIRST BRÂHMANA.

1. Verily, the guest-offering is the head of the sacrifice, and the Prâyanîya and Udayanîya are its arms. But the arms are on both sides of the head: therefore those two oblations, the Prâyanîya and Udayanîya, are on both sides of the guest-offering.

2. Now as to why it is called 'guest-offering.' He, the purchased Soma, truly comes as his (the sacrificer's) guest,—to him (is offered) that (hospitable reception): even as for a king or a Brâhman one would cook a large ox or a large he-goat—for that is human (fare offered to a guest), and the oblation is that of the gods—so he prepares for him that guest-offering.

3. Here now they say, 'Let him first walk past (Soma) and take out (the material for offering)!' For (they argue) where people do not show respect

to a worthy person (arhant) who has come to them, he becomes angry,—and in this way he (Soma) is indeed honoured.

4. Then only one (of the oxen) is to be unyoked, and the other to be left unyoked[1]; and thereupon he is to take out (the material for offering): for (they argue) in that one of them is unyoked, thereby he (Soma) has arrived; and in that the other is left unyoked, thereby he is honoured.

5. Let him, however, not do this; but let him take out (the material for offering) only after unyoking (both oxen) and after making (Soma) enter (the hall); for the ways of men are in accordance with those of the gods. And accordingly, in human practice, so long as (a guest) has not unyoked, people do not bring water to him and show him no honour, for so long he has not yet arrived; but when he has unyoked, then they bring him water and show him honour, for then he has indeed arrived: let him therefore take out (the material for offering) only after unyoking and after making (Soma) enter (the hall).

6. Let him take it out with all speed, for thus he (Soma) is honoured. The housewife holds on to it from behind[2]; for the sacrificer holds on to him (Soma), while he is driven around, and here his wife does so. Thus they enclose him on the two sides by a (married) couple: and, indeed, wherever a

[1] This is the practice recognised by the Taittirîyas (T. S. VI, 2, 1, 1), on the ground that, if one were to unyoke both oxen, he would interrupt the sacrifice; and if he were to leave them both unyoked, it would be as if a hospitable reception were given to one who has not actually arrived.

[2] That is, by touching the Adhvaryu while he takes out the sacrificial food. See p. 79, note 3.

worthy person comes, there all the inmates of the house bestir themselves, for thus he is honoured.

7. Let him take out (the material) with a different formula from that wherewith (one takes out) any other oblations[1], since, when he (Soma) is bought, he is bought for one special destination,—for the sovereignty of the metres, for the supreme sovereignty of the metres. The metres act as attendants about him; even as the non-royal king-makers, the heralds and headmen, (attend upon) the king, so do the metres act as attendants about him (Soma).

8. In no wise, then, is it befitting that he should take out any (material for offering) solely 'for the metres[2];' for whenever people cook food for some worthy person[3], then the attendants about him, the non-royal king-makers, the heralds and headmen, have their share (of the food) assigned to them after (or along with their master): hence, when he takes out that (oblation to Soma), let him assign the metres a share in it along with (the deity).

9. He takes it out, with the text (Vâg. S. V, 1), 'Thou art Agni's body,—thee (I take) for Vishnu!' the Gâyatrî is Agni: to Gâyatrî he thus assigns her share.

10. 'Thou art Soma's body,—thee for Vishnu!' Soma is the nobility, and the Trishtubh

[1] For the ordinary formula with which material for offering is taken out at an ishti, 'At the impulse of the divine Savitri, I take thee with the arms of the Asvins, with the hands of Pûshan, thee well-pleasing to—!' see I, 1, 2, 17.

[2] According to Taitt. S. VI, 2, 1, the five portions are taken out for the metres Gâyatrî, Trishtubh, Gagatî, Anushtubh, and Gâyatrî, with the texts, 'Thou art Agni's hospitable feast, for Vishnu (I take) thee,' &c.

[3] 'Arhant' seems rather to mean 'ruler' here.

is the nobility: to Trishtubh he thus assigns her share.

11. 'Thou art the guest's hospitable entertainment[1],—thee for Vishnu!' This is his (Soma's) special share: as there is a special share for a chief, so is this his special share apart from the metres.

12. 'Thee for the Soma-bearing falcon! thee for Vishnu!' thereby he assigns to Gâyatrî her share. Because Gâyatrî, in the form of a falcon, carried off Soma from the sky, therefore she is the Soma-bearing falcon: in virtue of that heroic deed he now assigns to her a second share.

13. 'Thee for Agni, the bestower of prosperity! thee for Vishnu!' Prosperity means cattle, and the *G*agatî (the moving, living one) means cattle: to *G*agatî he thereby assigns her share.

14. Now as to his taking five times;—the sacrifice is of equal measure with the year, and five seasons there are in the year: the latter he gains in five (divisions);—for this reason he takes five times. And as to his taking it with 'For Vishnu (I take) thee! for Vishnu thee!' it is because he who takes out (material) for the sacrifice, takes it for Vishnu.

15. It is a sacrificial cake on nine potsherds;—for the guest-offering is the head of the sacrifice, and the Gâyatrî consists of nine syllables[2]: eight (syllables) are those he recites and the sacred syllable[3] is the ninth; and the Gâyatrî is the fore-part of the

[1] Atither âtithyam, 'the guest's guest-meal.'

[2] According to Taitt. S. VI, 2, 1, 4, it is because the head has nine seams, 'navadhâ siro vishyûtam.'

[3] The final syllable of the prayers recited in offering is protracted and nasalized, a final 'a' becoming ô*m*,—this drawing out of the syllable is called 'pranava.'

sacrifice[1], and so is that (cake) the fore-part of the sacrifice: therefore it is a cake on nine potsherds.

16. The enclosing-sticks are of kârshmarya wood (Gmelina Arborea[2]), for the gods, once upon a time, perceived that one, the kârshmarya, to be the Rakshas-killer among trees. Now, the guest-offering being the head of the sacrifice, the enclosing-sticks are of kârshmarya wood, in order that the evil spirits may not injure the head of the sacrifice.

17. The prastara-bunch[3] is of a*s*vavâla-grass (Saccharum Spontaneum). For, once upon a time, the sacrifice escaped from the gods. It became a horse (a*s*va) and sped away from them. The gods, rushing after it, took hold of its tail (vâla) and tore it out; and having torn it out, they threw it down in a lump, and what had been the hairs of the horse's tail then grew up as those plants (of a*s*vavâla-grass). Now the guest-offering is the head of the sacrifice, and the tail is the hind-part (of animals): hence by the prastara being of a*s*vavâla-grass he encompasses the sacrifice on both sides.

18. There are two vidh*ri*tis[4] of sugar-cane, lest

---

[1] Because the Gâyatrî metre is connected with the prâta*h*savana or morning pressing. See IV, 2, 5, 20 seq.; Ait. Br. III, 27 seq.

[2] See I, 3, 3, 19–20, where the approved kinds of wood for the paridhis at an ish*t*i are enumerated.

[3] For the prastara, or bunch of reed-grass, representing the sacrificer, see I, 3, 3, 5 seq.; 8, 3, 11 seq. The a*s*vavâla (horse-tail) grass (generally called kâ*s*a) is said to resemble horse-hair, and is used for twine, mats, thatch, &c. Sir H. M. Elliot, 'Races of the N. W. Prov.,' II, pp. 371, 372, describes it as growing from three to fifteen feet high, and flowering in great profusion after the rains; the base of the flowers being surrounded with a bright silvery fleece, which whitens the neighbouring fields so much as frequently to resemble a fall of snow.

[4] For the vidh*ri*ti or stalks laid across the barhis (sacrificial

the barhis and the prastara should become mixed up together. Having then purified the ghee[1], he takes all the butter-portions in four ladlings[2], for at this (sacrifice) there are no after-offerings.

19. When he has placed the sacrificial dishes (on the altar)[3], he churns the fire. For the guest-offering is the head of the sacrifice; and in churning (the fire) they produce that (sacrifice); and one who is born is born with the head first: hence he thereby makes the sacrifice to be produced with the head first. Further, Agni means all the gods, since offering is made in the fire to all gods; and the guest-offering is the head of the sacrifice: hence, through all the deities, he secures success to the sacrifice from the very head (beginning). This is why he churns the fire[4].

20. He takes the bottom piece of wood[5], with the text (Vâg. S. V, 2), 'Thou art the birth-place of Agni;' for it is thereon that Agni is produced: hence he says, 'Thou art the birth-place of Agni.'

21. Thereon he lays two sprouts of a kusa stalk (with the tops towards the east), with, 'Ye are

grass covering the altar), to keep the prastara separate from the latter when laid upon it, see I, 3, 4, 10. As no special mention is made of the barhis, the same material has to be used for it as at the model ishti (New and Full-moon sacrifice), viz. Kusa grass (Poa Cynosuroides).

[1] See I, 3, 1, 22-23.

[2] See I, 3, 2, 8-9.

[3] See I, 3, 4, 14.

[4] On the production of the fire by 'churning,' see part i, p. 294, note 3.

[5] The adhimanthana sakala is a chip of wood used for the lower churning-stick (adhararani), wherein the upper churning-stick is drilled, to rest upon. It is laid down on the altar-grass (barhis) from south to north. According to Sâyana it is a chip obtained in rough-hewing the sacrificial stake.

males[1];' thereby these two are as two (sons) born together here from a woman.

22. Thereon he lays the lower churning-stick (with the top to the north), with, 'Thou art Urvasî!' He then touches the (ghee in the) ghee-pan with the upper churning-stick, with, 'Thou art Âyu,' he puts it down (on the lower arani) with, 'Thou art Purûravas.' For Urvasî was a nymph, and Purûravas was her husband; and the (child) which sprung from that union was Âyu[2]: in like manner does he now produce the sacrifice from that union. Thereupon he says (to the Hotri), 'Recite to Agni, as he is churned[3]!'

23. He churns, with the texts, 'With the Gâyatrî metre I churn thee!—With the Trishtubh metre I churn thee!—With the Gagatî metre I churn thee!' For it is with the metres that he churns him (Agni, the fire); the metres he recites to him when he is churned, whereby he attaches the metres to the sacrifice, even as the rays (are attached) to yonder sun.—'Recite to the born one!' he says,

---

[1] In this sense 'vrishanau' is taken by Mahîdhara (sektârau, from vrishan), Sâyana, and apparently also by our author. Perhaps it means 'testicles' (vrishana) in the text. See III, 6, 3, 10; and part i, p. 389, note 3.

[2] The myth of Purûravas and Urvasî is given at length XI, 5, 1, 1–17. Compare also Max Müller, Chips, vol. ii, p. 102 seq.; A. Kuhn, Herabkunft des Feuers, p. 78 seq.

[3] The verses which the Hotri has to recite are (a) one to Savitri (the Vivifier, viz. Rig-veda I, 24, 3); (b) to Heaven and Earth (IV, 56, 1); (c) a triplet to Agni (VI, 16, 13–15). If fire has not appeared by this time, he recites the so-called Rakshas-killing verses (X, 118), repeating them until fire has been produced. See Ait. Br. I, 17; Âsv. Sr. II, 16.

when he (Agni) is produced[1]; and 'To him who is thrown[2]!' when he throws him (on the old Âhavanîya fire).

24. He throws (the fire on the hearth), with the text (Vâg. S. V, 3), 'For our sake be ye two (fires) friendly to one another, of one mind, unblemished! Injure not the sacrifice, nor the lord of the sacrifice! be gracious unto us this day, ye knowers of beings!' He thus bespeaks peacefulness between them, that they may not injure each other.

25. He then takes out some clarified butter with the dipping-spoon, and pours it on the fire, with the text (Vâg. S. V, 4), 'Agni resorteth to Agni, he the son of the seers that shieldeth us from curses: graciously offer thou for us now with good offering, never withholding the oblation from the gods, Hail!' For the purpose of offering they have produced him, and by this offering he has now gratified him: that is why he thus makes offering unto him.

26. It (the guest-offering) ends with the Idâ; no after-offerings are performed. For the guest-offering is the head of the sacrifice, and the head is the fore-part: he thus fits him up as the head of the sacrifice. But were he to perform the after-offerings, it would be as if, by reversing, he were to put the feet in the place of the head. Hence it ends with the Idâ, and no after-offerings are performed.

---

[1] The Hotri recites the two verses, Rig-veda I, 74, 3; VI, 16, 40.

[2] The verb is 'pra-hri,' which is also the common term for the hurling of the thunderbolt. The six verses, recited by the Hotri, are Rig-veda VI, 16, 41–42; I, 12, 6; VIII, 43, 14; VIII, 73, 8; I, 164, 50.

THE TÂNÛNAPTRA, OR COVENANT OF TANÛNAPÂT[1].

SECOND BRÂHMANA.

1. When the gods had performed the guest-offering, discord befell them. They separated into four different parties, unwilling to yield to each other's excellence,—Agni with the Vasus, Soma with the Rudras, Varuna with the Âdityas, and Indra with the Maruts. Brihaspati with the All-gods, say some[2], but, indeed, those who separated into four parties were 'all the gods.' When they were separated, the Asura-Rakshas came after them and entered between them.

2. They became aware of it,—'Forsooth, we are in an evil plight, the Asura-Rakshas have come in between us: we shall fall a prey to our enemies. Let us come to an agreement and yield to the excellence of one of us!' They yielded to the excellence of Indra; wherefore it is said, 'Indra is all the deities, the gods have Indra for their chief.'

3. For this reason let not kinsmen fall out, for any (enemy) of theirs, be he ever so far away, steps in between them; they do what pleases their enemies and fall a prey to their enemies: therefore let them not fall out. For he who, knowing this, quarrels not, does what displeases his enemies and

[1] The Tânûnaptra is a solemn covenant made by the sacrificer and his priests, in the name of Tanûnapât, and while touching sacrificial butter; thereby pledging themselves not to injure each other.

[2] Thus Ait. Br. I, 24, where moreover the Rudras are assigned to Indra, (the Vasus to Agni, and the Âdityas to Varunâ.)

falls not a prey to his enemies: let him therefore not quarrel.

4. They said, 'Well then, let us contrive so that this (concord) of ours shall be for ever imperishable!'

5. The gods laid down together[1] their favourite forms and desirable powers[2], one after another, and said, 'Thereby he shall be away from us, he shall be scattered to the winds, whosoever shall transgress this (covenant) of ours!'—Whose (is it) as witness[3]?'—'Tanûnapât, the mighty!'—Now the mighty Tanûnapât indeed is yonder blowing (wind), he is the witness of living beings, entering thus as the in-breathing and out-breathing.

6. Wherefore they say, 'The gods know the mind of man.' In his mind he proposes; it passes on to the breath, and the breath to the wind, and the wind tells the gods what the mind of man is.

7. Hence it was in regard to this what was said by the *Ri*shi, 'In his mind he proposeth, and it goeth on to the wind[4]; and the wind telleth the gods what thy mind is, O man.'

8. The gods laid down together their favourite forms and desirable powers, and said, 'Thereby he shall be away from us, he shall be scattered to the winds, whosoever shall transgress this (covenant) of ours!' And even now the gods do not transgress that (covenant), for how would they fare, were they

[1] Literally, 'cut off together, part by part.'

[2] Or, attributes, resources, 'dhâmâni.'

[3] Kasya upadrash*t*ur; the Kâ*n*va text has, Tasya na*h* ka upadrash*t*â, 'who (shall be) the witness of this (covenant) of ours?'

[4] Cp. Atharva-veda XII, 4, 31, 'In his mind he proposes and it goes forth to the gods.'

to transgress it?—they would speak untruth, and verily there is one law which the gods do keep, namely, the truth. It is through this that their conquest, their glory is unassailable: and so, forsooth, is his conquest, his glory unassailable whosoever, knowing this, speaks the truth. Now, the Tânûnaptra is really that same (covenant of the gods).

9. The gods laid down together their favourite forms and desirable powers. Now it is by taking portions of butter that they (the priests) lay down together the desirable forms and favourite powers. Let him, then, not covenant with any one and every one, lest his favourite forms and desirable powers should be mixed up (with those of others). But let him not deceive one with whom he makes a covenant; for thus it is said, 'Let there be no deceiving of him with whom one has made the covenant of Tanûnapât.'

10. In the first place he takes (butter) therefrom[1], with the text (Vâ*g*. S. V, 5), 'For him that rushes onward, for him that rushes about, I take thee.' He that blows yonder (the wind) does indeed rush onward and rush about; and it is for him that he takes (the butter): therefore he says, 'for him that rushes onward, for him that rushes about, I take thee.'

11. 'For Tanûnapât, the mighty.' The mighty Tanûnapât truly is yonder blowing (wind), and it is for him that he takes (the butter): therefore he says, 'For Tanûnapât, the mighty.'

[1] Viz. the butter in the dhruvâ spoon, pouring it into the 'vratapradâna,' or vessel in which the fast-milk is handed to the sacrificer.

12. 'For the powerful, the most strong!' He is indeed powerful and most strong; and for him he takes it: therefore he says, 'For the powerful, the most strong.'

13. They then touch it at the same time. Now the gods were fully agreed on this point, 'Verily, so and thus shall he of us fare who shall transgress this (covenant) of ours!' And so are these (priests and sacrificer) now agreed on this,—'Verily, so and thus shall he of us fare who shall transgress this (covenant) of ours!'

14. They touch it simultaneously, with the text, 'Thou art the strength of the gods, unassailed and unassailable; for the gods were indeed unassailed and unassailable while being together, and speaking with one accord and holding together. 'The strength of the gods' doubtless means the favourite forms and desirable powers of the gods, 'uncursed, curse-averting, uncursable,' for the gods have overcome every curse;—'May I straightway go to the truth!' whereby he means to say, 'May I speak the truth, may I not transgress this (covenant);'—'Establish me in welfare!' for in welfare the gods indeed established themselves by speaking the truth, by performing the truth: therefore he says, 'Establish me in welfare!'

15. Now those favourite forms and desirable powers which the gods put together, they then deposited in Indra[1];—Indra verily is he that burns yonder (the sun); but he indeed did not burn in the beginning, but as now everything else is dark, so was he then; and it is by that very energy (derived

[1] According to Ait. Br. I, 24 the gods deposited their forms in the house of king Varuna.

from those divine objects) that he burns. Hence, if many persons perform the consecration[1], let it (the Tânûnaptra butter), after pouring the fast-milk to it, be handed only to the master of the house, since he, among them, is the representative of Indra. And if he perform the consecration by means of an (offering) with a dakshinâ, let them hand it (the butter) to the sacrificer, after pouring the fast-milk to it, for thus it is said,—'The Sacrificer is Indra.'

16. Now what favourite forms and desirable powers the gods then laid together, all that was wrought together and became the Sâman: wherefore they say, 'The Sâman is the truth, the Sâman is born of the gods.'

THE AVÂNTARADÎKSHÂ, OR INTERMEDIARY CONSECRATION.

THIRD BRÂHMANA.

1. When the gods had performed the guest-offering, discord arose between them. They allayed it by means of the Tânûnaptra (oaths). They desired an atonement for having spoken evil to one another; for they had appointed no other consecration-ceremony till the expiatory bath. They perceived this intermediate consecration[2].

2. By means of fire they enveloped (the body) with a skin. Now, fire being fervour, and the consecration being fervour, they thereby underwent an intermediate consecration; and because they underwent that

[1] That is, in a Sattra or sacrificial session, where all the officiating priests are consecrated and 'sacrificers;' the Yagamâna proper being styled Grihapati (master of the house). See IV, 6, 8, 1 seq.

[2] The Avântaradîkshâ extends to the end of the sixth Brâhmana.

intermediate consecration, therefore this intermediary consecration (avântaradîkshâ, is performed). They turned in their fingers more tightly and drew[1] their zone tighter, whereby they (again) put round them what had been put round them before[2];—and so does he thereby make atonement for what heretofore he has done injurious to the vow, for what he has spoken injurious to the vow.

3. By means of the fire they (the priests) envelop him with a skin. Now, fire being fervour, and the consecration being fervour, he thereby undergoes an intermediate consecration. He turns in his fingers more tightly and draws the zone tighter, whereby he (again) puts round himself what was put round him before. Moreover, it was offspring the gods thereby obtained.

4. By means of Agni (fire) they enveloped (the body) with a skin. Now, Agni being the causer of sexual union, the progenitor, they thereby obtained offspring. They turned in their fingers more tightly and drew their zone tighter, whereby they produced offspring for themselves. And in like manner does he (the sacrificer) thereby obtain offspring.

5. By means of Agni he envelops himself with a skin. Now, Agni being the causer of sexual union, the progenitor, he thereby[3] obtains offspring. He turns in his fingers more tightly and draws his zone tighter, whereby he produces offspring for himself.

6. Now, while the gods were consecrated, whichever of them fetched fire-wood or uttered his appointed texts, him the Asura-Rakshas endeavoured to

[1] Our text has no verb; the Kâṇva recension reads 'auhanta.'

[2] Viz. the dîkshâ, as symbolised by the zone (or the skin).

[3] Viz. through Agni, or the Avântaradîkshâ.

strike—the one by (assuming) the form of this one, and the other by that of another. They came together, upbraiding one another, saying, 'See, what thou hast done to me! see, how thou hast struck me!' But Agni alone did not speak thus to any one, nor did any one speak thus to Agni.

7. They said, 'Have they spoken thus to thee also, Agni?' He said, 'Verily, I have not spoken to any one, nor has any one spoken to me.'

8. They became aware,—'He verily is the greatest repeller of the Rakshas among us; let us be like him: thereby we shall escape from the Rakshas, thereby we shall attain to the heavenly world.' They accordingly became like Agni, and thereby escaped from the Rakshas and attained to the heavenly world. And in like manner does this one now become like Agni, and thereby escape from the Rakshas and attain to the heavenly world. It is in putting a kindling-stick on (the Âhavanîya fire[1]) that he enters upon the Avântaradîkshâ.

9. He puts on the kindling-stick, with the text (Vâ*g*. S. V, 6), 'O Agni, protector of vows; on thee, O protector of vows—' for Agni is lord of vows to the gods; wherefore he says, 'O Agni, protector of vows, on thee, O protector of vows—' 'what bodily form[2] there is of thine, (may that be) here on me; and what bodily form there is of mine, (may that be) on thee! May my vows be bound up with thine, O lord of vows!' whereby he envelops himself with the skin by means of Agni. 'May the lord of consecration approve my

[1] The sacrificer's wife performs silently on and near the Gârhapatya fire the same ceremonies as her husband.

[2] Tanu, see p. 10, note 4.

consecration, and the lord of penance my penance!' Thereby he enters upon the intermediary consecration. More closely he turns in his fingers, and closer he draws the zone; whereby he (again) puts round himself what was put round him before.

10. They then attend on him with the boiling lustral water (madantî);—fire is heat, and the lustral water is heat: that is why they attend on him with the lustral water.

11. Having touched the lustral water, they (the priests and sacrificer) therewith strengthen[1] the king (Soma). The reason why, after touching the lustral water, they strengthen the king is this;—ghee is a thunderbolt, and Soma is seed: hence they strengthen the king after touching the lustral water, lest they should injure the seed, Soma, by the thunderbolt, the ghee.

12. Here now they say, 'Him, Soma, for whom that strengthening (meal), the guest-offering, is prepared, they ought first to strengthen, and then (ought to be performed) the Avântaradîkshâ, and thereupon the Tânûnaptra.' But let him not do this. For such indeed was the course of the sacrificial performance: discord arose between them (the gods) thereat; they attained to their former tranquillity; then the Avântaradîkshâ and finally the strengthening.

13. Then as to why they strengthen (Soma). Soma is a god, since Soma (the moon) is in the sky. 'Soma, forsooth, was Vritra; his body is the same as the mountains and rocks: thereon grows that plant called Usânâ,'—so said Svetaketu Auddâlaki;

[1] On the 'âpyâyana' (â-pyai, 'to swell, make swell,' to strengthen, become strong, increase, fill), see part i, p. 178, note 2. According to Âpastamba and other authorities, they tie a piece of gold to their nameless (gold) finger, and touch the Soma with their moist hands.

'they fetch it hither and press it; and by means of the consecration and the Upasads, by the Tânûnaptra and the strengthening they make it into Soma.' And in like manner does he now make it into Soma by means of the consecration and the Upasads, by the Tânûnaptra and the strengthening.

14. 'It is bees' honey,' they say; for bees' honey means the sacrifice, and the bees that make the honey are no other than the officiating priests; and in like manner as the working-bees make the honey increase, so do they (the priests) thereby strengthen the sacrifice.

15. By means of the sacrifice the gods gained that supreme authority which they now wield. They spake, 'How can this (world) of ours be made unattainable to men?' Having sipped the sap of the sacrifice, as bees would suck out honey, and having drained the sacrifice and scattered it by means of the sacrificial post, they disappeared; and because they scattered (yopaya) therewith, therefore it is called yûpa (post).

16. Now this was heard by the *Ri*shis. They collected the sacrifice; and as that sacrifice was collected, so does he collect the sacrifice who is consecrated. The sacrifice is speech: hence he thereby again supplies what part of the sacrifice here has been sucked out and drained.

17. They strengthen (the Soma), being six[1];—there are six seasons: having become the seasons, they strengthen it[2].

18. They strengthen him with (Vâg. S. V, 7),

---

[1] Viz. the five priests—Brahman, Udgât*ri*, Hot*ri*, Adhvaryu, and Âgnîdhra—and the sacrificer.

[2] That is, as the seasons make the Soma-plant grow.

'Let stalk after stalk of thine wax strong, O divine Soma!' whereby they strengthen (increase) stalk after stalk of his;—'for Indra, the winner of the ekadhanas[1];' Indra indeed is the deity of the sacrifice: therefore he says, 'For Indra, the winner (or bestower) of the ekadhanas.' For verily every one of those stalks swells to fill a hundred or ten[2] ekadhana cups for the several gods. 'May Indra wax strong for thee, and wax thou strong for Indra!' for Indra is the deity of the sacrifice: he thus strengthens him who is the deity of the sacrifice. By saying, 'Wax thou strong for Indra,' he instils that invigorating draught into him. 'Strengthen us friends with gain and understanding!' 'With gain' he says with reference to what he gains; and 'with understanding' he says with reference to what he recites. 'Mayest thou thrive, O divine Soma, and may I attain to the Soma-feast!' They, the priests and sacrificer, have one prayer in common, 'May we reach the end of the sacrifice!' hence he thereby means to say, 'May I reach the end of the sacrifice!'

19. Thereupon they make amends on the prastara. For the sacrifice requires a northward attend-

---

[1] Ekadhana-vid; the meaning of 'ekadhana' (apparently 'one prize' or 'one part of the booty or goods') in this compound is not clear. The author of the Brâhmana seems to take it in its technical sense, viz. the ekadhana pitchers in which the ekadhanâ water, used for mixing with the Soma juice, is kept, see III, 9, 3; 16; 27; 34. According to Haug, Transl. Ait. Br. p. 114 notes, they are so called because the Adhvaryu throws one stalk of Soma (eka-dhana) into each pitcher to consecrate it.

[2] This anticlimax is rather curious. The Kânva text reads: dasa dasa vâ ha smaisha ekaiko 'msur devân pratîndrâyaikadhanân âpyâyayanti (!) satam satam vâ tasmâd âhaikadhanavida iti.

ance; but now they strengthen (Soma) after going, as it were, towards the right (south)[1]; and, the sacrifice being the fire, they thereby turn their back on the sacrifice and thus do wrong and are cut off from the gods. Now the prastara also is (part of) the sacrifice, and by (touching) it they again get hold of the sacrifice. And this is his expiation of that (transgression); and so no wrong is committed by them and they are not cut off from the gods: for this reason they make amends on the prastara.

20. Here now they say, 'On the anointed?—let them rather make amends on the unanointed[2]!' They should indeed make amends on the unanointed (prastara), since anointed it is thrown into the fire.

21. They make amends[3] with, 'Desirable treasures (may come) forth for strength and well-being—the right for the right-saying'—whereby

[1] Soma's throne stands south of the Âhavanîya fire, and in going to perform the âpyayanam upon him, the priests and sacrificer have to move round the fire, along the east side of it towards the south (the region of the Fathers).

[2] This seems to be Sâyana's interpretation of the passage 'akte nihnuvîrã̄n anaktã̄i.' The two words, with their final syllable protracted, being intended to strongly contradict the preceding 'akte.' It is hardly possible to take the latter absolutely, 'it being anointed (when thrown into the fire), let them make amends on it while unanointed.' On the throwing of the prastara into the fire, see I, 8, 3, 17. The prastara referred to is that of the guest-offering (âtithyeshti), which was broken off after the Idâ ceremony (see III, 4, 1, 26) and has to be completed after the present ceremony. Neither the prastara nor the barhis is burnt on this occasion.

[3] In performing this propitiatory rite, the priests and sacrificer lay their hands on the prastara, either both of them with the palms upwards, or only the right one, and the left in the opposite way. Kâty. VIII, 2, 9. The latter mode is the one practised by the Taittirîyas. Sây. on Taitt. S. I, 2, 11.

he means to say, 'the truth for the truth-speaking;'—'Homage be to Heaven and to the Earth!' whereby they make amends to these two, heaven and earth, on whom this All is founded.

22. Having then picked up the prastara, he says, 'Agnîdh, does the water boil?'—'It boils,' replies the Agnîdh[1]. 'Come hither with it!' He holds (the prastara) quite close over the fire. The reason why he does not throw it into the fire is that he (the sacrificer) is to perform therewith[2] during the days that follow; and in that he holds it quite close over the fire, thereby it is for him as if it were really thrown into the fire. He hands it to the Agnîdh, and the Agnîdh puts it aside (in a safe place).

THE UPASADS, OR HOMAGES.

FOURTH BRÂHMANA.

1. Verily the Upasads (homages or sieges) are the neck of the sacrifice, and the Pravargya is its head. Hence when it is performed with the Pravargya[3],

[1] According to the Kânva text, this conversation takes the place of the colloquy (samudita) held by the Adhvaryu and the Âgnîdhra, after the prastara has been thrown into the fire at the normal ishti; see I, 8, 3, 20.

[2] Or, 'in the shape of it (tena),' the prastara representing the sacrificer himself. This sentence seems also to imply, that the sacrificer thereby continues to live during the days that follow.

[3] The Pravargya, an offering of heated milk, which precedes each performance of the Upasads,—except at the first performance of the Soma-sacrifice, when it is prohibited by many authorities,—seems originally to have been an independent ceremony, and as such it is treated by most ritualistic books apart from the exposition of the Soma-cult. The Satapatha-brâhmana deals with it in XIV, 1–3 (Vâg. S. XXXIX). Its mystic significance appears to have been that of supplying the sacrificer with a new celestial body. There seems to have been a tendency towards exalting its

they perform the Upasads[1] after performing the Pravargya, and thereby they put the neck in its place.

2. The anuvâkyâs (invitatory prayers) in the forenoon are the yâgyâs (offering prayers) in the afternoon; and the yâgyâs are the anuvâkyâs[2]. He thus interlinks them, whence those joints and those bones of the neck are interlinked.

3. Now the gods and the Asuras, both of them sprung from Pragâpati, were contending against each other[3]. The Asuras then built themselves castles in these worlds,—an iron one in this world, a silver one in the air, and a golden one in the sky.

4. The gods then prevailed. They besieged them by these sieges (upasad); and because they besieged (upa-sad) them, therefore the name Upasads.

importance—if not, indeed, towards making it take the place of the Soma-cult. The hot milk (gharma) is even styled 'Samrâg' or supreme king—as against the title 'râgan' or king, assigned to Soma; and a throne is provided for it, just as for the latter. The rules for its performance, according to the Âpastamba Srauta-sûtra, have been published, with a translation, by Professor Garbe (Zeitsch. der D. M. G. XXXIV, p. 319 seq.). See also Haug's Transl. of the Ait. Br. pp. 41–43; Weber, Ind. Stud. IX. pp. 218–220.

[1] The Upasadah, consisting of three offerings of ghee to Agni, Soma, and Vishnu, followed by a Homa, have to be performed twice daily, for at least three days (the normal number at the Agnishtoma). The first day's performance is called (from the corresponding Homa) the 'ayahsayâ' (lying in iron, made of iron), the second day's 'ragahsayâ' (silvern), and the third day's 'harisayâ' (golden). If there are six, or twelve Upasad days, each of the three varieties of performance has assigned to it an equal number of successive days; and if there are more than twelve the three varieties are to be performed alternately.

[2] For the anuvâkyâs and yâgyâs, as well as the kindling-verses (sâmidhenîs) to be recited at the Upasads, see Ait. Br. I, 26; Âsv. IV, 8.

[3] For other versions of this myth, see Ait. Br. I, 23; Taitt. S. VI, 2, 3.

They clove the castles and conquered these worlds. Hence they say, 'A castle is conquered by siege;' for it is indeed by beleaguering that one of these human castles is taken.

5. By means of these sieges, then, the gods clove the castles and conquered these worlds. And so does this one (the sacrificer) now,—no one, it is true, builds for himself castles against him in this world; he cleaves these same worlds, he conquers these worlds: therefore he offers with the Upasads.

6. They have clarified butter for their offering material. For ghee is a thunderbolt, and by that thunderbolt, the ghee, the gods clove the strongholds and conquered these worlds. And so does he cleave these worlds by that thunderbolt, the ghee, and conquer these worlds; therefore they (the Upasads) have ghee for their offering material.

7. He takes eight times (ghee) in the *g*uhû, and four times in the upabh*ri*t; or conversely, they say, he is to take of it only four times in the *g*uhû and eight times in the upabh*ri*t[1].

8. He takes eight times in the *g*uhû, and four times in the upabh*ri*t. He thereby makes the thunderbolt heavy in front, and with that thunderbolt heavy in front he cleaves these worlds, and conquers these worlds.

9. Agni and Soma verily are yoke-fellows among the gods: for these two he takes (ghee) in common[2]. For Vish*n*u (he takes) singly. He makes only the one libation (âghâra) which (he makes) with the dipping-spoon (sruva)[3]. For when he has made

---

[1] This would be the regular mode of ladling. See I, 3, 2, 8 seq.

[2] See p. 108, note 1.

[3] For the two âghâra, or libations of ghee, made with the

the northern (higher) libation he retires[1]: 'May I conquer for conquest' so he thinks, and therefore he makes only the one libation, that with the dipping-spoon.

10. When he has called (on the Âgnîdhra) for the *S*raushat, he does not elect the Hot*ri*[2]. 'Seat thee, O Hot*ri*!' he says. The Hot*ri* sits down on the Hot*ri*'s seat. Having sat down he urges the Adhvaryu; and he, thus urged, takes the two offering-spoons[3].

11. While passing over (to the south side of the fire and altar) he says[4] (to the Hot*ri*), 'Recite the invitatory prayer to Agni!' and having called for the *S*raushat, he says, 'Pronounce the offering prayer to Agni!' and pours out the oblation when the Vashat is uttered.

12. Thereupon he says, 'Recite the invitatory prayer to Soma!' and having called for the *S*raushat, he says, 'Pronounce the offering prayer to Soma!' and pours out the oblation when the Vashat is uttered.

13. Thereupon, while pouring the ghee which is in the upabh*ri*t[5], together (with what is left in the *g*uhû), he says, 'Recite the invitatory prayer to Vish*n*u!' and, having called for the *S*raushat, he says, 'Pronounce the offering prayer to Vish*n*u!'

sruva north of the fire and *g*uhû south of the fire respectively, see I, 4, 4, 1 seq. At the Upasad-ish*t*i neither fore-offerings (prayâ*g*a) nor after-offerings (anuyâ*g*a) are performed.

[1] Viz. to the offering place on the south side of the fire. The covert meaning is that, were he to make the second libation, he would have to recede from the higher (uttara, northern) position already gained.

[2] See I, 5, 1, 1 seq. [3] See I, 5, 2, 1 seq. [4] See I, 7, 2, 1 seq.

[5] Of the ghee in the *g*uhû (obtained from eight ladlings with the

and pours out the oblation when the Vashat is uttered.

14. The reason why in offering he remains standing in one and the same place, and does not move about as he is wont to do here in performing, isthat he thinks 'I will conquer for conquest[1]!' And the reason why he offers to those deities is that he thereby constructs the thunderbolt: Agni (he makes) the point (anîka), Soma the barb (salya), and Vishnu the connecting piece (kulmala)[2].

15. For the thunderbolt is the year: the day is Agni, the night Soma, and what is between the two, that is Vishnu. Thus he makes the revolving year.

16. The thunderbolt is the year: by that year, as a thunderbolt, the gods clove the strongholds and conquered these worlds. And so does he now by that year, as a thunderbolt, cleave these worlds, and conquer these worlds. This is why he offers to those gods.

17. Let him undertake three Upasads; for, there being three seasons in the year, it is thereby made of the form of the year: he thus makes up the year. He performs twice each.

---

sruva) he first offers one half each to Agni and Soma. Thereupon he pours the ghee from the upabhrit (obtained from four ladlings with the sruva) into the guhû and offers it to Vishnu.

[1] 'It is for conquest that he does not move about as he (does when he) performs here in any other sacrifice.' Kânva recension.

[2] ? The socket; compare Ait. Br. I, 25, 'The gods constructed that arrow, the Upasads: Agni was its point (? anîka, shaft, Haug), Soma its barb (salya, steel, H.), Vishnu its shaft (teganam, point, H.), and Varuna its feathers (parna) . . . . For the arrow consists of three parts, anîka, salya, and tegana . . . . For the arrow consists of two parts, salya and tegana.' Here salya would seem to be the barbed head-piece (with the point, anîka), and tegana the shaft or reed of the arrow.

18. These amount to six; for, there being six seasons in the year, it is thereby made of the form of the year: he thus makes up the year.

19. And should he undertake twelve Upasads,—there being twelve months in the year, it is thereby made of the form of the year: he thus makes up the year. He performs twice each.

20. These amount to twenty-four;—there being twenty-four half-moons in the year, it is thereby made of the form of the year: he thus makes up the year.

21. As to his performing in the evening and in the morning,—it is because only thus completeness is obtained. When he performs in the forenoon, then he gains the victory;—and when he performs in the afternoon, he does so that it may be a good (complete) victory;—and when he offers the Homa, (it is as if) people fight here for a stronghold, and having conquered it, they enter it as their own.

22. When he performs (the upasads), he fights; and when (the performance) is completed, he conquers; and when he offers the Homa[1], he enters that (stronghold) now his own.

23. He offers it (with the verse) with which he

---

[1] On the completion of each performance of the Upasad offerings, after the anointing of the prastara (see I, 8, 3, 11–14) and previously to taking up the enclosing-sticks (ib. 22), a homa (or *gu*hoti) offering (part i, p. 263, note 2), called Upasad-homa, has to be performed with the dipping-spoon; the sacrificer holding on to Adhvaryu from behind, while the ghee is poured into the fire. Its performance over, the Upasads are brought to an end by a repetition of the ceremony with the prastara (which is not burnt) described above, III, 4, 3, 22, and the minor concluding ceremonies (I, 8, 3, 23 seq.; 9, 2, 19 seq.); whereupon the Subrahma*n*yâ litany (III, 3, 4, 17) is recited.

will have to perform twice in one day[1] (Vâg. S. V, 8), 'What most excellent iron-clad body is thine, O Agni, established in the deep, it hath chased away the cruel word, it hath chased away the fearful word; Hail!' for such-like it was, it was indeed iron.

24. Again he offers (with the verse) with which he will have to perform twice in one day, 'What most excellent silver-clad body is thine, O Agni, established in the deep, it hath chased away the cruel word, it hath chased away the fearful word; Hail!' for such-like it was, it was indeed silver.

25. And again he offers (with the verse) with which he will have to perform twice in one day, 'What most excellent gold-clad body is thine, O Agni, established in the deep, it hath chased away the cruel word, it hath chased away the fearful word; Hail!' for such-like it was, it was indeed golden. If he undertakes twelve Upasads, let him perform each of them for four days.

26. Now then of the fast-homages. Some Upasads get wider and wider, others narrower and narrower: those at which he milks out one (teat)[2] on the first day, then two, and then three, are those that get wider and wider; and those at which he

[1] While the Hotri, as we saw (parag. 2, above), uses the same two verses twice in one day, viz. one for the anuvâkyâ in the morning and for the yâgyâ in the afternoon; and the other for the yâgyâ in the morning and for the anuvâkyâ in the evening,—the Adhvaryu is to use the three formulas here mentioned on the three Upasad days respectively, both at the morning and afternoon performances.

[2] Viz. of the vratadughâ, or cow supplying his fast-milk. The milk so obtained is to be his only food during the Upasad days.

milks out three on the first day, then two, and then one, are those that get narrower and narrower. Those getting narrower and narrower are (as good as) those getting wider and wider; and those getting wider and wider are (as good as) those getting narrower and narrower.

27. Verily, the world is conquered by austere devotion. Now, his devotion becomes ever and ever wider, he conquers an ever and ever more glorious world and becomes better even in this world, whosoever, knowing this, undertakes the Upasads that get narrower and narrower[1]: let him, therefore, undertake the Upasads that get narrower and narrower. And should he undertake twelve Upasads, let him have three (teats) milked out for four days, two for four days, and one for four days.

PREPARATION OF THE SOMA ALTAR WITH THE HIGH ALTAR[2].

FIFTH ADHYÂYA. FIRST BRÂHMA*N*A.

1. From that post which is the largest on the east side (of the hall)[3] he now strides three steps forwards (to the east), and there drives in a peg,—this is the intermediate (peg)[4].

---

[1] The simile is apparently taken from the arrow, which pierces the deeper the more pointed it is; cf. parag. 14, above; Ait. Br. I, 25. Also Taitt. S. VI, 2, 3, 5, where a goad (âra?) is compared.

[2] The preparation of the special altars—viz. the large Soma altar (mahâ-vedi, or saumikî-vedi) and the 'high altar' (uttara-vedi) on the former—takes place on the last but one Upasad day, after the morning performance of the Upasads.

[3] This post stands in the middle of the east door of the hall or Prâ*k*îna-va*ms*a, just in front of the Âhavanîya-fire. See p. 3, note 2.

[4] Anta*h*pâta, lit. 'falling within or between,' because it stands

2. From that middle peg he strides fifteen steps to the right, and there drives in a peg,—this is the right hip.

3. From that middle peg he strides fifteen steps northwards, and there drives in a peg,—this is the left hip.

4. From that middle peg he strides thirty-six steps eastwards, and there drives in a peg,—this is the fore-part[1].

5. From that middle peg (in front) he strides twelve steps to the right, and there drives in a peg,—this is the right shoulder.

6. From that middle peg he strides twelve steps to the north, and there drives in a peg,—this is the left shoulder. This is the measure of the altar.

7. Now the reason why it is thirty steps broad behind is this: the Virâg metre consists of thirty syllables, and by means of the Virâg the gods obtained a firm footing in this world; and even so does he now, by means of the Virâg, obtain a firm footing in this world.

8. But there may also be thirty-three (steps); for of thirty-three syllables also consists the Virâg; and by means of the Virâg he obtains a firm footing in this world.

9. Then as to why the 'easterly line[2]' is thirty-six steps long;—the Brihatî consists of thirty-six syllables, and by means of the Brihatî the gods obtained

between the (new) altar and the Prâkîna-vamsa fires and altar. See III, 5, 2, 2.

[1] That is, the middle of the front side of the altar, or, as it were, its head, where the 'high altar' is to be raised.

[2] The 'prâkî' is the line drawn from the middle of the west side to that of the front side of the altar, forming as it were the spine (prishthyâ) of the altar.

the heavenly world: and so does he now, by means of the B*ri*hatî, obtain the heavenly world and that offering-fire (Âhavanîya) of his is in the sky.

10. And as to (the altar) being twenty-four steps broad in front;—the Gâyatrî consists of twenty-four syllables, and the Gâyatrî is the fore-part of the sacrifice: this is why it is twenty-four steps broad in front. This is the measure of the altar.

11. And why it is broader behind,—'Wider behind, broad-hipped,' thus they praise a woman. And by its being wider behind, he makes that womb at the hind-part (of the altar) wider, and from that wider womb these creatures are born.

12. That high altar (Uttaravedi[1]) is the nose of the sacrifice; because they throw it up so as to be higher than the altar, therefore it is called 'high altar.'

13. Now, in the beginning there were two kinds of beings here, the Âdityas and the Aṅgiras. The Aṅgiras then were the first to prepare a sacrifice, and having prepared the sacrifice they said to Agni, 'Announce thou to the Âdityas this our to-morrow's Soma-feast, saying, "Minister ye at this sacrifice of ours!"'

14. The Âdityas spake (to one another), 'Contrive ye how the Aṅgiras shall minister unto us, and not we unto the Aṅgiras!'

15. They said, 'Verily by nothing but sacrifice is there a way out of this[2]: let us undertake another

[1] On the uttara-vedi (lit. 'higher, upper altar'), now about to be raised on the fore-part of the great altar (mahâ-vedi or saumikî vedi) described in the preceding paragraphs, see also part i, p. 392 note.

[2] The Kâ*n*va MS. reads, nâpakrama*n*am astv iti, which, if correct,

Soma-feast!' They brought together the (materials for) sacrifice, and having made ready the sacrifice, they said, 'Agni, thou hast announced to us a Soma-feast for to-morrow; but we announce to thee and the Aṅgiras a Soma-feast even for to-day: it is for us that thou art (to officiate as) Hot*ri*[1]!'

16. They sent back some other (messenger) to the Aṅgiras; but the Aṅgiras going after Agni, were exceeding angry with him, saying, 'Going as our messenger, why didst thou not mind us[2]?'

17. He spake, 'The blameless chose me: as the chosen of the blameless, I could not go away.' And let not therefore the chosen (priest) of a blameless man turn away from him. The Aṅgiras then officiated for the Âdityas in the sacrifice with Soma bought (krî) on the same day (sadyas); whence this Sadya*h*krî[3].

18. They brought Vâ*k* (speech) to them for their sacrificial fee. They accepted her not, saying, 'We shall be losers if we accept her.' And so the performance of that sacrifice was not discharged (completed), as it was one requiring a sacrificial fee.

19. Thereupon they brought Sûrya (the sun) to them, and they accepted him. Wherefore the Aṅgiras say, 'Verily, we are fit for the sacrificial office, we are worthy to receive Dakshi*n*âs; yea, even he that burns yonder has been received by us[4]!'

---

would mean, 'Let there be no going away!' i.e. 'Let us not go (to the Aṅgiras)!' or perhaps, 'Do not thou (Agni) go away!'

[1] Teshâ*m* nas tva*m* hotâsîti, perhaps 'thou wilt sacrifice for us.'

[2] 'Sent by us, why didst thou not return?' Kâ*n*va rec.

[3] An ekâha (one day's) performance of the Soma-sacrifice at which the consecrations, buying and pressing of Soma, are compressed into one day.

[4] Api vâ asmâbhir esha pratig*ri*hîta*h*, 'Ist doch jener von uns empfangen worden.'

Hence a white horse is the sacrificial fee for the Sadya*h*krî.

20. On the front of this (horse) there is a golden ornament, whereby it is made an image of him that burns yonder.

21. Now Vâ*k* was angry with them: 'In what respect, forsooth, is that one better than I,—wherefore is it, that they should have accepted him and not me[1]?' So saying she went away from them. Having become a lioness she went on seizing upon (everything[2]) between those two contending parties, the gods and the Asuras. The gods called her to them, and so did the Asuras. Agni was the messenger of the gods, and one Saharakshas for the Asura-Rakshas.

22. Being willing to go over to the gods, she said, 'What would be mine, if I were to come over to you?'—'The offering shall reach thee even before (it reaches) Agni.' She then said to the gods, 'Whatsoever blessing ye will invoke through me, all that shall be accomplished unto you!' So she went over to the gods.

23. And, accordingly, when he pours ghee on the high altar[3], while the fire is held (over it)—since the gods said to her on that occasion, 'The offering shall reach thee even before Agni'—then that offering does reach her even before (it reaches) Agni; for this (high altar) is in reality Vâ*k*. And when he raises

---

[1] The Kâ*n*va text reads, Na mad esha kena *k*ana *s*reyân iti na bandhunâ na kena *k*ana katham eta*m* pragr*i*h*n*îyur na mâm iti; 'That one is not my superior by anything, not by kinship, not by anything, why should they accept him and not me?'

[2] Âdadânâ *k*a*k*âra=*g*ighatsayâ samîpastha*m* sarva*m* svîkurvatî, Sây.

[3] See III, 5, 2, 9-11.

the high altar, it is for the completeness of the sacrifice, for the sacrifice is Vâ*k* (speech) and that (high altar) is Vâ*k*.

24. He measures it with the yoke and pin;—namely with the yoke (that place) whither they take (the earth); and with a yoke-pin that, from whence they take (the earth[1]), for the team is harnessed with the yoke and the pin: it is because she (Vâ*k*), as a lioness, at that time roamed about unappeased that he thus yokes her here at the sacrifice.

25. One must not therefore accept a Dakshi*n*â (sacrificial fee) that has been refused (by another priest[2]), for, having turned into a lioness, it destroys him;—nor must he (the sacrificer) take it home again, for, having turned into a lioness, it destroys him;—nor must he give it to any one else, as he would thereby make over the sacrifice to some one other than himself. Hence if he have any wretched kinsman, let him give it to him; for in that he gives it away, it will not turn into a lioness and destroy him; and in that he gives it to a kinsman, he does not make over (the sacrifice) to one other than himself: and this is the settling of a refused Dakshi*n*â.

26. He now takes the yoke-pin and the wooden sword; and from where the northern peg of the front side is, he strides three steps backwards and there marks off the pit (*k*âtvâla). The measure for the pit is the same (as for the high altar)[3]; there

[1] That is to say, the pit (*k*âtvâla) whence the earth for the high altar is taken is measured with the yoke-pin, and the high altar with the yoke. Sâya*n*a seems to take it differently: Yatra yasmin de*s*e yugena haranti yato yasmât tatra *s*amyayâpi haranti.

[2] Or perhaps, one must not take back a Dakshi*n*â, refused by a priest.

[3] The earth taken from the pit being used for constructing the

is no (other) measure in regard to it: wherever he himself may think fit in his mind (to fix it), in front of the heap of rubbish (utkara), there let him mark off the pit.

27. From the (north) edge of the altar he lays down the pin from south to north, and draws the (western) outline, with the text (Vâg. S. V, 9), 'Thou art for me the resort of the afflicted!' Thereby he means this (earth), for it is thereon that he walks afflicted.

28. Thereupon he lays down the pin in front from south to north, and draws the outline with, 'Thou art my wealth-resort.' Thereby he means this (earth), for it is thereon that he walks having acquired (wealth).

29. He then lays down the pin along the (north) edge of the altar from west to east, and draws the outline with, 'Preserve me from being in want[1]!' Thereby he means this (earth): 'Wherever there is want, from that preserve me!'

30. He then lays down the pin on the north side from west to east, and draws the outline with, 'Preserve me from being afflicted[1]!' Thereby he

high altar, both are of the same size or cubic content. The pit is to measure thirty-two aṅgulas (about two feet) on each side. As to the exact distance of the pit from the north-east peg, this is to be left to the discretion of the Adhvaryu, provided it be in front of the utkara, or heap of rubbish formed in making the large altar (on which the high altar is raised), and a passage be left between the utkara and the pit. The latter is contiguous to the north edge of the large altar. As described in the succeeding paragraphs, the west side is marked off first (by drawing the wooden sword along the inner side of the yoke-pin), then successively the front, the south, and the north sides.

[1] For 'nâthitât' and 'vyathitât,' the Kânva text, as the Taitt. S. VI, 2, 7, 2, has the readings 'nâthitam' and 'vyathitam.'

means this (earth): 'wherever there is affliction, from that preserve me!'

31. He then flings (the wooden sword)[1]; at the place where he flings[2], the Agnîdh sits. He flings while mentioning the names of the Agnis[3]. For those (three) Agnis whom the gods at first chose for the office of Hotri passed away: they crept into these very earths,—namely, into this one and the two beyond it. It is really with this one[4] that he now flings.

32. He flings with the texts, 'May the Agni called Nabhas[5] know (thee)! Go thou, O Agni, Angiras, with the name of Âyu (life)!' What life they passed away from[6] that he bestows, that he re-animates. Having with, 'Thou who art in this earth,' taken (the loose soil dug up by the wooden sword), he puts it down (on the altar[7]), with, 'Whatever inviolate, holy name of thine,

[1] Compare the Stambayagur-haranam (which has also to be performed on the present occasion, in preparing the large altar), I, 2, 4, 8 seq.

[2] That is, at the place where the uttaravedi is to be raised, whence the Adhvaryu throws the sphya to where the pit is to be dug. While he throws (or thrusts in) the wooden sword, the sacrificer has to take hold of him from behind.

[3] See I, 2, 3, 1.

[4] I. e. with the Agni who entered into this earth.

[5] Apparently 'vapour, welkin.' The Kânva rec. reads, 'Mayest thou know Agni's name Nabhas' (Vider Agner, &c.). The Taitt. S., on the other hand, reads 'vider Agnir nabho nâma,' which Sâyana explains by 'the Agni of the vedi (!) is Nabhas by name.'

[6] Yat prâdhanvams tad âyur dadhâti. Perhaps we ought to read with the Kânva text, Yat prâdhanvat tad asminn âyur dadhâti tad enam samîrayati, 'the life which passed away (?), that he bestows on him, therewith he re-animates him.'

[7] He throws it on the fore-part of the altar, close to the peg marking the middle of the front side, where the 'high altar' is to be raised on it.

therewith I lay thee down!' whereby he means to say, 'whatever holy name, unviolated by the Rakshas, is thine, thereby I lay thee down[1].'—With 'Thee, moreover, for the delight of the gods,' he takes (earth) a fourth time[2]; whereby he means to say, 'I take thee well-pleasing to the gods.' He takes that (high altar) from a quadrangular pit, for there are four quarters: thus he takes it from all the four quarters.

33. Thereupon he shifts (the earth) asunder, with the text (Vâ*g*. S. V, 10), 'Thou art a lioness, overcoming the enemies; be thou meet for the gods!' Inasmuch as, on that occasion, she became a lioness and roamed about unappeased, therefore he says to her, 'Thou art a lioness;' and by 'overcoming the enemies' he means to say, 'Through thee may we worst our enemies.' 'Be thou meet for the gods' he says, because the high altar is a woman: her he thus renders meet for the gods.

34. He makes it on each side either of the size of the yoke, or ten feet of the sacrificer's[3]; for the

---

[1] He repeats the same ceremony a second and a third time with the same texts, except that, instead of 'Thou who art in this earth,' he says, 'Thou who art in the second (third) earth.'

[2] He takes with the spade as much as is required to make the high altar of the proper size.

[3] This statement seems to have greatly puzzled the later ritualists, as Kâty. V, 3, 32–35 and the comments thereon show. In rule 32 it is laid down, in accordance with paragraph 26 above, that the Adhvaryu is to make the high altar of the size of the yoke-pin and the pit, i.e. about two feet square. The next rule then leaves an option between four other measurements, viz. he may make it either one third of the area of the large altar, or of unlimited size, or of the size of the yoke (86 aṅgulas=c. 5–5½ feet) or of ten of the sacrificer's feet. This latter measurement is explained rather ingeniously by Harisvâmin, as meaning that the high altar is to form

Virâg consists of ten syllables, and the Virâg is speech, and the sacrifice is speech. In the middle[1] he makes, as it were, a navel, thinking, 'Seated in one and the same place, I shall sprinkle (ghee) all round[2].'

35. He sprinkles it with water: inasmuch as, on that occasion, she became a lioness and roamed about unappeased—water being (a means of) appeasement—he appeases her with water. And, the high altar being a woman, he thereby fits her for the gods: this is why he sprinkles it with water.

36. He sprinkles it with, 'Thou art a lioness, overcoming the enemies: get thee pure for the gods!' He then bestrews it with gravel. Now gravel certainly is an ornament, because gravel is rather shining. And that gravel being the ashes of Agni Vaisvânara, he is now about to place Agni thereon, and so Agni does not injure it: this is why he bestrews it with gravel. He bestrews it with, 'Thou art a lioness, overcoming the enemies: array thee for the gods!' He then covers it[3], and thus covered it remains during that night.

---

an oblong of three feet by one foot, when, in counting the number of sides of the three squares thus obtained, we obtain ten sides of one foot each. However, the repetition of 'dasa' in our text—which can only mean 'ten feet on each side'—does not favour this explanation. The last two alternatives, according to rules 34-35, only apply to the Soma-sacrifice, because otherwise the altar (as in the case of the 'northern altar' at the Kâturmâsya, cf. part i, p. 392) would not be large enough to contain a 'high altar' of that size.

[1] The Kânva text wants it to be made at the back (gaghanena).

[2] When he makes the libation of ghee on the high altar (III, 5, 2, 9-11), he pours it on the four corners of the 'navel' and thereby, as it were, on the whole 'high altar.'

[3] Viz. with branches of udumbara or plaksha (see III, 8, 3, 10), or with darbha grass.

THE AGNI-PRANAYANA, OR LEADING FORWARD OF THE FIRE[1] TO THE HIGH ALTAR.

SECOND BRÂHMANA.

1. They put fire-wood on (the Âhavanîya fire), and prepare the underlayer (of gravel[2]). He (the Adhvaryu) puts the butter on (the Gârhapatya to melt), and cleans both the dipping-spoon and the offering-spoon. Having then clarified the ghee, he ladles five times thereof (into the offering-spoon). When the fire-wood is ablaze—

2. They lift the (burning) fire-wood, and place it on the underlayer[3]. Thereupon he says (to the Hotri), 'Recite for Agni as he is taken forward[4]!' (and to the Pratiprasthâtri), 'Come up after me with the single sword(-line)!' The Pratiprasthâtri goes up after him with the single sword(-line) as far

---

[1] The transferring of the Âhavanîya fire to the high altar takes place in the forenoon of the last Upasad day (that is, on the day preceding the pressing day, and called upavasatha, or preparation day). It is preceded by the double or combined performance of the Upasad offerings (one of which took place in the afternoon on the two preceding days).

[2] Some gravel is put in a pan for the burning wood to lie upon, when it is to be transferred from the Âhavanîya to the new altar. The Taittirîyas mix with the gravel one-fourth part of the dust of the foot-print of the Soma-cow (III, 3, 1, 6), the other three parts being used respectively for anointing the axle of the Soma-cart (III, 5, 3, 13), for the underlayer of the Âgnîdhra fire (III, 6, 3, 4), and for scattering about behind the Gârhapatya (III, 6, 3, 4–7).

[3] Lit. they lift the underlayer underneath (the burning wood).

[4] For the eight verses (or twelve, the first and last being recited thrice each) which the Hotri has to repeat while the fire is carried eastward and laid down on the high altar, see Ait. Br. I, 28; Âsv. Sr. II, 17. For the Brahman's duties, see Kâty. XI, 1, 9.

as that middle peg on the hind-part of the altar[1]: whatever part of the Gârhapatya[2] is cut off from the altar by that intermediate (peg), that he thereby carries on to (connects with) it.

3. Now some walk up behind (and draw a line) as far as the high altar; but let him not do that: let him walk up only as far as that middle peg. They proceed and come up to the high altar[3].

4. The Adhvaryu takes the sprinkling-water. He first sprinkles (the high altar) in front, while standing (south of it) facing the north, with the text (Vâg. S. V, 11), 'May Indra's noise[4] shield thee in front with the Vasus!' whereby he means to say, 'May Indra's noise protect thee in front with the Vasus.'

5. He then sprinkles it behind with, 'May the Wise[5] shield thee from behind with the Rudras!' whereby he means to say, 'May the Wise One protect thee from behind with the Rudras!'

6. He then sprinkles on the right (south) side with, 'May the Thought-swift shield thee with the Fathers on the right!' whereby he means

---

[1] See III, 5, 1, 1.

[2] The Âhavanîya or offering fire being now transferred to the new altar, the old Âhavanîya hearth is henceforward used as Gârhapatya; and a line is drawn from it up to the antahpâta, marking the middle of the west side of the great altar.

[3] In 'leading forwards' the fire they proceed along the north side of the large altar.

[4] Indraghoshá, perhaps 'Indra's name;' Mahîdhara and Sâyana take it as 'he who is noised abroad as Indra' (i.e. called Indra), which, however, would require the accent 'Índraghosha.' Perhaps 'the noise of Indra' means Agni, the roaring fire: for Agni and the Vasus, see III, 4, 2, 1.

[5] Praketas, here Varuna according to Mahîdhara and Sâyana. Cf. III, 4, 2, 1.

to say, 'May he swift as thought[1] protect thee on the right with the Fathers!'

7. He then sprinkles on the left side with, 'May Visvakarman (the All-shaper) shield thee with the Âdityas on the left!' whereby he means to say, 'May Visvakarman protect thee on the left with the Âdityas!'

8. The sprinkling-water which is left he pours outside the altar close to where is the southern of those two front corners (of the high altar) with, 'This burning water I dismiss from the sacrifice.' Because she (Vâk—the altar) on that occasion became a lioness and roamed about unappeased[2], he thus dismisses from the sacrifice that sorrow of hers,—if he do not wish to exorcise. But should he wish to exorcise, let him indicate it by saying, 'This burning water I dismiss from the sacrifice against so and so!' He then smites him with that sorrow, and sorrowing he goes to yonder world.

9. Now as to why he pours ghee on the high altar, while the fire is held (over it). Because the gods said to her on that occasion, 'The offering shall reach thee before Agni,' therefore the offering now does reach her before (it reaches) Agni. And because she said to the gods, 'Whatsoever blessing ye will invoke through me, all that shall be accomplished unto you!' therefore the priests now invoke through her that blessing upon the sacrificer, and it is fully accomplished unto him.

10. When he pours ghee on the high altar, he

---

[1] 'Manogavas' is taken by Mahîdhara and Sâyana as referring to Yama.

[2] 'Sokantî (sorrowing),' Kânva rec.

does it twofold even while doing it in one[1]. Now that which is the southern of the two front corners of that navel, so to say, which is in the middle of these (sides of the high altar)—

11. On that[2] he pours ghee, with the text (Vâ*g*. S. V, 12), 'Thou art a lioness, Hail!' Then on the northern of the two back corners with, 'Thou art a lioness, winning the Âdityas[3], Hail!' Then on the southern of the two back corners with, 'Thou art a lioness, winning the Brahman, winning the Kshatra, Hail!' Manifold, verily, is the prayer for blessing in the sacrificial texts: by this one he prays[4] for the Brahman (priesthood) and the Kshatra (nobility), those two vital forces.

12. Then on the northern of the front corners with, 'Thou art a lioness, winning abundant offspring, winning growth of wealth, Hail!' In that he says, 'winning abundant offspring,' he prays for offspring; and in that he says, 'winning growth of wealth'—growth of wealth meaning abundance—he prays for abundance.

13. He then pours ghee into the middle with, 'Thou art a lioness, bring thou hither the gods for the sacrificer! Hail!' whereby he causes the gods to be brought to the sacrificer. He then raises the offering-spoon with, 'To the

[1] Viz. by pouring the ghee cross-wise on the corners of the 'navel' of the altar.

[2] The south-east is sacred to Agni, the north-west to Vâyu.

[3] Because the Âdityas brought her as a Dakshi*n*â, Kâ*n*va rec.; cf. III, 5, 1, 18.

[4] But for the lack of a demonstrative pronoun with â*s*î*h* one would like to take the passage thus: 'Plenteous, forsooth, is this prayer for blessing among sacrificial texts: he thereby prays for the priesthood and the nobility.' Cf. I, 2, 1, 7.

beings thee! Hail!'—beings meaning offspring—he thereby means to say, 'To offspring thee!'

14. He then lays the enclosing-sticks[1] round (the navel); with the text (Vâg. S. V, 13), 'Thou art firm, steady thou the earth!' the middle one; with, 'Thou art firmly settled, steady thou the air!' the right one; with, 'Thou art immovably settled, steady thou the sky!' the left one. With, 'Thou art Agni's provision' he throws the 'equipments' upon (the high altar). Wherefore are the equipments?—for Agni's completeness.

15. The pine-wood, namely, is his body[2]: hence in that there are enclosing-sticks of pine-wood, thereby he supplies him with a body, makes him whole.

16. And the bdellium, forsooth, is his flesh: hence in that there is bdellium, thereby he supplies him with flesh, makes him whole.

17. And the fragrant reed-grass (sugandhi-tegana), forsooth, is his fragrance: hence in that there is fragrant reed-grass, thereby he supplies him with fragrance, makes him whole.

18. And as to why there is a wether's hair-tuft,—Agni, forsooth, dwelt once for one night between the two horns of a wether: 'Whatever of Agni's nature is inherent therein, let that be here too,' so he thinks, and therefore there is a wether's hair-tuft. Let him, therefore, cut off that (tuft) which is nearest to the head, and bring it; and if he be unable to procure that, let him bring any kind (of wether's hair). And why there are enclosing-sticks?—for the

[1] They are of pîtudâru (Pinus Deodora) wood, a span (of thumb and fore-finger) long.

[2] The Kânva text makes it his bones.

protection (of Agni): for it is somewhat long before the next enclosing-sticks will come nigh to him[1].

CONSTRUCTION OF SHEDS, AND PREPARATION OF PRESSING-PLACE AND HEARTHS (DHISHNYAS).

THIRD BRÂHMANA.

1. The sacrifice is a man; it is a man for the reason that a man spreads (prepares) it. In being spread it is made just as large[2] as a man: this is why the sacrifice is a man.

2. The Soma-cart (shed) is no other than his head, and has Vishnu for its deity[3]. And because Soma is therein—Soma being havis (material for offering) for the gods—therefore it is called Havirdhâna (receptacle of havis).

3. The Âhavanîya is no other than his mouth: hence, when he offers on the Âhavanîya, it is as if he poured (food) into the mouth.

4. The sacrificial stake is no other than his crest-lock; and the Âgnîdhrîya and Mârgâlîya[4] are his arms.

---

[1] Ordinarily the laying round of the paridhis takes place immediately before the fire is kindled for the offering; but as the next offering is not to come off for some time, the fire would be without a protection, if he were to leave it without the enclosing-sticks. Sâyana takes 'dûre' in the sense of 'in a long time,' as above; but it might be taken of space 'far off,' when the passage would refer to the offering about to be performed on the old Âhavanîya (III, 5, 3, 10 seq.); and it may be noticed in reference to this point, that, according to Kâty. VIII, 3, 30, that fire does not become the Gârhapatya till immediately after that offering.

[2] Yâvat-tâvat would rather seem to mean here 'of corresponding (or relatively the same) proportions' as a man, viz. as the respective sacrificer. 'Sa vai tâyamâno yâvân eva purushas tâvân vidhîyate, purushasyaiva vidhâm anu.' Kânva rec.

[3] Soma himself is Vishnu.

[4] See III, 6, 1, 23; 2, 21.

5. The Sadas[1] (tent for the priests) is no other than his belly: wherefore they feed in the Sadas, for whatever food is eaten here on earth all that settles down here in the belly. And because all the gods sat (sad) in it therefore it is called Sadas: and so do these Brahmans of every family now sit therein.

6. And the two fires which are behind[2] it are his feet. In being spread it is made just as large as a man: this is why the sacrifice is a man.

7. The cart-shed has doors on both sides; and so has the Sadas doors on both sides: hence this man is perforated from one end to the other. He steps to the Soma-carts when they have been washed down.

8. They turn them round, the southern one on the south side, and the northern one on the north side[3]. The larger of the two should be the southern (or right) one[4].

9. Over them, having been turned round (and placed on the altar), they put a mat of reed-grass; or, if he cannot procure a reed-mat, a frame of split cane

---

[1] See III, 6, 2, 21.

[2] That is, the (old) Âhavanîya and Gârhapatya fires of the Prâ*k*îna-va*m*sa.

[3] The southern (and larger) cart is under the charge of the Adhvaryu and the northern one under that of his assistant, the Pratiprasthât*ri*. Each now drives his cart westward along the south and north sides respectively; and when they are opposite the hall (*s*âlâ), they make the carts turn round from left to right; whereupon they drive back to the altar, and place them thereon with the shafts towards the east, near the anta*h*pâta ('intermediate' peg, see III, 5, 1, 1), south and north of the 'spine' (cf. p. 112, note 2), each at the distance of one cubit from the latter.

[4] In order to make the shed incline towards the north, cf. III, 1, 1, 2.

made in like manner as a reed-mat. They fasten a front-band (to the posts of the front door[1]). They enclose (the carts) within two upright hurdles; and lay a (second) reed-mat, or a frame of split cane made in like manner as a reed-mat, behind (the first mat[2]).

10. Now[3], having again entered (the hall), and

[1] It is not clear to me whether the arrangements mentioned in this paragraph refer to the carts in the first place, and have then to be repeated after the shed has been erected, or whether, as I think, some of them refer to the shed only. Even at the time of the Kâty. Sûtras there seems to have been some confusion in this respect, and the rules VIII, 4, 7–12 (10–15, in edition) were entirely misunderstood by the commentator. It is, however, certain that the carts were covered with mats, previously to being shifted from the back to the front part of the altar. As regards the shed, it seems to have been constructed in the following way. In front of the carts, as well as behind them, beams are driven into the ground, six on each side, according to Sâya*n*a on T. S. I, 2, 13; the two middle ones, one cubit north and south of the 'spine' respectively, forming a gateway on each side (Kâty. VIII, 4, 24 scholl.). On these two rows of beams other beams are laid, running from south to north, and forming, as it were, the lintels of the gates; and thereon the tie-beams rest (west to east). This frame of timber is to form a square of nine (or ten) cubits. Over the tie-beams three mats of reed-grass (*k*adis)—measuring nine (or ten) cubits by three (3½)—are spread, from south to north; first the middle one and then the two others, behind and in front of it. Upright hurdles (or reed-mats) are then stretched between the respective corner-posts, so as to form the south and north sides of the shed; and are 'sewn' to the corner-posts. Between the tops of the two front door-posts a band or garland of plaited reed-tufts (or, according to Haug, a bunch of Darbha grass, consisting of dry and green stalks) is hung up, to represent either a fillet or wreath worn on the forehead (?), or as a door-garland.

[2] This remark would seem to imply that there are only two mats (cf. parags. 23, 24), but perhaps it is merely intended to show that two mats are spread behind and in front of the first mat (i. e. from south to north, and not west to east); not that there are only two mats.

[3] If the preceding paragraph refers (at least partly) to the shed,

taken ghee in four ladlings, he makes offering to Savitri for his impulsion, for Savitri is the impeller (prasavitri) of the gods: 'We will perform the sacrifice, for one impelled by Savitri,' thus (the priest thinks and) therefore he makes offering to Savitri.

11. He offers with the text (Vâg. S. V, 14; Rigveda V, 81, 1), 'They harness the mind and they harness the thoughts'—with the mind and with speech they truly perform the sacrifice. When he says, 'They harness the mind,' he harnesses the mind; and when he says, 'and they harness the thoughts (dhî),' he harnesses speech; for it is thereby[1] that people seek to make their living in accordance with their respective intelligence (dhî), either by reciting (the Veda), or by readiness of speech, or by songs,—with these two thus harnessed they perform the sacrifice.

12. 'The priests of the priest, of the great inspirer of devotion,'—the learned Brâhmans versed in sacred writ, truly, are the priests: it is regarding them that he says this. And 'of the great inspirer of devotion[2],'—the great inspirer of devotion, truly, is the sacrifice: it is regarding the sacrifice that he says this. 'The knower of rites alone hath assigned the priestly offices,' for, in per-

---

then the atha here means 'Now, in the first place,' thereby introducing details preliminary to what has just been stated.

[1] See III, 2, 4, 16. I now refer 'etayâ' to 'vâkam,' as does Sâyana,—yadâ buddhir gâyate tadâ khalv etayâ vâkâ gugyûshanti. He explains 'prakâmodya' by 'mlaikkhikam laukikam bhâshanam,' barbarous, worldly speech.

[2] Vipaskit, probably 'thinker of hymns.' It remains doubtful what meaning our author assigned to the word. Mahîdhara explains it by sarvagña, 'all-knowing.' Sâyana, on Taitt. S. I, 2, 13, refers 'viprasya brihato vipaskitah' to the sacrificer.

forming the sacrifice, they indeed assign the priestly offices. 'Great is the praise of the divine Savitri; Hail!' Thus he offers to Savitri for his impulsion.

13. Having then taken ghee a second time in four ladlings, he walks out (of the hall by the front door). The (sacrificer's) wife is led out by the south door. He then lays down a piece of gold in the right wheel-track of the southern Soma-cart, and offers thereon, with (Vâg. S. V, 15; Rig-veda I, 22, 17), 'Vishnu strode through this (universe), thrice he put down his foot: it is enveloped in his dust; Hail!' The residue (of ghee) he pours into the wife's hand. She anoints the burning (part) of the axle[1] with (Vâg. S. V, 17), 'Audible to the gods, announce ye unto the gods!' He hands to his assistant both the offering-spoon and the melting-pot. They lead the wife round by the back of the two fires[2].

14. Having taken ghee in four ladlings, the assistant lays down a piece of gold in the right wheel-track of the northern Soma-cart, and offers thereon, with (Vâg. S. V, 16; Rig-veda VII, 99, 3), 'Be ye too abundant in food and milch kine and pastures, through benevolence to man! Thou proppedst asunder these two worlds, O Vishnu; with beams of light didst thou hold fast[3] the earth on all sides; Hail!' The residue (of ghee) he pours into the wife's hand. She anoints the burning (part) of the axle with,

[1] That is, the iron pins driven into the axle, round which the naves of the wheels revolve. See also p. 121, note 2.

[2] They make her enter the hall by the south door and walk round by the back of the (old) Gârhapatya fire-place to the wheel-tracks on the north side where the Pratiprasthâtri is about to offer.

[3] The rays of the sun are apparently likened to ropes wherewith he keeps the earth straight and firm.

'Audible to the gods, announce ye unto the gods!' Then as to why he thus offers.

15. Now, once on a time, the gods, while performing sacrifice, were afraid of an attack on the part of the Asura-Rakshas; and, the ghee being a thunderbolt, they kept off the evil spirits from the south by that thunderbolt, the ghee; and thus they came not after them on their way. And in like manner does he now keep off the evil spirits from the south by that thunderbolt, the ghee; and thus they do not come after him on his way. And the reason why he offers with two verses relating to Vishnu, is that the Soma-cart belongs to Vishnu.

16. And in that the wife anoints the burning (part) of the axle, thereby a productive union is effected; for when woman and man become heated, the seed flows, and thereupon birth takes place. She anoints in a direction away (from the cart), for away the seed is cast. He then says (to the Hotri), 'Recite to the Soma-carts as they are wheeled forward[1]!'

17. He makes (the sacrificer) say, 'Go ye both forward, furthering the cult!' The cult, namely, is the sacrifice: 'go ye both forward, furthering the sacrifice' he thereby means to say. 'Convey ye the sacrifice upward; lead it not astray[2]!' whereby he means to say, 'convey this sacrifice upward to the world of the gods;' and by saying 'lead it not astray,' he prays for this (sacrificer) that he may not

[1] While reciting his hymn of eight verses (brought up, as usual, to twelve by repetitions of the first and last verses) the Hotri has to follow the carts so as to have the north wheel-track of the south cart between his feet. Cf. p. 79, note 1. For the verses recited by him, see Ait. Br. I, 29; Âsv. Sr. IV, 9.

[2] Or, 'falter not!'

stumble. Let them wheel (the carts) forward, as it were lifting them, so that they may not creak; for of the Asuras is that voice which is in the axle[1]: 'Lest the Asuras' voice should speak here!' so he thinks. But if they should creak,—

18. Let him make (the sacrificer) say this, 'Speak ye unto your own cow-pen, ye divine resorts; speak not my life away, speak not my offspring away!' This, then, is the expiation thereof.

19. As to this they say, 'Let him stride three steps from the high altar westward and make the Soma-carts stop there: this is the measure for the Soma-carts.' But there is no (fixed) measure in this; wherever he himself may think fit in his mind, only not too near[2], nor too far (from the high altar), there let him stop them.

20. He salutes them with, 'May ye rejoice here on the height of the earth!' for this (altar) is verily the height[3] (top) of the earth, since his offering-fire is in the heaven. He makes them rest on their naves[4] for that is the appearance of repose.

---

[1] The Taitt. S. VI, 2, 9 refers it to Varuna, on account of the axle being bound firmly with strings (thongs), resembling Varuna's noose.

[2] Rather, 'not so very near,' 'nicht allzu nahe, nicht gar zu nahe.'

[3] Both here, and on Taitt. S. I, 2, 13, Sâyana takes 'varshman' in the sense of 'body (sarîra).'

[4] Or rather, 'nave-boards (nabhya).' The cart wheels are described as consisting, after the fashion prevalent in Mâlava (Kâty. VIII, 4, 5 scholl.), of three parallel boards: the two outer ones form segments, and the middle and largest one has the nave fixed to it, the axle-pin running through its centre. It is on this middle board that he is to make the carts stand. Perhaps 'kshema' should be taken in the sense of 'security, firm position,' instead of 'repose, rest,' in which case the upright position of the middle board would seem to be compared with a man in upright position; 'nâbhi (nâbhya)' meaning both 'navel' and 'nave.'

21. The Adhvaryu, having gone round along the north side (of the carts), props the southern cart, with (Vâ*g*. S. V, 18; Rig-veda I, 154, 1), 'Now will I declare the heroic deeds of Vish*n*u, who measured out the earthly regions; who propped the upper seat, striding thrice, the wide-stepping! For Vish*n*u (I prop) thee!' He fixes the prop in a different place from where (it is fixed) in ordinary practice[1].

22. The assistant then props the northern cart, with (Vâ*g*. S. V, 19), 'Either from the heaven, O Vish*n*u, or from the earth, or from the great, wide airy region, O Vish*n*u, fill both thine hands with wealth and bestow on us from the right and the left! For Vish*n*u thee!' He fixes the prop in a different place from where (it is fixed) in ordinary practice. The reason why he performs with prayers to Vish*n*u is that the Soma-cart belongs to Vish*n*u.

23. He then makes (the sacrificer) say, after touching the middle reed-mat[2] (Vâ*g*. S. V, 20; Rig-veda I, 154, 2), 'Let Vish*n*u then be praised for his power, terrible like a wild beast prowling about the mountains, on whose three wide strides all beings abide!' Now that (mat-covering) indeed is his (Vish*n*u, the shed's) upper skull-bone[3]

[1] Sâya*n*a, on Taitt. S. I, 2, 13, remarks:—'The southern and northern parts of the yoke represent the ears of the cart. Through a hole (is effected) the firm tying (of the yoke parts) to the shafts. At the juncture (sandhi) at the (place of) fastening of the southern (part of the yoke) the prop is fixed.' In ordinary practice the prop is put up to support the extreme end of the shafts or pole.

[2] See p. 128, note 1.

[3] Apparently the parietal bone is meant; or perhaps the frontal bone. The Kâ*n*va text reads: 'He then touches that reed-mat, or

for thereon, as it were, the other skull-bones rest: this is why he says 'they abide on.'

24. Thereupon he makes him say, after touching the front-band (Vâg. S. V, 2), 'Thou art Vishnu's fillet;' for it indeed is his fillet. He then makes him say, after touching the two upright hurdles, 'Ye are the corners of Vishnu's mouth;' for they indeed are the corners of his mouth. Then that mat which is behind there, that indeed is that skull-bone of his here behind (viz. the occiput).

25. With 'Thou art Vishnu's sewer[1],' he sews (the hurdles to the four door posts) with cord by means of a wooden pin. With, 'Thou art Vishnu's fixed (point)[2],' he then makes a knot, 'lest it should fall asunder.' That same (knot) he undoes when the work is completed; and thus disease[3] befalls not either the Adhvaryu or the Sacrificer. The completed (cart-shed) he touches with, 'Thou art Vishnu's own,' for the Soma-cart (and shed) belongs to Vishnu.

---

cane-frame, above, with "Let Vishnu . . ." for that is for him (Vishnu, the shed) what that skull-bone is up here. And when he says "they abide upon," it is because that rest on the other skull-bones [? adhi hy etad anyeshu kapâleshu kshiyanti !]. Then what two reed-mats there are on the two carts, they indeed are for him what the two skull-bones are here on both sides. And that reed-mat, or cane-frame, which he puts on there behind (or behind that one), that is for him what the skull-bone behind is.'

[1] Syû, explained by Sâyana as 'thread, cord,' by Mahîdhara as 'needle.'

[2] ? Dhruvah, the 'firm one,' (? 'pole-star.') The St. Petersburg Dictionary gives the tentative meaning 'knot.' The Taitt. S. reads 'dhruvam.'

[3] Grâha, lit. 'seizing.' For Varuna, whose attribute the knot is (I, 3, 1, 16), seizing upon men by means of disease; see II, 5, 2, 2.

FOURTH BRÂHMANA.

1. It is for a twofold reason that the sounding-holes are dug. The cart-shed, truly, is the head of the sacrificer; and what four holes there are here in the head—namely, these two and these two[1]—those he thereby makes: for this reason he digs the sounding-holes.

2. Now the gods and the Asuras, both of them sprung from Pragâpati, were contending. The Asuras then by way of witchcraft buried charms[2] within these worlds, thinking, 'Peradventure we may thus overcome the gods.'

3. The gods then prevailed. By means of these (sounding-holes) they dug up those magic charms. Now, when a charm is dug up, it becomes inoperative and useless. And in like manner, if any malicious enemy buries here charms by way of witchcraft for this (sacrificer), does he thereby dig them up: this is why he digs sounding-holes. He digs just beneath the fore-part of the shafts of the southern cart.

4. He takes up the spade[3], with the text (Vâg. S.

---

[1] Viz. the ears and nostrils.

[2] Krityâm valagân nikakhnuh, 'they dug in, as a charm, secret (magic) objects.' Valaga is explained as charms, consisting of bones, nails, hair, foot-dust, and similar objects, tied up in a piece of worn matting or cloth, or the like, and dug into the ground arm-deep, for causing injury to enemies. See Taitt. S. VI, 2, 11, where Professor Weber refers to Wuttke, Der Deutsche Volksaberglaube, § 492 seq.

[3] The instrument used seems to be a kind of scoop or trowel,

V, 22), 'At the impulse of the divine Savitri, I take thee with the arms of the Asvins, with the hands of Pûshan: thou art a woman.' The significance of this formula is the same (as before). That spade (abhri, fem.) is indeed a female: therefore he says 'thou art a woman.'

5. He draws their outlines, saving[1] the measure of a span, with, 'Here do I cut off the necks of the Rakshas!' For the spade is the thunderbolt: it is with the thunderbolt that he thus cuts off the necks of the Rakshas.

6. Let him first mark off the right (southern) one of the two that are in front; then the left one of the two behind; then the right one of those behind; then the left one of those in front.

7. But they say conversely, that he should mark off first the left one of the two behind; then the right one of those in front; then the right one of those behind; and then the left one of those in front. Or he may also mark them off in one and the same direction[2]: but let him, in any case, mark off last of all the one which is on the left of those in front.

8. He digs them, in the very same order in which they have been marked off, with, 'Thou art great,

---

sharpened on one side. For a fuller description, see VI, 3, 1, 30 seq.

[1] Vinâ, i.e. leaving that space between each two adjoining uparavas. They are themselves to be round, a span in diameter. Hence by connecting the four centres by lines, a square of two spans (of thumb and forefinger), or one cubit, is obtained. See Baudh. Sulvas. 101.

[2] That is, successively the south-eastern, the south-western, the north-western, and last, the north-eastern hole.

of great sound!'—he praises and extols them, when he says, 'Thou art great, of great sound;'—'Utter thou the great voice unto Indra!'—Indra, forsooth, is the deity of the sacrifice; and the cart-shed belonging to Vishnu, he thereby makes it to be connected with Indra: therefore he says, 'Utter thou the great voice unto Indra!'

9. 'The Rakshas-killing, charm-killing (voice),' for it is indeed for the killing of the charms of the Rakshas that these (holes) are dug;—'Of Vishnu;' for that voice in the cart-shed is indeed Vishnu's.

10. He throws out (the earth from) them in the order in which he has dug them, with (Vâg. S. V, 23), 'Here do I cast out the charm which the alien, which the inmate of my house has buried for me!' Either an alien or an inmate of his house buries charms by way of witchcraft: these he thereby casts out.

11. 'Here do I cast out the charm which my equal, which my unequal has buried for me!' Either one equal, or one unequal, to him buries charms by way of witchcraft: these he thereby casts out.

12. 'Here do I cast out the charm which the kinsman, which the stranger has buried for me!' Either a kinsman or a stranger buries charms by way of witchcraft: these he thereby casts out.

13. 'Here do I cast out the charm which the countryman, which the foreigner has buried for me!' Either a countryman or a foreigner buries charms by way of witchcraft: these he thereby casts out. With 'I cast out witchcraft!' he finally

throws out (the earth remaining in the several holes[1]), whereby he casts out witchcraft.

14. Let him dig them arm-deep; for that being the end (extreme limit to which he can reach) he thereby in the end brings witchcraft to naught. He connects them crossways by (underground) channels[2]; or, if he cannot crossways, he may do so in one and the same direction. This is why these (openings of the) vital airs are connected by channels farther (inside).

15. In the same order in which he has dug them he makes (the sacrificer) touch them, with the texts (Vâg. S. V, 24), 'Self-ruling thou art, a slayer of enemies! Ever-ruling thou art, a slayer of haters! Man-ruling thou art, a slayer of Rakshas! All-ruling thou art, a slayer of foemen!' This is the blessing of that work: he thereby invokes a blessing.

16. The Adhvaryu and Sacrificer then touch one another (with their right hands through the holes), the Adhvaryu is at the right one of those in front, and the Sacrificer at the left one of those behind. The Adhvaryu asks, 'Sacrificer, what is here?'—'Happiness!' he says.—'(Be) that ours in common!' says the Adhvaryu in a low voice.

17. Thereupon the Adhvaryu is at the right one of those behind, and the Sacrificer at the left one of those in front. The Sacrificer asks, 'Adhvaryu, what is here?'—'Happiness!' he says.—'(Be) that mine!' says the Sacrificer. Now in that they thus

---

[1] That is, these words are to be pronounced at the end of each of the preceding four formulas, and the remaining loose soil is therewith to be removed from the respective hole.

[2] Lit. he inter-perforates, inter-channels.

touch one another, thereby they make the vital airs yoke-fellows: hence these vital airs meet together farther (inside). And in that, when asked, he replies, 'Happiness (bhadram),' thereby he utters the wish of 'prosperity (kalyânam)' of ordinary speech: that is why, being asked, he replies, 'Happiness.' Thereupon he sprinkles (the holes with water): one and the same forsooth is the significance of sprinkling; he thereby renders them pure.

18. He sprinkles, with the text (Vâg. S. V, 25), 'You, the Rakshas-killers, the charm-killers;' for they are indeed Rakshas-killers as well as charm-killers; 'Vishnu's own, I sprinkle;' for they indeed belong to Vishnu.

19. What remains of the sprinkling-water he then pours out into the pits;—what moisture there is here in the vital airs[1], that he thereby puts into them: hence that moisture in the vital airs.

20. He pours it out with, 'You, the Rakshas-killers, the charm-killers, Vishnu's own, I pour out.' Thereupon he spreads barhis-grass, both such as is turned with its tops to the east and such as is turned to the north[2]; what hair there is here at (the openings of) the vital airs, that he thereby bestows: hence that hair at (the openings of) the vital airs.

21. He spreads it with, 'You, the Rakshas-killers, the charm-killers, Vishnu's own, I spread.' He, as it were, covers the bodies on the top, for that (grass) is indeed his (Vishnu's) hair[3].

---

[1] The Kânva text has kidra ('holes, openings') instead of prâna.

[2] Cp. I, 3, 3, 7 seq.

[3] Or, the hair of the sacrificial man; see III, 5, 3, 1 seq.

22. Thereon he lays two pressing-boards[1] with, 'You, the Rakshas-killers, the charm-killers, Vishnu's own, I lay down;' they are indeed his (Vishnu's) jaws. He surrounds them (with earth) with, 'You, the Rakshas-killers, the charm-killers, Vishnu's own, I surround;' he thereby steadies them, makes them immovable.

23. Now the pressing-skin is cut straight all round and (dyed) red all over, for it is his (Vishnu's) tongue: the reason, then, why it is quite red, is because this tongue is, as it were, red. He lays it down with, 'Thou art Vishnu's own;' for it indeed belongs to Vishnu[2].

24. He then brings down the (five) press-stones. The press-stones, doubtless, are his (Vishnu's) teeth: hence, when they press (the Soma) with the stones it is as if he chewed with his teeth. He puts them down with, 'Ye are Vishnu's own;' for they indeed belong to Vishnu. Thus, then, the head of the sacrifice is complete.

SIXTH ADHYÂYA. FIRST BRÂHMANA.

1. The Sadas[3] is no other than his (Vishnu, the sacrifice's) belly; therefore they feed (drink) in the

[1] The pressing-boards are a cubit long, and somewhat broader behind than in front. They are placed one south of the other, and so as to lie close together behind (sambaddhânte, Kânva rec.), or the space of two inches between them. The space between them is filled up with earth.

[2] East of the 'sound-holes' he raises a square mound (khara), covered with gravel, for placing vessels on, Kâty. VIII, 5, 28.

[3] The Sadas is a shed or tent, facing the east with its long side, which is to measure eighteen (or twenty-one, or twenty-four, or, according to the Sulva-sûtra, twenty-seven) cubits, the breadth by

Sadas; for whatever food is eaten here on earth, all that settles down in the belly. And because all the gods sat (sad) in it, therefore it is called sadas: and so do these Brâhmans of every family now sit therein. By way of deity it belongs to Indra.

2. In the middle of it he puts up a (post) of udumbara wood (Ficus Glomerata); for the udumbara means strength and food; now the Sadas being his (Vishnu's belly), he thereby puts food therein; this is why he puts up an udumbara (post) in the middle of it.

3. From the peg[1] which stands in the middle on the hind-part of the altar, he strides six steps eastwards (along the 'spine'); the seventh he strides away from it to the right, for the sake of completeness, and there marks off a pit.

4. He takes the spade with (Vâg. S. V, 26), 'At the impulse of the divine Savitri, I take thee with the arms of the Asvins, with the hands of Pûshan: thou art a woman;' the significance of this formula is the same (as before). That spade, indeed, is a female (feminine): therefore he says 'thou art a woman.'

5. He then marks off the pit with, 'Herewith

six cubits (or ten, or one half that of the long side). The udumbara post, according to some, is to stand exactly in the centre of the shed; or, according to others, at an equal distance from the (long) east and west sides; the 'spine' (cf. p. 112, note 2) in that case dividing the building into two equal parts, a northern and a southern one. In the middle the shed is to be of the sacrificer's height, and from thence the ceiling is to slant towards the ends where it is to reach up to the sacrificer's navel. According to the Black Yagus, the erection of the Sadas precedes the digging of the Uparavas, described in the preceding Brâhmana. Taitt. S. VI, 2, 10, 11.

[1] The antahpâta, see III, 5, 1, 1.

I cut off the necks of the Rakshas!' for the spade is the thunderbolt: it is with the thunderbolt that he cuts off the necks of the evil spirits.

6. Thereupon he digs: eastwards he throws up the heap of earth. Having made the udumbara (post) of the same size as the sacrificer[1], he cuts it smooth all round, and lays it down, with the top to the east, in front (of the pit). Thereon he lays barhis-grass of the same length.

7. Now the sprinkling-water (used on this occasion) contains barley-corns. For the essence (sap) of plants is water; wherefore plants when eaten alone do not satiate; and the essence of water, on the other hand, are the plants; wherefore water when drunk alone does not satiate; but only when the two are united they satiate; for then they are sapful: 'with the sapful I will sprinkle,' so he thinks.

8. Now, the gods and the Asurus, both of them sprung from Pragâpati, were contending. Then all the plants went away from the gods, but the barley plants alone went not from them.

9. The gods then prevailed: by means of these (barley-grains) they attracted to themselves all the plants of their enemies; and because they attracted (yu) therewith, therefore they are called yava (barley).

10. They said, 'Come, let us put into the barley whatever sap there is of all plants!' And, accordingly, whatever sap there was of all plants, that they put into the barley: therefore the latter thrives lustily where other plants wither, for in such wise

[1] It is the part which is to stand above ground that is to be of the sacrificer's size.

did they put the sap into them. And in like manner does this one now by means of those (barley-grains) attract to himself all the plants of his enemies: this is why the sprinkling-water contains barley-corns.

11. He throws the barley-corns into it, with, 'Thou art barley (yava): keep thou (yavaya) from us the haters, keep from us the enemies!' In this there is nothing obscure. He then besprinkles (the post);—the significance of the sprinkling is one and the same: he thereby renders it sacrificially pure.

12. He sprinkles (the top, middle, and bottom parts), with, 'For the sky—thee! for the air—thee! for the earth—thee!' He thereby endows these worlds with strength and sap, bestows strength and sap on these worlds.

13. And the sprinkling-water which remains he pours into the hole, with, 'Be the worlds pure wherein the Fathers reside!' for a pit that is dug is sacred to the Fathers: this he thereby renders sacrificially pure.

14. He now strews barhis-grass therein, both eastward-pointed and northward-pointed with, 'Thou art the seat of the Fathers;' for that part of it (the post) which is dug into the ground is sacred to the Fathers: as though it were (naturally) established[1] among plants, and not dug in, so does it become established among those plants.

15. He raises it, with the text (Vâg. S. V, 27), 'Prop thou the sky! fill the air! stand firm on the earth!' Thereby he endows these worlds with strength and sap, bestows strength and sap on these worlds.

---

[1] Svâruh, 'naturally grown,' Taitt. S. VI, 2, 10, 4.

16. He then sinks it (in the hole, with), 'May Dyutâna, the son of the Maruts, plant thee!—' Dyutâna the son of the Maruts, doubtless, is he that blows yonder (the wind): by means of him he thus plants it;—'Mitra and Varuna with firm support!' Mitra and Varuna are the in-breathing and out-breathing: he thus plants it with the in-breathing and out-breathing.

17. He then heaps up (earth) round it, with, 'I enclose thee, winner of the priesthood, winner of the nobility, winner of growth of wealth!' Manifold, verily, is the prayer for blessing in the sacrificial texts: by this one he prays for the priesthood and nobility, those two vital forces[1]. 'Winner of growth of wealth,'—growth of wealth means abundance: he thereby prays for abundance.

18. He then presses it firmly all round, with, 'Uphold thou the priesthood! uphold the nobility, uphold our life, uphold our progeny!' this is the blessing of this rite: that blessing he thereby invokes. He presses it so as to be level with the ground: with an (ordinary) hole (round trees for watering) it is higher than the ground, but in this way it is with the gods;—and thus it is not planted in an (ordinary) hole.

19. He then pours water thereon;—wherever, in digging, they wound or injure this (earth),—water being a means of soothing,—there he soothes it by that means of soothing, water, there he heals it by water: therefore he pours water thereon.

---

[1] See III, 5, 2, 11 with note. The Kânva text has, bahvî vâ âsîr yagúhshu te asmâ ete âsishâ vâ sâste yad brahma ka kshatram ka.

20. He then makes (the sacrificer) say, while touching it thus (Vâg. S. V, 28), 'Thou art firm: may this sacrificer be firm in this homestead through progeny'—or, 'through cattle!' thus whatever wish he entertains that wish is accomplished unto him.

21. Thereupon, having taken clarified butter with the dipping-spoon, he pours it upon the (forked) top[1], with 'O Heaven and Earth, be ye full of ghee!' whereby he endows the heaven and the earth with strength and sap, bestows strength and sap on them: upon them thus full of sap and affording subsistence, these creatures subsist.

22. He then lays on a mat[2], with, 'Thou art Indra's mat,'—for the Sadas belongs to Indra,—'a shelter to every one,' for Brâhmans of all families sit therein. He adds two mats, one on each side thereof, and three north of them and three further (to the north): these make nine. For the sacrifice

---

[1] The post is to be furcate at the top, and between the branch-stumps (forming as it were its ears) he is to put a piece of gold and pour the ghee thereon; when the ghee reaches the ground, he is to pronounce the final 'Svâhâ!' in accordance with the practice at the homas; the gold representing, as it were, the sacrificial fire. Sâyana on Taitt. S. I, 3, 1; Kâty. VIII, 5, 37 seq.

[2] That is, after putting up the posts of the front and back doors, and laying the beams on, both longways and crossways, in the same way as was done in erecting the Prâkinavamsa and Havirdhâna, he is to spread over the beams the nine mats that are to form the ceiling,—viz. first the middle, and then the two others, of the three southern ones, thereupon three alongside these, across the central part of the shed, and finally the three across the north side. According to some authorities the central mats are laid down first, and then those on the south and north sides. See Sâyana on Taitt. S. I, 3, 1 (p. 450).

is threefold and nine also is threefold: for this reason there are nine.

23. That Sadas has its tie-beams running (from south) to north, and the cart-shed (from west) to east. For this, the cart-shed, belongs exclusively to the gods: hence neither food nor drink is taken therein, because it belongs exclusively to the gods; and were any one either to eat or to drink therein, his head would verily burst asunder. But those two, the Âgnîdhra and the Sadas, are common (to the gods and men): hence food and drink is taken in these two, because they are common (to the gods and men). Now the north is the quarter of men: therefore the Sadas has its tie-beams running (from south) to north.

24. They enclose it[1], with the text (Vâg. S. V, 29; Rig-veda I, 10, 12), 'May these songs encompass thee on every side, O thou that delightest in songs! May these favours be favourably received by thee, invigorating the vigorous!' He that delights in songs, forsooth, is Indra, and songs mean the people: he thus surrounds the nobility with the people, and therefore the nobility is here surrounded on both sides by the people.

25. Thereupon he sews (the hurdles to the posts) with a needle and cord[2], with the text (Vâg. S. V, 30), 'Thou art Indra's sewer.' With, 'Thou art Indra's fixed (point),' he then makes a knot, 'lest it should fall asunder.' He undoes it again, when the work is completed; and thus disease befalls not either the Adhvaryu or the Sacrificer. When completed, he

[1] Viz. with hurdles, or upright grass-mats, fastened to the door-posts by means of cord.

[2] See III, 5, 3, 25.

touches it (the Sadas) with, 'Thou art Indra's own!' for the Sadas belongs to Indra.

26. In the north—with regard to the back part of the Soma-carts[1]—he then raises the Âgnîdhra (shed). One half of it should be inside the altar, and one half outside; or more than one half may be inside the altar and less outside; or the whole of it may be inside the altar. When completed, he touches it with, 'Thou art the All-gods' own!' To the All-gods it belongs, because on the day before (the Soma feast) the All-gods abide in it by the Vasatîvarî water.

27. Now, once on a time, the gods, while performing sacrifice, were afraid of an attack on the part of the Asura-Rakshas. The Asura-Rakshas attacked them from the south and forced them out of the Sadas, and overturned those hearths (dhishnya) of theirs which are within the Sadas.

28. For, indeed, all of those (hearths) at one time burnt as brightly as this Âhavanîya and the Gârhapatya and the Âgnîdhrîya; but ever since that time when they (the Asuras) overturned them they do not burn. They forced them (the gods) back to the Âgnîdhra (fire) and even won from them one half of the Âgnîdhra. From there the All-gods gained immortality[2],—whence it (the Âgnîdhra fire) is sacred to the All-gods.

[1] North of the clog (apâlamba) of the carts, Kânva rec.

[2] They gained it, as would seem, by means of the other half of the Âgnîdhra fire. Cf. Ait. Br. II, 36. Sâyana interprets 'tân apy ardham âgnîdhrasya gigyus' by, '[They forced those (gods) back to the Sadas;] and they (the gods), having reached the side (ardham=samîpam) of the Âgnîdhra (fire), conquered the Asuras and won immortality.' The Kânva rec. reads:—'Te hâpy âgnîdhrasyârdham gigyus te 'rdhân (! read 'rdhâd) etad visve devâ amritatvam apâgayan.'

29. The gods kindled them again, as one would (light the fire where he is going to) stay. Therefore they are kindled at every Soma feast. Wherefore the duties of the Agnîdh should be discharged by one who is accomplished. Now he who is known and learned in sacred lore[1] is truly accomplished: hence they take to the Agnîdh his Dakshinâ first[2], since it is from thence (from the Agnîdh's fire) that the gods gained immortality. And if weakness were to come upon one of those that are consecrated, let (the Adhvaryu) say, 'Lead him to the Âgnîdhra!'—thinking 'that is unscathed, there he will not meet with affliction[3].' And because the All-gods gained immortality from there, therefore it is sacred to the All-gods.

Second Brâhmana.

1. The Dhishnya-hearths[4], forsooth, are no other

[1] Or, as Sâyana takes it, 'he who is known (as well-conducted) and a repeater (reader) of the Veda.'

[2] See IV, 3, 4, 19 seq.

[3] Or, 'that (fire) will not suffer evil' (ârtim na labheta, Sâyana).

[4] There are altogether eight dhishnyas, two of which, viz. the Âgnîdhra and the Mârgâlîya, are raised north and south of the back part of the cart-shed (havirdhâna) respectively; while the other six are raised inside the Sadas along the east side of it, viz. five of them north of the 'spine,' belonging (from south to north) to the Hotri, Brâhmanâkhamsi, Potri, Neshtri, and Akhâvâka respectively; and one south of the spine, exactly south-east of the Udumbara post, for the Maitrâvaruna (or Prasâstri) priest. These six priests, together with the Âgnîdhra, are called the 'seven Hotris.' The Âgnîdhra and Mârgâlîya have square sheds with four posts erected over them, open on the east side and on the side facing the cart-shed. The Âgnîdhra hearth is thrown up first, and the Mârgâlîya last of all; and the Maitrâvaruna's immediately after that of the Hotri. For the formulas by which they are consecrated, see Vâg. S. V, 31, 32.

than its (the sacrifice's) congeners[1]. They have the same marks, and those which have the same marks are congeners; and these, then, are those (corresponding limbs) of its trunk.

2. Now Soma was in heaven, and the gods were here on earth. The gods desired, 'Would that Soma might come to us; we might sacrifice with him, when come.' They produced those two illusions, Suparnî and Kadrû[2]; Suparnî, forsooth, was Vâk (speech)[3], and Kadrû was this (earth). They caused discord between them.

3. They then disputed and said, 'Which of us shall spy furthest, shall win the other[4].'—'So be it!' Kadrû then said, 'Espy thou!'

4. Suparnî said, 'On yonder shore of this ocean there stands a white horse at a post, that I see; doest thou also see it?'—'I verily do!' Then said Kadrû, 'Its tail was just now hanging down; there, now the wind tosses it, that I see.'

5. Now when Suparnî said, 'On yonder shore of this ocean,' the ocean, forsooth, is the altar, she thereby meant the altar; 'there stands a white horse at a post,' the white horse, forsooth, is Agni, and the post means the sacrificial stake. And when Kadrû said, 'Its tail was just now hanging down;

---

[1] That is, the parts of the body corresponding to one another, as arms, loins, &c.

[2] See III, 2, 4, 1 seq.; Oldenberg, Zeitsch. d. Deutsch. Morg. Ges. XXXVII, p. 67 seq.; Weber, Ind. Stud. VIII, p. 31.

[3] In Taitt. S. VI, 1, 6; Kâth. XXIII, 10, suparnî, 'the well-winged,' is identified with the sky.

[4] Lit. 'she shall win both of us,' i.e. each saying that the other would win herself.

there, now the wind tosses it, that I see;' this is nothing else than the rope.

6. Suparnî then said, 'Come, let us now fly thither to know which of us is the winner.' Kadrû said, 'Fly thou thither; thou wilt tell us, which of us is the winner.'

7. Suparnî then flew thither; and it was even as Kadrû had said. When she had returned, she (Kadrû) said to her, 'Hast thou won, or I?' —'Thou!' she replied. Such is the story called 'Suparnî-Kâdrava[1].'

8. Then said Kadrû, 'Verily I have won thine own self; yonder is Soma in the heaven: fetch him hither for the gods, and thereby redeem thyself from the gods[2]!'—'So be it!' She brought forth the metres; and that Gâyatrî fetched Soma from heaven.

9. He was enclosed between two golden cups[3]; sharp-edged they closed together at every twinkling of the eye; and these two, forsooth, were Consecration and Penance. Those Gandharva Soma-wardens watched over him; they are these hearths, these fire-priests.

10. She tore off one of the two cups, and gave it to the gods,—this was Consecration: therewith the gods consecrated themselves.

---

[1] 'And because these two there disputed, therefore the story called "Sauparnakâdrava" is here told,' Kânva text. It is difficult to see how this statement came to be inserted here, unless it be because of a division in the text,—this paragraph being the nineteen hundreth in the Mâdhyandina recension. This explanation would not, however, apply to the Kânva text.

[2] 'Therewith redeem thee from death,' Kânva rec.

[3] Kusî?=kosî, 'pod' (or case). Sâyana explains it by 'âyudha' (? weapon, or vessel, sheath).

11. She then tore off the second cup, and gave it to the gods,—this was Penance: therewith the gods underwent penance, to wit the Upasads, for the Upasads are penance.

12. She took possession (â-*k*akhâda)[1] of Soma by means of (a stick of) khadira wood (Acacia Catechu), whence (the name) Khadira; and because she thereby took possession of him, therefore the sacrificial stake and the wooden sword (sphya) are of khadira wood. She then carried him off while he was under the charge of the A*kh*âvâka, wherefore this A*kh*âvâka priest was excluded (from drinking Soma).

13. Indra and Agni preserved him for the production of creatures, whence the A*kh*âvâka priest belongs to Indra and Agni.

14. Therefore the consecrated keep charge of the king (Soma), 'lest (the Gandharvas) should carry him off.' Let him therefore guard him diligently, for verily in whosesoever charge they carry him off, he is excluded (from the Soma).

15. Wherefore the students guard their teacher, his house, and cattle, lest he should be taken from them. Let him therefore guard him (Soma) diligently in that place, for verily in whosesoever charge they carry him off, he is excluded therefrom. By means of him Supar*n*î redeemed herself from the gods; wherefore they say, 'He who has sacrificed shares in the world of bliss.'

[1] Sâya*n*a takes it in the sense of 'she swallowed (khâd),' but I should feel inclined to refer it to the same verb 'khid' (? khad) as 'âkhidat' coming immediately after it. Could Pâ*n*ini's Sûtra VI, 1, 52 refer to this passage? [Kâ*s*. V., Benares edition *k*ikhâda; MS. Indian Office *k*akhâda.] The Kâ*n*va text has the same reading: â*k*akhâda-âkhidat.

16. Verily, even in being born, man, by his own self, is born as a debt (owing) to death. And in that he sacrifices, thereby he redeems himself from death, even as Suparnî then redeemed herself from the gods.

17. The gods worshipped with him. Those Gandharva Soma-wardens came after him; and having come up they said, 'Do ye let us share in the sacrifice, exclude us not from the sacrifice; let there be for us also a share in the sacrifice!'

18. They said, 'What will there be for us, then?'—'Even as in yonder world we have been his keepers, so also will we be his keepers here on earth!'

19. The gods spake, 'So be it!' By saying, '(Here are) your Soma-wages . . .' he assigns to them the price of the Soma[1]. They then said unto them, 'At the third pressing an offering of ghee shall fall to your share, but not one of Soma, for the Soma-draught has been taken from you, wherefore ye are not worthy of a Soma-offering!' And accordingly, when he pours ghee on the hearths by means of fagots[2], at the evening libation, that same offering of ghee falls to their share, but not one of Soma.

20. 'And what they will offer in the fire that will satiate you;' hence that which they offer in the fire satiates them. 'And when they will move about, holding the Soma over each[3], that will satiate you;' hence when they move about, holding the Soma over each (hearth), that satiates them.

[1] See III, 3, 3, 11.

[2] For these oblations poured upon burning bundles of chips and grass held over the several hearth-fires, see IV, 4, 2, 7.

[3] Yad vâ uparyupari somam bibhratah samkarishyanti, Kânva rec. (? holding the Soma close above the dhishnyas). This passage

Wherefore let not the Adhvaryu pass between[1] the hearths, for the Adhvaryu carries the Soma, and they sit waiting for him (Soma) with open mouths, and he would enter into their open mouths; and either Agni would burn him, or else that god who rules over beasts (Rudra) would seek after him; hence whenever the Adhvaryu should have business in the hall, let him pass north of the Âgnîdhra shed.

21. Now it is for the protection of Soma that those (hearths) are thrown up, to wit the Âhavanîya in front (on the high altar), the Mârgâlîya in the south, and the Âgnîdhrîya in the north; and those that are in the Sadas (protect him) from behind.

22. They are in part raised[2], in part they are assigned[3]. And, in truth, they themselves insisted thereon, saying, 'They shall in part raise us, and in part they shall assign us; thus we shall know again that heavenly world from which we have come, thus we shall not go astray.'

23. And whichever of them are raised they are

---

apparently refers to the *K*amasa-Adhvaryus or cup-bearers, who at the time of the Savanas hold up their cups filled with Soma, which, after libations have been made of it on the fire, is drunk by the priests.

[1] Samayâ; the Kâ*n*va text has 'pratyań (in going to the back)' instead.

[2] That is, bestrewed with gravel.

[3] When the dhish*n*yas have been completed, the Adhvaryu, standing east of the front door of the Sadas, has to point at the Âhavanîya, the Bahishpavamâna-place, the pit whence the earth for the hearths and high altar was taken, the slaughtering place, the Udumbara post, the Brahman's seat, the (old Âhavanîya at the) hall-door, the old Gârhapatya, and the Utkara (heap of rubbish) one by one with the texts, Vâ*g*. S. V, 32, 2, &c. Kâty. VIII, 6, 23, 24.

thereby visibly in this world; but whichever of them are assigned they are thereby visibly in yonder world.

24. They have two names; for, in truth, they themselves insisted thereon, saying, 'We have not prospered with these names, since Soma has been taken away from us; well, then, let us take each a second name!' They took each a second name, and therewith prospered, inasmuch as they from whom the Soma-draught had been taken had a share in the sacrifice assigned to them; hence they have two names. Wherefore let a Brâhman, if he prosper not, take a second name, for verily he prospers, whosoever, knowing this, takes a second name.

25. Now what he offers in the fire, that he offers unto the gods, thereby the gods exist; and what (Soma) is consumed in the Sadas, that he offers unto men, thereby men exist; and in that the Nârâsamsa[1] (cups of Soma) stand with the Soma-carts, thereby he offers unto the Fathers, thereby the Fathers exist.

26. But those creatures which are not admitted to the sacrifice are forlorn; wherefore he now admits to the sacrifice those creatures here on earth that are not forlorn; behind[2] the men are the beasts; and behind the gods are the birds, the plants, and

[1] Nârâsamsa, 'pertaining to Narâsamsa (man's praise, i.e. Agni, or Soma, or the Fathers),' is the name given to certain remains of Soma-libations (or potations) sacred to the Fathers, which, in the nine Soma-cups, are temporarily deposited under the axle of the southern Soma-cart, till they are drunk by the priests at the end of the libation.

[2] Or, alongside of, corresponding to, included in, them (anu).

the trees; and thus whatsoever exists here on earth all that is admitted to the sacrifice. And verily both the gods and men, and the Fathers drink together[1], and this is their symposium; of old they drank together visibly, but now they do so unseen.

THE VAISARGINA OFFERINGS AND LEADING FORWARD OF AGNI AND SOMA.

THIRD BRÂHMANA.

1. Verily he who consecrates himself, consecrates himself for the sake of this All; for he consecrates himself for the sacrifice, and this All indeed results from[2] the sacrifice; having prepared the sacrifice for which he consecrates himself, he now sets free (or produces) this All.

2. The reason why he performs the Vaisargina offerings is this. They are called Vaisargina, because he sets free (vi-sarg) this All; wherefore let him who takes part in the rite[3] touch (the sacrificer) from behind; but if he have to go elsewhere (on business) he need not heed this. When he sacrifices, he sets free this All.

3. And again why he performs the Vaisargina offerings. Vishnu, forsooth, is the sacrifice; by his strides he obtained (vi-kram) for the gods that all-pervading power (vikrânti) which now belongs to them; by his first step he gained this same (earth); by the second, the region of air; and by the last,

[1] 'Sma' does not seem here to have its usual force, which it has in the next sentence, combined with 'purâ.'

[2] Or, corresponds to (anu).

[3] That is, a blood-relation of the sacrificer, dwelling together with him. Cf. also p. 40, note 1.

the heaven. And that same pervading power Vishnu, the sacrifice, obtains by his strides for this (sacrificer) when he sacrifices: this is why he performs the Vaisargina offerings.

4. In the afternoon, having covered the altar (with sacrificial grass), and handed (to the sacrificer and his wife) one half of the fast-milk, they enter (the hall), put fire-wood on[1], and prepare the underlayer (of gravel). He (the Adhvaryu) puts the butter on (the old Gârhapatya), and cleans the spoons. The sacrificer takes the king (Soma) on his lap. He (the Adhvaryu) scatters about the (dust of the) foot-print of the Soma-cow behind the (new) Gârhapatya for the sake of a firm standing, for it is with the foot that one stands firmly.

5. Now some divide it (the dust) into four parts[2]: one fourth part (they put) into the underlayer whereon they take up the Âhavanîya (for transferring it to the high altar); with one fourth part they anoint the axle; one fourth part (they put) into this underlayer (for taking out the Âgnîdhrîya fire); and one fourth part he scatters about behind the Gârhapatya.

6. But let him not do this; let him rather scatter it about entirely behind the Gârhapatya. Having then purified the ghee, he takes thereof four ladlings (with the sruva), both in the guhû and in the upabhrit; and clotted ghee[3] in five ladlings, with (Vâg.

---

[1] Viz. on the Âhavanîya of the Prâkînavamsa (hall) now serving as the Gârhapatya, and generally called sâlâdvârya, i.e. the one near the (front or eastern) hall-door.

[2] See p. 121, note 2.

[3] Prishad-âgya (lit. mottled butter) is clarified butter mixed with sour milk.

S. V, 35), 'Thou art a light endowed with all forms, the flame of the All-gods;' for the clotted ghee belongs to the All-gods. When the wood is well kindled, they hold the spoons for him.

7. He then offers[1], with, 'Thou, O Soma, wilt widely withhold thy protection from the life-injuring[2] hatreds put forth by others, Hail!' Thereby he takes a firm stand on this resting-place, the earth, and gains this world.

8. He then offers the second oblation to (Soma) the Nimble, with, 'May the Nimble graciously accept the butter, Hail!' For he (Soma) spake upon that time, 'Verily I am afraid of the Rakshas: do ye make me to be too small for their deadly shaft, so that the evil spirits (the Rakshas) shall not injure me on the way; and take me across in the form of a drop, for the drop is nimble.' And accordingly, having made him too small for the deadly shaft, they lead him safely across in the form of a drop, from fear of the Rakshas, for the drop is nimble: this is why he offers the second oblation to (Soma) the Nimble.

9. They lift the (burning) fire-wood, and place it on the support. He then says (to the Hotri), 'Recite for Agni, taken forward!' or (say some), '— for Soma, led forward.' But let him say, 'Recite for Agni, taken forward[3]!'

---

[1] He offers some ghee from a substitute spoon (prakaranî), as the proper offering-spoons now filled with ghee and clotted ghee have to be carried with the fire to the Âgnîdhra.

[2] Mahîdhara explains 'tanûkrit' by 'tanûm krintanti kindanti.' It ought rather to mean 'body-making,'—? from the enemies that assume (various) forms.'

[3] The Kânva text, on the contrary, enjoins that he is to say, 'Recite for Soma . . .!' In the Hotri's ritual this is called the

10. They take the pressing-stones, the Soma-trough (drona-kalasa); Vâyu's cups[1], the (twenty pieces of) fire-wood, the enclosing-sticks of kârshmarya wood (Gmelina Arborea), one prastara of asvavâla grass[2], and the two Vidhritis of sugar-cane; that barhis (which was used before[3]) is tied up therewith. Further, the two spits for (roasting) the omenta[4], the two ropes (for binding the stake and victims), the two churning-sticks (for producing fire), the adhimanthana chip, and the two vrishana[5], —having taken up all these they go forward (to the Âgnîdhra): thus the sacrifice goes upwards[6].

11. While they proceed thither, he makes (the sacrificer) say the text (Vâg. S. V, 36; Rig-veda I, 189, 1), 'O Agni, lead us on a good path unto wealth, thou, O God, that knowest all works! keep thou from us the sin that leadeth astray, and we will offer unto thee most ample adoration!' He thereby places Agni in front, and Agni marches in front repelling the evil spirits; and they take him thither on a (way) free from danger and

Agnîshoma-pranayana. For the seventeen verses (brought up to twenty-one by repetitions) of the Hotri, see Ait. Br. I, 30 (Haug, Translation, p. 68); Âsv. IV, 10. The Soma is carried either by the Brahman himself or by the sacrificer. Kâty. XI, 1, 13, 14.

[1] The 'Vâyavya' are wooden cups shaped like a mortar. It seems here to include all the Soma-cups, see IV, 1, 3, 7–10; Kâty. VIII, 7, 5.

[2] See III, 4, 1, 17–18.

[3] Viz. at the guest-offering, see p. 103, note 3. It was tied up with the three objects mentioned immediately before.

[4] The vapâsrapanî are sticks of kârshmarya wood.

[5] For these objects, see p. 90, note 5.

[6] 'Thus that sacrifice goes upwards to yonder heavenly world, and, the sacrifice being the sacrificer, the sacrificer thus goes thither,' Kânva text. See III, 6, 1, 28, where the gods are said to have attained immortality from the Âgnîdhrîya.

injury. They proceed, and reach the Âgnîdhra; and he (the Adhvaryu) puts (the fire) down on the Âgnîdhra hearth.

12. Thereon, when laid down, he offers with the text (Vâg. S. V, 37), 'May this Agni make wide room for us; may he march in front smiting the haters! May he gain riches in the winning of riches: may he, fiercely rushing, conquer the enemies, Hail!' By means of him (Agni) he thus takes a firm stand in that resting-place, the aerial region, and gains that world.

13. In the same place they deposit the pressing-stones, the Soma-trough, and Vâyu's cups[1]. Having then taken up the other (objects), they proceed and deposit them north of the Âhavanîya.

14. The Adhvaryu takes the sprinkling-water, and sprinkles first the fire-wood, and then the altar. They then hand to him the altar-grass. He puts it down with the knot towards the east, and sprinkles it. Having poured (the remaining sprinkling-water) upon (the root ends of the altar-grass), and untied the knot,—the Prastara-bunch of asvavâla grass is tied together (with the altar-grass),—he takes that; and having taken the Prastara, he spreads the altar-grass in a single layer. Having spread the altar-grass, he lays the enclosing-sticks of kârshmarya-wood round (the fire). Having laid the enclosing-sticks around, he puts two kindling-sticks (on the fire); and having put on the two kindling-sticks,

15. He offers with the text (Vâg. S. V, 38), 'Stride thou widely, O Vishnu, make wide room for our abode! drink the ghee, thou born of ghee,

[1] Also the two fringed filtering-cloths (dasâpavitre), according to the Kânva rec.

and speed the lord of the sacrifice ever onwards, Hail!' Thereby he takes a firm stand in that resting-place, the sky: he thus gains that world by offering with that (verse).

16. And as to his offering with a verse addressed to Vishnu, it was thus that they made him (Soma) to be too small for the deadly shaft and led him safely across in the form of a drop, for the drop is nimble. And having attained to safety, he now makes him the one he really is, namely, the sacrifice, for Vishnu is the sacrifice: therefore he offers with a verse addressed to Vishnu.

17. After depositing the spoons[1] and touching water, he makes the king (Soma) enter (the Havirdhâna shed). The reason why he makes the king enter, after depositing the spoons and touching water, is this. The ghee is the thunderbolt, and Soma is seed: hence it is after depositing the spoons and touching water that he makes the king enter, lest he should injure the seed Soma with the thunderbolt, the ghee.

18. He spreads the black deer-skin on the enclosed part of the southern Soma-cart, and sets him down thereon with (Vâg. S. V, 39), 'O divine Savitri, this is thy Soma: shield him; may they not injure thee!' whereby he makes him over to the God Savitri for protection.

19. Having quitted his hold of him, he (the sacrificer) renders homage to him with, 'Now, O divine Soma, hast thou, a god, joined the gods, and

[1] 'He then deposits the Prastara on the mound (p. 140, note 2), deposits there the guhû and the upabhrit and the prishadâgya; and having touched the sacrificial materials and touched water, he takes the king and enters (the cart-shed),' &c. Kânva rec.

here I the men with increase of wealth.' Now Agni and Soma have seized him who consecrates himself between their jaws[1], for that consecration-offering belongs to Agni and Vish*n*u, and Vish*n*u forsooth is no other than Soma; and he himself that consecrates himself is the food of the gods: thus they have seized him between their jaws, and he now expressly redeems himself from Soma, when he says, 'Now, O divine Soma, hast thou, a god, joined the gods, and here (have I joined) the men with increase of wealth;'—increase of wealth means abundance: 'with abundance' he thereby means to say.

20. He then walks out (of the cart-shed), with, 'Hail! I am freed from Varu*n*a's noose!' For he, truly, is in Varu*n*a's noose who is in another's mouth: he now frees himself from Varu*n*a's noose, when he says, 'Hail! I am freed from Varu*n*a's noose.'

21. He then puts a kindling-stick on the Âhavanîya in this way[2], 'O Agni, protector of vows, on thee, O protector of vows—' for Agni is lord of vows to the gods, wherefore he says, 'O Agni, protector of vows, on thee, O protector of vows'—'what bodily form of thine hath been on me, (may) that (be) on thee; what bodily form of mine has been on thee, (may) that (be) here on me! Our vows, O lord of vows, (have been performed) rightly: the lord of consecration hath

[1] See III, 3, 4, 21.

[2] Thus (iti), viz. with the following modifications of the corresponding formula, used at the 'intermediary consecration,' III, 4, 3, 9. Perhaps 'iti' may mean 'thus,' i. e. while still keeping his fingers turned in; or, it may mean 'as such' (as a free man).

approved my consecration; the lord of penance hath approved my penance.' Thereby he frees himself visibly from Agni, and sacrifices with a self (body) now his own: hence they now partake of his food, for he is a man (again); hence they now use his (real) name, for he is a man. And as to their not eating (of his food) heretofore, it is as one would not eat of sacrificial food, before offering has been made thereof: therefore let no one partake of the food of one consecrated. He now loosens his fingers.

THE ANIMAL SACRIFICE[1] TO AGNI AND SOMA.

FOURTH BRÂHMAṆA.

A. THE SETTING UP OF THE SACRIFICIAL STAKE.

1. Being about to cut the sacrificial stake, he offers[2] with a verse addressed to Vishṇu. For the stake belongs to Vishṇu; therefore he offers with a verse addressed to Vishṇu.

2. And again, why he offers with a verse addressed to Vishṇu—Vishṇu being the sacrifice, he thus approaches the stake by means of the sacrifice: therefore he offers with a verse addressed to Vishṇu.

3. If he offers with the offering-spoon, he offers after taking ghee by four ladlings; and if he offers with the dipping-spoon, he offers after 'cutting out' (some ghee from the pot) with the dipping-spoon;—with the text (Vâg. S. V, 41), 'Stride thou widely,

[1] On the Animal Sacrifice, cp. Dr. J. Schwab's dissertation, 'Das altindische Thieropfer,' 1882.

[2] This oblation is called yûpâhuti, or 'stake-offering.'

O Vishnu, make wide room for our abode! drink the ghee, thou born of ghee, and speed the lord of the sacrifice ever onwards! Hail!'

4. He takes the ghee which is left (in the melting-pot). Whatever chopping-knife the carpenter uses, that the carpenter now takes. They then proceed (to the wood). Whatever (tree) they select for the stake,

5. That he touches while muttering (Vâg. S. V, 42),—or he salutes it while standing behind it with his face towards the east,—'I have passed over the others, I have not gone nigh the others—' he does indeed pass over others and does not go near to others: wherefore he says, 'I have passed over the others, I have not gone nigh the others.

6. 'Thee have I found on the nearer side of the farther, and on the farther side of the nearer;' he does indeed fell it on the nearer side of the farther, of those that are farther away from it; and 'on the farther side of the nearer,' he says, because he does fell it on the farther side of the nearer, of those that are on this side of it. This is why he says, 'Thee have I found on the nearer side of the farther, and on the farther side of the nearer.'

7. 'Thee do we favour, O divine lord of the forest[1], for the worship of the gods.' As for the good work, he would favour (select) one from amidst many (men) and he (the chosen) would be well-disposed to that work, even so does he now, for the good work, favour that (tree) from amidst many, and it becomes well-disposed to the felling.

[1] 'Vanaspati' is a common synonym of vriksha, tree.

8. 'Thee may the gods favour for the worship of the gods!' for that is truly successful which the gods favour for the good work: therefore he says, 'Thee may the gods favour for the worship of the gods!'

9. He then touches it with the dipping-spoon, with, 'For Vishnu, thee!' for the stake belongs to Vishnu, since Vishnu is the sacrifice, and he fells this (tree) for the sacrifice: therefore he says, 'For Vishnu, thee!'

10. He then places a blade of darbha-grass between[1], with, 'O plant, shield it!' for the axe is a thunderbolt; but thus that thunderbolt, the axe, does not hurt it (the tree). He then strikes with the axe, with, 'O axe, hurt it not!' for the axe is a thunderbolt, but thus that thunderbolt, the axe, does not hurt it.

11. The first chip[2] which he cuts off, he takes (and lays aside). Let him cut (the tree) so as to cause no obstruction to the axle[3]. For, indeed, it is on a cart that they convey it, and in this way he does not obstruct the cart.

[1] Viz. he places or holds it against where he is about to strike the tree, so as first to cut the grass.

[2] For the destination of this chip of the bark, see III, 7, 1, 8.

[3] That is to say, he is not to cut the tree too high from the ground, so that the axle of the cart might readily pass over the remaining stump without touching it. The Kânva text reads, 'tam anakshastambhe vrisked uta hy enam anasâ vakshyanto bhavanty uto svargam hâsya lokam yate (sic) 'kshastambhah syât tasmâd anakshastambhe vrisket.' Nothing is said anywhere about the yûpa being conveyed on a cart to the sacrificial ground, if, indeed, that statement refer to the yûpa at all. Sâyana's comment is very corrupt here, but he seems to interpret the passage to the effect that some people might convey the stake on the cart (pakshe anasâ yûpam nayeyuh) and that in that case the cart would be obstructed.

12. Let him cut it so as to fall towards the east, for the east is the quarter of the gods; or towards the north, for the north is the quarter of men; or towards the west. But let him take care to keep it from (falling towards) the southern quarter, for that is the quarter of the Fathers: therefore he must take care to keep it from the southern quarter.

13. The falling (tree) he addresses with the text (Vâg. S. V, 43), 'Graze not the sky! hurt not the air! unite with the earth!' for verily that (tree) which they cut for the stake is a thunderbolt, and these worlds tremble for fear of that falling thunderbolt; but he thereby propitiates it for these worlds, and thus propitiated it injures not these worlds.

14. Now when he says, 'Graze not the sky,' he means to say, 'Injure not the sky!' In the words 'hurt not the air' there is nothing obscure. By 'Unite with the earth,' he means to say, 'Be thou in harmony with the earth!' 'For this sharp-edged axe hath led thee forward unto great bliss,' for this sharp axe indeed leads it forward.

15. Upon the stump he then offers ghee, 'lest the evil spirits should rise therefrom after (the tree):' ghee being a thunderbolt, he thus repels the evil spirits by means of the thunderbolt, and thus the evil spirits do not rise therefrom after it. And ghee being seed, he thus endows the trees with that seed; and from that seed (in) the stump trees are afterwards produced[1].

16. He sacrifices with, 'Grow thou out of this, O lord of the forest, with a hundred shoots!

[1] Or, 'hence trees grow up again from the stump (? after felling, "â vraskanât") out of seed.'

May we grow out with a thousand shoots!' There is nothing obscure in this.

17. Thereupon he cuts it (the stake of the proper length): of whatever length he cuts it the first time, so long let it remain.

18. He may cut it five cubits long; for fivefold is the sacrifice and fivefold is the animal (victim), and five seasons there are in the year: therefore he may cut it five cubits long.

19. He may cut it six cubits long; for six seasons there are in the year; and the year is a thunderbolt, as the sacrificial stake is a thunderbolt: therefore he may cut it six cubits long.

20. He may cut it eight cubits long, for eight syllables has the Gâyatrî, and the Gâyatrî is the fore-part of the sacrifice, as the sacrificial stake is the fore-part of the sacrifice: therefore he may cut it eight cubits long.

21. He may cut it nine cubits long, for threefold is the sacrifice, and 'nine' is threefold: therefore he may cut it nine cubits long.

22. He may cut it eleven cubits long, for eleven syllables has the Trishṭubh, and the Trishṭubh is a thunderbolt, as the sacrificial stake is a thunderbolt: therefore he may cut it eleven cubits long.

23. He may cut it twelve cubits long, for twelve months there are in the year, and the year is a thunderbolt, as the sacrificial stake is a thunderbolt: therefore he may cut it twelve cubits long.

24. He may cut it thirteen cubits long, for thirteen months there are in a year, and the year is a thunderbolt, as the sacrificial stake is a thunderbolt: therefore he may cut it thirteen cubits long.

25. He may cut it fifteen cubits long, for the

fifteen-versed chant is a thunderbolt[1], as the sacrificial stake is a thunderbolt: therefore he may cut it fifteen cubits long.

26. The sacrificial stake of the Vâgapeya sacrifice is seventeen cubits long. Indeed, it may be unmeasured[2], for with that same unmeasured thunderbolt did the gods conquer the unmeasured; and in like manner does he now conquer the unmeasured with that unmeasured thunderbolt: therefore it may even be unmeasured.

27. It is (made to be) eight-cornered, for eight syllables has the Gâyatrî, and the Gâyatrî is the fore-part of the sacrifice, as this (stake) is the fore-part of the sacrifice: therefore it is eight-cornered.

Seventh Adhyâya. First Brâhmana.

1. He takes the spade, with (Vâg. S. VI, 1), 'I take thee, at the impulse of the divine Savitri, with the arms of the Asvins, with the hands of Pûshan: thou art a woman.' The significance of that formula is the same (as before); and that spade (abhri, fem.) is indeed female: therefore he says 'thou art a woman.'

2. He thus draws the outline of the hole (for the stake[3]), with, 'Herewith I cut off the necks of

---

[1] On the connection of the Pañkadasa-stoma with Indra, the wielder of the thunderbolt, see part i, introduction, p. xviii.

[2] The Kânva text leaves an option first between stakes six, eight, eleven, fifteen (and for the Vâgapeya seventeen) cubits long; and finally lays down the rule that no regard is to be had to any fixed measure.

[3] According to the Kânva text, one half of it is to be within, and one half outside of the altar. See Kâty. VI, 2, 8.

the Rakshas!' The spade is the thunderbolt: with the thunderbolt he thus cuts off the necks of the Rakshas.

3. He then digs, and throws up a heap of earth towards the east. He digs the hole, making it equal (in depth) with the (unhewn) bottom part (of the stake). In front of it he lays down the stake with the top towards the east. Thereon he puts sacrificial grass of the same size, and thereupon he puts the chip of the stake. In front on the (north) side (of the stake) he puts down the head-piece[1]. The sprinkling-water has barley-corns mixed with it: the significance of this is the same (as before[2]).

4. He throws the barley-corns in with, 'Thou art barley (yava), keep thou (yavaya) from us the haters, keep from us the enemies!' There is nothing obscure in this. He then sprinkles: the significance of the sprinkling is one and the same: he thereby renders it sacrificially pure.

5. He sprinkles (the top, middle, and bottom parts) with, 'For the sky—thee! for the air—thee! for the earth—thee!' the stake being a thunderbolt (he does so) for the protection of these worlds[3]: 'I sprinkle thee for the protection of these worlds,' is what he thereby means to say.

6. The sprinkling-water that remains he then pours into the hole with, 'Be the worlds pure

[1] Of the part of the tree cut off from the sacrificial stake, a top-piece or head-ring (*k*ashâla) is made some eight or nine inches high, eight-cornered (like the sacrificial stake); narrower in the middle like a mortar, and hollowed out so as to allow its being fixed on the stake.

[2] See III, 6, 1, 7 seq.

[3] For the construction, see p. 15, note 3.

wherein the Fathers reside!' for a pit that is dug is sacred to the Fathers: this he thereby renders sacrificially pure.

7. Thereupon he strews barhis-grass therein, both eastward-pointed and northward-pointed, with, 'Thou art the seat of the Fathers!' for that part of it (the stake) which is dug into the ground is sacred to the Fathers: as though it were (naturally) established among plants, and not dug in, so does it become established among those plants.

8. He then throws in the (first) chip[1] of the stake. Now that chip of the outer (bark) doubtless is the vigour of trees; hence, when a chip of their outer (bark) is cut off they dry up, for it is their vigour. Hence, when he throws in the chip of the stake, he does so thinking, 'I will plant it (the stake) full of vigour.' The reason why it is this (chip) and no other, is that this one has been produced with a formula, is sacrificially pure: therefore he throws in the chip of the stake.

9. He throws it in with (Vâg. S. VI, 2), 'Thou art a leader, easy of access to the Unnetris[2];' for that (chip) is cut from it in front, wherefore he says, 'Thou art a leader, easy of access to the Unnetris.' 'Be thou mindful of this: it will stand upon thee!' for it (the stake) will indeed stand on it, wherefore he says, 'Be thou mindful of this: it will stand upon thee.'

10. Having then taken out ghee with the dipping-spoon, he offers it into the hole, 'lest the evil spirits should rise from below:' ghee is a thunderbolt, he

---

[1] See III, 6, 4, 11.

[2] The Unnetris are the priests that have to draw the Soma.

thus repels the evil spirits by means of the thunderbolt, and thus the evil spirits do not rise from below. Having then gone round to the front, he sits down facing the north and anoints the stake. He says (to the Hotri), 'Recite to the stake as it is anointed[1]!'

11. He anoints it with, 'The divine Savitri anoint thee with sweet drink (milk)!' for Savitri is the impeller (prasavitri) of the gods, and that stake is in reality the sacrificer himself; and sweet drink is everything here; he thus puts it in connection with all that, and Savitri, the impeller, impels it for him: therefore he says, 'The divine Savitri anoint thee with sweet drink!'

12. Having then anointed the top-ring on both sides, he puts it on (the stake) with, 'To the full-berried plants—thee!' for that (top-ring) is as its berry. And as to its being, as it were, contracted in the middle, the berry[2] here on trees is fastened (to the stalk) sideways; what connecting part there is between (the fruit and stalk) pressed in, as it were, that he thereby makes it. This is why it is, as it were, contracted in the middle.

13. He anoints from top to bottom the (corner) facing the fire; for the (corner) facing the fire is the sacrificer, and the ghee is sap: with sap he thus anoints the sacrificer; therefore he anoints from top to bottom the (corner) facing the fire. He then

---

[1] 'Recite to the stake being anointed!' or, 'we anoint the stake: Recite!' Kânva rec. The latter is the formula mentioned Ait. Br. II, 2 (but 'añgmo yûpam,' for Kânva 'yûpam añgmo'); where the seven verses recited by the Hotri (brought up to eleven as usual) are given. See also Âsv. III, 1, 8.

[2] Pippala refers especially to the berry or fruit of the Ficus Religiosa.

grasps the girding-part all round, and says (to the Hot*ri*), 'Recite to the (stake) being set up!'

14. He raises it with, 'With thy crest thou hast touched the sky; with thy middle thou hast filled the air; with thy foot thou hast steadied the earth;'—the sacrificial stake being a thunderbolt, (he raises it) for the conquering of these worlds; with that thunderbolt he gains these worlds, and deprives his enemies of their share in these worlds.

15. He then plants it (in the hole) with (Vâ*g*. S. VI, 3), 'To what resorts of thine we long to go where are the swift-footed, many-horned kine; there, forsooth, was imprinted wide-striding Vish*n*u's highest mighty foot-step.' With this trish*t*ubh verse he plants it; the trish*t*ubh is a thunderbolt, as the sacrificial stake is a thunderbolt; therefore he plants it with a trish*t*ubh verse.

16. That (corner which was) facing the fire he places opposite the fire; for the (corner) facing the fire is the sacrificer, and the sacrifice is fire. Hence were he to turn the fire-corner aside from the fire, the sacrificer would assuredly turn aside from the sacrifice; therefore he places the (corner which was) facing the fire opposite the fire. He then heaps up (earth) round it and presses it firmly all round, and pours water thereon[1].

17. Thereupon he makes (the sacrificer) say while touching it (Vâ*g*. S. VI, 4; Rig-veda I, 22, 19), 'See ye the deeds of Vish*n*u, whereby he beheld the sacred ordinances, Indra's allied

[1] The same formulas are used on this occasion as at III, 6, 1, 17–18.

friend!' For he who has set up the sacrificial stake has hurled the thunderbolt: 'See ye Vishnu's conquest!' he means to say when he says, 'See ye the deeds of Vishnu, whereby he beheld the sacred ordinances, Indra's allied friend.' Indra, forsooth, is the deity of the sacrifice, and the sacrificial stake belongs to Vishnu; he thereby connects it with Indra; therefore he says, 'Indra's allied friend.'

18. He then looks up at the top-ring with (Vâg. S. VI, 5; Rig-veda I, 22, 20), 'The wise ever behold that highest step of Vishnu, fixed like an eye in the heaven.' For he who has set up the sacrificial stake has hurled the thunderbolt: 'See ye that conquest of Vishnu!' he means to say when he says, 'The wise ever behold that highest step of Vishnu, fixed like an eye in the heaven.'

19. He then girds (the stake with a rope of kusa-grass). Now it is to cover its nakedness that he girds it; wherefore he girds it in this place (viz. on a level with the sacrificer's navel), for it is thus that this (nether) garment is (slung round)[1]. He thereby puts food into him, for it is there that the food settles; therefore he girds it at that place.

20. He girds it with a triple (rope), for threefold is food, and food means cattle; and (there is) the father and the mother, and what is born is the third; therefore he girds it with a triple (rope).

21. He girds it with (Vâg. S. VI, 6), 'Thou art enfolded; may the heavenly hosts enfold

[1] According to the Kânva text it is to be slung round nîvîdaghne, 'on a level with the nether garment' (nâbhidaghne, Taitt. S. VI, 3, 4, 5). According to Kâty. VI, 3, 1, the girding is preceded by a call on the Hotri to recite to the post being anointed; but neither recension mentions this.

thee! may riches enfold this sacrificer among men!' He invokes a blessing on the sacrificer, when he says, 'May riches enfold this sacrificer among men.'

22. Thereupon he inserts a chip of the stake (under the rope) with, 'Thou art the son of the sky.' For it is doubtless the offspring of that (sacrificial stake); hence if there be the full number of eleven stakes[1], let him insert in each its own (chip) without confounding them; and his offspring is born orderly and not foolish. But whosoever inserts them in confusion, not its own in each, verily his offspring is born disorderly and foolish; therefore let him insert its own in each without confounding them.

23. Moreover, that chip of the stake is made an ascent to the heavenly world; there is this girdle-rope; after the rope the chip of the stake; after the chip of the stake the top-ring; and from the top-ring one reaches the heavenly world.

24. And as to why it is called svaru ('very sore'),—that (chip) is cut off from that (stake), and thus is its own (sva) sore (arus); therefore it is called 'svaru.'

25. With that part of it which is dug in, he gains the world of the Fathers; and with what is above the dug-in part, up to the girdle-rope, he gains the world of men; and with what is above the rope, up to the top-ring, he gains the world of the gods; and what (space of) two or three fingers' breadths

[1] When, instead of a single he-goat to Agni, eleven victims are slaughtered, they are either bound to one stake each, or all to one and the same. See III, 9, 1, 4 seq. The chip alluded to is one of those obtained in rough-hewing the stake and making it eight-cornered.

there is above the top-ring,—the gods called the 'Blessed[1],'—their world he therewith gains; verily, whosoever thus knows this, he becomes one of the same world with the blessed gods.

26. That (sacrificial stake) he sets up on the fore-part (of the altar); for the stake is a thunderbolt, as the club is a thunderbolt. But in hurling the club one takes hold of its fore-part; and that (stake) is the fore-part of the sacrifice; therefore he sets it up on the fore-part (of the altar).

27. Verily, by means of the sacrifice the gods gained that supreme authority which they now wield. They spake, 'How may this (world) of ours be made unattainable to men?' They sipped the sap of the sacrifice, as bees would suck out honey, and having drained the sacrifice and scattered it by means of the sacrificial stake, they disappeared. And because they scattered (yopaya) therewith, therefore it is called yûpa (sacrificial stake). At the head stands intelligence, at the head swiftness of thought; therefore he sets it up on the fore-part (of the altar).

28. It is eight-cornered; for the gâyatrî metre consists of eight syllables, and the gâyatrî is the fore-part of the sacrifice, as this (stake) is the fore-part of the sacrifice; therefore it is eight-cornered.

29. Now the gods once threw it after (the prastara into the fire) even as now some throw it after, thinking, 'So the gods did it.' Thereupon the Rakshas sipped the sacrifice (Soma) after (the gods).

30. The gods said unto the Adhvaryu, 'Offer thou only a chip of the stake; thereby this (sacri-

[1] On the 'sâdhyas' see Weber, Ind. Stud. IX, p. 6, note 2.

ficer) will be bid good-speed[1]; and thus the Rakshas will not hereafter sip the sacrifice, thinking, "that (stake) surely is a raised thunderbolt."'

31. The Adhvaryu, then, offered up only a chip of the stake, and thereby that (sacrificer) was bid good-speed; and thus the Rakshas did not thereafter sip the sacrifice, thinking, 'that surely is a raised thunderbolt.'

32. And in like manner does he now only offer up that chip of the sacrificial stake[2]; thereby this (sacrificer) is bid good-speed; and thus the Rakshas do not thereafter sip the sacrifice, thinking, 'that surely is a raised thunderbolt!' He offers it[3] with the text (Vâg. S. VI, 21), 'May thy smoke rise up to the sky, thy light to the heavens! fill the earth with ashes, Hail!'

SECOND BRÂHMANA.

1. Verily, as large as the altar is, so large is the earth. The sacrificial stakes are thunderbolts; and by means of these thunderbolts he obtains possession of this earth, and excludes his enemies from sharing therein. Hence there are eleven stakes, and the twelfth lies aside rough-hewn; he puts it down south (of the altar). The reason why the twelfth lies aside is this.

2. Now the gods, while performing this sacrifice,

[1] See I, 8, 3, 11 seq.

[2] See Ait. Br. II, 3.

[3] The offering of the chips does not take place till the end of the after-offerings (see note to III, 8, 5, 6). It is somewhat strange that it should be anticipated in this place, both in this and the Kânva recensions.

were afraid of an attack from the Asura-Rakshas. Those raised (sacrificial stakes), then, were as a discharged arrow,—therewith one either smites or smites not; as a hurled club,—therewith one either smites or smites not. But that twelfth (stake) lying aside,—even as an arrow drawn but not discharged, as (a weapon) raised but not hurled, so was that a thunderbolt raised for repelling the evil spirits on the south; therefore the twelfth (stake) lies aside.

3. He lays it down with (Vâg. S. VI, 6), 'This is thy place on earth; thine is the beast of the forest.' There are the animal (victim) and the sacrificial stake; to this one he thereby assigns of animals that of the forest, and thus it, too, is possessed of an animal (victim). That setting up of the eleven sacrificial stakes is said to be of two kinds,—some, namely, set (them all) up (on the previous day) for the morrow's Soma feast, and others set up (one) stake for the preparation[1] of the morrow's Soma feast.

4. Let him, however, not do this; but let him only set up the one opposite the fire. For after setting it up the Adhvaryu does not quit his hold of it till the girding; but those (others) remain

---

[1] No satisfactory explanation of 'prakubratâ' occurs to me. It seems to be derived from 'kubra,' to which the dictionaries assign the meanings 'hole for sacrificial fire' and 'thread' (besides those of 'forest,' 'earring,' and 'cart'). Unâd. II, 28, derives this from a root 'kub,' to cover, shelter. ? For the safe foundation (or the protraction) of to-morrow's Soma feast. The Kânva text, on the other hand, reads: 'Some, now, raise all (the stakes) on the upavasatha (day before the Soma feast) for the sake of quickening (? prakudratâyai) the work, thinking, 'we will quickly bring the sacrifice to a close.'

ungirt during that night. Thus there would be an offence, since it is for the victim that the stake is set up, and the victim is (only) slaughtered on the next morning: let him therefore set up (the others) on the next morning.

5. Let him first set up that (stake) which stands (immediately) north of the one opposite the fire, then the one on the south, then a northern one,—last of all the one on the southern flank: thus it (the row of stakes) inclines to the north.

6. But they also say conversely[1], 'Let him first set up that which is south of the one opposite the fire, then the northern one, then a southern one,—last of all the one on the northern flank: and thus indeed his work attains completion towards the north.'

7. Let the largest be the one forming the southern flank; then shorter and shorter; and the one forming the northern flank the shortest: thus (the row of stakes) inclines to the north.

8. Thereupon they set up the wife-stake for the wives. It is for the sake of completeness, forsooth, that the wife-stake is set up: there they seize (and bind) the victim for Tvash*tri*, for Tvash*tri* fashions the cast seed, and hence he fashions the seed now cast. It (the victim to Tvash*tri*) is an animal with testicles, for such a one is a begetter. Let him not slay that one, but let him set it free after fire has been carried round it. Were he to slay it, there would assuredly be an end to offspring, but in this way he sets free the offspring. Therefore let him not

---

[1] The Kâ*n*va text first mentions the practice set forth in the preceding paragraph, as the teaching of 'some,' but then rejects it in favour of the second alternative.

slay it, but let him set it free after fire has been carried round it.

Third Brâhma*n*a.

B. The Killing of the Victim.

1. There are both an animal and a sacrificial stake, for never do they immolate an animal without a stake. And as to why this is so:—well, animals did not at first submit thereto that they should become food, as they are now become food; for just as man here walks two-footed and erect, so did they walk two-footed and erect.

2. Then the gods perceived that thunderbolt, to wit, the sacrificial stake; they raised it, and from fear thereof they (the animals) shrunk together and thus became four-footed, and thus became food, as they are now become food, for they submitted thereto: wherefore they immolate the animal only at a stake and never without a stake.

3. Having driven up the victim, and churned the fire, he binds it (to the stake). And as to why this is so:—well, animals did not at first submit thereto that they should become sacrificial food, as they are now become sacrificial food and are offered up in the fire. The gods secured them: even thus secured they did not resign themselves.

4. They spake, 'Verily, these (animals) know not the manner of this, that it is in fire that sacrificial food is offered, nor (do they know) that secure resort (the fire): let us offer fire into the fire after securing the animals and churning the fire, and they will know that this truly is the manner of sacrificial food,

this its resort; that it is truly in fire that sacrificial food is offered: and accordingly they will resign themselves, and will be favourably disposed to the slaughtering.'

5. Having, then, first secured the animals, and churned the fire, they offered fire into the fire; and then they (the animals) knew that this truly is the manner of sacrificial food, this its resort; that it is truly in fire that sacrificial food is offered. And accordingly they resigned themselves, and became favourably disposed to the slaughtering.

6. And in like manner does he now offer fire into the fire, after securing the animal and churning the fire. It (the animal) knows that this truly is the manner of sacrificial food, this its resort; that it is truly in fire that sacrificial food is offered; and accordingly it resigns itself and becomes favourably disposed to the slaughtering. Therefore having driven up the victim and churned the fire, he binds it (to the stake).

7. As to this they say, 'Let him not drive up (the victim), nor churn the fire; but having taken the rope and straightway gone thither and put (the rope) round it, let him bind it.' Let him, however, not do this; for it would be as if he intended to commit secretly some lawless action. Let him therefore go round there.

8. Then, taking a straw, he drives it up, thinking, 'having a companion, I will secure it;' for he who has a companion is strong.

9. He takes the straw with (Vâ*g*. S. VI, 7), 'Thou art a cheerer!' for a companion does cheer one: therefore he says, 'Thou art a cheerer.' 'The celestial hosts have approached the gods;'

the celestial hosts, forsooth, are those beasts: 'they have submitted to the gods' he means to say, when he says, 'The celestial hosts have approached the gods.'

10. 'The considerate[1], best of leaders;' for the gods are wise: therefore he says, 'The considerate, best of leaders.'

11. 'O divine Tvashtri, settle the wealth!' for Tvashtri is lord of beasts (cattle), and wealth means cattle, it is with regard to those which did not submit that the gods then said to Tvashtri, 'Quiet them,' when he says, 'O divine Tvashtri, settle the wealth!'

12. 'May the offerings be relished by thee!' Since they themselves submitted thereto that they should become sacrificial food, therefore he says, 'May the offerings be relished by thee!'

13. 'Rejoice, ye prosperous!' for cattle are prosperous: therefore he says, 'Rejoice ye prosperous.' 'O Lord of prayer, preserve our goods!' The Lord of prayer, forsooth, is the Brahman; and goods mean cattle: those, which did not submit, the gods on that occasion enclosed with the Brahman on the farther side, and they did not pass over it. And in like manner does he now enclose them with the Brahman on the farther side, and they do not pass over it: therefore he says, 'O Lord of prayer, preserve our goods!' Having made a noose he throws it over (the victim)[2]. Now then as to the binding itself.

---

[1] Usig rather means 'willing, loving, devoted.'

[2] According to the Taitt. authorities (Sâyana on Taitt. S. I, 3, 8), the rope is wound round the right fore-leg and then passed upwards

Fourth Brâhmana.

1. Having made a noose, he throws it over (the victim) with (Vâg. S. VI, 8), 'With the noose of sacred order I bind thee, O oblation to the gods!' for that rope, forsooth, is Varuna's: therefore he thus binds it with the noose of sacred order, and thus that rope of Varuna does not injure it.

2. 'Be bold, O man[1]!' for at first man dared not[2] to approach it (the victim); but now that he thus binds it with the noose of sacred order, as an oblation to the gods, man dares to approach it: therefore he says, 'Be bold, O man!'

3. He then binds it (to the stake) with (Vâg. S. VI, 9), 'At the impulse of the divine Savitri, I bind thee with the arms of the Asvins, with the hands of Pûshan, thee agreeable to Agni and Soma!' Even as on that occasion[3], when taking out an oblation for a deity, he assigns it, so does he now assign it to the two deities. He then sprinkles it,—one and the same, forsooth, is the

to the head. From Kâty. VI, 3, 27, on the other hand, it would seem that the rope is passed either between the horns (and under the neck?), or round the horns.

[1] Thus the author appears to take the formula 'dharshâ mânushah.' It would rather seem to mean, 'Be bold: [I am (or he, the slaughterer, is)] a man.' Mahîdhara interprets, 'May he (the Samitri) be bold enough!' Either the Kânva reading 'dharshân mânushah' or that of the Taittiriyas 'dharshâ mânushân' would seem preferable.

[2] The Kânva text has 'dhrishnoti' for 'adhrishnot,' which renders it more simple: 'At first the man (the slaughterer) dares not approach it, but when he thus binds it, &c.'

[3] Viz. at the Haviryagña; see I, 1, 2, 17.

significance of sprinkling: he thereby makes it sacrificially pure.

4. He sprinkles with, 'For the waters—thee, for the plants!' whereby it (the victim) exists, thereby he thus makes it sacrificially pure. For when it rains, then plants are produced here on earth; and by eating plants and drinking water that sap originates, and from sap seed, and from seed beasts: hence whereby it exists, wherefrom it springs, thereby he thus makes it sacrificially pure.

5. 'May thy mother grant thee permission, and thy father—;' for it is from its mother and father that it is born: hence wherefrom it is born, thereby he thus makes it sacrificially pure; '—thine own brother, thy fellow in the herd;' whereby he means to say, 'whatever kin there is of thine, with their approval I slay thee.' 'I sprinkle thee, agreeable to Agni and Soma;' he thus makes it pure for those two deities for whom he slays it.

6. With (Vâg. S. VI, 10), 'Thou art a drinker of water,' he then holds (the lustral water) under (its mouth), whereby he renders it internally pure. He then sprinkles it underneath (the body), with, 'May the divine waters make it palatable, a true palatable offering to the gods!' he thus makes it sacrificially pure all over.

7. Thereupon he says (to the Hotri), 'Recite to the fire being kindled!' when he has made the second libation of ghee[1], and returned (to his former place) without letting the two spoons touch one another[2], he anoints the victim with the (ghee in the)

[1] For the course of performance, see I, 3, 5, 1 seq.; I, 4, 4, 1 seq.

[2] See I, 4, 5, 5.

*g*uhû. For the second libation is the head of the sacrifice, and the sacrifice here indeed is that victim: hence he thereby puts the head on the sacrifice and therefore anoints the victim with the *g*uhû.

8. With 'May thy breath unite with the wind!' he anoints it on the forehead; with 'Thy limbs with those worthy of sacrifice' on the shoulders; with 'The lord of sacrifice with (the object of) his prayer!' the loins; whereby he means to say, 'For whatsoever object the animal is slain, do thou obtain that!'

9. For, indeed, the breath of the victim when slain here passes into the wind: 'Obtain thou that thy breath may pass into the wind!' is what he thereby means to say. 'Thy limbs with those worthy of offering' he says, because it is with its limbs that they sacrifice: 'Obtain thou that they may sacrifice with thy limbs' is what he thereby means to say. 'The lord of sacrifice with his prayer,' hereby they invoke a blessing on the sacrificer: 'Obtain thou that through thee they may invoke a blessing on the sacrificer' is what he thereby means to say. He then deposits the two spoons and calls for the *S*ausha*t* with a view to the Pravara (election of the Hot*ri*)[1]. The significance of this is the same (as before).

10. Thereupon he calls a second time for the *S*rausha*t*, for on this occasion there are two Hot*ri*s: it is with regard to the Maitrâvaru*n*a[2] that he now calls for the *S*rausha*t*. But it is the sacrificer whom

[1] See I, 5, 1, 1 seq. (also note to part i, p. 115).

[2] The Maitrâvaru*n*a or Pra*s*âst*ri* is the Hot*ri*'s chief assistant. He receives, as the badge of his office, the staff which the sacrificer

he chooses, saying, 'Verily, Agni is the leader of the divine hosts,' for Agni is the head of the deities; wherefore he says, 'Verily, Agni is the leader of the divine hosts;'—'this sacrificer of the human;' for that community wherein he sacrifices is behind (inferior to) him; wherefore he says, 'This sacrificer (is the head) of the human.' 'May the household of these two shine brightly, not (like a cart yoked) with one bullock, for a hundred winters,—two yoke-fellows!' whereby he means to say, 'May their household matters be free from calamities for a hundred years[1].'

11. 'Uniting blessings, not uniting bodies;' whereby he means to say, 'Unite ye your blessings only, but not also your bodies;' for were they also to unite their bodies, Agni (the fire) would burn the sacrificer. Now when this one sacrifices in the fire, he gives gifts to Agni; and whatever blessing the priests here invoke upon the sacrificer, all that Agni accomplishes. Thus they unite only their blessings, but not also their bodies: wherefore he says, 'Uniting blessings, not uniting bodies.'

Eighth Adhyâya. First Brâhmana.

C. The Oblations.

1. Thereupon the Hotri, having sat down on the Hotri's seat whereon he sits down after being chosen[2],

held while he was consecrated, and has, at the instance of the Adhvaryu, to call on the Hotri for the offering-prayers,—his summons (praisha) beginning with Hotâ yakshat, 'let the Hotri worship (or, pronounce the offering-prayer) . . .,'—and occasionally himself to pronounce the invitatory prayer.

[1] See I, 9, 3, 19.

[2] Viz. at the north-west corner (or left hip) of the altar. For the formulas used by him, see I, 5, 1, 24–2, 1.

urges, and thus urged the Adhvaryu takes the two spoons.

2. They then proceed with the Âprî (verses). The reason why they proceed with the Âprîs is this. With his whole mind, with his whole self, forsooth, he who consecrates himself prepares and endeavours to prepare the sacrifice. His self is, as it were, emptied out; with those Âprîs they fill it again; and because they fill[1] it therewith, therefore they are called Âprî. For this reason they proceed with the Âprîs.

3. Now there are here eleven fore-offerings; for here in man there are ten vital airs, and the eleventh is the self wherein those vital airs are contained; this is the whole man; thus they fill his whole self, and therefore there are eleven fore-offerings.

4. [The Adhvaryu] having called (on the Âgnîdhra) for the *S*raushat, he says (to the Maitrâvaruna), 'Prompt (the Hotri to recite to) the kindling-sticks[2]!' Thus he proceeds with ten fore-offerings,

---

[1] The text has only 'âpyâyayanti,' but the verb with which the author connects the verb 'âprî' is either â-prinâti, he fills; or (more correctly) 'â-prînâti,' he gratifies, propitiates, corresponding to the Zand âfrînaiti. Perhaps some words have been lost here. The Kânva text has: sa yad etâbhir âprîbhih punar âpyâyata etâbhir enam âprînâti tasmâd âpriyo nâma. On the Âprî verses, which form the offering-prayers (yâgyâs) at the fore-offerings of the animal sacrifice, and vary according to different families, see Ait. Br. II, 4; Max Müller, Hist. of A. S. L., p. 463 seq.; Haug, Essays, p. 241.

[2] See I, 5, 3, 8. The Adhvaryu calls out to the Agnîdh, 'O srâvaya (make listen)!' The Agnîdh calls out, 'Astu *s*raushat (yea, may one hear)!' The Adhvaryu calls on the Maitrâvaruna, 'Preshya samidhah (prompt as to the kindling-sticks)!' [or, 'Preshya Tanûnapâtam or Narâsamsam' &c. in the succeeding fore-offerings.] The Maitrâvaruna calls out, 'Hotâ yakshat samidham [Tanûnapâtam, &c.], (let the Hotri pronounce the offering-prayer to the kindling-sticks, &c.!)' Each offering-prayer (Âprî) is introduced

saying, 'Prompt . . .' at each, and pouring the ghee together at every fourth fore-offering[1]. Having performed ten fore-offerings, he says, 'Bring the slayer!' 'Slayer,' namely, the (butcher's) knife is called.

5. He then takes the (svaru) chip of the sacrificial stake, and having anointed both (the slaughtering-knife and the chip) at the top (with ghee) from the guhû-spoon, he touches the forehead of the victim with them, saying (Vâg. S. VI, 11), 'Anointed with ghee, protect ye the animals!' for the chip of the stake is a thunderbolt, and the slaughtering-knife is a thunderbolt, and ghee is a thunderbolt; having thus fitted together the entire thunderbolt[2] he appoints it the keeper of this (victim), lest the evil spirits should injure it. He again conceals the chip of the stake (under the girding-rope of the stake). In handing the slaughtering-knife to the butcher, he says, 'Be this thine approved edge!' and deposits the two spoons.

6. Thereupon he says (to the Hotri), 'Recite to Agni circumambient[3]!' Having taken a firebrand,

with the formula 'Ye yagâmahe, &c.' See part i, p. 148 note. The divine objects of these oblations of ghee are: 1. the Samidhs or kindling-sticks; 2. either Tanûnapât or Narâsamsa; 3. the Idas; 4. the Barhis (sacrificial grass on the altar); 5. the gates (of heaven and worshipping-ground); 6. Dawn and Night; 7. the two divine Hotris; 8. the three goddesses (Sarasvatî, Idâ, and Bhâratî); 9. Tvashtri; 10. Vanaspati (the tree, or lord of the forest); 11. the Svâhâkritis (calls of 'All-hail,' which at this, the last offering-prayer, are repeated before the names of the principal deities of the sacrifice). For this last fore-offering, see III, 8, 2, 23 seq.

[1] See I, 5, 3, 16.

[2] For the three parts of the thunderbolt, see p. 108, note 2.

[3] The Hotri recites the triplet, Rig-veda IV, 15, 1-3.

the Agnîdh carries the fire round (the victim). Why he carries the fire round, is that he encircles it (the victim) by means of the fire with an unbroken fence, lest the evil spirits should seize upon it; for Agni is the repeller of the Rakshas; therefore he carries the fire round. He carries it round the place where they cook it (the victim[1]).

7. As to this they say, 'Let him take back that firebrand (to the Âhavanîya); and having there (at the *S*âmitra) churned out a new fire, let them cook it (the victim) thereon. For this (firebrand), surely, is âhavanîya (fit to offer upon); it is not for the purpose that they should cook uncooked (food) thereon, but for this that they should sacrifice cooked (food) thereon.'

8. Let him, however, not do this. For in that he carries fire round it, it (the victim) becomes as food swallowed by that (firebrand), and it would be as if he were to seize and tear out food that has been swallowed and offer it to some one else; let them, therefore, crumble some coals off that same firebrand, and thereon cook that (victim).

9. Thereupon the Agnîdh, taking a (new) firebrand, walks in front: whereby he places Agni in front, thinking, 'Agni shall repel the evil spirits in front!' and

[1] Sâya*n*a seems to take 'abhipariharati' in the sense of 'he takes it round to the place where they cook.' According to Kâty. VI, 5, 2, 3, the Agnîdh circumambulates thrice from left to right, either the place comprising the victim, the ghee, the slaughtering-place, the sacrificial post, the *k*âtvâla, and Âhavanîya; or only the ghee, the victim, and slaughtering-place. He then throws the firebrand back on the Âhavanîya, and performs the circumambulation as many times in the opposite direction. On the Paryagnikara*n*a, see also part i, p. 45 note.

they lead the victim after him (to the slaughtering-place) on a (way) free from danger and injury. The Pratiprasthât*ri* holds on to it from behind by means of the two spits[1], and the Adhvaryu (holds on to) the Pratiprasthât*ri*, and the Sacrificer to the Adhvaryu.

10. As to this they say, 'That (victim) must not be held on to by the sacrificer, for they lead it unto death; therefore let him not hold on to it.' But let him nevertheless hold on to it; for that (victim) which they lead to the sacrifice they lead not to death; therefore let him hold on to it. Moreover he would cut himself off from the sacrifice, were he not to hold on to it; therefore let him hold on to it. It is held on to in a mysterious way; by means of the spits the Pratiprasthât*ri* (holds on to it); to the Pratiprasthât*ri* the Adhvaryu, to the Adhvaryu the Sacrificer; thus then it is held on to in a mysterious way.

11. Thereupon the Adhvaryu takes two stalks of grass from the covered altar, and having called for the *S*rausha*t*, he says (to the Maitrâvaru*n*a), 'O Hot*ri*, prompt again (the Hot*ri* to recite for) the offerings to the gods[2]!' This is what belongs to the All-gods at the animal offering.

12. He then makes (the Sacrificer) say the text (Vâ*g*. S. VI, 11), 'O thou prosperous! upon

[1] For the two omentum-spits, see note on III, 8, 2, 16.

[2] The Maitrâvaru*n*a's additional cue or order (upapraisha) is 'Agni has been victorious; he has won wealth!' On the Hot*ri*'s recitation—the so-called Adhrigu litany—commencing 'Ye divine quieters (slaughterers), commence, as well as ye that are human!' and consisting of formulas usually pronounced by the Adhvaryu (and hence perhaps going back to a time when the Hot*ri* had to perform all but the menial parts of the sacrificial service), see Ait. Br. II, 6–7; Roth, Yâska XXXVII seq.

the Sacrificer,'—the prosperous one, forsooth, is Speech, it is because she speaks much, that Speech is prosperous,—'bestow thou what is agreeable unto him! Approach thou,'—thereby he means to say, 'Approach thou an existence free from affliction,'—'from the wide air, along with the divine wind;' for the Rakshas moves about the air rootless and unfettered on both sides, even as man here moves about the air rootless and unfettered on both sides: he means to say, 'Meeting together with the wind, protect thou this one from the wide air,' when he says 'from the wide air, along with the divine wind.'

13. 'Offer thou with the self of this oblation!' whereby he means to say to Speech, 'Offer thou with the soul of this unblemished oblation;'—'Unite thou with its body!' whereby he means to say to Speech, 'Unite thou with the body of this unblemished oblation!'

14. In front[1] of the place where they cut it up, he throws down a stalk of grass, with, 'O great one, lead the lord of sacrifice unto greater sacrifice!' he thus strews barhis (an underlayer of sacrificial grass) for it, that no sacrificial food may be spilt; whatever may now be spilt of it when it is cut up, that settles thereon and thus is not lost.

15. They then step back (to the altar) and sit down turning towards the Âhavanîya, 'lest they should be eye-witnesses to its being quieted (strangled).' They do not slay it on the frontal bone[2], for that is human

[1] According to Kâty. VI, 5, 15, the stalk is put down behind the *S*âmitra (i. e. the fire at the slaughtering-place) with the top towards the east.

[2] Lit. 'by means of the frontal bone.' Sâya*n*a explains it by 'in

manner; nor behind the ear, for that is after the manner of the Fathers. They either choke it by merely keeping its mouth closed, or they make a noose. Therefore he says not, 'Slay! kill!' for that is human manner, but, 'Quiet it! It has passed away!' for that is after the manner of the gods. For when he says, 'It has passed away,' then this one (the Sacrificer) passes away to the gods: therefore he says, 'It has passed away.'

16. When they hold it down, then, before the strangling, he offers with 'Hail, to the gods!' And when (the butcher) says, 'Quieted is the victim,' he offers with, 'To the gods, Hail!' Thus some of the gods are preceded by 'Hail,' and others followed by 'Hail;' he thereby gratifies them, and thus gratified both kinds of gods convey him to the heavenly world. These are the so-called 'paripasavya[1]' oblations; he may offer them if he choose; or, if he choose, he need not mind them.

Second Brâhmana.

1. When he (the slaughterer) announces, 'The victim has been quieted!' the Adhvaryu says, 'Neshtar, lead up the lady!' The Neshtri leads up the (sacrificer's) wife bearing a vessel of water for washing the feet.

2. He makes her say (Vâg. S. VI, 12), 'Homage be to thee, O wide-stretched!'—the wide-stretched one, forsooth, is the sacrifice; for they stretch the sacrifice (over the sacrificial ground):

seizing it by the horn;' Professor Weber, Ind. Stud. IX, p. 222, 'by striking it with a horn.' The Kânva text reads, tasya na kûtena praghnanti mânusham ha kuryâd yad asya kûtena prahanyuh.

[1] That is, surrounding, relating to, the victim.

hence the wide-stretched one is the sacrifice. But that wife, forsooth, is the hind-part of the sacrifice, and he wants her, thus coming forward, to propitiate the sacrifice. Thereby, then, she makes amends to that sacrifice, and thus that sacrifice does not injure her: therefore she says, 'Homage be to thee, O wide-stretched!'

3. 'Advance, unresisted!' whereby she means to say, 'Advance on (a way) free from injury!' 'Unto the rivers of ghee, along the paths of sacred truth!' whereby she means to say, 'Unto good.' [Vâg. S. VI, 13], 'Ye divine, pure waters, carry ye (the sacrifice) to the gods, well-prepared! May we be well-prepared preparers!' Thereby she purifies the water.

4. Thereupon the wife cleanses with the water the (openings of the) vital airs of the victim. The reason why she thus cleanses with water the (openings of the) vital airs is this: the food of the gods is living, is immortal (ambrosia) for the immortals; but in quieting and cutting up that victim they kill it. Now the vital airs are water; hence she now puts into it those vital airs, and thus that food of the gods becomes truly living, becomes immortal for the immortals.

5. Then as to why it is the wife that cleanses. The wife is a woman, and from woman progeny is born here on earth; thus he causes that (creature) to be born from that woman; and therefore the wife cleanses (the victim).

6. With (Vâg. S. VI, 14) 'Thy speech I cleanse' she wipes the mouth; with 'Thy breath I cleanse,' the nostrils; with 'Thine eye I cleanse,' the eyes; with 'Thine organ of hearing I cleanse,' the

ears; with 'Thy navel I cleanse,' that mysterious (opening of a) vital air; or with 'Thy sexual organ I cleanse;' with 'Thy hind-part I cleanse,' that (opening of a) vital air behind. Thus she puts the vital airs into it, revives it. Thereupon, holding the legs together, (she wipes them) with 'Thy feet I cleanse;' for it is on its feet that it stands firmly; she thus makes it stand (on its feet) for the sake of a firm position.

7. With one half or the whole of the water that is left, he (the Adhvaryu) and the Sacrificer[1] then sprinkle it, beginning from the head; thereby they put those vital airs into it, and revive it (beginning) from that part.

8. Thus, wherever they wound it[2], wherever they hurt it—water being a means of soothing—there they soothe it by that means of soothing, water, there they heal it with water.

9. They sprinkle with (Vâ*g*. S. VI, 15), 'May thy mind grow full! may thy speech grow full! may thy breath grow full! may thine eye grow full! may thine ear grow full!' Thus they put the vital airs into it and revive it: 'Whatever is sore, whatever hurt in thee, may that fill up and become firm.'

10. Thus, wherever they wound it, wherever they hurt it—water being a means of soothing—they soothe it by that means of soothing, water, there

[1] Or, perhaps, she and the sacrificer, as Sâya*n*a takes it (ya*g*amâna*h* patnî *k*a). Kâty. VI, 6, 4 leaves it doubtful; but the commentator interprets the rule as referring to the Adhvaryu and Sacrificer, in accordance with the reading of the Kâ*n*va text—'atha yâ*h* pari*s*ish*t*â âpo bhavanti tâbhir adhvaryu*s* *k*a ya*g*amâna*s* *k*ânushi*ñk*ata*h*.'

[2] Âsthâpayanti = sa*mgñ*apayanti, Sâya*n*a.

they heal it with water: 'May that become pure in thee!' thereby they render it sacrificially pure. With 'Auspicious be the days!' they pour out (the remaining water) behind the victim.

11. Thus, wherever they wound it, wherever they hurt it,—lest thereafter the days and nights should be inauspicious[1],—they pour out (the water) behind the victim with, 'Auspicious be the days.'

12. Thereupon they turn the victim over so as to lie on its back. He (the Adhvaryu) puts the (other) stalk of grass thereon, with, 'O plant, protect!' for the knife is a thunderbolt, and thus that thunderbolt, the knife, does not injure it (the victim). He then applies the edge of the knife to it (and cuts through it) with, 'Injure it not, O blade!' for the knife is a thunderbolt, and thus that thunderbolt, the knife, does not injure it.

13. He applies that approved edge of his, for that has been made sacrificially pure by a text[2]. That which is the top part of the stalk he puts in his left hand, and that which is the bottom part he takes with his right hand.

14. And where he skins (the victim), and whence the blood spirts out, there he smears it (the bottom part with blood) on both ends with (Vâg. S. VI, 16), 'Thou art the Rakshas' share!' for that blood is indeed the Rakshas' share.

15. Having thrown it away (on the utkara), he treads on it with, 'Herewith I tread down the Rakshas! herewith I drive away the Rakshas! herewith I consign the Rakshas to the

---

[1] Ned idam anv ahorâtrâni sokân iti, Kânva recension.

[2] See III, 8, 1, 5.

nethermost darkness!' Thus it is by means of the sacrifice that he drives away the evil spirits, the Rakshas. And as to its being rootless and severed on both sides,—rootless, forsooth, and severed on both sides, the Rakshas moves about in the air, even as man here moves about in the air rootless and severed on both sides: therefore it (the grass-end) is rootless and severed on both sides.

16. Thereupon they pull out the omentum, and envelop the two spits[1] therein with, 'May ye envelop heaven and earth with ghee!' whereby he endows those two, heaven and earth, with strength and sap, and puts strength and sap into them; and upon those two, thus filled with sap and affording the means of subsistence, these creatures subsist.

17. The two omentum-spits are made of kârshmarya wood. For when the gods in the beginning seized (slew) a victim, then, as it was drawn upwards, its sacrificial essence[2] flowed downwards, and from it sprang a tree; and because it flowed down from the (victim) as it was drawn (karsh) upwards, therefore (it became) a kârshmarya tree[3]. With that

---

[1] The two vapâsrapanîs (omentum-roasters) consist of sticks of kârshmarya wood (Gmelina Arborea), one of them being quite straight, while the other is bifurcate at the top, thus resembling a prop.

[2] Or, its flesh-juice, medha. The Kânva text reads throughout medhas.

[3] The Kânva text has the preferable reading,—Sa yat krishyamânât samabhavat tasmât kârshmaryo nâma, 'and because it sprang from that drawn-up (victim), therefore it is called kârshmarya.'

same sacrificial essence he now perfects it, and makes it whole; therefore the two omentum-spits are of kârshmarya wood.

18. He cuts it (the omentum) off on all sides (from the belly) and heats it at the cooking-fire: thus it becomes cooked for him already at this (fire)[1]. The Agnîdh again takes a firebrand (from the *S*âmitra, and walks in front). They go behind the pit (*k*âtvâla) and proceed to the Âhavanîya. The Adhvaryu throws that (top part of the) grass-stalk into the Âhavanîya with, 'O Vâyu, graciously accept the drops!' for this is the kindler (samidh) of the drops[2].

19. Thereupon he heats the omentum while standing on the north side; for he is about to pass by the fire and to roast (the omentum) after walking round to the south side. Hereby then he propitiates it, and thus that fire does not injure him while passing by; this is why he heats the omentum while standing on the north side.

20. They take it along between the sacrificial stake and the fire. The reason why they do not take it across the middle (of the altar)[3], where they take other sacrificial dishes, is lest they should bring the sacrifice in the middle into contact with the uncooked (omentum). And why they do not take it there outside (the altar) along the front of the sacrificial stake, is that they would thereby put it outside the sacrifice; therefore they take it along

---

[1] [He does so, thinking], 'Lest I should cook it on the Âhavanîya uncooked.' Kâ*n*va rec.

[2] 'For it is for the drops that he thus lights it.' Kâ*n*va rec.

[3] That is, across the altar immediately behind the fire or high altar.

between the sacrificial stake and the fire. Having gone round to the south side, the Pratiprasthâtri roasts it.

21. Thereupon the Adhvaryu, having taken ghee with the dipping-spoon, pours it upon the omentum, with, 'May Agni graciously accept the ghee, Hail!' Thus those drops thereof reach the fire after becoming cooked offerings, made with Svâhâ (hail)!

22. He then says (to the Maitrâvaruna[1]), 'Recite to the drops!' He recites to the drops verses addressed to Agni[2]. The reason why he recites to the drops verses addressed to Agni, is that rain originates from gifts made from this earth, for from here it is that Agni obtains the rain; by means of these drops (falling from the omentum) he obtains those (rain) drops, and those drops rain down; therefore he recites to the drops verses addressed to Agni. When it is roasted,—

23. The Pratiprasthâtri says, 'It is roasted: proceed[3]!' The Adhvaryu, having taken the two spoons and stept across (to the north side of the fire) and called for the Sraushat, says (to the Maitrâvaruna), 'Prompt for the Svâhâs[4]!' and offers (the ghee) when the Vashat has been pronounced[5].

[1] Thus according to the commentator on Kâty. VI, 6, 18. See also note on IV, 2, 5, 22, and Haug, Transl. Ait. Br. p. 101 note.

[2] The (invitatory) formulas are Rig-veda I, 75, 1, and III, 21, 1–5; Ait. Br. II, 12; Âsv. Sr. III, 4, 1.

[3] The Pratiprasthâtri withdraws the omentum from the fire, and takes it (between fire and stake) to the north of the pit, where the Adhvaryu in the first place performs the so-called prânadâna (vol. i, p. 438 note), after which he deposits it on the altar. Kâty. VI, 6, 20.

[4] That is, for the offering-prayer or yâgyâ of the last fore-offering, being the last verse of whatever âprî hymn may be used; followed by a number of Svâhâs, each with the name of some deity or deities (cf. I, 5, 3, 22–23).

[5] Cf. Haug, Transl. Ait. Br. p. 100, note 4.

24. Having offered, he bastes first the omentum, then the clotted ghee. Now the *K*araka-Adhvaryus, forsooth, baste first the clotted ghee, arguing that the clotted ghee is the breath; and a *K*araka-Adhvaryu, forsooth, cursed Yâ*gñ*avalkya for so doing, saying, 'That Adhvaryu has shut out the breath; the breath shall depart from him!'

25. But he, looking at his arms, said, 'These hoary arms—what in the world has become of the Brâhman's word[1]!' Let him not heed that (objection of the *K*arakas); for this is the last fore-offering,—and this being a havis-offering, at the last fore-offering he first pours ghee into the dhruvâ, being about to offer the first two butter-portions with it[2]. Now, on the present occasion, he will first offer the omentum; therefore let him first baste the omentum, then the clotted ghee. And though he does not baste the victim with ghee, 'lest he should baste the uncooked,' that whole victim of his yet becomes (as it were) basted with ghee in that he bastes the omentum; let him therefore first baste the omentum, then the clotted ghee.

26. Thereupon he makes an 'underlayer' of ghee (in the *g*uhû-spoon), and lays a piece of gold thereon. Then, cutting off the omentum (from the spits and putting it into the spoon), he says (to the Hot*ri*), 'Recite (the invitatory prayer) to Agni and Soma

[1] That is, so much time has gone by since I first adopted that practice, and here I am grown old and still in full vigour, Sây. 'But he, lying old and worn out, said, "These two arms have become gray—what in the world has become of the Brâhman's word!"' Kâ*n*va text.

[2] On the two butter-portions to Agni and Soma, succeeding the fore-offerings, see part i, p. 174 note.

for the omentum and fat of the buck!' He then lays (another) piece of gold on (the omentum) and bastes it twice with ghee above.

27. The reason why there is a piece of gold on both sides is this. When they offer the victim in the fire they slay it; and gold means immortal life: hence it (the victim) rests in immortal life. And so it rises from hence, and so it lives; for this reason there is a piece of gold[1] on both sides. Having called for the *S*rausha*t*, he says (to the Maitrâvaru*n*a), 'Prompt (the Hot*ri* to recite the offering-prayer[2] on) the omentum and fat of the buck for Agni and Soma!' He does not say, '... (the omentum and fat) brought forward;' when the Soma has been pressed he says, 'brought forward[3].' He offers when the Vasha*t* has been pronounced.

28. Having offered the omentum, he lays the two spits together and throws them after (the omentum into the fire), with, 'Consecrated by Svâhâ, go ye to Ûrdhvanabhas[4], son of the Maruts!' He does so, thinking, 'Lest these two wherewith we have cooked the omentum should come to nought.'

29. The reason why they perform with the omentum is this. For whatever deity the victim is seized, that same deity he pleases by means of that fat (part); and that same deity, thus pleased with that fat, waits

---

[1] The Kâ*n*va text has 'hira*n*ya*s*alká (masc.)' here and elsewhere.

[2] The anuvâkyâ and yâ*g*yâ for the omentum are Rig-veda I, 93, 1 and 5 respectively.

[3] At the animal offerings on the Soma-days he adds to his praisha (order) the word 'prasthitam,' lit. standing before (the altar). Kâty. VI, 6, 27. See also *S*. Br. IV, 4, 3, 9.

[4] Ûrdhvanabhas, 'he who drives the clouds upwards' (or, keeps the clouds above), or, perhaps, 'he who is above (in) the welkin,' is apparently a name of Vâyu, the wind. Cf. III, 6, 1, 16.

patiently for the other sacrificial dishes being cooked; this is why they perform with the omentum.

30. They then cleanse themselves over the pit[1]. For in quieting and cutting up (the victim) they wound it; and water being a means of soothing, they now soothe it by means of water, heal it by means of water; therefore they cleanse themselves over the pit.

Third Brâhmana.

1. For the same deity for which there is a victim, he subsequently prepares a sacrificial cake[2]. The reason why he subsequently prepares a cake is this. Rice and barley, truly, are the sacrificial essence of all animals (victims)[3]; with that same essence he now completes that (victim) and makes it whole. This is why he subsequently prepares a sacrificial cake.

2. And why he proceeds with that cake after performing (offering) with the omentum is this. It is from the middle (of the victim) that this omentum is pulled out, and from the middle he now completes that (victim) by means of that sacrificial essence and makes it whole; therefore he proceeds with that cake after performing with the omentum. The relation of

---

[1] They do so with the mantra, Vâg. S. VI, 17 (Atharva-veda VII, 89, 3; cf. Rig-veda I, 23, 22; X, 9, 8).

[2] The technical name of this cake to Indra and Agni is pasupurodâsa (animal-cake). The anuvâkyâ and yâgyâ for the chief oblation, are Rig-veda I, 93, 2 and 6 respectively; for the Svishtakrit, III, 1, 23, and III, 54, 22; Âsv. III, 8, 1; 5, 9. For a similar performance, described in detail, see note on III, 2, 5, 22.

[3] On the sacrificial essence passing successively from man into the horse, the ox, the goat, and finally into the rice and barley, see I, 2, 3, 6–7.

this (cake to the animal offering), indeed, is one and the same everywhere; that cake is prepared after (and supplementary to) a victim.

3. Thereupon he cuts up the victim: 'Move thrice[1], and make the heart the uppermost of the thrice-moved!' thus (he says to the slaughterer), for threefold is the sacrifice.

4. He then instructs the slaughterer: 'If one ask thee, "Is the sacrificial food cooked, O Samitar?" say thou only "Cooked!" not "Cooked, reverend sir!" nor "Cooked, forsooth!"'

---

[1] The order of proceeding is not quite clear from the context, and seems to have puzzled the later ritualists. From Kâty. VI, 7–8 it would seem that the author of the Sûtras means the performance of the cake-offering to go on simultaneously with the cutting up of the victim (and the cooking of the portions and roasting of the beast). The comm. on Kâty. VI, 7, 29, however, protests against this arrangement as contrary to the order laid down in the Brâhmana; and insists especially on the 'atha (now)' at the beginning of this paragraph. This particle is, however, often used in a vague sense; as very frequently when, after sketching the chief course of performance, the author turns back to fill in the details. There seems also a difference of opinion as to the exact meaning of the above direction given by the Adhvaryu to the Samitar after (as would seem) the portions have been cooked. The commentator on Kâty. VI, 8, 1 apparently takes 'trih prakyâvaya' in the sense of 'shake thrice' or 'turn thrice.' Sâyana, on the other hand, explains it as meaning that the Samitri is to divide the portions into three parts, according to whether they are destined for the chief offerings, or the Svishtakrit, or the by-offerings (?). As the direction cannot refer to the taking out of the portions from the cooking-vessel (ukhâ) it would seem that the Samitar is either to move (shake) the vessel itself, or to stir the contents, perhaps hereby separating the respective portions. The Kânva text reads, Trih prakyâvayâd ity uttame prakyâva uttamârdhe hridayam kurutâd iti. The heart, when done, is to be removed from the spit and laid on the portions; whereupon the Adhvaryu pours ghee on the portions (paragraph 8).

5. Having then taken clotted ghee with the *g*uhû, the Adhvaryu, stepping up (from the altar) to (the *S*âmitra), asks, 'Is the sacrificial food cooked, O *S*âmitar?' 'Cooked,' he says. 'That is of the gods,' says the Adhvaryu in a low voice.

6. The reason why he asks is this. Cooked, forsooth, not uncooked (must be) the gods' food; and the *S*amit*ri* indeed knows whether it is cooked or uncooked.

7. And again, why he asks. 'I will perform with cooked (food),' so he thinks; and if that sacrificial food be uncooked, it is yet cooked food for the gods, and is cooked as regards the Sacrificer; and the Adhvaryu is guiltless; on the slaughterer that guilt lies. Thrice he asks, for threefold is the sacrifice. And as to his saying, 'That is of the gods,' that which is cooked, indeed, belongs to the gods; therefore he says, 'That is of the gods.'

8. The heart he bastes (with clotted ghee) first of all; for the heart is the self (soul), the mind; and the clotted ghee is the breath; he thus puts the breath into its (the victim's) self, into its mind; and thus it verily becomes the living food of the gods, and immortal for the immortals.

9. He bastes it with (Vâ*g*. S. VI, 18), 'May thy mind unite with the mind; thy breath with the breath!' He utters no Svâhâ ('hail'), for this is not an oblation. They remove the victim (from the cooking-fire)[1].

10. They take it along the back of the pit, and

[1] The Adhvaryu removes the dish northwards from the fire, takes the portions out of it, puts them into some kind of basket, and performs 'prâ*n*adâna' (p. 196, note 3) on them.

between the sacrificial stake and the (Âhavanîya) fire. The reason why, though it is cooked, they do not take it across the middle (of the altar), as they take other sacrificial dishes, is 'lest they should bring the sacrifice in the middle in connection with that which is cut up by limbs and mangled.' And why they do not take it outside (the altar) in front of the stake, is that they would thereby put it outside the sacrifice: therefore they take (the flesh) along between the stake and the fire. When they have put it down south (of the fire), the Pratiprasthâtri cuts off (the portions). There are Plaksha branches[1] (Ficus Infectoria) by way of an upper barhis (covering of altar); thereon he cuts. The reason why there are Plaksha branches by way of an upper barhis is this.

11. For when the gods, at first, seized an animal (to sacrifice), Tvashtri first spat upon its head, thinking, 'Surely, thus they will not touch it!' for animals belong to Tvashtri. That (spittle became) the brain in the head and the marrow in the neck-bone[2]: hence that (substance) is like spittle, for Tvashtri spat it. Let him therefore not eat that, since it was spitten by Tvashtri.

12. Its sacrificial essence flowed down and there a tree sprang up. The gods beheld it; wherefore it (was called) 'prakhya' (visible), for 'plaksha,'

[1] Or, the Plaksha branches with which the altar was covered on the preceding night. See p. 120, note 3. The Kânva text (as Taitt. S. VI, 3, 10, 2) speaks of one Plaksha branch put on the barhis.

[2] Anûka, of which anûkya is the adjective, means 'the fore-part of the spinal column.' The Kânva text reads,—yan mastishko yad anûke maggâ.

doubtless, is the same as 'prakhya.' With that same sacrificial essence he now completes it (the victim), and makes it whole: hence there are Plaksha branches as an upper covering.

13. He then makes an 'underlayer' of ghee both in the guhû and the upabhrit, and in the vasâhomahavanî[1], and the samavattadhânî[2]; and puts a piece of gold[3] both in the guhû and the upabhrit.

14. Thereupon he addresses (the Hotri) for the recitation on the havis to the manotâ deity[4]. The reason why he addresses him for the recitation on the havis to the manotâ deity is this. All the deities draw nigh to the victim while it is immolated, thinking, 'My name he will choose, my name he will choose!' for the animal victim is sacrificial food for all deities. The minds (manas), then, of all those deities are fixed upon (ota) that victim; those (minds of theirs) he thereby satisfies, and thus the minds of the gods have not drawn nigh in vain. For this reason he addresses him for the recitation on the havis to the manotâ deity.

---

[1] That is, the ladle used (as a substitute for the guhû) for offering the fat-liquor or gravy. See paragraph 20.

[2] That is, the vessel used for holding the cuttings (samavatta) of the idâ; also called idâpâtrî, see part i, p. 219, note 3.

[3] See p. 198, note 1.

[4] Thereupon he says, 'Recite to the manotâ (deity) the invitatory prayer for (of) the havis which is being cut in portions (havisho 'vadîyamânasya).' Kânva text; cf. Ait. Br. II, 10.—While the sacrificial portions are being cut into the respective spoons, the Hotri recites the Hymn to Agni, Rig-veda VI, 1, 1-13, beginning, 'Thou, O wondrous Agni, the first thinker (manotri) of this hymn, wert verily the priest. . . .' From the occurrence of this word manotâ, the latter has come to be the technical name both of the hymn itself and of the deity (Agni) to whom it is recited.

15. He first makes a portion of the heart[1]. The reason why he first makes a portion of the heart which is in the middle, is that the heart is the breath, since it is from there that this breath moves upward[2]; and the animal is breath, for only so long does the animal (live) as it breathes with the breath; but when the breath departs from it, it lies there useless, even (as) a block of wood.

16. The heart, then, is the animal; thus he first makes a portion of its very self (or soul). And, accordingly, if any portion were omitted, he need not heed this, since it is of his entire animal victim that the first portion is made which is made of the heart. He therefore first makes a portion of the heart, that being in the middle. Thereupon according to the proper order.

17. Then of the tongue, for that stands out from its fore-part. Then of the breast, for that also (stands out) therefrom[3]. Then of the simultaneously moving (left) fore-foot[4]. Then of the flanks. Then of the liver. Then of the kidneys.

18. The hind-part he divides into three parts; the broad piece (he reserves) for the by-offerings[5]; the middle one he cuts into the *g*uhû after dividing it in two; the narrow piece (he reserves) for the

---

[1] Literally, he makes a cutting of the heart (h*ri*dayasya-avadyati), that is to say, he puts the entire heart into the *g*uhû as an offering-portion.

[2] Etasmâd dhy ayam ûrdhva*h* prâ*n*a u*kk*arati, Kâ*n*va rec.

[3] Or, that (comes) after that (tongue): tad dhi tato 'nvak, Kâ*n*va rec.

[4] According to Kâty. VI, 7, 6, it is the foremost (or upper) joint (pûrvana*d*aka) of the left fore-foot which is taken. The Kâ*n*va text has simply 'atha dosh*n*a*h*.'

[5] See III, 8, 4, 9 seq.

tryaṅga[1]. Then of the simultaneously moving (right) haunch[2]. This much, then, he cuts into the *g*uhû.

19. Then into the upabh*ri*t, he makes a portion of the upper part of the fore-foot belonging to the tryaṅga (viz. the right one); of the (narrow piece of the) hind-part, after dividing it in two; and of the haunch belonging to the tryaṅga (viz. the left). Thereupon he puts two pieces of gold on (the flesh oblations in the spoons) and pours ghee thereon.

20. He then takes the oblation of gravy[3] with (Vâ*g*. S. VI, 18), 'Thou art trembling,' for quivering, as it were, is the broth: hence he says, 'Thou art trembling;'—'May Agni prepare[4] thee!' for the fire does indeed cook it: hence he says, 'May Agni prepare thee!'—'The waters have washed thee together,' for the water indeed gathers together that (fat) juice from the limbs: hence he says, 'The waters have washed thee together.'

21. 'For the sweeping of the wind—thee!' for verily yonder blower sweeps along the air, and for the air he takes it: hence he says, 'For the sweeping of the wind (I take) thee.'

22. 'For the speed of Pûshan,'—Pûshan's speed, forsooth, is yonder (wind)[5], and for that he takes it: hence he says, 'For the speed of Pûshan.'

---

[1] Literally, the three-limbs, the technical name of the portion for Agni Svish*t*akr*i*t.

[2] For 'athaika*k*arâyai *s*ro*neh*' the Kâ*n*va text reads 'áthā́dhyû-dhasa*h* *s*ró*neh*,' of the hip above the udder.

[3] Vasâ, i.e. the melted fat (and juice) mixed with the water in which the portions have been cooked, and forming a rich gravy, offered with the Vasâhomahavanî.

[4] Literally, 'mix'—*s*rî, this root being here, as usual, confounded with *sri*, to cook.

[5] Esha vâva pûshâ yo 'yam pavata etasmâ u hi g*ri*h*n*âti, Kâ*n*va recension.

23. 'From the hot vapour may totter—;' the hot vapour, namely, is yonder (wind), and for that he takes it: hence he says, 'From the hot vapour may totter—.' Thereupon he bastes it twice with ghee above.

24. He then mixes it either with the crooked knife or with the chopping-knife[1], with '—Confounded hatred[2]!' whereby he chases away from here those evil spirits, the Rakshas.

25. The broth which is left he pours into the Samavattadhânî, and therein he throws the heart, tongue, breast, the broad piece (of the back part), the kidneys, and the rectum. He then bastes it twice with ghee above.

26. The reason why there is a piece of gold on each side is this. When they offer up the victim in the fire, they slay it, and gold means immortal life: thereby then it rests in immortal life; and so it rises from hence, and so it lives. This is why there is a piece of gold on each side.

27. And because he cuts crossways,—of the left fore-foot and the right haunch; and of the right fore-foot and the left haunch,—therefore this animal draws forward its feet crossways. But were he to cut straight on, this animal would draw forward its feet (of the same side) simultaneously: therefore he cuts crossways. Then as to why he does not make cuttings of the head, nor the shoulders, nor the neck, nor the hind-thighs.

---

[1] *S*âsena vâ pârsvena vâ, Kâ*n*va text.

[2] This forms part of the preceding formula (as subject to the verb 'may totter'), though the author seems to separate it therefrom, as does Mahîdhara. The meaning of the formula seems to be, 'May the enemies perish, confounded by (?) the hot vapour!'

28. Now the Asuras, in the beginning, seized a victim. The gods, from fear, did not go near it[1]. The Earth[2] then said unto them, 'Heed ye not this: I will myself be an eye-witness thereof, in whatsoever manner they will perform this (offering).'

29. She said, 'Only one oblation have they offered, the other they have left over.' Now that which they left over are these same portions. Thereupon the gods made over three limbs to (Agni) Svish*t*ak*ri*t, whence the Tryaṅga oblations. The Asuras then made portions of the head, the shoulders, the neck, and the hind-thighs: therefore let him not make portions of these. And since Tvash*tri* spat upon the neck, therefore let him not make a portion of the neck. Thereupon he says (to the Hot*ri*), 'Recite (the invitatory prayer) to Agni and Soma for the havis of the buck!' Having called for the *S*rausha*t*, he says (to the Maitrâvaru*n*a), 'Prompt (the Hot*ri* to recite the offering-prayer[3] for) the havis of the buck to Agni and Soma!' He does not say '(the havis) made ready:' when the Soma has been pressed he says 'made ready.'

30. In the interval between the two half-verses of the offering-prayer he offers the oblation of gravy. It is from out of this that that essence (juice) has risen upwards here,—that sap of this earth whereby creatures exist on this side of the sky[4]; for the

[1] The St. Petersburg Dict. takes 'Na-upâveyu*h*' in the sense of 'they did not fall in therewith; they did not feel inclined for it;' as above, III, 7, 3, 3. Sâya*n*a explains it by 'nopâgatâ*h*' (MSS. nâpâgatâ*h*).

[2] That is, Aditi, according to the Kâ*n*va recension.

[3] The yâ*g*yâ and anuvâkyâ are I, 93, 3 and 7 respectively.

[4] Ito vâ ayam ûrdhva u*kkhri*to raso yam idam imâ*h* pra*g*â upa*g*îvanty arvâg divo 'sminn antarikshe, Kâ*n*va recension.

oblation of gravy is sap, and essence is sap: thus he renders the sap strong by means of sap, whence this sap when eaten does not perish.

31. And as to why he offers the oblation of gravy in the interval between the two half-verses of the offering-prayer,—one half-verse, forsooth, is this earth, and the other half-verse is yonder sky. Now between the sky and the earth is the air, and it is to the air that he offers: therefore he offers the oblation of gravy between the two half-verses of the offering-prayer.

32. He offers with (Vâ*g*. S. VI, 19), 'Drink the ghee, ye drinkers of ghee! Drink the gravy, ye drinkers of gravy! thou art the havis of the air, Hail!' With this prayer to the All-gods he offers, for the air belongs to the All-gods: because creatures move about here in the air breathing in and breathing out therewith, therefore it belongs to the All-gods. As the Vasha*t* (of the offering-prayer for the meat portions) is pronounced, he offers the portions that are in the *g*uhû.

33. Thereupon, while taking clotted ghee with the *g*uhû, he says (to the Hot*ri*), 'Recite (the invitatory prayer) to the Lord of the forest!' Having called for the *S*rausha*t*, he says (to the Maitrâvaru*n*a), 'Prompt (the Hot*ri* to recite the offering-prayer) to the lord of the forest!' and offers, as the Vasha*t* is pronounced[1]. The reason why he offers to the lord of the forest (the tree) is,—he thereby makes that thunderbolt, the sacrificial stake, a sharer (in the sacrifice); and, the lord of the forest being Soma[2],

[1] For the formulas used with this oblation, as well as the Svish*t*a-k*ri*t, see Haug, Transl. Ait. Br. pp. 95–96 notes.

[2] Or, Soma being a tree (plant).

he thereby makes the victim to be Soma. And as to his offering (to the tree) between the two oblations, he thus fills both completely: therefore he offers between the two oblations.

34. Thereupon, while pouring together the meat portions that are for the upabh*ri*t, he says (to the Hot*ri*), 'Recite (the invitatory prayer) to Agni Svish*t*ak*ri*t (the maker of good offering)!' Having called for the *S*rausha*t*, he says (to the Maitrâvaru*n*a), 'Prompt for Agni Svish*t*ak*ri*t!' and offers as the Vasha*t* is pronounced.

35. With what is left of the offering of gravy, he then sprinkles the quarters, with, 'The regions,—the fore-regions,—the by-regions,—the intermediate regions,—the upper regions,—to the regions, Hail!' For the offering of gravy is sap: thus he imbues all the regions with sap, and hence sap is obtained here on earth in every region.

36. Thereupon he touches (what remains of) the victim[1]: now is the time for the touching. And whether he has touched it before, fearing 'those (evil spirits) that hover near will tear it about,' or whether he be not afraid[2] of its being torn about, let him in any case now touch (the victim).

---

[1] This touching takes place either before or after the invocation of I*d*â (see I, 8, 1, 1 seq.), whereupon the priests and sacrificer eat their respective portions; the straight gut being the Agnîdh's, the part above the udder (adhyûdhnî) the Hot*ri*'s, the kloman (apparently the right lung) the Brahman's, the pericardium (? purîtat) the Adhvaryu's, and the spleen the sacrificer's share, while the I*d*â is eaten by all of them.

[2] Or perhaps,—And as to his touching it before this, (he did so) fearing lest those (evil spirits) that hover near would tear it about; and even if he be not (any longer?) afraid of its being torn about, let him now touch it in any case. The Kâ*n*va text has simply,—

37. [Vâ*g*. S. VI, 20], 'To Indra belongeth the out-breathing: may it attend[1] to every limb! To Indra belongeth the in-breathing: it is attended to in every limb.' Where it has been cut up limb by limb, there he heals it by means of the out-breathing and in-breathing.—'O divine Tvash*tri*, let thine ample (forms) closely unite together, that it be uniform what is of different shape:' whereby he makes it completely enclosed (in its limbs and flesh). 'May thy friends, thy father and mother[2], to please thee, joyfully welcome thee going to the gods!' Thus, having made it whole wherever he has offered (a piece of) it, he afterwards unites it firmly, and that body (self) of it is complete in yonder world.

FOURTH BRÂHMA*N*A.

1. Now there are three elevens at the animal offering,—eleven fore-offerings, eleven after-offerings, and eleven by-offerings: ten fingers, ten toes, ten vital airs, and the out-breathing, in-breathing and through-breathing—this much constitutes man, who is the highest of animals, after whom[3] are all animals.

This is the time for touching; but if he think, 'Those standing about here will meddle with it,' he may also touch it before: but this is certainly the time for touching.

[1] The St. Petersburg Dictionary suggests that 'nidîdhyat' and 'nidhîta' are probably corruptions of forms from 'dhâ;' the Taitt. S. (I, 3, 10) having 'ni dedhyat—vi bobhuvat' instead. Mahîdhara also takes 'nidîdhyat' from 'dhî' in the sense of 'dhâ,'—'Indra's out-breathing is infused into every limb; Indra's in-breathing has been infused into every limb.' The Kâ*n*va text has '-nidhîta*h*, -nidîdhe.'

[2] Rather, 'the mothers (or mother) and fathers.' The Taitt. S. separates mâtâ pitara*h*, the mother and the fathers.'

[3] That is, inferior to whom, or, after the manner of whom.

2. Now they say, 'What, then, is done at the sacrifice whereby the vital air is kindly to all the limbs?'

3. When he divides the hind-part into three portions,—the hind-part being (an opening of the) vital air, and that (animal) extending from thence forward, that vital air pervades it all through.

4. And in that he cuts the hind-part into three portions,—one third for the by-offerings, one third into the guhû, and one third into the upabhrit,—thereby the vital air is kindly to all the limbs.

5. He alone, however, may slay an animal who can supply it with the sacrificial essence[1]. And if it be lean, let him stuff into the hind-part whatever may be left of the fat of the belly: the hind-part being (an opening of) the vital air, and that (animal) extending from thence forward, that vital air pervades it all through. The animal, forsooth, is breath; for only so long (does) the animal (live), as it breathes with the breath; but when the breath departs from it, it lies there useless, even (as) a block of wood.

6. The hind-part is (part of) the animal, and fat means sacrificial essence[2]: thus he supplies it with the sacrificial essence. But if it be tender (juicy), then it has itself obtained the sacrificial essence.

7. Thereupon he takes clotted ghee; for twofold indeed is this (clotted ghee),—to wit, both ghee

[1] Sâyana takes 'medham' as apposition to 'enam,' and explains it by 'medhârha, pravriddha,' and 'upanayet' by 'prâpnuyât' (it is, doubtless, 'zuführen'). The Kânva text, however, reads,—Tad âhuh sa vai pasum labheteti ya enam medha upanayed iti.

[2] Gudo vai pasuh, medo vai medhas; this is one of many exceptions to the rule laid down by Professor Delbrück regarding the order of subject and predicate, Synt. Forsch., III, p. 26. Copulative sentences with a tertium comparationis likewise do not generally conform to that rule.

and sour milk[1],—and a productive union means a couple: thus a productive union is thereby effected.

8. Therewith they perform at the after-offerings. The after-offerings mean cattle, and clotted ghee means milk: hence he thereby puts milk into the cattle, and thus milk is here contained (or beneficial, hita) in the cattle; for clotted ghee means breath, because clotted ghee is food, and breath is food.

9. Therewith he (the Adhvaryu) performs in front (on the Âhavanîya) at the after-offerings,—whereby he puts into (the victim) that vital air which is here in front;—and therewith he (the Pratiprasthâtri) performs behind (the altar) at the by-offerings[2],—whereby he puts into it that vital air which is here behind: thus two vital airs are here contained (or beneficial) on both sides, the one above and the one below.

10. Here now, one (Hotri) pronounces the Vashat for two,—for the Adhvaryu (who performs the after-

---

[1] See p. 156, note 3.

[2] When the priests and sacrificer have eaten their portions of the Idâ, the Agnîdh fetches hot coals from the Sâmitra (or, at the animal offering connected with the Soma-sacrifice), optionally from the Âgnîdhra, and puts them on the Hotri's hearth (p. 148, note 4),—or at the ordinary animal offering (nirûdha pasu), on the north hip (north-west corner) of the altar after removing the sacrificial grass. On these coals the Pratiprasthâtri performs the by-offerings (upayag), while the Adhvaryu performs the after-offerings (anuyâga) on the Âhavanîya. For the by-offerings the Pratiprasthâtri cuts the respective part and the hind-quarter (III, 8, 3, 18) into eleven parts, and at each Vashat throws one piece thereof with his hand into the fire. The recipients of the first eight and the last after-offerings, on the other hand, are the same as those of the nine after-offerings at the Seasonal sacrifices (part i, p. 404). The Hotri's formulas for the additional two offerings, inserted before the last, are: 9. The divine lord of the forest [10. The divine barhis of water-plants] may graciously accept (the offering) for abundant obtainment of abundant gift! Vaushat!' (cf. part i, p. 235; Âsv. Sr. III, 6, 13.)

offerings) and for him (the Pratiprasthâtri) who performs the by-offerings. And because he offers them by (in addition to) the offering (Adhvaryu), therefore they are called by-offerings. And in performing the by-offerings, he produces (offspring)[1], since he performs the by-offerings behind (the altar), and from behind offspring is produced from woman.

11. He offers the by-offerings with (Vâg. S. VI, 21), 'Go thou to the sea, Hail!' The sea is water, and seed is water: he thereby casts seed.

12. 'Go thou to the air, Hail!' It is into (along) the air that offspring is born: into the air he produces (offspring).

13. 'Go thou to the divine Savitri, Hail!' Savitri is the impeller of the gods: impelled by Savitri he thus produces creatures.

14. 'Go thou to Mitra and Varuna, Hail!' Mitra and Varuna are the out-breathing and in-breathing: he thus bestows out-breathing and in-breathing on the creatures.

15. 'Go thou to the day and the night, Hail! It is through (along) day and night that offspring is born: through day and night he causes creatures to be born.

16. 'Go thou to the metres, Hail!' There are seven metres; and there are seven domestic and seven wild animals: both kinds he thus causes to be produced.

17. 'Go thou to heaven and earth, Hail!' For, Pragâpati, having created the living beings,

[1] Praivainam tag ganayati, 'he causes it (the victim) to be born (again),' Kânva rec. The above passage has apparently to be understood in a general sense, 'he causes birth to take place among living creatures

enclosed them between heaven and earth, and so these beings are enclosed between heaven and earth. And in like manner does this (offerer), having created living beings, enclose them between heaven and earth.

18. He then makes additional by-offerings (atiupayag). Were he not to make additional by-offerings, there would only be as many living beings as were created in the beginning; they would not be propagated; but by making additional by-offerings he indeed propagates them; whence creatures are again born here repeatedly[1].

Fifth Brâhmana.

1. He makes the additional by-offerings:—with 'Go thou to the sacrifice[2], Hail!' The sacrifice is water, and seed is water: he thus casts seed.

2. 'Go thou to Soma, Hail!' Soma is seed: he thus casts seed.

3. 'Go thou to the heavenly ether, Hail!' The heavenly ether is water, and seed is water: he thus casts seed.

4. 'Go thou to Agni Vaisvânara, Hail!' Agni Vaisvânara ('belonging to all men') is this earth, and she is a safe resting-place: upon that safe resting-place he thus produces (creatures).

5. He then touches his mouth, with, 'Give me mind and heart!' thus indeed the by-offerer does not throw himself after (the oblations into the fire).

6. Thereupon[3] they perform the Patnîsamyâgas

---

[1] Or, 'by making additional by-offerings he reproduces them: whence creatures are born here returning again and again' (metempsychosis).

[2] The Kânva text (as the Taitt. S.) reverses the order of this and the following formula. Nor does it begin a new Brâhmana here.

[3] Having completed the last after-offering, the Adhvaryu, in the

with the tail (of the victim), for the tail is the hind-part, and from the hind-part of woman offspring is produced: hence offspring is produced by the Patnîsamyâgas being performed with the tail.

7. For the wives of the gods he cuts portions from the inside, since it is from the inside of woman that offspring is produced; for Agni the householder from above, since it is from above that the male approaches the female.

8. Thereupon they betake themselves, with the heart-spit, to the purificatory bath[1]. Now, the anguish of the victim, in being slaughtered, concentrates itself into the heart, and from the heart into the heart-spit; and whatever part of cooked (food) is pierced that becomes palatable[2]: therefore let him roast it on the spit after piercing it. Uppermost on the thrice-moved (portions of the) victim he places that heart after pulling it off (the spit).

9. He (the slaughterer) then hands the heart-spit (to the Adhvaryu). Let him not throw it on the

first place, throws the first chip of the sacrificial stake into the fire, in accordance with III, 7, 1, 32. For the four Patnîsamyâgas, the deities of which are Soma, Tvashtri, the wives of the gods, and Agni the householder, see part i, p. 256. The first two offerings may consist only of ghee, or, as the last two, of a piece of the tail.

[1] The technical term for this purificatory ceremony is sûlâvabhritha, or 'spit-bath.' On the present occasion it is not performed (see paragraph 11), but it is inserted here because it forms the conclusion of the ordinary animal offering, not connected with the Soma-sacrifice (nirûdha-pasu), as well as of the offering of a sterile cow (termed anûbandhyâ) to Mitra and Varuna, which concludes the Soma-sacrifice. See part i, p. 379, note 1, and IV, 5, 2, 1 seq.

[2] ? Alamgusha, 'sufficient for eating,' Sâyana; 'sufficient in itself,' St. Petersburg Dict. The Kânva text has the probably preferable reading,—atha alamgusham sritam eva paritrindanti,—'they then pierce (with the spit) what is already sufficiently cooked.

ground, nor into the water; for were he to throw it on the ground, that anguish would enter into the plants and trees; and were he to throw it into the water, that anguish would enter into the water: hence neither on the ground, nor into the water.

10. But on going down to the water, let him bury it at the place where the dry and the moist meet. But if he feel disinclined to going down (to the water), he pours out a vessel of water in front of the sacrificial stake and buries (the spit) at the place where the dry and the moist meet, with (Vâg. S. VI, 22), 'Injure thou not the waters nor the plants!' thus it injures neither the waters nor the plants; 'From every fetter[1]—therefrom deliver us, O king Varuna! That they say, we swear by the "Inviolable (cows)," by "Varuna[2],"

[1] This is a doubtful rendering in accordance with the suggestion in the St. Petersburg Dict., that 'dhâmno-dhâmnah' in this passage is an old corruption of 'dâmno-dâmnah.' The Taitt. S. has the same reading. Sâyana and Mahîdhara take it in the sense of 'from every place (infested by enemies, or, rendered fearful by thy noose) deliver us!' Could 'dhâmno-dhâmnah' be taken as gen. to 'râgan?'

[2] ? Or, 'That they say (i.e. mention the word) "Cows,"—that we swear by "Varuna,"—therefrom deliver us, O Varuna!' If the mentioning of words for cow (as well as the taking in vain of Varuna's name) is meant to be censured in this passage, Sat. Br. II, 2, 4, 14 (part i, p. 326 note) may be compared. It seems, however, doubtful whether the author of the Brâhmana took the term aghnyâh as referring to 'cows' here. The St. Petersburg Dict., s.v. sap, translates, 'when we swear by the name of Varuna.' Instead of 'Yad âhur aghnyâ iti varuneti sapâmahe,' the Taitt. S (I, 3, 11, 1) reads 'Yad âpo aghniyâ varuneti sapâmahe,' which Sâyana explains by 'O ye waters, O ye Aghnyâh (? inviolable ones, cows, waters), O Varuna! thus we solicit thee (to avert evil from us);' adding a passage to the effect that he who approaches his better (addressing him) by name, wishes him 'punyârti;' while in the present mantra, he contends there is no mere 'taking the name of Varuna in vain.'

therefrom deliver us, O Varuna!' Thereby he delivers him[1] from every noose of Varuna, from all (guilt) against Varuna.

11. He then addresses (the water)[2] with, 'May the waters and plants be friendly unto us, unfriendly to him who hateth us, and whom we hate!' For when they proceed with that (spit), the waters, forsooth, as well as the plants, keep as it were receding from him; but hereby he now makes a covenant with them, and so they again approach to him, and that expiation is performed (to them). He does not perform (the spit-bath) at the animal offering to Agni and Soma, nor at that to Agni, but only at that of the Anûbandhyâ-cow[3], for therewith the whole sacrifice attains to completion. And in that they perform (the ceremony) with the heart-spit at the cow (offering), thereby indeed it comes to be performed also for the animal offering to Agni and Soma, as well as for that to Agni.

NINTH ADHYÂYA. FIRST BRÂHMANA.

1. Now Pragâpati (the lord of creatures), having created living beings, felt himself as it were exhausted[4]. The creatures turned away from him; the creatures[5] did not abide with him for his joy and food.

2. He thought within him, 'I have exhausted

[1] I. e. the sacrificer (or the victim representing the sacrificer).

[2] According to the Kânva text and Kâty. VI, 10, 5 they (the priests and sacrificer) touch the water while muttering the formula—'From every fetter . . . . and whom we hate.'

[3] See IV, 5, 1, 5 seq.

[4] Ririkânah, lit. 'emptied,' as âpyây means 'to fill.'

[5] 'Pragâ' has likewise here the meaning of 'people, subjects, constituting the power or glory (srî) of the king.

myself, and the object for which[1] I have created has not been accomplished: my creatures have turned away from me, the creatures have not abode with me for my joy and food.'

3. Pra*g*âpati thought within him, 'How can I again strengthen myself: the creatures might then return to me; the creatures might abide with me for my joy and food!'

4. He went on praising and toiling, desirous of creatures (or progeny). He beheld that set of eleven (victims). By offering therewith Pra*g*âpati again strengthened himself; the creatures returned to him, his creatures abode for his joy and food. By offering he truly became better.

5. Therefore, then, let him offer with the set of eleven (victims), for thus he truly strengthens himself by offspring and cattle; the creatures turn unto him, the creatures abide with him for his joy and food;—he truly becomes better by offering: therefore, then, let him offer with the set of eleven (victims).

6. In the first place he seizes[2] a victim for Agni. For Agni is the head, the progenitor of the gods, he is the lord of creatures: and thereby the sacrificer truly becomes Agni's own.

7. Then one for Sarasvatî. For Sarasvatî is speech: by speech Pra*g*âpati then again strengthened himself; speech turned unto him, speech he made subject to himself. And so does this one now become strong by speech, and speech turns unto him, and he makes speech subject to himself.

8. Then one for Soma. For Soma is food: by

---

[1] For 'asmâ u kâmâya' we ought to read 'yasmâ u kâmâya,' with Sâya*n*a and the Kâ*n*va text.

[2] Âlabh, to touch, seize, is a euphemistic term for immolating.

food Pragâpati then again strengthened himself; food turned unto him, and he made food subject to himself. And so does this one now become strong by food; food turns unto him, and he makes food subject to himself.

9. And as to why it comes after that for Sarasvatî,—Sarasvatî is speech, and Soma is food: he who is incomplete by (having only) speech, now becomes indeed an eater of food.

10. Then one for Pûshan. For Pûshan means cattle; by means of cattle Pragâpati then again strengthened himself; cattle turned unto him, he made cattle subject to himself. And so does this one now become strong by means of cattle; the cattle turn unto him, and he makes the cattle subject to himself.

11. Then one for Brihaspati. For Brihaspati means the priesthood (brahman); by means of the priesthood Pragâpati then again strengthened himself; the priesthood turned unto him, he made the priesthood subject to himself. And so does this one now become strong by means of the Brahman; the priesthood turns unto him, he makes the priesthood subject to himself.

12. And as to why it comes after that for Pûshan,—Pûshan means cattle, and Brihaspati the priesthood; hence the Brâhmana (priest) has the most power over beasts, because they are placed in front (are protected) by him[1], because they are placed at the head (or in his mouth); therefore

[1] Purâhitâh (pura-âhitâh, Kânva rec.) has both the general meaning of 'put before him (as food)' and that of 'being placed next in order before him.'

having given all that, he walks clad in sheepskin[1].

13. Then one for the Visve devâh. For the All-gods mean everything (or the All); with everything Pragâpati then again strengthened himself; everything turned unto him, and he made everything subject to him. And so does this one now become strong by everything; everything turns to him, and he makes everything subject to himself.

14. And as to why it comes after that for Brihaspati,—Brihaspati means the priesthood, and the All-gods this All; he then makes the priesthood the head of this All; wherefore the Brâhman is the head of this All.

15. Then one for Indra. For Indra means power (indriya) and vigour; by power and vigour Pragâpati then again strengthened himself; power and vigour turned unto him, and he made power and vigour subject to himself. And so does this one now become strong by means of power and vigour; power and vigour turn to him, and he makes power and vigour subject to himself.

16. And as to why it comes after that for the All-gods,—Indra is the nobility, and the All-gods are the clans (people); he thus places the food before him.

17. Then one for the Maruts. For the Maruts mean the clans, and a clan means abundance; with abundance Pragâpati then again strengthened himself; abundance turned unto him, and he made abundance subject to himself. And so does this one now become strong by abundance; abundance

[1] 'Since the lordship over cattle belongs to the Brâhman, therefore (the sacrificer) having given all his property to the Brâhmans,' &c. Sây.

turns unto him, and he makes abundance subject to himself.

18. And as to why it comes after that for Indra,—Indra is the nobility, and the All-gods are the clans, and the Maruts are the clans; he thus guards the nobility by the clan, and hence the nobility here is on both sides guarded by the clan.

19. Then one for Indra and Agni. For Agni means penetrating brilliance, and Indra means power and vigour; with these two energies Pragâpati then again strengthened himself; both energies turned unto him, and he made both energies subject to himself. And so does this one now become strong by both these energies; both energies turn unto him, and he makes both energies subject to himself.

20. Then one for Savitri. For Savitri is the impeller (prasavitri) of the gods; and so all those wishes become accomplished for him, impelled as they are by Savitri.

21. Then finally he seizes one for Varuna; thereby he delivers him (the sacrificer) from every noose of Varuna, from every (guilt) against Varuna[1].

22. Hence if there be eleven sacrificial stakes, let him bind Agni's (victim) to the one opposite the fire; and let them lead up the others one by one in the proper order.

23. But if there be eleven victims[2], let them only immolate at the stake that for Agni, and after that the others in the proper order.

---

[1] Varunyâd evaitat sarvasmât kilbishâd enaso 'ntato varunapâsât pragâh pramuñkati, Kânva rec.

[2] That is, if there be eleven victims and only one stake, in that case Agni's victim is tied to the stake, and each succeeding victim is tied to the neck of the preceding one. Kâty. VIII, 8, 28.

24. When they lead them northwards, they lead the one for Agni first, and then the others in the proper order.

25. When they throw them down, they throw down first the one for Agni, as the southernmost; then the others after leading them round northwards in the proper order.

26. When they perform (offerings) with the omenta, they perform first with the omentum of Agni's (victim); then with those of the others in the proper order.

27. When they perform with those (chief oblations), they perform first with that to Agni; then with the others in the proper order.

THE VASATÎVARÎ WATER.

SECOND BRÂHMANA.

1. Now, when the head of the sacrifice (victim) was struck off, its sap, running, entered the waters. It is by that very sap that those waters flow; that very sap is believed to be flowing there[1].

2. And when he goes for the Vasatîvarî water, he fetches that same sap and puts it into the sacrifice, and makes the sacrifice sapful; this is why he goes for the Vasatîvarî water.

3. He distributes it over all the Savanas (Soma-pressings)[2]; thereby he imbues all the pressings

[1] Yatra vai yagñasya siro 'khhidyata tasya raso drutvâpah prâvisat sa esha rasa eti yâ etâ âpah syandante tenaivainâ etad rasena syandamânâ manyante yah sa yagñasya rasas tam evaitad rasam syandamânam manyante, Kânva rec.

[2] 'He divides it into three parts for all the pressings,' Kânva text. See note on IV, 2, 3, 4.

with that sap, makes all the pressings sapful: this is why he distributes it over all the pressings.

4. Let him take it from flowing (water); for that sap of the sacrifice was moving[1]: let him therefore take it from flowing (water).

5. Moreover, it is taken for the purpose of protection. Now, everything else here on earth, whatever it be, takes rest, even yonder blowing (wind); but these (waters) alone take no rest: therefore let him take it from flowing (water).

6. Let him take it by day, thinking, 'Seeing, I will take the sap of the sacrifice[2]:' therefore let him take it by day. For it is for him that burns yonder (the sun) that he takes it, since he takes it for all the gods, and all the gods are his rays of light: therefore let him take it by day. For it is by day alone that he (shines): therefore, then, let him take it by day.

7. And again, all the gods, forsooth, now come to the sacrificer's house; and if one takes the Vasatîvarî water before the setting of the sun, it is as when one's better comes to visit one, he would honour him by trimming his house. They draw nigh to that sacrificial food, and abide (upa-vas) in that Vasatîvarî[3] water,—that is the Upavasatha (preparation-day).

8. And if the sun were to set on any one's (Vasatîvarîs) not having been taken, then expiation is made. If he have performed a (Soma-)sacrifice before this, let him (the Adhvaryu) take it from his tank[4], since

---

[1] Aid hi; see p. 222, note 1.

[2] Or perhaps, 'I will take it while I see the sap of the sacrifice.'

[3] 'Vasatîvarî' seems to mean 'affording dwelling;' or perhaps, 'that (water) which abides, remains (over night).' Cf. par. 16.

[4] 'Ninâhya' (ninā́hyah kumbháh, Kânva rec. each time); a vessel or cistern, dug into the ground for keeping water cool.

that (water) of his has been taken before (sunset) by day. But should he not have offered before, if there be one who has offered (Soma) settled close by or somewhere thereabout[1], let him take it from his tank, since that (water) of his has been taken before, by day.

9. But if he cannot obtain either kind (of water), let him seize a firebrand and betake himself (to the flowing water), and let him take thereof while holding that (firebrand) close above it; or let him take it while holding a piece of gold close above it: thus it is made like yonder burning (sun).

10. He takes therefrom with the text (Vâ*g*. S. VI, 23), 'Rich in havis are these waters,'—for the sap of the sacrifice entered into them, wherefore he says, 'Rich in havis (sacrificial food) are these waters;'—'One rich in havis wooeth for (them),' for the sacrificer, rich in havis, woos for (wishes to obtain) them; wherefore he says, 'One rich in havis wooeth for (them).'

11. 'Rich in havis (may be) the divine cult;' cult, namely, means the sacrifice; thus he makes the sacrifice for which he takes it rich in sacrificial food, therefore he says, 'Rich in havis is the divine cult.'

12. 'May Sûrya be rich in havis!' For he takes it for yonder burning (sun), since he takes it for all the gods, and all the gods are his (the sun's) rays of light; therefore he says, 'May Sûrya (the sun) be rich in havis!'

13. Having fetched it, he deposits it behind the Gârhapatya[2], with (Vâ*g*. S. VI, 24), 'I seat you in

---

[1] Upâvasito vâ paryavasito (prátive*s*o, Kâ*n*va text instead) vâ.

[2] That is, behind the old Âhavanîya of the Prâ*k*înava*m*sa, where the altar would be prepared at the ordinary haviryag*ñ*a.

the seat of Agni, the safe-housed;' whereby he means to say, 'I seat you (waters) in the seat of Agni, whose house is unimpaired.' And when the animal offering to Agni and Soma comes to a close, then he carries (the Vasatîvarî water) round. He says (thrice), 'Disperse!' The sacrificer is seated in front of the Soma-carts (holding Soma on his lap[1]). He (the Adhvaryu) takes it (the water standing behind the Gârhapatya).

14. He walks out (of the hall) by the south (door), and puts it down on the south hip (of the high altar), with, 'Ye (waters) are Indra and Agni's share!' for he takes it for all the gods, and Indra and Agni are all the gods. He takes it up again and puts it down in front of the lady (who, seated behind the Gârhapatya, touches the water-jar). Walking round behind the lady he (again) takes it.

15. He walks out (of the hall by the east door), along the north side (of the altar), and puts down (the water) on the north hip (of the high altar), with, 'Ye are Mitra and Varuna's share!' Let him not put it down in this way[2], that is redundant, and no fitting conclusion is thus attained. Let him rather (here also) say, 'Ye are Indra and Agni's share!' only thus there is nothing redundant, and so a fitting conclusion is obtained.

16. That (Vasatîvarî water) is carried round for the sake of protection; Agni is in front (of the sacrificial ground), and now that (water) moves about all round, repelling the evil spirits. He puts it

[1] According to Kâty. VIII, 9, 16.

[2] 'Some put it down with this (formula), but let him not put it down so, for thus completeness is left behind (or, has a surplus, sampad rikyate).' Kânva text.

down in the Âgnîdhra (fire-house) with, 'Ye are all the gods' share!' whereby he makes all the gods enter it. It is a desirable object (vara) to the dwellers (vasat), hence the name Vasatîvarî[1], and verily he who knows this, becomes a desirable object to the dwellers.

17. Now there are here seven formulas; with four he takes (the water), with one he puts it down behind the Gârhapatya, with one he carries it round, with one (he puts it down) in the Âgnîdhra,—this makes seven. For when the metres were produced from Vâk (speech), the one consisting of seven feet, the Sakvarî, was the last (highest) of them;—that completeness (he brings about): hence there are seven formulas.

THE SOMA FEAST.

THIRD BRÂHMANA.

A. PRÂTAR-ANUVÂKA (MORNING-PRAYER) AND PREPARATORY CEREMONIES.

1. They (the priests) are wakened (towards morning). Having touched water[2], they proceed together to the Âgnîdhra (fire-house) and take the portions of ghee (for the Savanîya animal offerings). Having taken the portions of ghee, they betake themselves (to the high altar). When they have deposited the ghee,—

[1] Cf. Taitt. S. VI, 4, 2, 'devâh . . . abruvan, vasatu nu na idam iti, tad vasatîvarînâm vasatîvaritvam.'

[2] After performing their ablutions they have to perform the preliminary work and ceremonies, such as preparing the Gârhapatya, fetching and arranging the vessels, cleaning of spoons, &c. up to the depositing of the ghee, near the high altar.

2. He (the Adhvaryu) takes down the king (Soma)[1]. Now this (earth) is a safe resting-place, and the birth-place of living beings; it is to this safe resting-place that he now takes him down; he spreads him thereon, produces him therefrom.

3. He takes him down between the shafts; for the cart is (a means of) the sacrifice, and thus alone he does not put him outside the sacrifice. He puts him on the pressing stones lying there with their heads (mukha, mouths)[2] towards each other; for Soma is the nobility, and the stones are the clans (people); he thereby raises the nobility over the clan. And as to why they are lying with their heads together,—he thereby makes the clan of one head (or mouth) with, and uncontentious towards, the nobles; therefore they are lying with their heads towards each other.

4. He takes (Soma) down, with (Vâg. S. VI, 25), 'Thee for the heart, thee for the mind!' This he says for the (accomplishment of the) sacrificer's wish, since it is with the heart and mind that the sacrificer entertains the wish for which he sacrifices; therefore he says, 'Thee for the heart, thee for the mind!'

5. 'Thee for the sky, thee for the sun!' This, on the other hand, he says with a view to the world of the gods. When he says, 'Thee for the sky, thee

[1] According to Kâty. VIII, 9, 24–25, on the previous evening,—immediately after the carrying round and depositing of the Vasativarî water,—the Soma is placed on a seat (âsandi) in the Âgnîdhra fire house, where the sacrificer has to watch over it during that night. This is not mentioned in the Brâhmana, and from what follows it would rather seem that the Soma is taken down from the cart (see III, 6, 3, 17 seq.). Otherwise we might translate, 'He brings him down (from the Âgnîdhra).'

[2] That is, with their broad sides turned towards each other.

for the sun,' he means to say, 'Thee for the gods!' 'Upwards convey thou to the sky, to the gods, this cult, these invocations!' Cult, doubtless, means sacrifice: he thereby means to say, 'Upwards carry thou this sacrifice to the sky, to the gods!'

6. [Vâg. S. VI, 26], 'O Soma, king, descend unto all thy people!' whereby he brings him down for the lordship, for the sovereignty of these people (creatures).

7. Having quitted his hold (of Soma) he sits down by him, with, 'May all thy people descend to thee.' Now, in saying, 'Descend unto all thy people,' he does what is unseemly, for Soma being the nobility, he thereby, as it were, confounds good and bad[1],—and, indeed, in consequence thereof, people now confound good and bad. But in this (formula) he does what is right and according to order,—in saying, 'May all thy people descend to thee,' he makes all his subjects go down (on their knees) before him; and hence when a noble approaches, all these subjects, the people, go down before him, crouch down by him on the ground[2]. Sitting near (Soma), the Hotri is about to recite the morning-prayer.

8. Then, while putting a kindling-stick (on the fire), he (the Adhvaryu) says, 'Recite to the gods

[1] 'He commits a pâpavasyasam, i. e. according to Haug, Ait. Br. p. 413, 'a breach of the oath of allegiance' (where Sâyana explains it by 'exceedingly bad'); or 'an (act of) perversity,' Weber, Ind. Stud. IX, p. 300. Sâyana, to our passage, explains it by 'mixing the bad with the good (or better).' The literal translation is 'a bad-bettering.' What is chiefly implied in the term is evidently the showing of disrespect by an inferior to a superior person.

[2] Tasmât kshatriyam upary âsînam adhastâd visa imâh pragâ upâsate. Kânva text.

the early-coming!' Now the early-coming gods are the metres, as the after-offerings are the metres; and the after-offerings are performed with, 'Prompt (the Hotri to recite) to the gods! Recite (the offering-prayer) to the gods!'

9. And so some say, 'Recite to the gods[1]!' But let him not say so; for the early-coming gods are the metres, as the after-offerings are the metres, and the after-offerings are performed with, 'Prompt—to the gods! Recite (the offering-prayer) to the gods!' therefore let him say, 'Recite to the gods, the early-coming!'

10. And when he puts on a kindling-stick, it is the metres he thereby kindles. And when the Hotri recites the morning-prayer[2], he thereby

---

[1] Here now, some say only, 'Recite to the early-coming!' not 'to the . . . gods!' but let him not say this. Kânva text.

[2] The Prâtar-anuvâka, or morning-prayer (matin chant), has to be recited by the Hotri in the latter part of the night before any sound (of birds, &c.) is to be heard. It may begin immediately after midnight, and conclude as soon as daylight appears. When called upon by the Adhvaryu to recite the morning-prayer, the Hotri first makes an oblation of ghee on the Âgnîdhra fire, with the mantra, 'Protect me from the spell of the mouth, from every imprecation, Hail!' and then two oblations on the Âhavanîya with appropriate mantras. Thereupon he betakes himself to the Havirdhâna (cart-shed), in entering which, by the east door, he touches successively the front-wreath (rarâtâ, cf. III, 5, 3, 9) and the door-posts, with formulas. He then squats down between the yoke-pieces of the two Soma-carts, and begins his recitation with Rig-veda X, 30, 12, 'Ye, O wealthy waters, verily possess good things; ye confer desirable energy and immortality; ye command riches with abundant offspring: may Sarasvatî (the river S., and Speech) bestow on the bard that vital vigour!' The 'early-coming' deities to whom the recitation is successively addressed, are Agni, Ushas (the dawn), and the two Asvins (the precursors of the sun); the prayer thus consisting of three sections, termed kratu (Agni-

again strengthens the metres, makes them to be of unimpaired vigour; for the metres had their vigour impaired by the gods, since it was through the metres that the gods reached the heavenly worlds; they neither sing praises (chants) nor recite (*s*astras) here. Hereby he now again strengthens the metres and makes them to be of unimpaired vigour; and by means of them, thus unimpaired in vigour, they

---

kratu, &c.). The hymns and detached verses making up these sections are arranged according to the seven metres (thus forming seven sub-sections of each), viz. gâyatrî, anush*t*ubh, trish*t*ubh, b*ri*hatî, ush*n*ih, *g*agatî, and paṅkti. The prayer may consist of as many verses as can be recited between midnight and daybreak; but there should be at least one hymn in each of the seven metres to each of the three deities; nor should the recitation consist of less than a hundred verses. From the beginning of the recitation up to the end of the last hymn but one, Rig-veda I, 112, there is to be a gradual modulation of the voice so as to pass upwards through the seven tones (yama) of the deep scale (mandrasvara). Moreover, that hymn is to be repeated (if necessary) till daylight appears. As soon as this is the case, he passes on without any break from the last (25th) verse to the last hymn (v. 75, 1–9), which he intones in the lowest tone of the middle scale, after shifting his place further east towards the gate. The recitation of the first eight verses of this hymn again gradually ascends through the whole of the middle scale; when—after once more shifting his place so as to be seated between the two door-posts—he intones the last verse—'The Dawn hath appeared with her shining kine, Agni hath been kindled at his appointed time: your car hath been yoked, ye mighty, mead-loving(?) A*s*vins, showerers of wealth, hear my call!' in reciting which he makes his voice pass through the several tones of the high scale. The Subrahma*n*yâ, likewise, has to chant the Subrahma*n*yâ litany (see III, 3, 4, 17 seq.)—as he had to do on the previous evening—inserting in it the names of the sacrificer's father and son. The Agnîdh, in the meantime, prepares the five havis-oblations (savanîyâ*h* puro*d*â*s*â*h*) to be offered at the morning-pressing (cf. IV, 2, 4, 18), and the Unnet*ri* puts the numerous Soma-vessels in their respective places on the khara, and about the Soma-carts.

perform the sacrifice; this is why the Hotri recites the morning-prayer.

11. Here now they say, 'What is the (Adhvaryu's) response to the morning-prayer[1]?' The Adhvaryu should wait through (the prayer) waking, and when he blinks, this is his response. But let him not do this; if he fall asleep (again) he may as well sleep. When the Hotri brings his morning-prayer to a close[2],—there is an offering-spoon called Prakaranî,—having therein taken ghee in four ladlings, he (the Adhvaryu) offers it.

12. For when the head of Yagña (the sacrifice) was struck off, his sap, running, entered the waters; that (sap) he fetched yesterday with the Vasatîvarî water; and he now goes for what sap of the sacrifice remains therein.

13. And when he offers that offering, he pours out (the ghee) towards that same sap of the sacrifice (in the water) and draws it to him. And, indeed, he pleases those deities to whom he offers that offering, and thus satisfied and pleased, they fit that sap of the sacrifice together[3] for him.

14. He offers with, 'May Agni, with his flame, hear my prayer;' whereby he means to say, 'May he hear this prayer of mine, may he vouchsafe it to me;'—'May the waters and the Soma-bowls hear, the divine!' whereby he means to say, 'May the waters hear this (prayer) of mine, may they vouchsafe it to me.'—'Hear me, ye stones,

---

[1] Cf. IV, 3, 2, 1 seq.

[2] That is, when he recites the last verse, 'Ushas hath appeared,' &c.

[3] Literally, 'Bend together (sam-nam),' which refers to the 'bending together' of the cups at the Aponaptrîya ceremony.

as knowing the sacrifice!' whereby he means to say, 'May the (pressing) stones hear this (prayer) of mine, may they vouchsafe it to me;' and 'as knowing the sacrifice,' he says, because the stones are indeed knowing[1]. 'May the divine Savitri hear my prayer, Hail!' whereby he means to say, 'May the divine Savitri hear this (prayer) of mine, may he vouchsafe it to me;' for Savitri is the impeller of the gods; impelled by him he goes for that sap of the sacrifice.

15. Having then a second time taken ghee by four ladlings, he says, while going forth towards the north, 'Summon the waters!' whereby he means to say, 'Desire the waters, O Hotar!' The reason why the Hotri then recites[2] is this: by that

[1] The text has rather to be construed, 'Ye stones, hear (my prayer) as (of one) knowing the sacrifice.'

[2] While the Adhvaryu and assistants go to the water to fill the Ekadhana pitchers, the Hotri recites the so-called Aponaptrîya hymn (Rig-veda X, 30) to the waters, omitting verse twelve, which was already recited as the opening verse of the morning-prayer. The first verse is recited thrice, and the tenth verse is recited after the eleventh, while the priests are returning with the water. As soon as they are in sight, the Hotri recites verse 13, followed by Rig-veda V, 43, 1; and (when the Ekadhanâ and Vasatîvarî waters meet together, paragraph 29) Rig-veda II, 35, 3; and, in case some of the water is actually poured over into the Hotri's cup, I, 83, 2. When the water is brought to the Havirdhâna, the Hotri addresses the Adhvaryu as stated in paragraph 31; whereupon he pronounces a 'nigada' (for which see Ait. Br. II, 20; Âsv. Sr. V, 1, 14–17), followed by Rig-veda I, 23, 16; while the Ekadhana pitchers are carried past him. The water in the Maitrâvaruna cup and one third of both the Vasatîvarî and Ekadhanâ water having been poured into the Âdhavanîya trough (standing on the northern cart), the pitchers with the remaining water are then deposited in their respective places behind the axle of the northern cart, whereupon the Hotri recites the two remaining verses (14 and 15) of the

(oblation) he (the Adhvaryu) pours out (the ghee) towards that sap of the sacrifice (in the water), and draws it to him; and he (the Hotri) then stands by those (Ekadhana pitchers) lest the evil spirits should injure them on the way.

16. He (the Adhvaryu) then gives directions, 'Come hither, cup-bearer of the Maitrâvaruna! Neshtar, lead up the wives! Ye bearers of the Ekadhana (cups), come hither! Agnîdh, step over against the pit with the Vasatîvarî water and the Hotri's cup!' this is a composite direction.

17. They walk northwards out (of the sacrificial ground)—by the back of the pit and the front side of the Âgnîdhra; whereupon they proceed in the direction in which the water is. They go thither together with the wives. The reason why they go thither with the wives is this.

18. When the head of the sacrifice was struck off, its sap, running, entered the waters; those Gandharva Soma-wardens watched it.

19. The gods then said, 'Those Gandharvas, surely, are a great danger to us here, how can we carry off the sap of the sacrifice to a place free from danger and injury?'

20. They said, 'Well, the Gandharvas are fond of women; let us go together with the wives! The Gandharvas, surely, will hanker after the wives, and we shall carry off that sap of the sacrifice to a place free from danger and injury.'

21. They went with the wives; the Gandharvas did indeed hanker after the wives, and they (the

---

Aponaptrîya hymn, and sits down in front of the Soma, behind the northern door-post of the Havirdhâna (cart-shed).

gods) carried off that sap of the sacrifice to a place free from danger and injury.

22. And so does that (Adhvaryu) now go (to the water) with the wives; the Gandharvas hanker after the wives, and he carries off that sap of the sacrifice to a place free from danger and injury.

23. He offers (the ghee) upon the water; for that sap of the sacrifice, indeed, draws near to that oblation, when offered; it rises (to the surface) to meet it; and having thus brought it to light, he seizes it.

24. And again why he offers this oblation: he thereby pours out (ghee) towards that sap of the sacrifice, and draws it to him, and craves it of the waters. And, indeed, he pleases those deities to whom he offers that oblation, and thus satisfied and pleased they fit that sap of the sacrifice together for him.

25. He offers with (Vâg. S. VI, 27), 'Ye divine waters,—the son of waters;' the waters are indeed divine, hence he says, 'Ye divine waters,—the son of waters;' 'That wave of yours, suitable for offering;' whereby he means to say, 'That wave of yours which is suitable for the sacrifice;' 'Mighty, most grateful;' by 'mighty' he means to say 'powerful,' and by 'most grateful' he means to say 'most sweet;' 'Give ye that unto those gods among the gods,' in saying this he has craved it of them; 'The drinkers of the pure (Soma);' the pure, doubtless, is the truth; in saying, 'the drinkers (pa) of the pure,' he means to say, 'the defenders (pa) of the truth;' 'Whose portion ye are, Hail!' for this indeed is their portion.

26. Thereupon he makes that oblation (ghee) float away by means of the Maitrâvaruna's cup, with (Vâg. S. VI, 28), 'Thou art furrowing!' Even

as a coal is consumed by Fire, so is that oblation consumed by that deity. Now that water, which is in the Maitrâvaruna's cup, he will have to pour on the king (Soma); and ghee being a thunderbolt, and Soma seed, he makes (the ghee) float away lest he should injure that seed, Soma, by that thunderbolt, the ghee.

27. He then takes (water) with, 'I draw thee up for the imperishableness of the ocean;' for the ocean is water; he thus confers imperishableness upon the waters; wherefore, in spite of so much food (and drink) being consumed, the waters are not diminished. Thereupon they draw (water in) the Ekadhana pitchers, and thereupon the vessels for washing the feet[1].

28. The reason why he takes (water) with the Maitrâvaruna's cup is this. When the sacrifice escaped from the gods, the gods endeavoured to call it up by means of (sacrificial) calls (praisha)[2]; by means of the puroruk ('shining before') formulas[3] they pleased it (pra-rokaya), and by the nivids they made (their wishes) known (ni-vid) to it. Therefore he takes (water) with the Maitrâvaruna's cup.

29. They come back. The Agnîdh takes up his position opposite to the pit with the Vasatîvarî water and the Hotri's cup. Close over the pit he

---

[1] These are filled by the sacrificer's wife, or, if there be more than one sacrificer (or, if the sacrificer have more than one wife), by all the wives, each having two vessels. For the use of this water, see note on IV, 4, 2, 18.

[2] The praishas or sacrificial directions to the Hotri, for the recitations of offering-formulas, are given by the Maitrâvaruna; see p. 183, note 2.

[3] See note on IV, 1, 3, 15; the nivids, part i, p. 114, note 2.

(the Adhvaryu) makes the Vasatîvarî water and the Maitrâvaruna's cup touch one another, with, 'Water hath united with water, plants with plants!' the sap of the sacrifice which was fetched yesterday and that fetched to-day, both kinds he thereby mixes together.

30. Now some indeed pour (some of) the Vasatîvarî water into the Maitrâvaruna's cup, and from the Maitrâvaruna's cup (back) to the Vasatîvarî water, arguing, 'Thereby we mix together both the sap of the sacrifice which was fetched yesterday and that fetched to-day.' But let him not do this; for when he pours (the water) together into the Âdhavanîya trough[1], then both kinds of sap are mixed together. Thereupon he pours the Vasatîvarî water into the Hotri's cup for the Nigrâbhyâs[2]. And as to why he makes them touch one another close over the pit, it was from thence, forsooth, that the gods rose to heaven; he thus makes the sacrificer look along the road to heaven.

31. They return (to the Havirdhâna). The Hotri asks him, 'Adhvaryu, hast thou gained the waters?' whereby he means to say, 'Hast thou obtained the waters?' He replies to him, 'Yea, they have yielded themselves!' whereby he means to say, 'I have obtained them and they have yielded to me.'

32. And if it be an Agnishtoma, and there be left a residue (of ghee poured together) in the prakaranî

---

[1] See p. 232, note 2 to paragraph 15.

[2] Nigrâbhyâh is the technical name the Vasatîvarî water in the Hotri's cup henceforth bears. It is handed to the sacrificer to carry to the Havirdhâna; and is afterwards used for moistening the Soma plants (or, for being poured thereon) at the time of the pressing. See III, 9, 4, 14 seq.

spoon sufficient for an oblation, let him offer that. But if it be not sufficient for an oblation, he takes another portion of ghee in four ladlings and offers it, with (Vâ*g*. S. VI, 29; Rig-veda I, 27, 7), 'Whatever mortal thou favourest in battles, whomsoever thou speedest in the race, he winneth unfailing strength, Hail!' He offers with (a prayer) to Agni, because the Agnish*t*oma ('Agni's praise') means Agni; thus he establishes the Agnish*t*oma in Agni. [He offers] with (a verse) containing the word 'mortal,' because the Agnish*t*oma is of the same measure as man. Let him then offer in this manner, if it be an Agnish*t*oma.

33. And if it be an Ukthya, let him touch the middle enclosing-stick,—there are three enclosing-sticks and three recitations (uktha)[1]; and by means of them the sacrifice is there established. And if it be either an Atirâtra or a Sho*d*a*s*in[2], let him neither make an oblation nor touch the middle enclosing-stick; having merely muttered (the above verse), let him silently betake himself (to the Havirdhâna) and enter it[3]. In this way he duly distinguishes the forms of sacrifice from one another.

34. The Ekadhana pitchers are always of uneven number,—either three, or five, or seven, or nine, or eleven, or thirteen, or fifteen[4]. Now two and two

[1] See note on IV, 4, 2, 18; Haug, Ait. Br., Transl. p. 251.

[2] And if it be a Sho*d*a*s*in, or an Atirâtra, or a Vâ*g*apeya. Kâ*n*va rec. See note on IV, 5, 3, 1.

[3] According to Kâty. IX, 3, 20–21 he may, while muttering that verse, touch the front wreath at the Sho*d*a*s*in, and the side-mat at the Atirâtra.

[4] The original has,—either three, or five, or five, or seven, or seven, or nine, &c. The Kâ*n*va text, on the other hand, has merely,—either three, or five, or seven, or nine, or nineteen.

(an even number) means a productive pair; and the one that remains over, remains over for the sacrificer's prosperity. And, moreover, that which remains over for the sacrificer's prosperity is the common property (sa-dhana) of these (others); and because it is the common property of these, therefore they are called Ekadhana (having one as their common property).

FOURTH BRÂHMANA.

B. THE PRÂTAHSAVANA, OR MORNING-PRESSING.

I. UPÂMSU-GRAHA.

1. Thereupon they sit down round the two press-boards[1]. He (the Adhvaryu) then ties a piece of gold to that (nameless finger). For twofold, verily, is this; there is no third, namely, the truth and the untruth; the gods, forsooth, are the truth, and men are the untruth. And the gold has sprung from Agni's seed: 'With the truth I will touch the stalks, with the truth I will take hold of Soma,' thus he thinks, and therefore he ties a piece of gold to that (ring-finger).

2. He then takes a press-stone[2]. Now those

[1] The Adhvaryu and sacrificer sit north of them, looking towards the south; and the assistants of the former—viz. the Pratiprasthâtri, Neshtri, and Unnetri—on the south side, looking northwards. The press-boards were laid down on the 'sound-holes,' under the fore-part of the southern Soma-cart, and the pressing-skin was spread over them; see III, 5, 4, 22–23. The Udgâtris, or chanters, are seated behind the carts.

[2] Viz. the upâmsusavana, or 'low-voiced pressing (stone),' (see paragraph 6,) with which the Soma for the Upâmsu libation (or cup, graha) is pressed.

press-stones are of rock, and Soma is a god—for Soma was in the sky, Soma was V*ri*tra; those mountains, those rocks are his body—he thus perfects him by means of his body, makes him whole; therefore they are of rock. Moreover, in pressing him they slay him, they slay him by means of that (stone, Soma's own body); thus he rises from thence, thus he lives; therefore the press-stones are of rock.

3. He takes it with (Vâ*g*. S. VI, 30), 'At the impulse of the divine Savit*ri* I take thee with the arms of the A*s*vins, with the hands of Pûshan; thou art a giver!' For Savit*ri* is the impeller of the gods; thus he takes it, impelled by Savit*ri*. 'With the arms of the A*s*vins,' he says,—the A*s*vins are the Adhvaryus (of the gods): with their arms he thus takes it, not with his own. 'With the hands of Pûshan,' he says,—Pûshan is the distributor of portions: with his hands he thus takes it, not with his own. Moreover, that (stone) is a thunderbolt, and no man can hold it: by means of those deities he takes it.

4. 'I take thee: thou art a giver,' he says; for when they press him by means of that (stone), then there is an oblation; and when he offers an oblation, then he gives sacrificial gifts,—thus, then, that (stone) gives twofold, oblations and sacrificial gifts; wherefore he says, 'Thou art a giver.'

5. 'Perform thou this deep cult!' Cult means sacrifice; he thereby means to say, 'Perform thou this great sacrifice!'—'well-gotten for Indra;' by 'well-gotten' he means to say, 'well-produced;' and Indra is the deity of the sacrifice, wherefore he says, 'for Indra;'—'by the most excellent bolt,'

for he, Soma, is indeed the most excellent bolt[1], therefore he says, 'by the most excellent bolt;'—'the (cult) rich in food and sweetness and drink,' whereby he means to say, 'the (cult) rich in sap.'

6. Thereupon he restrains speech. For once on a time, the gods, while performing sacrifice, were afraid of an attack from the Asura-Rakshas. They said, 'Let us sacrifice in a low voice, let us restrain speech!' They sacrificed (with formulas muttered) in a low voice and restrained speech.

7. He then fetches the Nigrâbhyâs (waters), and makes him (the sacrificer) mutter over them[2], 'Ye are the Nigrâbhyâs, heard by the gods; satisfy me, satisfy my mind, satisfy my speech, satisfy my breath, satisfy mine eye, satisfy mine ear, satisfy my soul, satisfy mine offspring, satisfy my flocks, satisfy my followers, let not my followers thirst!' For water is sap, and over it he invokes this blessing, 'Satisfy ye my whole self, satisfy my offspring, satisfy my followers, let not my followers thirst!' Now that Upâ*ms*usavana (stone), forsooth, is in reality Âditya Vivasvant (the sun), it is the pervading vital air (vyâna) of this (sacrifice).

8. Thereon he metes out (the Soma). For in pressing him they slay him, they slay him by means of that (stone); thus[3] he rises from hence, thus he

[1] It is doubtful what 'pavi' may mean here. It seems to mean originally a metallic mounting, especially of a shaft. The commentators explain it by 'thunderbolt.'

[2] The sacrificer holds the Hot*ri*'s cup with the Nigrâbhyâ*h* to his breast.

[3] Viz. by being placed upon the stone, which is identical with the sun (?); but cf. III, 8, 2, 27.

lives. And because he metes him out, therefore there is a measure,—both the measure among men[1], and what other measure there is.

9. He metes out with (Vâ*g*. S. VI, 32), 'Thee for Indra, with the Vasus, with the Rudras!' For Indra is the deity of the sacrifice: therefore he says, 'Thee for Indra;' and by saying 'with the Vasus, with the Rudras,' he assigns a share, along with (or after) Indra, to the Vasus and the Rudras.—'Thee for Indra, with the Âdityas!' whereby he assigns a share to the Âdityas along with Indra.—'Thee for Indra, the slayer of foes!' a foe is an enemy: 'Thee for Indra, the slayer of enemies,' he means to say. This is his (Indra's) special share: as there is a special share for a chief, so is this his special share apart from the (other) gods.

10. 'Thee for the Soma-bearing falcon!' this he metes out for Gâyatrî.—'Thee for Agni, the bestower of growth of wealth!' Now Agni is Gâyatrî: he metes this out for Gâyatrî. And since Gâyatrî, as a falcon, fetched Soma from heaven, therefore she is (called) the Soma-bearing falcon: for that prowess of hers he metes out (for her) a second portion.

11. Now as to why he metes out five times[2],—the sacrifice is of the same measure as the year, and there are five seasons in the year: he takes possession of it in five (divisions); hence he metes out five times.

---

[1] Tasmâd v iya*m* manushyeshu mâtrâ yat kaush*th*o yat kumbhî yeya*m* kâ *k*a manushyeshu mâtrâ. Kâ*n*va text.

[2] According to Taitt. S. VI, 4, 4 he metes out five times with the above texts, and five times silently.

12. He touches it with (Vâg. S. VI, 33), 'What light of thine there is in the heavens, O Soma, what on earth, and what in the wide air, therewith make wide room for this sacrificer, for his prosperity: speak thou for the giver!' Now when he (Soma) first became sacrificial food for the gods, he thought within himself, 'I must not become sacrificial food for the gods with my whole self!' Accordingly he deposited those three bodies of his in these worlds.

13. The gods then were victorious. They obtained those bodies by means of this same (formula), and he became entirely the sacrificial food of the gods. And in like manner does this (priest) now thereby obtain those bodies of his, and he (Soma) becomes entirely the food of the gods: this is why he thus touches it.

14. He then pours Nigrâbhyâ water on it. Now the waters, forsooth, slew Vritra and by virtue of that prowess of theirs they now flow. Wherefore nothing whatsoever can check them when they flow; for they followed their own free will, thinking, 'To whom, forsooth, should we submit (or stop), we by whom Vritra was slain!' Now all this (universe), whatsoever there is, had submitted[1] to Indra, even he that blows yonder.

15. Indra spake, 'Verily, all this (universe), whatsoever there is, has submitted unto me: submit ye also to me!'—They said, 'What shall be our (reward) then?'—'The first draught of king Soma shall be yours!'—'So be it!' thus they submitted to

[1] The Kânva MS. has twice 'tatsthâna,' as Ait. Br. VI, 5, and twice 'tasthâna;' cf. Weber, Ind. Stud. IX, p. 295.

him; and they having submitted, he drew (ni-grabh) them to his breast; and because he thus drew them to his breast, therefore they are called Nigrâbhyâs. And in like manner does this sacrificer now draw them to his breast: and this is their first draught of king Soma, in that he pours Nigrâbhyâ water thereon.

16. He pours it with (Vâ*g*. S. VI, 34), 'Ye are grateful, the subduers of V*ri*tra;'—the waters indeed are propitious: therefore he says, 'Ye are grateful;' and 'the subduers of V*ri*tra' he says because they did slay V*ri*tra;—'the beneficent wives of the immortal (Soma);' for the waters are immortal;—'Ye goddesses, lead this sacrifice to the gods!' there is nothing obscure in this;—'Invited, drink ye of Soma!' Thus invited they drink the first draught of king Soma.

17. Being about to beat (the Soma with the pressing-stone), let him think in his mind of him he hates: 'Herewith I strike N. N., not thee!' Now whosoever kills a human Brâhman here, he, forsooth, is deemed guilty[1],—how much more so he who strikes him (Soma), for Soma is a god. But they do kill him when they press him;—they kill him with that (stone): thus he rises from thence, thus he lives; and thus no guilt is incurred. But if he hate no one, he may even think of a straw, and thus no guilt is incurred.

18. He beats with (Vâ*g*. S. VI, 35), 'Fear not, tremble not!' whereby he means to say, 'Be not afraid, do not tremble, it is N. N. I strike, not thee!'—'Take thou strength!' whereby he means to say, 'Take sap!'—'Both ye bowls, that are

[1] 'Pari*k*akshate' ought rather to mean 'they despise him.'

firm, remain firm, take strength!'—'Surely, it is those two (pressing-)boards that are thereby meant,' so say some;—what, then, if one were to break those two boards[1]? But, forsooth, it is these two, heaven and earth, that tremble for fear of that raised thunderbolt (the stone): hereby now he propitiates it for those two, heaven and earth; and thus propitiated it does not injure them. By 'Take strength!' he means to say, 'Take sap!'—'The evil is slain, not Soma!' he thereby slays every evil of his.

19. Thrice he presses[2], thrice he gathers together,

[1] That is to say, in that case the formula would prove to have been a failure. According to the Taitt. Kalpas., quoted to Taitt. S. I, 4, 1 (p. 590), he presses the skin down upon the two press-boards while muttering this formula. The Kânva text argues somewhat differently,—ime evaitat phalake âhur iti haika âhus tad u kim âdriyeta yad athaite bhidyeyâtâm eveme haiva dyâvâprithivyâv etasmâd vagrâd udyatât samregete,—'Some say those two boards are thereby meant; but who would care if they should get broken; for it is rather those two, heaven and earth,' &c.?

[2] The pressing of the Upâmsu-graha—also called the 'small' pressing, distinguished from the 'great pressing' (mahâbhishava) for the subsequent cups or libations (graha)—consists of three turns of eight, eleven, and twelve single beatings respectively. Before each turn Nigrâbhyâ water is poured upon the Soma plants by the sacrificer from the Hotri's cup. After each turn of pressing the Adhvaryu throws the completely-pressed stalks into the cup, and when they have become thoroughly soaked, he presses them out and takes them out again; this being the 'gathering together' referred to above. At the same time he mutters the Nigrâbha formula (paragraph 21); after which the pressed-out juice, absorbed by the water, is poured into the Upâmsu vessel in the following manner. Before the pressing the Pratiprasthâtri had taken six Soma-stalks, and put two each between the fingers of his left hand. After each turn of pressing he takes the Upâmsu vessel with his right hand and holds one pair of the Soma-stalks over it (or, according to others, all six at the same time), through which (as through

four times he performs the Nigrâbha,—this makes ten, for of ten syllables consists the virâg, and Soma is of virâg nature: therefore he completes (the ceremony) in ten times.

20. Then as to why he performs the Nigrâbha. Now when he (Soma) first became sacrificial food for the gods, he set his heart on those (four) regions, thinking, 'Could I but consort with those regions as my mate, my loved resort!' By performing the Nigrâbha, the gods then made him consort with the regions as his mate, his loved resort; and in like manner does this (sacrificer) now, by performing the Nigrâbha, make him (Soma) consort with those regions as his mate, his loved resort.

21. He performs with (Vâg. S. VI, 36), 'From east, from west, from north, from south—from every side may the regions resort to thee!' whereby he makes him consort with the regions as his mate, his loved resort. 'O mother, satisfy (him)! may the noble meet together[1]!' A mother

a strainer) the Adhvaryu then pours the Soma-juice from the pressing-skin into the vessel. After the third turn the pressing-stone itself is put into the Hotri's cup, either with or without the muttering of the Nigrâbha formula. According to the commentary on Kâty. IX, 4, 27, the Soma-juice is transferred from the skin to the Upâmsu cup, by the straining-cloth being made to imbibe the juice and then being pressed out so as to trickle down through the plants between the Pratiprasthâtri's fingers. The description given by Haug, Ait. Br., Transl. p. 489, is somewhat different.

[1] The interpretation of this formula is very doubtful. The author evidently takes 'arîh' as nom. plur. of 'ari' (= ârya); but it does not appear how he takes 'nishpara,' while Mahîdhara explains it by 'pûraya (give him, Soma, his fill).' The St. Petersburg Dict. suggests that 'nishpara' may mean 'come out!' and that 'arîh' seems to be a nom. sing. here. I take the last part of the formula to mean, 'May he (Soma) win (or, perhaps, join) the longing (waters)!'

(ambâ) is a woman, and the regions (dis, fem.) are women: therefore he says, 'O mother, satisfy (him)!—May the noble meet together!' The noble doubtless means people (creatures, offspring): he thus means to say, 'May the people live in harmony with each other!' Even the people that are far away (from each other) live in harmony with each other: therefore he says, 'May the noble meet together.'

22. Now as to why he is called Soma. When he first became sacrificial food for the gods, he thought within him, 'I must not become sacrificial food for the gods with my whole self!' That form of his which was most pleasing he accordingly put aside. Thereupon the gods were victorious; they said, 'Draw that unto thee, for therewith shalt thou become our food!' He drew it to him even from afar, saying, verily, that is mine own (svâ me): hence he was called Soma.

23. Then as to why he is called Yagña (sacrifice). Now, when they press him, they slay him; and when they spread him[1], they cause him to be born. He is born in being spread along, he is born moving (yan gâyate): hence yan-ga, for 'yañga,' they say, is the same as 'yagña.'

24. Also this speech did he then utter (Vâg. S.

some of the Nigrâbhyâ water being poured on the Soma at each turn of pressing; and small stalks of Soma being, besides, thrown into the Hotri's cup containing that water. As to the first part of the formula, it may perhaps mean, 'Well, pour out (or, pour forth, intrans.).' Professor Ludwig, Rig-veda IV, p. xvi, thinks that 'nishpara' is a correction of the Taitt. reading 'nishvara,' which Sâyana interprets, 'O mother (Soma), come out (from the stalks, in the form of juice),' and according to the Sûtra quoted by him, the sacrificer is at the same time to think of the wife he loves.

[1] That is, when they perform the Soma-sacrifice.

VI, 37; Rig-veda I, 84, 19), 'Verily thou, a god, shalt extol the mortal, O most mighty! than thee there is no other giver of joy[1], O lord! unto thee do I speak this word, O Indra!' For it was indeed as a mortal that he uttered this, 'Thou alone wilt produce (me) from here, no other but thee!'

25. And from the Nigrâbhyâ water they draw the several grahas (cups or libations of Soma). For it was the waters that slew V*ri*tra, and in virtue of this prowess they flow; and it is from flowing water that he takes the Vasatîvarî water, and from the Vasatîvarî the Nigrâbhyâ water; and from the Nigrâbhyâ water the several grahas are drawn. In virtue of that prowess, then, the grahas are drawn from the Hot*ri*'s cup. Now the Hot*ri* means the *Ri*k (fem.), a woman; and from woman creatures are born here on earth: hence he makes him (Soma) to be born from that woman, the *Ri*k, the Hot*ri*; wherefore (he takes the grahas) from the Hot*ri*'s cup.

---

1 This is the traditional meaning (sukhayit*ri*) assigned to mar*d*ayit*ri* (the merciful, comforter); but it is not quite clear how the author of the Brâhma*n*a interprets it.

FOURTH KÂNDA.

First Adhyâya. First Brâhmana.

1. The Upâmsu (graha), forsooth, is the out-breathing of the Sacrifice[1], the Upâmsu-savana (press-stone) the through-breathing, and the Antaryâma (graha) the in-breathing.

2. Now as to why it is called Upâmsu. There is a graha called Amsu[2], that is Pragâpati: his out-breathing is this (graha); and because it is his out-breathing, therefore it is called Upâmsu.

3. This (graha) he draws without a strainer[3]: whereby he puts the out-breathing into him as one tending away from him, and thus this forward-tending out-breathing of his streams forth from him. He purifies it with sprigs of Soma, thinking 'it shall be pure.' He purifies it with six (sprigs), for there are six seasons: it is by means of the seasons that he thus purifies it.

4. As to this they say, 'When he purifies the Upâmsu by means of sprigs, and all (other) Soma-

[1] That is, the sacrificial man, or the sacrifice personified in Soma and the sacrificer.

[2] Lit. 'the Soma-plant,' hence the (Soma)-sacrifice itself, or Pragâpati. See IV, 6, 1, 1 seq.

[3] Bahishpavitrât, lit. from (a vessel, or Soma) having the strainer outside (away from) it. While no proper strainer is used for the Upâmsu-graha, the Soma-juice being poured through Soma-plants (see p. 244, note 2); at the great pressing it is passed through a fringed straining-cloth (dasâpavitra) spread over the Dronakalasa (the largest of the three Soma-troughs, the others being the Âdhavanîya and Pûtabhrit). See IV, 1, 2, 3.

draughts are purified by means of a strainer, whereby, then, do its sprigs become pure?'

5. He throws them down again (on the unpressed plants) with (Vâg. S. VII, 2), 'What inviolable, quickening name is thine, to that Soma of thine, O Soma, be Hail!' Thus his sprigs become purified by means of the Svâhâ ('Hail!'). But this graha means everything, for it is the type of all the pressings[1].

6. Now, once on a time, the gods, while performing sacrifice, were afraid of an attack from the Asura-Rakshas. They said, 'Let us completely establish the sacrifice: if the Asura-Rakshas should then attack us, our sacrifice will at least be completely established.'

7. Even at the morning Soma-feast they then completely established the entire sacrifice[2],—at this same (upâmsu) graha by means of the Yagus; at the first chant (stotra) by means of the Sâman; and at the first recitation (sastra) by means of the *Ri*k: with that sacrifice thus completely established they subsequently worshipped. And in like manner does this sacrifice now become completely established,—by means of the Yagus at this same graha; by means of the Sâman at the first chant; and by means of the *Ri*k at the first recitation; and with this sacrifice thus completely established he subsequently worships.

8. He presses (the Soma) eight times; for of eight

[1] Viz. inasmuch as the Upâmsu-graha is obtained by three turns of pressing, and each of the three Savanas (pressings, Soma-feasts) consists of three rounds of pressing of three turns each. See p. 256, note 1.

[2] Cf. Taitt. S. VI, 4, 5, where this theory (divested of its legendary form) is ascribed to Aruna Aupavesi.

syllables consists the Gâyatrî, and the morning Soma-feast belongs to the Gâyatrî; thus this (first turn of pressing) is made to be the morning Soma-feast.

9. He draws (the juice of the first turn of pressing into the cup) with (Vâg. S. VII, 1), 'Grow thou pure for Vâkaspati!' for Vâkaspati (lord of speech) is the out-breathing, and this (Upâmsu) graha is the out-breathing: hence he says, 'Grow thou pure for Vâkaspati!'—'purified by the hands with the sprigs of the bull;' for he purifies it with sprigs of Soma: hence he says, 'with the sprigs of the bull;' and 'purified by the hands (gabhasti-pûta[1]),' he says; for—'gabhasti' being the same as 'pâni' (hand)—he indeed purifies it with his hands.

10. He then presses eleven times; for of eleven syllables consists the Trishtubh, and the midday Soma-feast belongs to the Trishtubh: thus this (second turn of pressing) is made to be the midday Soma-feast.

11. He draws (the juice into the cup) with, 'Grow thou pure, a god, for the gods—;' for he (Soma) is indeed a god, and for the gods he becomes pure;—'whose portion thou art;' for he indeed is their portion.

12. He then presses twelve times; for of twelve syllables consists the Gagatî, and the evening Soma-feast belongs to the Gagatî: thus this (third turn of pressing) is made to be the evening Soma-feast.

---

[1] Sâyana, on Taitt. S. I, 4, 2, interprets it, 'Having been purified by the ray of the sun (while growing in the forest), do thou now become pure for the gods through the sprigs of the bull!' Cf., however, Taitt. S. VI, 4, 5, 'gabhastinâ hy enam pavayati,' where 'gabhasti' would seem to be taken in the sense of 'hand' (? the forked one). See p. 244, note 2.

13. He draws (the juice) with, 'Make thou our draughts sweet!' whereby he imbues him (Soma) with sap, and renders him palatable for the gods: hence, when slain, he does not become putrid[1]. And when he offers (that graha) he thereby completely establishes him.

14. 'For one desirous of spiritual lustre (brahmavarkasa) he should press eight times at each (turn),' so they say;—for of eight syllables consists the Gâyatrî, and the Gâyatrî is the Brahman: he indeed becomes endowed with spiritual lustre.

15. Thus the pressing amounts to twenty-four times (of beating). Now there are twenty-four half-moons in the year; and Pragâpati (the lord of creatures) is the year, and the sacrifice is Pragâpati: thus as great as the sacrifice is, as great as is its measure, so great he thereby establishes it.

16. 'For one desirous of cattle he should press five times at each (turn),' so they say;—the cattle (animal victims) consist of five parts: he indeed gains cattle; and there are five seasons in the year; and Pragâpati is the year, and the sacrifice is Pragâpati: thus as great as the sacrifice is, as great as is its measure, so great he thereby establishes it. This, however, is mere speculation: it is the other (manner) which is practised.

17. Having drawn the graha, he wipes (the vessel) all round, lest any (Soma-juice) should trickle down. He does not deposit it; for this is his out-breathing, whence this out-breathing passes unceasingly. Should he, however, desire to exorcise, he may

[1] The Kânva text adds, 'while whosoever else is slain becomes putrid.'

deposit it[1] with, 'I put thee down, the out-breathing of N. N.!' Thus, forsooth, inasmuch as he (the Adhvaryu) does not quit his hold of it, it is not again in that (enemy); and thus both the Adhvaryu and the Sacrificer live long.

18. Or he may merely cover (the vessel by his hand) with, 'I shut thee off, the out-breathing of N. N.!' Thus, forsooth, inasmuch as he does not deposit it, it is not again in that enemy; and thus he does not disorder the vital airs.

19. While he is still inside (the Havirdhâna) he utters 'Hail!' For the gods were afraid lest the Asura-Rakshas should destroy what part of this graha was previous to the offering. They offered it (symbolically) by means of the Svâhâ, while they were still inside (the cart-shed), and what was thus offered they afterwards offered up in the fire. And in like manner does he now offer it up by means of the Svâhâ, while he is still inside, and what has thus been offered he afterwards offers up in the fire.

20. He then walks out (of the Havirdhâna) with, 'I walk along the wide air[2].' For along the air

[1] That is, he may set it down on the khara for a moment without quitting his hold of it. While the subsequent cups of Soma are deposited in their respective places after they have been drawn, the Upâ*ms*u and Antaryâma are offered immediately.

[2] With the Taittirîyas the order of proceeding is somewhat different: The Adhvaryu pours the Soma through the Soma-plants into the Upâ*ms*u cup after each turn of pressing, with, 'Become pure for Vâ*k*aspati, O courser!'—'The bull purified by the hand with the plants of the bull!'—'Thou, a god, art a purifier of the gods whose share thou art: thee, to them!' respectively. He then takes the cup from the Pratiprasthât*ri* with, 'Thou art self-made!' eyes it with, 'Make our drinks sweet;' and wipes it clean upwards with, 'Thee for all powers, divine and earthly!' He then rises with, 'May the mind obtain thee!' steps to the Âhavanîya with, 'I move

the Rakshas roams rootless and unfettered on both sides, even as man here roams along the air, rootless and unfettered on both sides[1]; and, that formula being the Brahman (prayer), a slayer of the Rakshas, he, by means of that Brahman, renders the air free from danger and injury.

21. Thereupon he (the Sacrificer) asks a boon. For the gods, forsooth, greatly desire to obtain the offering of that graha, and they grant to him that boon, in order that he may forthwith offer that graha to them: this is why he asks a boon.

22. He (the Adhvaryu) offers with (Vâg. S. VII, 3), 'Self-made thou art,' for, this graha being his (Yagña's) out-breathing, it is indeed made by itself, born of itself[2]: hence he says, 'Self-made thou art;'—'for all powers, divine and earthly,'—for it is born of itself for all creatures[3];—'May the mind obtain thee!'—the mind being Pragâpati, he thereby means to say, 'may Pragâpati obtain thee!' 'Hail! thee, O well-born, for Sûrya!' thus he utters the second[4]

along the wide air,' and offers, while the sacrificer holds on to him from behind, with, 'Hail! thee, O well-born, to Sûrya!'

[1] See III, 1, 3, 13.

[2] 'For this libation is the out-breathing, and the out-breathing is he that blows yonder (the wind); and he indeed is made by himself, begotten (*gâta*) of himself, since there is no other maker nor begetter of him.' Kânva text.

[3] Perhaps we ought to translate the passage, 'from all the powers, divine and earthly,' for it is born by itself from all the creatures. But cf. Taitt. S. VI, 4, 5: 'Thereby he puts out-breathing both into gods and men.'

[4] While, in its force of 'subsequent,' avara here refers back to the first Svâhâ, pronounced by the Adhvaryu (par. 19); it also has here the meaning of 'lower,' and, developed out of this, that of 'preceding' (in which meaning it occurs in the *Ri*kprâtisâkhya). Hence it is quite impossible adequately to render this play on the words avara, 'subsequent, lower, preceding,' and para, 'higher, subsequent.'

(or inferior) 'Hail!' with regard to a subsequent[1] (or higher; the highest) deity.

23. Now it is in him that burns yonder (the sun) that he has just offered that (libation); and the latter is the All: hence he makes that (sun) the highest of the All. But were he to utter the second (or higher) 'Hail!' with regard to a preceding (or lower) deity[2], then it would be even higher than yonder sun: therefore he utters the second 'Hail!' with regard to a subsequent deity.

24. And, having offered, he wipes the (vessel of the) graha upwards; whereby he puts that out-breathing into him as one tending away from him. Thereupon he rubs (the wiped-off Soma) upon the middle enclosing stick from west to east with the palm of his hand turned upwards[3]—whereby he puts that out-breathing into him as one tending away from him—with, 'Thee to the gods sipping motes of light!'

25. For in that orb which burns yonder he has just offered this (libation), and those rays thereof are the gods sipping motes of light: it is these he thereby gratifies; and thus gratified those gods convey him to the heavenly world.

26. For this same graha there is neither an invitatory prayer nor an offering prayer[4]: he offers it

---

[1] That is, coming after Svâhâ in the formula.

[2] The Kâ*n*va text reads: etasmin vâ etan ma*nd*ale 'haushîd ya esha tapati; sarvam u vâ esha graha*h*; sarvasmâd evaitad asmâd enam uttara*m* karoti ya esho 'smât sarvasmâd uttaro yad dhâvarâ*m* devatâ*m* kuryât para*m* svâhâkâram anyad dhaitasmâd uttara*m* kuryât.

[3] That is to say, he is to pass his hand, palm upwards, under the middle enclosing stick.

[4] Such (*Ri*k verses) as are ordinarily recited by the Hot*ri*. When

with a (Yagus) formula, and thereby it becomes for him supplied with both an invitatory and an offering prayer. And if he desire to exorcise, let him offer some spray (of Soma) which may adhere either to his arm, or to his breast, or to his garment, with, 'O divine plant, let that be true wherefore I pray thee: let N. N. be struck down by destruction falling from above, crash!' Even as one of (enemies) that are being slain might escape, so does this (sprig) fly away from those that are being pressed: thus nothing (hostile)—either running thither or running away[1]—remains to him for whom he performs this. He deposits that (cup) with, 'Thee for the out-breathing!' for this (graha) indeed is his out-breathing.

27. Now some deposit it on the south part (of the khara[2]), for, they say, it is in that direction that

the Upâmsu cup is drawn, the Hotri says, 'Restrain the out-breathing (prâna)! Hail! thee, O well-calling one, to Sûrya!' whereupon he breathes into (or towards) the cup with, 'O out-breathing, restrain my out-breathing!' After that he remains silent till the Antaryâma is drawn, when he addresses that graha with, 'Restrain the in-breathing (apâna)! Hail! thee, O well-calling one, to Sûrya!' whereupon he draws in his breath over the cup, and says, 'O in-breathing, restrain my in-breathing!' He then touches the pressing-stone with, 'Thee to the through-breathing!' and therewith frees his speech from restraint. Ait. Br. II, 21. On the terms out-breathing (prâna) and in-breathing (apâna, or up-breathing, udâna) see part i, p. 19, note 2; J. S. Speijer, Jâtakarma, p. 64; Sâyana on Taitt. S. I, 4, 3 (vol. i, p. 603); Taitt. S. VI, 4, 6. Different Haug, Ait. Br. Transl. p. 118.

[1] 'Na dhâvan nâpadhâvat parisishyate;' perhaps we ought to read 'nâpadhâvan;' unless indeed 'tasya' refers to Soma, as Sâyana seems to take it. The Kânva text has: tathâ ha teshâm nâpadhâvañs kana mukyate yebhyas tathâ karoti.

[2] According to the Sûtras of the Black Yagus (cf. Sâyana on Taitt. S. I, 4, 2, p. 598), the Upâmsu cup is 'deposited' on the south-east and the Antaryâma cup on the north-east corner of the

yonder (sun) moves. Let him, however, not do this, but let him deposit it on the north (uttara) part (of the khara), because there is not any higher (uttara) graha than this. He deposits it with, 'Thee for the out-breathing!' for this (graha) is indeed his out-breathing.

28. He then takes the Upâmsu-savana (pressing-stone). He neither touches it with the fringe nor with the straining-cloth, for that would be like rinsing it in water. If there be any spray adhering to it, let him remove it with his hand, and then lay down (the stone) beside (the Upâmsu cup), with the face towards the north, with, 'Thee for the through-breathing!' for this (stone) is indeed his (Yagña's) through-breathing.

Second Brâhmana.

II. The Great Pressing[1].

1. The Upâmsu (graha), forsooth, is his out-breathing, the Upâmsu-savana (stone) his through-

khara or mound; the Upâmsu-savana stone being placed between them. Before depositing the vessel, the Adhvaryu pours some of the residue of Soma-juice from the Upâmsu cup into the Âgrayana-sthâlî, and having put a large twig of Soma into it for the evening pressing (? the Adâbhya graha, cf. Sây. on Taitt. S. I, 603), he 'deposits' it on the mound.

[1] The 'Great Pressing' (mahâbhishava) from which the Antaryâma and following libations are obtained is performed by the four priests, viz. the Adhvaryu and his three assistants, Pratiprasthâtri, Neshtri, and Unnetri, each having an equal portion of Soma-plants and one of the four remaining pressing-stones assigned to him. The ceremonies mentioned in III, 9, 4, 1 seq. are repeated on the present occasion, each of the priests tying a piece of gold to his ring-finger. The pressing is performed in three rounds of three turns each, the number of single strokes of the several turns

breathing, and the Antaryâma (graha) his in-breathing.

2. Now as to why it is called Antaryâma. That which is the out-breathing is also the in-breathing and the through-breathing. Now, in drawing the Upâmsu (graha), he puts into him that out-breathing which tends away from him; and in drawing the

being, however, not limited, as was the case at the pressing of the Upâmsu. Only before the first turn of each round Nigrâbhyâ water is poured on the plants. After each turn the scattered plants are gathered together on a heap. At the end of each round (of three turns) the Soma is touched (or 'strengthened'); whereupon the completely pressed-out stalks are thrown into the Hotri's cup and the Nigrâbha formula is pronounced (III, 9, 4, 21). The stalks which are still juicy are then 'gathered together' (see III, 9, 4, 19) into the so-called sambharanî and poured into the Âdhavanîya trough, and having been stirred about therein by the Unnetri, are taken out, pressed out, and thrown on the skin, when the same process is repeated. On the completion of the third round the Dronakalasa is brought forward (from behind the axle of the southern cart) by the Udgâtris (for the mantras used by them see Tândya Br. I, 2, 6–7) and placed on the four stones covered with the pressed-out Soma husks, the straining-cloth being then stretched over it, with the fringe towards the north. The Hotri's cup (held by the sacrificer and containing the remaining Nigrâbhyâ water) having then been filled up by the Unnetri with the Soma-juice in the Âdhavanîya trough, the sacrificer pours it in one continuous stream from the Hotri's cup upon the straining-cloth, spread over the Dronakalasa by the chanters (Udgâtris), muttering a mantra (Tândya Br. I, 2, 9) all the time. From this stream the first eight (at the midday pressing the first five) libations are taken, by the respective cups being held under, the remaining libations or cups being drawn either from the strained (or 'pure,' sukra) Soma-juice in the Dronakalasa, or from the Âgrayanasthâlî or the Pûtabhrit. Sâyana on Ait. Br. II, 22, 1 seems to exclude the Antaryâma graha from the 'great pressing:' antaryâmagrahahomâd ûrdhvam mahâbhishavam kritvâ. Also in II, 21, 1 he mentions the Dadhi graha, Amsu graha, and Adâbhya graha (see p. 255, n. 2) as intervening between the Aponaptrîya ceremony and the drawing of the Upâmsu graha.

Antaryâma, he puts into him that in-breathing which tends towards him. But this same in-breathing is confined within his self; and because it is confined (yam) within (antar) his self, or because these creatures are sustained (yam) by it, therefore it is called Antaryâma.

3. He draws it from inside the strainer[1], whereby he puts that in-breathing into him as one tending towards him, and that in-breathing of his is placed (or beneficial) within his self. And thereby also that Upâ*ms*u (libation) of his comes to be drawn from inside the strainer (i. e. from the pure Soma), for one and the same are the Upâ*ms*u and Antaryâma, since they are the out-breathing and in-breathing. And thereby, moreover, that (vital air) of his comes to be unceasing also at the other grahas.

4. Now as to why he purifies the Soma by means of a strainer (pavitra). When Soma had oppressed his own family-priest B*ri*haspati, he restored to him (his property); and on his restoring it, he (B*ri*haspati) became reconciled to him. Still there was guilt remaining, if only for having contemplated oppressing the priesthood.

5. The gods purified him by some means of purification (or a strainer, pavitra), and, being cleansed and pure, he became the (sacrificial) food of the gods. And

[1] Anta*h*pavitrât, lit. from (the vessel or stream of Soma) which has the strainer inside it; the straining-cloth being spread over the Dro*n*akala*s*a, into which the pressed-out Soma-juice is poured. The Petersburg Dictionary assigns to it the meaning 'the Soma within the filtering vessel' (see IV, 1, 1, 3). Perhaps it means 'from that which has a strainer between,' i. e. from the poured-out stream from which the libation is taken, and which is separated from the Dro*n*akala*s*a by the straining-cloth.

in like manner does he now purify him by means of that strainer, and, being cleansed and pure, he becomes the food of the gods.

6. Then as to why the grahas are drawn with the Upayâma[1]. Now Aditi is this (earth), and hers was that prâya*n*îya oblation, that Âditya rice-pap[2]. But that was, as it were, previous to the Soma feast: she desired to have a share along with the gods in the Soma feast, and said, 'Let there be for me also a share of the pressed Soma!'

7. The gods said, 'This sacrifice has already been distributed among the deities: by means of thee the grahas shall be taken and offered to the deities!'—

[1] The term Upayâma, lit. 'foundation, substratum,' referring properly to 'that which is held under' while taking the libation, that is, the cup of the respective graha (and hence also identified with the earth, as the substratum of everything, cf. Sây. on Taitt. S. I, 4, 3), has come to be applied likewise to the formula 'upayâma-g*ri*hîto 'si,' i.e. 'thou art taken with (or on) a support,' which is repeated at those libations before the formulas muttered while they are drawn into the respective vessels or cups (see par. 15). Haug, Transl. Ait. Br. p. 118 note, makes the following distinction between the graha (cup) and pâtra (vessel) of the Antaryâma (and Upâ*m*su) libation: 'The pâtra is a vessel resembling a large wooden jar with but a very slight cavity on the top, in which the Soma-juice is filled. The graha is a small cup, like a saucer, made of earth, and put over the cavity of the Soma vessel, in order to cover the "precious" juice. The bottom of it is first put in water, and a gold leaf placed beneath it. There are as many grahas as there are pâtras; they belong together just as cup and saucer, and are regarded as inseparable. The word graha is, however, taken often in the sense of the whole, meaning both graha and pâtra.' I doubt, however, whether this distinction is in accordance with the old authorities. The graha vessels or cups are described as resembling the shape of a mortar. For other peculiarities, see IV, 1, 5, 19. With some libations there is both a pâtra (cup) and a sthâlî (bowl).

[2] See III, 2, 3, 1 seq.

'So be it!' This, then, is her share of the pressed Soma.

8. And, again, why the grahas are drawn with the Upayâma. The Upayâma indeed is this (earth), since it is this (earth) that bears (upa-yam[1]) food here for cattle and men and trees; and the gods are above this, for the gods are in heaven.

9. The reason, then, why the grahas are drawn with the Upayâma, is that they are drawn by means of this (earth); and why he deposits them in the womb[2], is that this earth is the womb of everything, that it is from her that these creatures have sprung.

10. That same Soma the priests carry about as seed. And seed which is cast outside the womb is lost; but that which he deposits in the womb is indeed deposited in this earth.

11. Now these two grahas are his out-breathing and in-breathing; one of them he offers after sunrise and the other before sunrise, in order to keep the out-breathing and in-breathing distinct from each other. He thus keeps the out-breathing and in-breathing distinct from each other: hence these two, even while being one and the same, are yet called differently 'out-breathing' and 'in-breathing.'

12. Now those two grahas are for him day and night; one of them he offers after sunrise and the

[1] Lit. forms the support or basis for it. The sentence could also be translated, 'this earth doubtless is an upayâma (support), since she bears food.' Apparently he means to say that, as the gods are above, the food to be offered to them requires some support, something to 'hold it up' by for the gods to reach it.

[2] This refers to the formula 'This is thy womb,' with which most libations, after being drawn, are deposited in their proper place on the khara until they are used for offering. See IV, 1, 3, 19.

other before sunrise, in order to keep day and night distinct from each other: he thus keeps day and night distinct from each other[1].

13. The Upâmsu, being the day, he offers in the night; and thus he puts the day into the night: whence even in the deepest darkness one distinguishes something[2].

14. The Antaryâma, being the night, he offers after sunrise, and thus he puts the night into the day: whence that sun, on rising, does not burn up these creatures; whence these creatures are preserved.

15. He draws (the Antaryâma graha) therefrom[3] with (Vâg. S. VII, 4), 'Thou art taken with a support!'—The significance of the Upayâma has been told[4].—'Restrain thou, O mighty (Indra), guard Soma!' the mighty, forsooth, is Indra; and Indra is the leader of the sacrifice: wherefore he says 'O mighty!' and by 'guard Soma' he means to say 'protect Soma!' 'Preserve the riches! gain thee food in the sacrifice!'—riches mean cattle: 'Protect the cattle' he thereby means to say. 'Gain thee food in the sacrifice!'—food means creatures: he thus makes these eager to sacrifice, and these creatures go on sacrificing and praising and toiling.

---

[1] 'Were he to offer both after sunrise, there would only be day, and no night; and were he to offer both before sunrise, there would only be night, and no day.' Kânva text.

[2] Tasmâd v idam râtrau tamasi sati nirgñâyata iva kimkid iva. Kânva text.

[3] Viz. from the stream of Soma poured from the Hotri's cup on the straining-cloth. See p. 256, note 1.

[4] See paragraph 6, with note.

16. 'Into thee I lay day and night[1]; into thee I lay the wide air: allied with the gods, the lower and the higher,'—thereby he makes this (graha) one belonging to all the gods: because by means of it these creatures move about in the air breathing out and breathing in, therefore it belongs to all the gods.—'Delight thyself in the Antaryâma, O mighty one!' the mighty one is Indra, and Indra is the leader of the sacrifice, wherefore he says 'O mighty one!' and in that he draws it with 'into—into,' thereby he means to say 'I lay thee into his (Indra's) self.'

17. Having drawn it, he wipes (the vessel) all round, lest (any Soma-juice) should trickle down. He does not deposit it; for this is the in-breathing: hence this in-breathing passes unceasingly. But should he desire to exorcise, let him deposit it with 'I put thee down, the in-breathing of N. N.!'

18. If he deposits the Upâ*ms*u, let him also deposit this (Antaryâma cup)[2]; and if he does not deposit the Upâ*ms*u, let him also not deposit this. And if he covers the Upâ*ms*u (with his hand), let him also cover this; and if he does not cover the Upâ*ms*u, let him also not cover this: as the performance regarding the Upâ*ms*u, so regarding this (graha); for one and the same are these two, the Upâ*ms*u and Antaryâma, since they are the out-breathing and in-breathing.

19. Now the *K*arakas, forsooth, offer these two

[1] Mahîdhara offers the alternative interpretation, 'through thee I place day and night between (Soma and the enemies),' which is also Sâya*n*a's interpretation on Taitt. S. I, 4, 3; as apparently that of the Taitt. S. itself, VI, 4, 6.

[2] See IV, 1, 1, 17–18.

(libations) with two different formulas[1], saying, 'These two are his out-breathing and in-breathing: we make the out-breathing and in-breathing of varied vigour.' But let him not do this, for they disorder the sacrificer's out-breathing and in-breathing. Now, one might also[2] offer this one silently:—

20. But, as he offers the Upâmsu with a formula, even thereby this (libation) also comes to be offered with a formula. How then could one offer it silently, for these two, the Upâmsu and Antaryâma, are one and the same, since they are the out-breathing and in-breathing?

21. With the very same formula with which he offers the Upâmsu, he offers this (libation),—'Self-made thou art: for all powers divine and earthly: may the mind obtain thee! Hail!—thee, O well-born, for Sûrya!' The significance of this formula has been told.

22. And, having offered[3], he wipes the cup clean downwards. For even now, after offering the Upâmsu, he wiped (the cup) upwards; but here he wipes it downwards; whereby he puts the in-breathing into him as one tending towards him.

23. He then rubs (the wiped-off Soma) upon the middle enclosing stick from east to west with the palm of his hand turned downwards. For even now, after offering the Upâmsu, he rubbed it upon the

---

[1] This does not appear to refer to the Taittirîyas, since by them the same order of proceeding is prescribed for the Antaryâma as for the Upâmsu (p. 252, note 2); cf. Sâyana on Taitt. S. I, p. 603. See, however, Maitrây. Samh. I, 3, 4–5.

[2] 'Apîd (vai)' seems to have much the same meaning ('perhaps') as the later 'api nâma.' Cf. I, 9, 1, 19.

[3] He offers the entire Soma in the Antaryâma cup, without leaving any, or pouring any juice into the Âgrayanasthâlî.

middle enclosing stick from west to east with the palm of his hand turned upwards; but here he does so from east to west with the palm of his hand turned downwards—whereby he puts the in-breathing into him as one tending towards him—with, 'Thee for the gods sipping motes of light!' The significance is the same as before.

24. Having returned (to the cart-shed), he deposits that (cup) with, 'Thee for the in-breathing!' for this is indeed his in-breathing. He deposits them[1] so as to touch one another; whereby he makes out-breathing and in-breathing touch one another, joins the out-breathings and in-breathings together.

25. Now these (cups and stone) repose without being moved until the evening Soma feast, whence men sleep here on earth; and at the evening Soma feast they are used again, whence these men, having slept, awake and are bustling and restless;—this, forsooth, is after the manner of the sacrifice, for the sacrifice is fashioned like a bird: the Upâmsu and Antaryâma (grahas) are its wings, and the Upâmsu-savana (stone) its body.

26. They repose without being moved until the evening Soma feast. The sacrifice is spread along; but what is spread along moves, whence those birds fly spreading their wings, not drawing them in. At the evening Soma feast they are again used; whence

[1] According to the Kânva text he is to place the Antaryâma cup on the south-east corner (dakshinârdhe) of the khara (see p. 255, n. 2); while, according to Kâty. IX, 2, 1, both the Upâmsu and Antaryâma are to be placed on the north-east corner, the former south of the latter. This arrangement, however, would scarcely agree with IV, 1, 1, 27–28. The Upâmsu-savana stone, doubtless, is to lie between the two cups, with its face towards the Upâmsu.

these birds fly drawing in their wings to fold them: this indeed is after the manner of the sacrifice.

27. The Upâmsu, forsooth, is this (earth), for the Upâmsu is the out-breathing, and breathing out one breathes upon this (earth). And the Antaryâma is yonder (sky), for the Upâmsu is the in-breathing (up-breathing), and in breathing up one breathes towards yonder world. And the Upâmsu-savana (stone) is the air, for the Upâmsu-savana is the through-breathing, and he who breathes through (in and out), breathes through this air.

Third Brâhmana.

1. The Aindra-vâyava (graha), forsooth, is his speech; and as such belonging to his self[1]. Now Indra, when he had hurled the thunderbolt at Vritra, thinking himself to be the weaker, and fearing lest he had not laid him low, hid himself. The gods also hid themselves away in the same place.

2. The gods then said, 'Verily, we know not if Vritra be slain or alive: come, let one of us find out, if Vritra be slain or alive!'

3. They said unto Vâyu—Vâyu, forsooth, is he that blows yonder—'Find thou out, O Vâyu, if Vritra be slain or alive; for thou art the swiftest among us: if he lives, thou indeed wilt quickly return hither.'

4. He spake, 'What shall be my reward then?'—'The first Vashat of king Soma!'—'So be it!' so Vâyu went, and lo[2] Vritra slain. He spake, 'Vritra is slain: do ye with the slain what ye list!'

---

[1] That is, to Yagña's body (madhyadeha, Sây.) as distinguished from his limbs. The Petersb. Dict. takes adhyâtmam in the sense of 'in regard to the self (or person).' See IV, 1, 4, 1, with note; IV, 2, 2, 1 seq.

[2] At I, 6, 2, 3; II, 2, 3, 9, I erroneously supplied a verb of

5. The gods rushed thither,—as (those) eager to take possession of their property, so (it fared with) him (V*ri*tra—Soma)[1]: what (part of him) one of them seized, that became an ekadevatya (graha, belonging to one deity), and what two of them, that became a dvidevatya[2], and what many (seized), that became a bahudevatya;—and because they caught him up each separately (vi-grah) by means of vessels, therefore (the libations) are called graha.

6. He stank in their nostrils,—sour and putrid he blew towards them: he was neither fit for offering, nor was he fit for drinking.

7. The gods said to Vâyu, 'Vâyu, blow thou through him, make him palatable for us!' He said, 'What shall be my reward then?'—'After thee they shall name those cups.'—'So be it!' he said, 'but blow ye along with me!'

8. The gods dispelled some of that smell, and laid it into the cattle,—this is that foul smell in (dead) cattle: hence one must not close (his nose) at that foul smell, since it is the smell of king Soma.

9. Nor must one spit thereat[3]; even though he should think himself ever so much affected, let him

motion with the particle ed, following the original interpretation in the Petersb. Dict. and Weber's Ind. Stud. IX, 249. I now adopt the later explanation put forth in the 'Nachträge.' Professor Whitney, Amer. Journ. of Phil., III, p. 399, apparently draws from the same source.

[1] 'As (those) wishing to take possession of their property, so did they seize upon him each for himself (eva*m* ta*m* vyag*ri*h*n*ata);' Kâ*n*va text. The construction of our text is quite irregular.

[2] The dvidevatya grahas (libations belonging to two gods) at the morning Soma feast are the Aindra-vâyava (Indra and Vâyu), the Maitrâ-varu*n*a (Mitra and Varu*n*a), and the A*s*vina.

[3] That is, because of it, or away from it. Perhaps, however, it belongs to the next clause, 'therefore, even ....'

go round it windward[1]; for Soma means eminence, and disease meanness: even as at the approach of his superior the meaner man would get down (from his seat), so does disease go down before him (Soma).

10. Then Vâyu blew a second time through him and thereby made him palatable; whereupon he was fit for offering and fit for drinking. Hence those (vessels), though belonging to various deities, are called 'vâyavya (Vâyu's vessels)[2].' His (Vâyu's) is that first Vasha*t* of king Soma, and, moreover, those vessels are named after him.

11. Indra then thought within himself:—'Vâyu, forsooth, has the largest share of this our sacrifice, since his is the first Vasha*t* of king Soma, and, moreover, those vessels are named after him: nay, but I, too, will desire a share therein!'

12. He said, 'Vâyu, let me share in this cup!'—'What will then be?'—'Speech shall speak intelligibly[3]!'—'If speech will speak intelligibly, then will I let thee share!' Thus that cup henceforward belonged to Indra and Vâyu, but theretofore it belonged to Vâyu alone.

13. Indra said, 'One half of this cup is mine!'—'Only one fourth is thine!' said Vâyu.—'One half is mine!' said Indra.—'Only one fourth is thine!' said Vâyu.

14. They went to Pra*g*âpati for his decision. Pra*g*âpati divided the cup (of Soma) into two parts and said, 'This (half) is Vâyu's!' Then he divided the (other) half into two parts and said, 'This is

[1] That is, in order to inhale as much of the strong smell of the Soma as possible (?).

[2] See p. 158, note 1.

[3] Or, articulately, distinctly (niruktam).

Vâyu's!—This is thine!' then he assigned to Indra a fourth part for his share—one fourth is the same as a quarter: henceforward that cup belonged, one fourth of it, to Indra.

15. Now with this libation there are two puroruk[1]—formulas,—the first belonging to Vâyu alone, and the second to Indra and Vâyu; and two invitatory prayers (anuvâkyâ),—the first to Vâyu alone, and the second to Indra and Vâyu; and two praisha (directions),—the first belonging to Vâyu alone, and the second to Indra and Vâyu; and two offering prayers (yâgyâ),—the first to Vâyu alone, and the second to Indra and Vâyu: thus he assigns to him (Indra) each time a fourth part for his share.

16. He said, 'If they have assigned to me a fourth part each time for my share, then speech shall speak intelligibly only one fourth part!' Hence only that fourth part of speech is intelligible which men speak; but that fourth part of speech which beasts speak is unintelligible; and that fourth part of speech which birds speak is unintelligible; and that fourth part of speech which the small vermin here speaks is unintelligible.

17. Wherefore it has been thus spoken by the *Ri*shi (Rig-veda I, 164, 45):—'Four are the measured grades of speech; the Brâhmans that are wise know them: three, deposited in secret, move not; the fourth grade of speech men speak.'

18. He now draws (the graha) from that (stream of Soma)[2], with (Vâg. S. VII, 7; Rig-veda VII, 92, 1), 'Come nigh to us, O Vâyu, sipping of

[1] Puroruk (lit. 'fore-shining') is the designation of the formulas preceding the Upayâma, 'Thou art taken with a support, &c.'

[2] See p. 256, note 1.

the pure (Soma)! Thine are a thousand steeds, O bestower of all boons! Unto thee hath been offered the gladdening juice whereof thou, O God, takest the first draught!—Thee for Vâyu!'

19. And, having withdrawn (the cup), he again fills it[1], with (Vâg. S. VII, 8; Rig-veda I, 2, 4), 'O Indra and Vâyu, here is Soma-juice: come ye hither for the refreshing draught, the drops long for you!—Thou art taken with a support[2]!—Thee for Vâyu, for Indra and Vâyu!'—with 'This is thy womb[3]: thee for the closely united!' he deposits (the cup). As to why he says, 'Thee for the closely united,'—he who is Vâyu, is Indra; and he who is Indra, is Vâyu: therefore he says, 'This is thy womb: thee for the closely united!'

FOURTH BRÂHMANA.

1. Mitra and Varuna, forsooth, are his intelligence and will; and as such belonging to his self: whenever he desires anything in his mind, as 'Would that this were mine! I might do this!' that is intelligence; and whenever that is accomplished, that is will[4]. Now intelligence indeed is Mitra, and will is

[1] When the cup is half-filled he withdraws it for a moment from the stream of Soma flowing from the Hotri's cup into the Dronakalasa trough; after which he again holds it under to have it filled completely. For the shape of this cup, see IV, 1, 5, 19.

[2] See IV, 1, 2, 6, with note. [3] See IV, 1, 2, 9, with note.

[4] The Kânva text adds, tad asyaitâv âtmanah, 'and these two are of his self,' which seems to be intended to explain the preceding adhyâtmam, 'belonging to his self.' See IV, 1, 3, 1, with note.

Varuna; and Mitra is the priesthood, and Varuna the nobility; and the priesthood is the conceiver, and the noble is the doer.

2. Now in the beginning these two, the priesthood and the nobility, were separate: then Mitra, the priesthood, could stand without Varuna, the nobility.

3. Not Varuna, the nobility, without Mitra, the priesthood: whatever deed Varuna did unsped by Mitra, the priesthood, therein, forsooth, he succeeded not.

4. Varuna, the nobility, then called upon Mitra, the priesthood, saying, 'Turn thou unto me that we may unite: I will place thee foremost, sped by thee, I will do deeds!'—'So be it!' So the two united; and therefrom resulted that graha to Mitra and Varuna.

5. Such, then, is the office of Purohita (placed foremost, domestic priest). Wherefore let not a Brâhman desire to become the Purohita of any one Kshatriya (he may meet with), as thereby righteousness and unrighteousness unite; nor should a Kshatriya make any Brâhman (he may meet with) his Purohita, as thereby righteousness and unrighteousness unite.—Whatever deed, sped by Mitra, the priesthood, Varuna thenceforward did, in that he succeeded.

6. Hence it is quite proper that a Brâhman should be without a king, but were he to obtain a king, it would be conducive to the success (of both). It is, however, quite improper that a king should be without a Brâhman, for whatever deed he does, unsped by Mitra, the priesthood, therein he succeeds not. Wherefore a Kshatriya who intends to do a deed ought by all means to resort to a Brâhman, for

he verily succeeds only in the deed sped by the Brâhman.

7. Now he draws (the Maitrâ-varuna graha) from that (stream of Soma)[1], with (Vâg. S. VII, 9; Rig-veda II, 41, 4), 'This Soma, O Mitra and Varuna, hath been pressed for you; ye holy, now hear my cry!—Thou art taken with a support[2]!—Thee for Mitra and Varuna!'

8. He mixes it with milk. The reason why he mixes it with milk is this. Soma, forsooth, was Vritra. Now when the gods slew him, they said to Mitra, 'Thou also slayest!' But he liked it not and said, 'Surely, I am every one's friend (mitra): being no friend, I shall become an enemy (or, other than Mitra, Amitra).'—'Then we shall exclude thee from the sacrifice!'—Then said he, 'I, too, slay!' Thereupon the cattle went from him, saying, 'Being a friend, he has become an enemy!' Thus he was deprived of the cattle. By mixing (the Soma) with milk, the gods then supplied him with cattle; and in like manner does this (priest) now supply him (the sacrificer or Mitra) with cattle by mixing (the Soma) with milk.

9. As to this they say, 'Surely he liked it not to slay!' Thus, what milk there is in this (mixture) that belongs to Mitra, but the Soma belongs to Varuna: therefore one mixes it with milk.

10. He mixes it with (Vâg. S. VII, 10; Rig-veda IV, 42, 10), 'May we delight in the wealth we have gained, the gods in the offering, the kine in pasture! that unfailing milch cow,

[1] See p. 256, note 1. For the shape of this cup, see IV, 1, 5, 19.

[2] See IV, 1, 2, 6, and note.

O Mitra and Varuna, grant ye unto us day by day!'—with 'This is thy womb: thee for truth and life[1]!' he deposits it. Now as to why he says, 'Thee for truth and life,'—the truth is Mitra[2], since Mitra is the Brahman, and the truth is the Brahman (sacerdotium or sacred writ);—and life is Varuna, since Varuna is the year, and life is the year: therefore he says, 'This is thy womb: thee for truth and life!'

FIFTH BRÂHMANA.

1. The Âsvina graha[3], forsooth, is his organ of hearing; hence in drinking it he turns (the cup) all round[4], since with that ear of his he hears all round.—Now when the Bhrigus, or the Añgiras, attained the heavenly world, *K*yavana the Bhârgava, or *K*yavana the Âñgirasa, was left behind here (on earth) decrepit and ghostlike[5].

---

[1] This is a false analysis of ritâyu, 'righteous, holy.'

[2] The text has 'Brahman,' which must be wrong. The Kânva recension has, correctly, mitro vâ ritam, brahma hi mitro, brahma hy ritam.

[3] The Âsvina graha is not actually taken at this time, but later on, after the oblation of drops and the chanting of the Bahishpavamâna stotra; see IV, 2, 5, 12. The reasons for inserting it here are given in parag. 15–16.

[4] Lit. 'he drinks it while turning it all round,' in accordance with the regular Sanskrit idiom. The Âsvina cup has three mouths, from which the Soma is drunk by turns. See Haug, Transl. Ait. Br. p. 132.

[5] On this legend, and its probable connection with that of Medea's cauldron, and the Germanic 'quecprunno' (Jungbrunnen, well of renovation), see A. Kuhn, 'Herabkunft des Feuers und des Göttertranks,' p. 11. For other translations, see Weber, Ind. Streifen, i. p. 13 seq.; Muir, O. S. T. v. p. 250 seq.; Delbrück ii. p. 121. For

2. But *S*aryâta, the Mânava, just then wandered about here with his tribe, and settled near by that same place. His boys[1], while playing, setting that decrepit, ghostlike man at nought, pelted him with clods.

3. He was wroth with the *S*âryâtas, and sowed discord among them: father fought with son, and brother with brother.

4. *S*aryâta then bethought him[2],—'This has come to pass for something or other I have done!' He caused the cowherds and shepherds to be called together, and said—

5. He said, 'Which of you has seen anything here this day?'—They said, 'Yonder lies a man, decrepit and ghostlike: him the boys have pelted with clods, setting him at nought.' Then *S*aryâta knew that this was *K*yavana.

6. He yoked his chariot, and putting his daughter Sukanyâ thereon, he set forth, and came to the place where the *Ri*shi was.

7. He said, 'Reverence be to thee, O *Ri*shi;

---

another version, apparently more modern, of the same legend, found in the *G*aiminîya (Talavakâra) Brâhma*n*a, see Professor Whitney, Proceedings Amer. Or. Soc. 1883, p. ix.

[1] That is, youths of his clan.

[2] *S*aryâta then bethought him, 'From something I have done, thence (has come) so great a calamity.' It then occurred to him, 'Surely, *K*yavana, the Bhârgava, or Âṅgirasa, was left behind here, decrepit: him I (must) have somehow offended sorely, thence so great a calamity.' He called his tribe together. Having called the tribe together, he said, 'Who, be he cowherd or shepherd, has noticed anything here?' They said, 'Yonder in the wood lies a decrepit, ghostlike man; him the boys have this day pelted with clods: that is the only thing we have descried (? tad evâdarishma),' &c. Kâ*n*va text.

because I knew thee not, therefore have I offended thee; here is Sukanyâ[1], with her I make atonement to thee: let my tribe live at peace together!' And from that same time his tribe lived at peace together. But Saryâta, the Mânava, departed[2] forthwith, lest he should offend him a second time.

8. Now the Asvins then wandered about here on earth performing cures. They came to Sukanyâ, and desired to win her love; but she consented not thereto.

9. They said, 'Sukanyâ, what a decrepit, ghostlike man is that whom thou liest with; come and follow us!' She said, 'To whom my father has given me, him will I not abandon, as long as he lives!' But the *Ri*shi was aware of this.

10. He said, 'Sukanyâ, what have those two said to thee?' She told him all; and, when she had told him, he said, 'If they speak to thee thus again, say thou to them, "But surely, ye are neither quite complete nor quite perfect, and yet ye deride my husband!" and if they say to thee, "In what respect are we incomplete, in what respect imperfect?" say thou to them, "Nay, make ye my husband young again, and I will tell you!"' They came again to her, and said to her the same thing.

11. She said, 'But surely ye are neither quite complete nor quite perfect, and yet ye deride my husband!' They said, 'In what respect are we incomplete, in what respect imperfect?' She said, 'Nay, make ye my husband young again, and I will tell you!'

---

[1] That is, 'the fair maiden.'

[2] That is, 'he broke up his camp and departed with his tribe' (so 'payuyuge grâmah, Kânva recension).

12. They said, 'Take him down to yonder pool[1], and he shall come forth with whatever age he shall desire!' She took him down to that pool, and he came forth with the age he desired.

13. They said, 'Sukanyâ, in what respect are we incomplete, in what respect imperfect?' The *Ri*shi himself answered them,—'In Kurukshetra yonder the gods perform a sacrifice and exclude you two from it: in that respect ye are incomplete, in that respect imperfect!' And the A*s*vins departed forthwith, and came to the gods, as they were performing a sacrifice, after the chanting of the Bahishpavamâna.

14. They said, 'Invite us thereto!' The gods said, 'We will not invite you: ye have wandered and mixed much among men, performing cures.'

15. They said, 'But surely ye worship with a

---

[1] Or, according to the Petersburg Dictionary, 'Throw him into yonder pool.' In the Kâ*n*va text no mention is made of a pool (hrada), but merely of water to which the *Ri*shi is taken by his wife. I subjoin Professor Whitney's translation of the corresponding passage of the *G*aiminîya Br. version: 'They (the A*s*vins) said to him: "Sage, make us sharers in the Soma, Sir." "Very well," said he; "do you now make me young again." They drew him away to the *s*ai*s*ava of the Sarasvatī. He said: "Girl, we shall all come out looking alike; do you then know me by this sign." They all came out looking just alike, with that form which is the most beautiful of forms. She, recognising him .... "This is my husband." They said to him: "Sage, we have performed for you that desire which has been your desire; you have become young again; now instruct us in such wise that we may be sharers in the Soma." ....

'Then *K*yavana the Bhārgavan, having become young again, went to *K*aryāta the Mānavan, and conducted his sacrifice on the eastern site. Then he gave him a thousand; with them he sacrificed. Thus *K*yavana the Bhārgavan, having praised with this sāman (the *k*yāvana), became young again, won a girl for wife, sacrificed with a thousand,' &c.

headless sacrifice!'—'How with a headless (sacrifice)?'—'Nay, invite us, and we will tell you!'—'So be it!' so they invited them. They drew this Âsvina cup for them; and those two became the Adhvaryu priests of the sacrifice, and restored the head of the sacrifice. Then, in the chapter of the divâkîrtyas[1], it is explained how they did restore the head of the sacrifice. Hence this libation is drawn after the chanting of the Bahishpavamâna, for it was after the chanting of the Bahishpavamâna that they arrived.

16. They said, 'Well, but we two, being the Adhvaryus, are the heads (leaders) of the sacrifice: transfer ye that graha of ours to this earlier time, to those belonging to two deities[2]!' Accordingly they transferred that graha for them to a former time, to those belonging to two deities: hence that graha is drawn in the tenth place, and is consecrated by Vashat in the third place. And as to (the significance of) the Asvins,—the Asvins are manifestly[3] those two, heaven and earth[4], for it is those two

[1] Certain verses which are 'to be chanted by day.' According to Benfey (Ind. Stud. III, p. 228) also called mahâdivâkîrtya, and consisting of eleven verses (not in Sâma-veda), the first of which is called 'siras (head),' the second 'grîvâh (neck),' &c. The term is also applied to Sâma-veda II, 803–5 (Rig-veda X, 170, 1–3) in the Uhyagâna II, 12. The reference in the text seems to be to Sat. Br. XIV, 1, 1, 8 seq. See, however, Weber, Ind. Streifen, I, p. 15, note 4. The Kânva MSS. read 'divâkîrteshu.'

[2] One might expect the dual 'dvidevatyau,' as, besides the Âsvina graha, there are only two dvidevatya (belonging to two gods) grahas, viz. the Aindra-vâyava and Maitrâ-varuna. See p. 266, note 3.

[3] Or, in their visible form (pratyaksham).

[4] See Muir, O. S. T. v, p. 234. The identification of the Asvins with heaven and earth may have been suggested by Rig-veda VI, 70, 5,

that have obtained possession of everything here;—'the lotus-crowned' they (the Asvins) are called: Agni, forsooth, is the lotus of this earth, and the sun that of yonder sky.

17. Thus he takes (the Âsvina graha) from that (stream of Soma)[1], with (Vâg. S. VII, 11; Rig-veda I, 22, 3), 'Mix ye the sacrifice, O Asvins, with that goad of yours, rich in honey and joyfulness!—Thou art taken with a support[2]! thee for the Asvins!' with 'This is thy womb: thee for the honey-loving[3] (Asvins)!' he deposits it. Now as to why he takes (the graha) with a verse containing (the word) 'honey (madhu),' and deposits it with 'thee for the honey-loving!'

18. Dadhyañk, the Âtharvana, imparted to them (the Asvins) the brâhmana called Madhu[4]: that (Madhu) is their favourite resort, and with that (favourite resort) of theirs he now approaches them;—hence he takes (their graha) with a verse containing (the word) 'honey,' and deposits it with 'thee for the honey-loving!'

19. Now those vessels (other than those of the three dvidevatya grahas) are smooth[5]. The vessel of the graha for Indra and Vâyu has a (wooden)

---

where heaven and earth are called upon to mix the sweet drink, just as is the case with the Asvins in the verse with which their libation is taken.

[1] See p. 256, note 1.

[2] See IV, 1, 2, 6, and note.

[3] The real meaning of this epithet (mâdhvî) is uncertain.

[4] ? 'The mystery called Madhu (sweet drink, Soma).' See part i, Introd. p. xxxiv; Weber, Ind. Stud. I, p. 290.

[5] It might also mean, that those (three dvidevatya) vessels are smooth, straight, save the peculiarities noticed above. The Kânva text, however, reads, takkhlakshnâny anyâni pâtrâni bhavanti.

'belt' round it: this is its second (peculiarity of) shape, and therefore it belongs to two deities. The vessel of the graha for Mitra and Varuna is goat-like[1]: this is its second shape, and therefore it belongs to two deities. The vessel of the graha for the Asvins is lip-shaped: this is its second shape, and therefore it belongs to two deities. And the reason why (this belongs to) the Asvins is that the Asvins are the heads (mukhya, viz. of the sacrifice), and this head (mukha[2]) is supplied with lips: hence the vessel of the Âsvina graha is lip-shaped.

Second Adhyâya. First Brâhmana.

1. The Sukra and Manthin (grahas), forsooth, are his eyes. Now the Sukra, indeed, is he that burns yonder (the sun); and because it burns there[3], therefore it is (called) Sukra ('bright'). And the Manthin, indeed, is the moon.

2. He mixes it with (barley) meal: thus he makes it to be gruel (mantha), whence it is (called) Manthin. Now those two (sun and moon), forsooth, are the eyes of these creatures; for were those two not to rise, these (creatures) could not distinguish even their own hands.

3. One of them is the eater, and the other the

[1] Or rather, according to the commentary on Kâty. IX, 2, 6, it resembles the breast of the goat (agakâ).

[2] Lit. 'mouth.'

[3] This is how Sâyana takes the passage: sukragrahas tapati sokati dîpyata iti tasya sukranâmadheyam. It is doubtless the correct interpretation, though the pronouns 'esha' and 'etad' might lead one to refer them to the sun.

food[1]; to wit, the *S*ukra is the eater, and the Manthin the food.

4. To one of them corresponds the eater, and to the other the food; to wit, the eater corresponds to the *S*ukra, and the food to the Manthin. Now these two (cups) are drawn for one (person) and offered to another. There are two Asura-Rakshas, *S*a*nd*a and Marka: for them they are drawn; and to deities they are offered. The reason for this is as follows.

5. Now when the gods drove away the Asura-Rakshas, they could not drive away these two; but whatever (sacrificial) work the gods performed, that these two disturbed, and then quickly fled.

6. The gods then said, 'Contrive ye how we shall drive away these two!' They said, 'Let us draw two cups (of Soma-juice) for them: they will come down to us, and we shall seize them and drive them away.' They accordingly drew two cups (of Soma) for them, and they both came down, and, having seized them, they (the gods) drove them away[2]. This is why (the two cups) are drawn for *S*a*nd*a and Marka, but are offered to deities.

7. Also Yâ*gñ*avalkya said, 'Should we not rather draw them for the deities, since that is, as it were, the sign of conquest[3]?' In this, however, he merely speculated, but he did not practise it.

---

[1] The one that is to be eaten (âdya*h*).

[2] Muir, O. S. T. ii, p. 386, translates apa-han by 'to smite,' which would seem to suit this passage much better than the ordinary meaning 'to beat off, repulse, eject;' but see paragraph 20. The corresponding version of the legend in Taitt. S. VI, 4, 10 has 'apa-nud (to drive away).'

[3] Thus this passage is interpreted by Sâya*n*a, who refers to Pâ*n*. III, 3, 161 (sampra*s*ne liṅ) and VIII, 2, 97 (vi*k*âryamâ*n*ânâm

8. Now some make this the puroruk formula of the Sukra, 'He, the longing, light-enveloped, urged the daughters of the dappled (cloud) along the measurer of the welkin,'—saying, 'We thus make it like him that burns yonder, in that he says "the light-enveloped."'

9. But let him make this one the puroruk formula of the Sukra (Vâg. S. VII, 12; Rig-veda V, 44, 1), 'In the olden way, in the former way, in every way, in this way (drawest thou) supremacy from him, the barhis-seated, and the bliss-attaining,'—for the eater corresponds to this (Sukra cup), and the eater is supreme: hence he says, 'Supremacy from him, the barhis-seated, bliss-attaining,'—'and onward strength drawest thou from him, the roaring[1], the swift, that winneth those[2] through which thou waxest strong.—Thou art taken with a support: thee for Sanda!'—With 'This is thy womb: protect manhood!' he deposits (the cup); for to this one corresponds the eater, and the man (hero) is the eater: hence he says, 'This is thy womb: protect manhood!' He deposits it on the south part (of the mount), for it is in that direction that yonder (sun) moves.

10. Thereupon he draws the Manthin with (Vâg.

plutah). Possibly, however, 'no svid' may have to be separated from what follows: 'by no means! for deities we should draw them,' &c. The Kânva text reads, 'no svit khalu devatâbhya eva grihnîyâmeti viditam hîdam iti, tad u tan mîmâmsâm eva kakre nety u tak kakâra.'

[1] The Rig-veda reads 'girâ (through song)' instead of 'dhunim.'

[2] Viz. waters, juice, sap. Professor Ludwig supplies 'plants.' This verse is extremely obscure.

S. VII, 16; Rig-veda X, 123, 1), 'He, the longing[1], light-enveloped[2], urged the daughters of the dappled[3] on the measurer of the welkin[4]: him the bards kiss like a child with songs at the union of the waters and the sun.—Thou art taken with a support: thee to Marka!'

11. He mixes it with (barley) meal: the reason why he mixes it with meal is this. Varuna once struck king Soma right in the eye, and it swelled (asvayat): therefrom a horse (asva) sprung; and because it sprung from a swelling, therefore it is called asva. A tear of his fell down: therefrom the barley sprung; whence they say that the barley belongs to Varuna. Thus whatever part of his eye was injured on that occasion in (that part he now restores him and makes him whole by means of this (barley): therefore he mixes (the libation) with meal.

12. He mixes it with (Vâg. S. VII, 17; Rig-veda X, 61, 3), 'At whichever offerings ye two, rushing swiftly as thought, accept with favour the songs—he, the manly, who by the reeds of this (one) hath seasoned[5] in the hand the

---

[1] Vena, according to Roth and Grassmann, refers to the Gandharva, as the representative of the rainbow. This view is, however, rejected by Ludwig. The entire hymn is extremely and purposely obscure.

[2] *G*yotir-*g*arâyu, lit. 'having light for his chorion, or placenta.'

[3] P*ri*snigarbhâ*h*, lit. 'those who have the dappled (cloud) for their womb (or, are contained therein);' apparently the rain-drops.

[4] Ludwig identifies the measurer of the welkin with the moon (Soma). Grassmann takes it in the sense of 'in measuring through the air.'

[5] The verse is manifestly corrupt. Professor Ludwig omits the accent in 'asrînîta,' thus taking it out of the relative clause; but

(object of his) desire;'—with 'This is thy womb: protect the creatures!' he deposits it (on the north part of the mound); for to this (graha) corresponds the food, and these creatures, the people, are food: hence he says, 'This is thy womb: protect the creatures!'

13. There are two sprinkled and two unsprinkled chips of the sacrificial stake[1]: the Adhvaryu takes a sprinkled and an unsprinkled one; and in like manner the Pratiprasthâtri takes a sprinkled and an unsprinkled one. And the Adhvaryu takes the Sukra, the Pratiprasthâtri the Manthin.

14. The Adhvaryu cleanses (his cup) with the unsprinkled chip, with, 'Swept away is Sanda!' In like manner the Pratiprasthâtri with, 'Swept away is Marka!' Thus even while drawing (the cups), they drive away the two Asura-Rakshas. With 'May the Sukra-sipping gods lead thee forward!' the Adhvaryu walks out (of the cart-shed); with 'May the Manthin-sipping gods lead thee forward!' the Pratiprasthâtri: thus they lead forward those two (libations) to the deities.

15. Behind the Âhavanîya fire they put their (right) elbows together, and deposit (the cups) on the high altar: the Adhvaryu on the right hip, and the Pratiprasthâtri on the left—without quitting their hold of them—with 'Unassailable art

even thus, no satisfactory sense, it seems to me, can be extracted from this line. When the Soma is mixed with milk or some other substance (as meal) two stalks of (kusa) reed-grass are laid on the cup, the accessory substance being then poured through them. Kâty. IX, 6, 9–10.

[1] In paragraphs 13–31 the libations from the Sukra and Manthin cups are anticipated. For their proper place in the actual performance, see note to IV, 3, 1, 1.

thou!' whereby they make the high altar unassailable by evil spirits; for they are about, in walking round it, to pass by the fire: hereby, then, they propitiate it, and so the fire does not injure them, while they walk round it on different sides[1].

16. The Adhvaryu walks round it (on the north side) with (Vâg. S. VII, 13), 'Abounding in heroes, producing heroes'—for to this (libation) corresponds the eater, and the hero is the eater: hence he says, 'Abounding in heroes, producing heroes!'—'encompass thou[2] the sacrificer with growth of wealth!' By saying 'Encompass thou the sacrificer with growth of wealth!' he invokes a blessing upon the sacrificer.

17. And the Pratiprasthâtri walks round (on the south side) with (Vâg. S. VII, 18), 'Abounding in creatures, producing creatures'—for to this (libation) corresponds the food, and the creatures, the people, are the food: hence he says, 'Abounding in creatures, producing creatures,'—'encompass thou the sacrificer with growth of wealth!' By saying 'Encompass thou the sacrificer with growth of wealth!' he invokes a blessing on the sacrificer.

18. They step out (from the altar) after closing the two (cups with their hands): thereby they make them invisible; whence no one sees yonder sun and moon when they go forward (eastwards). Having gone round to the front (of the stake), they uncover (the cups), and offer them while standing in front: thereby they make them visible; whence every one

---

[1] The Petersburg Dictionary takes 'vi-pari-i' in the sense of 'to turn round.' Cf. Kâty. IX, 10, 8; 'vividham dakshina uttaratas ka paribhogam ishyantau (!),' Sâyana.

[2] Or, 'walk round to the sacrificer.'

sees yonder sun and moon when they go backwards. Hence also no one sees the seed which is cast forwards, but every one sees what is produced backwards.

19. They put their elbows together behind the sacrificial stake, unless the fire should blaze up[1]; but if the fire blaze up, they may join their elbows in front of the stake,—the Adhvaryu with, 'The *S*ukra (bright), uniting with the sky, with the earth, with the brightly shining;' the Pratiprasthât*ri* with, 'The Manthin, uniting with the sky, with the earth, with the manthin-shining.' Thus they make these two (cups) the resting-places of the eyes, and join the two eyes together: whence these two eyes are joined together with bones all round[2].

20. The Adhvaryu throws the unsprinkled stake-chip outside (the altar) with, 'Cast out is *S*a*nd*a!' and in like manner the Pratiprasthât*ri* with, 'Cast out is Marka!' Thus they drive away the two Asura-Rakshas before the offerings.

21. Thereupon the Adhvaryu throws the sprinkled stake-chip on the Âhavanîya with, 'Thou art the abode of the *S*ukra!' and in like manner the Pratiprasthât*ri* with, 'Thou art the abode of the Manthin!' These two (chips), forsooth, are the kindlers of the eyes,—he kindles the eyes therewith; whence these eyes are kindled.

22. Thereon he mutters (Vâ*g*. S. VII, 14), 'May

---

[1] The sacrificial stake stands immediately in front of the high altar and fire. 'Yadi tato 'gnir nodbâdheta,' Kâ*n*va text.

[2] That is, the cups represent the sockets of the eyes, and the libations the eyes themselves. Perhaps, however, we ought to translate, 'whence these eyes are joined together (so as to be) on both sides of the bone,' the sacrificial stake representing the bone or bridge of the nose. See paragraph 25.

we be the preservers of thine unbroken manhood and prosperity, O divine Soma!' This is the benediction of that performance: he thereby invokes a blessing.

23. He then calls (on the Agnîdh) for the *S*raushat, and says, 'Urge thou for Indra the Soma-draughts brought forward, the pure, sweet-flowing, of the morrow's morning feast!' As the Vashat is uttered, the Adhvaryu offers; then the Pratiprasthât*ri*; then the cup-bearers (*k*amasâdhvaryu).

24. Those two offer while standing in front (of the fire); for these two (libations) are the eyes: thus they put those eyes in the front; and hence these eyes are in the front.

25. They offer while standing on both sides of the stake; for what the nose is, that is the sacrificial stake: hence these two eyes are on both sides of the nose.

26. Being consecrated by Vashat, these two (libations) are offered with a prayer. Now it is because the entire Savana is offered after these two (libations) that they attain to this (distinction)[1]; and the reason why the entire Savana is offered after them, is that they are most distinctly Pra*g*âpati's own: for they are the eyes, and the eye is the truth, and Pra*g*âpati is the truth;—this is why the entire Savana is offered after them.

27. He offers with, 'This is the first consecration, assuring all boons: he is the first, Varu*n*a,

[1] 'And because these two (libations), having been consecrated by Vashat, are offered with a mantra, therefore they attain this (distinction) that the entire Savana is offered after them; and the reason why the entire Savana is offered after them, is that these two are its eyes,' &c.

Mitra, Agni;—he is the first, Brihaspati, the wise: to that Indra offer ye the liquor, Hail[1]!'

28. Now when he offers with, 'This is the first—he is the first,' it is just as with cast seed; for the eyes doubtless are formed first[2]: hence he offers with, 'This is the first—he is the first.'

29. He then gives directions:—'Let the Hotri's cup advance! let the Brahman's, the Chanters', the Sacrificer's (cups) advance! Ye cup-bearers of the fire-priests[3], approach and fill up (the cups) with pure Soma!'—this is a composite direction. Having gone round (to behind the high altar) the Pratiprasthâtri pours his residue (of Soma) into the Adhvaryu's (Sukra) vessel; whereby he makes the food pay tribute to the eater. The Adhvaryu pours it into the Hotri's cup for drinking; because the draught belongs to the utterer of the Vashat; for the Vashat is the breath, and that breath has, as it were, departed from him while uttering the Vashat. Now the draught is breath: thus he puts that breath back into him.

30. And the reason why they do not take those

---

[1] Or, according to Mahîdhara, 'To that Indra offer ye the liquor with Svâhâ!' The Pratiprasthâtri makes his libation after the Adhvaryu. The Kânva texts read, 'When the Vashat has been uttered, the Adhvaryu offers, then the Pratiprasthâtri, then the others offer;' and, according to Kâty. IX, 11, 2, the Kamasâdhvaryus make libations from the cups of the nine Kamasins (see note 2, next page) with, 'This to Indra' at the Vashat, and 'This to Agni' at the Anu-vashat. These libations are evidently referred to in paragraph 31.

[2] ? Sasvad dha vai retasah siktasya sambhavatas kakshushî eva prathame sambhavatas tasmâd v evam gapati; Kânva rec.

[3] 'Sadasyânam hotrânam.' The subordinate priests to whom the dhishnyas (except that of the Hotri) belong, both those in the Sadas and the Âgnîdhra. See page 148, note 4.

two (cups) behind[1], but do so take the other cups, is that those two are the eyes. The residue (of Soma), then, he pours into the Hotri's cup.

31. They now fill up the cups of the fire-priests. For those residues[2] are remains of oblations, insufficient for offering: he now fills them up again, and thus they become sufficient for offering: therefore they fill up the cups of the fire-priests.

32. Thereupon they make the fire-priests offer together[3]. Now the fire-priests combined convey

---

[1] That is, to the Sadas, for the priests to drink from.

[2] Viz. the residues in the *k*amasas of the Hotrakas. The filling (by the Unnetri) of the cups of the *K*amasins—Hotri, Brahman, Udgâtri, (and Sacrificer); Prasâstri, Brâhmanâ*kh*amsin, Potri, Neshtri, and Âgnîdhra; that of the A*kh*âvâka remains empty for the present—takes place before the libations from the *S*ukra and Manthin grahas. Their cups are filled by the Unnetri with Soma-juice from the Pûtabhrit, with an 'underlayer' and final 'sprinkling' or 'basting' of 'pure' Soma from the Dronakalasa. Previous to the filling, the Adhvaryu calls on the Maitrâvaruna to 'recite to (those cups) being drawn,' the latter then reciting the hymn, Rig-veda I, 16, while the cups are filled. When the *S*raushat is about to be pronounced by the Agnîdh for the *S*ukra and Manthin libations, the cup-bearers lift (udyam) the cups, and, after the Pratiprasthâtri has made his libation, they also pour some Soma-juice into the fire. The cup-bearers of the first four *K*amasins do so twice (and then take their cups back to the Sadas), the others only once. Thereupon the cup-bearers of these last five—the so-called Hotrakas, or subordinate Hotris—are summoned again, and their cups having been filled up with 'pure' Soma, the Adhvaryu makes, after the *S*raushat, two more libations from each at the Vashat and Anuvashat respectively. For the offering-formulas and Anuvashatkâras, see Âsv. V, 5, 18–19. Holding the Agnîdh's cup in his hand, he then goes to the Sadas and sits down facing the Hotri, whereupon they drink together the Soma in the dvidevatya cups.

[3] The phrase 'hotrâh (fem.) samyâgayanti' is apparently analogous to the 'patnîh samyâgayanti' [they perform the Patnîsamyâgas, or, make the wives (of the gods) participate in the sacrifice] of the

the sacrifice to the gods,—it is them he thereby satisfies together, thinking, 'Satisfied and pleased they shall convey the sacrifice to the gods:' therefore they make the fire-priests offer together.

33. When (the libation of) the first, or last[1] fire-priest has been offered, he addresses them (Vâg. S. VII, 15), 'Let the priests' offices be satisfied, they that have obtained a good sacrifice of sweet drink; they that are well-pleased, when they have obtained good offering with Svâhâ!' for this is the satisfaction of the priests' (offices). Thereupon he approaches (to the Hotri's hearth) and sits down with his face to the west, with 'The Agnîdh hath sacrificed!' for on this occasion the Agnîdh sacrifices last of those that sacrifice: hence he says, 'The Agnîdh hath sacrificed.'

SECOND BRÂHMANA.

1. The Âgrayana graha, forsooth, is his self (body, trunk), and as such it is his all; for this self is one's all. Therefore he draws it by means of this (earth), for of her is the bowl[2], and with a bowl he draws this (libation); and this (earth) is all, as this

---

Haviryagña. See part i, p. 256. Indeed Mahîdhara identifies the hotrâs with the metres of the offering-formulas, thus treating them as a kind of deities.

[1] The order of the dhishnya-priests is (1. Hotri), 2. Prasâstri (Maitrâvaruna), 3. Brâhmanâkhamsin, 4. Potri, 5. Neshtri, 6. Akhâvâka—the fires of all of whom are in the Sadas—and 7. the Agnîdh (in the Âgnîdhra fire-house). The Akhâvaka, however, is for the present excluded from offering.

[2] Viz. inasmuch as the bowl is made of clay,—asyâh prithivyâh sakâsât sthâlî bhavati utpadyate; Sây. The Âgrayana, Ukthya, and Dhruva grahas are drawn in a sthâlî (pot or bowl).

graha is all: hence he takes it by means of this (earth).

2. He draws it full; for the 'full' means all, and this graha is all: therefore he draws it full.

3. He draws it for the All-gods; for the All-gods are all, and this graha is all: therefore he draws it for the All-gods.

4. He draws it at all (three) Soma feasts; for the (three) feasts mean all, and this graha is all: therefore he draws it at all the feasts.

5. And if the king (Soma) become exhausted, they extend him from out of that (bowl), make him issue therefrom; for the Âgrayana is the body, and from the body all these limbs issue. Therefrom they draw at the end the Hâriyogana cup[1]: whereby the sacrifice is established at the end in this resting-place, the body (or its own self).

6. Then as to why it is called Âgrayana. His speech which he restrains, on taking up that press-stone[2], spoke out again first at this (libation); and because it spoke out first (agre) at this (libation), therefore this is called the Âgrayana[3].

7. It was from fear of the evil spirits that (the gods) restrained their speech. Previously to this he draws six grahas, and this is the seventh: for there are six seasons in the year, and the year is all.

8. And all being conquered and free from danger and injury[4], the gods now first uttered speech; and

---

[1] See IV, 4, 3, 2.

[2] The Upâmsusavana, cf. III, 9, 4, 6.

[3] The primary meaning seems to be 'firstling.' For the Âgrayaneshti, or offering of first-fruits, see part i, p. 369.

[4] Or perhaps, 'and their entire conquest being free from danger and injury;' or, 'security and peace (abhayam anâshtram) having

in like manner does he first utter speech now that everything is conquered and free from danger and injury.

9. He now draws it from that (stream of Soma[1]) with (Vâg. S. VII, 19; Rig-veda I, 139, 11), Ye Gods, who are eleven in heaven, who are eleven on earth, and who are eleven dwelling in glory in the (aerial) waters: do ye graciously accept this sacrifice!—Thou art taken with a support: thou art Âgrayana, a good firstling (sv-âgrayana)!' Hereby he makes that speech of renewed vigour; whence he speaks therewith in a different way, while yet the same, in order to avoid sameness; for were he to take it with, 'Thou art Âgrayana, thou art Âgrayana,' he would commit (the fault of) sameness: therefore he says, 'Thou art Âgrayana, a good âgrayana.'

10. 'Guard the sacrifice! guard the lord of the sacrifice!' whereby he utters freed speech, meaning to say, 'Protect the sacrifice! protect the sacrificer!' for the lord of the sacrifice is the sacrificer. 'May Vishnu guard thee with his might! guard thou Vishnu!' whereby he utters freed speech—Vishnu being the sacrifice—'May the sacri-

been completely gained.' Cf. IV, 3, 3, 5; also III, 6, 3, 11; 8, 1, 9; 8, 2, 3.

[1] The Âgrayana is taken rather from two streams of Soma, viz. from that poured by the sacrificer from the Hotri's cup into the Dronakalasa, and from another poured out by the Unnetri, and consisting either of Soma taken from the Âdhavanîya or, according to others, of the residue of the Upâmsu libation, which had been temporarily kept in the Âgrayana bowl (see p. 255, note 2), and has to be emptied by the Unnetri into some other vessel, when that bowl is about to be used for the Âgrayana libation. See Kâty. IX, 6, 15 comm.

fice protect thee with its power! protect thou the sacrifice!'—'Guard thou the Soma feasts all around!' whereby he means this very graha, because that belongs to all (three) Soma feasts[1].

11. Having then wrapped up (the bowl in) a fringed filtering-cloth, he utters 'Hiṅ!' Now that same speech (Vâ*k*, fem.), being unsupported, lay exhausted. By means of the 'Hiṅ' the gods infused breath into that exhausted speech, for the 'Hiṅ' is breath, the 'Hiṅ' is indeed breath: hence one cannot utter the sound 'hiṅ' after closing his nostrils. By means of that breath she rose again, for when one who is exhausted takes breath, he rises again. And in like manner does he now infuse breath into the exhausted speech by means of the 'Hiṅ,' and through that breath she rises again. Thrice he utters the 'Hiṅ,' for threefold is the sacrifice.

12. He then says (Vâ*g*. S. VII, 21), 'Soma becometh pure!' For that (speech) which, for fear of the Asura-Rakshas, they (the gods) did not utter, he now utters and reveals when all is conquered and free from danger and injury: therefore he says, 'Soma becometh pure.'

13. 'For this priesthood, for this nobility'—whereby he means to say, 'for the priesthood as well as for the nobility;'—'for the Soma-pressing sacrificer he becometh pure;' whereby he means to say, 'for the sacrificer.'

14. Here now they say, 'Having said this much, let him deposit (the cup); for as much as the priesthood, and the nobility, and the people are, so much

[1] The Âgraya*n*a libation is repeated at the midday as well as at the evening feast.

means this All, since Indra and Agni are this All[1]: hence, having said this much, let him deposit (the cup).'

15. Let him, nevertheless, say this more, 'For sap and pith he becometh pure,'—by saying 'for sap' he means to say 'for rain;' and 'for pith' he says with a view to that pith or juice which springs from rain;—'for the waters and plants he becometh pure,' this he says for the waters and plants;—'for heaven and earth he becometh pure,' this he says for those two, heaven and earth, whereon this All rests;—'for well-being he becometh pure,' whereby he means to say 'for good.'

16. Here now some say, 'for spiritual lustre he becometh pure;' but let him not say so, for in saying 'for this priesthood,' he says it with a view to spiritual lustre. With, 'Thee for the All-gods! this is thy womb: thee for the All-gods!' he deposits (the cup); for it is for the All-gods that he draws it. He deposits it in the middle (of the mound); for this is his trunk, and that trunk is, as it were, in the middle. On the right (south) side of it is the Ukthya bowl, and on the left side the Âditya bowl.

THIRD BRÂHMAN̲A.

1. That Ukthya (graha), forsooth, is his undefined breath (vital air)[2], and as such it is that self of his; for the undefined breath is the self; it is his

---

[1] On Indra and Agni, as the divine representatives of the two privileged castes, see part i, Introd. p. xvi seq.

[2] We ought doubtless, with the Kânva text, to read 'prân̲ah' instead of 'âtmâ.'

vital energy. Hence he draws it by means of this (earth), because of her is the bowl, and he draws it with a bowl;—for undecaying and immortal is this (earth), and undecaying and immortal is the vital energy; therefore he draws it by means of this (earth or bowl).

2. He draws it full; for full means all, and the vital energy means all: therefore he draws it full.

3. That Dhruva (graha)[1], forsooth, (also) is his vital energy; by it his body is held together, and the joints are knit together. For (when) the last cup has not yet been drawn from that (Soma juice in the Ukthya vessel) for the A*kh*âvâka priest,

4. Then he takes the king (Soma) down (from the cart)[2], and pours one third of the Vasatîvarîs (into the Âdhavanîya trough). Thus the joint unites; for, indeed, he makes (the Ukthya cup) the first of the second pressing (Soma feast), and the last of the first: that which belongs to the second pressing he makes first, and that which belongs to the first he makes last. Thus he interlocks them; whence these joints are interlocked: this one overlapping thus, and this one thus.

5. In like manner at the midday pressing: (when)

---

[1] See IV, 2, 4, 1 seq.

[2] At the end of the morning feast the Soma in the Ukthya bowl (sthâlî) is poured into the Ukthya cup (pâtra) in three portions; and part of each having been offered, the remaining juice is drunk by the Hotri's assistants, viz. the Pra*s*âst*ri*, Brâhma*n*â*kh*a*m*sin, and A*kh*âvâka. Each of these potations is preceded by the chanting of an âgya-stotra, and the recitation of the âgya-*s*astra (see next page, note 2). But before the portion of the last-named priest is poured into his cup (*k*amasa), fresh Soma-plants are taken down from the cart for the midday pressing; one half of the remaining Vasatîvarî water (or one third of the original quantity) being also poured into the Âdhavanîya trough. See III, 9, 2, 3.

the last cup has not yet been drawn therefrom for the A*kh*âvâka priest, he pours (the remaining) one-third of the Vasatîvarî (into the Âdhavanîya). Thus the joint unites; for, indeed, he makes it the first of the second pressing, and the last of the first pressing[1]: that which belongs to the second pressing he makes first, and that which belongs to the first he makes last. Thus he interlocks them; whence these joints are interlocked: this one overlapping thus, and this one thus. And because his body is thereby held together, therefore this (graha) is his vital energy.

6. This (Ukthya graha) is the cow of plenty, Indra's special portion. At the morning feast he (the Adhvaryu) divides it for three songs of praise[2], and at the midday feast for three,—this makes six times, for there are six seasons, and the seasons mature all wishes here on earth: for this reason, then, this (libation) is the cow of plenty, Indra's special portion.

7. He draws it without (reciting) a puroru*k*; for the puroru*k* is a song of praise, since the puroru*k* is a *Rik*, and the song of praise is *Rik*; and the libation is Sâman; and what other (formula) he mutters, that is Ya*g*us. Formerly these same (puroru*k* verses) were apart[3] from the *Rik*s, apart from the Ya*g*us, and apart from the Sâmans.

---

[1] That is to say, the last (thing) of the first of the last two pressings, or of the midday pressing.

[2] Uktha, lit. 'recitation,' is the old term for '*s*astra' (IV, 3, 2, 1 seq.). Regarding the three *s*astras of the Hotrakas, for the recitation of which the Ukthya graha is divided between those priests, see notes on IV, 3, 1, 25; 3, 3, 19.

[3] The Kâ*n*va text reads thrice 'abhyardhe.' Regarding the puroru*k* formulas see p. 268, note 1.

8. The gods said, 'Come, let us place them among the Yagus: thus this science will be still more manifold.' Accordingly they placed them among the Yagus, and thenceforward this science was still more manifold.

9. And the reason why he draws this (graha) without a puroruk, is that the puroruk is praise, (being) a *Rik*, and the song of praise is *Rik*; and in that he divides it for recitations, thereby indeed it becomes possessed of a puroruk: hence he draws it without a puroruk.

10. Now he draws it from that (stream of Soma[1]), with (Vâg. S. VII, 22), 'Thou art taken with a support: thee for Indra, possessed of the great (chant), possessed of vigour,'—for Indra is the deity of the sacrifice; wherefore he says 'thee for Indra;' and by 'possessed of the great (chant), possessed of vigour,' he means to say 'for him, the strong;'—'I take (thee) the song-pleasing,' for he indeed takes it for songs of praise;—'what great vigour is thine, O Indra'—whereby he means to say, 'what strength is thine, O Indra'—'for that (I take) thee! for Vishnu—thee!' for he takes it for the life of the sacrifice: hence he says, 'for that—thee! for Vishnu—thee!' With, 'This is thy womb: thee for the songs of praise!' he deposits it; for he indeed takes it for songs of praise.

11. He distributes it[2] with, 'Thee, the god-

---

[1] See p. 256, note 1.

[2] That is, he pours, for each of the three assistant priests, his respective portion into the Ukthya-pâtra. This distribution does not however take place till the end of the morning performance; see note to IV, 2, 2, 4; 3, 1, 25.

pleasing[1], I take for the gods, for the life of the sacrifice.' He who would perform it in this manner would assume the command[2]; but let him rather distribute it to the respective deities.

12. With, 'Thee, the god-pleasing, I take for Mitra and Varu*n*a, for the life of the sacrifice!' (he takes the portion) for the Maitrâvaru*n*a priest;—for in verses to Mitra and Varu*n*a they (the Udgât*ri*s) chant praises for this (libation); and he (the Hot*ri*) afterwards recites verses to Mitra and Varu*n*a for the *s*astra, and offers with a verse to Mitra and Varu*n*a.

13. With, 'Thee, the god-pleasing, I take for Indra, for the life of the sacrifice!' (he takes the portion) for the Brâhma*n*â*kh*am*s*in; for in verses to Indra praises are chanted for this (libation); and verses to Indra are afterwards recited as a *s*astra, and offering is made with a verse to Indra.

14. With, 'Thee, the god-pleasing, I take for Indra and Agni, for the life of the sacrifice!' (he takes the portion) for the A*kh*âvâka; for in verses to Indra and Agni praises are chanted for this (libation); and verses to Indra and Agni are afterwards recited as a *s*astra, and offering is made

[1] Or, the god-prospering (i. e. the one prospering the gods), devâvî.

[2] Pra*s*âsana*m* kuryât. The same phrase occurs I, 9, 1, 14, where I translated 'will ensure dominion,'—probably wrongly, though I am by no means sure of the correct meaning. Sâya*n*a there seems to take it in the sense of 'he bids (the gods grant his request), thus having chiefly his own interest in view'—'pra*s*âsyante 'to devâ*h* prârthyamânâ iti pra*s*âsanam parusha*m* syât sâkshât svârthaparatva*m* kuryâd ity artha*h*.' The Kâ*n*va text reads, 'let him not divide (the libation) with this (formula), for he who divides it thus—pra*s*âsana*m* kuryât.' Perhaps he means to say, that by using that formula one would put oneself above the gods. At I, 9, 1, 14 'one would give orders (to the gods)' is probably the right translation.

with a verse to Indra and Agni. With, 'Thee.... for Indra,' he performs at the midday feast, for the midday feast is sacred to Indra.

15. Now the *K*arakâdhvaryus[1] divide (the Ukthya libation into three portions), with 'Thou art taken with a support: thee, the god-pleasing, I take for the gods; (thee) the praise-pleasing, for praises,—agreeable to Mitra and Varu*n*a!'—with 'This is thy womb: thee to Mitra and Varu*n*a!' he (the *K*arakâdhvaryu) deposits it; and with 'Thou art a re-offering' he touches the sthâlî.

16. 'Thou art taken with a support: thee, the god-pleasing, I take for the gods; (thee) the praise-pleasing, for praises,—agreeable to Indra!—This is thy womb: thee to Indra!' thus he deposits it; and with 'Thou art a re-offering' he touches the sthâlî.

17. 'Thou art taken with a support: thee, the god-pleasing, I take for the gods; (thee) the praise-pleasing, for praises,—agreeable to Indra and Agni! —This is thy womb: thee for Indra and Agni!' thus he deposits it. He does not at this (third portion) touch the sthâlî with 'Thou art a re-offering.' '.... Thee for Indra!' he says each time at the midday feast, for the midday feast is sacred to Indra. Twice he touches the sthâlî with 'Thou art a re-offering;' and silently he puts it down the third time.

18. But, in order to avoid sameness (of performance), let him not take it out with the 'support;' nor let him deposit it in the 'womb;' for this (Ukthya

[1] 'Such is the rule (sthiti); but the *K*arakâdhvaryus divide it in this way.' Kâ*n*va text. The formulas of the Taitt. S. I, 4, 12, and Maitrây. S. I, 3, 14, differ from the above; perhaps the Kâ*th*aka is referred to; see v. Schroeder, M. S. I, p. 36, note 3.

libation) has at first been taken with the 'support,' and it has at first been deposited in the womb;—and were he now also to take it with the 'support,' and deposit it in the 'womb,' he would assuredly commit (the fault of) sameness. And as to his touching the sthâlî with 'Thou art a re-offering,' he will indeed again take a libation therefrom. Let him not heed this, but let him put down (the vessel) silently.

FOURTH BRÂHMA*N*A.

1. That (opening of) vital air of his which is in front, that, forsooth, is the Vai*s*vânara (graha); and that which is behind is the Dhruva. Formerly, indeed, both these grahas, the Dhruva and Vai*s*vânara, were drawn; and even now one of them is still drawn, to wit, the Dhruva[1]. And if he acquire a knowledge of that (Vai*s*vânara graha) either from the *K*arakas, or from anywhere else, let him pour it into the sacrificer's cup; but this (Dhruva graha he pours) into the Hot*ri*'s cup[2].

2. Now, what part of him there is below the navel, that part of his self, that vital energy of his, is this (Dhruva): hence he draws it by means of this (earth), because of her is the bowl (sthâlî)[3], and with a bowl he draws it;—for undecaying and immortal is this (earth), and undecaying and immortal is the vital energy: therefore he draws it by means of this (earth).

---

[1] 'Formerly they took these two separately, as Dhruva and Vai*s*vânara; but now they take them as one only.' Kâ*n*va text.

[2] Both these libations are reserved for the evening feast.

[3] See p. 288, note 2.

3. He draws it full; for full means all, and the vital energy means all: therefore he draws it full.

4. He draws it for (Agni) Vai*s*vânara; for Vai*s*vânara ('he that belongs to all men') is the year, and the vital energy (life) is the year: therefore he draws it for Vai*s*vânara.

5. Having been drawn at the morning pressing, it reposes apart from that time: thus he guides him (the sacrificer) safely through all the pressings.

6. Let him not pour it (into the Hot*ri*'s cup) during the chanting; for, verily, were he to pour it out during the chanting, the sacrificer would not live through the year.

7. He pours it out during the recitation of the *s*astra; whereby he guides him safely over the twelvefold chant of praise: thus he obtains ever continued life, and thus does the sacrificer live long. Therefore the Brâhman should sit through the praise of Agni (Agnish*t*oma)[1]; till the offering of this (libation) he must not slip away[2]—nor must he

---

[1] ? Tasmâd brâhma*n*o 'gnish*t*omasat syât. The obvious meaning of this sentence is, 'hence the celebrator of the Agnish*t*oma should be a Brâhman,' or, perhaps, 'hence a Brâhman should celebrate the Agnish*t*oma;' but I do not see how it can have that meaning here, without at least a double-entendre in the term 'agnish*t*omasad,' Agnish*t*oma in that case ('the praise of Agni') referring both to the sacrifice generally and to the chanting (stoma or stotra). See next note. My MS. of Sâya*n*a's commentary (from the library of the Mahârâ*g*a of Bikaner) has unfortunately an omission here.

[2] Viz. from the Sadas; 'ni*h*sarpet,' Kâ*n*va text. The verb sarp, 'to glide or creep,' is used technically of a peculiar noiseless mode of leaving (ni*h*sarp) the Sadas and returning thither (prasarp or pratisarp, see paragraph 10), and respectfully approaching the dhish*n*ya fires. If it has to be taken here in that sense, the first prohibition would seem to refer to the Hot*ri* (cf. Ait. Br. II, 22, where the question is argued whether or not the Hot*ri* ought to

discharge urine: thus he obtains the full life—for this (libation) is his life—thus he reaches the full (measure of) life.

8. For, what part of him there is below the navel, that part of his self is this (Dhruva libation). Hence were he to slip away or discharge urine before the offering of this (libation), he would discharge the Dhruva (the firm, constant one): hence, lest he should discharge the Dhruva, he sits through the praise of Agni. This, indeed, applies only to the sacrificer[1], for this (libation) is part of the sacrificer's self.

9. He sits through the praise of Agni[2];—for Soma is glory: hence they both approach, he who partakes of the Soma and he who does not,—they approach, forsooth, to behold that glory. And thus indeed the Brâhmans, having crept near together, take unto them that glory, when they drink (the Soma);—and verily whosoever, knowing this, drinks (Soma), becomes glorious[3] indeed.

10. Now, those same (priests) having, while gliding along[4], deposited that glory in him who sits through (celebrates) the praise of Agni, they glide along and turn away from that glory[5]: having thus encompassed it, he again takes that glory unto him-

---

proceed to the chanting-place with the other priests, and is decided in the negative); since the sacrificer, to whom the second prohibition refers (Kâty. IX, 6, 23), goes along with them, according to IV, 2, 5, 4. According to the commentary on Kâty. IX, 6, 33, in performing the sarpa*n*a the priests and sacrificer should move along sitting at the morning feast; walking with bent bodies at the midday feast; and walking upright at the evening feast.

[1] Tad u tad ya*g*amânasyaiva. Kâ*n*va text.

[2] Or, he indeed becomes a celebrator of the Agnish*t*oma.

[3] The Kâ*n*va text has 'ya*s*asvî.'

[4] See p. 299, note 2.

[5] The Kâ*n*va MS. (W.) reads, 'agnish*t*omasad etad yá*s*a*h* sanni-

self;—verily, whosoever, knowing this, sits through (celebrates) the praise of Agni, he passes away after becoming the most glorious of these (men).

11. Now, the gods and the Asuras, both of them sprung from Pragâpati, were contending for this sacrifice—their father Pragâpati, the year,—saying, 'Ours he shall be! ours he shall be!'

12. Then the gods went on singing praises and toiling. They devised this Agnishtoma feast, and by means of this Agnishtoma feast they appropriated the entire sacrifice and excluded the Asuras from the sacrifice. And in like manner does this (sacrificer), by means of this Agnishtoma feast, now appropriate the entire sacrifice, and exclude his enemies from the sacrifice: therefore he celebrates the Agnishtoma.

13. Having drawn it (the Dhruva graha), he deposits it with the northern cart[1], lest he should confound the vital airs, for the grahas are vital airs: now the other grahas he deposits on the raised (mound), but this one (he deposits) after pushing (the dust) aside without leaving as much as a blade of grass between[2].

14. For those (other cups of Soma) are that part of his body from the navel upwards, and above, as it were, is what is from the navel upwards, and above, as it were, is what is raised: therefore he deposits

dhâyata etasmât parâñko yasáso (sic) bhavanti' ('they turn away from that glorious one').

[1] The dhruva-sthâlî is placed just in front of the northern prop.

[2] Lit. not putting a blade of grass between (the sthâlî and the ground on which it stands). Cf. Kâty. IX, 2, 18. Apparently he is to shift the sthâlî along the ground from the khara to the place where it is to stand, all grass and other objects being thus removed between this vessel and those standing on the mound ('vyuhyaitam na trinam kanântardhâya,' Kânva text).

(the others) on the raised (mound), and this one (he deposits) after pushing (the dust) aside without leaving as much as a blade of grass between.

15. For this (cup of Soma) is that part of his body from the navel downwards; and below, as it were, is what is from the navel downwards; and below, as it were, is what (one deposits) after pushing (the dust) aside and leaving not so much as a blade of grass between: therefore he deposits this (Dhruva graha) after pushing (the dust) aside, without leaving so much as a blade of grass between.

16. Now, that sacrifice which is being performed is Pragâpati, from whom these creatures on earth have been born,—and indeed even now they are born after this (sacrifice). The creatures that are born therefrom after those (libations) which he deposits on the raised (mound), stand on this (earth) with something different from their own self,—for those which stand on hoofs indeed stand on this (earth) with something different from their own self. And when he deposits this (Dhruva cup) after shifting aside (the dust), and not leaving so much as a blade of grass between,—the creatures that are born thereafter from this (sacrifice), stand on this (earth) with their own self, namely, men and wild beasts[1].

17. Moreover, on the one hand, in throwing up (the mound) he puts upon this (earth) something different from it; and those creatures that are born from this (sacrifice) after those (libations) which he deposits on the raised (mound), they stand on this (earth) with something different from their own self, namely, with hoofs.

[1] Svâpada, lit. 'dog-footed' beasts.

18. And, on the other hand, they offer in the Âhavanîya[1] a sacrificial cake, parched barley-grains, porridge, sour curds, and clotted curds,—this is like pouring (food) into one's mouth. But this (libation) remains apart, (being) of one form like water. Hence while he eats the multiform food with that mouth (the fire), he lets flow from that opening the uniform (libation) like water. Then as to why it is called Dhruva.

19. Now, once on a time, the gods, while performing sacrifice, were afraid of an attack from the Asura-Rakshas. The Asura-Rakshas assailed them from the south, and overturned those southern cups of Soma,—even that southern Soma-cart they overturned; but that other (cart) they could not overturn: the northern cart then kept the southern cart steady[2]. And because they could not overturn that (northern cup) therefore it is called Dhruva (firm)[3].

20. They indeed watch over it; for this (cup of Soma) is the head of Gâyatrî, Gâyatrî being the sacrifice,—there are twelve chants (stotra) and twelve recitations (*s*astra): that makes twenty-four, and of twenty-four syllables consists the Gâyatrî. This cup of Soma is her head; but the head means excellence, for the head indeed means excellence: hence people say of him who is the best man of a place, that 'so and so is the head of such and such a place.' And, indeed, the best man would come to harm, if this

---

[1] See IV, 2, 5, 15 seq.

[2] 'They (the gods) then made the southern cart firm from (or by means of) the northern cart.' Kâ*n*va text.

[3] It is more probable that the Dhruva (firm, constant) derives its name from the fact that it remains intact till the very end of the Agnish*t*oma, as suggested in the Petersburg Dictionary.

(cup) were to come to harm; and, the best man being the sacrificer, they watch (this cup) lest the sacrificer should come to harm.

21. Moreover, this (graha) is Gâyatrî's calf, Gâyatrî being the sacrifice,—there are twelve chants and twelve recitations: that makes twenty-four, and of twenty-four syllables consists the Gâyatrî. This is her calf;—when they watch it, then they watch these calves for the sake of the milking: 'as they yield this milk, even so may this Gâyatrî yield all the sacrificer's wishes,'—this is why they watch it.

22. And when both the Adhvaryu and the Pratiprasthât*ri* walk out (of the cart-shed) and (afterwards) enter (again)[1], it is as if (a cow) were to come with the calf tied to her. They come to this cup of Soma, and he (the Adhvaryu) pours it out; whereby he lets loose the Gâyatrî: 'Made over to the sacrificer, may this Gâyatrî yield all his desires!' for this reason he pours it out.

23. He pours it (into the Hot*ri*'s cup[1]) with (Vâ*g*. S. VII, 25), 'The firm Soma I pour out—or, I take—with firm mind and speech: now may Indra make our people of one mind, free from enemies!' whereby he means to say, 'so that Indra may make these our creatures, the people, of one mind and free from enemies, for their happiness and glory and nourishment!'

24. Here now he draws it from that (stream of Soma)[2], (Vâ*g*. S. VII, 24; Rig-veda VI, 7, 1), 'Agni

[1] Viz. at the evening feast, when the Adhvaryu pours the Soma from the Dhruva-sthâlî into the Hot*ri*'s cup (paragraph 23).

[2] See p. 256, note 1. The preceding paragraphs anticipate the future rites regarding this libation, the original drawing of which is only now described.

Vaisvânara, the crest of heaven, the disposer of the earth, born in the sacred rite, the wise all-ruler, the guest of men,—him the gods have begotten as a vessel for their mouth. Thou art taken with a support: thou art firm (Dhruva), of firm abode, the firmest of the firm, the most solidly founded of the solid! This is thy womb—thee for Vaisvânara!' therewith he deposits it after pushing (the dust) aside, and not leaving so much as a blade of grass between: for he indeed takes it for (Agni) Vaisvânara.

FIFTH BRÂHMANA.

1. Having drawn the cups of Soma, and gone out (of the cart-shed to the high altar)[1], he offers the oblation of drops[2]. The reason why he offers the oblation of drops is this. Whatever drops of that (Soma) are spilt here, to them he now wishes a safe journey to the Âhavanîya, for the Âhavanîya is the resting-place of offerings: this is why he offers the oblation of drops.

2. He offers with (Vâg. S. VII, 26; Rig-veda X, 17, 12), 'Whatever drop of thine leapeth

[1] The libations (grahas) having been taken, and the remaining Nigrâbhyâ water, mixed with Soma-juice, poured from the Hotri's cup into the Dronakalasa (p. 256, note 1), the Adhvaryu, Pratiprasthâtri, Prastotri, Udgâtri, Pratihartri, and Sacrificer walk out of the Havirdhâna shed, each following one touching the hem of the garment of the one before him, and betake themselves to the altar.

[2] The viprud-homa, an expiatory oblation for the Soma spilt during the pressing, consists of a prakaranî spoon full of ghee. According to Âsv. V, 2, 6, and Lâty. I, 11, 9, it would seem that each of those taking part in the Sarpana (see p. 299, note 2) makes two oblations (called 'pravritta-homa' by Lâty. Sr. and Pañkavimsa Br.).

away, whatever stalk of thine,'—whatever particle (of Soma) is spilt, that is a drop, that indeed he means; and by 'whatever stalk of thine' he mentions the stalk;—'stone-pressed, from the lap of the press-bowls;' for pressed by the stone[1] it leaps away from the two press-bowls;—'be it from the Adhvaryu or from the strainer,'—for it leaps away either from the Adhvaryu's hands or from the strainer,—'that I offer unto thee in my mind consecrated by Vashat, Hail!' whereby it becomes for him as an offering consecrated by Vashat.

3. Thereupon the Adhvaryu takes two stalks of grass from the covered altar. The two Adhvaryus[2] proceed first (to the chanting-place beside the pit), as the out-breathing and in-breathing of the sacrifice; then the Prastotri, as the voice of the sacrifice; then the Udgâtri, as the self (or body), the Pragâpati, of the sacrifice; then the Pratihartri, either as the physician or the through-breathing[3].

4. The Sacrificer holds on to those five priests from behind[4], for as much as those five priests are, so much is the whole sacrifice, the sacrifice being fivefold: hence the Sacrificer thereby holds on to the sacrifice.

5. He (the Adhvaryu) then throws one of the two

---

[1] 'Grâva-kyuta' seems to be taken by the author in the sense of 'set in motion by the (pressing) stone.' The Rig-veda reads 'bâhu-kyuta;' also 'dhishanâyâh' instead of 'dhishanayoh.'

[2] That is, the Adhvaryu and his assistant, the Pratiprasthâtri.

[3] Ait. Br. II, 20 enumerates Adhvaryu, Prastotri, Pratihartri, Udgâtri, and Brahman (see also Âsv. V, 2, 4–5); the Lâtyây. Sûtra I, 11, Adhvaryu, Prastotri, Udgâtri, Pratihartri, Brahman, and Sacrificer.

[4] That is, each holds on to the hem of the garment of the one who precedes him.

stalks of grass forward towards the pit[1], with, 'Thou art the ascent of the gods!' for when the gods through the sacrifice attained to the heavenly world, it was from that pit that they went upwards to the heavenly world: he thus makes the sacrificer look along the road to heaven.

6. He then throws down the other stalk in front of the chanters, silently, for those chanters represent the hymn of praise (stotra), Pragâpati (the sacrifice),—he (Pragâpati) draws to himself everything here, and takes possession of everything here: it is to him that that stalk is offered, and thus he does not draw the Adhvaryu to himself, and take possession of him. And when they mutter[2],—for the chanters mutter now[3],—

7. Then he bespeaks the chant, saying, 'Soma becometh pure!' He bespeaks the chant right off[4], and they chant right off; for these chants, the Pavamânâh[5], are directed towards the gods, since

[1] The Udgâtris (chanters) also throw stalks of grass to the south with their left hands, with the text, Pañkav. I, 3, 3.

[2] And when he thinks 'they have muttered' (atha yadâ manyate 'gâpishur iti)—for the chanters mutter now. Kânva text.

[3] For the mantras the Udgâtris have to mutter on this occasion, previous to the chanting, see Tândya Br. I, 3, 4-6. The recitation of the Âgyasastra, by the Hotri, succeeding the chanting of the Bahishpavamâna-stotra, is likewise preceded by a prayer muttered by that priest, for which see Ait. Br. II, 38; Âsv. V, 9.

[4] That is, without repeating that formula, in the same way as the Pavamâna chants are performed without repeating single verses. See p. 308, note 2.

[5] The first stotra at each pressing is called pavamâna (purifying, i.e. during the chanting of which the Soma becomes clarified), viz. the Bahishpavamâna at the morning, the Mâdhyandina pavamâna at the midday, and the Ârbhava (or tritîya) pavamâna at the evening pressing. The other stotras are called Dhurya, 'to be harnessed, belonging to or forming a team.' For the correspondence between the stotra and sastra, see p. 325, note 2.

the gods thereby attained to the heavenly world right off (straightway): therefore he bespeaks the chant right off, and right off they chant.

8. With 'Turn ye back[1]!' (he bespeaks) the other chants (viz. the Dhuryas), and turning back (or repeating) they chant the Dhuryas[2], for the latter

---

[1] This is Sâya*n*a's interpretation of 'upâvartadhvam,' instead of 'draw near,' as translated by me at I, 5, 2, 12. He is probably right in connecting it with the repetitions which certain verses have to undergo in the dhurya-stotras.

[2] There are many different stomas, or forms of chanting stotras, named from the number of verses produced in each form (generally by repetitions of certain verses). Those required for the Sha*d*aha and Dvâda*s*âha (see IV, 5, 4, 1 seq.) are: trivr*i*t (9), pañ*k*ada*s*a (15), saptada*s*a (17), ekavi*ms*a (21), tri*n*ava (27), trayastri*ms*a (33), *k*aturvi*ms*a (24), *k*atus*k*atvâri*ms*a (44), and ash*t*a*k*atvâri*ms*a (48). The first four of these are those most frequently used, and the only ones used at the Agnish*t*oma. All these stomas, with one exception (24), have two or more different varieties or arrangements, called vish*t*uti, differing from one another either in the order in which the several verses are to be chanted, or in regard to the number of repetitions which the corresponding verses have to undergo. Besides, stomas are generally performed in three turns or rounds, paryâya, consisting of a triplet of verses (some of which may have to be repeated more than once), and preceded by the sound 'hu*m*' (Hiṅkâra). Thus the first Â*g*yastotra, Sâmav. II, 10–12, (consisting of three verses, a, b, c,) is to be performed in the pañ*k*ada*s*a-stoma; that is, the three verses have to be so treated, by repetitions, as to produce fifteen verses in three turns. Now, as there are three different varieties of performing the pañ*k*ada*s*a-stoma, the stotra might be chanted in one or other of the following three arrangements:—

1.	Hu*m*	a a a	b	c	this form is called 'pañ*k*a-pañ*k*inî,' i. e. consisting of five in each row.
	Hu*m*	a	b b b	c	
	Hu*m*	a	b	c c c	
Or 2.	Hu*m*	a a a	b	c	('aparâ' or 'other, second').
	Hu*m*	a	b	c	
	Hu*m*	a	b b b	c c c	

are directed towards these creatures: whence creatures are produced here repeatedly.

9. And as to why they chant the Bahishpavamâna here (near the *k*âtvâla). In the beginning, forsooth, yonder sun was here on earth[1]. The seasons embraced him and ascended from hence to the heavenly world: there he burns firmly established

Or 3. Hu*m*	a	b	c	this form is called 'udyatî,' or the ascending one.
Hu*m*	a	b b b	c	
Hu*m*	a a a	b	c c c	

The three paryâyas of a stoma (or vish*t*uti) show each three subdivisions (viz. a a a—b—c, being those of the first paryâya above), called vish*t*âva. When the Udgât*ri*s are about to commence a chant, the Prastot*ri* spreads in their midst a cloth, doubled up so that the unwoven fringe lies over the selvage, either towards the east or north. Thereon he marks the subdivisions of the rounds, by means of sticks (ku*s*â), a span long, of some kind of wood suitable for sacrifice, split lengthways along the pith (the bark being left outside) and somewhat pointed at one end, then smeared over with some fragrant substance, and wrapped up singly in pieces of the same kind of cloth as that spread on the ground. The marking of the vish*t*âvas, or subdivisions, takes place at the end of the prastâva or prelude (see next page, note 1) in this way, that each vish*t*âva is marked by as many sticks as the corresponding verse has to be repeated; those of the first vish*t*âva being laid down with the point to the north, then behind or west of them those of the second turn with the point to the west, and behind them those of the third turn with the point to the north. Thereupon those of the other two rounds are laid down in the same way, each turn north of the preceding one. Hence the arrangement of sticks for the first of the above varieties of the pa*ñk*ada*s*a-stoma would be three straight, one across, one straight; one straight, three across, one straight; one straight, one across, three straight.

With the exception of the Bahishpavamâna, the chanting is performed in the Sadas by the side of the Udumbara post (see III, 6, 1, 2 seq.), the latter being likewise enclosed in a cloth of the above description, wrapt round it from left to right, with the unwoven fringe towards the top.

[1] Cf. Tâ*nd*ya Br. VI, 7, 24.

in the seasons. And in like manner do the priests thereby embrace the sacrificer and ascend from hence to the heavenly world: this is why they chant the Bahishpavamâna here.

10. The Bahishpavamâna[1] chant truly is a ship

[1] The Bahishpavamâna-(stotra), or 'outside-pavamâna,'—so called because (on the first day of a Soma-sacrifice) it is performed outside the altar (commentary on Pañkav. Br. VI, 8, 10–11; or outside the Sadas, Sây. on Sâmav. S. p. 47),—is chanted in the Trivrit, or threefold, stoma; consisting, as it does, of three gâyatrî triplets (Sâmav. II, 1–9 for the Agnishtoma), and none of its verses being chanted more than once. This stoma has three different varieties, viz. the udyatî, or ascending mode, the first turn of which consists of the first verses of the three triplets, the second turn of the second verses, and the third turn of the last verses, hence a^1 a^2 a^3—b^1 b^2 b^3—c^1 c^2 c^3; the parivartinî, or reverting mode, following the natural order, a^1 b^1 c^1—a^2 b^2 c^2—a^3 b^3 c^3; and the kulâyinî, or web-like mode, performed in the order a^1 b^1 c^1—b^2 c^2 a^2—c^3 a^3 b^3. Cf. Haug, Transl. Ait. Br. p. 237, where, however, these forms are described quite differently. The term used for the natural order of verses in the parivartinî vishtuti is 'parâkî,' i. e. thitherwards, straight off. From the statement in paragraph 7 above, that 'they chant straight off (parâk),' one might therefore infer that that particular mode of chanting ought to be used for the Bahishpavamâna-stotra; but the term 'parâk' may also be taken as referring to each of the several verses being chanted 'straight off,' without any repetition. Haug, Transl. Ait. Br. p. 120 note, remarks: 'Each of these verses is for the purpose of chanting divided into four parts: *Prastâva*, i. e. prelude, the first being preceded by *hum*, to be sung by the Prastotar; *Udgîtha*, the principal part of the Sâman, preceded by *Om*, to be chanted by the Udgâtar; the *Pratihâra*, i. e. response [? rather check, stop; cf. IV, 3, 4, 22], introduced by *hum*, to be chanted by the Pratihartar; and the *Nidhana*, i. e. finale, to be sung by all three. To give the student an idea of this division, I here subjoin the second of these rikas in the Sâman form, distinguishing its four parts:—

[The connected *rik* form is: Abhi te madhunâ payo—atharvâno asisrayur—devam devâya devayu.]

'*Prastâva:* abhi te madhunâ payom.

'*Udgîtha:* om âtharvâno asisrâdeyurvam devâyadâ.

bound heavenwards: the priests are its spars and oars, the means of reaching the heavenly world. If there be a blameworthy one, even that one (priest) would make it sink: he makes it sink, even as one who ascends a ship that is full would make it sink. And, indeed, every sacrifice is a ship bound heavenwards: hence one should seek to keep a blameworthy (priest) away from every sacrifice.

11. Thereupon, when the chanting is over[1], he

'*Pratihâra:* hum âvâyo.

'*Nidhana:* sâm.

'The Nidhanas, i.e. finales, are for the nine Pavamâna-stotra verses the following ones: sât, sâm, suvâh, idâ, vâk, and â (for the four last verses).' See also Burnell, Ârsheyabr. p. xlv seq.

[1] Lâty. I, 12; II, 1; Tândya Br. VI, 7 seq. give the following details: The Prastotri takes the prastara (bunch of grass, representing the Sacrificer) from the Adhvaryu and says, 'Brahman, we will chant, O Prasâstar!' The Brahman and Maitrâvaruna having given their assent (Âsv. V, 2, 12–14), the Prastotri hands the prastara to the Udgâtri. The latter touches his right thigh with it (or bends his right knee thereon) and 'harnesses' (introduces) the chant by the formula, 'With Agni's fire, with Indra's might, with Sûrya's brilliance, may Brihaspati harness thee,' &c. (Tândya Br. I, 3, 5); whereupon he mutters, 'I will make food,' &c. (ib. 6); and after looking towards the pit and a vessel of water and the sun, he commences the chant. The three chanters are seated west of the Adhvaryu and Pratiprasthâtri (who look towards them), viz. the Udgâtri facing the north, the Prastotri the west, and the Pratihartri the south (or south-east). To the west of them are seated three, four, or six subordinate singers, or choristers (upagâtri), who accompany the chanting in a deep voice with the sound 'Ho.' When the chant is completed, the Udgâtri says, 'I have made food,' and makes the sacrificer mutter the formula, 'Thou art a falcon,' &c. (Pañk. Br. I, 3, 8); whereupon he takes a stalk of grass from the prastara, cuts off the top and bottom, so as to make it of the length of four thumbs' breadths, and throws it into the pit with, 'If it has been chanted,' &c. (ib. II, 1, 8). They then pour out the vessel of water into the pit, with, 'I send you to the sea,' &c., and make 3, 5, 7 or 9 steps northwards outside the altar.

utters this speech,—'Agnîdh, spread the fires! strew the barhis! Prepare the cakes! go on with the victim!' The Agnîdh spreads the fires, that is to say, kindles them[1]; he strews that barhis[2], thinking, 'When the barhis is strewn, I will offer to the gods on the kindled (fire).'—'Prepare the cakes,' he says, because he is about to proceed with the cakes; and, 'Go on with the victim,' because he is about to get ready the victim[3].

12. Having again entered (the cart-shed) he draws the Âsvina graha[4]. Having drawn the Âsvina graha he goes out and girds the sacrificial stake[5]; and having girt the stake he gets ready the victim: he thereby puts flavour (juice) into him (Soma—the sacrificer).

13. Having been slain at the morning feast, it continues being cooked till the evening feast; whereby he puts flavour (juice) into the whole sacrifice, imbues it with flavour.

14. Let him therefore, at the Agnishtoma, slay a (victim) sacred to Agni, for there is harmony when, at the Agnishtoma, he slays a (victim) for Agni. If

---

whereupon they betake themselves to the Âgnîdhrîya. During the chanting, the Unnetri pours the Soma-juice from the Âdhavanîya trough through the strainer into the Pûtabhrit.

[1] The Agnîdh takes burning coals from the Âgnîdhrîya fire, and puts them on the dhishnya hearths, in the order in which they were raised. See p. 148, note 4.

[2] He spreads a layer of (ulapa) grass along the 'spine' (the line from the middle of the back to the middle of the front side) of the altar.

[3] Pasum hy âlipsyamâno (!) bhavati. Kânva MS.

[4] Having taken this cup of Soma or libation (with the formula, Vâg. S. VII, 11) from the Drona-kalasa or the Pûtabhrit, he makes the sacrificer eye the several cups and Soma vessels, as set forth IV, 5, 6, 1 seq.; the Âsvina being looked at sixth in order (or fourth of the grahas), not tenth (as was its order of drawing). See IV, 1, 5, 16.

[5] See III, 7, 1, 19 seq.

it be an Ukthya sacrifice, let him slay one to Indra and Agni in the second place, for songs of praise (uktha)[1] refer to Indra and Agni. If it be a Shodasin sacrifice, let him slay one to Indra in the third place, for the sixteenfold chant (shodasin)[2] means Indra. If it be an Atirâtra, let him slay one to Sarasvatî in the fourth place, for Sarasvatî is speech, and speech (vâk, fem.) is female, as the night (râtri, fem.) is female: he thus duly distinguishes the forms of sacrifice[3].

---

[1] Or, the (three) Uktha-stotras (Sâmav. II, 55–62) and sastras, the characteristic feature of the Ukthya sacrifice. Cf. p. 325, note 2; and IV, 6, 3, 3.

[2] The Shodasi-stotra (Sâmav. II, 302–304) chanted in the ekavimsa stoma is the characteristic stotra of the Shodasin sacrifice. The term meaning 'having a sixteenth' (viz. stotra), it evidently refers originally to the sacrifice, and has then also been applied to the stotra and sastra. See also Haug, Ait. Br. Transl. p. 255, note 2.

[3] On this occasion the same rites are performed as at the sacrifice of the Agnîshomîya buck (III, 6, 4, 1 seq.), viz. from the girding of the stake (III, 7, 1, 19) to the election of the Hotri (III, 7, 4, 9). Then the other priests are elected, viz. Adhvaryu (and Pratiprasthâtri), the Prasâstri (Maitrâvaruna), the Brâhmanâkhamsin, the Potri, the Neshtri, the Âgnîdhra, and finally the sacrificer himself; after which each of them makes two election-oblations (pravrita-homa) of ghee, the first with, 'May I be well-pleasing to Speech, well-pleasing to the Lord of speech: O divine Speech, what sweetest, most pleasing speech is thine, therewith endow me! Hail to Sarasvatî!' the second with, 'May the holy Sarasvatî, of abundant powers, rich in devotion, accept favourably our sacrifice!' Thereupon they proceed with the animal offering up to the offering of the omentum (vapâ) and cleansing (III, 8, 2, 30); after which all the eighteen priests and the sacrificer perform the Sarpana (see p. 299, note 2), that is, they step up to the eight dhishnya hearths (with formulas Vâg. S. V, 31 a–d; 32 a–d respectively), the Adhvaryu then pointing out the Âhavanîya, the Bahishpavamâna place, the Kâtvâla, &c. (with Vâg. S. V, 32 e seq.); and touching the Sadas and its door-posts, and addressing Sûrya (the sun), the Ritvigs (officiating priests) and dhishnya hearths (with V, 33–34). Kâty. IX, 8, 8–25. For the duties of the Udgâtris, see Lâty. Sr. II, 2, 10 seq.

15. Thereupon he proceeds with (the offering of) the cakes of the Soma feast. Now Soma is a god, for Soma was in the heaven;—'Soma, forsooth, was Vritra; the mountains and stones are his body: thereon grows that plant called Usânâ,' said Svetaketu Auddâlaki; 'that they bring hither and press.'

16. Now when he slays the victim, he thereby puts flavour into it; and when he proceeds with (the offering of) the Soma feast cakes, he puts sap into it: thus it becomes Soma for him.

17. They all belong to Indra; for Indra is the deity of the sacrifice: that is why they all belong to Indra.

18. And as to why there are a cake, parched barley-grain, a porridge, sour curds, and clotted curds,—it is that those who are the deities of the sacrifice shall be well-pleased.

19. For, when one has eaten cake here, he wishes, 'I should like to take parched grains, I should like to eat porridge, I should like to eat sour curds, I should like to eat clotted curds!' All these (are objects of one's) wishes: it is in order that those who are the deities of the sacrifice shall be well-pleased. Now as to why that offering of clotted curds (payasyâ) is prepared only at the morning libation, and not at the two other libations (Soma feasts).

20. The Gâyatrî, forsooth, bears the morning libation (to the gods), the Trishtubh the midday libation, and the Gagatî the evening libation,—but, then, the Trishtubh bears the midday libation, not alone, (but) with both the Gâyatrî and the Brihatî[1]; and the Gagatî (bears) the evening libation, not alone,

[1] For the metres of which the Mâdhyandina-pavamâna stotra is composed, see p. 333, note 1.

(but) with the Gâyatrî, the Kakubh, and Ushnih, and the Anushtubh[1].

21. The Gâyatrî alone bears singly the morning libation,—with those two sets of five (pankti)[2], the set of five chants, and the set of five oblations: there are four Âgya (chants)[3] and the Bahishpavamâna is the fifth,—the Pankti metre is five-footed—with that pankti of chants, not alone, the Gâyatrî bears the morning libation.

22. To Indra belongs the cake, to the two bay steeds the parched grains (dhânâh)[4], to Pûshan the porridge (karambha), to Sarasvatî the sour curds (dadhi), and to Mitra and Varuna the clotted curds (payasyâ)[5],—the Pankti is five-footed—with that pankti of oblations, not alone, the Gâyatrî bears the

[1] The Ârbhava or Tritîya-pavamâna stotra, Sâmav. II, 39–52 (see note on IV, 3, 5, 24), is made up of five parts, composed chiefly in the Gâyatrî, Kakubh, Ushnih, Anushtubh, and Gagatî metres respectively. It is chanted in the Saptadasa-stoma, the seventeen verses being obtained in the following way. The Gâyatrî triplet (II, 39–41) is chanted twice, in the Gâyatra and Samhita tunes, making six verses. Then verses 42 and 44 once each, in the Sapha and Paushkala tunes respectively. Then the triplet II, 47–49 twice, in the Syâvâsva and Ândhîgava tunes (six verses). And finally the triplet II, 50–52 once, in the Kâva tune (three verses). This makes together seventeen verses. Verses 43, 45, and 46 of the Samhita are omitted in the chanting.

[2] Pankti means both 'a set of five,' and the pankti metre, consisting of five octosyllabic feet.

[3] See p. 325, note 2.

[4] Taitt. Br. I, 5, 11 assigns them to the Asvins, for the reason that they performed cures therewith.

[5] These five sacrificial dishes, called savanîyâh (or aindrâh) purodâsâh, are placed together in one vessel (pâtrî)—the purodâsa proper, or rice-cake to Indra, being placed in the centre—and oblations are made from them to the respective deities at one and the same time, two pieces being cut from each dish into the guhû for the chief offering, and one piece from each into the upabhrit

morning libation (to the gods): for the sake of completing that paṅkti, that oblation of clotted curds to Mitra and Varuna is prepared only at the morning libation, and not at the two other libations.

Third Adhyâya. First Brâhmana.

1. Having drunk (Soma)[1] and said, 'We are

spoon, for the svishtakrit. While cutting the portion he calls on the Maitrâvaruna to 'Recite (the invitatory prayer) of the cakes of the morning feast for Indra!' The anuvâkyâ (Rig-veda III, 52, 1) having been recited by the Maitrâvaruna, the Adhvaryu steps to the fire, calls on the Âgnîdhra for the Sraushat formula (see I, 5, 2, 16, with note), and thereupon on the Maitrâvaruna to 'Urge the cakes of the morning feast brought forward for Indra!' That priest then urges, 'Let the Hotri pronounce the offering prayer to Indra! May Indra with his bays eat the grain! [O Hotar, pronounce the offering prayer!]' Whereupon the Hotri recites, 'We who worship (part i, p. 142, note),—May Indra with his bays eat the grains, with Pûshan the porridge; with Sarasvatî, with Bhâratî, the sour curds, with Mitra and Varuna the clotted curds! [cf. Ait. Br. II, 24; Taitt. Br. I, 5, 11; Âsv. V, 4, 3] Vaushat!' when the Adhvaryu pours the oblation into the fire. For the oblation to Agni Svishtakrit the invitatory prayer is Rig-veda III, 28, 1, and the offering formula 'Havir agne vîhi,' 'graciously accept the offering, O Agni!' The offerings completed, the dishes of sacrificial food are placed on the Hotri's hearth.

[1] The Purodâsa offerings, described in the preceding paragraphs, are followed by libations from the dvidevatya cups, viz. the Aindravâyava, Maitrâvaruna, and Âsvina. Each time the Adhvaryu is about to make a libation, the Pratiprasthâtri draws Soma-juice into the Âditya cup (pâtra) and makes libations therefrom immediately after the Adhvaryu on the north side of the fire. And each time he pours the remains from the Âditya cup into the Âditya sthâlî with, 'Thee to the Âdityas!' finally covering the latter with the former (see IV, 3, 5, 6). Then follows the filling of the cups of the Kamasins (see p. 287, note 2), and the libations from the Sukra and Manthin grahas (already anticipated in IV, 2, 1, 13–31) and from the cups of the Kamasins. Thereupon the Adhvaryu goes to the Sadas and sits down opposite the Hotri; and in alternate draughts and with mutual 'invitations' they empty the

invited together[1],' he (the Adhvaryu) rises. He takes a piece of the cake, and at the place where the Akhâvâka, being seated, is now (about to) recite, he puts the piece of cake in his hand and says, 'O Akhâvâka, say what thou hast to say!' Now, the Akhâvâka was excluded (from the Soma)[2].

2. Indra and Agni preserved him for the production of creatures, whence the Akhâvâka priest belongs to Indra and Agni. But it is by means of that sacrificial food, the piece of cake which he now puts in his hand, and by means of that (saying) of the seers which he now recites, it is thereby they (Indra and Agni) preserve him.

3. When the Akhâvâka has (again) taken his seat

dvidevatya cups. The remains are poured into the Hotri's cup, and portions of the purodâsas having then been put into those cups, they are deposited in the left track of the southern cart. The Adhvaryu and Pratiprasthâtri then drink the remains of the Sukra and Manthin cups; the other priests also drinking from their cups, without, however, quite emptying them, after which the cup-bearers deposit them in the Havirdhâna, behind the axle of the southern cart. Henceforward, till the Vaisvadeva cup is drawn (IV, 3, 1, 25), those cups are called nârâsamsa. The Adhvaryu then takes a piece of the sacrificial cake and rises, calling out, 'We are invited together;' after which follows the rehabilitation of the Akhâvâka, referred to above. Being called upon by the Adhvaryu, he recites the verse Rig-veda V, 25, 1 (beginning with 'akhâ,' whence perhaps his name), 'Hither will I sing Agni the god for your protection,' &c., and then says, 'Ye Brâhmans, invite us Brâhmans also!' whereupon the Adhvaryu says, 'This Brâhman desires an invitation: invite him, Hotri!' Being then invited, he pronounces an anuvâkyâ, and his cup-bearer fills his cup, which henceforth ranks last but one, thus preceding that of the Âgnîdhra. He now drinks from his cup, and the latter is then deposited along with the other Kamasas; whereupon the priests, who have taken part in the offering of the purodâsas, and the sacrificer eat the Idâ in the Âgnîdhra fire-house.

[1] Or rather, we have been mutually invited.

[2] See III, 6, 2, 12.

(behind his hearth), he (his Adhvaryu) proceeds with the libations of the seasons (*Ri*tugraha). The reason why he proceeds with the libations of the seasons when the A*kh*âvâka is seated, is that the A*kh*âvâka represents a sexual union, since the A*kh*âvâka belongs to Indra and Agni, and Indra and Agni are two, and a productive union means a pair: from that same productive union he produces the seasons, the year.

4. And again why he proceeds with the libations of the seasons, when the A*kh*âvâka is seated. The seasons, the year, are everything; he thus produces everything: this is why he proceeds with the libations of the seasons when the A*kh*âvâka is seated.

5. Let him draw twelve of them,—twelve months there are in the year: therefore he should draw twelve (cups of Soma). But he may also draw thirteen, for, they say, there is a thirteenth month[1]. Let him nevertheless draw twelve only, for such is completeness.

6. He draws them from the Dro*n*akala*s*a (Soma trough), for the Dro*n*akala*s*a is Pra*g*âpati, and from out of that Pra*g*âpati he produces the seasons, the year.

7. He draws them by means of double-mouthed cups[2];—for where is the end of those two (cups) that are double-mouthed? Hence this year revolves without end. When he has drawn this (libation), he does not deposit it: whence this year is ceaseless.

8. He recites no invitatory prayer; since one

---

[1] See part i, p. 321, note 6.

[2] The two *Ri*tu vessels are made of kârshmarya or a*s*vattha wood, of the shape of spoon-bowls, with spouts on both sides. Kâty. IX, 2, 13.

invites with an invitatory prayer, and the present season has already come, either by day or by night. Nor does he utter a second Vashat, lest he should turn away the seasons. Simultaneously they (the Adhvaryu and Pratiprasthâtri) draw the two first and the two last libations: thus they embrace everything here by means of the year, and everything here is embraced within the year.

9. Out (of the Havirdhâna shed) walks the one, in steps the other, whence these months pass following one another. But were both to walk out together, or were both to enter together, these months would assuredly pass separated one from the other: therefore while out walks the one, in steps the other.

10. Six times they perform[1] with, 'With the

[1] The twelve Ritugrahas are drawn alternately by the Adhvaryu and Pratiprasthâtri—the first two and the last two simultaneously, the others singly, so that the one enters the cart-shed while the other leaves. Both in entering and leaving the Pratiprasthâtri passes by the Adhvaryu on the north side, and for a moment encircles him by passing his arms round him and holding his own vessel south of him. With the exception of the last two libations, the libations are offered up entire (holocausts). When either of them is about to offer one of the first six libations, he calls on the Maitrâvaruna to 'Prompt (the Hotri, &c.) by the season!'—and at the four succeeding ones (after turning round the vessels so as to put the other mouth in front) to 'Prompt by the seasons!' For the last two libations they again reverse the vessels to the previous position and call on him to 'Prompt by the season!' The Maitrâvaruna's formula runs thus: 'Let the Hotri pronounce the offering prayer to Indra!—From the Hotri's cup, from heaven to earth, may he drink Soma together with the season (or, seasons)! O Hotri, pronounce the offering prayer!' Whereupon the Hotri (Potri, &c.) recites—'We who worship,—From the Hotri's cup, from heaven to earth, may he drink Soma together with the season (or, seasons)! Vaushat!' These formulas are slightly varied according to the deity to whom the libation is offered, and the priest who pronounces the offering prayer and Vaushat. The

season'—thereby the gods created the day; and four times with, 'With the seasons'—thereby they created the night. And, assuredly, were only this much (used), there would be nothing but night: it would never pass away.

11. Over and above they perform twice with the formula 'With the season;' thereby the gods subsequently gave the day (again), whence it is now day here, then it will be night, and to-morrow day.

12. By 'With the season' the gods forsooth created the men, and by 'With the seasons' the beasts; and because they created the beasts in the middle of those (men), therefore these beasts (cattle), being shut in on both sides, have come into the power of men.

13. And having performed six times with, 'With the season,' they both turn round their vessels to the other side; and having performed four times with, 'With the seasons,' they turn round their vessels to the other side: from the one side (or mouth) indeed the gods created the day, and from the other side the night; from the one side the gods created men, and from the other beasts.

14. Now he draws the cups (for the seasons)

deities and offering priests of the twelve libations are: 1. Indra—the Hotri; 2. the Maruts—the Potri; 3. Tvashtri and the wives of the gods—the Neshtri; 4. Agni—the Âgnîdhra; 5. Indra-Brahman—the Brâhmanâkhamsin; 6. Mitra-Varuna—the Maitrâvaruna; 7–10. Deva Dravinodas—the Hotri, Potri, Neshtri, and Akhâvâka respectively; 11. the Asvins—the Hotri; 12. Agni Grihapati—the Hotri. For this last libation, the Maitrâvaruna in the first place calls on the sacrificer with, 'O lord of the house, pronounce the offering prayer!' and the sacrificer then again on the Hotri with, 'O Hotri, pronounce the offering prayer upon this!' whereupon the Hotri pronounces the (sacrificer's) offering prayer. Kâty. IX, 13; Sâṅkhâyana Sr. VII, 8; Haug, Transl. Ait. Br. p. 135.

therefrom[1], with (Vâ*g*. S. VII, 30), 'Thou art taken with a support: thee for Madhu!' the Adhvaryu takes (the first); with 'Thou art taken with a support: thee for Mâdhava!' the Pratiprasthât*ri* (the second). These two are the spring (months[2]): because in spring plants sprout and trees are brought to ripeness, therefore these two are Madhu (sweet) and Mâdhava.

15. With 'Thou art taken with a support: thee for *S*ukra!' the Adhvaryu draws (the third); with 'Thou art taken with a support: thee for *S*u*k*i!' the Pratiprasthât*ri* (the fourth). These two are the summer (months): because during them it burns fiercest, therefore these two are *S*ukra (clear) and *S*u*k*i (bright).

16. With 'Thou art taken with a support: thee for Nabhas!' the Adhvaryu draws (the fifth); with 'Thou art taken with a support: thee for Nabhasya!' the Pratiprasthât*ri* (the sixth). These two are (the months) of the rainy season: it rains from yonder sky, and hence these two are Nabhas (mist, cloud) and Nabhasya.

17. With 'Thou art taken with a support: thee for Ish (sap)!' the Adhvaryu draws (the seventh); with 'Thou art taken with a support: thee for Ûr*g* (food)!' the Pratiprasthât*ri* (the eighth). These two are the autumn (months): because in autumn food (ûr*g*) and juice, (namely) plants, ripen, therefore these two are Isha and Ûr*g*a.

18. With 'Thou art taken with a support: thee for Sahas!' the Adhvaryu draws (the ninth); with 'Thou art taken with a support: thee for

[1] Viz. from the Dro*n*akala*s*a trough; see paragraph 6.

[2] The Kâ*n*va text adds *ri*tû in each case.

Sahasya!' the Pratiprasthâtri (the tenth). These two are the winter (months): because the winter by force (sahas) brings these creatures into his power, therefore these two are Saha and Sahasya.

19. With 'Thou art taken with a support: thee for Tapas!' the Adhvaryu draws (the eleventh); with 'Thou art taken with a support: thee for Tapasya!' the Pratiprasthâtri (the twelfth). These two are (the months) of the dewy season: because during them it freezes most severely, therefore these two are Tapas and Tapasya.

20. With 'Thou art taken with a support: thee to Amhasaspati (lord of trouble)!' he (the Adhvaryu) draws the thirteenth libation, if he draw a thirteenth. The Pratiprasthâtri then pours his residue into the Adhvaryu's vessel, or the Adhvaryu pours his residue into the Pratiprasthâtri's vessel. He (the Adhvaryu) takes it (to the Sadas) for the purpose of drinking it[1].

21. Thereupon the Pratiprasthâtri draws the Aindrâgna graha with the vessel not used for the drinking. The reason why he draws the Aindrâgna libation with the vessel not used for drinking is that

[1] The Kânva text has 'bhakshyam' instead of 'bhaksham.' Each of the priests who have pronounced the offering prayer and Vaushat partakes of this Soma in his respective order,—the Hotri thus taking four draughts; and the Adhvaryu and Pratiprasthâtri (who, after drawing the Aindrâgna cup, join them in the Sadas) drinking alternately from the same vessel with those Hotri priests, who pronounced the Vashat at their libations. As at the drawing of the libations, the vessel is turned round after the sixth and tenth offering priests have drank. The vessel having been emptied, the Adhvaryu takes it outside the Sadas, and then sits down in front of the Hotri's hearth, with his face to the east, till the recitation of the Sastra (IV, 3, 2, 2).

no second Vasha*t* is pronounced on the *Ri*tugrahas, and for them he is about to take the Aindrâgna graha: thus they become consecrated for him by a second Vasha*t* through the Aindrâgna.

22. And again, why he draws the Aindrâgna graha. By drawing the libations to the seasons he has generated this All, and having generated this All, he now establishes it on the out-breathing and in-breathing: hence this All is established on the out-breathing and in-breathing, for Indra and Agni are the out-breathing and in-breathing, and these two, heaven and earth, are the out-breathing and in-breathing, and within these two this All is established.

23. And again, why he draws the Aindrâgna cup. By drawing the libations to the seasons he has generated this All, and having generated this All, he lays the out-breathing and in-breathing into this All: hence these two, the out-breathing and in-breathing, are laid into (or beneficial, hita, in) this All.

24. He now draws it from that (dro*n*akala*s*a trough) with (Vâ*g*. S. VII, 3, 1; Rig-veda III, 12, 1), 'O Indra and Agni, through our songs come ye hither to the Soma, to the agreeable fume: drink thereof, urged by our hymn!—Thou art taken with a support: thee to Indra and Agni!'—with 'This is thy womb: thee to Indra and Agni!' he deposits it (on the mound), for it is for Indra and Agni that he draws it.

25. Thereupon he draws the Vai*s*vadeva cup[1].

[1] According to Kâty. IX, 13, 33 seq. the order of performance is as follows. In the first place the first Â*g*ya-*s*astra is recited. Thereupon the Adhvaryu fetches the Aindrâgna cup from the Havirdhâna (where it was deposited by the Pratiprasthât*ri*), makes a libation from it—after calling on the Hot*ri*, as at all libations accompanied

For by drawing the *Ri*tugrahas he has generated this All; but were there nothing but that, there would indeed be only as many creatures as were created in the beginning: no (more) would be generated.

26. Now, in that he draws the Vai*s*vadeva graha, thereby he sends forth this All, these creatures in due order: whence these creatures are generated again repeatedly. He draws it with the *S*u*k*ra cup, for the *S*u*k*ra (bright) is yonder burning (sun), and

by a *s*astra, 'Singer of praises, recite Soma's offering prayer;' the nârâ*s*a*m*sa cups being shaken by the cup-bearers at the same time —and then drinks the remaining Soma with the Hot*ri*. Thereupon he draws the Vai*s*vadeva cup from the Dro*n*akala*s*a, pours the remaining juice from the latter into the Pûtabh*ri*t, and spreads the straining-cloth over the empty vessels for the midday pressing. He also prepares the Savanîya purodâ*s*as (see p. 315, note 4), for the midday feast, omitting however the dish of clotted curds (payasyâ). Then follows the chanting of the first Â*g*ya stotra by the Udgât*ri*s, and the recitation of the Praüga-*s*astra by the Hot*ri*, after which takes place the Vai*s*vadeva libation (and emptying of the cup) in the same way as with the Aindrâgna—the *k*amasas being also drained of their contents by the respective priests. Then follows the distribution—already referred to IV, 2, 3, 11 seq. —of the Soma in the Ukthya bowl into three parts for the three Hotrakas, now about to recite their *s*astras (preceded by their respective stotras). The Adhvaryu takes one portion of the Soma, calls on the Udgât*ri*s to chant the stotra, and afterwards on the Pra*s*âst*ri* (Maitrâvaru*n*a) to recite his *s*astra; after which he makes a libation from the portion of Soma, and pours the remainder into the Pra*s*âst*ri*'s cup, to be drunk by that priest. In the same way the Pratiprasthât*ri* then proceeds with the portions of the two other Hotrakas, viz. the Brâhma*n*â*kh*a*m*sin and A*kh*âvâka. Each time also the ten *k*amasas are filled, and after libations therefrom, are emptied by the *K*amasins. See also p. 287, note 2. At the end of the performance the priests pass silently out (ni*h*sarp, see p. 299, note 1) of the Sadas by the back-door and out of the Vedi; the midday performance afterwards beginning with the pratisarpa*n*a, or 'creeping back' to the Sadas, with homage to the dhish*n*ya hearths, &c.

what rays of his there are, they are the All-gods: therefore he draws it with the *S*ukra cup.

27. He draws it from that (Soma in the Dro*n*a-kala*s*a) with (Vâ*g*. S. VII, 33; Rig-veda I, 3, 7), 'Ye protectors and supporters of men, O All-gods, come hither, ye givers, to the giver's liquor!— Thou art taken with a support: thee to the All-gods!' with 'This is thy womb: thee to the All-gods!' he deposits it[1], for it is for the All-gods that he draws it.

SECOND BRÂHMA*N*A.

1. Now truly when the Hot*ri* praises (recites the *s*astra[2]), he sings, and to him thus singing the

---

[1] Viz. in the place of the *S*ukra cup, on the south-east corner of the khara or mound.

[2] Every chant or hymn (stotra) of the Udgât*ri*s is followed by a 'song of praise' (*s*astra) recited by the Hot*ri* or one of his three assistants (Maitrâvaru*n*a, Brâhma*n*â*kh*a*m*sin, and A*kh*âvâka); the first two *s*astras at each savana being recited by the Hot*ri*, and the three additional ones at the morning and midday feast by his assistants (Hotrakas). The exact correlation between the stotras and *s*astras at the three savanas will appear from the following table:—

I. Prâta*h*-savana.

Stotras		Sastras	
1. Bahish-pavamâna-stotra.		1. Â*g*ya-*s*astra (Hot*ri*).	
2. Â*g*ya-stotra	dhuryas.	2. Praüga-*s*astra (Hot*ri*).	
3. "	dhuryas.	3.	Â*g*ya-*s*astras (Hotrakas).
4. "	dhuryas.	4.	Â*g*ya-*s*astras (Hotrakas).
5. "	dhuryas.	5.	Â*g*ya-*s*astras (Hotrakas).

II. Mâdhyandina-savana.

Stotras		Sastras	
6. Mâdhyandina-pavamâna-stotra.		6. Marutvatîya-*s*astra (Hot*ri*).	
7. P*ri*sh*th*a-stotra	dhuryas.	7. Nishkevalya-*s*astra (Hot*ri*).	
8. "	dhuryas.	8. " "	(Hotrakas).
9. "	dhuryas.	9. " "	(Hotrakas).
10. "	dhuryas.	10. " "	(Hotrakas).

Adhvaryu responds (prati-â-gar), whence the name response (pratigara).

2. [The Hotri] calls upon that (Adhvaryu) seated (before him) with his face towards the east[1]. For all

III. Tritîya-savana.

11. Ârbhava (or Tritîya)-pavamâna.	11. Vaisvadeva-sastra (Hotri).
12. Agnishtoma-sâman (Yagñâyagñîya).	12. Âgnimâruta-sastra (Hotri).

These are the twelve stotras and sastras of the Agnishtoma. At the Ukthya sacrifice, the performance of the evening feast is completed by the addition of three uktha stotras and sastras, one for each Hotraka.

[1] While the Adhvaryu sits before the Sadas, with his back to the Hotri (p. 322, note 1), the latter performs the (tûshnîm-) gapa—i.e. the muttering of the formula 'May Father Mâtarisvan grant flawless (verse-) feet! may the bards sing flawless hymns!' &c. Ait. Br. II, 38; Âsv. Sr. V, 9, 1—after which he addresses to the Adhvaryu his call (âhâva), 'sõmsâvõm (let us two recite, Om)!'—which formula is used at all sastras, except that, at the midday and evening libations, it is preceded by 'Adhvaryo' (O Adhvaryu); while at the evening savana the first syllable of the verb is repeated, thus 'sosomsâvo.'—The Adhvaryu rises, turns round so as to face the Hotri, and responds by 'somsâmo daiva (we recite, O divine one)!' According to Ait. Br. III, 12, the Âhâva and Pratigara together are to consist of the number of syllables corresponding to the metre of the respective libation, viz. 8, 11, 12 respectively. Then follows the Hotri's Tûshnîm-samsa or 'silent praise;' viz. 'Earth! Agni is the light, the light is Agni, Om!—Indra is the light, Ether! the light is Indra, Om! Sûrya is the light, the light, Heaven! is Sûrya, Om!'—This is followed by a Puroruk, or preliminary invocation of a deity, recited in a loud voice, and consisting of twelve short formulas resembling the Nivid (part i, p. 114, note 2; ib. I, 4, 2, 5 seq.), which, indeed, takes its place in the sastras of the midday and evening libations, being inserted in the middle or before the last verse of the hymn of the sastra; viz. 'Agni kindled by the gods, Agni kindled by man, Agni the well-kindling, the Hotri chosen by the gods, the Hotri chosen by men, the carrier of offerings, the leader of sacrifices, the irresistible Hotri, the swift carrier of oblations: may he, the god,

others except the Udgâtri perform their priestly duties while facing the east, and in this manner that priestly duty of his is performed towards the east.

3. Now the Udgâtri is Pragâpati, and the Hotri, (being) the Rik (fem.), is a female. And when he chants, then the Udgâtri, Pragâpati, implants seed in the female Hotri, the Rik; this the Hotri brings forth by means of the sastra (recitation), he sharpens

---

bring hither the gods! may Agni, the god, worship the gods! may (Agni), the knower of beings, perform the sacrificial rites!' (Ait. Br. II, 34.) Then follows the hymn, the Âgya-sûkta, the chief part of the sastra, viz. Rig-veda III, 13, 'To him, your god Agni, will I sing with loudest voice; may he come hither to us with the gods; may he, the best offerer, sit down on our sacred grass!' &c.; the seven (anushtubh) verses of which are recited in the order 1, 5, 4, 6, 3, 2, 7. The first and last verses being, however, repeated thrice, the number is thus raised to eleven. The recitation of the hymn is followed by the so-called ukthavîrya ('the strength of the praise'), consisting of the formula uktham vâki, 'praise hath been sung,' with some words added to it differing at different sastras,—at the present sastra 'ghoshâya tvâ,' 'thee (I have recited) for sound (praise)!' [for school-differences as to these formulas, see Haug, Transl. Ait. Br. p. 177],—to which the Adhvaryu responds, Om ukthasâh, 'yea, singer of praise!' The Ukthavîrya, together with the response, is again to consist of as many syllables as the characteristic metre of the respective libation. Then follows the recitation, by the Âgnîdhra (Ait. Br. VI, 14), of the yâgyâ or offering prayer, viz. Rig-veda III, 25, 4.—As regards the term 'âgya,' the Pañk. Br. VII, 2, 1, 2, derives it from âgi, a race, in accordance with the following legend: When Pragâpati offered himself as a sacrifice to the gods, the latter could not agree as to which of them should have the first share. Pragâpati then proposed that they should run a race for it. In this race Agni came off first, then Mitravaruna, then Indra. To each of these three divinities an âgya was thereupon assigned; and, by a secret understanding between Indra and Agni, these two divided the fourth âgya between them. Hence the âgneya, maitrâvaruna, aindra, and aindrâgna sastra (and stotra), belonging to the Hotri, Maitrâvaruna, Brâhmanâkkhamsin, and Akhâvâka priests respectively.

it even as this man is sharpened[1], and because he thereby sharpens (so) therefore it is called sastra.

4. Having turned round (so as to face the Hotri, the Adhvaryu) then responds: thereby he quickens[2] that implanted seed. On the other hand, were he to respond while standing with his face turned away (from the Hotri), that implanted seed would assuredly perish away, and would not be brought forth; but thus facing each other (the male and female) bring forth the implanted seed.

5. Now the strength of the metres was exhausted by the gods, for it was by the metres that the gods attained the world of heaven. And the response (song) is ecstasy (mada[3])—what ecstasy there is in the *rik* and that which there is in the Sâman, that is sap: this sap he now lays into the metres, and thus makes the metres of restored strength; and with them of restored strength they perform the sacrifice.

6. Hence if (the Hotri) recites by half-verses, let (the Adhvaryu) respond at each half-verse; and if he recites by pâdas (hemistichs), let him respond at each pâda. For whenever, in reciting, he (the Hotri) draws breath, there the Asura-Rakshas rush into the sacrifice: there he (the Adhvaryu) closes it up by means of the response, so that the evil spirits, the Rakshas, cannot rush in; and thus he destroys the world of the sacrificer's enemies.

---

[1] That is, fashions him, or makes him slender. A fanciful derivation of sastra (sams, to recite, praise, cf. carmen), from the root sâ (so), to sharpen (? or from sas, to cut, carve). 'Yathâyam purovartî purushas tîkshnakritah, avaya(va)vibhâgena spashtîkritas tathâ sastrenaitad retah syati spashtam karoti,' Sây.

[2] Upanimadati, 'cheers;' the Kânva text (W.) has 'upanivadati.'

[3] Or, intoxication, intoxicating drink. See paragraph 10, and p. 330, note 1.

7. Now, in the beginning the metres consisted of four syllables. Then *G*agatî flew up for Soma and came back, leaving behind three syllables. Then Trish*t*ubh flew up for Soma and came back, leaving behind one syllable. Then Gâyatrî flew up for Soma, and she came back bringing with her those syllables as well as Soma. Thus she came to consist of eight syllables: wherefore they say, 'Gâyatrî is octosyllabic.'

8. With her they performed the morning feast of the Soma-sacrifice,—whence the morning feast pertains to Gâyatrî. With her they performed the midday feast. Trish*t*ubh then said to her, 'To thee will I come with three syllables: invite me, and exclude me not from the sacrifice!'—'So be it!' she said and invited her. Thus the Trish*t*ubh came to consist of eleven syllables, and therefore they say, 'The midday Soma feast pertains to Trish*t*ubh.'

9. With her (Gâyatrî) indeed they performed the evening feast. *G*agatî then said to her, 'To thee will I come with one syllable: invite me, and exclude me not from the sacrifice!'—'So be it!' she said and invited her. Thus the *G*agatî came to consist of twelve syllables; and therefore they say, 'The evening Soma feast pertains to *G*agatî.'

10. As to this they say, 'Surely all the Soma feasts pertain to Gâyatrî, since Gâyatrî alone went on increasing.' At the morning feast he should therefore respond with a complete (formula), for complete[1] Gâyatrî returned. At the midday feast

[1] Or perhaps, successful, sa*m*siddhâ [svakîyâny aksharâ*n*y aparityag*y*âvik*ri*tâ (? avik*ri*ttâ), Sây.]. The response (pratigara) here alluded to, is probably the one ordinarily used by the Adhvaryu, whenever the Hot*ri* pauses in his recitation, at the end of half-

(he responds with a formula) containing once (the verb) 'to rejoice (mad)[1],' for she (Trishtubh) came back, leaving one syllable behind; and with that same (formula) he then completes her, makes her whole,—

11. When trishtubh verses were recited. At the evening Soma feast (the Adhvaryu responds with a formula) containing thrice (the verb) 'to rejoice[2],' for she (Gagatî) came back leaving three syllables behind; and with these (formulas) he then completes her, makes her whole,—

12. When (the hymn) to Heaven and Earth is recited[3]. Now these creatures subsist on those two,

---

verses (or pâdas), nivids, &c., viz. 'Othâmo daiva,'—or, Ôthâvo daivom, whenever the Hotri puts in the sacred syllable 'om.' 'Tasmât kâranâd gâyatra-prâtahsavane samsiddham avikritam vidhâsyamânam omantam prati-grihnîyât,' Sây. For the Adhvaryu's response, 'samsâmo daiva,' to the Hotri's summons (âhâva), see p. 326, note 1.

[1] When the first verse of the trishtubh hymn, Rig-veda X, 73, is recited by the Hotri in the Marutvatîya Sastra at the midday feast, the Adhvaryu's response is 'madâmo daiva' (we rejoice, O divine one). Kâty. X, 3, 8; cf. Weber, Ind. Stud. X, p. 37.

[2] According to Kâty. X, 6, 6 'madâmo daiva' is optionally the Adhvaryu's response at the recitation in the Âgnimârutra Sastra of three of the so-called Anupânîya (or Svâdushkilîya) trishtubh verses VI, 47, 1–4 (see note on IV, 4, 2, 18). Possibly the present paragraph may refer to those verses, in which case the words 'when trishtubh verses are recited' would begin a fresh paragraph. Sâyana, however, seems to take it in the same way as above; cf. also the Kânva reading in next note.

[3] This is the (Gagatî) hymn I, 159 recited in the Vaisvadeva Sastra. According to Kâty. X, 6, 5, the response is to be thrice (after each of the three first verses) 'madâmo daiva.' The Kânva has for paragraphs 10–12, 'At the morning feast he responds by a complete (formula), for complete Gâyatrî returned. At the midday feast he responds once with one containing "mad," when he

the heaven and the earth—he thereby imbues those two, heaven and earth, with vigour; and upon those two, thus vigorous and affording the means of subsistence, these creatures subsist. Let him respond with 'Om!' only, for that is truth, that the gods know.

13. Now some respond with 'Othâmo daiva vâk,' saying, 'The response is speech (vâk): thus we obtain speech.' But let him not do this; for surely, in whichsoever way he may respond, speech is obtained by him, since he responds by speech. Let him therefore respond with 'Om[1]!' only, for that is truth, that the gods know.

THIRD BRÂHMANA.

C. THE MÂDHYANDINA SAVANA, OR MIDDAY SOMA FEAST.

1. He presses out (the Soma-juice) with 'Ihã! Ihã[2]!' (hither), whereby he draws Indra nigh; and

recites trish*t*ubh verses, for she (Trish*t*ubh) returned leaving one syllable behind: hereby now he completes her, makes her whole. At the evening feast with something containing thrice "mad," for she (*G*agatî) returned leaving three syllables behind: hereby now he completes her, makes her whole. At the (hymn) to Heaven and Earth he responds with one that contains "mad;" when he recites (the hymn) Heaven and Earth—these creatures subsisting on those two, Heaven and Earth—he thereby puts juice into them, and upon those two, thus rendered juiceful, these creatures subsist. He responds with "Om," for that is truth, that the gods know.'

[1] That is, instead of 'vâk,' hence 'Othâmo daivom.' 'Om' pure and simple is the response at the end of the *s*astra.

[2] 'Iha' (here, hither) with the last syllable protracted. The Hot*ri*'s cup with the Nigrâbhyâ (vasatîvarî) water having been handed to the sacrificer, and the fillet or band (ush*n*îsha) with which the Soma-plants are tied together, to the Grâvastut, the pressing is performed in the same way as the 'great pressing,' at

with 'Brihat! Brihat!' (great), whereby he draws Indra[1] nigh.

2. The Sukra and Manthin grahas he draws first, for thereby the Soma feast comes to be supplied with pure Soma (sukra). Thereupon the Âgrayana, for that (cup) is drawn at all (three) feasts. Then the Marutvatîya cup; then the Ukthya, for here also there are songs of praise (Uktha)[2].

3. Now some draw the Marutvatîya after they have drawn the Ukthya; but let him not do this,—let him rather draw the Ukthya after he has drawn the Marutvatîya.

---

the Prâtahsavana (see p. 256, note 1). Meanwhile the Grâvastut takes the band, and winds it thrice round his head and face from left to right. And whenever Soma-stalks are taken out for pressing he extols the stones by chanting the Grâva-stotra or 'praise of the stones.' According to Âsv. Sr. V, 12; Ait. Br. VI, 7, 2, this chant consists of the verses Rig-veda I, 24, 3; V, 81, 1; VIII, 81, 1; VIII, 1, 1, followed by the hymn X, 94, ascribed to the serpent Rishi Arbuda. Before the last verse of this hymn he inserts the hymns X, 76 and X, 175 (ascribed to the serpents Garatkarna and Arbuda respectively); and either before, or between, or after these two hymns he throws in the pâvamânîh (Rig-veda IX) according to requirement, till the pressing is completed, or the libations are to be drawn, when having wound up with the last verse of the first Arbuda hymn, he makes over the band to the sacrificer. The five cups mentioned in paragraph 2 are filled from the stream of Soma flowing from the Hotri's cup into the Dronakalasa; the Âgrayana (p. 290, note 2) however being taken (in the Âgrayana sthâlî or bowl) from that and two other streams, poured by the Unnetri from the Âdhavanîya, and by the Pratiprasthâtri from some vessel containing the Soma previously kept in the Âgrayana sthâlî.

[1] Probably on account of the connection of the Brihat-sâman with Indra; see part i, p. 196, note 2.

[2] See p. 294, note 2. Sâyana here curiously explains the term by 'stotrâni.'

4. These, then, are five grahas he draws; for that midday Pavamâna chant is a thunderbolt: hence it is a fifteenfold five-hymned chant[1], for the thunderbolt is fifteenfold[2]. He is so by means of these five grahas (cups of Soma[3]): for five are these fingers, and with the fingers he hurls (the thunderbolt).

5. Indra hurled the thunderbolt at Vritra; and having smitten Vritra, the wicked, and safety and peace being secured[4], he led forth the dakshinâs (gifts to priests). Wherefore now also, when they (the Udgâtris) chant the midday Pavamâna, and safety and peace are secured, the dakshinâs are led forth. And so, forsooth, does he now by means of those five cups of Soma hurl the thunderbolt at the wicked, hateful enemy, and having smitten Vritra, the wicked, and safety and peace being

[1] The Mâdhyandina-pavamâna-stotra, Sâmav. II, 22–29, is made up of three hymns (sûkta), consisting of three gâyatrî (22–24), two brihatî (and satobrihatî, 25, 26), and three trishtubh verses (27–29) respectively. These are chanted in such a way as to produce five Sâman hymns (i. e. a hymn of three verses), viz. the gâyatrî triplet is chanted twice, in the Gâyatra and Âmahîyava tunes;—the brihatî-satobrihatî couplet is likewise chanted twice, in the Raurava and Yaudhâgaya tunes, the two verses being as usual (by the repetition of certain pâdas) made into three. These, with the addition of the trishtubh hymn, chanted in the Ausana tune, make five Sâman hymns of three verses each, or altogether fifteen verses (pañkadasastoma).

[2] Or consists of the fifteenfold (chant), as Sâyana takes it. Regarding the connection between the pañkadasa-stoma (the characteristic stoma of the midday pressing) and Indra (the deity of the midday pressing), see part i, introd. p. xviii.

[3] Perhaps 'graha' has here a double meaning, viz. 'that which is taken, a draught, cup of Soma,' and 'the taker, seizer.'

[4] See p. 289, note 4.

secured, he leads forth the dakshinâs. This is why he draws those five cups.

6. Then as to why he draws the Marutvatîya cups. Now this, the midday pressing feast, is Indra's special (nishkevalya) feast: thereby he strove to smite Vritra, thereby he strove to vanquish him. But the Maruts, having on that account[1] withdrawn, were standing on an Asvattha tree[2] (Ficus Religiosa). Now Indra is the nobility, and the Maruts are the people, and through the people the noble becomes strong: therefore the two Ritu cups (they say)[3] may be of asvattha wood; but in reality they are of kârshmarya wood.

7. Indra called on them, saying, 'Do ye join me that with you as my force I may smite Vritra!' They said, 'What will be our (reward) then?' He drew those two Marutvatîya cups for them.

8. They said, 'Having put aside this one (cup) for our vigour, we will join thee.' Having accordingly put it aside for their vigour[4], they joined him. But Indra sought to obtain it, thinking, 'They have come to me after putting aside their vigour.'

---

[1] Lit. 'thus;' 'itisabdenâpakramanaprakâro 'bhinayena pradarsyate,' Sây.

[2] This passage would seem to be based on a mistaken interpretation of Rig-veda I, 135, 8, where the bard says that 'the victorious (gâyavah) have come nigh to the asvattha,' the 'gâyavah' here evidently referring (not to the Maruts, as in I, 119, 3), but to the powerful draughts of Soma flowing into the asvattha vessel. The Kânva text reads, Sâ (i.e. vis, the people or Maruts) hâsvatthe tishthate.

[3] The Kânva text inserts 'ityâhuh.'

[4] The context seems to be purposely ambiguous, as it may also be construed thus: They said, 'After putting aside this (cup), we will come (attain) to strength.' Having accordingly put it aside, they came to strength.

9. He said, 'Do ye join me with vigour!'—'Then draw a third cup for us,' they said. He drew a third cup for them, with, 'Thou art taken with a support,—thee for the vigour of the Maruts!' They then joined him with vigour,—and he conquered with them, and smote Vritra with them;—for Indra is the nobility, and the Maruts are the people, and through the people the noble becomes strong. Hence he now bestows that strength on the nobility, and therefore he draws the Marutvatîya cups.

10. Let him draw them for Indra Marutvat (accompanied by the Maruts), and not for the Maruts likewise. For were he also to draw cups for the Maruts, he would make the people refractory to the nobility. He thus assigns to the Maruts a share therein after Indra, whereby he makes the people subservient and obedient to the nobility: therefore let him draw the cups for Indra Marutvat, and not for the Maruts likewise.

11. But he was afraid of their desertion,—'Lest they should desert me, lest they should take to some other (party)[1],' so thinking, he by that (share in the libation) made them unwilling to desert him. This is why he should draw the grahas for Indra Marutvat.

12. He draws them with the two vessels of the seasons, for the year, the sacrifice, means the seasons. There, at the morning Soma feast, they are overtly attended to, in that he draws the grahas for the seasons[2]; and now they are covertly attended

[1] For the construction, see p. 33, note 1.

[2] See IV, 3, 1, 3 seq.

to, in that he draws the Marutvatîya grahas with the two vessels of the seasons.

13. He draws (the first) from that (stream of Soma)[1], with (Vâg. S. VII, 35; Rig-veda III, 51, 7), 'O Indra, leader of the Maruts, drink thou the Soma here, as thou drankest of the liquor at (the sacrifice of) the Son of Saryâti: by thy guidance, in thy protection, O Lord, do the wise serve thee with good offerings!—Thou art taken with a support: thee to Indra Marutvat!—This is thy womb: thee to Indra Marutvat!'

14. [The second he draws[2] with Vâg. S. VII, 36;

---

[1] See p. 331, note 2.

[2] Here the author again anticipates, important parts of the performance being not even referred to. On the present occasion only one Marutvatîya cup is drawn and deposited on the mound (khara). The Ukthya cup having then been drawn and deposited, the priests leave the Havirdhâna in the same way as at the morning performance (see IV, 2, 5, 1, with note), and perform the Viprud-homas, or drop-offerings. Thereupon the priests 'creep' (sarp), with their upper bodies bent parallel to the ground, to the Sadas, where, near the Udumbara post, the chanting of the midday Pavamâna-stotra now takes place after the necessary preliminaries. If the Pravargya has been performed on the preceding day (see III, 4, 4, 1, with note), the Dadhi-gharma, or libation of hot milk mixed with sour milk, is now made. Then follow the oblations from the Savanîya-purodâsa (see IV, 2, 5, 15 seq., and p. 323, note 1). Thereupon filling of the cups of the ten Kamasins, and the libations from (and drinking of) the Sukra and Manthin cups. After the eating of the Idâ of the purodâsas, the Dâkshina-homas and distribution of the sacrificial fees take place, as set forth in the next Brâhmana. Thereupon the Adhvaryu calls on the Maitrâvaruna to pronounce the invitatory prayer to Indra Marutvat (viz. Rig-veda III, 51, 7), 'O Indra, attended by the Maruts, here drink the Soma,' &c., followed by the order (praisha), 'Let the Hotri pronounce the offering prayer to Indra Marutvat!'

Rig-veda III, 47, 5], 'The mighty bull, followed by the Maruts, the bountiful, divine ruler Indra,—him, the all-subduing, the terrible bestower of victory, do we now invoke for new favour.—Thou art taken with a support: thee to Indra Marutvat!—This is thy womb: thee to Indra Marutvat!'—with 'Thou art

---

The Pratiprasthâtri now draws a second Marutvatîya cup in the other *Ri*tu-pâtra. The offering prayer (Rig-veda III, 47, 2, 'United with the host of Maruts, O Indra, drink the Soma, O wise hero!' &c.) having meanwhile been pronounced by the Hotri, the Adhvaryu makes libations from the first cup at the Vashat and Anuvashat. Then pouring the remains of the juice into some other vessel, to be taken to the Sadas, he enters the Havirdhâna and draws the third Marutvatîya graha with the cup just emptied. Having deposited it, he betakes himself to the Sadas to drink with the Hotri the remains of the first libation. Thereupon the Hotri recites the Marutvatîya *S*astra.

The Marutvatîya *S*astra consists of the following parts. After the summons (âhâva) to the Adhvaryu, and the response (pratigara) of the latter, the Hotri intones the

Pratipad (opening triplet), Rig-veda VIII, 57, 1–3, followed by the Anu*k*ara (sequel), VIII, 2, 1–3.

Then the Indranihava pragâtha (VIII, 53, 5) and the Brâhma*n*aspatya pragâtha (I, 40, 5).

Then follow the three Dhâyyâs (complementary verses), III, 20, 4; I, 91, 2; I, 64, 6; and the Marutvatîya pragâtha, VIII, 89, 3, succeeded by the hymn X, 73, the chief part of the *S*astra, in the middle of which (after the sixth verse), the Nivid ('Let us sing, Om! may Indra with the Maruts drink of the Soma,' &c.) is inserted.

Having recited the last verse (paridhânîyâ or closing verse) of the hymn, he concludes the *S*astra by the Ukthavîrya, 'Praise has been sung to Indra who hears thee!' Thereupon the offering prayer III, 47, 4 is pronounced, and libations are made, both at the Vashat and Anuvashat, by the Adhvaryu from the third, and after him each time, by the Pratiprasthâtri from the second graha.

The priests having drank in the Sadas the Soma remaining from the grahas and in the *k*amasas, the Mâhendra cup is drawn.

taken with a support: thee for the strength of the Maruts!' he draws the third cup.

15. Thereupon he draws the Mâhendra cup. For Indra was then bound up with evil, in the shape of the people, the Maruts; as one might, for the sake of victory, eat from the same vessel with the people[1], so it was when they drew a cup for him in common with the Maruts.

16. When all was conquered and free from danger and injury, the gods plucked him from out of all evil—even as one might pluck out a reed from its sheath—when they drew the cup for the Great Indra. And even as the reed becomes leafless, so is he thereby freed from all evil, when one draws the Mâhendra cup.

17. And again, why he draws the Mâhendra cup. Before the slaughter of V*ri*tra, he was indeed Indra; but when he had slain V*ri*tra, he became the Great Indra, even as one who has conquered all around, becomes a Great King (mahârâ*g*a): therefore he draws the Mâhendra cup. And, moreover, he forsooth makes him great for the slaughter of V*ri*tra: therefore also he draws the Mâhendra cup. He draws it in the *S*ukra vessel, for bright (*s*ukra) and great indeed is he (the sun) that burns yonder: therefore he draws it in the *S*ukra vessel.

18. He thus draws it from that (Dro*n*akala*s*a or Pûtabh*ri*t), with (Vâ*g*. S. VII, 39; Rig-veda VI, 19, 1), 'Great is Indra and hero-like, gladdening the people, of double stature and unimpaired in power. For our sake he waxed strong for heroic deed,—great and broad was he, and

[1] That is, as a chief, or lord, might do so with a clansman (vai*s*yena, Kâ*n*va text); or as the master of a house with his servants.

well-shapen by the shapers[1].—Thou art taken with a support: thee to Mahendra!'—with 'This is thy womb: thee to Mahendra!' he deposits it; for it is indeed for the Great Indra that he draws it.

19. And having bespoken (the chant[2]), he says this speech,—'Pressers, press ye! make the mortars

[1] Or, according to Ludwig, 'rendered favourable by the performers (priests).'

[2] That is, the (first) P*ri*sh*th*a-stotra, consisting of the Rathantara-sâman, Sâmav. II, 30–31. For the way in which the two verses are manipulated (by repetition of the last pâda of the first, and of the second pâda of the second verse), so as to yield a three-versed choral, see Haug, Ait. Br. II, p. 198; Weber, Ind. Stud. VIII, p. 25. These chants derive their name from the circumstance that the Sâmans employed in them are capable of being used as 'p*ri*sh*th*as,' that is, of being chanted twice with another Sâman inserted between them,—or, to speak symbolically, to serve as the womb for the reception of an embryo. For this purpose the Rathantara and B*ri*hat Sâmans are chiefly used. See note on IV, 5, 4, 13. Whenever the P*ri*sh*th*as are chanted in this way (which they are not at the ordinary Agnish*t*oma), it is chiefly at this very place in the Soma performance, at the midday libation. The chant is succeeded by the recitation, by the Hot*ri*, of the Nishkevalya *S*astra, consisting of the following parts. The Âhâva (and pratigara) is followed by the Stotriya (Rig-veda VII, 32, 22–23, identical with the Rathantara) and Anurûpa (VIII, 3, 7–8) pragâthas; then a dhâyyâ, X, 74, 6; the Sâma-pragâtha, VIII, 3, 1, and the hymn (to Indra) I, 32, with the Nivid inserted in the middle (after the eighth verse). Finally the Hot*ri* pronounces the Ukthavîrya, and the offering prayer, VII, 22, 1, after which the Mâhendra libation is poured into the fire.

Then follows the distribution of the Ukthya graha among the three assistants of the Hot*ri*, and the recitation of their (nishkevalya) *s*astras—each preceded by a P*ri*sh*th*a-stotra [Sâmav. II, 32–34 (chanted to the Vâmadevya-sâman); 35–36 (Naudhasa); 37–38 (Kâleya) respectively]—as at the conclusion of the morning performance; see p. 295, note 2. Thereupon he addresses the above summons to the respective priests, for the preparations necessary for the evening pressing.

resound! Agnîdh, stir the sour milk! be thou mindful of Soma's (pap)!' It is for the evening's press-feast that those pressers press out (the Soma-juice), for the evening feast they make the mortars resound, for the evening feast the Agnîdh stirs the sour milk, for the evening feast he boils the pap for Soma. For these two press-feasts, the morning feast and the midday feast, are indeed rich in pure Soma, are rich in juice; but that third press-feast is emptied of the pure Soma. Hence he forms it from out of this midday feast; and thus that third press-feast becomes for him rich in pure Soma, rich in juice: this is why he now speaks that speech.

FOURTH BRÂHMANA.

1. Now, they slay the sacrifice, when they spread (perform) it:—to wit, when they press out the king (Soma), they slay him; when they quiet the victim, they slay it; and with mortar and pestle, with the upper and nether millstone, they slay the havis offering.

2. When slain, that sacrifice was no longer vigorous. By means of dakshinâs (gifts to the priests) the gods invigorated it: hence the name dakshinâ, because thereby they invigorated (dakshay) it. Whatever, therefore, fails in this sacrifice, when slain, that he now invigorates by means of gifts to the priests; then the sacrifice becomes indeed successful: for this reason he makes gifts to the priests.

3. Now at the Haviryagña, indeed, they give as little as six or twelve (cows[1]), but no Soma-sacrifice should have dakshinâs of less than a hundred. For

[1] See II, 2, 2, 3-5.

he, Pragâpati[1], forsooth, is the visible sacrifice; and man is nearest to Pragâpati, and he has a life of a hundred years, a hundred powers, a hundred energies. Only by a hundred he invigorates him, and not by less than a hundred: wherefore no Soma-sacrifice should have dakshinâs of less than a hundred; nor should any one officiate as a priest for a sacrificer at a (Soma-sacrifice) where less than a hundred are given,—'lest he should be an eyewitness when they will but slay and not invigorate him (Soma).'

4. Now, truly, there are two kinds of gods; for the gods, forsooth, are the gods; and the learned Brâhmans versed in sacred lore are the human gods. And the sacrifice to them is twofold, oblations (being the sacrifice) to the gods, and gifts to the priests being that to the human gods, to the learned Brâhmans versed in sacred lore. With oblations, forsooth, one gratifies the gods, and with gifts to the priests the human gods, the learned Brâhmans versed in sacred lore. These two kinds of gods, when gratified, convey him to the heavenly world.

5. But it is to the officiating priests, forsooth, that these gifts of his belong, for they prepare him another self,—to wit, this sacrifice, consisting of *Rik* and Yagus and Sâman and oblations,—that becomes his self in yonder world: 'It is they that have generated me,' from this (consideration) he should give the gifts to officiating priests and not to non-officiating.

6. Having gone back to the Gârhapatya fire[2], he

[1] 'For he, Soma, doubtless is the visible Pragâpati (pratyaksham pragâpatih).' Kânva text.

[2] That is, the fire at the front door of the hall (the old Âhavanîya fire). Each priest has to perform two such dâkshina-homas

offers the gift offerings. Having tied a piece of gold in a fringed cloth[1], and laid it (into the spoon), he offers. 'May there be a place for me in the world of the gods!' With this hope he offers whoever offers: that same sacrifice of his goes to the world of the gods; and behind it goes the gift he gives to the priests, and holding on to the gift follows the sacrificer.

7. Now, there are four (kinds of) gifts to priests,—gold, the cow, cloth, and the horse. But it is not proper that he should lay a horse's foot or a cow's foot (into the spoon): hence he ties up a piece of gold in a fringed cloth, and having laid it (into the spoon) he offers.

8. He offers with two verses to the Sun. For yonder world is shut off by darkness; and dispelling the darkness by that light he reaches the heavenly world: therefore he offers with two verses to the Sun.

9. He offers with this gâyatrî verse (Vâg. S. VII, 41; Rig-veda I, 50, 1), 'The lights bear on high that divine knower of beings, Sûrya, that all may see him,—Hail!'—for the gâyatrî is this earth, and she is a safe resting-place: hence he thereby stands firmly on this safe resting-place.

10. He then makes the second offering with this trishtubh verse (Vâg. S. VII, 42; Rig-veda I, 115, 1), 'The brilliant front[2] of the gods hath risen,

---

of ghee. For the Hotri's formulas, see Âsv. Sr. V, 13, 14. For the proper place of these offerings in the performance, see p. 336, note 2.

[1] Or rather, in a cloth such as is used at a dasâhoma, or oblation at which the fringe (or unwoven end) of a cloth is used (dasâhomîya).

[2] That is, either 'face' or 'van-guard,' anîka.

the eye of Mitra, Varu*n*a, and Agni: Sûrya, the soul of the movable and immovable, hath filled the heaven and the earth and the air,—Hail!' whereby he approaches the world (of the gods).

11. He then makes either one or two oblations on the Âgnîdhra (fire). The reason why he makes one or two oblations on the Âgnîdhra fire is that Agni rules over beasts (cattle)[1], and they lie round about him on every side: it is him he pleases by this oblation, and thus pleased he is gracious unto this (sacrificer), and the latter offers (to the priests a cow) graciously given up by him (Agni).

12. He offers with (Vâ*g*. S. VII, 43; Rig-veda I, 189, 1), 'O Agni, lead us on a good path unto wealth; thou, O god, that knowest all works! keep thou from us the sin that leadeth astray, and we will offer unto thee most ample adoration,—'Hail!' Thereupon, if he intends to give away a horse, harnessed or unharnessed, let him make a second oblation; but if not, he need not attend to this.

13. He offers with (Vâ*g*. S. VII, 44), 'May this Agni make wide room for us: may he march in front smiting the haters! May he gain riches in the winning of riches: may he, fiercely rushing, conquer the enemies! Hail!' for the horse is a winner of riches (spoils, prizes).

14. Thereupon, taking some gold, (the sacrificer)

---

[1] For this usurpation, on the part of Agni, of one of Rudra's functions, Sâya*n*a refers to a legend in the Taittirîyaka (Taitt. S. I, 5, 1), where Agni is identified with Rudra, Agni being so called because he roared (rud). See also *S*at. Br. I, 7, 3, 8.

goes to the hall. South of the altar stand the Dakshinâ (cows). Standing in front of the hall, he respectfully addresses them[1] with (Vâg. S. VII, 45), 'By your beauty have I come to beauty.' Now at first cattle did not submit to being given away. Laying aside their own beauteous forms[2] they approached with their (bare) bodies. The gods then went up to them from the offering ground with their (the animals') own forms; and they, knowing their own forms, resigned themselves and became well-disposed to being given away. And in like manner does he now go up to them from the offering ground with their own forms; and they, knowing their own forms, resign themselves and become well-disposed to being given away.

15. 'May the all-knowing Tutha distribute you!'—Now, Tutha is the Brahman: he thus distributes them by means of the Brahman. And the Brahman knows who is fit to receive a dakshinâ and who is unfit: thus these (cows) of his are given away only to him who is fit to receive a dakshinâ and not to him who is unfit.

16. 'Go ye forward in the way of truth,'—for whosoever walks in the way of the gods, walks in the way of truth;—'ye of shining (kandra) gifts!' whereby they walk with that light (kandra, the moon).

---

[1] The cows are driven past him along the back of the altar, between the hall and Sadas, and then along the north side of the altar, south of the Âgnîdhra and between the pit (kâtvâla) and heap of rubbish (utkara), the sacrificer following them as far as the Âgnîdhra. At the same time the Subrahmanyâ litany (see III, 3, 4, 17 seq.) may be recited.

[2] Sâyana explains 'rûpâni' by 'sâmarthyâni,' capabilities, powers.

17. He then goes to the Sadas, saying, 'Behold thou the heaven, behold the air!' whereby he means to say, 'May I through thee, the dakshinâ, see the (heavenly) world.'

18. Thereupon he looks on the Sadas, with, 'Unite with the Sadas-priests!' whereby he means to say, 'May the Sadas-priests not go beyond thee!'

19. He then takes the gold and goes up to the Âgnîdhra (fire-house), saying (Vâg. S. VII, 46), 'May I this day obtain a Brâhman who has a father and forefathers!'—for he who is renowned and of renowned family, is one who has a father and forefathers; and by the gifts which he gives to a renowned (priest), though they be but few, he gains great things.—'A *Ri*shi, the scion of *Ri*shis,' for he who is renowned as learned in sacred lore, is a *Ri*shi, the scion of *Ri*shis;—'of well-bestowed gifts,' for he indeed is one on whom gifts are well-bestowed.

20. Having thus respectfully sat down by the Agnîdh, he gives him the gold, with 'Given (râta) by us, go ye to the gods!'—for whatever sacrificial gift he gives unhesitatingly, with a liberal (râta) mind, thereby he gains great things, 'Go ye to the gods,' he says, for he who sacrifices, sacrifices with the hope, 'May there be a place for me in the world of the gods;' and he thus makes him a sharer in the world of the gods.—'Enter ye to the Giver!' whereby he means to say, 'Enter ye into me!' and thus those (cows)[1] do not get lost to him. And as to his giving

[1] The cows (and other gifts) are presented at the same time, viz. either a hundred to each officiating priest, or to each his proportionate share of an aggregate of a hundred cows, viz. twelve cows

a dakshinâ first to the Agnîdh, it was from thence (from the Âgnîdhra)[1] that all the gods gained immortality: therefore he gives the dakshinâ first to the Agnîdh.

21. Then, approaching in the same way, he gives some gold to an Âtreya[2]. For, at the time[3] when they recite the morning prayer, they were once upon a time singing praises here in front[4]. Now Atri was the Hotri of the Rishis. Then the darkness of the Asuras came rushing into the Sadas. The Rishis said to Atri, 'Come back here, and dispel this darkness!' He dispelled that darkness; and thinking, 'He indeed is the light who has dispelled this darkness,' they brought him this light, gold, for a sacrificial gift,—for gold is indeed light; and by that same splendour and energy the Rishi dispelled the darkness. And so does he now also dispel the darkness by that light: therefore he bestows gold on an Âtreya.

---

to each of the first four priests, six to each of the second four (Brâhmanâkhamsin, &c., see § 22), four to each of the third four, and three cows to each of the remaining four priests.

[1] See III, 6, 1, 27–28.

[2] That is, one of Âtreya descent, who does not officiate as a priest, and who is seated in front of the Sadas. According to the Kânva text (and Kâty. X, 2, 21) the Adhvaryu approaches him with 'Ka Âtreyam'—who (? sees) the Âtreya?—thrice repeated. Kâtyâyana specifies some subdivision of the (female line of) the Âtreya race—also mentioned in the same order in the Pravarâdhyâya—as excluded from this privilege. On this legend cf. V, 3, 2, 2; Taitt. S. II, 1, 2, 2; Tândya Br. VI, 6, 8; Ind. Stud. III, p. 464.

[3] Viz. early in the morning of the sutyâ day, when the Prâtaranuvâka is recited. See p. 229, note 2.

[4] I take 'purâ' in the sense of 'in front' (cf. III, 9, 1, 12), that is, in the havirdhâna shed, and not in that of 'formerly' (Ind. Stud. X, 158). The Kânva text brings out the meaning still more clearly: Sa yad âtreyâya hiranyam dadâty, atrir hi vâ rishînâm hotâ sa yatro

22. Then to the Brahman, for the Brahman watches over the sacrifice from the south. Then to the Udgâtri (chanter); then to the Hotri; then to the two Adhvaryus, seated in the cart-shed. Then, having returned (to the Sadas he presents gold) to the Prastotri; then to the Maitrâvaruna; then to the Brâhmanâkhamsin; then to the Potri; then to the Neshtri; then to the Akhâvâka; then to the Unnetri; then to the Grâvastut; then to the Subrahmanyâ. To the Pratihartri he presents it last, since he is the restrainer (pratihartri)[1]: he thus in the end restrains (the cows) for him, and so they do not become lost to him.

23. Thereupon he (the Adhvaryu) says (to the Maitrâvaruna), 'Recite (the invitatory prayer) to Indra, followed by the Maruts!' Now when, in the beginning, Pragâpati gave gifts, Indra thought within himself, 'Everything here, forsooth, he will give away, and not anything will he leave for us.' He then, to stop the giving, raised up that thunderbolt 'Recite to Indra Marutvat!' and thereafter he (Pragâpati) gave no more. And in like manner is that thunderbolt 'Recite to Indra Marutvat!' now raised up to stop the giving, and thereafter he (the sacrificer) gives no more.

24. There are, then, four (kinds of) sacrificial gifts: Gold—thereby indeed he preserves his own life, for gold is life. That he (Pragâpati or Varuna) gave

---

ha vâ ada âsînah prâtaranuvâkam anvâha tad dha smaitat purâsîno hotâ samsaty atha paskât tamah sado 'bhipupluve. Te hokus tamo vâ idam sado 'bhyaproshteti pratyañ prehîti pratyañ prehîti sa pratyañ prait sa tat tamo 'pâhan, &c. Sâyana also interprets it by 'pûrvasmin pradese âhavanîyasya samîpe.'

[1] For the part taken by the Pratihartri in the chanting of stotras, see p. 310, note 1.

to Agni, performing the office of the Agnîdh (fire-kindler): wherefore now also gold is given to the Agnîdh.

25. Then the Cow—thereby he preserves his own breath, for the cow is breath, since the cow is food, and breath also is food: her he gave to Rudra, the Hotri.

26. Then Cloth—thereby he preserves his own skin, for the cloth is skin: this he gave to Brihaspati, who chanted.

27. Then the Horse—for the horse is a thunderbolt: he thereby makes the thunderbolt the leader. And, moreover, he who sacrifices, sacrifices with the hope 'May there be a place for me in Yama's world!' He thus makes him a sharer in Yama's world. This he gave to Yama, the Brahman.

28. The (proffered) gold he (the Adhvaryu) goes to meet (accepts) with (Vâg. S. VII, 47), 'Let Varuna give thee to me (who am) Agni!' for to Agni Varuna gave it. 'May I obtain immortality! be thou life to the giver, joy (mayas) to me, the receiver!'

29. And the cow he accepts with, 'Let Varuna give thee to me, Rudra!' for to Rudra Varuna gave her. 'May I obtain immortality! be thou breath to the giver, strength (vayas) to me, the receiver!'

30. And the cloth he accepts with, 'Let Varuna give thee to me, Brihaspati!' for to Brihaspati Varuna gave it. 'May I obtain immortality! be thou a skin to the giver, joy to me, the receiver!'

31. And the horse he accepts with, 'Let Varuna give thee to me, Yama!' for to Yama Varuna

gave it. 'May I obtain immortality! be thou a steed (hayah) to the giver, strength (vayas) to me, the receiver!'

32. And whatever other gift he gives that he gives with the hope, 'May I also have this in yonder world!' That he accepts with (Vâg. S. VII, 48), 'Who hath given it? to whom hath he given it? Hope hath given it, for Hope hath he given it: Hope is the giver, Hope the receiver. This to thee, O Hope!' Thus he assigns it to a deity.

33. Here they say[1],—Let him not assign it to any deity; for whatsoever deity he here kindles, that deity, being kindled, becomes ever more glorious from one day to the morrow; and to whatever fire he here adds fuel, that fire, being kindled, becomes ever more glorious from one day to the morrow; and ever more glorious does he become, whosoever, knowing this, accepts (a gift): even as one offers in kindled fire, so does he offer that (gift) which he gives to one learned in the scriptures. Therefore he who is learned in the scriptures need not assign (the gift to a deity).

---

[1] The Kânva text of this paragraph seems more correct: Thus he assigns it to deities; for when he bestows (abhyâdhâ) anything on a deity, that deity thereby shines ever more brilliantly; and whatever (fuel) he adds to the fire, thereby it shines ever more brilliantly: and more glorious does he become from day to day whosoever, knowing it, accepts it thus. Here now Âsuri said, 'But he who is learned in the scriptures need not regard this; for as one puts fuel on kindled fire, and offers on kindled fire, thus he gives who gives gifts to one learned in the scriptures.'

FIFTH BRÂHMANA.

D. THE TRITÎYA SAVANA, OR EVENING PRESSING.

1. Now there are three kinds of gods,—the Vasus, the Rudras, and the Âdityas. Between them the press-feasts are divided: the morning pressing belongs to the Vasus, the midday pressing to the Rudras, and the third pressing to the Âdityas. But the morning pressing belonged to the Vasus exclusively, and the midday pressing to the Rudras exclusively, and the third pressing to the Âdityas conjointly (with others).

2. The Âdityas then said, 'As that morning pressing belongs exclusively to the Vasus, and that midday pressing exclusively to the Rudras, so offer ye now to us a libation before the common (pressing).' The gods said, 'So be it!' After the completion of the midday pressing, they offered that (libation) previous to the third pressing[1]. And in like manner is that libation offered to this day after the completion of the midday pressing and previous to the third pressing.

3. The Âdityas said, 'Neither in the one pressing have we a share nor in the other: we fear lest the Rakshas might injure us!'

4. They said to the (cups) belonging to two deities (dvidevatya[2]), 'We are afraid of the Rakshas: pray, let us enter into you!'

---

[1] The Âditya-graha, with which the succeeding paragraphs deal, is considered as not belonging to the Tritîya Savana proper, but as a preliminary ceremony.

[2] For the three dvidevatya grahas (Aindravâyava, Maitrâvaruna, and Âsvina), see Brâhmanas IV, 1, 3–5.

5. The Dvidevatyas said, 'What will be our reward then?'—'By us ye shall be supplied with the Anuvashat[1]!' said the Âdityas.—'So be it!'—They entered into the dvidevatya cups.

6. Hence, when at the morning pressing he (the Adhvaryu) proceeds with the dvidevatya cups, the Pratiprasthâtri draws Soma-juice from the Dronakalasa into the Âditya vessel, with this much (of the formula, Vâg. S. VIII, 1), 'Thou art taken with a support!' The Adhvaryu calls for the (Agnîdh's) Sraushat, and after the Adhvaryu's libation the Pratiprasthâtri pours (his juice into the fire), and with this much 'Thee to the Âdityas!' he pours the remains (into the Âditya-sthâlî). In the same way at all (three dvidevatya libations).

7. Thus, the reason why the Pratiprasthâtri draws the Soma-juice, is that they entered into the dvidevatya cups. And the Âdityas then said, 'By us ye shall be supplied with the Anuvashat!' For, that second libation which he (the Pratiprasthâtri) makes, he makes to (Agni) Svishtakrit, and by means of the Svishtakrit these (dvidevatyas) are supplied with the Anuvashat; and thus those (libations) of

[1] At the three dvidevatya libations no Anuvashatkâra is permitted; that is to say, the Hotri is not to pronounce the words, 'O Agni, accept of the Soma!' after the Vashat, with which the offering prayer (yâgyâ) concludes. But as the libation, ordinarily made at the Anuvashat, corresponds to the oblation to Agni Svishtakrit made after each chief oblation at the haviryagña (see I, 7, 3; Ait. Br. III, 5), there is apparently no such Svishtakrit oblation at the dvidevatya libations. Now, as each of these chief libations, made by the Adhvaryu, is followed by one made by the Pratiprasthâtri from the Âditya vessel (see p. 316, note 1), these latter libations are here, as it were, identified with the Svishtakrit and the Anuvashatkâra.

his are supplied with the Anuvasha*t*, having the (oblation to Agni) Svish*t*ak*ri*t performed for them. He offers on the north part (of the fire), for that is the region of that god[1]: hence he offers on the north part.

8. And again, why the Pratiprasthât*ri* draws the Soma. They entered into the Dvidevatyas; and from those which they entered he thereby draws them out. He then covers it[2]—for they were afraid of the Rakshas—with 'O Vish*n*u, Far-strider, here is thy Soma, protect it lest they should injure it!' For Vish*n*u is the sacrifice: to the sacrifice he thus makes it over for protection. Now, after the completion of the midday Soma feast and before the evening feast he says, 'Come hither, Sacrificer!'

9. They enter (the Havirdhâna) together,—the Adhvaryu, Sacrificer, Âgnîdhra, Pratiprasthât*ri*, Unnet*ri*, and whatever other attendant (of the Adhvaryu) there is[3]. They close both doors,—for they (the Âdityas) were afraid of the Rakshas. He (the Adhvaryu) takes up the Âditya-sthâlî and Âditya-pâtra, and holds them close over the Pûtabh*ri*t, 'lest (any Soma-juice) should be spilt.'

10. He then draws (the juice from the sthâlî into the pâtra) with (Vâ*g*. S. VIII, 2; Rig-veda VIII, 51, 7), 'At no time art thou barren, and never failest thou the worshipper, O Indra; but

---

[1] See I, 7, 3, 20.

[2] The remains of Soma-juice he pours after each libation from the Âditya-pâtra into the Âditya-sthâlî, and finally puts the former on the latter by way of a lid. See p. 316, note 1.

[3] While they enter by the front door, the mistress of the house enters by the back (west) door. Kâty. X, 4, 2.

more and ever more is thy divine gift increased, O mighty lord!—Thee to the Âdityas!'

11. Let him not draw it with a 'support'—for it was originally drawn with a support—to avoid a repetition (of sacrificial performance); but were he now also to draw it with a support, he would certainly commit a repetition.

12. Having withdrawn (the cup for a moment from the flowing juice), he again pours it in with (Vâg. S. VIII, 3; Rig-veda VIII, 52, 7), 'At no time art thou heedless, but watchest over both generations; the Soma feast[1] is thy strength, O fourth Âditya: the ambrosia is ready for thee in the heavens!—Thee to the Âdityas!'

13. Thereupon he takes sour milk; for the evening pressing belongs to the Âdityas, and cattle are after (the manner of) the Âdityas[2]: he thereby puts milk into the cattle, and thus that milk in cattle is beneficial[3]. 'He should put it right in the centre (of the Âditya cup),' they say, 'for that milk is right in the centre of cattle.' But let him rather put it in the back part (of the cup), for that milk is in the hind part of cattle.

14. And the reason why he takes sour milk is that those remains (of Soma) poured together are the leavings of offerings, and insufficient for an oblation: he now increases those (remains), and thus they

[1] The Rig-veda reads 'havanam' (invocation) instead of 'savanam.'

[2] Or, cattle correspond, stand in relation, to the Âdityas. Sâyana takes 'anu' in the sense of 'behind, inferior to, dependent upon (hîna).' The cattle are inferior to, or dependent upon, the Âdityas, inasmuch as the Âdityas give the rain on which the cattle depend for their food.

[3] Or, 'put' (hita) into them.

become sufficient for an oblation. This is why he takes sour milk.

15. He takes it with (Vâg. S. VIII, 4; Rig-veda I, 107, 1), 'The sacrifice draweth nigh to the glory of the gods: be ye merciful, O Âdityas! Let your favour incline unto us, that it may set us free from all trouble!—Thee to the Âdityas!'

16. He mixes it by means of the Upâmsusavana stone[1]. For, indeed, that Âditya Vivasvat (the sun) is really the same as the Upâmsusavana, and this is the Âditya libation: thus he makes him delight in his own share.

17. He touches it neither with the fringe nor with (the woven part of) the straining-cloth; for those two pressings, the morning pressing and midday pressing, forsooth are rich in pure Soma, rich in juice, but this, the third pressing, is emptied of its pure Soma. Now, in that he does not touch it either with the fringe or the straining-cloth, thereby that third pressing of his also becomes rich in pure Soma and juice: therefore he touches it neither with the fringe nor with the straining-cloth.

18. He mixes it with (Vâg. S. VIII, 5), 'O Âditya Vivasvat, this is thy draught of Soma: feast thou upon it!' Thereupon he hands the Upâmsusavana to the Unnetri. Then he says to the Unnetri, 'Drop in the pressing-stones!' He drops them either into the Âdhavanîya or into a cup[2].

---

[1] See p. 238, note 2.

[2] 'Into the Âdhavanîya trough or into a kamasa cup containing Soma-juice,' Kâty. X, 4, 10; 'into the Âdhavanîya or the Sambharanî,' Kânva text; 'into the Âdhavanîya or into the graha,' Weber, Ind. Stud. X, 386. Perhaps the next paragraph has to

19. After drawing the king (Soma)—the third press-feast belonging to the Âdityas, and the pressing-stones being after (the manner of[1]) the Âdityas, he thus makes them delight in their own share—they open the doors.

20. He now walks out, covering (the cup with his hand or the sthâlî); for they (the Âdityas) were afraid of the Rakshas. He then says (to the Maitrâvaruna), 'Recite (the invitatory prayer) to the Âdityas!' If he likes, he may now enumerate (their qualities); but let him rather enumerate them, after he has called for the *S*raushat,—'Prompt (the Hotri to recite the offering prayer) to the Âdityas, the beloved, rite-loving, law-loving lords of the great abode, the rulers of the wide air.' He offers, as the Vashat is pronounced. He (the Hotri) pronounces no Anuvashat, lest he should consign the cattle to the fire. The remains (of juice in the sthâlî and graha) he (the Adhvaryu) hands to the Pratiprasthâtri.

21. Thereupon he again enters (the Havirdhâna) and draws the Âgrayana graha[2]. They spread (over the Pûtabhrit) a straining-cloth with the fringe towards the north. The Adhvaryu pours out (the

be taken along with this: 'Or into a *k*amasa, after drawing Soma (into it).' According to Kâty., the stones are taken out again immediately and laid down in their places on the pressing-skin.

[1] See p. 353, note 2. Sâyana again takes 'anu' in the sense of 'after, behind,' apparently on the ground that, in the above formulas, the stones are mentioned after the Âditya. The text of my manuscript is, however, rather corrupt at this place.

[2] The Âgrayana Soma was originally drawn into the Âgrayana bowl (sthâlî) and deposited in its place in the centre of the khara. It is now poured from the bowl into some other vessel, and thence through a straining-cloth into the Pûtabhrit.

juice) of the Âgrayana; the Pratiprasthâtri holds out (and pours in) the two residues (of the Âditya graha[1]); the Unnetri adds thereto (some juice from the Âdhavanîya) by means of a *k*amasa cup or a dipping-vessel (udañ*k*ana).

22. Thus he draws the Âgrayana graha from four streams; for the evening pressing belongs to the Âdityas, and cows are after the manner of the Âdityas; whence this milk of cows is of a fourfold nature: therefore he draws the Âgrayana from four streams[2].

23. And as to why the Pratiprasthâtri holds out the two residues: this is (the remains of) the Âditya libation, and for the Âditya libation he pronounces no Anuvashat; and from that (Âgrayana graha) he intends to draw the Sâvitra graha,—so that the Anuvashat is performed for it by means of the Sâvitra graha.

24. And again why the Pratiprasthâtri holds out the two residues. Previous to that mixed (press-feast), previous to the evening feast, they have offered that (unmixed or special) libation to those (Âdityas); but this libation is taken for the evening feast: thereby the Âdityas take part in the evening feast, and thus they are not excluded from the sacrifice. This is why the Pratiprasthâtri holds out the two residues[3].

---

[1] 'Sampraskandayati pratiprasthâtâdityapâtrayo*h* samsravam,' Kânva text.

[2] In drawing the Âgrayana cup he uses the same formula as at the morning pressing. See IV, 2, 2, 9 seq.

[3] In the actual performance of the Agnish*t*oma the drawing of the Âgrayana graha is followed by sour milk being poured to the Soma-juice left in the Pûtabhrit, the compound being consecrated by the lady eying it with an appropriate mantra. Thereupon they leave the Havirdhâna shed in the same way as at the morning feast

FOURTH ADHYÂYA. FIRST BRÂHMANA.

1. Savitri, forsooth, is his[1] mind: therefore he draws the Sâvitra cup. And, forsooth, Savitri is his breath (vital air);—when he draws the Upâmsu cup, then he puts into him that vital air in front; and when he draws the Sâvitra cup, then he puts into him that vital air behind: thus those two vital airs on both sides are beneficial (or, put into him), both that which is above and that which is below.

2. And the sacrifice, forsooth, is the seasons, the year. There, at the morning feast, they are overtly attended to, in that he draws the cups for the seasons; and at the midday feast they are covertly attended to, in that he takes the Marutvatîya libations by means of the two Ritu vessels[2]. Now here (at the evening feast) they neither draw any libation expressly for the seasons, nor is any libation taken with the two Ritu vessels.

(see IV, 2, 5, 1, with notes), and perform the Viprud-homas, followed by the Sarpana and chanting of the Ârbhava, or Tritîya Pavamâna stotra (for an account of which, see p. 314, note 2). Then follow the oblations from the victim (which has been cooking since the morning, see IV, 2, 5, 13), &c., up to the eating of the pasvidâ (see III, 8, 3, 4 seq.); and offering of the four Savanîya-purodâsas, likewise up to the eating of the idâ. Previous to the eating, small pieces of rice-cake are thrown into the kamasa cups, as an oblation to the sacrificer's deceased ancestors, with naming of his father, grandfather, and great-grandfather (as at the Pindapitriyagña, II, 4, 2, 19 seq.); whereupon the pieces are eaten along with the idâ.

[1] Viz. that of Yagña, the sacrificial man, representing the sacrificer himself, with a view to the preparation of a new body in a future existence.

[2] See IV, 3, 3, 12.

3. But Savitri, forsooth, is he that burns yonder (the sun); and he indeed is all the seasons: thus the seasons, the year, are overtly attended to at the evening feast,—for this reason he draws the Sâvitra cup.

4. He draws it with the Upâmsu vessel. For Savitri is his mind, and the Upâmsu is his breath: therefore he draws it with the Upâmsu vessel; or with the Antaryâma vessel, for that is one and the same, since the Upâmsu and Antaryâma are the out-breathing and in-breathing[1].

5. He draws it from the Âgrayana graha; for Savitri is his mind, and the Âgrayana is his body (or self): he thus puts the mind into the body. Savitri is his breath, and the Âgrayana is his body: he thus puts the breath into the body.

6. He thus draws it therefrom with (Vâg. S. VIII, 6; Rig-veda VI, 71, 6), 'Bring thou forth boons for us this day, O Savitar, boons to-morrow, boons day by day: O God, through this our prayer may we be sharers of boons, of a good and plenteous abode!—Thou art taken with a support!—Thou art Savitri's joy-giver, thou art a joy-giver: give me joy!" speed the sacrifice; speed the lord of the sacrifice to (receive) his share!'

7. Having drawn it, he does not deposit it; for Savitri is his (Yagña's) mind, and hence this mind is restless. And Savitri is his breath: hence this breath passes to and fro unrestingly. He then says (to the Maitrâvaruna), 'Recite (the invitatory prayer) to the god Savitri!' Having called for the

[1] See IV, 1, 1 1.

*S*raushat, he says, 'Prompt (the Hot*ri* to recite the offering prayer) to the god Savit*ri*!' The Vashat having been pronounced, he offers. He (the Hot*ri*) pronounces no Anuvashat[1],—for Savit*ri* is his mind,—'lest he should consign his mind to the fire;' and Savit*ri* being his breath,—'lest he should consign his breath to the fire.'

8. Then with the (same) vessel, without drinking therefrom[2], he draws the Vai*s*vadeva graha. The reason why he draws the Vai*s*vadeva graha with the (same) vessel, without drinking therefrom, is this: on the Sâvitra graha he (the Hot*ri*) pronounces no Anuvashat, and it is therefrom that he is about to draw the Vai*s*vadeva graha,—thus it is by means of the Vai*s*vadeva that it becomes supplied with the Anuvashat for him.

9. And further why he draws the Vai*s*vadeva graha. Savit*ri*, forsooth, is his mind, and the Vi*s*ve Devâ*h* (All-gods, or all the gods[3]) are everything here: he thus makes everything here subservient and obedient to the mind, and hence everything here is subservient and obedient to the mind.

10. And again why he draws the Vai*s*vadeva graha. Savit*ri*, forsooth, is his breath, and the All-gods are everything here: he thereby puts the out-breathing and in-breathing into everything here, and

[1] See p. 351, note 1.

[2] Lit. 'with the not-drunk-from vessel.' He is not to drink with the Hot*ri* the remains of the Sâvitra graha, which is to be offered up entirely (holocaust).

[3] In Ait. Br. III, 31 five classes of beings, viz. the gods and men, the Gandharva-Apsaras, the serpents and the manes, are included in the term Vi*s*ve Devâ*h*.

thus the out-breathing and in-breathing become beneficial (or put) in everything here.

11. And again why he draws the Vaisvadeva graha. The evening feast belongs to the All-gods: thus indeed it is called on the part of the Sâman, in that the evening feast is called Vaisvadeva on the part of the *Rik*[1], and in the same way on the part of the Yagus, by way of preparatory rite, when he draws that Mahâ-vaisvadeva graha.

12. He draws it from the Pûtabh*ri*t; for the Pûtabh*ri*t belongs to the All-gods, because therefrom they draw (Soma-juice) for the gods, therefrom for men, therefrom for the Fathers: hence the Pûtabh*ri*t belongs to the All-gods.

13. He draws it without a puroru*k*[2], for he draws it for the All-gods, and the All-gods are everything, the *Rik* and Yagus and Sâman; and even in that he draws it for the All-gods, thereby it becomes supplied with a puroru*k* for him: therefore he draws it without a puroru*k*.

14. He thus draws it therefrom with (Vâg. S. VIII, 8), 'Thou art taken with a support: thou art well-guarded, well-established,'—for well-guarded and well-established is the breath,—'homage to the great bull!'—the great bull is Pragâpati (the lord of creatures): 'homage to Pragâpati,' he thereby means to say.—'Thee to the All-gods! this is thy womb,—thee to the All-gods!' Therewith he

---

[1] The first sastra of the T*ri*tîya-savana, now about to be recited by the Hot*ri* (Rig-veda priest), is the Vaisvadeva sastra; hence also, he argues, it is Vaisvadeva on the part of the Sâman, because of the intimate connection of the Sâman chants (here the T*ri*tîya, or Ârbhava, pavamâna stotra; see p. 325, note 2) with the sastras.

[2] See p. 268, note 1.

deposits it; for it is for the All-gods that he draws it. Thereupon he goes (to the Sadas) and sits down (in front of the Hotri) with his face to the east[1].

15. And when he (the Hotri) recites this (verse), 'With one and ten for thine own sake, with two and twenty for offering, with three and thirty for up-bearing (the sacrifice to the gods); with thy teams, O Vâyu, do thou here unloose them!'—during (the recitation of) this verse to Vâyu the drinking-vessels are unyoked[2], for beasts have Vâyu for their leader; and Vâyu

---

[1] He remains thus seated till the Hotri utters the Âhâva 'Adhvaryo sosamsâvom' (Adhvaryu, let us sing!), when he turns round and makes his response (pratigara) 'Samsâmo daivom.' See p. 326, note 1.

The Vaisvadeva sastra consists of the following parts:—

Pratipad (opening triplet), Rig-veda V, 82, 1-3.

Anukara (sequel), ib. 4-7.

Sûkta (hymn) to Savitri, IV, 54. Before the last verse the Nivid ('May the god Savitri drink of the Soma!' &c.) is inserted; to which the verse to Vâyu, referred to in paragraph 15, is added.

Sûkta to Heaven and Earth, I, 159, with the Nivid 'May Heaven and Earth delight in the Soma!' &c., inserted before the last verse; the Adhvaryu's response being thrice 'Madâmo daiva,' see p. 330, note 3.

Dhâyyâ verse, I, 4, 1.

Sûkta to the Ribhus, I, 111; with Nivid before the last verse.

Three Dhâyyâs, X, 123, 1; X, 63, 3; IV, 50, 6.

Sûkta to Visve Devâh, I, 89; with Nivid before the last verse.

The concluding verse (paridhânîyâ) is recited thrice; the first time with stops at every half verse, the second and third time at every pâda.

Ukthavîrya, 'Praise has been sung to Indra, to the gods, to hear thee!'

Then follows the recitation of the offering prayer VI, 52, 13, after which the libation is made, the remaining juice being then drunk, as well as that in the kamasas.

[2] That is, having been rinsed in the Mârgâlîya, the three dvidevatya are deposited on the khara by the Pratiprasthâtri.

(wind) is breath, since it is by means of the breath that beasts move about.

16. Now once on a time he went away from the gods with the beasts. The gods called after him at the morning pressing,—he returned not. They called after him at the midday pressing,—but he returned not. They called after him at the evening pressing.

17. Being about to return, he said, 'If I were to return to you, what would be my reward?'—'By thee these vessels would be yoked, and by thee they would be unloosed!'—Hence those vessels are yoked by that (Vâyu), when he (the Adhvaryu) draws the (cups) for Indra and Vâyu and so forth [1]. And now those vessels are unloosed by him, when he says, 'with thy teams, O Vâyu, do thou here unloose them;'—teams mean cattle: thus he unlooses those vessels by means of cattle.

18. Now, had he returned at the morning pressing—the morning pressing belonging to the Gâyatrî, and the Gâyatrî being the priesthood [2]—then cattle would have come to be with priests only. And had he returned at the midday pressing—the midday pressing belonging to Indra, and Indra being the nobility—cattle would have come to be with nobles only. But in that he returned at the evening pressing—the evening pressing belonging to the All-gods, and the All-gods being everything here—therefore there are cattle everywhere here.

---

[1] See IV, 1, 3–10.

[2] Perhaps we ought to read, with the Kânva text, gâyatram vai prâtahsavanam gâyatram agnes khando brahma vâ agnir, brâhmaneshu haiva pasavo 'bhavishyan, 'the morning pressing relating to the gâyatrî, and the gâyatrî metre belonging to Agni, and Agni being the priesthood.'

SECOND BRÂHMANA.

1. He proceeds with (the offering of) Soma's rice-pap; for Soma is the sacrificial food of the gods; and here now sacrificial food is prepared for Soma on his part; and thus Soma is not excluded therefrom. It is a rice-pap (*k*aru), for rice-pap is food for the gods, since rice-pap is boiled rice, and boiled rice is clearly food: therefore it is a rice-pap.

2. Neither at the morning feast, nor at the midday feast does he offer it, for those two press-feasts, the morning feast and the midday feast, are the exclusive feasts of the gods; and Soma is sacred to the Fathers[1].

3. But were he to offer it at the morning feast, or at the midday feast, he would cause discord between the gods and Fathers. He offers it at the evening feast, because the evening feast belongs to the All-gods[2]: thus he does not cause discord. He recites no invitatory prayer (but only an offering prayer), for the Fathers have passed away once for all: hence he recites no invitatory prayer.

4. Having, in the first place, taken ghee in four ladlings, and having called (on the Agnîdh) for the *S*raushat, he says, 'Recite the offering prayer of the ghee!' and offers as the Vashat is uttered. Whatever oblations have been offered previous to this (*k*aru), therefrom he separates this one (to Soma), and thus he causes no discord.

---

[1] Probably, because Soma is slain in being sacrificed (see IV, 3, 4, 1), and therefore belongs to the Fathers or Departed Spirits.

[2] And the All-gods (or all the gods) mean everything. See IV, 4, 1, 4.

5. Having poured (into the spoon) an 'underlayer' of ghee, he makes two cuttings from the rice-pap; and bastes them with ghee above. Having called for the Sraushat, he says, 'Recite the offering prayer of the Saumya (rice-pap)!' and offers as the Vashat is uttered.

6. He then takes ghee a second time by four ladlings, and having called for the Sraushat, he says, 'Recite the offering prayer of the ghee!' and offers as the Vashat is uttered. From whatever oblations he intends to offer hereafter, he thereby separates this one (to Soma), and thus he causes no discord. If he chooses, he may offer (ghee) on both sides (before and after the Soma's rice-pap); or, if he chooses, he may offer on one side only[1].

7. Now there is an offering-spoon called 'prakaranî.' Therein the Adhvaryu takes ghee by four ladlings (with the dipping-spoon) and pours it on the Dhishnya hearths by means of fagots (held over them). The reason why he pours ghee on the hearths by means of fagots is this. Because, on a former occasion[2], the gods said to those (Gandharva

---

[1] The homa of ghee, made before the rice-pap oblation to Soma, belongs to Agni, and the one made after the oblation, to Vishnu. If only one homa be made, it belongs to Agni and Vishnu. The Kânva text reads, 'Tad vâ âhur anyatarata eva pariyaget purastâd eveti,' now they say, 'He should offer on one side only, and that in front (previously to the karu).' For the offering formulas, see Âsv. V, 19, 3; Ait. Br. III, 32. After the completion of these offerings, the Adhvaryu pours ordinary ghee on the rice-pap and presents it to the Hotri, who looks at it while pronouncing some formulas (Âsv. V, 19, 4, 5), and he smears his eyes with the ghee on the pap, after which the latter is handed to the chanters (udgâtri) to be eaten by them.

[2] See III, 6, 2, 19.

Soma-wardens), 'At the third pressing an offering of ghee shall fall to your share, but not one of Soma, for the Soma-draught has been taken from you, wherefore ye are not worthy of a Soma-offering,' that same offering of ghee now falls to their share at the evening pressing, but not one of Soma, in that he pours ghee on the hearths by means of fagots. One after another, in the order in which they were thrown up, and with the same formulas[1], he pours ghee upon them; on the Mârgâlîya last of all.

8. Now some make a second pouring on the Âgnîdhrîya hearth, thinking, 'In the North (or upwards) shall this sacred work of ours be accomplished!' but let him not do it in this way, but rather the Mârgâlîya last[2].

9. Now, while the Adhvaryu pours ghee on the hearths by means of fagots, the Pratiprasthâtri draws the Pâtnîvata[3] cup. For from the sacrifice creatures are produced; and being produced from the sacrifice, they are produced from union; and being produced from union, they are produced from the hind part of the sacrifice;—hence he thereby produces them from a productive union, from the hind part of the sacrifice: therefore he draws the Pâtnîvata cup.

10. He draws it with the Upâmsu vessel. If he

---

[1] Viz., Vâg. S. V, 31, 32. The Âgnîdhra hearth is prepared first, and the Mârgâlîya last of the eight dhishnyas. See p. 148, note 4.

[2] Or, uppermost (uttamam; the Kânvas read 'antamâm').

[3] The meaning of the term pâtnîvata is 'relating to the patnîvant (i. e. wived or mated one),' the 'patnîvant' being probably Soma with the water mixed with it; or Agni with the wives of the gods, (with special reference to the sacrificer's wife); cf. Taitt. S. VI, 5, 8, 1, 2. According to the Kânva text, Agni associated with the goddess Speech (Vâk patnî) seems to be understood.

draws the Sâvitra libation with the Upâmsu vessel, (he draws) this one with the Antaryâma vessel; and if he draws the Sâvitra with the Antaryâma vessel (he draws) this one with the Upâmsu vessel;—for one and the same indeed are the Upâmsu and Antaryâma, being breath, and that which is the out-breathing is also the in-breathing. Now the breath (prâna, masc.) is male, and the wife is female: a productive union is thus brought about.

11. He draws it without a puroruk[1],—the puroruk being manhood,—lest he should bestow manhood on women: therefore he draws it without a puroruk.

12. He thus draws it from that (Âgrayana graha) with (Vâg. S. VIII, 9), 'Thou art taken with a support: Of thee, divine Soma, begotten by Brihaspati'—Brihaspati is the priesthood: 'of thee, divine Soma, the priest-begotten' he thereby means to say—'Of thee, the potent juice'—'of the powerful (manly) juice' he means to say when he says 'of thee, the potent juice'—'May I prosper the draughts of thee, the mated one[2]!' he does not now draw it for the wives, lest he should bestow manhood on women: therefore he does not now draw it for the wives.

13. He (the Adhvaryu) then mixes it with the residue (of ghee) which is left in the prakaranî spoon. Now other libations he completes by mixing, but this one he diminishes; for ghee is a thunderbolt,

---

[1] See p. 268, note 1.

[2] In the St. Petersburg Dictionary 'patnîvatah' seems to be taken as qualifying 'grahân;' but cp. Rig-veda VIII, 82, 22, 'United with their wives (i.e. the water mixed with the Soma-juice?) these Soma-draughts (sutâh) go longing to the rejoicing.'

and by that thunderbolt, the ghee, the gods smote the wives and unmanned them, and thus smitten and unmanned they neither owned any self nor did they own any heritage. And in like manner does he now, by that thunderbolt, the ghee, smite the wives and unman them; and thus smitten and unmanned, they neither own[1] any self nor do they own any heritage.

14. He mixes it, with (Vâg. S. VIII, 9), 'I am above, I am below; and what space there is between, that was my father;—I saw the sun on both sides: I am what is highest to the gods in secret.' In that he mixes with 'I—I,' thereby he bestows manhood on men.

15. He then says, 'Agnîdh, pronounce the offering prayer of the Pâtnîvata!' The Agnîdh is male, and the wife is female: thus a productive union is brought about. He offers with (Vâg. S. VIII, 10), 'O Agni, wife-leader[2]!'—Agni is male, and the wife is female: thus a productive union is brought about.

16. 'Together with the divine Tvash*tri*'—for Tvash*tri* transforms the cast seed: thus he thereby transforms the cast seed;—'drink the Soma, Hail!' therewith he offers on the north (left) part (of the fire); what other offerings there are, they are the gods, and these are the wives: thus alone it is a proper union, since the woman lies on the left (north) side of the man. The Adhvaryu takes a draught of Soma to the Agnîdh, and the latter says, 'Adhvaryu, invite me!' [It might be said

---

[1] 'îs,' etymologically connected with 'own.'

[2] Or, wived, mated one, 'patnîvan;' the Kânva text reads 'Agne Vâk patni.' See preceding page, note 2.

that] he should not invite him, since how can there be an invitation of one smitten and unmanned? He should nevertheless invite him: they offer in his fire, and utter the Vasha*t*,—therefore he should invite him.

17. He then gives orders, 'Agnîdh, sit in the Nesh*tri*'s lap! Nesh*tri*, lead up the lady, and make her exchange looks with the Udgât*ri*! Unnet*ri*, fill up the Hot*ri*'s cup, and let no Soma-juice remain!' Thus, if it be an Agnish*t*oma sacrifice.

18. But if it be an Ukthya[1], let him say, 'Lengthen out the Soma!'—Holding the same vessel (from which the Pâtnîvata libation was made, the Agnîdh) sits down in the Nesh*tri*'s lap,—for he, the Agnîdh, is in reality Agni, and the Nesh*tri* is female: the Agnîdh is male, and the Nesh*tri* female,—a productive union is thus brought about. The Nesh*tri* leads up the lady and makes her exchange looks with the Udgât*ri*[2], with 'Thou art Pra*g*âpati, the

[1] 'But if it be an Ukthya, or Shoda*s*in, or Atirâtra, or Vâ*g*apeya, Kâ*n*va text. See towards the end of next note.

[2] Kâty. X, 7 and schol. supply the following details. The Unnet*ri* puts down the *k*amasa cups behind the high altar, and pours into them the entire Soma-juice remaining in the Pûtabh*ri*t, putting but little into the Hot*ri*'s cup, to leave room in it for the dhruva libation. Besides this the Âgraya*n*a is the only Soma that remains. The Adhvaryu then, by touching the Soma in the Hot*ri*'s cup with two stalks of grass, gives the signal for the chanting of the Agnish*t*oma Sâman (viz. the Ya*gñ*âya*gñ*îya, Sâmav. II, 53, 54), wrapping up his head, if he chooses, in the same way as the Udgât*ri*s. Meanwhile the Nesh*tri* leads up the lady through the back door into the Sadas, makes her sit down north of the Udgât*ri* and exchange looks with the latter three times (at the 'Hi*m*,' see p. 308, note 2). Three times also (at every Nidhana) she uncovers her right leg and pours on it some of the pânne*g*anî water fetched by her in the morning (see III, 9, 3, 27),

male, the bestower of seed: lay thou seed into me!' The Udgâtri is Pragâpati, and the lady is a woman: a productive union is thus brought about.

THIRD BRÂHMANA.

1. The metres, forsooth, are the (draught) cattle of the gods. Even as harnessed cattle here on earth

whereupon she returns to her own tent. Then follows the recitation of the Âgnimâruta sastra, consisting of the following parts:—

Sûkta (hymn), Rig-veda III, 3, to Agni Vaisvânara, with Nivid ('May Agni Vaisvânara feast on this Soma,' &c.) inserted before the last verse.

Dhâyyâ, I, 43, 6; or (verse to Rudra) II, 33, 1.

Sûkta, I, 87, to Maruts, with Nivid ('May the Maruts feast on this Soma,' &c.) before the last verse.

{ Stotriya pragâtha, VI, 48, 1–2 (identical with the text of the Yagñâyagñîya Sâman).
{ Anurûpa pragâtha, VII, 16, 11–12 (antistrophe).

Sûkta to Agni Gâtavedas, I, 143, with Nivid before the last verse.

Tristich to Âpah (waters), X, 9, 1–3, recited in breaks, the Hotri having previously uncovered his head (as do the other priests) and touched water, and the others holding on to him from behind. This and the following parts also have the Âhâva ('somsâvom') before each of them.

Verse VI, 50, 14 to Agni Budhnya.

Verses V, 46, 7–8 to wives of gods.

Verses II, 32, 4–5 to Râkâ.

Verse VI, 49, 7 to Pâviravî (daughter of lightning).

Verse X, 14, 4 to Yama.

Verse X, 14, 3 to Kavyas (manes).

Verses X, 15, 1, 3, 2 to Pitarah (fathers), with the Âhâva before each verse.

Anupânîya (or Svâdushkilîya) verses VI, 47, 1–4 to Indra. After each of the first three the Adhvaryu may respond to the Hotri's Âhâva, with 'madâmo daiva' (instead of 'samsâmo daiva'). See note on IV, 3, 2, 11.

Verse to Vishnu and Varuna (Atharva-veda VII, 25, 1).

draw for men, so do the harnessed metres draw the sacrifice for the gods. And whenever the metres gratified the gods, then the gods gratified the metres. Now it has been previous to this, that the harnessed metres have drawn the sacrifice to the gods, that they have gratified them[1]:

2. He now draws the Hâriyogana[2] graha—the Hâriyogana being the metres—it is the metres he thereby gratifies: this is why he draws the Hâriyogana graha.

3. He draws it as an additional (libation); since

Verse to Vishnu, Rig veda I, 154, 1.

Verse to Pragâpati, X, 53, 6.

Paridhânîyâ (concluding verse) IV, 17, 20, in reciting which the Hotri touches the ground; and during the recitation of the last pâda the Dhruva graha is poured into the Hotri's cup.

Ukthavîrya, 'Praise has been sung to Indra, to the gods, for hearing (?) thee!'

Yâgyâ (offering prayer) V, 60, 8, at the conclusion of which libations are made to Agni and the Maruts, both at the Vashat and Anuvashat.

Then follow the after-offerings of the animal sacrifice (see III, 8, 4, 1 seq.).

At the Ukthya (and other Soma-sacrifices) the Ukthya graha is drawn immediately after the drawing of the Âgrayana (see IV, 3, 5, 24, with note). Previous to the after-offerings the Ukthya graha is divided, as at the morning and midday performances (see p. 293, note 2), between the three Hotrakas, with a view to the recitation of their sastras which form the distinctive feature of the Ukthya sacrifice, bringing up the number of sastras (and stotras) from twelve (of the Agnishtoma) to fifteen. Besides, the Ukthya requires the immolation of at least two victims on the Soma-day, viz. a he-goat to Indra and Agni, besides the one to Agni.

[1] See I, 8, 2, 8; the translation has been amended in accordance with Professor Whitney's suggestions, American Journal of Philology, III, p. 406.

[2] That is, referring to the 'hari-yogana,' or (Indra's) team of bay steeds.

he draws it when he (the Hotri) pronounces the 'All-hail and blessing[1].' For there are here the gods, and the metres in addition to them; and there are men, and beasts in addition to them: therefore he draws it as an additional one.

4. He draws it in the Dronakalasa. Now Soma was Vritra. When the gods slew him, his head rolled off[2]: it became the Dronakalasa. Thereinto flowed together so much of the juice as it could hold[3]; that was in excess; and so is this graha in excess: he thus puts the excess to the excess,—therefore he draws it in the Dronakalasa.

5. He draws it without a puroruk-formula, for he draws it for the metres; and in that he draws it for the metres, even thereby that (graha) of his becomes supplied with a puroruk: therefore he draws it without a puroruk.

6. He now draws it from that (Âgrayana graha) with (Vâg. S. VIII, 11), 'Thou art taken with a support: of bay colour art thou, meet for the team of bay steeds,—thee to the pair of bay steeds!' Now, the two bay horses are the *Rik* and Sâman: it is for the *Rik* and Sâman that he draws it.

7. He then pours parched grain into it with, 'Ye are the bays' grains, united with the Soma for

---

[1] For the Sam-yos, see part i, p. 254, note. The pronunciation of that formula takes place after the offering proper is completed.

[2] ? Or burst (udvavarta), as the St. Petersburg Dictionary takes it. The Kânva text reads,—Vritro vai soma âsît tam yatra devâh pâtreshu vyagrihnata tasya mûrdhno (!) vyavartta sa dronakalaso 'bhavat.

[3] Yâvân vâ yâvân vâ rasah, (? some indeterminate quantity of the juice.) Cf. IV, 4, 5, 13.

Indra!' Whatever metres there are, both measured and unmeasured, they all thereby drink (of the Soma[1]).

8. For this (libation) the Unnetri[2] calls for the Sraushat;—for the Unnetri is in excess (additional), since he does not call for the Sraushat for any other (libation); and this libation also is in excess: thus he puts the excess to the excess,—therefore the Unnetri calls for the Sraushat.

9. Placing (the Dronakalasa) on his head, he calls for the Sraushat,—for this (vessel) is his (Soma's) head. He first says (to the Maitrâvaruna), 'Recite (the invitatory prayer) for the Soma-draughts with grains!' Having called for the Sraushat, he says, 'Prompt (the Hotri to pronounce the offering prayer on) the Soma-draughts with grain brought forward[3]!' and offers as the Vashat and Anuvashat are uttered. They then divide the grain between them for the sake of the Soma-draught.

10. Now some take the Dronakalasa over to the Hotri, on the ground that 'the draught belongs to the utterer of the Vashat.' But let him not do it thus; for the other draughts are (taken by the respective priests) according to the kamasa cups, but this one is in excess: therefore there is a draught in it for all of them,—for this reason they divide the grain between them for the sake of the Soma-draught.

---

[1] The text might also be taken in the sense of 'Whatever metre there is, both measured and unmeasured, all that he thereby consumes.' The libation is, however, taken out for the metres or cattle, represented by the grain.

[2] Instead of the Âgnîdhra, see I, 5, 2, 16, with note.

[3] Regarding 'prasthitam,' see p. 198, note 3.

11. They must not bite them with their teeth,—for these (grains) mean cattle,—thinking 'lest we should do aught to crush our cattle!' They only drink it in with their breath[1], with (Vâg. S. VIII, 12), 'What horse-winning, what cow-winning draught is thine[2];' for they are cattle: therefore he says, 'what horse-winning, what cow-winning draught is thine;'—'Of that draught, offered with Yagus, praised by chants[3],'—for Yagus-prayers have indeed been offered, and chants have been chanted;—'sung by hymns,'—for songs (sastras) have been sung;—'Of the invited[4] do I drink, invited,'—for invited, he now drinks of the invited.

12. They must not throw them into the fire, lest they offer remains (of offerings) in the fire. They rather throw them on the high altar: thus they are not excluded from the sacrifice.

13. Thereupon they touch the vessels filled (with water[5]) which some call Apsushomâh (Soma-draughts in water). For even as a yoked (animal) draws, so

---

[1] They are only to smell the grains steeped in the Soma-juice.

[2] The Kânva recension adds, 'O divine Soma!'

[3] Lit., having Yagus offered, and chants chanted for it.

[4] ? I.e. 'that to which I am invited.'

[5] That is, the ten Kamasins touch their respective kamasa cups, filled with water and placed in the proper order from south to north, behind the pit (kâtvâla), after putting fresh kusa stalks on them. Those priests who have no cups of their own touch the cups of those with whom they are most nearly connected, viz. the four Adhvaryus that of the Neshtri, the Udgâtri's assistants that of their principal, the Grâvastut that of the Hotri. Thereupon they touch their faces and betake themselves to the Âgnîdhra fire-house, to partake of sour milk. Then follow, on the Gârhapatya (at the front hall door), the Patnîsamyâgas of the cakes of the animal offering, followed by the Samishtayagus. See also Lâty. Sr. II, 11, 16 seq.

do they who perform the priestly duties. But the yoked (animal) galls or scratches itself; and water is a means of soothing, a medicine: thus wherever in this (sacrifice) they gall or scratch themselves—water being a means of soothing—they soothe by that means of soothing, water; they heal it by water. This is why they touch the vessels filled (with water).

14. They touch them with (Vâg. S. VIII, 14), 'With lustre, with sap, with bodies[1] have we united,—with the happy spirit: may Tvash*tri*, the dispenser of boons, grant us riches, and may he smooth what was injured in our body!' thus they heal what was torn.

15. They then touch their faces. There is a twofold reason why they touch their faces;—water, forsooth, is the elixir of immortality: it is with the elixir of immortality that they thus touch themselves. And, moreover, they thus deposit that holy work into their own self: therefore they touch their faces.

Fourth Brâhmana.

E. Concluding Ceremonies.

1. Now, it is nine Samish*t*ayagus[2] he offers on this occasion. The reason why he offers nine Samish*t*ayagus is that those stotra-verses at the Bahishpavamâna[3] chant amount to nine. Thus there is at both ends an inferior (incomplete) virâ*g*[4], for the

[1] See I, 9, 3, 6. Cf. Atharva-veda VI, 53, 3. The Tâ*nd*ya Br. I, 3, 9 reads 'sa*m* tapobhi*h*' (with fervour).

[2] See I, 9, 2, 25 seq.

[3] See p. 310, note 1.

[4] The virâ*g* consists of pâdas of ten syllables. For the same speculation, see II, 5, 1, 20.

sake of production: it was from that same inferior (lower) source of production on both sides that Pragâpati produced the creatures,—from the one (he created) the upright, and from the other those tending to the ground. And in like manner does he (the Adhvaryu) now create creatures from that lower source of production on both sides,—from the one the upright, and from the other those tending to the ground.

2. The call 'Him' is the tenth of stotra-verses, and the 'Svâhâ' (the tenth) of these (Samishtayagus): and thus does this incomplete virâg come to consist of tens and tens.

3. And as to why they are called Samishtayagus. Whatever deities he invites at this sacrifice, and for whatever deities this sacrifice is performed, they all are thereby 'sacrificed-to together' (sam-ishta); and because, after all those (deities) have been 'sacrificed-to together,' he now offers those (libations), therefore they are called Samishtayagus.

4. And as to why he offers the Samishtayagus. Now, the self of him who has sacrificed has, as it were, become emptied, since he gives away of whatever is his: it is him he fills again by three out of these (oblations).

5. And as to the three following which he offers,—whatever deities he invites at this sacrifice, and for whatever deities this sacrifice is performed, they continue waiting till the Samishtayagus are performed, thinking, 'These, forsooth, he must offer unto us!' It is these same deities he thereby dismisses in due form whithersoever their course lies.

6. And as to the three last which he offers,—in performing the sacrifice he has produced it, and,

having produced it, he firmly establishes it where there is a safe resting-place for it: this is why he performs the Samishtayagus.

7. He offers (the first) with (Vâg. S. VIII, 15; Rig-veda V, 42, 4), 'With thought lead us, O Indra, to meet with kine,'—'with thought:' him who was emptied he thereby fills with thought; 'with kine;' him who was emptied he thereby fills with kine;—'with patrons, O mighty Lord, with well-being; with prayer which is divinely inspired[1],'—'with prayer:' him who was emptied he thereby fills with prayer;—'with the favour of the adorable gods! Hail!'

8. [The second with Vâg. S. VIII, 16], 'With lustre, with sap, with bodies,'—'with lustre:' him who was emptied he thereby fills with lustre; 'with sap,'—sap is vigour—him who was emptied he thus fills with sap;—'We have united, with the happy spirit: may Tvashtri, the dispenser of boons, grant us riches, and may he smooth what was injured in our body!' Thus they heal what was torn.

9. [The third with Vâg. S. VIII, 17; Atharva-veda VII, 17, 4], 'May the gracious Dhâtri, Savitri, Pragâpati, the guardian of treasures, and the divine Agni accept this (offering); and Tvashtri and Vishnu: grant ye willingly to the sacrificer wealth together with children! Hail!' Him who was emptied he fills again, when he says, 'grant ye wealth to the sacrificer, Hail!'

---

[1] ? The author of the Brâhmana would rather seem to take it in the sense of 'with the priestly authority (sacerdotium) instituted by the gods.'

10. [The fourth with Vâg. S. VIII, 18[1]], 'Accessible homes have we prepared for you, O gods, who graciously came to this Soma feast;'—whereby he means to say, 'seats easy of access we have prepared for you, O gods, who have graciously come to this Soma feast;'—'Carrying and driving the offerings,' thereby he dismisses the several deities; 'Those forsooth who are without cars may go away carrying; and those who have cars may go away driving,' this is what he means to say; therefore he says, 'Carrying and driving the offerings;'—'bestow goods on him, ye good! Hail!'

11. [The fifth with Vâg. S. VIII, 19; Atharva-veda VII, 97, 3], 'The willing gods whom thou, O God, broughtest hither, speed them each to his own abode, O Agni!' For to Agni he said, 'Bring hither such and such gods! bring hither such and such gods!' and to him he now says, 'Whatever gods thou hast brought hither, make them go whithersoever their course lies!'—'Ye have all eaten and drunk,'—for they have eaten the cakes of the animal offering, and they have drunk the king Soma: therefore he says, 'ye have all eaten and drunk;'—'Draw ye nigh to the air, to the heat, to the light! Hail!' Hereby, then, he dismisses the deities.

12. [The sixth with Vâg. S. VIII, 20], 'Thee, O Agni, have we chosen here for our Hot*ri* at the opening of this sacrifice: severally hast thou offered to them, and severally hast thou toiled; well-knowing the sacrifice, draw thou nigh[2], thou the wise! Hail!' by this (verse) he releases Agni, dismisses Agni.

---

[1] Cf. Atharva-veda VII, 97, 4.

[2] That is, according to Mahîdhara, 'knowing that the sacrifice

13. [The seventh with Vâ*g*. S. VIII, 21], 'Ye path-finding gods,'—for the gods are, indeed, the finders of the path;—'having found the path,'—'having found the sacrifice,' he thereby means to say;—'go ye in the path!' therewith he dismisses them in due form;—'O divine Lord of mind, this sacrifice—Svâhâ!—give thou to the wind!' for the sacrifice, indeed, is yonder blowing (wind): having thus completed this sacrifice, he establishes it in that sacrifice, and thus unites sacrifice with sacrifice,—hence he says, 'Svâhâ! give (it) to the wind!'

14. [The eighth with Vâ*g*. S. VIII, 22], 'O sacrifice, go to the sacrifice, go to the lord of the sacrifice, go to thine own womb, Hail!'—the sacrifice, thus established, he thereby establishes in its own womb. [The ninth he offers with], 'This is thy sacrifice, O lord of the sacrifice, bestowing numerous heroes, together with the song of praise: do thou accept it, Hail!' the sacrifice, thus established, bestowing numerous heroes, together with the song of praise he thereby finally establishes in the sacrificer.

FIFTH BRÂHMA*N*A.

1. He now betakes himself to the expiatory bath (avabh*ri*tha). The reason why he betakes himself to the expiatory bath is this. What vital sap there has been in him (Soma and the sacrificer), that (sap) of his he (the priest) has produced (extracted) for the offerings. Now that body (of Soma, i.e.

is accomplished, go thou to thine own house!' Cf. Atharva-veda VII, 97, 1 ('draw near to Soma!').

the Soma-husks),—there is no sap in it; (yet) it is not to be cast away: they take it down to the water and—water being sap—he puts that sap into it. Thus he unites him with that sap, and thus he produces him from it,—he (Soma), even when produced, produces him (the sacrificer)[1]: and because they take it down (ava-hri[2]) to the water, therefore (the bath is called) avabhritha.

2. In the first place he performs the Samishtayagus offerings, for the Samishtayagus are the extreme end of the sacrifice. As soon as he has performed the Samishtayagus, they go together to the kâtvâla (pit) with whatever he (the sacrificer) has about him[3]: both the black-deer's horn[4] and the girdle he throws into the pit,—

3. With (Vâg. S. VIII, 23), 'Be thou nor adder nor viper!' Now when they take the Soma-husks down to the water, that forsooth is the wishing of 'good-speed[5]!' to it, and this now is the 'good-speed!' to him (the sacrificer); for snakes are like rope, and snakes' haunts are like wells (pits), and there is as it were a feud between men and snakes: 'Lest that should spring therefrom,' he thinks, and therefore he says, 'Be thou nor adder nor viper!'

---

[1] ? That is, as the Soma plants become juicy again, so the sacrificer has his vital sap or spirit restored.

[2] Or, according to the St. Petersburg Dictionary, 'they throw it into the water.'

[3] Or, whatever is connected with Soma (?). According to Kâty. X, 8, 12, 19 the throne (âsandî) and Audumbarî, as well as the Soma vessels, Dronakalasa, &c., are to be carried in the first place to the kâtvâla, and from there to the water.

[4] See III, 2, 1, 18. The Pratiprasthâtri is silently to throw after the lady's zone and peg (for scratching herself).

[5] For the 'svagâkâra,' see I, 8, 3, 11.

4. He then makes (the sacrificer) say (Rig-veda I, 24, 8), 'Broad forsooth is the path which king Varuna hath made for the sun to walk along,'—whereby he means to say, 'even as there is for the sun that broad path, free from danger and injury, so may there be for me here a broad path, free from danger and injury.'

5. 'For the footless hath he made feet to put down[1],' for, although he (the sun) is footless, yet he is able to walk;—'And the forbidder is he of all that woundeth the heart,'—thus he frees him from every guilt and evil of the heart.

6. He then says, 'Sing the Sâman!' or 'Speak the Sâman!' but let him rather say 'Sing,' for they do sing the Sâman. The reason why he sings the Sâman is that the evil spirits may not injure that body of his outside the sacrifice, for the Sâman is a repeller of the evil spirits.

7. He (the Prastotri) sings a (verse) to Agni, for Agni is a repeller of the evil spirits. He sings in the Atikkhandas; for this, the Atikkhandas, is all the metres[2]: therefore he sings in the Atikkhandas.

8. He sings, 'Agni burneth, Agni encountereth with flames,—Ahâvah! Ahâvah[3]!' Thus he drives the evil spirits away from here.

[1] Or, 'To the footless he has given to put down his feet:' in either sense it seems to be taken by the author of the Brâhmana (and the St. Petersburg Dictionary). Perhaps, however, 'apade' had better be taken, with Mahîdhara (and Sâyana?), in the sense of 'padarahite,' i. e. 'in the trackless (ether) he caused him (the sun) to plant his feet.' Similarly Ludwig, 'Im Ortlosen hat er sie die Füsse niedersetzen lassen.'

[2] 'Eshâ vai sarvam ati yad atikkhandah,' Kânva text. Atikkhandas, i. e. over-metre, redundant metre, is the generic term for metres consisting of more than forty-eight syllables.

[3] All the priests, as well as the sacrificer, are to join in the

9. They walk out (from the sacrificial ground) northwards, along the back of the pit and the front side of the Âgnîdhra: then they proceed in whatever direction the water is.

10. Where there is a standing pool of flowing water, there let him (the sacrificer) descend into the water—for whatsoever parts of flowing water flow not, these are holden by Varuna; and the expiatory bath belongs to Varuna—to free himself from Varuna. But if he does not find such, he may descend into any water.

11. While he makes him descend into the water, he bids him say, 'Homage be to Varuna: down-trodden is Varuna's snare!' thus he delivers him from every snare of Varuna, from every (infliction[1]) of Varuna.

12. Thereupon, taking ghee in four ladlings, and throwing down a kindling-stick (on the water), he offers thereon, with (Vâg. S. VIII, 24), 'The face of Agni, the waters, have I entered, escaping from the power of demons, O son of the waters! In every homestead offer thou the log, O Agni! let thy tongue dart forth towards the ghee,—Hail!'

13. Now, once on a time, the gods made so much of Agni, as would go in[2], enter the water, in order that the evil spirits should not rise therefrom; for Agni is the repeller of evil spirits. It is him he kindles by this kindling-stick and by this

nidhana (finale, or concluding word of the Sâman). According to Kâty. X, 8, 16, 17 the Sâman is chanted thrice, viz. in starting from the *k*âtvâla, midway, and at the water-side.

[1] Or guilt against Varuna. See p. 221, note 1.

[2] Agner yâvad vâ yâvad vâ. Cf. p. 371, note 3.

oblation, thinking 'On the kindled (fire) will I offer to the gods!'

14. Then, having taken ghee a second time in four ladlings, and having called for the (Âgnîdhra's) Srausha*t*, he says, 'Pronounce the offering prayer to the Kindling-sticks!' He offers four fore-offerings, omitting that to the Barhis[1]—the Barhis being offspring, and the expiatory bath belonging to Varu*n*a—lest Varu*n*a should seize upon his offspring. This is why he offers four fore-offerings, omitting that to the Barhis.

15. Then follows a cake on one potsherd for Varu*n*a. For whatever sap there had been in him (Soma), that sap of his he has produced (extracted) for the offerings. Now that body: there is no sap in it. But the cake is sap: that sap he puts into it. Thus he unites him with that sap, and so produces him from it,—he (Soma), even when produced, produces him (the sacrificer): hence there is a cake on one potsherd for Varu*n*a.

16. Having made an 'underlayer' of ghee (in the offering-spoon), he says, while making the cuttings from the cake[2], 'Recite (the invitatory prayer) to Varu*n*a!' Here now some make two cuttings from the Soma-husks, but let him not do so; for that (heap of husks) is an empty body, unfit for offering. He makes two cuttings (from the cake) and bastes them once with ghee, and anoints (replenishes the places whence) the cuttings (have been made). Having called for the Srausha*t*, he says, 'Recite the

[1] For the usual five prayâ*g*as, see I, 5, 3, 8–13.

[2] As a rule, cakes on one potsherd are to be offered entire. The present cake, however, is to be an exception, and the usual two portions are to be cut from it. See part i, p. 192, note.

offering prayer to Varuna!' and offers as the Vashat is uttered.

17. Then, having made an underlayer of ghee, he says, while putting the (remainder of the) cake (into the spoon), 'Recite the invitatory prayer to Agni and Varuna!' This is for (Agni) Svishtakrit[1]; and as to why he does not say 'To Agni,' it is lest Varuna might seize upon Agni. If before he has cut twice from the Soma-husks, he now does so once, but if (he did) not, he need not heed it. He then bastes it twice with butter on the upper side; and having called for the Sraushat, he says, 'Recite the offering prayer to Agni and Varuna!' and offers as the Vashat is uttered.

18. Now these are six oblations; for there are six seasons in the year, and Varuna is the year: hence there are six oblations.

19. This is the course of the Âdityas[2]; and these Yagus, they say, belong to the Âdityas. Let (the Adhvaryu) endeavour to perform as much of it as is his (the sacrificer's) wish. And if the sacrificer tell him to do otherwise, then he should do otherwise. He may also perform those same four fore-offerings, —omitting that to the Barhis—two butter-portions, (the oblations of cake) to Varuna and Agni-Varuna, and two after-offerings,—omitting the one to the Barhis;—this makes ten. Now the virâg consists

[1] See I, 7, 3, 7 seq.

[2] Professor Weber, Ind. Stud. X, p. 393, refers us to XIV, 9, 4, 33, where it is stated that the Vâgasaneyin Adhvaryu has to study the Yagus of the Âditya Rishi. One might also be inclined to think that, by 'Âdityânâm ayanam' and 'Angirasâm ayanam' the author intended to connect the Agnishtoma with the sacrificial sessions designated by those terms, for which see Âsv. Sr. XII, 1-2; Ait. Br. IV, 17, with Haug's notes.

of ten syllables, and the sacrifice is virâg: thus he makes the sacrifice to be like the virâg.

20. This is the course of the Aṅgiras. Having performed the offerings either way, (the Adhvaryu) makes the pot, in which the husks are, float with (Vâg. S. VIII, 25), 'In the ocean, in the waters, is thy heart (O Soma)'—for the ocean is the waters, and water is sap: that sap he now puts into him (Soma), and thus he unites him with that sap, and produces him therefrom; and he (Soma), even when produced, produces him (the sacrificer);—'May the plants and the waters unite with thee!'—thereby he puts two kinds of sap into him, that which is in plants, and that which is in water,—'that we may serve thee, O lord of the sacrifice, in the singing of praises and the utterance of worship[1], with Svâhâ!' Whatever is good in the sacrifice, that he thereby puts into him.

21. Thereupon, letting it go, he stands by it with (Vâg. S. VIII, 26), 'Ye divine waters, this is your child,'—for he (Soma) indeed is the child of the waters,—'bear ye him, well-beloved, well-nourished!' he thereby makes him over to the waters for protection—'This, O divine Soma, is thine abode: thrive thou well therein, and thrive thou[2] thoroughly!' whereby he means to say, 'Be thou therein for our happiness, and shield us from all inflictions!'

---

[1] See part i, p. 249, note 1.

[2] 'Vakshva' is by Mahîdhara (and apparently by the author of the Brâhmana) referred to 'vah;' by the St. Petersburg Dictionary to 'vas' for 'vatsva.' I have referred it to 'vaksh.' The Kânva text reads, Pari *k*a vakshi *sam k*a vakshîti pari *k*a no gopâya *sam k*a na edhîty evaitad âha.

22. He then immerses it with (Vâg. S. VIII, 27), 'O laving bath, laving thou glidest along: with the help of the gods may I wipe out the sin committed against the gods; and with the help of the mortals that committed against mortals!'—for the sin committed against the gods he has indeed wiped out with the help of the gods, namely, with the help of king Soma; and the sin committed against mortals he has wiped out with the help of mortals, namely, by means of the animal victim and the sacrificial cake:—'Preserve me, O god, from injury from the fiercely-howling (demon)!' whereby he means to say, 'Preserve me from all inflictions!'

23. Thereupon both (the sacrificer and his wife) having descended, bathe, and wash each other's back. Having wrapped themselves in fresh garments[1] they step out: even as a snake casts its skin, so does he cast away all his sin,—there is not in him even as much sin as there is in a toothless child. By the same way by which they came out (from the sacrificial ground), they return thither[2]; and, having returned, he puts a kindling-stick on the Âhavanîya (at the front hall-door) with, 'Thou art the kindler of the gods!' He thereby kindles the sacrificer him-

[1] According to the Mânava Sûtra, as quoted on Kâty. X, 9, 6, the sacrificer wraps himself in the cloth in which the Soma stalks were tied (somopanahana), and his wife in the outer cloth tied round the Soma bundle (paryânahana). The Soma vessels and implements are likewise thrown into the water.

[2] While going thither they all mutter the Âmahîyâ verse, Rig-veda VIII, 48, 3, 'We have drunk Soma, we have become immortal, we have gone to the light, we have attained to the gods: what now can the enemy do unto us, what the guile, O immortal, of the mortal?'

self, for along with the kindling of the gods the sacrificer is kindled[1].

Fifth Adhyâya. First Brâhmana.

1. He proceeds with the rice-pap to Aditi, as the concluding oblation. The reason why there is a rice-pap for Aditi is this. Because, on that former occasion[2], the gods said to her, 'Thine forsooth shall be the opening, and thine the concluding oblation,' therefore he prepares that share for her at both ends (of the Soma-sacrifice).

2. And because, on that occasion, he offers when about to go forth (upa-pra-i) to buy the king (Soma), therefore that (opening oblation) is called Prâyanîya. And because he now offers after coming out (ud-â-i) from the expiatory bath, therefore this (concluding oblation) is called Udayanîya[3]. For this indeed is one and the same oblation: to Aditi belongs the opening, to Aditi the concluding (oblation); for Aditi is this (earth).

3. To Pathyâ Svasti he offers first (at the opening sacrifice): then the gods, through speech, saw their way in what was unknown to them, for by speech the confused becomes known. But now that it is known, he performs in the proper order.

4. To Agni he offers first, then to Soma, then to Savitri, then to Pathyâ Svasti, then to Aditi. Now Pathyâ Svasti (the wishing of a 'happy journey')

---

[1] The sacrificer sits down behind the sâlâdvârya fire and spreads the black deer-skin over his knees; the Adhvaryu then making an oblation of ghee from the dipping-spoon.

[2] See III, 2, 3, 6.

[3] See p. 48, note 1.

is speech, and Aditi is this (earth): on her the gods thereby established speech, and thus established thereon speech speaks here.

5. Thereupon he slaughters a barren anûbandhyâ[1] cow for Mitra and Varuna. And this indeed is performed as a different sacrifice, and that an animal offering; for the Samishtayagus form the end of the sacrifice.

6. The reason why there is a barren cow for Mitra and Varuna is this. Whatever part of his (sacrifice)[2] who has offered is well-offered that part of his Mitra takes, and whatever is ill-offered that Varuna takes.

7. Then they say, 'What has become of the sacrificer?'—whatever well-offered part of his (sacrifice) Mitra here takes, that he now again surrenders to him, being pleased with this (cow); and whatever ill-offered part of his Varuna takes, that indeed he makes well-offered for him, being pleased with this (cow), and surrenders it again to him. This forsooth is his own sacrifice[3], his own merit.

8. And again, why there is a barren cow for Mitra and Varuna. Now, when the gods caused the cast seed to spring,—there is that sastra called Âgnimâruta[4]: in connection therewith it is explained how

[1] The meaning of this technical term would seem to be 'to be bound (or immolated) after' the sacrifice.

[2] Or, of him, the sacrificer.

[3] That is, the sacrifice of his own self.

[4] The same passage occurs at I, 7, 4, 4, where I erroneously supplied 'samabhavat.' It is a broken, incoherent construction. The explanation, referred to in these two passages, may be Ait. Br. III, 34, though in that case one might have expected a somewhat closer adherence to the order of production there proposed;

the gods caused that seed to spring. From it the coals (aṅgâra) sprung, and from the coals the Aṅgiras; and after that the other animals[1].

9. Then the dust of the ashes which remained: therefrom the ass was produced,—hence when it is dusty anywhere, people say, 'A very place for asses, forsooth[2]!' And when no sap whatever remained,—thence was produced that barren cow belonging to Mitra and Varuṇa; wherefore that (cow) does not bring forth, for from sap seed is produced, and from seed cattle. And because she was produced at the end, therefore she comes after the end of the sacrifice. Hence also a barren cow for Mitra and Varuṇa is the most proper here: if he cannot obtain a barren cow, it may also be a bullock[3].

10. Then the Viśve Devâḥ applied themselves[4] a second time: thence the Vaiśvadevî (cow) was produced; then the Bârhaspatyâ: that is the end, for Bṛihaspati is the end.

11. And whosoever gives a thousand or more

---

see part i, p. 210, note 1. Regarding the Âgnimâruta śastra, see above, p. 369 note.

[1] ? Or, the others, the animals (tad anv anye paśavaḥ). Cp. the French idiom, 'Les femmes et nous autres hommes.' The Kâṇva text reads, tad anu paśavaḥ.

[2] The Kâṇva reads, And when they (the coals) became dust of ashes, the ass was produced therefrom: hence they call 'asses' place' where the dust of the ashes (lies).

[3] Kâty. X, 9, 15 allows, in lieu of the animal offering, an oblation of clotted curds (payasyâ or âmikshâ). See also II, 4, 2, 14.

[4] ? They applied their minds, or, they took hold (amarîmṛiśanta): Tad u viśve devâ marîmṛiśâṃ kakrire tato dvitîyâ vaiśvadevî samabhavat.' Kâṇva text. Perhaps the verb has here the same meaning as 'dhû' in the passage of the Ait. Br. referred to, tad (reto) maruto 'dhunvan.

(cows to the priests), he will slaughter all these;—indeed, everything is obtained, everything conquered by him who gives a thousand or more. Those (three) cows are everything, (when offered) thus in the proper order: first one to Mitra and Varuna, then one to the All-gods, then one to Brihaspati.

12. And those who perform a long sacrificial session, for a year or more, they will slaughter all these[1];—indeed everything is obtained, everything conquered by those who perform a long sacrificial session, for a year or more: those (cows) are everything, (when offered) thus in the proper order.

13. Thereupon he performs the Udavasânîyâ ishti (completing oblation). He prepares a cake on five potsherds for Agni. Its invitatory and offering prayers are five-footed paṅktis[2]. For at this time the sacrifice of him who has sacrificed is, as it were, exhausted in strength: it, as it were, passes away from him. Now all sacrifices are Agni, since all sacrifices are performed in him, the domestic sacrifices as well as others. He thus takes hold again of the sacrifice, and thus that sacrifice of his is

[1] The immolation of the three anubandhyâ cows is prescribed at the end of the Gavâmayana (see note on IV, 5, 4, 14), and at other Sattras (sacrificial session) lasting at least a year, and endowed with fees of at least a thousand cows, except the Sârasvata Sattra. Kâty. XIII, 4, 4, 5.

[2] The Udavasânîyâ ishti is performed, with certain modifications, on the model of the Paunarâdheyikî ishti, or offering for the re-establishment of the sacred fire; for which see II, 2, 3, 4 seq., and especially the notes on part i, p. 317 seq. It is to be performed somewhere north of the sacrificial ground on a fire produced by the churning of the aranis or (pairs of) churning-sticks, with which the priests have previously 'lifted' their several fires. See p. 90, notes 4 and 5; and part i, p. 396, note 1.

not exhausted in strength, and does not pass away from him.

14. The reason why the cake is one on five potsherds, and the invitatory and offering prayers are paṅktis (verses of five feet), is that the sacrifice is fivefold. He thus takes hold again of the sacrifice, and thus that sacrifice of his is not exhausted in strength, and does not pass away from him.

15. The priests' fee for it is gold; for this is a sacrifice to Agni, and gold is Agni's seed: therefore the priests' fee is gold. Or an ox, for such a one is of Agni's nature as regards its shoulder, since its shoulder (bearing the yoke) is as if burnt by fire.

16. Or[1], he takes ghee in five ladlings, and offers it with the verse to Vishnu (Vâg. S. V, 38), 'Stride thou widely, O Vishnu, make wide room for our abode! drink the ghee, thou born of ghee, and speed the lord of the sacrifice ever onwards, Hail!' For Vishnu is the sacrifice: he thus takes hold again of the sacrifice, and thus his sacrifice is not exhausted in strength, and does not pass away from him. And let him on this occasion give as much as he can afford, for no offering, they say, should be without a Dakshinâ. When this Udavasânîyâ-ishti is completed, he offers the (ordinary) evening (milk-)offering[2],—but the morning offering at its proper time.

[1] According to Kâty. X, 9, 20 (as interpreted by the commentator) this (Vaishnavî) âhuti may optionally take the place of the Udavasânîyâ ishti. 'Atho' has evidently the force of 'or' here, as in IV, 6, 4, 5. The Kânva text has atho apy âhutim eva guhuyât; with the same meaning, cf. I, 1, 3, 3; also 'uto,' note to IV, 5, 2, 13.

[2] For the Agnihotra, or morning and evening libation of milk, see II, 2, 4; 3, 4. The performance being completed, the tempo-

SECOND BRÂHMA*N*A.

1. They lay hands on the barren cow[1], and having laid hands on it, they quiet it. It having been quieted[2], he says (to the slaughterer), 'Pull out the omentum!' The omentum having been pulled out[2], let him tell (the slaughterer) to search groping for an embryo. If they do not find one, why need they care? and if they find one, atonement is made therefore.

2. For surely it is not right that, thinking it to be one (cow), they should perform, as it were, with that one; or that, thinking them to be two, they should perform, as it were, with two[3]. Let him bid (the

---

rary erections, as the Sadas, cart-shed, Âgnîdhra fire-house, &c., are set on fire, and the sacrificer and priests go home.

[1] The order of this and the succeeding Brâhma*n*as differs considerably in the two recensions. In the Kâ*n*va recension the present Brâhma*n*a (the text of which also differs very much) is preceded by three others (V, 6, 1–3), corresponding to M. IV, 5, 3; IV, 5, 4 and IV, 5, 6, respectively.

[2] The text has simply, he (viz. the Samit*ri* or butcher) having quieted it, he (the Adhvaryu) says, (*S.*) having pulled it out, let him (A.) bid....

[3] The meaning of this would seem to be, that they should not content themselves with the supposition of its being a barren cow, but that they should ascertain whether she is not—as the term is—'ash*t*âpadî,' or eight-footed, i. e. a cow with calf (cf. par. 12), and should in that case make atonement. The Kâ*n*va text reads, Now when they thus proceed with that (animal offering), they, thinking it to be one (cow) only, pronounce the âprî verses (âprî*n*anti). They turn out to be two (te dve bhavata*h*); and surely it is not right that one should cast away that on which the âprî verses have been pronounced. Now that juice has flowed together from all the limbs: thus offering is also made with those sacrificial portions of that (embryo). And the sacrifice is as much as the havis and Svish*t*akr*i*t: he thus connects that whole (embryo) with that sacri-

slaughterer) get ready the pot (sthâlî) and the cloth (ush*n*îsha)[1].

3. They then perform with the omentum, just as its mode of performance is[2]. Having performed with the omentum, both the Adhvaryu and Sacrificer return (to the sacrificial ground). The Adhvaryu says, 'Pull out that embryo!' otherwise he would not pull it out from the womb, since it is only pulled out from the womb of a sick or dead (female); but when the embryo is full grown, then indeed it comes out through birth: let him bid him pull it out even after tearing asunder the thighs.

4. When it is pulled out, he addresses it with (Vâ*g*. S. VIII, 28), 'May the embryo of ten months move together with the caul!'—by saying, 'May it move,' he puts breath into it; and 'of ten months' he says, because when an embryo is full grown, then it is one of ten months: thus, even though it is not ten months old, he makes it one of ten months by means of the Brahman (prayer), the Ya*g*us.

5. 'Together with the caul'—this he says so that, like a ten months' (calf), it may go out with the caul[3],—'As yonder wind moveth, as the ocean moveth;'—thereby he puts breath into it;—'So hath this ten months' (calf) slipped out with the caul;'—this he means to say so that, like a ten months' calf, it may slip out with the caul.

6. Here now they say, 'What is he to do with

fice, and thus that which is superfluous (atirikta) becomes not superfluous.

[1] The comm. on Kâty. XXV, 10, 7, describes the ush*n*îsha, used on this occasion, as a small cloth, or kerchief.

[2] See III, 8, 2, 16 seq.

[3] Or, even as a ten months' calf moves with the caul, so he means to say (that) this (should take place).

that embryo?'—They might cut off a portion from every limb, even as (is done) the portioning of other portions. But let him not do so; for that (embryo) surely has its limbs undeveloped. Having cut it below the neck, they should let that fat juice drip into the pot; for that same juice drips from all its limbs, and thus it is a portion cut out from all its limbs. He then cuts the sacrificial portions of the cow in the same way in which they are (usually) portioned off.

7. They cook them on the cooking-fire of the animal offering: at the same time[1] they cook that fat juice. Having wrapped the embryo in the cloth, he lays it down by the side of the cooking-fire. When it (the victim) is cooked, he puts together[2] the (flesh) portions and bastes only them, but not that juice. They remove the victim (from the fire); and at the same time they remove that juice.

8. They take it along the back of the pit, between the sacrificial stake and the fire. It having been put down south (of the fire), the Pratiprasthâtri cuts off the sacrificial portions. He then makes an underlayer (of ghee) in both offering-spoons, and addresses (the Hotri) for the recitation to the Manotâ deity on the havis. Thereupon they make cuttings from the portions of the cow, in the same way in which cuttings are made from them[3].

9. Now there is an offering-spoon called prakaranî:

---

[1] Or, in the same place. The Kânva text reads, Having cut off the head, and let the juice (rasa) flow out, he cooks it by the side of (pratives*am) the (flesh) portions. And when they proceed with the havis, then having made an underlayer of ghee, and, taking twice from that juice, having basted (the portions therewith), he replenishes the (places of the) two portions.

[2] ? Read 'samuhya' for 'samudya.' See III, 8, 3, 5 seq.

[3] See III, 8, 3, 15 seq.

therein the Pratiprasthât*ri* makes an underlayer of ghee for the fat juice, takes two portions (from the juice), bastes them once (with ghee), and replenishes (the juice whence) both portions (have been taken). He (the Adhvaryu) then addresses (the Hot*ri*) for the recitation (of the invitatory prayer). Having called for the *S*raushа*t*, he says (to the Maitrâvaru*n*a), 'Prompt (the Hot*ri* to recite the offering prayer)!' As the Vasha*t* is uttered, the Adhvaryu offers (the flesh portions). After the Adhvaryu's oblation the Pratiprasthât*ri* offers (the fat juice)—

10. With (Vâ*g*. S. VIII, 29), 'Thou whose fruit is fit for sacrifice,'—for embryos are unfit for sacrifice: this one he thus makes fit for sacrifice by means of the Brahman, the Ya*g*us;—'thou who hast a golden womb,'—for on that former occasion[1], they rend the womb when they tear out (the embryo); and gold means immortal life; he thus makes that womb of her (the cow) immortal;—'Him whose limbs are unbroken, I have brought together with his mother, Hail!' Thus, if it be a male (embryo); but if it be a female one, with, 'Her whose limbs are unbroken, I have brought together with her mother, Hail!' And, if it be an indistinguishable embryo, let him offer in making it male, since embryos (garbha, masc.) are male, 'Him whose limbs are unbroken, I have brought together with his mother, Hail!' For on that former occasion, when they tear out (the embryo) they separate it from its mother: now, having rendered it successful by means of the Brahman, the Ya*g*us, he brings it again together with its mother in the midst of the sacrifice.

[1] See par. 3.

11. Thereupon the Adhvaryu makes the oblation to the Lord of the forest[1]. Having made the oblation to the Lord of the forest, the Adhvaryu, while pouring together the sacrificial portions that are for the upabh*ri*t, says (to the Hot*ri*), 'Recite the invitatory prayer to Agni Svish*t*ak*ri*t!' The Pratiprasthât*ri* comes and takes all that fat juice, and pours twice (ghee) thereon. Having called for the *S*rausha*t*, the Adhvaryu says, 'Prompt!' and offers as the Vasha*t* is uttered. After the Adhvaryu's oblation the Pratiprasthât*ri* offers,—

12. With (Vâ*g*. S. VIII, 30), 'The bountiful multiform juice[2],'—by 'bountiful' he means to say (the bestower) 'of numerous gifts;' and 'the multiform' he says, because embryos are, as it were, multiform,—'The strong juice hath invested itself with greatness:'—for it (the embryo) is indeed invested[3] in the mother.—'May the worlds spread along her, the one-footed, two-footed, three-footed, four-footed, eight-footed,—'Hail!' He thereby magnifies her (the cow): far more, forsooth, does he gain by offering an eight-footed one, than by one not eight-footed.

13. Here now they say, 'What is he to do with that embryo[4]?' They may expose it on a tree; for

[1] See III, 8, 3, 33.

[2] Indu, lit. 'droop,' a term usually applied to the draughts of Soma, a connection with which doubtless is here intended.

[3] A different simile is implied in the original 'antar mahimânam ânañ*g*a.'

[4] The Kâ*n*va text is much briefer here: He then ties up the head (*s*ira*h* pratinahya, ? with the body) either with a cloth (ush*n*îsha), or with bast (vakala), and having pushed asunder the cooking-fire of the animal offering, he lays it above them, with 'Verily, O Maruts ...,' for the common people are eaters of raw flesh, and the Maruts

embryos have the air for their support, and the tree is, as it were, the same as the air: thus he establishes it on its own support. But, say they, if, in that case, any one were to curse him, saying, 'They shall expose him[1] dead on a tree,' then verily it would be so.

14. They may throw it into the water, for water is the support of everything here: he thus establishes it in the water. But, say they, if, in that case, any one were to curse him, saying, 'He shall die in water!' then verily it would be so.

15. They may bury it in a mole-hill; for this (earth) is the support of everything here: he thus establishes it on this same (earth). But, say they, if, in that case, any one were to curse him, saying, 'They shall quickly prepare a burying-place for him, being dead!' then verily it would be so.

16. He may offer it to the Maruts on the cooking-fire of the animal sacrifice; for the Maruts, the clans (common people) of the gods, are not oblation-eaters (ahuta-ad)[2], and the uncooked embryo, as it were, is no oblation (ahuta); and the animal cooking-fire is taken from the Âhavanîya: thus indeed it (the embryo) is

are the people: he thus establishes it with the Maruts. Or (uto) with a verse to Heaven and Earth, 'The great Heaven and Earth . . .,' for additional superfluous (atirikta) is that (garbha), beyond these two, heaven and earth, nothing whatever remains (or, nothing surpasses them, atiri*k*yata): thus he establishes it within those two, heaven and earth; and while being superfluous, it comes to be no longer superfluous (or redundant).

[1] 'Enam' apparently refers both to the sacrificer and to the embryo (garbha, masc.).

[2] For the common people are eaters of raw flesh (âmâd), and the Maruts are the people. Kâ*n*va text. Neither a Kshatriya nor a Vai*s*ya can eat remains of offerings, but only a Brâhman is hutâd, Ait. Br. VII, 19.

not excluded from the sacrifice, and yet is not (offered) directly in the Âhavanîya (offering-fire). And the Maruts are of the gods: he thus establishes it with the Maruts[1].

17. As soon as he has performed the Samishtayagus offerings, when the coals are only just extinguished, he takes that embryo with the cloth, and standing with his face to the east, he offers it with a verse to the Maruts (Vâg. S. VIII, 31; Rig-veda I, 86, 1),—'Verily, O Maruts, in whosesoever house ye drink, the heroes of the sky, he is the best protected man.' He utters no Svâhâ (hail), for the Maruts, the clans of the gods are no oblation-eaters, and no oblation, as it were, is what is offered without Svâhâ. And the Maruts are of the gods: he thus establishes it with the Maruts.

18. He then covers it over with the coals with (Vâg. S. VIII, 32; Rig-veda I, 22, 13), 'The great Heaven and Earth may mix this our sacrifice, and fill us with nourishments!'

Third Brâhmana.

1. The Shodasin[2] (graha) forsooth is Indra. Now, at one time the beings surpassed (ati-rik)

---

[1] One might expect 'deveshu:' thus he establishes it with the gods; unless it is intended as the final decision: 'hence he consigns it to the Maruts.' The wording is, however, the same as in the preceding paragraphs.

[2] The author has now completed his exposition of the simplest form of Soma-sacrifice, viz. the Agnishtoma, the libations of which are accompanied by twelve chants (stotra) and as many recitations (sastra), and which (on the press-day) requires one victim to Agni (see IV, 2, 5, 14). He has also incidentally (IV, 4, 2, 18) touched upon the characteristic features of the Ukthya sacrifice, viz. its second victim, a he-goat to Indra-Agni, and three additional Uktha stotras and sastras (p. 370 note). He now proceeds to

Indra—the beings being the creatures—they were in a state of equality, as it were, with him.

2. Indra then bethought himself, 'How can I stand forth over everything here, and how may everything here be beneath me?' He saw that graha, and drew it for himself. Then he stood forth over everything here, and everything here was

---

consider another libation which, with its accompanying stotra and sastra, forms the distinctive feature of the Shodasin sacrifice, i.e. the one having sixteen or a sixteenth (hymn). This sacrifice also requires a third victim on the press-day, viz. a ram to Indra. By the addition, on the other hand, of the Shodasin graha, with its chant and recitation, to an ordinary Agnishtoma, another form of one day's (ekâha) Soma-sacrifice is obtained, viz. the Atyagnishtoma, or redundant Agnishtoma, with thirteen stotras and sastras. This form of sacrifice is, however, comparatively rarely used, and was probably devised on mere theoretic grounds, to complete the sacrificial system. A somewhat more common form is the Atirâtra, lit. 'that which has a night over and above,' differing as it does from the Shodasin in that—besides a fourth victim (a he-goat to Sarasvatî)—it has in addition a night performance of libations, with three rounds (paryâyas) of four stotras and sastras each (one for the Hotri and for each of his three assistants), and concluding at daybreak with one more stotra, the sandhi (twilight) stotra, and the Âsvina sastra and offering. These are the forms of Soma-sacrifice referred to in the present book, as required for the performance of sacrificial sessions (twelve days and more) of which its concluding portion treats. With another form, the Vâgapeya sacrifice, the author deals in the next Kânda. These—with the Aptoryâma, which to the Atirâtra adds another course of four Atirikta, or superadded stotras—constitute in the later official classification the seven fundamental forms (samsthâ) of Soma-sacrifice. This term, meaning properly 'termination, consummation,' probably applied originally to the concluding rites of the Soma-sacrifice proper, as the distinctive features of the several forms of sacrifice, but by a natural transition, became the generic terms for the complete forms of sacrifice. See Professor Weber's somewhat different explanation, Ind. Stud. IX, 229.

beneath him. And, verily, for whomsoever, knowing this, they draw that cup of Soma, he stands forth over everything here, and everything here is beneath him.

3. Wherefore it has been said by the *Ri*shi (Rig-veda III, 32, 11), 'The sky hath not reached thy greatness, when thou didst rest on the earth with thine other thigh,'—for, verily, yonder sky did not reach up to his other thigh[1]: so did he stand forth over everything here, and everything here was beneath him. And, verily, for whomsoever, knowing this, they draw that cup of Soma, he stands forth over everything here, and everything here is beneath him.

4. He draws it with a verse to the lord of the bay steeds (Indra Harivant); they (the Udgât*ri*s) chant verses to (Indra) Harivant, and he (the Hot*ri*) afterwards recites verses to (Indra) Harivant. For Indra seized upon the strength, the fury (haras) of his enemies, the Asuras; and in like manner does he (the sacrificer) now seize upon the strength, the fury of his enemies: therefore he draws the graha with a verse to (Indra) Harivant; they chant verses to Harivant, and he (the Hot*ri*) afterwards recites verses to Harivant.

5. He draws it with an Anush*t*ubh verse; for the morning press-feast belongs to the Gâyatrî, the mid-day feast to the Trish*t*ubh, and the evening feast to the *G*agatî. The Anush*t*ubh, then, is over and above[2] (ati-rikta), and he thus makes that (Soma of the

[1] ? Or either of his thighs. The situation depicted in this verse would seem that of the warrior Indra lying or kneeling on V*ri*tra, whom he has thrown on the ground.

[2] Or, additional, in excess; see IV, 4, 3, 4.

Sho*d*a*s*in) to remain over: hence he takes it with an Anush*t*ubh.

6. He draws it in a square cup; for there are three worlds: these same worlds he gains by three corners, and by the fourth corner he makes that (Soma) to remain over;—therefore he draws it in a square cup.

7. Let him draw it at the morning pressing, after drawing the Âgraya*n*a. Having been drawn at the morning pressing, it reposes apart from that time: he thus makes it to outlast all (three) pressings.

8. Or he may draw it at the midday pressing, after drawing the Âgraya*n*a,—but this is mere speculation: let him rather draw it at the morning pressing, after drawing the Âgraya*n*a: having been drawn at the morning pressing, it reposes apart from that time.

9. He thus draws it therefrom with (Vâ*g*. S. VIII, 33; Rig-veda I, 84, 3), 'Mount the chariot, O slayer of V*ri*tra, thy bay steeds have been harnessed by prayer! May the stone by its sound draw hitherward thy mind!—Thou art taken with a support: thee to Indra Sho*d*a*s*in (the sixteenfold)!—This is thy womb: thee to Indra Sho*d*a*s*in!'

10. Or with this (verse, Vâ*g*. S. VIII, 34; Rig-veda I, 10, 3), 'Harness thy long-maned, girth-filling bay steeds! Come hither to us, O Indra, drinker of Soma, to hear our songs! Thou art taken with a support: thee to Indra Sho*d*a*s*in!—This is thy womb: thee to Indra Sho*d*a*s*in!'

11. Thereupon he returns (to the sadas) and bespeaks the chant with, 'Soma has been left over:

Turn ye back[1]!' for he indeed causes it to remain over by that (Shodasin graha). He (the Adhvaryu) bespeaks it[2] before the setting of the sun; and after sunset he (the Hotri) follows it up by reciting the sastra: thus he thereby joins day and night together,—therefore he bespeaks (the stotra)[3] before the

---

[1] See IV, 2, 5, 8. The verb, here and elsewhere translated by 'to bespeak,' is upâ-kri, the proper meaning of which would seem to be 'to prepare, to introduce, to bring up' the chant. As the same verb is, however, also used for the 'driving up, or bringing up' of cattle (to the stable), it may perhaps have a similar meaning in connection with the stotra; the metres of the chant (which are often called the cattle of the gods) being, as it were, 'led up' (or 'put to') by the Adhvaryu, to be 'harnessed' or 'yoked' (yug) by the Udgâtri; see p. 311, note 1. Instead of the Prastara, handed to the Udgâtri on the occasion of the Pavamânas, two stalks of sacrificial grass are generally used with other chants; but certain stotras and sâmans require to be 'introduced' by special objects, such as a fan, or the two churning sticks (for producing fire), or water mixed with avakâ plants, or an arrow.

[2] ? Read 'tad' for 'tam;' or 'he calls upon him (the Udgâtri).'

[3] The Shodasi-stotra usually consists of the Gaurivîta Sâman (S. V. II, 302–4); but the Nânada Sâman (ib. II, 790–3) may be used instead. It is performed in the ekavimsa stoma, i.e. the three verses are chanted in three turns, so as, by repetitions, to produce twenty-one verses; the usual form being a a a - b b b - c; a - b b b - c c c; a a a - b - c c c. For some modifications in the present case, see Haug, Transl. Ait. Br. p. 258 note. The first turn is to be performed in a low voice, while the sun is going down; the second in a middle voice, when the sun has disappeared, but not entirely the daylight; and the third turn in a loud voice, when darkness is closing in. If, for some reason or other, the stotra is entirely performed after sunset, it is chanted with a loud voice throughout. During the chanting a horse (black, if possible), or a bullock, or he-goat is to stand at the front (or back) gate of the sadas, facing the latter. Besides, a piece of gold is to circulate among the chanters, each of them holding it, while his turn of chanting lasts, and the Udgâtri (or all three) doing so during the nidhana or finale.

setting of the sun, and after sunset he follows it up by reciting the sastra[1].

THE DVÂDASÂHA[2].

Fourth Brâhmaṇa.

1. Now, at first the gods were all alike, all good. Of them, being all alike, all good, three desired, 'May we be superior[3]!'—Agni, Indra, and Sûrya.

2. They went on praising and toiling. They saw those Atigrâhyas[4], and drew (grah) them for them-

---

[1] The Shodasi-sastra is minutely described in the Ait. Br. IV, 3 seq. The opening verses are in the Anushṭubh metre (of sixteen syllables), but otherwise also the Hotṛi has by means of pauses and insertions of formulas (nivid) to bring out its 'sixteenfold' character so as to accord with its designation.

[2] The Dvâdasâha, or twelve days' performance, forms the connecting link between the so-called Ahîna sacrifices (consisting of between two and twelve press-days) and the sattras, or sacrificial sessions (of twelve press-days and upwards); since it can be performed as one or the other. As a sattra (which seems to be its usual character) it consists of the Dasarâtra, or ten nights' (or days') period, preceded and followed by an Atirâtra, as the prâyaṇîya (opening) and udayanîya (concluding) days. The Dasarâtra, on its part, consists of three tryahas (or tridua), viz. a Pṛishṭhya shaḍaha (see note 4), and three Ukthya days, the so-called *Kh*andomas (on which see Haug, Ait. Br. Transl. p. 347). These are followed by an Atyagnishṭoma day, called Avivâkya (i. e. on which there should be 'no dispute, or quarrel').

[3] Ati-tishṭhâvânaḥ, lit. 'standing forth over (all others,' see IV, 5, 3, 2). In this, as in the preceding Brâhmaṇa, the prefix ati has to do service repeatedly for etymological and symbolical purposes.

[4] I. e. cups of Soma 'to be drawn over and above' (Weber, Ind. Stud. IX, 235; for a different explanation see Haug, Ait. Br. Transl. p. 490). These three grahas are required at the Pṛishṭhya shaḍaha, which forms part of the Dvâdasâha (see note 2), and of sacrificial sessions generally. The shaḍaha, or period of six Soma days, which (though itself consisting of two tryaha, or

selves over and above (ati): hence the name Atigrâhyas. They became superior, even as they are now superior[1]: and verily he becomes superior for whomsoever, knowing this, they draw those cups of Soma.

3. And at first there was not in Agni that lustre which is now in him. He desired, 'May that lustre be in me!' He saw this graha, and drew it for himself, and henceforth that lustre was in him.

---

tridua) may be considered as forming a kind of unit in sattras, or sacrificial sessions, is of two kinds, viz. the Abhiplava shadaha and the Prishthya shadaha. Both require (for the Hotri's prishtha-stotra at the midday pressing) the use of the Rathantara-sâman on uneven, and that of the Brihat-sâman on even days. The chief difference between them is that while the prishtha-stotras of the Abhiplava are performed in the ordinary (Agnishtoma) way, the Prishthya shadaha requires their performance in the proper prishtha form, see p. 339, note 2. Besides, while the Abhiplava shadaha consists of four Ukthya days, preceded and followed by one Agnishtoma day; the first day of the Prishthya shadaha is an Agnishtoma, the fourth a Shodasin, the remaining four days being Ukthyas. There is also a difference between the two in regard to the stomas, or forms of chanting, used; for while the Prishthya requires successively one of the six principal stomas (from the Trivrit up to the Trayastrimsa, as given p. 308, note 2) for each day, the Abhiplava requires the first four stomas (Trivrit to Ekavimsa) for each day, though in a different order. In this respect, three groups or forms are assumed for the performance of the stotras at the Agnishtoma and Ukthya, viz. the Gyotishtoma [a. Bahishpavavamâna in the Trivrit; b. Âgyastotras and c. Mâdhyandina-pavamâna in the Pañkadasa; d. the Prishtha-stotras and e. Ârbhava-pavavamâna in the Saptadasa; and f. the Agnishtoma sâman in the Ekavimsa stoma]; the Goshtoma [a. Pañkadasa; b. Trivrit; c. Saptadasa; e. f. (and g. Ukthastotras) Ekavimsa]; and Âyushtoma [a. Trivrit; b. Pañkadasa; c. d. Saptadasa; e. f. g. Ekavimsa]. These forms are distributed over the two tridua of the Abhiplava in the order: Gyotishtoma, Goshtoma, Âyushtoma; Goshtoma, Âyushtoma, Gyotishtoma.

[1] Lit. even as they are now the superiority, i.e. a superior power.

4. And at first there was not in Indra that power which is now in him. He desired, 'May that power be in me!' He saw this graha and drew it for himself, and henceforth that power was in him.

5. And at first there was not in Sûrya that splendour which is now in him. He desired, 'May that splendour be in me!' He saw this graha and drew it for himself, and henceforth that splendour was in him. And verily for whomsoever, knowing this, they draw those cups of Soma, he takes unto himself those same fires (energies), those same powers.

6. Let him draw them at the morning pressing, after drawing the Âgrayana; for the Âgrayana is the self (body), and many parts of this self are one each (and thus) over and above (the others), such as the lung[1] and heart, and others.

7. Or he might draw them from the Pûtabhrit, at the midday pressing, after drawing the Ukthya, or when about to bespeak (the chant), for the Ukthya indeed is the same as that undefined self of his. But this is mere speculation: let him rather draw them at the morning pressing, after drawing the Âgrayana.

8. They are offered after the offering of the Mâhendra graha; for that, the Mâhendra, is Indra's special cup; and so are the (Nishkevalya) stotra and sastra specially his. But the sacrificer is Indra; and for the sacrificer's benefit (these cups) are drawn: therefore they are offered after the offering of the Mâhendra graha.

9. He thus draws them therefrom [the first with

[1] That is, the right lung (kloman), the left lung being called by a different name. See St. Petersb. Dict. s. v.

Vâg. S. VIII, 38; Rig-veda IX, 66, 21][1], 'O Agni, skilful in works, become thou pure, bestowing upon us lustre and manly vigour, and upon me health and wealth!—Thou art taken with a support: thee to Agni, for lustre!—This is thy womb: thee to Agni, for lustre!'

10. [The second with Vâg. S. VIII, 39; Rig-veda VIII, 76, 10], 'Uprising by thy power didst thou move thy jaws, O Indra, drinking the cup-drawn juice!—Thou art taken with a support: thee to Indra for power!—This is thy womb: thee to Indra for power!'

11. [The third with Vâg. S. VIII, 40; Rig-veda I, 50, 3], 'His beacons have appeared, his beams, wide and far over the people, shining splendidly like fires!—Thou art taken with a support: thee to Sûrya for splendour!—This is thy womb: thee to Sûrya for splendour!'

12. The drinking of these (cups is performed by the sacrificers with the resp. texts), 'O lustrous Agni, lustrous art thou among the gods: may I be lustrous among men!—Most powerful Indra, most powerful art thou among the gods: may I be the most powerful among men!—Most splendid Sûrya, most splendid art thou among the gods: may I be the most splendid among men!' And, verily, these same splendours, these same powers he takes unto himself for whomsoever, knowing this, they draw these cups.

13. Let him draw them on the first three days of the P*ri*sh*th*ya sha*d*aha[2]; namely, the Agni cup on

[1] The Kâ*n*vas use a different formula, viz. Rig-veda IX, 66, 19. See Vâg. S. ed. Weber, p. 254 (XII).

[2] See page 402, note 4. In conjunction with the Rathantara

the first day, the Indra cup on the second, the Sûrya cup on the third—thus one day by day.

14. Some[1], however, draw them on the last three days; but let him not do so: let him rather draw them on the first three days. But should he intend to draw them on the last three days, let him first draw them on the first three days and let him then draw them on the last three days. In like manner they are drawn (all three) in their proper order, on one and the same day, at the Visvagit[2] with all the Prishthas.

Fifth Brâhmana.

1. Pragâpati, forsooth, is that sacrifice which is performed here, and from which these creatures have been produced: and in like manner are they produced thereafter even to this day.

2. After the Upâmsu cup goats are produced. Now that (cup) is again employed in the sacrifice: hence creatures are here produced again and again.

3. After the Antâryama cup sheep are produced. Now that (cup) is again employed at the sacrifice: hence creatures are here produced again and again.

(Sâma-veda II, 30–31) and Brihat (II, 159–60) sâmans, the other four principal prishtha sâmans—viz. the Vairûpa (II, 212–13), Vairâga (II, 277–9), Sâkvara (II, 1151–3; or Mahânâmnî, 1–3), and Raivata (II, 434–6)—are used respectively by the Hotri on the last four days of the shadaha. As regards the Hotri's assistants, while the Maitrâvaruna always uses the same sâman, as at the Agnishtoma, viz. the Vâmadevya (II, 32–34), the sâmans used by the other Hotrakas are given in the Sâma-veda immediately after the respective sâman of the Hotri, mentioned above.

[1] The Kânva text ascribes this practice to the Karakas.

[2] Regarding the sacrificial session, called Gavâm ayana, of which the Visvagit forms part, see p. 426, note 3.

4. And because of those two (cups) which are together he offers the Upâmsu first, therefore, of goats and sheep when they are together[1], the goats go first, and the sheep behind them.

5. And because, having offered the Upâmsu, he wipes (the vessel) upwards, therefore these goats walk like nimbly[2] climbing spokes.

6. And because, having offered the Antaryâma, he wipes (the vessel) downwards, therefore these sheep walk with their heads down, as if digging. Now they, the goats and sheep, are most conspicuously Pragâpati-like: whence, bringing forth thrice in the year, they produce two or three[3] (young ones).

7. After[4] the Sukra cup men are produced. Now that (cup) is again employed at the sacrifice: hence creatures are here produced again and again. But the Sukra (bright) is the same as he that burns yonder, and he indeed is Indra; and of animals, man is Indra-like[5]: whence he rules over animals.

8. After the *Ri*tu cup the one-hoofed species is produced. Now that (cup) is again employed in the sacrifice: hence creatures are here produced again and again. And such-like is the *Ri*tu cup[6], and such-like the head of the one-hoofed. The Âgrayana

[1] That is, in mixed flocks. In the compound 'agâvika' (Kânv. agâvayah, αἶγες καὶ ὄϊες) also the goats come first.

[2] Perhaps 'ara' has to be taken in the sense of 'quick, nimble,' instead of 'spokes,' and 'dîtara' might mean 'flying up,' 'popping up their heads,' as opposed to 'avâkînasîrshan.'

[3] ? Or, three (times) two, 'dvau trîn iti;' the Kânva text reads (of goats alone) 'trîms trîn.'

[4] Or, along with, correspondingly with, anu.

[5] Or, connected with Indra, Indra's own (aindra).

[6] The two *Ri*tupâtras are shaped like spoon-bowls, with spouts on both sides.

cup, the Ukthya cup, and the Âditya cup,—after them cows are produced. Now, these are again employed in the sacrifice: hence creatures are here produced again and again.

9. And because goats are produced after the fewest cups, therefore, though bringing forth thrice in a year, producing two or three, (they are) very few, for they are produced after the fewest cups.

10. And because cows are produced after the most cups, therefore, though bringing forth once in a year, and producing one each time, (they are) most numerous, for they are produced after the most cups.

11. Then, in the Dro*n*akala*s*a (trough) he finally draws the Hâriyo*g*ana graha. Now, the Dro*n*akala*s*a is Pra*g*âpati;—he turns unto these creatures, and fosters them, and kisses them[1]: he fosters them in that he produces them.

12. Now, these same cups after which creatures are produced, are five,—those of the Upâ*m**s*u and Antaryâma (counting as) one and the same, the *S*ukra cup, the *Ri*tu cup, the Âgraya*n*a cup, and the Ukthya cup; for there are five seasons in the year, and Pra*g*âpati is the year, and the sacrifice is Pra*g*âpati. But if there be six seasons in the year, then the Âditya cup is the sixth of them.

13. But indeed there is only that one cup after which creatures are produced here, to wit, the Upâ*m**s*u cup; for the Upâ*m**s*u is breath, and Pra*g*âpati is breath, and everything here is after Pra*g*âpati.

[1] Or, smells, sniffs at them (as a cow does the calf).

SIXTH BRÂHMANA.

1. Pragâpati, forsooth, is that sacrifice which is here performed, and whence these creatures have been produced, and in like manner are they produced therefrom even to this day. Having drawn the Âsvina graha, he makes (the sacrificer) eye (the several cups, while muttering) the Avakâsa formulas[1].

2. The Upâmsu cup he eyes first with (Vâg. S. VII, 27), 'For mine out-breathing, (a) giver of lustre[2], become thou pure for lustre!' Then the Upâmsusavana stone with, 'For my through-breathing, giver of lustre, become thou pure for lustre!' Then the Antaryâma cup with, 'For mine up-breathing, giver of lustre, become thou pure for lustre!' Then the Aindravâyava with, 'For my voice, giver of lustre, become thou pure for lustre!' Then the Maitrâvaruna with, 'For mine intelligence and will, giver of lustre, become thou pure for lustre!' Then the Âsvina with, 'For mine ear, giver of lustre, become thou pure for lustre!' Then the Sukra and Manthin with, 'For mine eyes, givers of lustre, become ye pure for lustre!'

3. Then the Âgrayana with (Vâg. S. VII, 28), 'For my mind, giver of lustre, become thou pure for lustre!' Then the Ukthya with, 'For

1 For the proper place of this ceremony in the actual performance of the Agnishtoma, see p. 312, note 4.

2 Either, thou who bestowest lustre on my out-breathing ..., or, Thou who art a bestower of lustre, become thou pure for lustre to my out-breathing.

my vigour, giver of lustre, become thou pure for lustre!' Then the Dhruva with, 'For my life, giver of lustre, become thou pure for lustre!' Then the two Soma-troughs (Pûtabhrit and Âdhavanîya) with, 'For all mine offspring, givers of lustre, become ye pure for lustre!' Now the two troughs belong to the All-gods, for therefrom they draw (Soma) for the gods, therefrom for men, therefrom for the Fathers: therefore the two Soma-troughs belong to the All-gods.

4. Then the Dronakalasa with (Vâg. S. VII, 29), 'Who (ka) art thou? Which one art thou?'—Ka is Pragâpati;—'Whose (kasya, or Ka's) art thou? who (ka) art thou by name?'—Ka ('who') by name is Pragâpati;—'Thou upon whose name we have thought,' for he indeed thinks upon his name;—'Thou whom we have gladdened with Soma;'—for he indeed gladdens him with Soma. Having drawn the Âsvina cup, he prays for blessing part after part (of the sacrifice) with, 'May I be abundantly supplied with offspring,' thereby he prays for offspring;—'abundantly supplied with men,' thereby he prays for men (heroes);—'abundantly supplied with food!' thereby he prays for prosperity.

5. He must not let every one eye them, but only him who is well known, or one who is his friend, or one who, being learned in sacred lore, may acquire these (texts) through study. Having drawn the Âsvina cup, he (thus) produces the whole sacrifice; and having produced the whole sacrifice, he deposits it in his own self, and makes it his own.

SEVENTH BRÂHMA*N*A.

1. Now, there are here thirty-four utterances, called expiations[1]. Pra*g*âpati, forsooth, is that sacrifice which is performed here, and from which these creatures have been produced,—and in like manner are they produced therefrom even to this day.

2. There are eight Vasus, eleven Rudras, twelve Âdityas; and these two, Heaven and Earth, are the (thirty-second and) thirty-third. And there are thirty-three gods, and Pra*g*âpati is the thirty-fourth;—thus he makes him (the sacrificer, or Ya*gñ*a) to be Pra*g*âpati[2]: now that[3] is, for that is immortal, and what is immortal that is. But what is mortal that also is Pra*g*âpati; for Pra*g*âpati is everything: thus he makes him to be Pra*g*âpati, and hence there are these thirty-four utterances, called expiations.

3. Now some call these (formulas) the 'forms of the sacrifice;' but, indeed, they are rather the joints of the sacrifice: this same sacrifice, in being performed, is continually becoming those deities.

4. Now should the cow, which supplies the gharma[4], fail (to give milk), let them go to another; and at the same place where they otherwise make that gharma (milk) flow[5], let them place her with her

---

[1] Viz. the formulas, Vâ*g*. S. VIII, 54–58, employed for making good any mishaps during the Soma-sacrifice. Cf. *S*at. Br. XII, 6, 1, 1 seq. In the Kâ*n*va recension, V, 7, 4, ka*nd*ikâs 5–10 correspond to the present Brâhma*n*a, while ka*nd*ikâs 1–4 contain the account of the Mahâvratîya graha corresponding to M. IV, 6, 4.

[2] ? Or, this then he makes Pra*g*âpati to be; but see IV, 6, 1, 5.

[3] ? I.e. that divine race or element. The Kâ*n*va text reads, etâvad vâ idam asty, etad dhy am*ri*tam, yad dhy am*ri*ta*m* tad asti.

[4] See p. 104, note 3.

[5] That is, when they milk the cow with the Mantras 'Flow thou

head towards the north, or in front of the hall with her face to the east.

5. And that which is the right one of the two bones with hair-tufts which protrude on both sides of her tail-bone,—thereon he offers those thirty-four oblations of ghee; for as much as are those thirty-four utterances, so much is the sacrifice: thus he lays the whole sacrifice entirely into her; for therefrom she lets the gharma (milk) flow, and this is the atonement therefore.

6. And if any part of the sacrifice were to fail, let him make an oblation with regard thereto on the Âhavanîya during the consecration and the Upasads, and on the Âgnîdhra during the Soma feast—for whatever point of the sacrifice fails, that breaks—and whichever then is the deity in that (special offering), through that one he heals it, through that he puts it together again.

7. And if anything[1] be spilt, let him pour water thereon—everything here being pervaded (or obtained) by water—for the obtainment of everything[2]; with a verse to Vishnu and Varuna,—for whatsoever distress one undergoes here on earth, all that Varuna inflicts[3],—(Vâg. S. VIII, 59; Atharva-veda VII, 25,

for the Asvins!' &c., see IV, 2, 1, 11 seq. Perhaps yasyâm velâyâm has to be taken in the sense of 'at the same time at which they make it flow,' as is done in the St. Petersb. Dict. Compare, however, the Kânva reading, tad yâm upasamkrâmeyus tâm agrena vâ dîkshitasâlâm yatra vainam etat pinvayanti tad enâm prâkîm vodîkîm vâ sthâpayitavai brûyât.

[1] Viz. any Soma, according to Kâty. XXV, 2, 9; or any clotted ghee (prishadâgya), according to the Kânva text.

[2] For this construction, see p. 15, note 3.

[3] Or, whatsoever undergoes (suffering) here on earth, all that Varuna causes to undergo it.

1), 'They by whose vigour the spheres were propped up, who are in strength the strongest and mightiest; who sway with powers unresisted, to Vishnu and Varuna hath it gone at the morning prayer!' For Vishnu is the sacrifice, and it is that (sacrifice) of his which now undergoes distress; and Varuna is the inflicter: thus by both these deities—that whose (sacrifice) undergoes distress, and that which inflicts it—he heals (the joint of the sacrifice), by both he puts it together.

8. And let him then touch (the spilt material) with (Vâg. S. VIII, 60), 'To the gods, to the sky hath the sacrifice gone: may wealth thence accrue to me! to the men, to the air hath the sacrifice gone: may wealth thence accrue to me! to the Fathers, to the earth hath the sacrifice gone: may wealth thence accrue to me!'—'To whatever world the sacrifice has gone, thence happiness has come to me[1]!' this is what he thereby means to say.

9. Here now Âruni said, 'Why should he sacrifice who would think himself the worse for a miscarriage of the sacrifice? I, for one, am the better for a miscarriage of the sacrifice[2]!' This, then, he said with reference to the adoption of those benedictions.

---

[1] This last sentence ('To whatever world . . .') is treated as if it belonged to the sacrificial formula, to which it is attached in the Samhitâ. The mistake (which doubtless there is) probably arose from the omission of the 'iti' in the Brâhmana. In the Kânva text of the Brâhmana, the analogous sentence appears clearly as belonging to the exposition, and not to the Samhitâ.

[2] Kim sa yagñena yageteti yo yagñah syât tena vyriddhena sreyo nâbhigakhed iti. Kânva text.

EIGHTH BRÂHMANA.

1. Now when at that Trirâtra[1] sacrifice he gives those thousand (cows), then that one is made the one-thousandth[2]. On the first day he brings three hundred and thirty-three; and likewise on the second day he brings three hundred and thirty-three; and likewise on the third day he brings three hundred and thirty-three. Then that one-thousandth is left over.

2. She should be three-coloured, they say, for that is the most perfect form for her. But let it be a red one, and spotted, for that indeed is the most perfect form for her.

3. Let it be one that has not been approached (by a bull), for she, the Sâhasrî, is in reality Vâk (speech); but Vâk, forsooth, is of unimpaired vigour, and so is one of unimpaired vigour which has not been approached: therefore it should be one that has not been approached.

4. He may lead her up (to the sacrificial ground) on the first day; for she, the Sâhasrî, is in reality Vâk, and hers, Vâk's, is that thousandfold progeny[3].

---

[1] The Sahasradakshina Trirâtra, or sacrifice of three (pressing) days, with a thousand cows as the priests' fee, is mentioned Kâty. XIII, 4, 15 seq. as, apparently, an independent Ahîna sacrifice. I do not, however, know whether it might not be added on to some other sacrificial performance, as, for instance, to the Prishthya shadaha, thus forming together with this the Navarâtra (or first nine days of the Dasarâtra, see p. 402, note 2). Kâty. gives no indication as to the particular forms of Soma-sacrifice required for the several days; but, guided no doubt by the Brâhmana, he confines his remarks to the manner of distribution of the dakshinâs.

[2] Sâhasrî, lit. 'she who makes the dakshinâ to consist of one thousand.'

[3] Or,—and from her, Vâk, those thousand (cows) were produced;

She walks at the head (of the other 333 cows), and behind her follows her progeny. Or he may lead her up on the last day; then her progeny precedes her, and she herself walks behind. This, however, is mere speculation: let him lead her up on the last day,—her progeny precedes her, and she herself walks behind.

5. North of the Havirdhâna shed, and south of the Âgnîdhra fire-house he makes her smell the Dronakalasa; for the Dronakalasa is the sacrifice; thus he makes her see the sacrifice.

6. With (Vâg. S. VIII, 42), 'Smell the trough: may the drops enter thee, O mighty one!' Now he who gives a thousand (cows) becomes, as it were, emptied: him, thus emptied, he thereby replenishes, when he says, 'Smell the trough: may the drops enter thee, O mighty one!'

7. 'Return again with sap!' him who is emptied he thus replenishes when he says, 'Return again with sap!'

8. 'And milk to us a thousandfold!' him who is emptied he thus replenishes with a thousand (forces), when he says, 'And milk to us a thousandfold!'

9. 'Broad-streamed, milk-abounding,—may wealth come back to me!' him who is emptied he thus replenishes when he says, 'May wealth come back to me!'

10. He then mutters in her right ear, 'O Idâ, blithesome, adorable, lovable, bright, shining, Aditi (inviolable), Sarasvatî (sapful), mighty,

---

or,—and from her (the thousandth cow) that thousandfold progeny of Vâk was produced; see IV, 6, 7, 3, where the thousandfold progeny of Vâk is identified with the Vedic texts generally.

glorious,—these are thy names, O cow: tell thou the gods of me as a doer of good!'—or, 'speak thou . . . .' These indeed are her names with the gods: he thus means to say, 'whatever thy names are with the gods, therewith tell the gods of me as a doer of good.'

11. They release her. If, not urged by any man, she goes eastwards, then let him know that this sacrificer has succeeded, that he has won the happy world. If she goes northwards, let him know that the sacrificer will be more glorious in this world. If she goes westwards, let him know that he will be rich in dependants and crops. If she goes southwards, let him know that the sacrificer will quickly depart from this world. Such are the ways of knowledge.

12. And what three (cows) there are each time over and above the (three hundred and) thirty, thereto they add that one[1]. Now, when they draw out a Virâ*g* (verse), they pull it asunder, and a Virâ*g* which is pulled asunder is torn in two;—and the Virâ*g* consisting of ten syllables, he thus makes the Virâ*g* complete. Let him give her to the Hot*ri*; for the Hot*ri* is a thousandfold[2]: therefore let him give her to the Hot*ri*.

[1] I am not certain whether I understand this passage rightly. According to paragraph 16, and Kâty. XIII, 4, 23, he is to give away the cows by tens. This would leave three each day, or nine on the three days. To them he is to add the Sâhasrî, and give the ten cows to the Hot*ri*.—A common Virâ*g* verse consists of three times ten syllables; but there are also such as consist of three times eleven syllables. These latter the sacrificer is thus represented (by withholding three cows out of thirty-three) to make into a proper Virâ*g*.

[2] That is, according to the St. Petersb. Dict., he possesses a

13. Or let him appoint two Unnetris, and let him give her to him, of the two, who does not call for the Sraushat; for defective, indeed, is he who, being an officiating priest, does not call for the Sraushat; and defective also is the Virâg which is pulled asunder: thus he puts the defective to the defective.

14. Now they say, one ought not to give anything above a thousand (cows), because by a thousand he obtains all the objects of his desire. But Âsuri said, 'Let him give according to his wish: by a thousand he indeed obtains all his wishes; and anything else (that he gives) is likewise given at his wish[1].'

15. And should he intend to give a cart yoked (with a team of oxen), or something else, let him give it either after the offering of the omentum of the barren cow, or at the concluding (udavasânîyâ) offering.

16. In bringing the dakshinâs, let him bring complete decads. If he intends to give one (cow) to any (priest), let him pass over a decad to ten such (priests). If he intends to give two to any one, let him pass over a decad to five such (priests). If he intends to give three to any one, let him pass over a decad to three such[2]. If he intends to give five to

thousand verses;—if it does not rather refer to the extent of the Rig-veda, consisting of rather more than a thousand (1028) hymns. Cp. also 'the thousandfold progeny of Vâk,' p. 414, note 3.

[1] The Kânva text has much the same reasoning, but does not ascribe it to any one.

[2] In this and all other cases the text has 'to those three (ten &c.).' It is not clear in what manner he is to divide the ten cows between the three priests, unless indeed he is to repeat the same process three times, giving the odd cow each time to another priest. The Kânva text only mentions two of the cases here given, viz. that if he intends to give one cow to each (ekaikâm),

any one, let him pass over a decad to two such. Thus up to a hundred: and thus this perfect Virâg of his becomes a cow of plenty for him in yonder world.

NINTH BRÂHMANA.

1. When he performs a twelve days' sacrifice with transposed metres (Dvâdasâha vyûdhakkhandas), then he (the Adhvaryu) transposes the grahas (cups of Soma); and both the Udgâtri and the Hotri transpose the metres. Now there is first that normal Tryaha (triduum), with settled metres[1]: there he draws the cup beginning with the Aindravâyava.

---

he is to give ten to ten such; and if he intends to give two to each, he is to give ten to five such. Professor Weber, Ind. Stud. X, 52, remarks that this paragraph is not clear to him, and suggests that it may be interpolated. It does not appear, what the exact proportion of the thousand cows is for each of the sixteen priests; but we may assume that it did not differ much from that given at the Agnishtoma (see p. 345, note), and that this result was brought about by repeated distributions among varied groupings of the priests.

[1] That is, three days, on which the order of the Agnishtoma is observed. Hence, having drawn the Upâmsu and Antaryâma cups (IV, 1, 1 and 2), which must always be drawn first, he draws the Aindravâyava cup (IV, 1, 3) and so on. The same order is preserved on the fifth, eighth, and last three days. On the fourth and ninth days, on the other hand, he follows up the Upâmsu and Antaryâma by the grahas of the third pressing, beginning with the Âgrayana (IV, 3, 5, 21 seq.); these being then succeeded by those of the morning and midday pressings; and on the sixth and seventh days the Upâmsu and Antaryâma cups are succeeded by the grahas of the midday pressing, beginning with the Sukra cup (IV, 3, 3, 2). This change of the proper order of performance, of course, involves a different arrangement of the stotras and sastras (or 'the metres,' as they are called in the texts). This dislocation of the three pressings is afterwards to be rectified by the various cups being 'deposited' on the khara in their normal order. In the last two paragraphs of the present Brâhmana the author, however,

2. Then, on the fourth day, he transposes the grahas, and they transpose the metres. There he draws the cups beginning with the Âgrayana,—for that fourth day is Pragâpati's own; and the Âgrayana is the self, and Pragâpati is the self: therefore he draws the cups beginning with the Âgrayana.

3. Having drawn that (Âgrayana) cup, he does not deposit it—the grahas being the vital airs—lest he should disorder the vital airs[1]; for he would indeed disorder the vital airs, were he to deposit it. They sit near holding that (cup)[2]; and (the Adhvaryu) draws (the other) cups; and while he draws the cups, then whenever the time of that cup (in the order of performance comes), he utters 'Him' and deposits it. Then follows that normal[3] fifth day; on that he draws the cups beginning with the Aindravâyava.

4. Thereupon, on the sixth day, he transposes the grahas, and they transpose the metres. There he draws the cups beginning with the Sukra; for that sixth day is Indra's own, and the Sukra (bright, clear) is he that burns yonder, and he (the sun) indeed is Indra: therefore he draws the cups beginning with the Sukra.

5. Having drawn that (cup), he does not deposit it—the grahas being the vital airs—lest he should disorder the vital airs; for he would indeed disorder the vital airs, were he to deposit it. They sit near

---

discountenances this practice of changing the natural order of drawing the cups.

[1] For this construction see p. 15, note 3.

[2] 'Having given it to some one else (to hold), he draws the other cups.' Kânva text.

[3] Or, that 'known' fifth day, i.e. performed in the manner known, or explained before (viz. at the Agnishtoma).

holding that (cup); and he draws (the other) cups; and while he draws the cups, then whenever the time of that (cup comes), he deposits it.

6. Then, on the seventh day, he transposes the grahas, and they transpose the metres. There he draws the cups beginning with the Sukra cup; for that seventh day belongs to the Brihatî ('great' metre); for the Sukra is he that burns yonder, and he indeed is great: therefore he draws the cups beginning with the Sukra.

7. Having drawn that (cup), he does not deposit it—the grahas being the vital airs—lest he should disorder the vital airs; for he would indeed disorder the vital airs, were he to deposit it. They sit near holding that (cup); and he draws the (other) cups; and while he draws the cups, then whenever the time of that (cup comes), he deposits it. Then follows that normal eighth day: there he draws the cups beginning with the Aindravâyava.

8. Then, on the ninth day, he transposes the grahas, and they transpose the metres. There he draws the cups beginning with the Âgrayana; for that ninth day belongs to the Gagatî (metre), and the Âgrayana is the self, and the self (soul) is this whole world (gagat): therefore he draws the cups beginning with the Âgrayana.

9. Having drawn it, he does not deposit it—the grahas being the vital airs—lest he should disorder the vital airs; for he would indeed disorder the vital airs, were he to deposit it. They sit near holding that (cup); and he draws the (other) cups; and while he draws the cups, when the time of that (cup comes), he utters 'Him' and deposits it.

10. Now they say, He should not transpose the

cups—the cups being the vital airs—lest he should disorder the vital airs; for he would indeed disorder the vital airs, were he to transpose them: therefore he should not transpose (the cups).

11. But let him, nevertheless, transpose them; for the cups are the limbs, and in sleeping one likes to turn[1] his limbs from one side to the other: therefore let him nevertheless transpose them.

12. Nevertheless, he should not transpose them—the cups being the vital airs—lest he should disorder the vital airs; for he would indeed disorder the vital airs, were he to transpose (the cups): therefore let him not transpose them.

13. What, then, is the Adhvaryu to do in that case, when both the Udgât*ri* and Hot*ri* transpose (change) the metres[2]? In that, at the morning pressing, he draws first the Aindravâyava cup; and at the midday pressing the *S*ukra cup; and at the evening pressing the Âgraya*n*a cup,—thereby forsooth the Adhvaryu transposes (the cups).

TENTH BRÂHMA*N*A[3].

1. If the Soma is carried off, let him say, 'Run about and seek!' If they find it, why should they care? But if they do not find it, atonement is made therefore.

2. Now there are two kinds of Phâlguna plants,

[1] In the text our subordinate clause is, as usual, the principal clause: 'one sleeps in turning his limbs from one side to the other.'

[2] The chanters and the Hot*ri* in any case use different metres, as the principal ones, at different pressings.

[3] In the Kâ*n*va text I have met with nothing corresponding to this Brâhma*n*a.

the red-flowering and the brown-flowering. Those Phâlguna plants which have brown flowers one may press; for they, the brown-flowering Phâlgunas, are akin to the Soma-plant: therefore he may press those with brown flowers.

3. If they cannot get brown-flowering (Phâlgunas), he may press the *S*yenah*ri*ta[1] plant. For when Gâyatrî flew up for Soma, a sprig of Soma fell from her, as she was bringing him: it became the *S*yenah*ri*ta plant: therefore he may press the *S*yenah*ri*ta plant.

4. If they cannot get the *S*yenah*ri*ta, he may press Âdâra plants. For when the head of the sacrifice was cut off, then Âdâra plants sprung from the sap which spirted from it: therefore he may press Âdâra plants.

5. If they cannot get Âdâras, he may press brown Dûb (dûrvâ) plants, for they, the brown Dûb plants, are akin to the Soma: therefore he may press brown Dûb plants.

6. If they cannot get brown Dûb plants, he may also press any kind of yellow Ku*s*a plants. In that case let him also give one cow; and, when he comes out of the purificatory bath, let him again become consecrated, for the atonement for that (use of plants other than Soma) is a second sacrifice. So much then as to those robbed of their Soma.

7. Now as to those who burst their Soma-trough (kala*s*a). If the trough bursts, let him say, 'Try to catch it!' If they catch a handful or a goupenful[2] (of Soma), let them perform, as far as is in their power[3],

[1] That is, the plant 'carried away by the falcon (or eagle).'

[2] Scotch for the measure of both hands placed side by side; Ags. geap, Low Germ. göpse.

[3] Yathâprabhâvam: Kâty. XXV, 12, 24 seems to take it in the

after pouring (water) to it from other ekadhana pitchers. But if they do not catch any, let them perform, as far as is in their power, after pouring out some of the Âgrayana and pouring (water) thereto from other ekadhana pitchers. And if the trough bursts before the dakshinâ (cows) have been led up, let him then give one cow; and after coming out from the purificatory bath, let him be consecrated again; for the atonement for that (mishap) is a second sacrifice. So much then as to those who burst the trough.

8. Then as to those by whom any Soma is left over. If any (Soma) be left after the Agnishtoma, let him draw the Ukthya cup from the Pûtabhrit. If any be left after the Ukthya, let him undertake the Shodasin. If any be left after the Shodasin, let them undertake a night (performance)[1]. If any be left after the night (performance), let them undertake a day (performance)[2]. But nothing, surely, remains after that[3].

SIXTH ADHYÂYA. FIRST BRÂHMANA.

1. Now, the Amsu (graha), forsooth, is no other than Pragâpati: that (cup) is his (Yagña's or the

sense of 'abundantly,' as he circumscribes it by 'prabhâvayantah' (which the commentator explains by 'distributing over the several vessels').

[1] That is, he is to perform an Atirâtra, see p. 397, note 2.

[2] Kâty. XXV, 13, 12–14, in that emergency, prescribes either the Brihat-sâman (by which a seventeenth stotra is obtained at the Vâgapeya sacrifice, for which see more in Kânda V), or the Mahâvrata (see IV, 6, 4, 1, with note), or the Aptoryâma (see p. 398, note).

[3] The meaning of this seems to be, that after the Aptoryâma, no other sacrifice remains at which he could dispose of any Soma that might be left (and hence one must finish it at that sacrifice). According to Kâty. ib. 15, he is to repeat the Aptoryâma, if any Soma remains after the first performance.

Sacrificer's) self[1], for Pragâpati is the self. Hence when they draw that (cup) they produce that self of his. Therein they lay these vital airs, according to as these vital airs, the grahas, are explained[2]; and verily the sacrificer is born with his whole body in yonder world.

2. Where they draw that (cup), then that is (like) having a hold[3]; and where they do not draw it, then that is (like) having no hold: therefore, then, he draws the Amsu.

3. He draws it with a vessel of udumbara wood; for that (cup) is Pragâpati, and the udumbara tree is Pragâpati's own: therefore he draws it with a vessel of udumbara wood.

4. He draws it with a square vessel; for there are here three worlds: these three worlds he obtains by three (corners). And Pragâpati is the fourth over and above these three worlds: thus he obtains Pragâpati by the fourth (corner): therefore he draws it with a square vessel.

5. Silently he takes up the pressing-stone; silently he throws down the Soma-plants (amsu); silently he pours water thereon; silently raising (the stone), he

---

[1] Or body (âtman); amsu meaning the Soma-plant, and hence the body of the Soma. This graha seems to consist of imperfectly pressed Soma-plants in water. Cf. Kâty. XII, 5, 6–12. See also Sat. Br. IV, 1, 1, 2; Taitt. S. VI, 6, 10; Sây. on Taitt. S. I, p. 603. In the Kânva text this Brâhmana is followed by one on the Adâbhya graha, which is identified with speech.

[2] Or, perhaps, according to as the grahas are explained as being these vital airs.

[3] Or, like something that has a handle. The Kânva text reads,—for whomsoever they draw that (cup), his vital airs are, as it were, supplied with a firmer hold, and, as it were, firmly established (ârambhanavattarâ iva pratishthitâ iva). And for whomsoever they do not draw it, his vital airs are, as it were, without any hold ('halt-loser') and quite unrestrained (anârambhanatarâ ivâsyâyatatarâ iva prânâh).

presses once; silently he offers that (libation) without drawing breath: thus he makes him (the sacrificer) to be Pragâpati.

6. Now there is a piece of gold in that (spoon): that he smells at. And if he either galls or scratches himself at this (sacrifice),—gold being immortal life,—he lays that immortal life into his own self.

7. As to this Râma Aupatasvini said, 'Let him freely breathe out and freely breathe in: if he but offers silently, thereby he makes him (the sacrificer) to be Pragâpati.'

8. Now there is a piece of gold in that (spoon): that he smells at. And if he either galls or scratches himself at this (sacrifice),—gold being immortal life,—he lays that immortal life into his own self.

9. As to this Budila Âsvatarâsvi said, 'Let him draw it after merely raising (the stone), and let him not press; for they do press for other deities: thus he does different from what he does for other deities; and in that he raises (the stone) thereby indeed the pressing takes place for him.'

10. As to this Yâgñavalkya said, 'Nay, let him press: "The unpressed Soma delighted not the mighty Indra, nor the outpressed draughts without prayer," thus spake the *Ri*shi (Rig-veda VII, 26, 1). For no other deity does he strike but once: thus he does different from what he does for other deities,—therefore let him press!'

11. Twelve heifers pregnant with their first calf are the priests' fee for this (graha). Now there are twelve months in the year, and Pragâpati is the year, and the A*ms*u is Pragâpati: thus he makes him (the sacrificer) to be Pragâpati.

12. They have twelve embryo calves,—that makes

twenty-four. Now there are twenty-four half-moons in the year, and Pragâpati is the year, and the Amsu is Pragâpati: thus he makes him to be Pragâpati.

13. Now Kaukûsta[1] indeed gave as many as twenty-four heifers with their first calf as dakshinâs, and a bull as the twenty-fifth, and gold; and truly that is what he gave.

14. This (graha) should not be drawn for every one, since this is his (Yagña's) self. It should only be drawn for one who is well known, or one who is his (the Adhvaryu's) friend, or one who, being learned in sacred lore, would acquire it by his study.

15. It should be drawn at a (sacrifice with) a thousand (cows as the priests' fee); for a thousand is everything, and this (graha) is everything. It should be drawn at (a sacrifice) where the entire property is given away, for the entire property is everything, and this (graha) is everything. It should be drawn at a Visvagit with all the Prishthas, for the Visvagit ('all-conquering') is everything, and this (cup) is everything. It should be drawn at a Vâgapeya and Râgasûya, for that is everything. It should be drawn at a sattra (sacrificial session), for the sattra means everything[2], and this (cup) means everything. These are the drawings.

THE GAVÂM AYANA[3].

SECOND BRÂHMANA.

1. Verily, they who sit (sacrificing) for a year, by means of six months go to him that burns yonder:

[1] The Kânva MSS. read 'Kaükthasta.'

[2] Perhaps the author here means to connect sattra (satra) with the adverbs satram, satrâ, 'altogether, always,' instead of with the verb sad, to sit; but cf. IV, 6, 8, 1.

[3] The great sacrificial session (sattra), called Gavâm ayana, or

so it is told on the part of the Sâman, in as much as it is made of the form of that (sun) it is told on the part of the Rik[1]; and now in like manner on the part of the Ya*g*us, by means of preparatory rite, when they draw that (graha)[2], they thereby also go to him (the sun).

---

cows' walk (or course), usually extends over twelve months (of 30 days), and consists of the following parts:

Prâya*n*îya Atirâtra, or opening day.

*K*aturvi*ms*a day, an Ukthya, all the stotras of which are in the *K*aturvi*ms*a stoma.

Five months, each consisting of four Abhiplava sha*d*ahas and one P*r*ish*th*ya sha*d*aha (= 30 days). Cf. p. 402, n. 2.

Three Abhiplavas and one P*r*ish*th*ya.
Abhi*g*it day.
Three Svarasâman days.
} 28 days, which, with the two opening days, complete the sixth month.

VISHUVANT or central day.

Three Svarasâman days.
Vi*s*va*g*it day.
One P*r*ish*th*ya and three Abhiplavas.
} 28 days, which, with the two concluding days, complete the seventh month.

Four months, each consisting of four Abhiplavas and one P*r*ish*th*ya.

{ Three Abhiplava sha*d*ahas.
One Gosh*t*oma (Agnish*t*oma, p. 403, n.).
One Âyush*t*oma (Ukthya).
One Da*s*arâtra (the ten central days of the Dvâda*s*âha, p. 402, note 2). } 30 days.

Mahâvrata day.

Udayanîya Atirâtra.

In imitation of the retrograde course of the sun, the order of the performance during the second part of the year is, generally speaking, the reverse of that of the former half.

[1] Ta eta*m* sha*d*bhir mâsair yanti, tasmât parâ*ññ*ko grahâ g*r*ihyante parâ*ññ*ki stotrâ*n*i parâ*ññ*ki *s*astrâ*n*i. Ta eta*m* shash*th*e mâse ga*kh*anti tad etasya rûpa*m* kriyate. Kâ*n*va text.

[2] Viz. the Atigrâhya cup to Sûrya (IV, 5, 4, 2 seq.), which has

2. He thus takes it therefrom with (Vâ*g*. S. VIII, 41; Rig-veda I, 50, 1)[1], 'The lights bear on high that divine knower of beings, Sûrya, that all may see him!—Thou art drawn with a support: thee to Sûrya for splendour!—This is thy womb: thee to Sûrya for splendour!'

THIRD BRÂHMA*N*A.

1. Now as to the manner of animal offerings. One may perform with the (ordinary) set of eleven victims. He seizes one for Agni as the first victim, and one for Varu*n*a (as the last); then again one for Agni: in this way let him perform with the set of eleven victims[2].

2. Or one may day after day seize a victim for Indra and Agni; for all the gods are Agni, since in Agni offering is made to all the deities; and Indra is the deity of the sacrifice: thus he neither offends any of the deities, nor does he offend him who is the deity of the sacrifice.

3. Then as to the manner (of animal offering) in accordance with the Stoma[3]. At the Agnish*t*oma

to be drawn on the Vishuvant or middle day of the Gavâm ayana; an animal sacrifice to the same deity being also prescribed.

[1] The Kâ*n*va text allows the alternative mantra, Rig-veda I, 50, 3; Vâ*g*. S. VIII, 40, Ad*ris*ram asya ketava*h*, &c. See IV, 5, 4, 11.

[2] See III, 9, 1, 5 seq. He is to sacrifice one victim each day, and if after the eleventh day, the performance is to go on (as at the Dvâda*s*âha), he is to begin anew with the first victim of the ekâda*s*inî. According to the Kâ*n*va text and Kâty. XII, 6, 17 he is on such an odd day to immolate all the remaining victims of the set of eleven. Thus on the last (twelfth) day of the Dvâda*s*âha—the Udayanîya Atirâtra—he would have to sacrifice the entire set of eleven victims.

[3] I. e. the particular form of the *G*yotish*t*oma, which is being performed.

let him seize a (victim) for Agni; for it is befitting that at the Agnish*t*oma ('Agni's praise') he should seize a victim for Agni. If it be an Ukthya sacrifice, let him seize as the second (victim) one for Indra and Agni, for the hymns (uktha)[1] belong to Indra and Agni. If it be a Sho*d*a*s*in sacrifice, let him seize as the third (victim) one for Indra; for the Sho*d*a*s*in (graha) is Indra. If it be an Atirâtra, let him seize as the fourth (victim) one for Sarasvatî; for Sarasvatî is Vâ*k* (speech), and Vâ*k* is a female, and so is râtri (fem., 'night') female. Thus he duly distinguishes between the sacrificial performances. Such are the three manners (of animal offering): he may perform in whichever manner he pleases. Two victims must needs be seized,—for Sûrya he seizes the second on the Vishuvant day, and for Pra*g*âpati at the Mahâvrata.

FOURTH BRÂHMANA.

1. Then as to the Mahâvratîya (graha)[2]. Now when Pra*g*âpati had created the living beings, his

[1] That is, the hymns of the Rig-veda, the single collections of which begin with the hymns to Agni, followed by those to Indra. The 'ukthâni' here can scarcely refer to the three additional *s*astras of the Ukthya sacrifice, as they are composed of hymns to Indra-Varu*n*a, Indra-B*ri*haspati, and Indra-Vish*n*u respectively. Â*s*v. *S*r. VI, 1; Ait. Br. III, 50. Cp. IV, 2, 5, 14.

[2] The drawing of this cup forms part of the performance of the last but one day of the Gavâm ayana, the so-called Mahâvrata (great vow) day, on which the following particulars are supplied by Kâtyâyana XIII, 2, 16 seq. The particular form of sacrifice prescribed for the day is the Agnish*t*oma. A victim to Pra*g*âpati is to be immolated. The Mahâvratîya-graha is drawn as an additional libation (like the Atigrâhyas, IV, 5, 4, 2). The signal for the chanting of the P*ri*sh*th*a-stotras is given by (a Brâhman) playing, with a rattan plectrum, on a harp with a hundred strings of

joints were relaxed: with his relaxed joints he was unable to raise himself. Then the gods went on praising and toiling. They saw this Mahâvratîya (cup) and drew it for him: thereby they restored his joints.

2. With his joints thus restored, he approached this food, what food of Pragâpati there is,—for what eating is to men, that the vrata (fast-food, or religious observance generally) is to the gods. And because (they say), 'Great, indeed, is this vrata whereby he has raised himself,' therefore it is called Mahâvratîya.

3. Now, even as Pragâpati then was, when he had created the living beings, so are those who sit (in sacrificial session) for a year; and as Pragâpati then, after a year, approached food, so do they now, after a year, approach food, for whomsoever that knows this, they draw that cup.

4. Let him draw it for Indra Vimridh (the Averter of scorn), for, verily, the scorners of those who sit for

Muñga grass. During the chanting and recitation, the Udgâtri sits on an arm-chair, the Hotri on a hammock or swing, the Adhvaryu on a board, and the other priests on cushions of grass. Then follow several curious ceremonies, performed partly inside and partly outside the Vedi. The performance of the Sattra is alternately lauded and vituperated by two persons [the one, a Brâhman, seated at the front door of the Sadas; the other, a Sûdra, at the back door; both facing each other;—thus Lâty. IV, 3, according to which authority, however, they are merely to say respectively, 'These Sattrins have not succeeded!'—'They have succeeded!'] At the same time a harlot and a theological student (brahmakhârin) upbraid one another (in front of the Âgnîdhrîya fire shed); while (south of the Mârgâlîya) a sham contest takes place between an Ârya (Vaisya) and a Sûdra for the possession of a round white skin, the Sûdra having to give in (after the third effort, when the Ârya beats him with the skin). Thereupon a couple is shut up in an enclosed space south of the Mârgâlîya (or behind the Âgnîdhrîya, Lâty.) for maithuna.

a year are smitten, and all is won by them: hence for Indra Vimridh,—with (Vâg. S. VIII, 44; Rig-veda X, 152, 4), 'Scatter thou our scorners, O Indra, lay them low that war against us, and send them, that persecute us, to the nethermost darkness!—Thou art taken with a support: thee to Indra Vimridh!—This is thy womb: thee to Indra Vimridh!'

5. Or for Visvakarman (the All-worker), for all work is done, everything is won by those who sit in session for a year: hence for Visvakarman,—with (Vâg. S. VIII, 45; Rig-veda X, 81, 7), 'Vâkaspati Visvakarman, the thought-speeder[1], let us invoke for protection in our struggle[2] this day: may he, the all-beneficient worker of good, delight in all our offerings[3] for our protection!—Thou art taken with a support: thee to Indra Visvakarman[4]!—This is thy womb: thee to Indra Visvakarman!'

6. But if he knows the (verse) referring to Indra (and) Visvakarman, let him draw it thus[5] (Vâg. S. VIII, 46), 'O Visvakarman, with strengthening libation madest thou Indra an invincible champion: to him did the people bow down of

[1] Or, the thought-swift (manogû).

[2] For the different meanings of 'vâga' see Max Müller, 'India, what can it teach us?' p. 164.

[3] Or, in all our invocations (havana).

[4] The identification of Visvakarman with Indra was probably suggested by the final pâda of the preceding verse of the hymn (Rig-veda X, 81, 6): 'May there be (or may he, Visvakarman, be) for us a Sûri Maghavan' (a rich patron; terms frequently applied to Indra). But cp. Muir, O. S. T. vol. iv, p. 7.

[5] The Kânva text does not give the verse, but remarks merely,—But if he can get (vindet) an aindrî vaisvakarmanî (verse), let him draw it therewith.

old, because[1] he, the mighty, is worthy of adoration.—Thou art taken with a support: thee to Indra Visvakarman!—This is thy womb: thee to Indra Visvakarman!'

Fifth Brâhmana.

1. Now the graha[2], forsooth, is he that burns yonder, since by him all these creatures are held (swayed). Hence they say, 'We take (grah) the grahas,' 'They walk, seized by the grahas.'

2. The graha, forsooth, is Vâk (speech); for by speech everything is swayed (grah) here[3],—what wonder, then[4], that Vâk is the graha?

3. The graha, forsooth, is the name, for everything is held (fixed) by a name here,—what wonder, then, that the name is the graha? We know the names of many, and are they not thereby held by us[5]?

---

[1] I see no other way of rendering 'yathâ-asat' in this passage.

[2] That is, the seizer, holder, swayer. According to the St. Petersb. Dict. the word 'graha' probably has not already in this passage the later meaning of 'planet' as the one holding or influencing man; but that of some demoniac being. The whole Brâhmana is a play on the word 'graha' in its active and passive meanings of seizer, holder, influence; and draught, libation. The corresponding Brâhmana of the Kânva text (V, 7, 1) differs widely from our text. Its general drift is as follows: The graha is the breath,—the graha of that breath is food,—the graha of that food is the water,—the graha of that water is fire,—the graha of the fire (Agni) is the breath,—thus the deities are seized by him, and he wins a place in the world of the deities.

[3] Perhaps with the double-entendre, 'everything (libation &c.) is drawn with speech here.'

[4] ? Kimu tad yad vâg grahah. The usual meaning of kim u, 'how much more,' 'still more so,' seems hardly to suit this passage.

[5] ? Or, 'are not those of us (that have a name) held (known) thereby?' In either case, however, the interrogative force of 'atha,' without any other particle, is rather unusual.

4. The graha, forsooth, is food; for by food everything is kept (grah) here: hence as many as eat our food, all those are kept by us. Such is the natural order of things.

5. And as to this graha of Soma, that is food; for whatever deity one draws this graha, that deity, being seized by this graha, fulfils that wish of his for which he draws it. He approaches either the rising or the setting sun, thinking, 'Thou art the seizer, seize thou N.N. by such and such a disease! may N.N. not obtain such and such!' (naming) him whom he hates; or with, 'May such and such a wish not be fulfilled to him!' and, assuredly, that wish is not fulfilled to him for whom he thus approaches (the sun).

SIXTH BRÂHMANA.

1. Now once on a time the gods, while performing sacrifice, were afraid of an attack from the Asura-Rakshas. They said, 'Who of us shall sit on the south side; we will then enter upon the sacrifice on the north side in a place free from danger and injury.'

2. They said, 'He who is the strongest of us, let him sit on the south side; we will then enter upon the sacrifice on the north side in a place free from danger and injury.'

3. They said, 'Verily, Indra is the strongest of us: let Indra sit on the south side; we will then enter upon the sacrifice on the north side in a place free from danger and injury.'

4. They said to Indra, 'Verily, thou art the strongest of us: sit thou on the south side; we will then enter upon the sacrifice on the north side in a place free from danger and injury.'

5. He said, 'What will be my reward then?'—'The office of Brâhma*n*â*k*/*h*am*s*in shall be thine, the

Brahmasâman[1] shall be thine!'—Hence one elects the Brâhmanâkkhamsin with, 'Indra is the Brahman, by virtue of the Brahmaship!' for to Indra belongs this (office). Indra sat on the south side, and they entered upon the sacrifice on the north side in a place free from danger and injury. Therefore let him who is the strongest sit on the south side, and let them then enter upon the sacrifice on the north side in a place free from danger and injury. Now he, forsooth, who is the most learned of Brâhmans, is the strongest of them; and as now any one is (able to become) a (superintendent) Brahman[2]—nay, does he not sit still?—therefore whosoever is the strongest

[1] That is, the Sâman which supplies the text for the Stotra chanted in connection with the Brâhmanâkhamsin's Sastra, and forming the Stotriya verse of the latter. Thus, at the midday savana, the (Prishtha) Stotra of that priest usually consists of the Naudhasa-sâman (Sâma-veda II, 35–36), if the Rathantara-sâman (Sâma-veda II, 30–31) is used for the Hotri's Stotra; but, if the Brihat-sâman (ib. II, 159–160) is used for the latter, then the Syaita-sâman (II, 161–2) is used as the Brahma-sâman. See p. 339, note 2. The reason, however, why special mention is made of the Brâhmanâkhamsin in this place, probably is that at the Gavâm ayana the Brahma-sâman is treated in a peculiar way. For, while on 142 days of the first half of the year,—viz. on the Katurvimsa, on all (6 × 23) Âbhiplavika days and on the three Svara-sâman days,—one and the same tune, the Abhîvarta-sâman, is to be used day by day, but each time with a different pragâtha stanza (thus the pragâtha S. V. II, 35–36, usually chanted to the Naudhasa tune, being on this occasion chanted to the Abhîvarta tune); on the corresponding days of the second half of the year, one and the same stanza, 'Indra kratum na â bhara' (S. V. II, 806–7), is to be used day by day, but with different tunes (six such being given in the Calc. ed. vol. iv, pp. 529–34). Tândya Br. IV, 3, 1 seq.

[2] According to XII, 6, 1, 40 only priests of the Vasishtha family could become Brahmans, or superintendent priests, in olden times; because they alone knew the Somabhâga mantras; but now every one learns them, and can therefore become a Brahman.

of them, let him sit on the south side, and let them then enter upon the sacrifice on the north side in a place free from danger and injury. Hence Brâhmans sit on the south side (of the vedi), and they enter upon the sacrifice on the north side in a place free from danger and injury.

6. When (the Prastot*ri*) says, 'Brahman, we will chant, O Pra*s*âstar!' then the Brahman mutters (Vâ*g*. S. II, 12), 'This thy sacrifice, O divine Savitar, have they announced unto B*ri*haspati (the lord of prayer), the Brahman[1]: therefore speed the sacrifice, speed the lord of the sacrifice, speed me[2]!—Praise ye at the impulse (prasava) of Savit*ri*!' The significance is the same (as before)[3]. With this (text) most probably enter upon (the chant).

7. But one may also enter upon it with, 'O divine Savitar; this, O B*ri*haspati, forwards!' Therewith he hastes to Savit*ri* for his impulsion, for he is the impeller (prasavit*ri*) of the gods; and 'O B*ri*haspati, forwards!' he says, because B*ri*haspati is the Brahman of the gods,—thus he announces it to him who is the Brahman of the gods: therefore he says, O B*ri*haspati, forwards[4]!'

8. The Maitrâvaru*n*a then mutters, 'Impelled

[1] Mahîdhara interprets, 'This sacrifice, O divine Savitar, they announce to thee and to B*ri*haspati, the Brahman.' Perhaps the correct meaning (though not that assumed by the Brâhma*n*a) is, 'This sacrifice they announce to thee as the B*ri*haspati, the Brahman!' and similarly the mantra in the next paragraph.

[2] The Kâ*n*va text adds here the verse Vâ*g*. S. II, 13; see *S*at. Br. I, 7, 4, 22, with the same various reading '*g*yotir.'

[3] See I, 7, 4, 21. Asau nvaivaitasya ya*g*usho bandhur ya evâsau dar*s*apûr*n*amâsayo*h*; Kâ*n*va text.

[4] On 'pra' see part i, p. 101 note.

by the divine Savitri, acceptable to Mitra and Varuna!' Therewith he hastes to Savitri for his impulsion, for he is the impeller of the gods; and 'acceptable to Mitra and Varuna' he says, because Mitra and Varuna are the deities of the Maitrâvaruna (Prasâstri),—thus he announces it to those who are the deities of the Maitrâvaruna: therefore he says, 'acceptable to Mitra and Varuna.'

Seventh Brâhmana.

1. Threefold, forsooth, is science; the *Rik*s, the Yagus, and the Sâmans. The *Rik*s are this (earth), since it is thereon that he who sings them, does sing them; the *Rik*s are speech, since it is by speech that he who sings them, does sing them. And the Yagus, forsooth, are the air, and the Sâmans the sky. That same threefold science is used in the Soma-sacrifice.

2. By the *Rik* he conquers this world, by the Yagus the air, and by the Sâman the sky. Therefore whosoever has learnt one of these sciences, let him endeavour to learn also what is contained in the two others: by the *Rik*, forsooth, he conquers this world, by the Yagus the air, and by the Sâman the sky.

3. This, then, is the thousandfold progeny of Vâk (speech)[1]. Indra (obtained for his share) two-thirds, and Vishnu one-third[2]: the *Rik*s and Sâmans are Indra, and the Yagus are Vishnu. Therefore in the Sadas they perform (the Sastras and Stotras) with the *Rik* and Sâman, for the Sadas is Indra's own.

4. And by means of these Yagus they, as it were, bring forward (puras) that Vishnu, the sacrifice: hence the name 'puraskarana' (preparatory ceremony).

[1] See IV, 5, 8, 4.

[2] Thus according to the Kânva text,—dvau bhâgâv indro 'bhagataikam vishnuh.

5. Both the *Rik*s and the Sâmans are Speech, and the Ya*g*us are the Mind. Now wherever this Speech was, there everything was done, everything was known; but wherever Mind was, there nothing whatever was done, nothing was known, for no one knows (understands) those who think in their mind.

6. The gods said to Speech, 'Go thou forward and make this known!' She said, 'What will be my reward then?'—'Whatever in the sacrifice is offered with Svâhâ, and without Vasha*t*, that shall be thine!' Hence whatever in the sacrifice is offered with Svâhâ, and without Vasha*t*, that belongs to Speech. She then went forward and made that known, saying, 'Do this so! do this so!'

7. Therefore they also perform with the *Rik* in the Havirdhâna: he (the Hot*ri*) recites the morning prayer, he recites the kindling-verses; he (the Grâvastut) praises the pressing-stones,—for thus, indeed, they (Speech and Mind) became yoke-fellows.

8. And hence they also perform with the Ya*g*us in the Sadas: they raise up the Udumbara post, they erect the Sadas, they throw up the dhish*n*ya hearths,—for thus they became yoke-fellows.

9. That same Sadas they enclose on all sides with a view to that generation, thinking, 'Quite secretly shall be carried on that generation!' for improper, indeed, is the generation which another sees · hence even when a husband and wife are seen, while carrying on intercourse, they run away from each other, for they give offence. Therefore to any one looking into the Sadas, except through the door, let him say, 'Look not!' for it is as if he were seeing intercourse being carried on. Freely (one may look) through the door, for the door is made by the gods.

10. In like manner they enclose the Havirdhâna on all sides with a view to that generation, thinking, 'Quite secretly this generation shall be carried on!' for improper, indeed, is the generation which another sees: hence even when a husband and wife are seen, while carrying on intercourse, they run away from each other, for they give offence. Therefore to any one looking into the Havirdhâna, except through the door, let him say, 'Look not!' for it is as if he were seeing intercourse being carried on. Freely (one may look) through the door, for the door is made by the gods.

11. Now there, in the Sadas, that male, the Sâman, longs after the female, the *Rik*. From that generation Indra was produced: from fire, indeed, fire is produced, viz. Indra from the *Rik* and the Sâman; for Indra they call him that burns yonder (the sun).

12. And there, in the Havirdhâna, that male, the Soma, longs after the female, the water. From that generation the moon was produced: from food, indeed, food is produced, viz. the moon from water and Soma; for the moon is the food of him that burns yonder[1]. Hence he thereby produces the sacrificer, and for him he produces food: from the *Rik* and Sâman he produces the sacrificer, and from water and Soma he produces food for him.

13. Now with the Ya*g*us the gods first performed sacrifice, then with the *Rik*, then with the Sâman; and in like manner do they now perform the sacrifice, first with the Ya*g*us, then with the *Rik*, then with the Sâman; for Ya*g*us, they say, is the same as Ya*g*as (worship).

14. Now when the gods milked (the objects of) their wishes from these sciences, the Ya*g*us science

[1] See I, 6, 4, 13 seq.

milked most wishes. It became, as it were, emptied the most; it was not equal to the other two sciences,—the air-world was not equal to the two other worlds.

15. The gods desired, 'How can this science become equal to the other two sciences; how can the air-world become equal to the two other worlds?'

16. They said, 'Let us perform in a low voice with the Yagus: then that science will become equal to the other two sciences; then the air-world will become equal to the two other worlds!'

17. They performed with them in a low voice, and thereby strengthened them; and henceforth that science was equal to the other two sciences, and the air-world was equal to the two other worlds. Therefore the Yagus, while being distinct, are yet indistinct; and therefore the air-world, while being distinct, is yet indistinct (indefinable).

18. He who performs with the Yagus in a low voice, strengthens them; and they, thus strengthened, strengthen him. But he who performs in a loud voice, weakens them, and, being weak, they weaken him.

19. The *Rik*s and Sâmans, forsooth, are speech, and the Yagus are the mind; and so those who perform with the *Rik* and Sâman are speech, and those who perform with the Yagus are the mind. Hence nothing whatever is done, unless ordered by the Adhvaryu: when the Adhvaryu says, 'Recite (the invitatory prayer)! Pronounce the offering prayer!' then those who perform with the *Rik* perform it. And when the Adhvaryu says, 'Soma becometh pure: turn ye back[1]!' then those who perform with the Sâman perform it,—for speech speaks not but what is conceived by the mind.

[1] See IV, 2, 5, 8.

20. Thus, then, the Adhvaryu, the mind, walks, as it were, in front (puras-karati): hence the name 'puraskarana[1];' and verily, he who knows this, stands, as it were, in front through prosperity and glory.

21. Now that same puraskarana (going before) is nothing else than yonder burning (sun): one ought to perform in accordance with his (the sun's) course. When he (the Adhvaryu) has drawn a cup of Soma, let him turn round in accordance with his course; when he has responded (to the Hotri's recitation), let him turn round in accordance with his course; when he has offered a graha, let him turn round in accordance with his course: he (the sun), verily, is the supporter; and whosoever, knowing this, is able to perform in accordance with his course, he, forsooth, is able to support his dependants[2].

Eighth Brâhmana.

1. Now the consecration-ceremony[3] (for the sacrificial session) is a sitting down, is a session (sattra): hence they say of them, 'they sit.' And when thereafter they perform the sacrifice, then they (under)go; then he, who is the leader, leads: hence they say of them, 'they (under)go[4].'

---

[1] That is, preparation, preparatory ceremony;—and hence also the 'taking the lead, being the precursor.'

[2] In the Kânva text this is the last Brâhmana of the (fifth) Kânda.

[3] For the Dîkshâ see III, 1, 1, 1 seq. In the Kânva text I have found nothing corresponding to the present Brâhmana.

[4] That is to say, the verb 'i' (to go; more especially its compound upa-i, to undergo, go through, undertake) is used of sacrificial performances in the Sattra lasting for twelve (pressing) days and upward, to distinguish the latter from the ahîna-sacrifices, lasting for from two to twelve (pressing) days.

2. The consecration-ceremony, then, is a sitting down, it is a session, it is an (under)going, it is the (under)going of a session. And when afterwards, having reached the end of the sacrifice, they rise, that is 'the rising:' hence they say of them, 'They have risen.' So much, then, for preliminary remark.

3. Now those who are about to consecrate themselves settle (the time and place) between them. If they intend to construct a fire-altar, they take up their (ordinary sacrificial) fires on churning-sticks[1] and betake themselves together to where they are about to perform the animal offering to Pra*g*âpati. Having churned (the fire), and put fire-wood on, they take out the Âhavanîya fire, and perform that animal offering to Pra*g*âpati.

4. Its head they keep[2]. If their consecration does not fall upon that same day (of the animal offering), then, taking up the fires (again) on the churning-sticks, they disperse to their several (homes) and perform the (daily) offerings.

5. But if their consecration falls upon that same day, then, taking up the fires (again) on the churning-sticks, they betake themselves to where they intend to perform the consecration-ceremony. The G*ri*hapati[3] churns (his fire) first somewhere about the centre of the hall; and one half of the others settle down south and one half north of him. Having

---

[1] That is to say, they hold their churning-sticks to the fires to get warm; see part i, p. 396, note 1.

[2] The head of the victim (or victims, see VI, 2, 1 seq.) will have to be put in the bottom layer of the fire-altar, to impart stability to the latter.

[3] See p. 97, note 1. At a Sattra the G*ri*hapati, as well as all the other *ri*tvig, should be a Brâhman; Kâty. I, 6, 13–16.

churned (their fires), and put on fire-wood, they take one fire-brand each and betake themselves together to the Grihapati's Gârhapatya fire. Having taken out the Âhavanîya from the Grihapati's Gârhapatya, they perform the consecration-ceremony. They have one and the same Âhavanîya, but different Gârhapatyas, during the consecration and the Upasads [1].

6. Then, on whatever day their purchase (of Soma-plants) takes place, on that day he raises the Gârhapatya hearth; and on the Upavasatha day [2] the dhishnya hearths for the others. At the time of the Vaisargina [3] offerings, the wives come forward together; and they (the sacrificers) abandon those other (Gârhapatya) fires [4]. As soon as the Vaisargina offering has been performed,—

7. He leads forward the king (Soma). That Âgnîdhrîya fire has just been taken up on the support [5], when they take one fire-brand each (from the fire at the hall-door) and disperse to their several dhishnya hearths: 'They who do so,' said Yâgñavalkya, 'slay with those fire-brands of theirs.' This now is one way.

---

[1] At Sattras there are usually twelve Upasad days. See p. 105, note 1. Ait. Br. IV, 24 enjoins twelve days for the Dîkshâ and as many for the Upasads of the Dvâdasâha. Kâty. XII, 1, 19; 2, 14 gives no special rule regarding the duration of the Dîkshâ, but enjoins twelve Upasads. See also Lâty. III, 3, 27; Âsv. VI, 1, 2.

[2] The day before the first pressing day.

[3] See III, 6, 3, 1 seq.

[4] Or, those minor (? western) fires, viz. they extinguish those south and north of the Grihapati's Gârhapatya, or (optionally) also the latter, it being again supplied by the fire-brand from the Sâlâdvârya fire. Cf. Kâty. XII, 1, 25–26.

[5] See III, 6, 3, 9 seq.

8. Then there is this second. Having taken up their fires on churning-sticks, they betake themselves to where they intend to perform the animal offering to Pragâpati. Having churned (the fire), and put on (fire-wood), they take out the Âhavanîya and perform that animal offering to Pragâpati.

9. Its head they keep. If their consecration does not fall upon the same day, then, taking up the fires (again) on the churning-sticks, they disperse to their several (homes), and perform (the ordinary) offerings.

10. But if their consecration falls upon the same day, then, taking up the fires (again) on the churning-sticks, they betake themselves to where they intend to perform the consecration-ceremony. The Grihapati churns first, and then the others churn, seated round about him, and throw each the (fire) produced by him on the Grihapati's Gârhapatya. Having taken out the Âhavanîya from the Grihapati's Gârhapatya, they perform the Dîkshâ. Theirs is the same Âhavanîya and the same Gârhapatya during the consecration and the Upasads.

11. Then, on whatever day their purchase (of Soma-plants) takes place, on that day he piles up the Gârhapatya hearth, and on the Upavasatha day the dhishnya hearths for the others. At the time of the Vaisargina offerings the wives come forward together; they (the sacrificers) abandon that (common Gârhapatya) fire. As soon as the Vaisargina offering has taken place,—

12. He leads forward the king. That Âgnîdhrîya fire has just been taken up on the support, when they take one fire-brand each and disperse to their several dhishnya hearths. But those who do it thus, raise

up strife, and strife comes upon them; they become contentious, and, moreover, strife comes upon that community where they sacrifice. This is the second way.

13. Then there is this third. They commune with each other over the Grihapati's churning-sticks,—'What fire shall be produced therefrom, be that ours in common! what we shall gain by this sacrifice, by this animal offering, be that ours in common! In common be our good work! whosoever shall do evil, be that his alone!' Having thus spoken, the Grihapati first takes up (the fire on the churning-sticks) for himself, then he takes it up for the others, or they take it[1] up for themselves. They betake themselves to where they intend to perform the animal offering to Pragâpati. Having churned (the fire) and put on (fire-wood), they take out the Âhavanîya and perform that animal offering to Pragâpati.

14. Its head they keep. If their consecration does not fall on the same day, then, taking up (again) the fires on the churning-sticks, they disperse to their several (homes), and perform (the ordinary) offerings.

15. But if their consecration falls on the same day, they commune with each other over the Grihapati's churning-sticks,—'What fire shall be produced therefrom, be that ours in common! what we shall gain by this sacrifice, by this session, be that ours in common! In common be our good work! Whosoever shall do evil, be that his alone!' Having thus spoken, the Grihapati first takes up (the fire) on the churning-sticks for himself, then he takes it up for

[1] Or, according to Kâty. XII, 2, 8–9, each takes up two fires, viz. his own and that of the Grihapati.

the others, or they take it up for themselves. They betake themselves to where they intend to perform the consecration-ceremony. Having churned (the fire) and put on (fire-wood), they take out the Âhavanîya and perform the consecration-ceremony. Theirs is the same Âhavanîya and the same Gârhapatya during the consecration and the Upasads.

16. And on whatever day their purchase (of Soma-plants) takes place, on that day he piles up the Gârhapatya hearth, and on the Upavasatha day the dhishnya hearths for the others. At the time of the Vaisargina offerings the wives come forward together; and they (the sacrificers) abandon that (Gârhapatya) fire. As soon as the Vaisargina offering has been performed,—

17. He leads forward the king. That Âgnîdhrîya fire has just been taken up on the support, when they take one fire-brand each and disperse to their several dhishnya hearths. Thus is this done, and not (left) undone. The reason why they have different dhishnyas, is that there may be wider space for moving about; and why they have different purodâsas[1], is that more sacrificial food may be left over for completeness.

18. Now then the sacrificial session is explained, whereby the gods quickly drove out evil, and gained the supreme authority which they now wield: having one Grihapati, one purodâsa, one dhishnya, they quickly drove out mischief and quickly were born again. And in like manner will these (sacrificers), by having one Grihapati, one purodâsa, one dhishnya, quickly drive out evil and be born again.

[1] The usual Savanîya-purodâsas (III, 8, 3, 1) are to be offered separately on each fire.

19. Now, in that former case, there is a hall with the roof-beams running from south to north [1],—that is human practice. There are one and the same Âhavanîya, and different Gârhapatyas—that is dissimilar. On the Grihapati's Gârhapatya they perform the Patnîsamyâgas with the tail (of the victim), and the others sit offering in response with ghee—that is dissimilar.

20. But here there is a hall with the roof-beams running from west to east [2]: that is as with the gods. There are the same Âhavanîya, the same Gârhapatya, and the same Âgnîdhrîya: thus this sacrificial session is successful, even as the one day's Soma-sacrifice was successful, there is no failure for it. Its course is one and the same in everything except the dhishnyas.

Ninth Brâhmana.

1. Now, once on a time, the gods were sitting [3] in a sacrificial session, thinking, 'May we attain excellence, may we be glorious, may we be eaters of food!' That same food, gained by them, wished to go away from them,—and, food being cattle, it was the cattle that wished to go away from them, thinking, 'It is to be feared lest they, being exhausted, may hurt us [4]: how, indeed, will they deal with us?'

2. They offered these two oblations in the Gâr-

[1] Viz. the Sadas, see p. 128, note 1.

[2] As in the case of the Prâkîna-vamsa of ordinary ishtis. See III, 1, 1, 6–7.

[3] The Kânva text has nisheduh, 'they sat down.' See IV, 6, 8, 1.

[4] See p. 31, note 1.

hapatya; and—the Gârhapatya being a house (griha), and a house being a resting-place—they thereby secured them in the house, and thus that food, gained by them, did not go away from them.

3. And in like manner do these Sattrins now sit through a sacrificial session, thinking, 'May we attain excellence, may we be glorious, may we be eaters of food!' That food, gained by them, wishes to go away from them,—and, food being cattle, it is the cattle that wish to go away from them, thinking, 'It is to be feared lest they, being exhausted, may hurt us: how, indeed, will they deal with us?'

4. They offer these two oblations[1] in the Gârhapatya; and—the Gârhapatya being a house, and the house being a resting-place—they thereby secure them in the house, and thus that food, gained by them, does not go away from them.

5. And in like manner that offered food wishes to go away from him, thinking, 'It is to be feared lest this one will hurt me: how, indeed, will he deal with me?'

6. He first eats a very little from the further (back) end of it;—thereby he encourages it: it knows, 'It was not so as I thought: he has in no wise hurt me.' Thus it becomes attached to him, and, indeed, whosoever, knowing this, is able to observe the vow thereof, he becomes an eater of food, dear to food.

7. This, then, is done at the Sattrotthâna (rising from the session) on the tenth day[2]. Each of them

---

[1] Viz. those referred to in paragraphs 8 and 9.

[2] That is, on the tenth day of the Dasarâtra, and hence either the last but one day of the sessional Dvâdasâha (p. 402, note 2), or the last day but two of the Gavâm ayana (p. 426, note 3), called

sits speechless, strengthening his voice[1]: with that (voice) strengthened and reinvigorated they perform the last day. Then the others are dismissed, either (for) fetching fuel or to their day's reading of the scriptures. Now also they take food.

8. In the afternoon, having come together and touched water, they enter the ladies' hall[2], and while the others hold on to him from behind, he[3]

Avivâkya. The ceremonies here described take place in the afternoon, after the regular performance of that day's (atyagnishtoma) Soma-sacrifice.

[1] 'Each of them (? or, one by one), speech-bound, guards Soma till the wakening,' Kâty. XII, 4, 1. According to the Kânva text only one (eko haishâm) does so (but perhaps at a time), while the others disperse (vitishthante).

[2] The Patnîsâla seems to be identical here with the Prâkînavamsa (see Kâty. XII, 4, 7), unless it be some shed or tent adjoining the latter, cf. Âpast. Sr. X, 5, comm. The sacrificial formula of the first offering seems to refer to the domestic hearth, the centre of the family life, as a source of joy and strength to the householder.

[3] According to the Kânva text, the Adhvaryu makes the oblations; but if he does not know how to perform them (i.e. if they are not recognised by his school as belonging to the Adhvaryu's duties), the Grihapati does so; and if he cannot do so, any one that knows them, may perform them. Regarding these oblations, and the order of the subsequent ceremonies, there is indeed considerable difference of opinion among the ritualistic authorities. According to Âsv. VIII, 13, 1–2 all of them offer, but only the first oblation is to be performed on the Gârhapatya, and the second on the Âgnîdhrîya. Lâty. III, 7, 8 seq., on the other hand, enjoins the Udgâtri to perform two oblations on the Gârhapatya; the first with the (somewhat modified) formula, assigned in our text to the second oblation, while the second oblation is to be made with 'Svâhâ' simply. [The first of the above formulas is, according to that authority, to be used by them, when they touch the Udumbara post, see IV, 6, 9, 22.] The oblations completed, they are to proceed to the Âhavanîya, where the Udgâtris are to chant thrice the Sâman II, 1126 (?); after which they enter the Sadas to perform the Mânasa-stotra.

offers (on the Sâlâdvârya fire) those two oblations; (the first) with (Vâg. S. VIII, 51), 'Here is joy: here rejoice ye! here is stability, here is (your) own stability,—Hail!' He thereby addresses the cattle; they thereby secure cattle for themselves.

9. And the second he offers with, 'Letting the sucking calf to the mother,'—he means to say by this, 'letting the fire go to the earth;'—'a sucking calf drinking from the mother,'—he thereby means the fire sucking the (moisture of the) earth; —'may he maintain increase of wealth among us,—Hail!' increase of wealth is cattle: they thus secure cattle for themselves.

10. They go out eastward, and enter the (shed of the) Havirdhâna carts from behind towards the front; for from the front towards the back (they enter) when about to perform the sacrifice, but thus (it is done) at the rising from the session.

11. On the hinder shaft of the northern cart[1] they sing the Sâman (Vâg. S. VIII, 52), called 'the completion of the session,'—there it is that they reach completeness; or on the northern hip of the high altar; but the other is the more usual,—

12. That is, on the hinder shaft of the northern cart. 'We have gone to the light, we have become immortal,'—for they who sit through a sacrificial session become indeed the light, they

[1] According to Kâty. XII, 4, 10 and comm., the southern shaft of the northern cart is intended. Similarly the Kânva text,—while touching the right shaft of the northern cart he sings thereon the Sâman 'the completion (success) of the session.' The words 'sattrasya riddhih' are doubtless the name of the Sâman, which has been erroneously made, with 'asi' appended to it in the Mâdhy. text of the Samhitâ, the beginning of the Sâman.

become immortal;—'to the sky have we ascended from the earth,'—for they who sit through a sacrificial session indeed ascend from the earth to the sky;—'we have attained to the gods,'—for they indeed attain to the gods;—'to heaven, to the light!' thrice they repeat the finale; for they indeed become (partakers of) heaven and bliss. Thus, whatever the nature of his Sâman is, that they come to be who sit through a sacrificial session.

13. They creep[1] along right under the axle of the southern cart: even as a snake frees itself from its skin, so do they free themselves from all evil. They creep along with an ati*kh*andas verse; for that, the ati*kh*andas (redundant metre), is all the metres;—thus evil does not overtake them: therefore they creep along with an ati*kh*andas verse.

14. They creep along with (Vâ*g*. S. VIII, 53; Rig-veda I, 132, 6), 'O Indra and Parvata, leaders in battle, smite ye every one that wars against us, smite him with the thunderbolt! him that is hidden may it please in the far retreat which he hath reached: our foes, O hero, on all sides may the tearer tear to pieces,—on all sides!'

15. They go out eastward, and enter the Sadas from the front towards the back; for from the back towards the front (they do so) when about to perform the sacrifice; but thus (they do) at the rising from the session.

16. They sit down by their several dhish*n*ya-hearths. Now, once on a time, the pith of Vâ*k* (speech) wished to desert the gods who had won it; it tried to creep away along this earth, for Vâ*k* is

[1] See p. 299, note 2.

this earth: her pith are these plants and trees. By means of this Sâman[1] they overtook it, and, thus overtaken, it returned to them. Hence upwards on this earth grow the plants, and upwards the trees. And in like manner does the pith of Vâk wish to desert these (sacrificers) who have won it, and tries to creep away along this earth,—for Vâk is this earth: her pith are these plants and trees. By means of this Sâman they overtake it, and, thus overtaken, it returns to them. Hence upwards on this earth grow the plants, and upwards the trees.

17. They chant verses of the queen of serpents; for the queen of serpents is this earth: through her they thus obtain everything. The prelude is performed by (the Udgâtri) himself[2], and the chant is not joined in (by the choristers[3]), lest some one else overhear it. For he would cause (the performance) to be in excess were another to chant; he would cause an excess, were another to join in it; he would cause an excess, were another to overhear it: therefore the prelude is performed by (the Udgâtri) himself, and the chant is not joined in.

---

[1] Viz. the so-called Mânasa-stotra (mental chant), Sâma-veda II, 726–8 (Rig-veda X, 189, 1–3, ascribed to the queen of serpents): 'The spotted bull has come up, &c.,' performed inaudibly. In connection with this Stotra, an imaginary libation to Pragâpati-Vâyu is performed, everything connected with which, from the upâkarana (or introduction, on the part of the Adhvaryu, see p. 401, note 1) up to the bhaksha, or drinking of the cup by the priests, is done 'mentally' (that is, as would seem, by gestures merely). According to Âsv. II, 13, 6, however, the Hotri recites the same hymn in a low voice (upâmsu), but not inaudibly, as a Sastra. But see p. 452, note 1.

[2] Not by the Prastotri, as is otherwise the case; see p. 310, note 1.

[3] See p. 311, note 1.

18. The Hot*ri* recites the Four-Hot*ri* formulas, whereby he follows up that chant by a *S*astra [1]. If the Hot*ri* does not know them, let the G*ri*hapati recite them; but it is the Hot*ri*'s recitation [2].

19. Then the Adhvaryu's response [3] is, 'These sacrificers have prospered: happiness hath accrued unto them!' whereby he bespeaks success to human speech.

20. Thereupon they utter the Brahmodya [4] in

[1] According to this (and Tâ*nd*ya Br. IV, 9, 13) it would seem that the Hot*ri* is not to recite the hymn of the Mânasa-stotra, as prescribed by the Ait. Br. and Â*s*v.

[2] The *k*aturhot*ri* formulas—so-called from four priests, Agnîdh, Adhvaryu, Hot*ri*, and Upavakt*ri*, being mentioned in them—are as follows: 'Their offering-spoon was (the power of) thinking; the ghee was thought; the altar was speech; the barhis was object of meditation; the fire was intelligence; the Agnîdh was understanding; the oblation was breath; the Adhvaryu was the Sâman; the Hot*ri* was Vâ*k*aspati; the Upavakt*ri* was the mind;'—at the end of each of these ten formulas the Adhvaryu, according to Â*s*v., responds, 'Yea (om), Hotar! So (it is), O Hotar!'—(the Hot*ri* proceeds), 'They forsooth took that (mânasa) graha; O Vâ*k*aspati! O disposer (or decree), O name! Let us praise thy name! Praise thou (and) by our name go to heaven! What success the gods have obtained with Pra*g*âpati as their g*ri*hapati, that success shall we obtain!'

[3] ? That is, at the conclusion of the *k*aturhot*ri*-mantras. Â*s*v., on the other hand, makes the Hot*ri* conclude the Brahmodya with the benediction, 'O Adhvaryu, we have succeeded!' to which the latter is to respond, 'We have succeeded, O Hotar!'

[4] That is, a discussion, or disputation, regarding the nature of the Brahman. According to Tâ*nd*ya Br. IV, 9, 14, as interpreted by the commentary, the performance consists rather in (or is followed by?) vituperative remarks on Pra*g*âpati, whom they have now safely got into their power (allusion being made, for instance, to his criminal relations to his daughter; to his having created thieves, gad-flies and mosquitos, &c.); but this, it seems to me, is probably a wrong interpretation of the 'parivadanti' in the text, which may mean that 'they discourse' upon Pra*g*âpati. So also Kâty. XII, 4,

(the form of a) dialogue. For everything, indeed, is obtained, everything gained by them that sit through a sacrificial session,—they have performed with Yagus prayers: these have obtained so much, have acquired so much; they have recited *Ri*k verses: these have obtained so much, have acquired so much; they have chanted Sâmans: these have obtained so much, have acquired so much. But this has not been obtained, this has not been acquired by them, namely, the (theological) discussion, the sacred discourse: this is what they thereby obtain, what they acquire.

21. Having 'crept' up to the Udumbara post, they restrain their speech. Now, they who perform the sacrifice with speech, milk and suck out the

---

21, Pragâpater agu*n*âkhyânam, 'agu*n*a' may have to be taken in the sense of 'nirgu*n*a' or 'nirgu*n*atvam' (unqualifiedness, unconditionedness), rather than in that of 'vice;' and it is worthy of note that the Pragâpati-tanu formulas, preceding the Brahmodya proper, consist chiefly in the enumeration of negative qualities. 'The twelve bodies of Prâgapati are qualified as follows:—the eater of food and the mistress of food; the happy and glorious; the abodeless and dauntless; the unattained and unattainable; the invincible and irresistible; the unpreceded and unmatched.' Then follows the Brahmodya:—'Agni is the house-lord (g*ri*hapati),' so say some: 'he is the house-lord of this world;'—'Vâyu is the house-lord,' so say some: 'he is the house-lord of the airy region;'—yonder (sun), forsooth, is the house-lord: he who burns yonder, he is the lord, and the seasons are the house. Verily, to whatsoever (sacrificers) he becomes the g*ri*hapati, who knows that divine g*ri*hapati, that g*ri*hapati prospers, and they, the sacrificers, prosper: to whatsoever (sacrificers) he becomes the g*ri*hapati, who knows the divine averter of evil, that g*ri*hapati averts evil, and they, the sacrificers, avert evil! See Ait. Br. V, 25. According to Âsv., the Hot*ri* alone would seem to repeat the Brahmodya. The expression vâkovâkya (dialogue) apparently refers to the controversial form of this discourse. See also A. Ludwig, Rig-veda, III, p. 390 seq.

sacrifice; for sacrifice is speech. And previously to this, each of them sits speechless, strengthening his speech [1], and with their speech thus strengthened and reinvigorated they perform the last day. But at this (disputation) the entire speech, thus obtained, becomes exhausted: that speech they all strengthen (by remaining) speechless, and with it thus strengthened and reinvigorated they perform the Atirâtra [2].

22. They sit touching the Udumbara post [3], for strength is food, and the Udumbara tree is strength: with strength he thus invigorates speech.

23. When the sun has set, they go out (of the Sadas) eastward, and sit down behind the Âhavanîya, in front of the Havirdhâna shed. Round them, sitting speechless, the Pratiprasthât*ri* carries the Vasatîvarî water [4]. For whatever object they perform the session, therewith let them release their speech. For in olden times the *Ri*shis were wont to hold sacrificial sessions for certain objects,—'such is our wish: may that be fulfilled!' And if they be desirous of different objects, desirous of subjects, desirous of offspring, desirous of cattle,—

---

[1] The construction of the text is quite irregular, and I am by no means certain whether 'tâm eshâm purâ' should not be separated from what follows, and have the verbs 'viduhanti' and 'nirdhayanti' supplied after them,—That (speech) of theirs (they milk and suck out) before this. Each now sits speech-bound, strengthening his speech, &c.

[2] That is, the last day of the Dvâda*s*âha, or of the Gavâmayana, the so-called Udayanîya-atirâtra.

[3] According to Lâty. III, 8, 11 they form a circle round the Udumbara post and touch it, muttering the mantra, 'Here is stability, here is (our) own stability! Here is joy: here rejoice ye!' or, 'In me is stability, in me is (your) own stability! in me is joy: in me rejoice ye!' or both. See p. 448, note 3.

[4] See III, 9, 2, 1 seq.

24. Let them release their speech with this (Vâg. S. VIII, 53), 'Earth! Air! Sky!' Thus they render their speech auspicious by means of the truth, and with that auspicious (speech) they pray for blessings,—'May we be abundantly supplied with offspring!'—thereby they pray for offspring;—'May we be abundantly supplied with men!'—thereby they pray for men;—'May we be abundantly supplied with food!' thereby they pray for prosperity.

25. Thereupon the Grihapati, or whomsoever the Grihapati may call upon, recites the Subrahmanyâ litany[1]. Some, indeed, recite the Subrahmanyâ each separately; but rather let the Grihapati, or whomsoever the Grihapati may call upon, recite the Subrahmanyâ. Having desired an invitation to that (Atirâtra feast), they put kindling-sticks on the fire[2].

---

[1] See III, 3, 4, 17 seq.

[2] According to the comm. on Kâty. XII, 4, 28 it is the reciter of the Subrahmanyâ who, having said 'O Subrahmanyâ, invite me thereto!' puts sticks on the fire.

INDEX TO PARTS I AND II.

(KÂ*ND*AS I—IV.)

â, Part I, page 101.
abhighâra*n*a, I, 192.
abhiplava-sha*d*aha, II, 403.
abhîvarta-sâman, II, 434.
abortion, causing of, II, 11.
adâbhya-graha, II, 424.
âdâra plant, a substitute for Soma-plants, II, 422.
âdhîtaya*g*us, II, 20, 22, 23.
adhrigu litany, II, 188.
adhvara, I, 114.
Adhvaryu, I, introd. xx seq., xxvi; must not pass between dhish*n*yas, II, 153; passes north of Âgnîdhra shed, ib.; his response (pratigara), 231, 326, 328, 330, 331; he is the head of the sacrifice, 276; goes in front, 440.
Aditi, I, 25, 73, 307; has seven or eight sons, II, 12; to her belong the Prâya*n*îya and Udayanîya-ish*t*i, II, 48, 386; is the earth, 51; two-headed, 57; her share in the Soma feast, 259.
Âditya, seven or eight Âdityas, sons of Aditi, II, 12; they accompany Varu*n*a, 93; Vivasvat (sun) the Âditya, 13; is the eye, 39; the vyâna, 240; Âdityâ*h* and Aṅgirasa*h*, 113; Indra with Vasus, Rudras, and Âdityas, 241, 350; evening feast is theirs, ib.; cattle after their manner, 353; the press-stones, 355; to them belong the ya*g*us, 383; Âdityânâm ayana, II, 383; twelve Âdityas, eight Vasus, and eleven Rudras, 411.
âditya-graha, II, 350, 352.
âghâra, two libations of ghee (to Pra*g*âpati and Indra), I, 91, 124; (to Agnîshomau and Vish*n*u), II, 106.
Agnâ-vish*n*û, cake to, II, 12; to them belongs dîksha*n*îyesh*t*i, 82.
Agni, representative of priestly caste (brahman), I, introd. xvi seq.; four different forms, I, 47, 136, 452; their names, II, 118; shuts out Asuras, I, 54; is the youngest, 108; messenger of gods, 110, 156; ancestral Hot*ri*, 115; repeller of Rakshas, 158; II, 99; best of gods, I, 163; seeks for Indra, 175; identified with Rudra, 201; II, 343; with Pra*g*âpati, I, 346, 386; with Rudra, Varu*n*a, Indra, Mitra, Brahman, 340 seq.; unites with waters, 277; gold is his seed, 277; milk ditto, 326; Agni first created by Pra*g*âpati, 323 seq., 342 seq., 389; the root and progenitor of deities, 386; II, 98; is te*g*as, I, 418, 419; originally alone immortal, 310; covets the beasts deposited with him, 347; all forms (rûpa) deposited with him, 314; Agni Vai*s*vânara, 104 seq.; oblations to Agni pavamâna, pâvaka, and *s*u*k*i, 304 seq.; Agni pavamâna and indumat, 320; Agni anîkavat, 408; Agni kavyavâhana, 430; the woof of cloth belongs to Agni, II, 9; Agni is all the deities, 12; the lower (Vish*n*u the upper) half of the sacrifice, 12; Indra, Soma, and Agni, 22; Agni is the brahman (sacerdotium) and sacrifice, 38; speech, 39; Vratapati, 44, 45; guardian of the east, 50; Agni attended by

the Vasus, 93; messenger to Aṅgiras and Âdityas, 113; Agni Vaisvânara's ashes is gravel, 120; Agni head of deities, 184; his victim, 218; the lotus of the earth, 277; Varuna, Mitra, and Agni, 285; Agni vaisvânara, 305; rules over beasts, 343; officiates as Agnîdh, 348; Agni with Vâyu and Sûrya, I, 325, 327; II, 453; Agni, Varuna, and Indra, leaders of the gods, I, 449 seq.; Agni, Soma, and Vishnu form the thunderbolt, II, 108; five-kapâla cake to Agni, 389; Agni, Indra, and Sûrya superior to the others, 402.

Âgnîdhra (Agnîdh), identical with Agni, I, 58; ought to be learned, and receives first the dakshinâ, II, 148; heads procession with a firebrand, 187, 195; with the vasatîvarî water, 235; sits in the Neshtri's lap, 368.

Âgnîdhrîya (Âgnîdhra) fire-shed, Yagña's arm, II, 126; erection of, 147, 148; from thence the gods gained immortality, 147; sacred to the All-gods, 148; the gods stay therein beside the vasatîvarî water, 226.

Agnihotra, I, 2, 320 seq.; is the Sun, 327; time of, 328 seq.; two libations each time, 332, 334; a domestic sacrifice, 333; first of sacrifices, 344; a heavenward sailing ship, 345; number of, in the year, 346.

agnihotra-havanî, ladle, I, 11, 67, 331.

âgnimâruta-sastra, I, 209; II, 369.

agni-pranayana, I, 298; II, 121 seq., 157 seq.; cf. fire.

agnirahasya, I, introd. xxx seq.

Agnîshomau, I, 169, 373 seq., 377, 379; Agni and Soma (offered to separately, I, 364); seize the Soma sacrificer between their jaws, II, 82, 161; are yoke-fellows, 106.

agnîshomîya he-goat, II, 82; black-spotted, 83; sacrifice of, 162 seq.

Agnishtoma, II, 301; stotras and sastras, 325, 326, 397.

agnishtoma-sâman, II, 368.

Agnyâdhâna (agnyâdheya), I, 1, 2, 274 seq.

agnyanvâdhâna, I, 2.

agnyuddharana, I, 2; time of, 328 seq.

agnyupasthâna, I, 339 seq.

âgrayana-graha, II, 288 seq., 332, 355; -sthâlî, ib.; drawn for All-gods, 289; at all three Savanas, ib.; mode of drawing, 290; depositing, 292.

Âgrayaneshti, offering of first-fruits, I, 369 seq.

âgur ('ye yagâmahe'), I, 142, 148.

âgyabhâga, butter portions to Agni and Soma, I, 159 seq.

âgya-sastra, II, 293; -stotra, 293, 324.

Ahalyâ, Indra as lover of, II, 81.

âhâva, II, 326, 361.

ahâvah, II, 380.

Âhavanîya, used for cooking, I, 18; when taken out from Gârhapatya, 328 seq.; is Yagña's mouth, II, 126.

âhavanîya, I, 208; II, 187.

âhuti (guhoti-offering), I, 263.

aindrâgna-graha, II, 322 seq.

aindravâyava (graha), II, 265 seq.; shape of cup, 277.

airs, vital, three, I, 19 seq.; nine, 140; seven, II, 17; ten, 25; ten (besides out-breathing, in-breathing, and through-breathing), 210; speech, out-breathing and in-breathing, eye and ear, 39.

Akhâvâka, priest, II, 317 seq.

âkhûtkara, mole-hill, I, 441; earth of (âkhukarîsha), 278.

âkhyânavidah, I, introd. xxiv.

Âkuli, Asura priest, I, 29.

akyuta, I, 156.

altar, see vedi.

Amarâvatî, I, 110.

amâvâsyâ, I, 172, 177.

amsu-graha = Pragâpati, II, 248, 423 seq.

Anasnat sâṅgamana (as the sabhya fire) resides with man, I, 338.

Aṅgiras and Âdityas perform a Soma-sacrifice, II, 113; a name of Agni, 118; Aṅgirasâm ayana, 384.

anîka, I, 408 seq.; II, 342.

animal (victim), fivefold, II, 24; sacrifice, 162 seq.
anointment of Dîkshita with fresh butter, II, 13; of his eyes with Traikakuda ointment, 14; of the sacrificial stake, 170; of the victim, 183.
antaḥpâta, peg, II, 111.
antaryâma (graha), II, 257 seq.; is the night and offered at sunrise, 261; offered entirely, 263.
anûbandhyâ, barren cow slaughtered at Soma-sacrifice, I, 379; II, 217; maitrâvaruṇî, 387, 391 seq.; vaiśvadevî and bârhaspatyâ, 388.
anumantraṇa, I, 124, 154.
anushṭubh, metre, is speech, II, 21, 24.
anuvâkyâ, invitatory prayer, I, 119, 135, 170 seq., 195.
anuvashaṭkâra, II, 351.
anuyâga, after-offering; three at haviryagña, I, 80, 230 seq., 445; nine at Vaiśvadeva, Varuṇapraghâsâḥ, &c., 390, 404, 418; eleven at animal offerings, II, 210.
anvâhârya, I, 7, 49.
anvâhâryapakana fire (dakshiṇâgni), I, 339; when taken out from Gârhapatya, 340.
anvâ-rabh, II, 40.
anvârambhaṇîyâ-ishṭi, I, 7, 386; II, 40.
apâna, I, 120.
apasalavi (apadakshiṇa), I, 441; referring to the Fathers, II, 29.
Âpastamba, I, introd. xxxix seq.
aponaptrîya sûkta, II, 232.
âprî-hymns, I, introd. xv; II, 185.
apsu-dîkshâ, II, 5.
apsushomâḥ, II, 373.
Aptoryâma, II, 398.
Âptya, I, 47 seq.
apûpa, cake, I, 317.
âpyâyana, strengthening of Soma-plants, I, 178; II, 100, 103.
araṇi, I, 275; are held while the prâkîna-vaṃśa is approved of, II, 5.
Araru, I, 57.
ârbhava, or tritîya pavamâna stotra, II, 315.
Argunî (phalgunî), nakshatra, I, 285.
ârsheya, I, 115.
Aruṇa Aupaveśi, I, introd. xli, 313, 452.
Âruṇi, I, 14; Takshan recites for him, 335; arranger of Subrahmaṇyâ litany, II, 82, 413.
Arunmukhas, I, 57.
Arurmaghas, I, 57.
Arvâvasu, I, 137.
Asat Pâṃsava, resides with man, I, 338.
Âshâḍha Sâvayasa, I, 4.
âs-pâtra, I, 117.
âśrâvaṇa (śraushaṭ), I, 132, 140, 142 seq.
Asuras, contend against gods, I, 54; by speech (numerals), 153; divide the world with gods, 59 seq.; have darkness and magic (mâyâ) assigned to them by Pragâpati, 362; defile plants, 370; deprived of (intelligible) speech, II, 31; build three strongholds, one in each world, 105; bury magic charms, 135; the blood spirting out from victims is their share, 193.
Âsuri, I, introd. xxxv, 169, 300, 432, 448; II, 349.
aśvavâla-grass, II, 89.
âśvina-graha, II, 272 seq.; drawn in the tenth place and offered in the third, 276, 312; shape of cup, 278.
Aśvins, Adhvaryus of gods, I, 16, 53; II, 276; wander about on earth performing cures, 274 seq.; are heaven and earth, 276.
Atharvâṅgirah, I, 38.
atigrâhya (graha), II, 402 seq.
atikkhandas, II, 66, 380.
Atirâtra, II, 398.
Âtithyeshṭi (guest-offering to Soma), II, 51, 85 seq.
Âtreya, II, 346.
Atri, etymology, I, 131; hotṛi of Ṛishis, II, 346.
Atyagnishṭoma, II, 398.
audgrabhaṇa, II, 20.
audumbarî. See udumbara post.
Aupoditeya (Tumiñga Vaiyâghapadya), I, 271.
austerity (tapas), world conquered by, II, 111.
avabhṛitha, expiatory bath, I, 406; II, 378; śûlâvabhṛitha, 215.
avadâna, portion, I, 191.

âvahana (devatânâm), I, 118, 157.
avakâ*s*a formulas, II, 409.
avântaradîkshâ, II, 97 seq.
avântaredâ, I, 221.
avara, II, 253.
avivâkya, II, 402, 448.
ayavan, I, 199.
Âyu, I, 389; II, 91; a name of Agni, 118.
âyush*t*oma, II, 403.

bahishpavamâna (stotra), II, 307, 309 seq.
bali, I, 329.
barhis, I, 84 seq., 147, 233.
Barku Vârsh*n*a, I, 5.
beasts, ruler of (Rudra), I, 201; II, 153; Tvash*t*ri, II, 180.
Bhaga, is blind, I, 210.
Bhâllaveya (Indradyumna), I, 206, 293.
Bhava (Rudra-Agni), I, 201.
Bh*ri*gu-Aṅgiras, I, 38.
bhûr bhuva*h* sva*h*, I, 296; II, 37.
Bhûtavat (Rudra), I, 209.
black-deer skin (k*ri*sh*n*â*g*ina), I, 23; two, representing heaven and earth, II, 25; Soma placed thereon, 160.
brahmabhâga, I, 214.
brahmahatyâ, I, 48.
Brahman priest, I, introd. xx seq., 223; II, 347, 434.
Brahman, the glowing fire, I, 341.
Brâhma*n*a, human god, I, 309, 374; follows the Kshatriya, 47, 452; may be without a king, but not vice versâ, II, 270.
brâhma*n*a, I, introd. xxii seq.
Brâhma*n*â*kh*am*s*in, is Indra, II, 433.
brahmanicide, I, 47; II, 243.
brahmasâdana, I, 6.
brahmasâman, II, 434.
brahmodya, II, 452.
B*ri*haspati, I, introd. xvi seq.; Aṅgirasa, I, 67; as Brahman priest, 211; the brahman (n.), II, 23, 59; is dyumna, 24; animal offering to, 219; B*ri*haspati the purohita of Soma, oppressed by Soma, 258; B*ri*haspati the wise, is the first, 286; officiates as Udgâtri, 348.
b*ri*hatî, metre, I, 175; II, 112.
b*ri*hatî-*s*astra, II, 430.
b*ri*hat-sâman, I, 196, 222; II, 339, 403.
Budila Â*s*vatarâ*s*vi, II, 425.
bull, at Sâkamedhâ*h*, representative of Indra, I, 416.
butter, fresh, used for anointing the Dîkshita, II, 14; melted: see ghee.

calf, first-born of season, dakshi*n*â at Âgraya*n*esh*t*i, I, 373; dakshi*n*â at Vai*s*vadeva (seasonal sacrifice), 390.
carpenter, unclean, I, 23.
cart, receptacle of havis, I, 12 seq.; bound with thongs, 452; turned round and placed on altar, II, 127 seq.; description of, 132.
caste, I, introd. xii, xviii, 28, 452; II, 4.
castles, three, built by the Asuras, II, 105.
cattle, threefold, II, 28.
charms, only effective when buried in the ground, II, 135; formulas against, 137.
chip, first of the sacrificial stake, II, 164, 169; svaru, 173, 186; four chips, 282.
cloth, its parts assigned to various deities, II, 9.
confession of sin, I, 397.
consecration (dîkshâ) for Soma-sacrifice, II, 1 seq.
covenant of Tanûnapât, not to be broken, II, 95 seq.
cow, when created, coveted by Agni, I, 326; her skin originally on man, II, 9; her flesh not to be eaten by the consecrated, 11; to be eaten according to Yâ*gñ*avalkya, ib.; her ten properties, 69.
creatures, of three kinds, I, 384; the upright and those tending downwards, 387, 404.

dadhigharma, II, 336.
Dadhya*ñk* Âtharvana, teaches the A*s*vins the madhu-brâhma*n*a, II, 277.
Daivya, messenger of Asuras, I, 111.
Daksha (Pra*g*âpati), I, 375.
Daksha Pârvati, I, 377.
Dâkshâya*n*as, I, 377.
Dâkshâya*n*a sacrifice, I, 374 seq.
dakshi*n*â, I, 48, 308; (the greater the better), 309, 322; not to be accepted, if refused by some one else, II, 116; different

kinds of, 340 seq.; are the sacrifice to human gods, 341, 417.
Dakshi*n*âgni (anvâhâryapa*k*ana), when taken out from Gârhapatya, I, 339 seq.; altar near it at pit*ri*yag*ñ*a, 422.
dâkshi*n*a-homa, II, 336, 341.
dakshi*n*îkara*n*a, I, 37.
Dânava (V*ri*tra), I, 166.
Danâyû, I, 166.
Danu, I, 166.
darbha grass, I, 84.
Dar*s*apûr*n*amâsa-ish*t*î, I, 1 seq.
darvihoma, oblation of spoonful of boiled rice, to Indra, I, 415.
da*s*âpavitra, straining-cloth, II, 248, 258.
da*s*arâtra, II, 402.
deasil (deiseil, dessel), I, 37.
death, identification with the sun, I, 343 seq.
debt, owed by man to *Ri*shis, fathers, and men, I, 190.
deva (Savit*ri*), I, 46.
Devabhâga *S*rautarsha, purohita to Kurus and S*riñ*gayas, I, 377.
dhâman, I, 74, 93.
dhânya, I, 39.
dhâyyâ, I, 112.
dhish*n*ya, hearth-mounds, represent the Gandharvas, II, 72; overturned by Asuras, 147; preparation of, 148 seq.; fagots held over them, 364.
dh*ri*sh*t*i, I, 33.
dhruva (graha), II, 293, 298 seq.; -sthâlî, 298.
dhruvâ, spoon, I, 67; II, 23.
dhurya (stotra), II, 307.
Dîkshâ, consecration, II, 1 seq.; apsu-d., 5; intermediate, 97 seq.
Dîksha*n*îyesh*t*i, II, 12 seq.
Dîkshita, consecrated, is an embryo, II, 19; is Vish*n*u, 29; (dhîkshita), 47.
doshâvastar, I, 354.
dro*n*a-kala*s*a, II, 257 seq., 268, 318; is V*ri*tra's head, 371.
drop, Soma as bindu, II, 157; oblation of drops (stoka), 195 seq.
durvâ (dûb) plant, a substitute for Soma-plants, II, 422.
dvâda*s*âha, II, 402; vyû*dh*a*kh*andas, 418.
dvidevatya grahas, II, 266; shape of cups, 277, 316, 351.
Dyâvâp*ri*thivî, heaven and earth, cake-offering to, at Âgraya*n*esh*t*i, I, 369 seq.; ditto at Vai*s*vadeva, 388; contain the universe, II, 19, 26; when agreeing (uniting) they give rain, I, 196, 241; hymn to, 330.
Dyutâna, son of the Maruts, II, 144.

Earth, trembling like lotus-leaf, I, 279; creation of, 280; goes to witness the Asuras' animal offering, II, 207.
east, quarter of gods, II, 1, 3, 4; (faultless) man offers, facing east, II, 3; assigned to Agni, 50.
ekâda*s*inî, set of eleven stakes, II, 173, 176 seq., 218 seq.
ekadhana, II, 102, 232, 233, 235, 237.
ekavi*ms*a (stoma), II, 401.
elephant, its origin, II, 13; not to be accepted as a gift, ib.
embryo, expulsion of, II, 11, 19; have their hands closed, 27; enveloped in the amnion and placenta, 28, 29, 73; found in cow slaughtered, 391; unfit for sacrifice, 394, 396.
ewe, image of, at Varu*n*apraghâsâ*h*, I, 395 seq.
eye, the truth, I, 78; man's eye is sore (secreting matter), II, 14; entered by *S*ush*n*a the Dânava, ib.

falcon (? eagle), Soma as falcon, II, 80; Gâyatrî, 88.
fast. See vrata.
fast-food, II, 37 seq.
Fathers (manes). See Pitara*h*.
fingers, bending in of, II, 18, 98; (nameless) ring-finger, eating with, I, 332; gold tied to it, II, 63; different fingers used in meting out Soma-plants, 67; loosening of fingers, 162.
Fire, kindling of, I, 95 seq.; production of (by churning, agni-manthana), 275, 294, 297, 311, 389; II, 90 seq.; carrying fire round (paryagnikara*n*a), I, 45; II, 187; leading forwards (agni-pra*n*ayana), I, 298; II, 121 seq., 157 seq.; homage to, at time of Agnihotra, I, 301, 322 seq., 348 seq.;

homage to, when leaving home, 360; mounting of (samâropa*n*a), 396; womb of the sacrifice, II, 19; serves as a skin to the sacrificer (as embryo), 98.
fire-place, fivefold lustration of, I, 2, 276, 359.
fish, accursed, I, 452; Manu's, 216 seq.
five, number, I, 16.
flood, legend of the, I, 216.
food, threefold (cattle), II, 28.
Full-moon sacrifice, I, 1, 17, 180.

*G*agatî, metre, means cattle, II, 88.
*G*anaka Vaideha, I, introd. xxxi, xlii seq.
Ga*nd*akî, I, 104.
Gandharvas, steal Soma, II, 52; fond of women, 53, 233; receive purchase price for Soma, 72, 152; Soma-wardens, 150 seq., 233.
Gârhapatya, used for cooking, I, 18; sacred to sacrificer, 339.
gata*s*rî, I, 98, 183.
*G*âtavedas, I, 119.
gaurivîta-sâman, II, 401.
Gavâm ayana, II, 426.
Gâyatrî, I, 80, 91, 97, 100; fetches Soma, 183; II, 52, 150, 329; as a falcon, 88, 241; by means of a khadira stick, 151; is the earth, I, 194; Agni, 234; II, 87; fore-part of the sacrifice, 89; her calf is the dhruva graha, 304.
gharma, I, 44; (samrâ*g*), II, 105, 411.
*gh*asha, I, 216.
ghee (gh*ri*ta), sap of heaven and earth, I, 372; a purifier, II, 8; belongs to the gods, 14; a thunderbolt, 106, 170.
girdle, hempen, putting on for consecration, II, 28, 98; of sacrificial stake, 172.
*G*îvala *K*ailaki, I, 336.
goat (he-) tied up at agnyâdhâna, I, 292; she-goat given for Soma, II, 71, 74; goat and sheep, 407.
gods, path to, I, 267; how they became immortal, 310 seq.; do not sleep, II, 44; thrice eleven, 290; three kinds of, 350; eight Vasus, eleven Rudras, and twelve Âdityas, 411.
gold, Agni's seed, I, 277; II, 59, 390; piece of gold used in offering, II, 54; tied to the ring-finger (as a symbol of truth), 63, 70; symbol of the sun, 115, 224; put in right wheel-track and offered on, 130; with oblation of omentum, 198.
gosh*t*oma, II, 403.
Gotama Râhûga*n*a, I, 104 seq.
Graha, cup of Soma, II, 247, 259; meanings of, 432 seq.
grâva-stotra, II, 332.
Grâvastut, assistant of Hot*ri*, I, 223, 332.
gravel (sikatâ), the ashes of Agni Vai*s*vânara, II, 120.
g*ri*hapati, II, 97, 441, 453, 455.
G*ri*hya-sûtra, I, introd. xlviii.
*g*uhû, offering-spoon, I, 67 seq., 139; II, 23; portions of victim for *g*uhû, 204.
*G*yotish*t*oma, II, 403.

harî, the two bay steeds, are the *Rik* and Sâman, II, 371.
Harivant (Indra), II, 399.
hâriyogana (graha), II, 289, 370 seq.
Hasta (nakshatra), I, 286.
havirdhâna, I, 14; Soma-cart shed, II, 126 seq.; sacred to Vish*n*u, 126, 131; belongs exclusively to the gods, 146; Soma placed there, 160.
haviryag*ñ*a, I, introd. xv, xlviii.
havis, I, 151.
havishk*ri*t, I, 27.
havishpaṅkti, I, 16.
havyadâti, I, 107.
heart, of victim, is roasted first, II, 201; offered, 204.
Heaven and Earth. See dyâvâ-p*ri*thivî.
hiṅ, I, 100, 325.
Hira*n*yagarbha, I, 271.
Hira*n*yastûpa, I, 175.
hira*n*yavatî-âhuti, II, 52 seq.
horn, of black antelope, used for scratching, II, 32, 33; taking up earth, 43.
horse, present at production and carrying forward of fire, I, 297 seq.; white horse (symbol of sun), dakshi*n*â at *S*unâsîrîya, 447; at the Sadya*h*krî, II, 115; at Soma-sacrifice, 348.

hotrâ (sa*m*yâgay-), II, 287.
Hotraka (Maitrâvaru*n*a, Brâhma*n*â*kkh*a*m*sin, and A*kkh*âvâka), II, 295 seq., 324.
Hot*ri*, seven, I, 223.

i*d*â, I, 216 seq.; II, 60.
I*d*a*h*, I, 147, 152.
immortality, gained by the gods, II, 147.
Indra, representative of the Kshatra, I, introd. xvi seq.; slays V*ri*tra, I, 20, 52, 166, 175, 416, 452; II, 265; slays Vi*s*varûpa, I, 47, 164; is deity of sacrifice, I, 129; the Vasu of gods, 176; overturns Asuras' fire-altar, 287; resides with man, 338; is the blazing fire, 340; Indra Vim*ri*dh, 375; II, 430; Indra and Maruts = Kshatra and Vi*s*, I, 399; Agni, Varu*n*a, and Indra, leaders of gods, 449 seq.; Indra, Soma, and Agni, II, 22; he is born of Yag*ñ*a and Vâ*k*, 32; the ruddy cow belongs to Indra v*ri*trahan, 62; Indra's amours, 81; called Kau*s*ika, Gautama, 82; attended by the Maruts, 93; Indra the chief of gods, 93; is the Sun, 96; delights in songs, 146; animal offering to, 220; Indra with the Vasus, Rudras, and Âdityas, 241; is assigned a special (chief's) share, 241; everything submits to him, even the wind, 242; leader of the sacrifice, 262; the cow of plenty (Kâmaduh) his special portion, 294; Indra marutvant, 335 seq., 347; stands over everything, 398; Indra harivant, 399; Indra sho*d*a*s*in, 400; Indra, Agni, and Sûrya, superior to others, 402; Indra vi*s*vakarman, 431; Indra, the strongest of gods, 433; is the Brâhma*n*â*kkh*a*m*sin, ib.; to Indra belong *Rik* and Sâman, 436; he is produced by them, 438; Indra and Parvata, leaders in battle, 450.
Indrâgnî, win the race, I, 371; cake to, at Âgraya*n*esh*t*i, ib.; at Dâkshâya*n*esh*t*i, 375, 378; at Varu*n*apraghâsâ*h*, 393; at Mahâhavis, 419; are the Kshatra, 371; outbreathing and inbreathing, 393; animal offering to, 221; are all the gods, 225; the universe, 292; cup to them, 323.
indra*s*atru, I, 165.
Indrâvish*n*û, divide one thousand by three, II, 62.
Irâvatî, I, 110.
ish*t*i (yagati-offering), I, 263.

Ka (Pra*g*âpati), I, 8, 395; II, 410.
Kadrû (and Supar*n*î), II, 52 seq., 149 seq.; is the earth, 149.
Kaho*d*a Kaushîtaki, I, 370.
kâmaduh, cow of plenty, Indra's special portion, II, 294.
*K*amasâdhvaryu, II, 287.
*K*amasins, enumerated, II, 287; touch the cups, 373.
kâmyesh*t*i, I, 97.
Kâ*n*va-*s*âkhâ, I, introd. xxviii seq., xxxviii, xliv seq.
kapâlas, I, 32; arrangement of, 34.
*K*arakas, I, introd. xxvi; a *K*araka Adhvaryu curses Yâg*ñ*avalkya, II, 197, 262, 297, 298.
karambha, porridge, I, 395; II, 303.
Karatoyâ, I, 104.
Karîra fruit, offered at Varu*n*apraghâsâ*h*, I, 394.
kârshmarya tree, Rakshas-killer, II, 89.
*k*aru (pap of whole rice-grains), I, 7, 211, 410.
Kâ*t*h*aka, I, introd. xxvi seq.
*k*aturhot*ri* formulas, II, 452.
*k*âturmâsya, seasonal sacrifice, I, 383 seq.; detached sacrifices, 407.
*k*atushprâ*s*ya, I, 275, 292, 373.
*k*âtvâla, pit, II, 116, 379.
Kâtyâyana, I, introd. xxxv seq., xl.
Kaukûsta (Kaükthasta), II, 426.
Kavasha Ailûsha (Ailushîputra), I, introd. xxxv.
khadira stick, therewith Soma carried off by Gâyatrî, II, 151.
*kh*andoma, II, 402.
Kilâta, Asura priest, I, 29.
kim-purusha, I, 51.
kim u, II, 432.
king, paying homage to (Soma as) supreme ruler, II, 79; attended by heralds and headmen, 87.
*K*itrâ (nakshatra), I, 286.

knot, attribute of Varuna, I, 73; II, 146.
Kosala-Videhas, I, introd. xlii.
Krisânu (Gandharva archer), I, 183; II, 72; footless archer, 78.
Krittikâs, I, 282.
Kshatra, served by the Vis, I, 393; Kshatra and Vis, Indra and Maruts, 399; Varuna and Maruts, 401.
Kshatriya, oppressor of Vaisya, I, 82; served by Vis, 94; lives on them, II, 66; before a Kshatriya approaching the people go down, 228; should always have recourse to a Brâhman, 270.
kukkuta, I, 30.
Kurukshetra, II, 275.
Kurus, I, introd. xliii, 377.
Kuru-Pañkâlas, I, introd. xli seq., 192; nature of their speech, II, 50.
kusa-plant, yellow, a substitute for Soma-plants, II, 422.
kusâ, II, 309.
Kusri Vâgasravasa, I, introd. xxxiii.
Kyavana Bhârgava (Âṅgirasa), II, 272 seq.

lines, drawing of, on hearth, I, 2, 276; round the altar (parigraha), 62; round foot-print of Soma-cow, II, 60; one line drawn with the sphya in following the fire carried to uttaravedi, 121.
lute, created by the gods, II, 53.

madantî, (hot) lustral water, II, 100.
madhukânda, I, introd. xxxiv; madhu-brâhmana, II, 277.
Mâdhuki, I, 300.
madhyama (kânda), I, introd. xxix.
Mâdhyandina, I, introd. xxviii seq.
mâdhyandina-pavamâna (stotra), II, 333, 336.
mâdhyandina-savana, belongs to Trishtubh, II, 250; to the Rudras, 330, 331 seq.
Maghavan, I, introd. xi.
mahâbhishava, great pressing, II, 244, 256.
mahad uktham, II, 430.
mahâhavis, great oblation, at Sâkamedhâh (offerings to Agni, Soma, Savitri, Sarasvatî, and Pûshan, Indrâgnî, Mahendra, and Visvakarman), I, 417 seq.
mahârâga, II, 338.
mahâvrata, II, 429.
mahâvratiya-graha, II, 429.
Mahendra, I, 182, 419; II, 338.
mâhendra, graha, II, 337 seq.
Maitrâvaruna (or Prasâstri), assistant of Hotri, I, 223, 224; II, 183; prompts the Hotri, 188; his cup meets the Vasatîvarî water, 235 seq.
Maitrâvaruna-graha, II, 269 seq.; mixed with milk, 271; shape of cup, 278.
Maitrâyanî-samhitâ, I, introd. xxvi.
man, the highest of animals, II, 210; his skin now on the cow, 9.
Manas (mind) and Vâk (speech), I, 124 seq.; II, 55; inherited by gods and Asuras respectively, 30; are heaven and earth, ib.
mânasa-stotra, II, 451.
Manâvî, wife of Manu, I, 29.
Manes (Fathers). See Pitarah.
Manotâ deity, offering to, II, 203, 393.
mantha, gruel, II, 278.
Manthin graha, II, 278 seq., 316 seq., 332.
Manu, his bull, I, 29; Manu and the fish, 216 seq.
Mârgâlîya, shed, in Yagña's arm, II, 126; erection, 148.
Marka and Sanda, two Asuras, II, 279 seq.
marriage between kinsfolk, I, 238.
Mârtânda, abortive child of Aditi, II, 12.
Maruts, representative of the Visah, I, introd. xvii, 387, 393, 399; divided into troups of seven each, 394; threaten to destroy creatures, 393, 394; Marutah sântapanâh, 409; Maruto grihamedhinah, 409; Marutah krîdinah, 416; Maruts accompany Indra, II, 93; Dyutâna, son of the Maruts, 144; Ûrdhvanabhas, son of the Maruts, 198; animal offering to Maruts, 220; assist Indra in smiting Vritra, 334; embryo of slaughtered cow offered to Maruts, 396.
marutvatîya (graha), II, 332, 334, 336; sastra, 337.

Mâtarisvan's cauldron, I, 186.
Medhâtithi's ram, Indra, II, 81.
Menâ (? wife) of Vrishanasva, II, 81.
metres, I, 80, 96; Soma supreme ruler of metres, II, 65; they are his attendants, 87; their part in the guest-offering, 88; in the production of fire, 91; at Soma-sacrifice, 314, 315, 329; are the draught cattle of the gods, 369 seq.
milk, should be cooked, I, 330; sustains creatures, 385 seq., 388; offered to Vâyu, 446.
mill-stones, I, 38 seq.
mind, is sacrifice, II, 30; heaven, ib.
Mitra, the waning fire, I, 341; the waning moon, 380; implants seed in Varuna, ib.; (friendly) tying of foot by Mitra, II, 57; what is of Mitra is not of Varuna, ib.; Mitra, priesthood, can exist without the Kshatra, but not vice versâ, 270; every one's friend, 271; Mitra is the brahman, the truth, 272; Varuna, Mitra, and Agni, 285.
Mitrâvarunau, offering of payasyâ to, at Dâkshâyaneshti, I, 375 seq., 378 seq.; they are the out-breathing and in-breathing, II, 39; intelligence and will, 269; brahman and kshatra, 270; anûbandhyâ cow to, 387.
Mlekkha, speaks barbarous, unintelligible language, II, 32.
mole-hill used for hearth, I, 278; for burying Rudra's oblation in, 441; for burying the embryo of a slaughtered cow, II, 396.
months, names of, II, 301.
moon, waxing and waning = Varuna and Mitra, I, 381.
Mrigasîrsha I, 284.
Mûgavantah, I, 443.
musala (mortar), I, 26.

Nabhas, a name of Agni, II, 118.
Nada Naishadha, resides with man, I, 338.
nails, cutting of, II, 6.
Nakshatra, etymology, I, 288, 452; lights of righteous men, 269; those suitable for agnyâdhâna, 282 seq.; the meshes of cloth belong to them, II, 10.
nâkshatra name, I, 251.
name, a second, to be taken, II, 154.
nânada-sâman, II, 401.
Narâsamsa, I, 136, 146, 233.
nârâsamsa cups, belong to Fathers, II, 154.
navarâtra, II, 414.
Neshtri, priest, leads up the Patnî, II, 190; takes the Agnîdh in his lap, 368.
nidhana, II, 310, 311.
nigada, I, 114, 202.
nigrâbha formula, II, 245.
nigrâbhyâ, the Vasatîvarî water poured into the Hotri's cup, II, 236; used for moistening the Soma-plants, 240, 242; etymology, 243, 247.
nirvapana, I, 168.
nishkevalya-sastra, II, 339.
nîvi, tuck of nether garment, sacred to Manes, I, 368, 435; (Soma), II, 29.
nivid, formulas, II, 235.
north, quarter of men, II, 2, ; of Pathyâ Svasti (speech), 50; sacrifice performed north, 102.
north-east, II, 8.

omentum. See vapâ.
oni, II, 66.
oshadhi, etymology, I, 323.
Otos and Ephialtes, myth of (piling of Ossa on Olympus, and Pelion on Ossa), I, 286.
ox, present at production and carrying forward of fire, I, 297; its flesh not to be eaten by consecrated, II, 11; to be eaten according to Yâgñâvalkya, ib.; black oxen, insure rain, 78; is of Agni's nature, 390.

pâkayagña, I, introd. xlviii, 333.
palâsa, tree, identified with the brahman, I, 90; central leaflet of palâsa leaf used for offering on to Rudra, 439; branch used for driving the calves from the cows, 183; for driving Soma, II, 78.
Pânini, I, introd. xxxv seq.
pañkadasa-stoma, I, 96; II, 308, 333.
Pañkâlas, I, introd. xli.
Pâñki, I, 61, 300.
pankti, II, 315.

pânnegana water, used by Patnî for cleansing the victim, II, 190.
parâk, II, 310.
Parâvasu, I, 137.
paridhi, enclosing-stick, I, 87 seq.; offering of, 245; II, 125.
parigraha, line of enclosure, I, 60 seq.
parna, I, 183; II, 78.
Parvata, Indra and Parvata, leaders in battle, II, 450.
paryagnikarana, I, 45; II, 187.
paryâya (turn of chanting), II, 308 seq.
pasupurodâsa, II, 199 seq.
Patañgali, I, introd. xxxvi seq.
path to Gods or Fathers, I, 267.
Pathyâ svasti, offering to, II, 49, 50, 386.
Patnî, girding of, I, 71 seq.; seat, 72; interrogated by Pratiprasthâtri as to her lovers, 396; the house her resting-place, II, 61; exchanges looks with Udgâtri, 368; touches (bids welcome to) Soma when he enters the hall, 87; anoints axle of Soma-cart, 130; is led up by Neshtri to cleanse the victim, 190 seq.
patnî-sâla, II, 448.
patnîsamyâga, I, 75, 256 seq.; not performed at Prâyanîyeshti, II, 52; at animal offerings performed with tail of victim, II, 215.
patnîvant, II, 365 seq.
pâtnîvata-graha, II, 365 seq.
pâtra, cup, II, 259.
pavamâna (stotra), II, 307.
pavamâneshti, I, 304.
pavitra (strainer, purifier), consisting of two stalks of grass, I, 19; II, 16; of one, three, seven, or twenty-one stalks, 17; (straining-cloth), 258.
payasyâ, clotted curds offered to Mitrâvarunau, 378 seq.; preparation, 381; sexual union with whey, 388, 394.
pebbles, used for hearth, I, 280.
phâlguna plants, a substitute for Soma-plants, II, 421.
Phalgunî, I, 285.
pinda, (round) rice-cakes to deceased ancestors, I, 366.
Pindapitriyagña, I, 361 seq.
pishta-peshana, I, 41.
Pitarah (Manes, Fathers); conditions of existence assigned to them by Pragâpati, I, 361; Pitarah somavantah, barhishadah, agnishvâttâh, 421; path to Pitarah, 267; the nîvi (tuck) sacred to Pitarah, 368, 435; the thrum of cloth sacred to, II, 9; ruddy cows with reddish-white eyes belong to Pitarah, 62; part of post dug into the ground is sacred to them, 143; pit ditto, 169.
pitritîrtha, I, 365.
Pitriyagña, oblation to Manes, I, 361 seq., 420 seq.
plaksha (ficus infectoria) branches used to cover the altar, II, 120, 202.
plants, are the vis, II, 65.
porcupine-quill used for shaving, I, 450.
pra, I, 101; II, 435.
pradakshina, I, 37, 45, 272, 442: cf. prasalavi, apas., dakshinîkâra.
Pragâpati, father of gods and Asuras, I, 54; II, 301; creates and becomes exhausted, I, 173; enamoured of his daughter, 208 seq.; creates Agni, 322 seq., 342; creates living beings, 384; heals the creatures stricken by Varuna, 391; assigns conditions of life to creatures, 361; identified with Agni, 346; with Agni and Savitri, 386; is Daksha, 375; is vasishtha, 376; man nearest to him, 384; Pragâpati, lord of thought and speech, II, 17; becomes an embryo, 28; is the sacrifice, the year, 37; exhausted, fortifies himself by animal offering, 217 seq.; arbiter between Indra and Vâyu, 268; is over and above the thirty-one gods and heaven and earth, 411; over and above the three worlds, 424; libation to Pragâpati-Vâyu, 451.
pragâpati-tanu formulas, II, 453.
prâkî, the easterly line, I, 63; II, 33; forms the back-bone of vedi, 112.
prâkîna-vamsa, II, 3; used for the consecrated, 4; approved of, 5.

prâna, I, 19, 120: cf. airs, vital.
prânadâna, I, 94, 438.
pranîtâh, I, 9, 23, 265; II, 12.
pra-ruk, I, 161.
prasalavi (pradakshina), I, 442; strings twisted, II, 29.
prâsitra, fore-portion (Brahman's), I, 212.
prâsitra-harana, I, 69, 212.
prastara, I, 84 seq., 92 seq.; (the sacrificer), 240 seq., 389, 405; II, 89; amends made on the prastara, 102; anointed when thrown into the fire, 103, 104.
prastâva, II, 310.
prasthita, II, 198, 372.
Prastotri, II, 310, 311.
Prâtahsavana, II, 238 seq.; belongs to Gâyatrî, 250; to the Vasus, 350.
Prâtaranuvâka, morning-prayer, II, 226 seq.
Pratîdarsa Svaikna, I, 376.
pratigara, Adhvaryu's response, II, 231, 326, 328, 361.
pratihâra, II, 310.
Pratihartri, II, 310, 347.
Pratiprasthâtri, assistant of Adhvaryu, roasts the omentum, II, 196.
pratyabhighârana, replenishing, I, 201, 414.
pratyâsrâvana, I, 132, 140.
praüga-sastra, II, 324.
pravara, I, introd. xvi, 95, 114 seq., 131 seq.
pravargya, I, 44; II, 104.
pravritta (pravrita) homa, II, 305.
prayâga (fore-offering), five at havirya*gña*, I, 138 seq., 318 seq., 445; four at avabhritha, II, 382; nine at Vaisvadeva, Varunapraghâsâh, &c., 390, 400, 418; eleven at animal offering, II, 185, 210.
Prâyanîyeshti, belongs to Aditi, II, 47; oblations to Pathyâ svasti, Agni, Soma, Savitri, and Aditi, 49-51.
press-board (adhishavana), II, 140.
pressing-skin, round and dyed red, II, 140.
press-stones (five), II, 140, 227.
priest, medium of worship, II, 3.
prishad-âgya, clotted butter, I, 404.
prishtha-stotra, II, 339, 403; -sâman, 406.
prishthya shadaha, II, 402, 403, 405.
prokshanî, sprinkling water, I, 20, 83; II, 122, 139, 142, 159, 168, 181.
Prometheus, I, 186.
Punarâdheya, I, 285, 313 seq.
Punarvasû, I, 285.
puraskarana, II, 436, 440.
purîsha, I, 64.
pûrnâhuti, full-offering, I, 302; II, 25.
purodâs, I, 32.
purodâsa, preparation of, I, 42 seq.; etymology, 162.
purohita, I, introd. xii, 377; II, 270.
puroruk, preliminary formula, II, 235, 280, 295.
Purûravas, I, 389; II, 91.
Pûshan, distributer of portions, I, 53; toothless, 211; identified with the earth, 418; II, 57; represents (prosperity) cattle, II, 22; guardian of paths, 57; Pûshan's speed is the wind, 205; animal offering to, 219.
pûti, II, 8.

Quarters (dis), oblation of whey to disah, pradisah, âdisah, vidisah, uddisah, I, 382; oblation of fat gravy, II, 209.

Rakshas, etymology, I, 8; roam about the air, ib.; II, 16; pursue women, 35.
ram, image of, at Varuna-praghâsâh, I, 395 seq.; Varuna's victim, ib.
Râma Aupatasvini, II, 425.
rathantara-sâman, I, 196, 222; II, 339, 403.
rauhina (fire-altar constructed by Asuras), I, 286.
razor, copper, I, 450; II, 7.
reed, used for anointing, being a thunderbolt, II, 15; for intertwining with zone, 28.
region (dis). See quarter.
repetition of sacrificial performance to be avoided, I, 80.
Ribhus, II, 361.
Rig-veda, arrangement of hymns, I, introd. xvi, xx seq.
riksha (ursa major), I, 283.
Rishi, the seven, I, 282.

ritu-graha, oblations for seasons, II, 318 seq.; -pâtra, 407.
Rohinî (nakshatra), I, 283.
Rudra, purification after mentioning his name, I, 3; identified with Agni (Sarva, Bhava, Pasûnam pati), 201; is the newly-kindled fire, 340; pierces Pragâpati, 209; to Rudra is due what is injured in the sacrifice, 211; pursues creatures, 340; Tryambaka oblations to Rudra, on a cross-road, 438; the mole sacred to him, 440; Rudra with Vasus, II, 59; the Rudras accompany Soma, 93; (pasûnâm îshte, 153. See Tvashtri); Indra with Vasus, Rudras, and Âdityas, 241, 350; Rudra officiates as Hotri, 348; eleven Rudras, eight Vasus, and twelve Âdityas, 411.

sabhya, hall-fire, I, 302; resides with man (as Anasnat sâṅgamana), 338; worship of, 339.
sacrifice, Indo-Iranian, I, introd. xv, 49; is man, 78; II, 25, 126; passes from priest to priest, I, 140 seq.; from father to son, 162; as tortoise, 161; place of, II, 1 seq.; Brâhman, Râganya, and Vaisya, able to sacrifice, 4; of equal measure with the year, 16; is invisible, 19; is speech, 23, 24; the Brahman, ib.; fivefold, 24; changed into a horse, 89; animal sacrifice, 162 seq.; the Sacrifice (Yagña) is Soma, 246; fashioned like a bird, 264.
sacrificer (yagamâna), is the victim, I, 49, 62, 78; his foot used for measuring uttara-vedi, II, 119.
sacrificial essence (medhâ), I, 50.
Sadânîrâ, I, introd. xlii, 104 seq.
Sadas (text), is Yagña's belly, II, 127; construction of, 140 seq.; sacred to Indra, 141; is common to gods and men, 146.
sadasya, II, 286.
sâdhyâh, 'blessed' gods, II, 174.
sadyahkrî, kind of Soma-sacrifice, II, 114.
Sahadeva Sârñgaya, I, 376.
Saharakshas, messenger of Asuras, I, 110; II, 115.
sâhasrî, II, 414.
Sâkamedhâh (seasonal sacrifice), I, 384, 408 seq.; cake to Agni Anîkavat, 408; karu to Marutah sântapanâh, 409; ditto grihamedhinâh, ib.; darvihoma, 415; cake to Maruts, 416; mahâhavis, 417 seq.; Pitriyagña, 420.
Sakvarî metre, II, 226.
sâlâ (hall), measure of, II, 3.
salt, used for hearth, I, 278.
sâman, I, 100; is the truth, II, 97.
samâropana, lifting or mounting of fire, I, 396.
samavatta, cuttings from idâ, I, 219; II, 203; -dhânî, 207.
sambhâra, I, 276 seq.
Sâmgîvî-putra, I, introd. xxxii seq.
samî leaves, offered at Varunapraghâsâh, I, 395.
samidh, I, 91 seq., 95 seq., 146, 152.
sâmidhenî, I, 95 seq.; II, 13.
samishtayagus, one, I, 262 seq., 445; three, 390, 406, 418; nine, II, 374; the end of the sacrifice, 13, 374 seq.
samitri, butcher, cooks the victim, II, 200.
samsrava, offering of, I, 236.
samsthâ, II, 398.
samyâ, yoke-pin, used as wedge, I, 29; II, 116 seq.
samyâgye, I, 164, 307.
Samyu Bârhaspatya, I, 254.
samyuvâka, I, 236, 247, 254 seq.
Sanda and Marka, two Asuras, II, 279 seq.
sandhyâ, twilight worship, I, 344.
Sândilya, I, introd. xxxi seq., xlvi.
sânnâyya, I, 162, 178 seq., 381.
saptahotr^, I, 223.
sarabha, I, 52.
Sarasvatî, river, I, 104 seq.
Sarasvatî, goddess, oblation to, I, 418; speech, II, 22; animal offering to, 218.
sarpana, II, 299.
sarparâgñî, II, 451.
Sarva (Rudra-Agni), I, 201.
Saryâta Mânava, II, 273 seq.
sasni, I, 15.
sastra, twelve at Agnishtoma, II, 303, 325 seq.

*S*atapatha-brâhma*n*a, I, introd. xxviii seq.
*S*atarudriya-homa, I, 346.
sattra, sacrificial session, II, 402, 426, 440; sattrasya *ri*ddhi, 449.
sattrotthâna, II, 441, 447.
Sâtyayag*ñ*a (Sâtyayag*ñ*i), II, 2.
saumya-adhvara, I, 26, 114.
saumya *k*aru, II, 364.
sautrâma*n*î, I, 165.
savanîya puro*d*â*s*a, II, 230, 314, 315, 324.
sâvitra-graha, II, 357.
Savit*ri*, the intermediate progenitor (Pragâpati), I, 386; is net*ri* (leader), II, 24; repres. cattle, 49; (the sun) guardian of the west, 50; animal offering to, 221; the sun, the mind, 358.
Sâvitrî (gâyatrî), I, 356.
seasons (*ri*tu), five, I, 98; II, 16, 24, 50, 241; six, I, 281; II, 101, 289; siding with Asuras, I, 155 seq.; identified with gods and fathers, 289; with the castes, 290; the divine coursers, 382; oblation of whey, ib.; consort with Soma, 245.
session, sacrificial. See sattra; rising from, sattrotthâna.
sha*d*aha, II, 402.
sha*d*avatta, I, 229.
shash*t*ipatha, I, introd. xxix, xxxii, xlvi.
shaving, II, 6.
sheep, goats and, II, 407.
sho*d*a*s*in, stotra, II, 313, 401; *s*astra, 402; graha and sa*m*sthâ, 398; Indra, 400.
silver, not suitable for dakshi*n*âs, I, 322.
sin, confession of, I, 397; expiation of, 398, 406; II, 385.
snakes, west their quarter, II, 4; the fore-edge (?) belongs to them, 10.
Soma, plant (juice) and moon, I, 176; fetched by Gâyatrî, 183, 452; II, 52, 241; establishes the fire, I, 313; offering to Soma (and Agni) at Pit*ri*yag*ñ*a, 364; Indra, Soma, and Agni, II, 22; purchase of, 63 seq.; Soma is seed, ib.; Soma-cloth, wrapper and head-band, 64; picking of Soma-plants, ib.; Soma the Kshatra, 65, 87; meting out of Soma, 66; tied up in the form of a man, 68; bargaining for Soma, 69 seq.; Soma driven on car, 74; grows on mountains, 77; seated on throne of udumbara wood, 84; enters the hall, ib.; guest-offering to Soma, 85 seq.; Soma attended by the Rudras, 93; Soma strengthened (â-pyai), 100; Soma is V*ri*tra, 100, 271, 314; Agni, Soma, and Vish*n*u form the thunderbolt, 108; Soma, when carried off by Gâyatrî, was enclosed in two golden cups, 150; Soma placed on sacrificer's lap, 156; Soma the nimble, 157; enters the Havirdhâna, 160; is Vanaspati, 208; animal offering to, 218; Soma taken down from cart, 227; watched in the Âgnîdhra, ib.; pressing of, 238 seq.; meting out, 240; deposits his three bodies (or lights) in the three worlds, 242; consorts with the seasons, 245; explanation of the name, 246; pressing, 249; great pressing, 256; oppresses his family-priest B*ri*haspati, 258; king Soma struck in the eye by Varu*n*a, 281; *k*aru to Soma, 363; substitutes of Soma-plants, 421 seq. — On Soma-myth generally, II, introd. xi seq.
Soma-kraya*n*î, cow, is Vâ*k*; II, 54, 56, 58; her seven foot-prints, 59; colour of, 62; her virtues, 69; dust of foot-print scattered behind Gârhapatya, 156.
Soma-sacrificer, sacred, II, 35.
Soma-seller, II, 69; beaten, 71.
south, quarter of Fathers, II, 2, 4, 165.
spaces, the six (urvî), I, 136.
speech. See Vâ*k*; four grades of speech, II, 268.
sphya (wooden sword), I, 6, 13, 54, 66; II, 60, 121.
spoons, sacrificial, I, 67 seq.; brushing of, 69 seq., 78 seq.; separation (vyûhana) of, 236, 404.
sprinkling (with lustral water), I, 2, 20, 83; II, 122, 139, 143, 159, 168, 181.
*s*râddha (pit*ri*yag*ñ*a), I, 361 seq., 420.

srausha*t*, I, 132, 140, 142, 239.
*S*rauta-sacrifices, I, 26.
S*riñg*ayas, a prosperous tribe, I, 376.
*sr*itâvadâna, I, 429.
sru*k*, offering-spoon, I, 67; II, 20, 23.
sruva, dipping-spoon, I, 68; II, 20.
staff, the Dîkshita's, a thunderbolt, II, 34; reaches up to his mouth, ib.
stambaya*g*ur-hara*n*a, I, 55; II, 118.
stoma, kinds of, II, 308.
stomayoga, II, 311.
stotra, twelve at Agnish*t*oma, II, 303; preparation (upâkara*n*a) for, 307 seq.; 325 seq.
strainer, straining-cloth. See pavitra, da*s*âpavitra.
Subrahma*n*yâ, priest, drives the Soma cart, II, 77; litany, 81, 230.
*S*ûdra, must not enter the prâ*k*inava*m*sa, II, 4.
Sukanyâ, daughter of *S*aryâta Mânava, II, 273.
*S*ukra graha, II, 278 seq., 316 seq., 332.
sûktavâka, I, 236 seq., 247 seq., 405.
*s*ûlâvabh*r*itha, spit-bath, II, 215.
Sun, rays of, are the righteous dead, I, 269; are purifiers, II, 18; they are the gods, 224; the sun is the final goal, I, 271; moving north and south, 289; (Vivasvat) is the Âditya, II, 13; the eye, 39; wards off evil spirits, 77; is Indra, 96; (sûrya) given as dakshi*n*â to the Aṅgiras, 114; its rays are the gods sipping motes of light, 254; the lotus of the heavens, 277; offering to, 342; the eye of Mitra, Varu*n*a, and Agni, 343.
*S*unâ*s*îrîya (seasonal sacrifice), I, 384, 444 seq.
sunwise circumambulation. Cf. pradakshi*n*a, dakshi*n*îkâra, prasalavi.
Supar*n*î (and Kadrû), II, 52 seq., 149 seq.; is Vâ*k*, 149.
Supar*n*îkâdrava (Saupar*n*akâdrava), II, 150.
Suplan Sâr*ñg*aya, I, 376.
*s*ûrpa, winnowing-basket, I, 11, 30, 398.
Sûrya (with Agni and Vâyu), I, 325, 327; II, 453; Sûrya is death, I, 343; his rays attached to creatures, ib.; wards off evil spirits, II, 77; given as dakshi*n*â to the Aṅgiras, 114; the soul of the universe, 343; Indra, Agni and Sûrya, superior to others, 402.
*S*ush*n*a, the Dânava, enters the eye of man, II, 14.
svagâ, I, 244, 259; II, 379.
svâhâ, I, 324 (derivation of), 148 seq., 153; II, 252.
svaru, chip, II, 173, 186.
*S*vetaketu (Auddâlaki), I, introd. xli seq.; II, 100, 314.
Svish*t*ak*r*it, I, 129, 151, 199 seq., 372.
*s*yenah*r*ita plant, a substitute for Soma-plants, II, 422.

Taittirîyas, I, introd. xxvi seq.
Takshan, recites for Âru*n*i, I, 335.
tanu, II, 10.
tanûhavir-ish*t*i, I, 304, 317.
Tanûnapât, I, 146 seq., 152; is Vâyu, II, 94, 95.
Tânûnaptra, covenant of Tanûnapât, II, 93 seq.
tapas (austerity), world conquered by, II, 111.
thousand, one, divided by three, II, 62.
thunderbolt, composed of anîka, *s*alya, and kulmala, II, 108.
Tittiri (*s*lokâ*h*), I, introd. xxxviii.
Traikakuda ointment, II, 15.
trayî vidyâ, II, 436.
trees, fit for sacrificial purposes, I, 90.
Trikakud, mount, originally V*r*itra's eye, II, 15.
trirâtra (sahasradakshi*n*a), II, 414.
Trish*t*ubh, is the sky, I, 195, 205; the air, 234; the kshatra, II, 87.
Trita, I, introd. xvii, 47 seq.
T*r*itîya-savana, II, 350 seq.; belongs to *G*agatî, 250.
Tryambakâ*h* (seasonal offerings), I, 437 seq.; offered to Rudra, 438.
tryaṅga, the three limbs, the portion of Agni svish*t*ak*r*it in animal offerings, II, 205, 207.
Tumi*ñg*a Aupoditeya, I, 271.
Tura Kâvasheya, I, introd. xxxi seq.
Tutha (the brahman), II, 344.
Tvash*t*ri, father of Vi*s*varûpa, I, 47.

164 seq.; offering to, 258; obtains the forms from Agni, 314; victim and stake for Tvash*t*ri, II, 177; pa*s*ûnâm îsh*t*e, (? 153), 180; spits upon the head of a victim, 202; fashions the seed, 367; dispenser of boons and healer, 374.
tyâga, dedicatory formula, I, 303.

udâna, I, 19, 76, 120.
udavasânîyesh*t*i, II, 389.
udayanîyesh*t*i, II, 48, 51, 386 seq.
Udgât*ri*, I, introd. xx seq.; chanting of, II, 307 seq., 310; exchanges looks with Patnî, 368.
udgîtha, II, 310.
udumbara post (in Sadas), II, 141; made of the sacrificer's size, 142; touching of, 448, 453, 454.
udumbara wood, food and strength, II, 34.
uktha (= *s*astra), II, 294, 313.
ukthavîrya, II, 327.
Ukthya-graha, II, 292 seq., 332, 336; distribution among hotrakas, 295 seq., 339, 370; -sthâlî and pâtra, 293.
Ukthya sacrifice, II, 326, 370, 397.
ulûkhala, I, 26.
Unnet*ri*, calls for the *s*raushat at the hâriyogana libation, II, 372; two Unnet*ri*s, 417.
upabh*ri*t, I, 67 seq., 139; portions of victim for upabh*ri*t, II, 205.
upakara*n*a, the introducing of the stotra, II, 401.
upâ*ms*u-graha, II, 238 seq., 244, 248; offered, 255; is the day, and offered at night, 261.
upâ*ms*u-savana, stone, II, 238; is Âditya Vivasvat, 240, 256, 354.
upâ*ms*uyâga (low-voiced offering), I, 118, 192, 372.
upanâmuka, I, 326.
uparava, sounding-hole, II, 135 seq.
upasad (homage or siege), II, 104 seq.; three, 108; or twelve, 109; the fasting connected with them, 110; at sattras, 442.
upasarganî, I, 42, 65.
upastara*n*a, I, 192.
upavakt*ri*, II, 452.
upavasatha, fast-day, I, 1, 5, 291; II, 223.
upavesha, I, 33, 125.
upayâ*g*a, by-offerings of Pratiprasthât*ri*, II, 204; eleven, 210, 212; four additional (aty-upaya*g*), 214.
upayâma, formula of 'support,' II, 259 seq.
Ûrdhvanabhas (? Vâyu), son of the Maruts, II, 198.
Urva*s*î, I, 389; II, 91.
urvî, I, 136.
ushânâ (the Soma-plant), II, 314.
ush*n*îsha, II, 392.
utkara, I, 25, 54.
utpavana, I, 76.
uttara, II, 2.
uttarâhi, II, 50.
uttaravedi, I, 388, 392, 393, 417; II, 113; is Vâ*k*, 115; measure of, 116; is a woman, 120.

Vâ*g*apeya, II, 398.
Vâ*g*asaneyaka, I, introd. xxxix.
Vâ*g*asaneyina*h*, I, introd. xxxvi seq.
Vaikar*n*au, I, introd. xlii.
vaisar*g*ina oblations, II, 155 seq., 442.
Vai*s*vadeva (seasonal sacrifice), I, 383 seq.; cake to Agni, 386; *k*aru for Soma, ib.; cake for Savit*ri*, ib.; *k*aru for Sarasvatî, ib.; cake for Maruts, 387; payasyâ to Vi*s*ve devâ*h*, 388; cake to Heaven and Earth, ib.
Vai*s*vadeva-graha, II, 323 seq., 359 seq.; (mahâ-), 360.
Vai*s*vadeva-*s*astra, II, 360 seq.
Vai*s*vânara-graha, II, 298.
Vâ*k* (speech) and Manas (mind), I, 124 seq.; II, 55 seq.; inherited by Asuras and gods respectively, II, 30; Vâ*k* wooed by Ya*gñ*a, 30 seq.; sent by the gods to the Gandharvas, 53; given as dakshi*n*â to the Aṅgiras, 114; becomes a lioness, 115; Vâ*k* speaks intelligibly in men, 267, 268; her thousandfold progeny, 414, 436; pith of Vâ*k*, 450.
Vâ*k*aspati, lord of speech, is the out-breathing, II, 250.
vâkovâkya, II, 453.
vakshva, II, 384.
Vâmadevya-sâman, I, 222.
va*ms*a (roof-beam), II, 3, 146.
va*ms*as, lists of, I, introd. xxxiv.

vanaspati (lord of forest, tree), oblation to, II, 208, 395; is Soma, 208.
vapâ, omentum, cut out and roasted, II, 194 seq.; offered, 198, 392.
vapâsrapanî, omentum-spit, II, 194.
varsha, varshâh, I, 315.
Vârshnya (Vârshna), II, 2.
Varuna, noose of, I, 72, 391; II, 161; (noose of sacred order), 181; knot, I, 73; rope, II, 57, 181; he establishes the fire and becomes king Varuna, I, 313; is the brightly-burning fire, 340; the waxing moon, 380 (cf. Mitra, the waning); seizes creatures by disease, 391, 398; is the Kshatra, 393, 401; the ram his victim, 395; Varuna guardian of conjugal vow, 397; Agni, Varuna, and Indra, leaders of gods, 449 seq.; oblation to Varuna and the Maruts, 394, 395; Varuna attended by Âdityas, II, 93; swearing by Varuna (?), 216; animal offering to, 221; Varuna the Kshatra, cannot exist without the priesthood, 270; strikes king Soma in the eye, 281; Varuna, Mitra, and Agni, 285; king Varuna has made a path for the sun, 380.
Varunapraghâsâh (seasonal sacrifice), I, 384, 391 seq.; cake to Indrâgnî, 393; payasyâ to Varuna and to the Maruts, 394; cake to Ka, 395; dishes of karambha (porridge) to Varuna and the Maruts, 395 seq.
vasâ, fat gravy, II, 205; offered (vasâhoma), 207.
vasâhomahavanî, II, 203.
vasatîvarî water, II, 147, 222 seq.; carrying around of, 225, 454; etymology, 226, 231; meets the water in Maitrâvaruna cup, 235; in the Hotri's cup it becomes the Nigrâbhyâh, 236, 293.
vashat (vaushat), I, 88, 135, 143, 171, 193 seq., 197 seq., 198.
Vasishthayagña, I, 376.
Vâstavya (Rudra), I, 200.
Vasu, I, 176; the Vasus accompany Rudra, 59, Agni, II, 93; Indra with Vasus, Rudras, and Âdityas, 241, 350; eight Vasus, eleven Rudras, twelve Âdityas, 411.
vâyavya, Soma-cups, II, 158, 267.
Vâyu (with Agni and Sûrya), I, 325, 327; II, 453; oblation of drops (stoka) to Vâyu, II, 195; sent by the gods to ascertain if Vritra be slain, 265; leader of beasts, 361; libation to Pragâpati-Vâyu, 451.
veda, bunch of grass, I, 41, 84.
vedi, etymology, I, 60; measure and construction of, 62 seq.; lustration of, 423; Soma-altars prepared, II, 111; vedi is as large as the earth, 175.
Vedic science, threefold, I, 24.
victim, kinds of, I, 50; killing of, II, 178 seq.; mode of killing, 189; skinning and cutting open, 193 seq.; cutting up, 200 seq.; offering of portions, 204 seq.; touching of, 209; the eleven, 218 seq.; those suitable for certain forms of sacrifice, 312, 313, 428, 429.
Videgha Mâthava, I, introd. xli seq., 104 seq.
Videhas, I, introd. xlii.
vidhriti, stalks of grass laid across the barhis, I, 93; II, 89.
vikankata tree, when created, I, 325.
virâg, I, 11; II, 68, 112; incomplete, I, 390; II, 374.
vis, serves the Kshatra, I, 393; eat no offerings, 398; is the Kshatriya's food, II, 66; go down before a Kshatriya, 228.
Vishnu, three steps of, I, 15, 268; II, 155; Vishnu a dwarf, I, 59; etymology, 73; is the upper (Agni the lower) half of the sacrifice, II, 12; is the consecrated, 29; formula referring to Vishnu used for atonement, 35; Agni, Soma, and Vishnu form the thunderbolt, 108; fixed like an eye in the heavens, 172; to Vishnu belong the Yagus, 436.
vishtâva, II, 309.
vishtuti, II, 308 seq.
vishuvant day, II, 427.
visvadhâyas, I, 188.
visvakarman, I, 188.
Visvakarman, offering to, I, 419; with the Âdityas, II, 123; Indra, 431.

Vi*s*varûpa, son of Tvash*tri*, I, 47, 164 seq.
Vi*s*vâvasu, Gandharva, I, 90; steals Soma from Gâyatrî, II, 52.
vi*s*vâyu, I, 188.
Vi*s*ve Devâ*h* (All-gods), representative of Vi*s*, I, introd. xvi, 204, 371; oblation of *k*aru at Âgraya*n*esh*t*i, 369 seq.; share with Indra and Agni, 371; the threads of cloth belong to them, II, 10; they are the ear, 39; the air belongs to them, 208; animal offering to, 220.
vîti, I, 107.
Vivasvat (the sun), is the Âditya, II, 13; Âditya Vivasvat, the vyâna of the Soma-sacrifice, 240.
vrata, I, 1 seq.; II, 6.
vrata-dughâ, cow, II, 40, 43.
vratopanîya, I, 2.
V*ri*sha*n*a*s*va's Menâ (wife?), II, 81.
V*ri*tra, slain by Indra, I, 20 seq.; 52, 452; II, 265; by the waters, II, 242, 243, 247; (Dânava), I, 166; V*ri*tra is Soma, II, 100.
vyâna, I, 19, 20, 120.
vyû*dh*a*kh*andas (dvâda*s*âha), II, 418.

water, a thunderbolt, II, 7; the waters slay V*ri*tra, 242, 243, 247.
west, quarter of snakes, II, 4; of Savit*ri* (the sun), 50; sleeping with head towards, forbidden, II, 4.
wether, hair-tuft of, II, 125.
whey, offering of, to divine coursers (seasons), I, 382; is seed, 388.
wind, tells the gods the thoughts of men, II, 94.
woman, given to vain things, II, 53.
worlds, three, II, 26.
worship, is truth, I, 313.

Ya*gñ*a (sacrifice) wooes Vâ*k*, II, 30 seq.
Yâ*gñ*avalkâni brâhma*n*âni, I, introd. xxxvi seq.
Yâ*gñ*avalkya, I, introd. xxx seq., 5, 76, 77, 271, 333, 370, 384 (contradicted); II, 2; (advocates the eating of the flesh of cows and oxen), 11, 14; cursed by a *K*araka Adhvaryu, 197, 279, 425, 442.
ya*gñ*âya*gñ*îya (sâman), II, 368.
ya*gñ*opavîtin, I, 361, 424.
Yagur-veda, I, introd. xxvii.
yâ*g*yâ, I, 119, 135, 142, 170 seq., 195.
Yama, king, resides with man, I, 338; chief of Fathers, 364; Yama aṅgirasvat pit*ri*mat, 429; officiates as Brahman priest, II, 348.
yava, II, 142, 168.
yavan, I, 199.
yâvihotra, I, 199.
yûpa, sacrificial stake, I, 160; II, 21, 36, 39, 46, 101; is Ya*gñ*a's crest-lock, 126; belongs to Vish*n*u, 162, 164; cutting of, 162 seq.; size of, 166; raising of, 167 seq.; anointing of, 170; girding, 172; means of ascending to the 'blessed' gods, 174; it is eight-cornered, 174; is not thrown into the fire, ib.; is a thunderbolt, 175, 176; wife-stake, 177; eleven: see ekâda*s*inî.
Yûpâhuti, stake-offering, II, 162 seq.

ADDITIONS AND CORRECTIONS.

PART I. (VOL. XII OF SERIES.)

Page vii, line 15. Read,—Stambhayagus.
P. xvi, l. 8. Read,—arrangement.
P. xxx, l. 2. Read,—'sixty' for 'forty.'
P. xliv, l. 28. Read,—'recensions' for 'relations.'
P. 3, l. 2 seq. I now take 'pûti' in the sense of 'foul,' and would translate thus,—The reason why he touches water is this: man forsooth is impure; in that he speaks untruth, thereby he is foul within. Now water is pure: 'Having become pure, I will enter on the vow,' &c. See Part II, p. 8, n. 1.
P. 9, paragraph 18. Cf. 'mas ignis, quod ibi semen, aqua femina, quod fetus alitur humore.' Varro, L. L. 5, 61.
P. 65, last line. Read,—a composite direction.
P. 94, l. 8. Read,—'vedi' for 'prastara.'
P. 142, l. 1. Read,—'Turn ye back!' for 'draw near!' see Part II, p. 308, n. 1.
P. 166, par. 13. Read,—Now while Indra, being thus pushed aside, was moving on, he addressed . . .
P. 183, l. 6. Dele,—(the moon).
P. 210, note 1. Read twice,—'sastra' for 'sâstra.'
P. 221, l. 4 seq. Instead of,—'Before the Rakshas (come),' B. R.'s Dict. interprets, perhaps rightly, 'Safely from the Rakshas.'
P. 263, par. 27.—These same deities . . .; for an improved rendering, cf. IV, 4, 4, 5-6.
P. 308, l. 21. For,—'and in pressing,' read 'to wit, in pressing.'
P. 323, l. 15. 'whom, surely, he would not eat;' for this construction, see Part II, p. 31, n. 1.
P. 338, l. 9. Read,—Verily, with him . . .
P. 389, l. 26. Read,—'Âyu' for 'Âyus.'

PART II. (VOL. XXVI.)

P. 2, l. 4. Read,—'sacrificer' for 'sacrifice.'
P. 31, note 3. Cf. J. Muir, O. S. T. II, p. 114 note.
P. 71, note 1. According to Âp. Sr. X, 20, 12 he is to buy the Soma from a Kautsa Brâhman; otherwise from any Brâhman; otherwise from one who is not a Brâhman.
P. 77, ll. 27, 32. Read,—Subrahmanyâ.
P. 103, note 1. Read,—âpyâyanam.
P. 128, l. 26. Read,—(*kh*adis).
P. 153, l. 6, to Rudra cf. III, 7, 3, 11.
P. 201, l. 4. Read,—Samitar.
P. 224, ll. 17-20. Dele thrice 'for.'
P. 267, par. 10. Cf. A. Bergaigne, La Réligion Védique, I, p. 171.
P. 286, note 3. Read,—sadasyânâm hotrânâm.
P. 305, last line. Cf. Âp. XI, 20, 1 (pravrita-homa).
P. 324, ll. 8, 9. Read,—Sukra.
P. 334, note 2. Cf. Atharva-veda V, 4, 3; Kuhn, Herabkunft, p. 126 seq.
P. 441, l. 15. Read,—all-beneficent.

PLAN OF SACRIFICIAL GROUND.

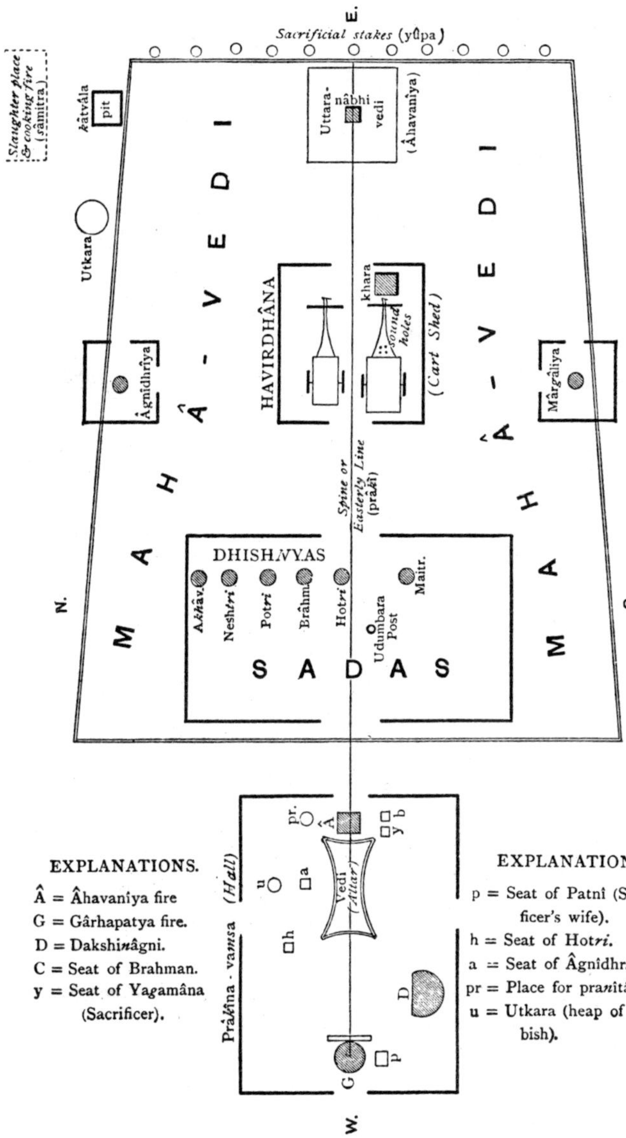

EXPLANATIONS.

Â = Âhavanîya fire
G = Gârhapatya fire.
D = Dakshinâgni.
C = Seat of Brahman.
y = Seat of Yagamâna (Sacrificer).

EXPLANATIONS.

p = Seat of Patnî (Sacrificer's wife).
h = Seat of Hotri.
a = Seat of Âgnîdhra.
pr = Place for pranîtâh.
u = Utkara (heap of rubbish).

Transliteration of Oriental Alphabets adopted for the Translations of the Sacred Books of the East.

CONSONANTS.	MISSIONARY ALPHABET. I Class.	II Class.	III Class.	Sanskrit.	Zend.	Pehlevi.	Persian.	Arabic.	Hebrew.	Chinese.
Gutturales.										
1 Tenuis	k	. . .	. . . .	क	𐬐	[illegible]	ک	ک	כּ	k
2 „ aspirata	kh	. . .	. . . .	ख	𐬑	[illegible]	. . .	. . .	כ	kh
3 Media	g	. . .	. . . .	ग	𐬔	[illegible]	گ	. . .	גּ	. . .
4 „ aspirata	gh	. . .	. . . .	घ	𐬖	[illegible]	. . .	. . .	ג	. . .
5 Gutturo-labialis	q	. . .	. . . .	. . .	. . . .	. . .	ق	ق	ק	. . .
6 Nasalis	ṅ (ng)	. . .	. . . .	ङ	{ 𐬧 (ng) / 𐬣 (N) }	. . .	. . .	. . .	. . .	. . .
7 Spiritus asper	h	. . .	. . . .	ह	𐬵 (𐬓 *hv*)	[illegible]	ه	ه	ה	h, hs
8 „ lenis	ʼ	. . .	. . . .	. . .	. . . .	. . .	ا	ا	א	. . .
9 „ asper faucalis	ʻh	. . .	. . . .	. . .	. . . .	. . .	ح	ح	ח	. . .
10 „ lenis faucalis	ʼh	. . .	. . . .	. . .	. . . .	. . .	ع	ع	ע	. . .
11 „ asper fricatus	. . .	*ʻh*	. . . .	. . .	. . . .	. . .	خ	خ	ח	. . .
12 „ lenis fricatus	. . .	*ʼh*	. . . .	. . .	. . . .	. . .	. . .	. . .	. . .	. . .
Gutturales modificatae (palatales, &c.)										
13 Tenuis	. . .	*k*	. . . .	च	𐬗	[illegible]	چ	. . .	. . .	*k*
14 „ aspirata	. . .	*kh*	. . . .	छ	. . . .	. . .	. . .	. . .	. . .	*kh*
15 Media	. . .	*g*	. . . .	ज	𐬘	[illegible]	ج	ج	. . .	. . .
16 „ aspirata	. . .	*gh*	. . . .	झ	. . . .	. . .	غ	غ	. . .	. . .
17 „ Nasalis	. . .	*ñ*	. . . .	ञ	. . . .	. . .	. . .	. . .	. . .	. . .

CONSONANTS (*continued*).	MISSIONARY ALPHABET. I Class.	II Class.	III Class.	Sanskrit.	Zend.	Pehlevi.	Persian.	Arabic.	Hebrew.	Chinese.
18 Semivocalis	y	. . .	. . .	य	𐬫, init. 𐬌 𐬌	𐭩	ي	ي	י	y
19 Spiritus asper	. . .	(*ẏ̔*)	. . .	. . .	. . .	. . .	. . .	. . .	. . .	. . .
20 „ lenis	. . .	(*ẏ̓*)	. . .	. . .	. . .	. . .	. . .	. . .	. . .	. . .
21 „ asper assibilatus	. . .	*s*	. . .	श	𐬱	𐭱	ش	ش	. . .	. . .
22 „ lenis assibilatus	. . .	*z*	. . .	. . .	𐬲	𐭦	ژ	. . .	. . .	*z*
Dentales.										
23 Tenuis	t	. . .	. . .	त	𐬙	𐭲	ت	ت	תּ	t
24 „ aspirata	th	. . .	. . .	थ	𐬚	. . .	. . .	. . .	ת	th
25 „ assibilata	. . .	. . .	TH	. . .	. . .	. . .	ث	ث	. . .	. . .
26 Media	d	. . .	. . .	द	𐬛	𐭣	د	د	דּ	. . .
27 „ aspirata	dh	. . .	. . .	ध	𐬜	. . .	. . .	. . .	ד	. . .
28 „ assibilata	. . .	. . .	DH	. . .	. . .	. . .	ذ	ذ	. . .	. . .
29 Nasalis	n	. . .	. . .	न	𐬥	𐭭	ن	ن	נ	n
30 Semivocalis	l	. . .	. . .	ल	. . .	𐭫	ل	ل	ל	l
31 „ mollis 1	. . .	*l*	. . .	ळ	. . .	. . .	. . .	. . .	. . .	. . .
32 „ mollis 2	. . .	. . .	L	. . .	. . .	. . .	. . .	. . .	. . .	. . .
33 Spiritus asper 1	s	. . .	. . .	स	𐬯	𐭮	س (ث)	س	שׂ	s
34 „ asper 2	. . .	. . .	s (ʃ)	. . .	. . .	. . .	. . .	. . .	ס	. . .
35 „ lenis	z	. . .	. . .	. . .	𐬰	𐭦	ز (ذ)	ز	ז	z
36 „ asperrimus 1	. . .	. . .	z (ʒ)	. . .	. . .	. . .	ص	ص	צ	ʒ, ʒh
37 „ asperrimus 2	. . .	. . .	ẓ (ʒ̣)	. . .	. . .	. . .	ض	. . .	. . .	. . .

Dentales modificatae (linguales, &c.)										
38 Tenuis	...	*t*	...	ट	...	...	ط	ط	ט	...
39 „ aspirata	...	*th*	...	ठ	...	...	ظ	ظ	...	...
40 Media	...	*d*	...	ड	𐬜	𐭣	...	...	...	...
41 „ aspirata	...	*dh*	...	ढ	...	...	...	ض	...	...
42 Nasalis	...	*n*	...	ण	𐬣	...	...	...	...	...
43 Semivocalis	r	...	...	र	𐬭	ו, ﻝ, ו	ر	ر	ר	...
44 „ fricata	...	*r*	...	...	...	...	...	...	...	*r*
45 „ diacritica	...	...	R	...	...	...	...	...	...	...
46 Spiritus asper	sh	...	...	ष	𐬴	𐭱	...	...	...	sh
47 „ lenis	zh	...	...	...	...	...	...	...	...	...
Labiales.										
48 Tenuis	p	...	...	प	𐬞	𐭯	پ	...	פּ	p
49 „ aspirata	ph	...	...	फ	...	...	...	...	פ	ph
50 Media	b	...	...	ब	𐬠	𐭡	ب	ب	בּ	...
51 „ aspirata	bh	...	...	भ	...	...	...	...	ב	...
52 Tenuissima	...	*p*	...	...	...	...	...	...	...	...
53 Nasalis	m	...	...	म	𐬨	𐭬	م	م	מ	m
54 Semivocalis	w	...	...	...	𐬡	...	...	...	...	w
55 „ aspirata	hw	...	...	...	...	...	...	...	...	...
56 Spiritus asper	f	...	...	...	𐬟	𐭯	ف	ف	...	f
57 „ lenis	v	...	...	व	𐬬	ו, 𐭥	و	و	ו	...
58 Anusvâra	...	*m*	...	अं	𐬅 ã	...	...	...	...	...
59 Visarga	...	*h*	...	अः	...	...	...	...	...	...

VOWELS.	MISSIONARY ALPHABET. I Class.	II Class.	III Class.	Sanskrit.	Zend.	Pehlevi.	Persian.	Arabic.	Hebrew.	Chinese.
1 Neutralis	0	. . .	. . . .	. . .	. . . .	. . .	. . .	. . .	ְ	ă
2 Laryngo-palatalis	ĕ	. . .	. . . .	. . .	. . . .	. . .	. . .	. . .	. . .	. . .
3 ,, labialis	ŏ	. . .	. . . .	. . .	. . . .	𐭠 fin.	. . .	. . .	. . .	. . .
4 Gutturalis brevis	a	. . .	. . . .	अ	𐬀	𐭠 init.	َ	َ	ַ	a
5 ,, longa	â	(*a*)	. . . .	आ	𐬁	𐭠	ـَا	ـَا	ָ	â
6 Palatalis brevis	i	. . .	. . . .	इ	𐬌	. . .	ِ	ِ	ִ	i
7 ,, longa	î	(*i*)	. . . .	ई	𐬍	𐭉	ـِي	ـِي	ִי	î
8 Dentalis brevis	*li*	. . .	. . . .	ऌ	. . . .	. . .	. . .	. . .	. . .	. . .
9 ,, longa	*lî*	. . .	. . . .	ॡ	. . . .	. . .	. . .	. . .	. . .	. . .
10 Lingualis brevis	*ri*	. . .	. . . .	ऋ	. . . .	. . .	. . .	. . .	. . .	. . .
11 ,, longa	*rî*	. . .	. . . .	ॠ	. . . .	. . .	. . .	. . .	. . .	. . .
12 Labialis brevis	u	. . .	. . . .	उ	𐬎	. . .	ُ	ُ	ֻ	u
13 ,, longa	û	(*u*)	. . . .	ऊ	𐬏	𐭅	ـُو	ـُو	וּ	û
14 Gutturo-palatalis brevis	e	. . .	. . . .	. . .	𐬈 (e) 𐬉 (*e*)	. . .	. . .	. . .	ֶ	e
15 ,, longa	ê (ai)	(*e*)	. . . .	ए	𐬉, 𐬊	𐭉	. . .	. . .	ֵ	ê
16 Diphthongus gutturo-palatalis	âi	(*ai*)	. . . .	ऐ	. . . .	. . .	ـَيْ	ـَيْ	. . .	âi
17 ,, ,,	ei (ĕi)	. . .	. . . .	. . .	. . . .	. . .	. . .	. . .	. . .	ei, êi
18 ,, ,,	oi (ŏu)	. . .	. . . .	. . .	. . . .	. . .	. . .	. . .	. . .	. . .
19 Gutturo-labialis brevis	o	. . .	. . . .	. . .	𐬋	. . .	. . .	. . .	ָ	o
20 ,, longa	ô (au)	(*o*)	. . . .	ओ	𐬌	𐭅	. . .	. . .	וֹ	. . .
21 Diphthongus gutturo-labialis	âu	(*au*)	. . . .	औ	𐬀𐬊 (*au*)	. . .	ـَوْ	ـَوْ	. . .	âu
22 ,, ,,	eu (ĕu)	. . .	. . . .	. . .	. . . .	. . .	. . .	. . .	. . .	. . .
23 ,, ,,	ou (ŏu)	. . .	. . . .	. . .	. . . .	. . .	. . .	. . .	. . .	. . .
24 Gutturalis fracta	ä	. . .	. . . .	. . .	. . . .	. . .	. . .	. . .	. . .	. . .
25 Palatalis fracta	ï	. . .	. . . .	. . .	. . . .	. . .	. . .	. . .	. . .	. . .
26 Labialis fracta	ü	. . .	. . . .	. . .	. . . .	. . .	. . .	. . .	. . .	ü
27 Gutturo-labialis fracta	ö	. . .	. . . .	. . .	. . . .	. . .	. . .	. . .	. . .	. . .